THE LAWS OF THE MEDIEVAL KINGDOM OF HUNGARY 2
1301-1457
DECRETA REGNI MEDIAEVALIS HUNGARIAE II
1301-1457

THE LAWS OF HUNGARY
SERIES I: *1000-1526*
Volume 2: *1301-1457*

THE LAWS OF EAST CENTRAL EUROPE
General Editor: Charles Schlacks, Jr.

THE LAWS OF HUNGARY
Editor-in-Chief: Peter I. Hidas

SERIES I: *1000-1526*
Edited by János M. Bak, Leslie S. Domonkos and James Ross Sweeney

THE LAWS OF THE MEDIEVAL KINGDOM OF HUNGARY

Volume 2

1301-1457

DECRETA REGNI MEDIAEVALIS HUNGARIAE

Tomus II

1301-1457

translated and edited by
critice recensuerunt et Anglice reddiderunt

János M. Bak, Pál Engel, James Ross Sweeney

in collaboration with
Paul B. Harvey, Jr.
adjuvante

Apud
CHARLES SCHLACKS, JR., PUBLISHER
Salt Lake City

Charles Schlacks, Jr., Publisher

Library of Congress Cataloguing-in-Publication Data:

The Laws of the medieval kingdom of Hungary / translated and edited by János M. Bak . [et al.] ; with a critical essay on previous editions by Andor Csizmadia.

(The Laws of east central Europe) (The Laws of Hungary. Series I, 1000-1526 ; v. 1-2)
English and Latin.
Vol. 2 has parallel title : Decreta regni mediaevalis Hungariae.
Includes bibliographical references and indexes.
Contents : v. 1. 1000-1301 — v. 2. 1301-1457.
1. Law—Hungary—Sources. I. Bak, János M. II. Hungary. III. Title : Decreta regni mediaevalis Hungariae. IV. Series. V. Series : Laws of Hungary ; ser. 1, v. 1, etc.
KKF13 1989a ser. 1, vol. 1, etc. 89-10492
[KKF129] 348.439'022 s 344.390822 s
348.439'022] [344.390822]

Suggested form of Reference: DRMH 2

János M. Bak is Professor of History at the University of British Columbia, Vancouver.

Pál Engel is Head, Department of Medieval History, in the Institute for Historical Research, Hungarian Academy of Sciences, Budapest.

James Ross Sweeney is Professor of Medieval History, and Paul B. Harvey, Jr. is Associate Professor of History and Classics, both at the Pennsylvania State University.

In memoriam
Georgii Bónis
(1914-85)

It is with great sadness that we dedicate this volume to the memory of the scholar who was instrumental in editing the first volume of Decreta Regni Mediaevalis Hungariae *and who was the chief editor of the Latin text for the present volume. We had the privilege of receiving his guidance for the selection and organisation of this volume, given to us when he was already fatally ill. But, alas, he did not live to see even the first volume in print. Yet, we hope to keep up the work to which he had devoted many years of his life by presenting the second volume and by doing our best to bring the entire series, of which he was to be one of the editors, to completion.*

TABLE OF CONTENTS

LIST OF MAPS AND ILLUSTRATIONS:

PUBLISHER'S PREFACE

Volume 2 of THE LAWS OF HUNGARY continues the format of its predecessor. The facing bilingual texts provide precise access to all the laws while the extensive notes and commentary reside at the back of the volume for exact reference. Taken together the material contained herein offers state of the art utility.

Charles Schlacks, Jr.
October 31, 1992

PREFACE

In view of the turbulent history of East Central Europe, it may be useful to define briefly what is meant by "Hungary" in the context of this collection. Centuries after leaving their ancestral Finno-Ugric home east of the Ural Mountains for the southern Eurasian steppe, the Hungarians eventually turned west and reached the Carpathian basin in the late ninth century. There, the loose alliance of tribes, led by the Magyars from whom the Hungarians derive their name, became a monarchy, first under a grand prince and, from 1000 A.D. under a king. The medieval kingdom of Hungary, from the eleventh to the mid-sixteenth century, comprised the entire Carpathian basin. Magyar conquest and settlement of the land proceeded gradually from the river valleys to the fertile plains and toward the mountainous border regions. To the east, Transylvania was incorporated in King Stephen's time but retained some measure of regional autonomy. The kings of Hungary annexed the formerly independent kingdom of Croatia and Dalmatia around 1100. From the twelfth to the fifteenth century Hungary extended her sovereignty along the Sava and lower Danube Rivers into border areas called banates, whose shifting frontiers depended on political conditions in the northern Balkans. From the later fourteenth century the country frequently shared rulers with Bohemia and Poland; yet, Hungary remained an independent unitary political entity. Even the vicious factional strife between competing aristocratic leagues in the fourteenth century could not shatter the cohesion of the state.

After the Ottoman Turks defeated the Hungarian royal army at the battle of Mohács (1526), the estates elected two rival kings: one native, another a Habsburg. During the ensuing civil wars the Turks occupied the central areas of the country and remained in control for a century and a half. Hungary was divided into three parts. Until the end of the seventeenth century Royal and Habsburg Hungary occupied the western and northern regions and a portion of western Croatia; the Principality of Transylvania, lying to the east and northeast, became a vassal state of the Ottoman Sultan; while the region in the center came

under the Turkish adminstration of the Pasha of Buda. The recovery of Hungary from the Turks in the late seventeenth century, however, did not result in reunification of the country. The Habsburg rulers preferred to govern Transylvania from Vienna rather than from the Hungarian "capital" Pozsony, continuing a practice which had begun with the separation of southern Hungary as a Military Frontier. The pre-1526 Kingdom of Hungary was only reestablished after the Compromise (*Ausgleich*) of 1867, although with increased autonomy for Croatia, and was maintained as part of the Austro-Hungarian Empire until 1918. Details of the complicated legal and constiutional status of Hungary within the Habsburg monarchy between 1868 and 1918 will be examined later in the appropriate volumes of Series II and III.

At the end of World War I Hungary became a republic from October 1918 to March 1919, and a soviet republic from March to July 1919. During these months most of historical Hungary was occupied by the successor states of the dissolved Habsburg Empire. Under the terms of the Treaty of Trianon in 1920 Hungary lost about 70 percent of her former territory and over 60 percent of her population, excluding Croatia-Slavonia, which land became part of the new South Slav state, Yugoslavia. The areas temporarily recovered by Hungary during World War II—mainly through the Vienna Arbitrations of Hitler and Mussolini—were later returned to Czechoslovakia, Romania, and Yugoslavia by the Paris Peace Treaty of 1946 which restored the borders essentially as they stood in 1920, except for Carpatho-Ukraine (Ruthenia) which became part of the USSR. In 1946 Hungary was declared a republic and from 20 August 1948 to 23 October 1989 it was called The People's Republic of Hungary.

* * *

The complex historical geography of Hungary is matched by the thorny problem of the definition of her law. In the course of a thousand years the notion of law, decree, statute or legal act underwent so many changes that a detailed legal history would be necessary to provide adequate definitions. The task of clarification is left to the introductory essays in the individual volumes where specific terms of reference valid for each age will be established. Only the main principles of selection need be stated here.

The Laws of Hungary widens the framework of the old *Corpus Juris Hungarici.* The laws presented are the ones which the supreme authorities of the Hungarian state or parts thereof have proclaimed as such and under which the population of Hungary was obliged to live at a given time. Consequently, we shall include in *The Laws of Hungary* enactments of rebel and revolutionary assemblies, rival assemblies, rump or otherwise, so long as they were able to impose their laws on a

significant part of contemporary Hungary and claim jurisdiction over the rest, as well as the laws (patents, and so forth) of rulers, regardless of their legitimacy in the eyes of later lawmakers or legal historians. Accordingly, the editors recognize the *de facto* as *de iure*. While the laws contained in the traditional collections may essentially be found here, they have been supplemented with acts uncovered by scholars in the last century and a half and with laws in effect but considered unconstitutional by the editors of previous collections. The texts, moreover, have been emended in light of modern critical textual analysis.

In another sense, however, this collection of statute law would still be an incomplete record of legal realities of the past ten centuries. As significant as royal legislation from the time of the first king may have been, custom and customary law reigned supreme well beyond the Middle Ages virtually to 1848. According to the legal historian J. Illés, "a statute cannot be upheld by its own force . . . it does not survive the legislator, only the force of custom keeps it alive." While this may have been literally the case until the close of the fifteenth century, the overwhelming force of custom continued well beyond that time. The clearest indicator of the ongoing role of legal custom is the preeminence enjoyed for centuries by a collection of customary law, namely, the compilation by the practical lawyer and high court judge István Werbőczy (1458-1541). The collection was never approved or promulgated by any ruler, but was clearly the summary of centuries of custom and hence regarded as the law of the land par excellence until 1848. Its inclusion in the editions of the laws of Hungary ever since the seventeenth century suggests the paramount significance of custom, not all of which was ever written down, not even in the *Tripartitum*.

* * *

The Laws of Hungary will consist of seven parts. The present volume is the second in Series I, which will contain the laws between 1000 and 1526. Series II contains the laws from 1526 to 1867; Series III from 1867 to 1919; Series IV from 1920 to 1945; Series V from 1945 to 1948. Series VI, the last historical set, will contain the laws of the People's Republic, and conclude with 1990. In Series VII we will present the living laws of Hungary passed by the freely elected parliament (from 1990 onward). In addition, we shall publish two supplementary sets: the laws of Transylvania and the laws of Croatia-Slavonia.

For first names and geographical terms our translators were encouraged to use the English equivalents. The editors prefer St. Stephen to Szt. István and Louis Kossuth to Lajos Kossuth. Less well-known Hungarian names are spelled in the Magyar manner, as people

addresssed each other at the time. Since we are publishing the laws of the state of Hungary, in the absence of English geographical terms Hungarian place names are used regardless of other names in use at the time (German or Latin) or presently (Romanian, Slovak, Serbian, Croatian, or Russian). If necessary, gazetteers will be added for orientation (see below, p. 294). The translators are encouraged to follow the original Latin or Hungarian texts, both in sense and style, as faithfully as possible, but never at the expense of clarity. *The Chicago Manual of Style,* Thirteenth Edition, Revised and Expanded (Chicago and London: The University of Chicago Press, 1982) serves as our main editorial guide.

* * *

We gratefully acknowledge the financial support we received for the preparation of this volume from the National Endowment for the Humanities, an independent agency of the United States Government and a number of individual donors. Thanks are also due to the universities and institutes of the editors (The University of British Columbia, the Historical Institute of the Hungarian Academy of Sciences and The Pennsylvania State University) for granting them time or covering minor expenses. The valuable assistance of many colleagues is noted at the suitable sections, but editor-in-chief and publisher also wish to extend their gratitude to all those who participated in this team-work.

Peter I. Hidas
Editor-in-Chief
Dawson College, Montréal

Charles Schlacks, Jr.
Publisher
Salt Lake City, Utah

ABBREVIATIONS

AUSBp, Sect. hist.	*Annales Universitatis Scientiarum Budapestinensis de Rolando Eötvös nominatae, Sectio historica.*
Bak, *Königtum*	J. M. Bak, *Königtum und Stände in Ungarn im 14.-15. Jh.* Wiesbaden: Steiner, 1973.
Bak, "Monarchie"	J. M. Bak, "Monarchie im Wellental: Materielle Grundlagen des ungarischen Königtums im späteren Mittelalter" in R. Schneider, ed. *Das spätmittelalterliche Königtum im europäischen Vergleich.* Sigmaringen: Thorbecke, 1987, pp. 347-87.
Bak-Király, *Hunyadi*	J. M. Bak and B. K. Király, ed. *From Hunyadi to Rákóczi: War and Society in Medieval and Early Modern Hungary.* Brooklyn: Social Science Monographs, 1982.
Bartal, *Glossarium*	A. Bartal, *Glossarium mediae et infimae latinitatis Regni Hungariae* Bp.: MTA, 1901 (repr. *ibid.*, 1981).
Biogr. Lex.	*Biographisches Lexikon zur Geschichte Südosteuropas.* M. Bernath *et al.*, eds. München: Oldenbourg, 1974–81, 4 vols.
Bp. *(as place of publication)*	Budapest
ch.	chapter
civ.	*civitas*, city
Co., com.	county, *comitatus*
DRH 1301-1457	F. Dőry, Gy. Bónis, V. Bácskai, eds. *Decreta regni Hungariae: Gesetze und Verordnungen Ungarns 1301-1457.* Bp.: Akadémiai K., 1978.

DRMH	*Decreta Regni Mediaevalis Hungariae 1000 to 1526: The Laws of the Medieval Kingdom of Hungary 1000-1526*. J. Bak, Gy. Bónis, J. R. Sweeney, L. S. Domonkos, eds., Bakersville-Salt Lake City: Charles Schlacks, Jr., Publisher, 1989- [*The Laws of Hungary*, ed. Peter I. Hidas. Series I, Vol. 1-] (the present volume is volume 2.)
Eckhart, Glaubw. Orte	F. Eckhart, "Die glaubwürdigen Orte Ungarns im Mittelalter," *MIÖG*, Ergänzungsband 9 (1913/15): 395-558.
f., ff.	following page(s)
Fejér, *Cod. dipl.*	G. Fejér, *Codex diplomaticus Hungariae ecclesiasticus ac civilis*. 11 vols. in 43 pts. Bp.: Regia Universitas, 1829-66.
Fügedi, *Kings*	E. Fügedi, *Kings, Bishops, Nobles and Burghers in Medieval Hungary*. ed. J. M. Bak. London: Variorum Reprints, 1986.
Hajnik, *Bir. szerv.*	I. Hajnik, *Bírósági szervezet és perjog az Árpád- és a vegyesházi királyok alatt* [Judicial System and Procedural Law under the Kings of the Árpád and the Diverse Dynasties]. Bp.: MTA, 1899.
Katona, *Hist. crit.*	St. Katona, *Historia critica regum Hungariae*. 42 vols. Pest: Weigand, 1779-1817.
K.	Kiadó [Publishing House]
Knauz, *MES*	N. Knauz, ed., *Monumenta ecclesiae Strigoniensis*. 2 vols. Esztergom: Horak, 1874-82.
Kovachich, *Vestigia*	M. G. Kovachich, *Vestigia comitiorum apud Hungaros ab exordio regni eorum in Pannonia, usque ad hodiernum diem celebratorum*. Buda: Regia Universitas, 1790.
Kovachich, *Supplementum*	M. G. Kovachich, *Supplementum ad vestigia comitiorum apud Hungaros ab exordio regni eorum in Pannonia, usque ad hodiernum diem celebratorum*. 3 vols. Pest: Regia Universitas, 1789-1801.

Kovachich, *Sylloge*	J. M. Kovachich, *Sylloge decretorum comitialium inclyti regni Hungariae, quae in vulgato corpore juris hungarici, hactenus, aut penitus desiderabantur, aut aliqua sui parte, manca referebantur. et oblivioni postliminio, recenter erepta sunt.* . . . Pest: Trattner, 1818.
Mályusz, *Sigismund*	E. Mályusz, *Kaiser Sigismund in Ungarn 1386–1437*. Transl. by A. Szmodits. Bp.: Akadémiai K., 1990.
Mályusz, "Rendi állam"	E. Mályusz, "A magyar rendi állam Hunyadi korában" [The Hungarian Corporatist State in the Age of Hunyadi], *Száz.* 91 (1957): 46-123, 529-602.
Marczali, *Enchiridion*	H. Marczali, *A magyar történet kútfőinek kézikönyve. Enchiridion fontium historiae Hungarorum.* Bp.: Athenaeum, 1901.
MTA	Magyar Tudományos Akadémia [Hungarian Academy of Sciences]
MTvt/CJH	*Magyar Törvénytár: Corpus Juris Hungarici.* D. Márkus *et al.* eds. Bp.: Franklin, 1896 ff. [Millennial edition]
MIÖG	*Mitteilungen des Instituts für österreichische Geschichtsforschung*
OL Dl.	Országos Levéltár, Diplomatikai levéltár [Hungarian National Archives, Budapest, Collectio Antemohacsiana]
Pray, *Annales*	G. Pray, *Annales regum Hungariae ab anno Christi CMXCVII ad annum MDLXIV deducti.* . . . 5 vols. Wien: Schulz/Trattner/Bernard, 1763-1770.
Száz.	*Századok: A Magyar Történelmi Társulat közlönye* [Centuries: Journal of the Hungarian Historical Association]
Szentpétery, *Scriptores*	E. [I.] Szentétery, ed. *Scriptores rerum Hungaricum tempore ducum regumque stirpis Arpadianae gestarum.* 2 vols. Bp.: MTA, 1937-38.

Theiner, *Vet. mon. hist.* — A. Theiner, *Vetera monumenta historica Hungariam sacram illustrantia*. I. Roma: Typis Vaticanis, 1859 (repr. Osnabrück: Zeller, 1968).

Tripartitum — I. Werbőczy, *Tripartitum opus iuris consuetudinarii regni Hungariae*. ed. K. Csiky. Bp.: Eggenberger, 1894.

Zs. O. — *Zsigmondkori Oklevéltár* [Calendar for the Age of Sigismund]. E. Mályusz, *et al.* eds. Bp.: Akadémiai K., 1954- (vols. 1 ff.)

REFERENCES TO THE LAWS

Following the practice of *DRH 1301–1457* the usual reference to the decrees is (as far as known) by full date—day, month, year—and section (paragraph) number, e.g., **11 December 1351:20** stands for the twentieth article (*articulum, törvénycikk, Gesetzartikel*) of the decree issued on 11 December 1351 A.D. However, since usually only one decree was issued in any given year, in notes and other cross-references we omit the month and day, except for the two decrees of the years 1404, 1405, and 1435. On 17 March 1427 two decrees were issued, these we abbreviate as **1427A** and **1427B.**

The documents printed in the Appendix are referred to by an abbreviation hinting at their character, thus: **CC 1342** for the cameral contract of 2 February 1342 and **Pro 1432/33** for the royal propositions of c. 1432/33 and its supplement.

The Notes always open by giving the *initia* of the laws, for it has been suggested that they should be used in international references.

LEGISLATION IN THE FOURTEENTH AND EARLY FIFTEENTH CENTURY
Editors' Introduction

This volume contains *decreta* of the medieval kingdom of Hungary from the accession of Charles I in 1301 to the death of Ladislas V Postumus in 1457. During that century and a half, Hungary experienced the re-establishment of monarchical authority under rulers of the Angevin dynasty (1301-86) after a decade of anarchy. The long reign of Sigismund of Luxemburg (1386–1437) also began after years of succession struggles and was followed by the contested reigns of the Habsburg Albert I (1437–39), of the Jagiello Wladislas I (1440–44), and finally of the Habsburg Ladislas V (1452–57), which closed this turbulent period. The second quarter of the fifteenth century was characterized by near civil war, only temporarily halted by the regency of János (John) Hunyadi and by the actions of the ever more influential noble diet. In contrast to the political and economic stability of the fourteenth century, Hungary became increasingly overtaxed by the task of parrying Ottoman advance in the Balkans. By the mid-fifteenth century the Ottoman Empire has reached the border of the kingdom and threatened its integrity.[1]

Relatively few, but nonetheless important, legislative acts have come down to us from the Angevin era, whereas a considerable body of legal records survives from the later time of Sigismund and his successors. Many of these laws were passed by the "estates" without royal participation, that is, by general assemblies of the nobility occasionally augmented by certain clergy and burghers in the absence

1. On the general history of the period, see B. Hóman, *Gli Angioini di Napoli in Ungheria, 1290–1403* (Roma: Reale Academia, 1938); Idem, "Hungary 1301–1490," in *The Cambridge Medieval History*, J. B. Bury, ed., 7 (Cambridge: Cambridge Univ. Press, 1936), pp. 587–619 with bibliography on pp. 961–64; *Handbuch der Europäischen Geschichte*, Th. Schieder, ed. (Stuttgart: Klett, 1971–81) 2: 1062–72, 3: 1103–24; J. M. Bak, "Hungary," in *Dictionary of the Middle Ages* 6 (New York: Scribner, 1985), pp. 344–48; D. Hay, *Europe in the Fourteenth and Fifteenth Centuries* 2nd ed. (London: Longman, 1988), pp. 214–51; *A History of Hungary* P. F. Sugár and P. Hanák, eds. (Bloomington: Indiana Univ. Press, 1989), pp. 34–70, all with bibliography. More extensive bibliography can be found in *Historische Bücherkunde Südosteuropa*, M. Bernath, ed. (München: Oldenbourg, 1980) 1: 842–1132.

of the monarch. The growth of non-royal legislation obliges us to define the *decreta* in this volume somewhat differently from the laws of the Árpádian epoch printed in the first volume of this series. All enactments of law, whether issued by the king, the reigning queen, or a particular institution acting in a sovereign capacity (the royal council, an ad-hoc council of magnates, a diet of one estate—the nobility—or more, or a regent installed by the community of the kingdom) must be regarded as valid legislation. Since the formal criteria of *decreta* were not yet definitely established before 1457, we have determined the character of legal documents, in keeping with modern scholarship, not by their external features but on the basis of their general validity for the inhabitants of the kingdom.[2]

The territorial applicability of the laws extended to the regions of historical Hungary comprising the entire Carpathian Basin. The frontiers were little changed from the preceding century. However, Hungarian sovereignty in Dalmatia and in the banats of the northern Balkans was intermittent, and by 1457 most of these territories were lost either to Venice or to the Ottomans. In the following historical overview these gains and losses will be noted in their chronological context.

The Historical Background

Interregnum and Angevin Rule (1301–82)

When King Andrew III, the last male member of the Árpád dynasty died in 1301, several candidates who had been gathering supporters in the country well before the king's demise advanced their claims to the throne of Hungary. The struggle of these candidates and their partisans brought years of civil war, anarchy throughout the country, and growth in the local power of a handful of oligarchs. The majority of the great families first installed Wenceslas III, the son of the Bohemian King Wenceslas II and a descendant of the kings of Hungary, on the throne. However, his situation soon became so hopeless that he returned home[3] and transferred his claims, in 1305, to the Bavarian

2. On this definition, see "Editor's Introduction," in *DRH 1301–1447*, pp. 15–18, also below, pp. xlii–xliii; cf. A. Wolf, "Die Gesetzgebung der entstehenden Territorialstaaten," in *Handbuch der Quellen und Literatur der neueren europäischen Privatrechtsgeschichte,* H. Coing, ed. (München: Beck, 1973) 1:721–62.

3. On this episode, see J. M. Bak, "Die Armrelique König Stefans im Ornat König Wenzels von Ungarn," in *Festschrift Percy Ernst Schramm zu seinem siebzigsten Geburtstag von Schülern und Freunden zugeeignet*, C.-P. Classen and P. Scheibert, eds. (Wiesbaden: Steiner, 1964) 1: 175–88.

Prince Otto of Wittelsbach, a grandson of Béla IV.[4] After being crowned, he was soon captured by László Kán, the voivode of Transylvania, and was lucky to return to Bavaria alive in 1307. His departure left only one candidate on the scene, the most persistent of them all, Charles (often called Charles Robert) of Anjou-Naples, also a descendant of the Árpáds in the female line. Because the Angevins had raised their claim as early as 1290, Charles was already an experienced claimant when he finally achieved his goal. Entering Hungary in 1301, he was quickly crowned in a somewhat impromptu ceremony. To gain the support of the Hungarian lords, he needed crucial assistance from the Church. Cardinal Gentile de Montefiore, who came to Hungary in 1308 as papal legate, removed the last obstacles barring Charles's way to the throne. After a species of election took place at a diet held under the guidance of the legate, Charles was crowned a second time with a crown specially prepared and consecrated by the legate in 1309, and finally, on 27 August 1310, he was crowned a third time with the "Holy Crown of St. Stephen," which had lately been recovered from Transylvania where it had been kept by the voivode since 1307. At last the country had a legal king and the interregnum came to an end.[5]

The third crowning was the beginning of the establishment of a new dynasty. Charles still had to fight long and hard before the country had a real master. His most difficult task was to end the anarchy that had prevailed for decades and to liquidate the power structure of the oligarchy before it became fully institutionalized. From his southern stronghold in Temesvár (today: Timişoara) Charles directed campaigns in every direction, expanding his rule over the entire country. The reunification of the country ended in 1323 when Pozsony (today: Bratislava) opened its gates to the ruler. Only then could Charles claim to be in full political control of the country.

During the following years Charles concentrated his energies on consolidating his power. Although during the first years of his reign he proved to be a capable military leader, he was primarily a politician not a soldier. Charles accepted without a fight Venice's lordship over the Dalmatian cities which the Árpáds had long claimed and did not even attempt the subjugation of the recalcitrant lords of southern Croatia. He concluded an alliance with the ban of Bosnia and was satisfied with Bosnia's nominal homage. He conducted few Balkan campaigns, one of

4. On his adventure, see *Handbuch der bayerischen Geschichte*, M. Spindler, ed. (München: Beck, [©1966]) 2: 110–16, with literature.

5. The records of these events are published as *Acta legationis Cardinalis Gentilis, 1307–1311* in *Monumenta Vaticana historiam regni Hungariae illustrantia*, vol. I/2, A. Pór, ed. (Bp.: Franklin, 1885); on the "election" and coronation, see Bak, *Königtum*, pp. 11–22.

which allowed him to re-establish the Banate of Macsó (Mačva) in northern Serbia (1319), but another in Walachia resulted in a major defeat which further justified Charles's cautious policy.[6]

Charles worked for peaceful relations with his northern and Western neighbors. With the Polish kings Wladislaw I the Short (Lokietek) and his son Casimir III (the Great), he maintained a firm alliance into which he tried also to include the Luxemburg rulers of Bohemia. To bring about such an alliance, he assumed the role of mediator between the Polish and Bohemian kings in their competition for territories and legitimacy. The outstanding issues were settled in 1335 when the three rulers met in Visegrád where they signed a formal alliance on the basis of the status quo.[7]

When Charles died on 16 July 1342, he was succeeded by the eldest of his three sons, Louis I (the Great), born in 1326, who ruled until 1382.[8] The preference of the Hungarian nobility, who for so long wanted a warrior king and who saw in war and not in peace the road to glory was now fulfilled. Louis offered them the promise of the status of a great power based on an aggressive foreign policy and a regular second income from the loot of yearly campaigns. It is not surprising that the epithet, the Great, was added to his name soon after his death, and for centuries his reign lived in the nation's memory as a period of greatness.

The foundations of Angevin power had been laid so solidly by Charles that nothing could shake them until after Louis' death. From what can be gleaned from the sources Louis was also free of financial worries. He certainly always had enough money for military ventures. The military balance sheet, however, showed more glory than profit. This negative feature is well illustrated by Louis's Neapolitan adventures, which were prompted by the fate of his brother Andrew, who was intended to inherit the paternal throne of Naples, but who was killed before he could do so. In 1352 Louis's two campaigns to Italy to punish his brother's murderers ended in failure.

6. See J. V. A. Fine, Jr. *The Late Medieval Balkans: A Critical Survey from the Late Twelfth Century to the Ottoman Conquest* (Ann Arbor: Univ. of Michigan Press [1987]), pp. 168–70, 184–87, 191–96, 230–36; J. R. Sweeney, "Walachia-Moldavia," in *The Dictionary of the Middle Ages* (New York: Scribner, 1989) 12: 497f.

7. See Paul W. Knoll *The Rise of the Polish Monarchy: Piast Poland in East Central Europe 1320–1370* (Chicago–London: Univ. of Chicago Press [©1972]), pp. 65–82.

8. A summary biography of Louis by M. Ferdinandy, "Ludwig I. von Ungarn" can be now found in S. B. Vardy, G. Goldschmidt, L. S. Domonkos, eds., *Louis the Great, King of Hungary and Poland* (Boulder, Co.: East European Monographs, 1986), pp. 3–48.

Louis's wars directed against his southern neighbors to gain their allegiance to Hungary brought similarly meagre results.[9] In most of the twenty Balkan campaigns the king led his armies in person. With the exception of the short-lived "annexation" of Bulgaria (1365–69), the expeditions were intended to force the various rulers into accepting more or less formal positions of vassalage. Only the Croatian and Dalmatian wars brought tangible results. In 1345 Louis defeated the lords of the south whom Charles had not dislodged from their power, and all of Croatia was ruled once more by a Hungarian ban as in the days of the Árpáds. It was more difficult to acquire the port cities of the Adriatic. Finally, the second Venetian war brought success (1356–58): with the help of allies from northern Italy Louis achieved the submission to Hungary of a number of Dalmatian cities.[10]

During the last years of his life Louis was increasingly preoccupied with the question of succession. Louis had no sons, only three daughters. He hoped that one of them, together with her future husband, would succeed him on the throne. Many marriage alliances with France and Hungary's neighbors were explored, but finally a dynastic marriage with the Bohemian Luxemburgs was concluded. Markgrave Sigismund of Brandenburg, the son of the Emperor Charles IV and brother of King Wenceslas IV of Bohemia, became the fiancé of Mary and hence heir presumptive. In Poland, where Louis was crowned king in 1370, the younger daughter, Hedwig/Jadwiga was accepted as her father's successor.[11]

Economy and Society

The six decades of stability under Charles and Louis constitute a period of apparent prosperity and economic development, at least in certain sectors of Hungary. The picture that emerges from our knowledge of Angevin Hungary presents a country which, in spite of great changes that took place in the late thirteenth century, nonetheless lagged behind contemporary Western and Central Europe in several respects. The

9. For these see Fine, *Balkans*, pp. 339–41, 367–70, 395–96; F. Szakály, "Phases of Turco-Hungarian Warfare before the battle of Mohács (1365–1526)," *Acta Orientalia Acad. Sc. Hung.*, 33 (1979): 67–75.

10. Louis's Dalmatian campaigns and the conquest of Zara/Zadar are discussed by V. Brunelli, *Storia dell città di Zara* 2nd. ed. (Trieste: Lint, 1974), pp. 483–89.

11. See now O. Halecki, *Jadwiga of Anjou and the Rise of East Central Europe*, Th. V. Gromada, ed. (Boulder, Co.–Highland Lakes, NJ: Social Science Monographs–Atlantic Research & Publications, 1991), pp. 77–112.

Figure 3. Gold Florins of Charles I (1325) and Louis I (1370)
Corpus Nummorum Hungariae, II: 1 and 66.

most obvious features were the low density of the population (about 25 per square mile) and the low level of urbanization.[12]

The country's most significant source of income was its mineral wealth. Mining of salt and silver had developed in the twelfth and thirteenth centuries. Around 1320 one rich gold mine after another was opened and silver production also increased. Modern estimates place the annual yield of Hungarian mines at the middle of the century at 4,500 to 5,000 pounds of gold and 22,000 pounds of silver. Both the promotion of mining and the regulation of the country's monetary system were the work of Charles I. His monetary reform ended the anarchy in minting practices which had characterized the Árpád period. The king abolished the practice of issuing new money yearly, which went hand-in-hand with a forced return of the old coins to the treasury, and issued silver coins with a constant value. The treasury's resulting loss was compensated by the introduction of a new tax which retained its name from the old system of coin devaluation, the "chamber's profit" (*lucrum camerae*). It became henceforth a direct tax, collected from each peasant household. The second lasting aspect of Charles's reform was the introduction of a gold coin, the *florenus*, modeled on its Florentine namesake, the fineness and weight of which would remain unaltered for centuries.

In terms of social development, the process of transformation from the archaic structure to a typical medieval stratified society, which began in the thirteenth century[13] had ended in the mid-fourteenth. Two more or less homogeneous strata, the major components of Hungarian society for centuries, emerged: the nobility (*nobiles*) and the personally free tenant peasants (*jobagiones*) subject to seigneurial dues and jurisdiction.

The Hungarian nobility was in many respects similar to the élite elsewhere in medieval Europe but differed in certain particular features. Hungarian nobles enjoyed a privileged position: noble status was inherited at birth and was protected by law and custom. From the fourteenth century onward the noble was by definition a landowner.[14] Nobles did not pay taxes and troops could not be quartered on their property. They were also exempted from paying the tithe.[15] The nobility did not owe feudal service and were obliged to follow a call to

12. See *Anonymi Descriptio Europae Orientalis ... anno MCCCVIII exarata*, O. Górka, ed. (Cracow: Academia Litterarum, 1916), esp. p. 49; cf. J. Deér, "Ungarn in der Descriptio Europae Orientalis," *MIÖG* 45 (1931): 1–22.

13. See DRMH 1:l–li.

14. See Gy. Bónis, *Hűbériség és rendiség a középkori magyar jogban* [Feudalism and Corporatism in Medieval Hungarian Law] (Kolozsvár: Erdélyi Tudományos Intézet, n.d. [1947]), pp. 139–45.

15. See the royal mandates referring to a lost decree from ca. 1405, *DRH 1301–1457*, p. 216, and the explicit renewal of this measure in 1439:28.

arms only if the country was under attack and the king personally took command of a "general levy" (*generalis exercitus*). Regardless of their historical origin, the nobility claimed descent from the conquerors of Hungary and considered ancestral lands as its share of the Magyar-occupied country. Consequently, all noble land was considered free and could not be encumbered. The major differences between Hungarian and Western or Central European nobility were that the former included a much larger proportion of the population than in any other country (save Poland) and that the majority of Hungarian nobles consisted of families which in fact lived like peasants.[16]

This relatively numerous nobility[17] resulted from the gradual merger of three pre-existing social elements: the richest, the descendants of the *ispánok*, had been the élite of the early Árpád period; others were descendants of an armed population called "castle warriors" (*jobagiones castri*) in the eleventh century; but the bulk of the Hungarian nobility originated in that stratum of free Hungarian warriors who were called "royal servants" (*servientes regis*) and had come to be recognized as nobles in the later thirteenth century. The noble estate also included the lower ranked and less privileged nobles of Transylvania and Slavonia.[18] The centuries-long process of integration was finally legalised by Louis I in 1351 through the renewal of the Golden Bull of 1222 (see below, pp. 8f.). This re-issue contained the additional statement that all "true" nobles living in the country were entitled to the same freedoms (*sub una et eadem libertate gratulentur*). This maxim, of course, was neither a description of social reality, nor was it intended to be as all-embracing as later generations preferred to understand it. It was a legal fiction, but in the Middle Ages legal fictions had real implications. The claim to equal status at law and in politics was in later centuries a powerful slogan and program for the lesser nobility.[19]

The development of a legally uniform dependent peasantry had also begun in the preceding century, when, after the devastation of the Mongol invasion and changes in agriculture, the status of "settlers"

16. A few comparative studies discuss this matter; see, e.g., F. Maksay, *Les pays de la noblesse nombreuse* (Bp.: Akadémiai K., 1980).

17. The nobility was, nonetheless, a small segment of the total population, not more than 3–5 percent (according to fifteenth-century estimates).

18. See DRMH 1:34–43, 97–110; E. Fügedi, "The Aristocracy in Medieval Hungary: Theses" in *Kings* ch. 4, pp. 3–6.

19. As this law also makes clear, in the fourteenth century not all nobles were "true" nobles. For example, those who lived on estates owned by the Church and were obligated to serve in perpetuity as soldiers had the status of nobles, but were not counted among those who enjoyed all the rights and freedom of the nobility.

(*hospites*), foreign and domestic, was granted increasingly to former serfs and other unfree elements on royal and seigneurial estates. This process—called the "first emancipation of the peasantry"—began with transformations in agricultural production, in settlement patterns and in administration of landed estates. The servile labor on the extensively cultivated vast lands and grazing fields, organized into *predia*, came to be less valuable than the dues in kind and money from peasants settled in villages and cultivating the arable on their own. The person and the physical labor of the tenant tended to be irrelevant once the village community's dues were properly collected. Fourteenth- and fifteenth-century evidence suggests that boon-work was minimal, but with the slow growth of markets money payments could be levied from the tenants, whose movement from one estate to another was not viewed as a problem, at any rate not in times of labor surplus.[20]

The Angevin State and the Royal Court.

The strength of the monarchy of the fourteenth century derived from a new cooperation between aristocracy and the crown. The immense energy expended by Charles I in the destruction of the oligarchy brought positive results. Conquered land became the king's and through these recovered royal estates he created a new ruling system. Whereas in the thirteenth century the royal domain diminished rapidly and constantly, in the fourteenth this process was reversed. The royal properties remained impressively extensive in comparison with even the largest private wealth. When Louis I died in 1382, the royal family owned 15 percent of the country's land. The royal castles, some 150 in all parts of the kingdom, guaranteed the stability of royal power, and the income derived from appurtenant estates was used to reward important royal officeholders.[21]

The élite of the court aristocracy consisted of the highest lay and ecclesiastical office holders: *praelati et barones regni*. Included in this group were the two archbishops and twelve bishops (sometimes more, including the Dalmatian sees); the chief justices of the realm (the count palatine, the judge royal, and the Master of the Treasury who, since the days of Charles I, was the chief judge of the chartered royal cities); the voivode of Transylvania, as well as the bans of the southern provinces of Slavonia, Croatia and Dalmatia, Macsó (Mačva), and Szörény (Severin); and, finally, the chief dignitaries of the royal household (*aula*)—the Master of the Horse, the butler, the steward, and the

20. See A. Kornjáthy, "Hungarian *jobbágyság* in the Fifteenth Century," *East European Quarterly* 10 (1976): 77–111; J. Held, *Hunyadi: Legend and Reality* (Boulder, Co.: East European Monographs, 1985), pp. 56–79.

21. See Fügedi, *Castle*, pp. 103–22.

Master of the Doorkeepers. In a wider sense the officers of the queen's household and all those who were charged with the command of royal castles or administration of the more important counties were also considered to be barons.[22] It was this circle of men who constituted the king's council which decided all political issues and represented the country in foreign affairs.

The king's household, fairly informal under the Árpád rulers, became well organized under the Angevins and played an important role in the running of affairs. From the time of Charles it was called the *aula regia*, possessing a hierarchic organization that included knights, squires, and pages. They made up the ruler's immediate entourage and were always in attendance to carry out his orders.[23] The queen had her own court, organized along identical lines. The queen's household became particularly important during the reign of Louis I because the queen-mother, Elizabeth Piast, had great influence on him and thus on the country's affairs until her death in 1380.

An office at court and the administration of counties and castles was usually referred to as *honor*. Its character has been compared to that of early medieval (Carolingian) royal officials rather than to feudal arrangements typical of high medieval Europe. An honor was held "at the king's pleasure" (*ad beneplacitum regis*) and did not become hereditary. The holders of honors seem to have collected all the revenues of their office, administered justice in the king's name, and commanded the armies of the territory entrusted to them. The honors of the barons and the employment of lesser nobles in the frame of *familiaritas* were the pillars on which Angevin power rested. The noble who became the retainer (*familiaris*) of a great lord entered into his service only as a person. His possessions and his noble privileges were not involved.[24]

The same twin pillars supported the Angevin army. During the numerous wars of Louis the Great, the royal, baronial, and ecclesiastical units played the major role; those who fought in these units were *familiares*. Prelates and barons possessed the right and duty

22. See Fügedi, "Aristocracy," p. 11; P. Engel, "Honor, vár, ispánság: Tanulmányok az Anjou-királyság kormányzati rendszeréről" [*Honor*, Castle, *Ispán*: Studies on the Governmental System of the Angevin Monarchy], *Száz.*, 116 (1982): 880–922, French summary p. 922.

23. See Á. Kurcz, *A lovagi kultúra Magyarországon a 13–14. században* [Knightly Culture in 13th-14th Century Hungary] (Bp. Akadémiai K., 1988) esp. pp. 121f.; E. Fügedi, "Tourniere im mittelalterlichen Ungarn" in *Das ritterliche Turnier im Mittelalter*, J. Fleckenstein, ed. (Göttingen: Vandenhoek & Ruprecht, 1986), pp. 390–400.

24. On the *familiaritas* there is still no better summary in a foreign language than that of Gy. Szekfü, "Die Servienten und Familaren im ungarischen Mittelalter," *Ungarische Rundschau für historische und soziale Wissenschaften* 2 (1912): 524–57; see also Fügedi, *Castle*, pp. 78–80, 129–30; Held, *Hunyadi*, pp. 17–19.

of commanding troops under their own banner (*vexillum* or *banderium*) in battle; whence the name: banderial system. The army was composed entirely of cavalry. Its core consisted of armored knights, but a major component was made up of lightly armed mounted archers. Special units were furnished by the free warrior settlers, the non-noble Cumans, Jazygians (*jászok*) and the Székely, the former borderguards of Transylvania. In the pursuit of loot and rewards numerous independent nobles also joined the royal army.

Although the administration of the country continued to depend mainly on orally transmitted orders and soldiers prevailed over clerks, the volume of written records increased significantly. Several tens of thousands of documents have survived from the fourteenth century, in sharp contrast to the few thousand from all previous centuries.[25] In the higher courts of law, especially, literacy became widespread in this period making legal procedure more professional and complicated. In 1342, Louis transferred to Visegrád those courts which had nation-wide jurisdiction: those of the palatine and the judge royal. In 1377, he created a third permanent court which operated in the name of the king in his "special presence" (*specialis praesentia regia*). It functioned under the supervision of the chancellor, now frequently referred to as archchancellor. In addition to the great seal of state entrusted to him, a secret seal was introduced by Charles I in a manner similar to that of many other rulers of Europe. In time diplomas issued under the secret seal became true expressions of royal will. For a while, under Louis I, the royal signet-ring was also used to authenticate documents. Around the secret seal a second chancellery was organized in 1374. Those serving in both chancelleries and the higher courts were recruited increasingly from the laity. They were usually not university graduates, but "practical lawyers," trained in the local and higher courts and thoroughly familiar with the "custom of the realm."[26]

25. A calendar of charters is at present being prepared under the editorship of Gyula Kristó and his team for the fourteenth century. Until it is finished, it is difficult to estimate the number of royal charters issued under the Angevins. The number of surviving royal charters in an annual average had risen to 75 under Andrew III (from ca. 20 p. a. in the preceding five decades). For the Anjou chancelleries this figure may very well go into the hundreds. Similar "jumps" were recorded for France and England in the late twelfth-early thirteenth centuries by M. Clanchy (*From Memory to Written Record* [London: Arnold, 1979], pp. 44 ff.).

26. See Gy. Bónis, *A jogtudó értelmiség a Mohács előtti Magyarországon* [Professionals Learned in the Law in Pre-Mohács Hungary] (Bp.: Akadémiai K., 1971), pp. 21–29, cf. Idem, "Men Learned in the Law in Medieval Hungary" *East Central Europe–L'Europe de centre-est,* 4, pt. 1 (1977): 183.

Sigismund of Luxemburg (1386–1437)[27]

After the death of Louis I the succession was anything but smooth. Mary, betrothed to Sigismund of Luxemburg, was crowned soon after her father's death, but her husband, Sigismund, was not given any recognition. Prior to the coronation she had confirmed the privileges of the nobility (see below, 22 June 1384); and from now on this became the accepted practice at every inauguration. However, Mary's rule, or in reality that of her mother and her favorites, was challenged by the adherents of Charles of Durazzo, king of Naples. Charles, supported by the great lords of Croatia and Slavonia, above all by the Horváti clan, and by a great many lesser nobles who thought inheritance in the female line to be an anomaly, landed in Dalmatia to vindicate his claims. He was crowned king of Hungary as Charles II on the last day of 1385, having forced the queens to acquiesce formally in his rule.

Years of civil strife followed. Only thirty-nine days after his coronation Charles was assassinated by the queens' men. Then the two royal ladies were taken captive, Palatine Nicholas of Gara was killed, and a few months later the queen mother was strangled by the rebels. The death of Charles and the capture of Mary turned the tide in favor of Sigismund. A group of great lords who had constituted themselves guardians of the realm, acting in the name of the *regnum*, and swearing to defend the interests of the kingdom even against its ruler (see below, 27 August 1386), offered the crown to the margrave. After signing an agreement with his followers, assuring them of a share of power in return for support, Sigismund was elected and crowned king. With the help of Venetian diplomacy, he soon secured the release of his wife. Theoretically he ruled "in concert" with her until her death in an accident in 1395.

For almost two decades Sigismund's hold on the kingship was tenuous at best. During the early years of the reign, still fighting for the throne and his wife's life, he could scarcely avoid giving away much of the royal domain. Through perpetual donations or mortgages (which were rarely redeemed) almost two-thirds of the castles and estates of the Angevins were transferred into the hands of the barons by the end of the century.[28]

27. For the following see Mályusz, *Sigismund*, passim.

28. See P. Engel, *Királyi hatalom és arisztokrácia viszonya a Zsigmond-korban* [Relationship of Royal Power and Aristocracy under Sigismund] (Bp.: Akadémiai K., 1977), p. 207, table 1, where the author demonstrates that by 1407, from the approximately 150 royal castles of the Angevin era only 57 remained in the king's hand. It should be noted that a number of southern counties were not included in the survey.

Sigismund was the first of the kings of Hungary to contemplate seriously the defense of the realm against Ottoman advances. After the Turkish occupation of the southern Balkans, the first skirmishes between Ottoman and Hungarian troops were fought under the Angevins, but the magnitude of the danger was not clear until the defeat of Serbian and allied troops at Kọsovo Polje in 1389. Following the traditions of Hungarian foreign policy and the mood in the country, Sigismund embarked on several offensive forays into the border areas in response to Ottoman incursions into Hungarian territory. In 1395 he called on the chivalry of Europe to confront the infidels. The defeat suffered by the crusaders at Nicopolis on 28 September 1396 cost the lives of many knights, while hundreds of thousands of ducats ended up in the Sultan's coffers as ransom for the notable captives.[29]

Although the defeat did not enhance the king's position at home, it gave him an occasion to propose serious reforms. Military reforms were enacted at a diet in Temesvár (October, 1397), to which, for the first time, so far as is known, the nobles sent regularly empowered deputies from every county. At the same diet Sigismund tried to build an alliance with the county nobles by confirming the privileges of 1222 and 1351 (omitting, however, the clause on the nobles' right of resistance) and by promising to dismiss his foreign counsellors, whom they resented. Their dislike was less motivated by "national" or "ethnic" motives than by the fact that these men owed their position to the king's pleasure and not to noble family connections. In 1401 the king's own party rebelled and took Sigismund captive. Meanwhile a baronial council administered the realm in the name of the "Holy Crown of Hungary." This device proved useful in giving the magnates a legal base of power. It also indicates the progress made during the interregna and under a weak king toward an abstract notion of a state distinct from the person of the ruler. Before the "council of the realm" was able to agree to offer the crown to another prince, Sigismund negotiated his release, making an alliance with his captors and marrying Barbara of Cilli, daughter of the powerful Slavonian lord Count Hermann of Cilli.

The last major challenge to Sigismund's rule came from King Ladislas of Naples (1386–1414), the son of the hapless Charles of Durazzo, who in 1403 tried to renew his father's claim to Hungary. Supported by Rome, where Pope Boniface IX disapproved of Sigismund's leaning towards his Avignonese rival, he landed in Dalmatia accompanied by a papal legate and had himself crowned. He could count on a good number of dissatisfied Hungarian lords who had sworn an oath on the relics of St. Ladislas to abandon Sigismund, but the king's league was more powerful and swiftly restored order. Ladislas

29. See A. S. Atiya, *The Crusade of Nicopolis* (London: Methuen, 1934); Fine, *Balkans*, pp. 408–414, and 424–25; Szakály, "Phases," pp. 74f.

returned to Naples. His Hungarian followers were pardoned by the victorious king, although in subsequent years they lost their offices and most of their properties as well.[30]

Papal support for the pretender offered Sigismund an occasion to proclaim the supreme royal right of patronage in the Hungarian church and to prohibit appeals to Rome. This so-called *placetum regium* (see below, 6 April 1404) was the first step in gaining control of the wealthy Hungarian prelacies. At the Council of Constance, a decade later, Sigismund negotiated an agreement with the college of cardinals confirming his rights over the Church. Although these were soon abrogated by the Holy See, future kings of Hungary wielded considerable *de facto* power in appointing their favorites to lucrative and influential prelatures.[31]

Government and Reforms Under Sigismund

Sigismund was finally in a position to stabilize his rule. In 1408 he united his faithful barons in a formal league, the Order of the Dragon. This knightly order, in the style of the chivalric age, was based on the new aristocracy—the great landowners whose power rested on extensive landed properties including several castles and thousands of tenant peasants. These aristocrats were henceforth regularly called barons, not because they held "baronial offices" (as their predecessors had under the Angevins), but merely because of their wealth and status. The domestic members of the Order of the Dragon held some 70 to 80 castles, far more than the king.[32]

In the subsequent decades Sigismund issued important laws on criminal jurisdiction, coinage and trade, and confirmed the right of peasant tenants to change their lord. He attempted to strengthen the legal and economic position of the towns whose deputies he had consulted on several occasions (see 15 April 1405). The increasing conflicts in Bohemia and Germany, however, often distracted Sigismund as his interests turned more to the west. For years the country was in reality reasonably well governed by the barons of his league. Sigismund's last decades were devoted more to European than to Hungarian matters. The impact on Hungary of the personal union with the Holy Roman Empire (1411-39) needs more study than it has hitherto received. The growing role of legally trained secretaries in the king's council and his secret chancellery, the attempt of Sigismund to centralise the administration of Hungary and his reliance on councillors

30. See Bak, *Königtum*, pp. 35–37.

31. See E. Mályusz, *Das Konstanzer Konzil und das königliche Patronatsrecht in Ungarn* (Bp.: Akadémiai K., 1959).

32. See Fügedi, *Castles*, pp. 123–28.

from burgher and lesser noble backgrounds derive in part from non-Hungarian, Western models.[33]

Sigismund's interest in the cities may have been influenced by his experiences in much more urbanized Bohemia and Germany but was essentially due to his need for regular income and also, once most royal castles had been lost, for fortified bases. Hungary had very few cities in the early fifteenth century: contemporary reports speak of altogether twenty walled ones. These were in fact that handful of urban settlements which enjoyed the privileges of Buda (the only one with more than five thousand inhabitants) and were directly subject to the Master of the Treasury. Each of them was regarded as a corporation and granted equal standing with a nobleman. They were later to be called "royal free cities" and retained their legal, even if not always their economic, privileges into modern times. They included Pozsony (Pressburg, Bratislava), Sopron, Nagyszombat (Tyrnau, Trnava), Kassa (Kaschau, Košice), Bártfa (Bartfeld, Bardejov) and Eperjes (Prešov). A dozen more unwalled cities with one to two thousand inhabitants approximated this status, and Sigismund encouraged the building of walls, e.g. in the case of Kolozsvár (Klausenburg, Cluj). The cities of the Saxon communities in Transylvania with Nagyszeben (Hermannstadt, Sibiu) and Brassó (Kronstadt, Braşov) at their head enjoyed similar rights. The mining towns of northern and northeastern Hungary were under the jurisdiction of the royal chamber, but many of them became alienated in the fifteenth century.

The above list, if projected on a map (see pp. lii-liii), immediately suggests that the limited urban development was motivated by external trade: cities of any importance grew at the gates of trade routes toward Austria, Poland, and the Balkans. There was no such network of cities in the central areas of the country; the old episcopal and comital sees here tended to decline. The close connection with external trade is also obvious from the internal structure of the cities. Their leadership came originally from German *Ritterbürger*, half-adventurers, half-traders, then was taken over by German families engaged in long-distance trade, and finally, occasionally, by mixed groups of merchants from Germany and Hungary. Under the Angevin kings the Italian presence in Buda was conspicuous, but at the end of the century south German entrepreneurs began to take over. Although Sigismund attempted to inhibit trade "with foreigners," the trend to conduct business to the advantage of the south Germans remained unchecked.

Royal support for urbanization was inconsistent. Sigismund's "urban decree" of 1405 attempted to introduce uniform weights and measures based on the custom of Buda and to strengthen urban

33. See E. Mályusz, "Die Zentralisationsbestrebungen König Sigismunds in Ungarn," in *Études historiques* (Bp.: Akadémiai K., 1960) 1: 317–58.

liberties by granting high justice to walled cities and urban privileges to some developing market centers. Yet, only a few years later Sigismund granted seigneurial rights over Debrecen, one of the towns that had just received new liberties, to one of his aristocratic followers. The cities were not united among themselves, were economically too weak to count for much, and, under baronial rule, had little chance to become a political force. Because the kings of the fifteenth century had to resort repeatedly to squeezing out additional revenues by taxing the cities (or imposing "loans" on them), the urban sector was essentially seen as a source of cash and also as valuable military support, without having been the target of conscious economic policies or of significant alliances with the crown.

While the development of "true" cities, in both legal and commercial-industrial terms, lagged behind the countries west of Hungary, the size and number of market centers, in fact overgrown villages, with weekly markets, and occasionally even annual fairs, had grown since the fourteenth century. These market-towns (in Hungarian: *mezővåros*, in the sources mostly *oppidum* in contrast to *civitas*-city, with charter of privilege and self-government) developed from the free villages and the centers of estates of the preceding centuries. They were situated along trade routes, the meeting points of plains and highlands and in specialized agrarian areas (such as stock breading or wine-growing districts). By 1440 about 300, and by 1520 about 800 settlements were so classified, even though probably only 300–400 of these were in any way genuine market centers. *Oppida* did not enjoy urban privileges, although some of them were granted certain autonomous rights by their secular or ecclesiastical lords, and the tenant farmers living in them were often permitted to pay their census in a lump sum. While a typical peasant village comprised not more than 20–30 *portae* (i.e., that many tax units, meaning perhaps twice that number of families), *oppida* counted at least 100 tax units, some even as many as 300–500 *portae*.[34]

Although the negative assessment of Sigismund's achievements which used to dominate textbooks has been revised in recent decades, the king's West European orientation undeniably resulted in losses to Hungary. Among the country's neighbors, Venice was the first to take advantage of the king's many absences to reconquer the Dalmatian territories, based on the claim that Ladislas of Naples "sold them" to

34. On urbanization in medieval Hungary, see Sugár–Hanák, *History*, pp. 57–60; also: E. Fügedi, "Die Ausbreitung der städtischen Lebensform—Ungarns *oppida* im 14. Jahrhundert," in *Stadt und Stadtherr im 14. Jh.*, W. Rausch, ed. (Linz: Wimmer, 1972), pp. 165–92; repr. in *Kings* as ch. 13.

the Signoria in 1409. In 1433 a truce was signed, in which Sigismund accepted the conditions he could not or would not alter. Thus after 300 years Hungary's intermittent presence along the Dalmatian coast ended.

The greatest losses were sustained beyond the Hungarian border. The Ottoman Empire, having recovered from succession struggles, expanded its control in the Balkans as far as the frontiers of the "buffer states" that had for decades protected Hungary from immediate Ottoman attack. The Turks became a direct threat to the kingdom. However, the defeat at Nicopolis showed that offensive actions had little chance of success, and Sigismund appears to have recognized this. Attempts at securing the loyalty of Balkan rulers during the time of Ottoman weakness were partially successful: the ruler of Serbia, the Despot Stephen Lazarević, was a true ally for decades. In Bosnia Prince Hrvoje was also for a time persuaded to join the anti-Ottoman alliance. But suspicion of Hungarian political aspirations prevented later rulers of Walachia and the many decentralized authorities in Bosnia from accepting Hungarian suzerainty or even being drawn in as allies.[35]

Faced with the limited Hungarian influence beyond the border, Sigismund and his barons, above all his Florentine financial councillor and commander, Pipo Scolari, concentrated on building up defenses along the southern frontier. Scolari was given the command over several counties and banats as well as the income of the salt monopoly (which he reformed) to rebuild and reorganize the fortresses of southeastern Hungary (with Temesvár at its center) and to establish a system of defenses along the entire southern border.[36] The keystone of this system, the castle of Belgrade, was acquired by Sigismund in negotiations with Despot Stephen. Scolari's successors, the Tallóci brothers, Ragusans by birth, managed to unify the command of the entire southern defense.[37] For its upkeep they held three banats, forty-four castles, the income from the salt mines, from direct taxes and from several vacant episcopal sees, plus the revenues from the estates of the Hospitallers. Under favorable circumstances the fortresses and the mobile defense forces permitted even offensive actions. Sigismund's achievements and those of his barons show foresight, careful planning, and a determined mastering of resources. The system they built

35. See Fine, *Balkans*, pp. 465–80; Sweeney, "Walachia," p. 501.

36. See Szakály, "Phases," pp. 72–85, Idem, "The Hungarian-Croatian Border Defense System" in Bak-Király, *Hunyadi*, pp. 141–58; on Scolari, see P. Engel "Ozorai Pipo," in *Ozorai Pipo emlékezete* [In Memory of Pipo of Ozora], F. Vadas, ed. (Szekszárd: Béri Balogh Múzeum, 1987), pp. 53–88.

37. See E. Mályusz, "Die vier Gebrüder Tallóci," *Studia Slavica Acad. Sc. Hung.* 28 (1982): 1–66.

protected Hungary from being overrun by the Ottoman army for almost a century.

Albert I (1437–39) and the Double Coronation of 1440

The death of Sigismund in late 1437 initiated a succession crisis, for he was the last member of the House of Luxemburg. Sigismund's only daughter, Elizabeth, was married to Albert V of Habsburg, Duke of Austria. Albert was "elected" king, but the diet insisted that their choice and not Elizabeth's hereditary right, was decisive. Elizabeth and Albert were crowned on New Year's Day 1438. Later, however, while Albert was absent on imperial and Bohemian business (he was, as Albert II, emperor of the Holy Roman Empire), the regiment of the queen and the Garai-Cillei clan triggered a noble reaction. The decree passed by the diet on 29 May 1439 reveals the rise of a new power in the realm: the assembled county nobility. The "election promises" Albert had made to the leading magnates, just like those of his father-in-law half a century before, had been formulated in the interest of the prelates and barons and aimed at dismantling whatever remained of Sigismund's reforms. The law passed at the diet of 1439 altered this agreement by including several clauses which guaranteed the rights of middle and lesser nobles, preserved Sigismund's ecclesiastical reforms, and strengthened the king's hand in granting offices and properties without the approval of the barons.[38]

In 1439 the Ottoman army attacked Serbia, Hungary's ally. The noble levy was called up, but too late to rescue the land of Djuradj (George) Branković, Despot Stephen's successor. Serbia fell, the despot fled to Hungary, and Albert died of dysentery in his camp barely more than two years after his accession to the throne. With the king's demise the smoldering conflict between the court and the county nobility flared up. A few months after Albert's death his widow bore a child, Ladislas, called Postumus. The queen's adherents, the courtly or Habsburg party, led by Ulrich of Cille were supporters of "legitimacy," a Western orientation, and the succession of the infant to the throne. Queen Elizabeth contrived to have the "Crown of St. Stephen" taken from its guardians and had her son crowned with it on 5 May 1440 in Székesfehérvár.

Opponents of the queen and the legitimists, the party of the "soldier barons," and the masses of the nobility in the counties, were more interested in meeting the challenge of Ottoman advance in the south and in the elective principle of kingship. They wanted to have a king on the throne who could actively lead the fight against the Ottomans. They turned to the king of Poland, the young and valiant

38. For this and the following, see Mályusz, "Rendi állam," passim.

Wladislas III, called Jagiełłonczyk. Their asking him to accept the crown was a further demonstration of the diet's claim to elect the monarch. The baronial electors made sure that the Polish king, known as Wladislas I in Hungary, first signed election promises and upon his coronation swore an oath to uphold a set of ancient privileges presented to him by the noble assembly. These privileges included not only the Golden Bull, but also a set of *decreta* issued in assemblies of the late thirteenth century, apparently forgotten for 150 years. These decrees of the time of Andrew III reflected the far-reaching political program of the lesser nobility and clergy, in opposition to the barons (see below 20 July 1440). Since the "Crown of St. Stephen" was in the hands of the queen and her party, Wladislas had to be crowned with another diadem. The estates issued a charter in which they argued that the validity of coronation did not depend on the insignia but on the "will of the gentlemen of the realm" and declared that the coronation of the infant Ladislas with the abducted crown was null and void.[39] Wladislas was crowned on 17 July 1440 with a crown that once adorned a head-reliquary of St. Stephen.

Wladislas I (1440–44) and the Interregnum

The double election led to civil war. When the majority of barons accepted Wladislas and the commanders of his troops, Nicholas of Újlak and John of Hunyad (János Hunyadi), defeated those of the Habsburg barons, a stalemate developed. Most of northeastern Hungary remained in the hands of a Habsburg supporter, Jan Jiskra (or Giskra) z Brandýsa, who ruled that rich territory for decades in the name of the Habsburgs.[40] Some Western towns acknowledged the queen and, after her untimely death, were taken over by her relative, Duke Frederick of Austria, who became the guardian of King Ladislas Postumus.

A decisive battle at Bátaszék (1441) in favor of Wladislas I was the first event of national significance connected with the name of János Hunyadi.[41] He and his son, the future King Matthias I ("Corvinus"), were to define to a great extent Hungary's fortunes for the half century that followed. Hunyadi was a descendant of a Vlach (Romanian) noble family that had moved to Hungary. His father received the estate of Hunyad from Sigismund in 1409. He grew up as

39. This charter, issued the same day as the coronation decree, contains very significant legal and constitutional ideas, but cannot be regarded as law, hence it is not contained in this volume. A new edition of it is in Bak, *Königtum*, pp. 141–43.

40. See *Biogr. Lex.* 2: 269–70.

41. On this and the following, see also P. Engel, "János Hunyadi: The Decisive Years of His Career, 1440–1444," in Bak-Király, *Hunyadi*, pp. 103–27; Held, *Hunyadi*, pp. 80–170.

a retainer of Hungarian barons and prelates, learning the craft of war in Italy and in Sigismund's entourage as "knight of the household." In cooperation with Francis Tallóci, he received commissions at the southern border, and in 1439 was made ban of Severin.

With the fall of Serbia the Ottoman Empire reached the border of Hungary. The defence system built up under Sigismund still protected the frontier, but the "glacis" in front of it shrank from year to year. In 1441–42 Hunyadi, understanding the offensive mood in the country, led counterattacks against the bey of Smederevo and won several battles in Transylvania and Walachia. After decades of defense, Hungarian troops were moving at last into enemy territory: Hunyadi became the idol of the nobility. During 1443–44, in the so-called "long campaign," Wladislas and Hunyadi led a Hungarian army, supported by allies from the Balkans, as far as the Rhodope Mountains, returning only with the onset of winter. This is not the place to rehearse the arguments for and against the decision about the campaign of 1444. The result is well known. On 10 November 1444 the Ottoman army confronted the Hungarian-Polish camp on the Black Sea coast at Varna. Within a few hours the young king and his Polish knights were dead and the greater part of the army fell with them. Hunyadi barely escaped with his life.

After the strong showing of corporate politics at the election of Wladislas it is not surprising that, once he was gone, power would devolve to the barons and nobles. The years that followed Varna witnessed the maturing of the idea of a noble-aristocratic polity and the establishment of aspects of an institutional framework that were to last, *mutatis mutandis*, to the end of Old Hungary in 1848. The underlying idea was that decisions, such as the election and coronation of a king, as in 1440, should be made by a gathering of all propertied men of the realm. The meaning of the term *regnicolae* (in our translation: "gentlemen of the realm"), which as late as the last years of Sigismund's reign could still refer broadly to nobles, freemen, peasants, and settlers, came to be limited to the *possessionati*: noble landowners, the church, the privileged royal cities, and the foreign communities, such as the Germans, called Saxons.

Congregationes generales or diets came to be virtually annual meetings of the upper strata of the nobility with secondary roles assigned to the county delegates, the urban deputies and churchmen. The nobles retained the right to appear personally (*viritim*) at the diet, a right frequently exercised. When major decisions were taken, such as Hunyadi's election to the governorship in 1446, thousands of noblemen assembled on the field of Rákos (at present the eastern side of Budapest).[42] The major cities sent their representatives to the earlier

42. See Gy. Bónis, "The Hungarian Feudal diet (13th to 18th Centuries)," *Receuils de la Société Jean Bodin pour l'histoire comparative des*

diets, but soon realised that it was not worth the expense: their word, a dozen "votes" against the hundreds of the nobles, carried little weight.[43] In fact, the term "estates" in late medieval Hungary should be used in the singular: the nobility counted, legally, as one estate and regarded themselves as the sole speakers for the nation, the representative of the "community of the realm" (*universitas regni*).

The practical power base that supported the corporate idea was the noble corporation of the counties. Since the beginnings of the assemblies of royal servitors in the thirteenth century, an increasing number of tasks of local administration, jurisdiction, peace-keeping, and the authentication of transactions were entrusted to these communities in the fifty-odd counties of Hungary and Slavonia. While the head of the county was still a royal appointee, though usually a local magnate, his deputy, the *vicecomes (alispán)*, tended to be as much a representative of the nobles as of his lord whose retainer he mostly was. He and the elected noble magistrates (*iudices nobilium, szolgabírák*) were in fact the administrators of the smaller units.

In the kingless years after Varna, when the party struggles between Habsburg supporters and their opponents came into the open again, the diet of 1445 worked out a compromise. Negotiators were sent to Frederick III, King of the Romans, to ask for the return of Ladislas Postumus and the territories occupied by the Habsburgs. Awaiting his answer a regency council was nominated and seven captains, including both the Hunyadi and the Habsburg party, were given commission to restore the peace (see below, 1445). The negotiations did not immediately yield fruit; therefore, the June 1446 diet decided to elect Hunyadi regent. He was given many royal rights, but was limited in capital jurisdiction and major donations; these sovereign rights remained with the council or were reserved for the king.

Ladislas V Postumus (1440/53–57)

In 1452 the Austrian estates rebelled against Frederick III and, in concert with the Czech nobility and finally also with the Hungarians, forced him to let his ward go. The Hungarian lords negotiated a settlement with Ladislas, which the diet approved (see below, 1453). A general amnesty was proclaimed, the donations of both King Wladislas and Queen Elizabeth were annulled, and the royal government was restored, but the council of barons retained. There was no talk about a

---

institutions 25 (1965): 287–307; J. Holub, "La représentation politique en Hongrie au Moyen Age," *Études présentés à la Commission Internationale pour l'Histoire des Assemblés d'États*, 18 (1958): 79–121.

43. See A. Kubinyi, "Der ungarische König und seine Städte im 14. und am Beginn des 15. Jahrhunderts," in *Stadt und Stadtherr*, pp. 193–220.

new election or coronation; the corporate program of 1440 was tacitly buried. Hunyadi retained most of his power as "captain general," including the administration of the royal revenues and was granted, instead of his regency, the title of perpetual count of Beszterce.

While in Hungary the rearrangement of forces preoccupied the public life of the realm, the fall of Constantinople in 1453 once more alerted all Europe to the fate of peoples threatened by the Ottoman advance. When in 1456 the Ottoman army besieged Belgrade, the key to Hungary's southern defense system, Hunyadi mobilized some 10,000 soldiers from his estates and retinue, while Giovanni Capestrano, papal legate and inquisitor, called for a crusade in Austria and Hungary. The relief of the castle by the crusaders became a legend in its own time.[44] The victory at Belgrade was the last deed of both Hunyadi and Capestrano. The hero of his country died two weeks later in an epidemic that broke out in the camp, and Capestrano—soon to be venerated as a saint—followed him in a few months.

The events of the following months were as melodramatic as they were historically consequential. In spite of promises to Hunyadi, the king named Ulrich of Cille captain general. Ladislas Hunyadi, elder son of János, seemed to accept the new commander, but on 9 November 1456, his men killed Ulrich in Belgrade. The king, virtually a prisoner of the Hunyadi party, promised amnesty, but as soon as he was able to act freely, he had Ladislas Hunyadi and his brother Matthias arrested; the former was tried in a hurry and executed in March 1457. Thereupon Hunyadi's widow, Elizabeth of Szilágy (Szilágyi), and her brother Michael, drawing upon the enormous economic and human resources, of the family rose against the "treacherous king." The young king fled to Prague, taking Matthias Hunyadi with him. On 23 November 1457, Ladislas Postumus died, not yet eighteen years old.

Legal Developments[45]

Influenced by the study of Roman Law, the last Árpáds were the first Hungarian kings to claim an independent right to issue laws. Beginning with the 1320s, King Charles consciously attempted to regulate legal practice based on his *plenitudo potestatis*. His chancellery announced that "laws spoken by the mouth of the ruler emanate from God" while

44. See Fine, *Balkans*, pp. 568–77.

45. The following is based on the "Einleitung" by Gy. Bónis in *DRH 1301–1457*, pp. 17–30.

his son, Louis, summoned the Neapolitan estates during his brief rule there, in traditional Hohenstaufen spirit, as *lex animata in terris*.[46]

Relatively few records of Angevin legislation have survived. The first legal enactment of the age (1320), for example, was transmitted through a formulary, without formal preface and closing paragraphs. Over centuries the vicissitudes of war, the Ottoman occupation, and pillaging have caused such losses in written records that only a fraction of actual legislation remains. Only references in charters and other records indicate the scope and character of lost legislation. Thus, we know only from passages in later records, citing these regulations, that in 1328 Charles issued some sort of general decree concerning the jurisdiction of seigneurial courts, or that some time before 1382 royal limitations were placed on the practice of granting male inheritance rights to women.

However, a major cause of the dearth of Angevin laws was that statute law (*statuta, decreta*) was still seen as much less important and more ephemeral than either custom, which governed almost the entire private and criminal legal sphere, or the occasional royal decision (*mandatum, edictum*) and privilege granted case by case. Even if fourteenth-century Hungarian rulers announced their right to issue general legal norms (that is, statute law), they did not attempt such wholesale reforms of justice as those of Frederick II in Sicily or of Charles IV in Bohemia. With the exception of the decree of 1351, the entire body of surviving Angevin legislation only treated the administration of justice and monetary issues.

King and Estates

Before the development of the corporate polity of estates (the *Ständestaat*) the circle of those whom the ruler consulted in his legislative function was left entirely to his pleasure. The presence and the participation of a relatively wide and influential segment of the ruling strata must have seemed useful, if only for gaining their support and cooperation in implementing the measures. But a decree issued by the king and his immediate council was not any less valid. The representation of the entire *regnum* (*ország, Land,* in the meaning of politically relevant people), that is, the participation of the diet, was seen as necessary only when matters concerned the renewal of the "liberty of the kingdom."

A kind of hierarchy can be detected among the *decreta*, with those containing the confirmation of liberties at the top. They begin with the

46. See Gy. Bónis, *Die Einflüsse des römischen Rechts in Ungarn* (Milano: Giuffre, 1964); Idem, "Petrus de Vinea leveleskönyve Magyarországon" [The Letter-Book of P. de V. in Hungary], *Filológiai Közlöny* 4 (1958): 188–90.

renewal and expansion of the Golden Bull of 1222 by Louis I in 1351, after the partly successful Neapolitan campaign at the request of "the entire community of the barons, lords, and nobles of our kingdom." After his death Queen Mary in 1384 re-issued that decree, at the request of "two emissaries" of the delegates to the diet, and in her decree of 1385 she renewed it in a general clause. From her charter these highly valued enactments found their way into the decree of the diet of Temesvár (1397), not in their original form, but embedded in other decisions and incorporated into a general ordinance. The older tradition of verbatim copy and re-issue of ancient liberties was again taken up by Albert on 29 May 1439, and continued by Wladislas I in his decree of 20 July 1440.

In contrast to these festive and elaborate privileges of liberty, the Angevin kings also issued decrees on administrative, financial, or other current matters in concert with the council *(prelati et barones)*, occasionally augmented by certain *nobiles* assembled for the occasion. Under Sigismund the circle of those involved in the passing of laws was even more varied. Because of the vagaries of the king-emperor's ecclesiastical policies, the clergy were frequently absent from such gatherings. On the other hand, the more powerful middle-rank nobility called *proceres* or "lords" appear ever more regularly in the preface to decrees, when no diet of county delegates was assembled. The so-called urban decree of 15 April 1405 was enacted "after having called together the emissaries and delegates of cities, towns and free villages;" the decree limiting the *ispán*'s jurisdiction was issued on 23 July 1421, "with prelates, barons and lords" sitting in judgment at the judicial assembly of County Pozsony.

The many absences of Sigismund, the interregna and the period of civil war gave the county nobles a chance to emerge as a necessary partner of the king in legislation; from the mid-fifteenth century onward they could no longer be ignored. In the decades after Sigismund's death one can follow, almost year by year, the development of the estates. The nobility's participation was still irregular in the fourteenth century. In 1351 and 1384 they are implicitly included in the "community of the realm," although we know only from 1385 and 1397 that every county sent four delegates with full powers of those absent. In the decree of 8 March 1435 they are grandly styled as *totum corpus regni representantes*. Nevertheless, urgent matters could be decided by king and council without the nobility, at least until mid-century. A few important *decreta* list the consenting "mightier nobles" individually (1439); from these we can see that they belong to the leading strata of county nobles, some of them even magnates. Delegates of the towns are listed only in decrees with immediate urban relevance (15 April 1405, 1445), although they did participate in the diets of the interregnum.

We have little evidence about the process of legislation from the initial intent to regulate a matter to the final issuing of a law. The initiative could come from the king, his council, or the diet. There is no way to reconstruct the debates of the council: in the records it is always the king's voice we hear, even if he refers to consultation with his lords. Under Sigismund one can begin to discern the profile of one or another influential councillor, not from *decreta*, but from relevant charters bearing their name in the commission-clause. Noble initiative is obvious when a decree is issued at the request of the levy (1324), or in privileges for the nobility (1351, 1384, 1439, 1440) where their *supplicatio* is always explicitly narrated. Clearly, these "requests," which, of course, had significant political weight, were supported in writing. In 1351 the nobles must have had a copy of the Golden Bull of Andrew II, for the confirmations of Louis's decree reproduce a copy of that text; and in 1440 we are told that they had submitted a "booklet" (*libellus*) containing not only the *decreta* of 1222 but also those of 1290, 1298 and 1351. The Hunyadi party arrived with a written program for the 1446 diet, and in 1453 the estates also "presented articles" to the young king. Since the noble community could hardly have had its own writing personnel, one might assume that protonotaries of the royal court helped them—as is proven from later instances—or that notaries in the counties, in convents or chapters, performed such services.

Even if the initiative came from the diet, the formulation of the law was shaped by the royal chancellery, apparently with considerable liberty. Thus the king was able not only to negotiate a compromise with the estates, but also to infuse major or minor corrections into the final text. A good example is the decree of 1397: the nobles at the diet of Temesvár were obviously keen on having their privileges renewed, while the king was more concerned with military and financial reforms. The compromise seems to have entailed the inclusion of the text of the 1222 Golden Bull (by that time barely understood), without its most obsolete parts. However, the final text also dropped the famous *ius resistendi*, so that once promulgated as a royal diploma no one could change it.

Form and Validity of Decrees

Just as the concept of royal legislation remained fluid in this period, so the name for legal enactments lacked uniformity. The vague *statutum seu decretum* in the undated (c. 1320) decree of Charles was used frequently throughout the following century. In the legal records of Charles I the king uses the verb *statuere* for legislating and calls the order of execution a royal edict. The *Decretum Maius* of Sigismund uses the rhetoric of "constitutions, statutes, and laws of eternal validity" (8 March 1435), but in mid-century the more practical *articuli* became

general, sometimes specifying "decreed articles" of law (1447). References to lost decrees often use the generic terms edict and mandate. A few *decreta* of the estates in the mid-fifteenth century (1439, 1444, 1445) contain a special clause in which the estates through their representatives expressly obligate themselves in addition to the sovereign to observe the law.

Similarly, the diplomatic form of the decrees was not uniform. The general will of the ruler appears in the usual form of a charter, as a privilege or letters patent. Full-dress privileges are usually issued for the guarantee of noble liberty: the originals of the decrees of 1351, 1384, and 1435 are sealed with the authentic double seal and contain a full list of dignitaries; however, the 1439 charter, of similar content, is authenticated merely with the privy seal (*sigillum secretum*) for Albert had no great seal. Most other laws of Sigismund (if their original is known) were issued as letters patent. In the turbulent years after 1440 decrees were issued as charters of privilege, but without lists of dignitaries. During the interregnum the charters were sealed with the *sigillum universitatis regni Hungariae* of the estates, but to assure their force, the lords present appended (or at least intended to append) their own seals as well. Hunyadi's decree of 1446 bears his seal as voivode of Transylvania, logically so, for it essentially contains his promise to observe the limits set on the regent's power by the diet. Ladislas V sealed his *decretum* of 1453 with the signet, as he did not have a great seal. The list of dignitaries is not used after 1435, but the clauses or additional charters of greater lords, appended to some mid-fifteenth-century *decreta* may be regarded as serving a similar purpose. All in all, the diplomatic situation is characterised by immaturity, trial and error, and search for forms. This holds true for the so-called commission notes, which begin to appear on mandates and charters around 1330. While the participation of a consultative body was not a prerequisite for validity, some decrees contain beyond the notation "on the lord king's own commission" (e.g., 1421), the additional words "from the deliberations of the prelates, barons, and gentlemen of the realm" (1443).

More frequent legislation, together with wider social participation, seems to have increased the importance of statute law in the fifteenth century. Whereas, references to decrees in charters and mandates are rare in the Angevin age, they increase after 1400 to the point where they become widespread from the 1430s onward. This observation suggests that written law gained in importance (within the limits set by the anarchic conditions of the early fifteenth century). The prerequisite for such a growth was effective promulgation of laws. Notations on the originals of several *decreta* indicate that the counties received copies of the laws and made their contents known. Decrees in council around 1400–20 also prescribed that these should be "proclaimed at large ... at fairs and other public places."

Statute Law and Custom

For an understanding of the place of statute law in the administration of justice we are in the fortunate position of having a near-contemporary treatise about the relationship of different sources of law. There is a three-paragraphs-long gloss on this topic in the so-called Somogyvár Formulary, compiled in the royal court around 1460, but containing texts of earlier origin.[47] The editor dates the passage, on the basis of internal evidence, as mid-fifteenth century. The short treatise establishes a typically medieval co-existence between different legal principles, much in the spirit of the well-known contradiction between old law and new law.[48] First, it prescribes that the judge should apply either local custom or *lex*—which here does not mean positive law, but merely general custom based on ancient legislation—according to the plea submitted by the plaintiff. Statute law cannot be expected to be familiar to all; hence, it may not be applied unless so requested, and no penalty is imposed for the lack of its knowledge. The text continues to explain that the plaintiff can request judgment according to received custom, local usage, royal *decretum*, or general justice. As we have seen, the plaintiff may chose between the first two; the choice between two others, however, is not up to him. Royal decisions, if called upon, have to be applied because of the obligatory submission to secular authority, even if, so it appears, they contradict "good" customary law. Finally, *ius*, divine or natural law, has to be followed above any other prescription, for it expresses those higher values which no medieval person would have challenged.

From these glosses one can appreciate that medieval Hungarian legal practice knew about both hierarchy and competition of sources of law. However, with the exception of *ius*, which probably rarely came into discussion, local and general custom on the one side and royal statute law on the other were pitted against each other. This struggle was not to be decided before the end of the Middle Ages, if then. That law (*lex*) was seen as established custom (*consuetudo*) is reflected frequently in formulae where the two are used synonymously or interchangeably (e.g., in 15 April 1405:17).

There were clear attempts in the fourteenth century to replace custom by statute law, expressed, for example, in the introductions to

47. See Gy. Bónis, "A Somogyvári Formuláskönyv" in *Emlékkönyv Kelemen Lajos születésének 80. évfordulójára* [L. Kelemen Festschrift] (Bucharest: Tudományos K., 1957), pp. 117–33; the MS is in the Bolyai-Library, Tîrgu-Mureş, MS 374; the cited passage on foll. 223v-224v.

48. See H. Krause, "Dauer und Vergänglichkeit im mittelalterlichen Recht" *Zeitschrift der Savigny-Stiftung für Rechtsgeschichte* 75, Germ. Abt. (1958): 206–51; Idem, *Kaiserrecht und Rezeption* Abh. d. Heidelberger Akad. d. Wiss., Phil.-hist. Kl. 1952/1.

Sigismund's decrees of 1405 and to his *Decretum Maius*. It is noteworthy that in the early 1400s the validity of decrees is often stipulated, not merely in terms of "eternal force" but, specifically, "until the present decree of ours is altered or revoked," as in 1404. Similar attempts at defining validity can be seen in 1447:16, where the *decreta* of the previous two years are to remain in force "excepting those which will be changed by more recent laws [*constitutiones*]."

Whether these programmatic statements were indeed able to overrule earlier tradition is highly doubtful. The gloss in the Somogyvár Formulary reflects traditional views: a *decretum* is certainly valid during the life of its author, for the subjects would not dare to oppose the ruling king, but after his death it is subject to the test of "ancient custom." If a royal decree conforms to it, the statute will become *lex*, ancient law and custom; but if not, custom will prevail. Those who wished to counteract this traditional view and enhance the force of statute law seem to have made significant progress toward the end of the fourteenth century. The noble and urban beneficiaries of royal statutes were eager to keep copies of them, as is evident from the surviving copies in the counties of the 1351 decree and from the town archives' retention of the urban decree of Sigismund. The preserved copies were put to good use. For example, 1397:61 mentions that the communities of the counties Zagreb and Körös produced the text of 1351, and 15 April 1405:3 notes that the burghers of Zagreb presented an original statute thirty years after its issue. Similarly, some barons, who—according to the endorsements of some originals—were given copies of laws, kept their originals as well: thus, in 1446 the count palatine was able to issue an authentic transcript of article 8 of the *Decretum Maius*, almost a decade after Sigismund's death.

The statutes most often cited by king and subjects, those which set a deadline, were mainly invoked in cases related to property rights. Thus references to the date for returning to the king's obedience in Sigismund's letter of pardon of 1403 can be found as late as 1409. Several charters mention the (lost) decree of 1405 (before 24 April) about the transumption and revalidation of records lost in the time of troubles, and in 1409 and 1412, general reviews were held on the basis of this decree in Hungary and Transylvania, respectively. Decrees of the diets in the turbulent years after 1440 are often referred to in connection with the repeated deadlines set for the return of usurped estates, which were, *mirabile dictu*, often observed even by powerful nobles. A lost *decretum* (from March 1451) is known to us only from such references. The lesser noble camp applied 1444:25, about the summary citations against violent trespass, again and again, and had some success against the "robber barons." Article 1447:15 was frequently cited even after the accession to the throne of Ladislas V.

Measures once decreed were often repeated in later laws of the fifteenth century, which may mean either that the earlier enactments were not kept or that the authority of the decree was worth something for those benefiting from it. In fact, these two aspects are not mutually exclusive. Such repetitions can be found concerning the right of tenants to change their lords (first in a charter of 3 August 1397, then in 15 April 1405:14–16, and in December 1405:6), concerning the fee for funerals (1351:2, March 1439:34), and regarding chancellery fees (1435:10, 1447:25). Beyond repetitions of particular measures, principles of law were repeated, suggesting that these must have had some impact on the administration of justice. For example, 1397:53 involved for the first time the noble county in the fight against violent trespass, and this article was often cited in later legal records; December 1435:3–4 and its renewal, March 1439:29–30, elaborated on the procedure and strengthened the hand of lesser nobles.

The application of the *non obstante* (notwithstanding) clause allows similarly contradictory conclusions: on the one hand, if the king had the right to issue laws, then he could also disregard them, but, on the other hand, the fact that he had to specify "overriding" a statute suggests the growing significance of the latter. An extreme example is a charter from 1436 in which Sigismund expressly put aside—thirty years later—the application of the above mentioned *deperditum* of April 1405, demanding instead that authentic deeds had to be produced in certain proceedings in favor of a loyal follower.

The increased weight of statute law is also reflected in the more abundant evidence of its implementation. Notes to the decrees contain references to legal practice. We can, for example, follow the implementation of several articles of the decree of 1397, which stipulate the return of illegally seized property. Naturally, in this and similar cases we should not expect strict observance of the law, as would be self-evident in an absolute monarchy or a modern state. Implementation always depended on the efficacy and size of the forces interested in making reality out of a program expressed in the decree. There is evidence for the application, albeit in a skewed way, of 21 December 1404:1 as late as 1437; the prohibition of sitting in judgment *in casu proprio* (1421) was soon interpreted in a much wider sense than originally meant. It is noteworthy that for the implementation of the decree of 1445, a special meeting of certain counties was held, and that this meeting decided upon some modifications, adjusting the law to local custom.

Finally, limitation was placed on all law, statute and customary, by the overriding force of *ius*, which appears in the *decreta* either as divine law or as natural law. The former is often cited in spiritual matters, the latter mostly in charters regarding the rights of women (dowry, filial quarter). To an extent the recurrent formula of the

authenticating chapters and convents, which testify to a legal matter *communi iustitia requirente* (or similar words), is also based on natural law. These institutions were not required by any law to act in this capacity, but did so in the spirit of *suum cuique*.

All in all, the hundred and fifty or so years of legal development reflected in the *decreta* of this volume contained many significant, yet still contradictory, elements that were to be consequential for the future and signalled major steps toward a formalised, professional, and modern system of justice.

Principles of This Edition

In contrast to the first volume of this series, there exists a critical edition of the *decreta* for the period 1301–1457, which was the first volume of the great project of a complete edition of medieval laws, along the lines of the *Monumenta Germaniae Historica, Leges* series. After nearly five decades of editorial preparation by Ferenc Dőry (1875–1960), it was edited by György Bónis and Vera Bácskai in 1976 as *Decreta regni Hungariae. Gesetze und Verordnungen Ungarns 1301–1457* (Budapest: Akadémiai Kiadó), in the series Publicationes Archivi Nationalis Hungariae II, Fontes vol. 11 [henceforth: *DRH 1301–1457*].

The editors of *DRH 1301–1457* decided to go the way of magnanimity, in opposition to the old *Corpus Juris Hungarici*, which contained only the major royal privileges and a few dietal decisions for this period. *DRH 1301–1457* contains all those legal decisions that fit our definition (which, in turn, is indebted to Bónis's understanding of the character of fourteenth-fifteenth-century *decreta*), and also includes surviving fragments of decisions of royal councils or references to lost decrees. By adding the deperdita to the texts that were part of the *CJH/MTvt* and those edited by other historians, the editors of *DRH 1301–1457* documented to the widest possible extent the legislative activity of the period. They interpreted the definition of decree so broadly that even contracts between the king and counts of the chamber for the farmage of the mint (admittedly, our only sources for the highly significant monetary reforms of the early fourteenth century) were included in the chronological sequence. Similarly, significant political documents, such as the draft treaty between the adherents of Queen Mary (and Sigismund of Luxemburg), on the one hand, and those of the Neapolitan claimants, on the other (in the period of contested succession 1385–87), were also deemed to be *decreta*. Only the royal propositions sent to the council or the diet for deliberation were relegated to an appendix, suggesting thus that they are of importance for the study of legal development, but not laws.

When preparing the present volume, we still had the benefit of the counsel of Professor Bónis, who, though seriously ill, assisted us in establishing a corpus according to our common definition of *decretum*, without overburdening this edition with incomplete texts. Since the *DRH 1301–1457*, with its German preface and calendars and Latin texts in critical edition is available for the researcher of details, we agreed to omit from the bilingual edition the fragments and deperdita, referring to them in notes if they are relevant to the understanding of the formally issued and promulgated decrees. Hence, our selection is narrower than that of the *DRH 1301–1457*. However, in order to conform to the principles of edition for Volume 1, we decided to shift from the chronological sequence to the appendix one more document, which Bónis kept among the "full dress" *decreta*: the 1342 cameral contract, deemed to be the most complete text of its kind. The other cameral contracts, preceding and following that of 1342, have been omitted, as they can be consulted in *DRH 1301–1457*. For the sake of economy, passages repeating older laws verbatim were either replaced by brief references to the original text or set in smaller type to indicate repetition.

The Latin text in this volume follows essentially the best reading offered in *DRH 1301–1457*, with the occasional correction of obvious misprints; here and there we opted for a variant listed by the editors as an alternative reading. An exception is the decree of 1411, for which a text, hitherto not utilized in previous editions, was recently discovered. Thanks to the collegial advice of Dr. Iván Borsa of the Hungarian National Archives, we were able to include the reading of this version, as it seems to contain the oldest text. Just as in the first volume, ours is a vulgate edition; the full critical apparatus can be found in *DRH 1301–1457*, where not only textual annotations are given but, in many cases also more detailed references to Hungarian legal practice. We, of course, have added many notes that may help the reader unfamiliar with medieval Hungarian institutions and historical circumstances better to understand text and translation. The Glossary serves the same purpose and is an extended version of that in the first volume adapted to the conditions of the fourteenth and fifteenth century. In the compilation of the Glossary, as well as in the formulation of many explanatory notes, the editors have been greatly assisted by the best expert of the period, Professor Erik Fügedi, whom they wish to thank for his help and critique. Professor Imre Bard, a student of the Sigismundian period, also assisted in the notations.

The English translation of the Latin original posed slightly different problems from those encountered in the first volume. While there we had to work with faulty, often fragmentary, but in the course of the centuries "corrected" texts, here we mostly had originals or near-contemporary copies. Nevertheless, the Latin of the fourteenth-century

and even more of the fifteenth-century writers of the royal chancellery tried our abilities to their utmost. On the one hand, their attempts at rhetorical flourishes, above all in the preambles (*arengae* and *narrationes*) of the laws, do not seem to have been matched by their training in elegant Latin, and many a sentence ended up highly convoluted and, strictly speaking, meaningless, but apparently sounding appropriately festive for their authors. More challenging were those formulae which are well known to us from the royal chancellery of the age and which may have also been mere rhetorical fillings, but may have had some specific meaning no longer obvious to us. An example of this is the recurrent clause regarding some royal decision, made *ex certa nostra scientia* and what we understand as referring in some way to the king's perception of his royal office. We translated it as "in accordance with our understanding of our office," but there is no indication anywhere what exactly is meant by these words.[49] Also, frequent repetitions or even a whole series of synonyms may have had specific legal significance, even if they sound to us as like rhetorical devices. We were obligated to keep these, even if they often cloud the meaning of the passage.

Our major problem of the first volume, the difficulty of rendering in English words, inevitably connected to legal and social development in the British Isles, institutions, social groups, or procedures of a country of widely different traditions, remained with us. True, by the fourteenth century, Hungary was in many respects similar to her Western neighbors, and under Angevin kings and queens, even ruled by a family related to the French, English and Sicilian and other dynasties of the age. Nevertheless, there remained many archaic and locally-grown features that did not resemble closely West European ones to permit naming them with words borrowed from the West. While the officers of the royal household can be called steward, butler, or Master of the Horse, the local representatives of the ruler in the counties were sufficiently specific Hungarian officers, derived from the eleventh century royal retainers, not to be called "counts" or "sheriffs" but rather *ispánok*, even though the Latin texts refer to them as *comites*. To make things more difficult, members of families which often had held the honor of *comes* tended to be called *comites*, whether in office or not: in this case the "title" *count* may reflect the implication well enough to use this translation, but it is still misleading, for there were no "titled nobles" in Hungary until modern times (unless they received a title from abroad).

49. Zs. Teke, in her preface to *Decreta Regni Hungariae 1458–1490* (Bp.: Akadémiai K., 1991), p. xix, suggests that this clause was meant to refer to the king's *absoluta potestas*, but not all instances of its use bear out this interpretation.

Just as in the first volume, we chose to avoid the insertion of an inordinate number of Latin or, for that matter, truly "original" Hungarian terms into the English text, but at the risk of simplification. As discussed above, we did our best to render every term by its closest English equivalent and retained a Latin or Hungarian word only if all our attempts were defeated. In this volume we decided to abandon a translation introduced, reluctantly, in the first, that of *regnicola* as "landed resident." This word was usually used not in its verbatim meaning comprising every inhabitant of the realm, but rather referring only to the politically and legally relevant inhabitants, that is nobles and higher clergy. However, at least until the 1440s this exclusive meaning is by no means consistently applied: *regnicolae* often include all subjects of the king or an undefined great number of them. Unless the context unequivocally suggests the latter, we call them "gentlemen of the realm."

***

While working on the English translation we received much assistance from younger collegues, above all from Thomas Hannon, M.A., who translated several *decreta* of the 1400–57 period in first draft and from Natalie Johnson, who did the same for the fourteenth century texts. However, the major credit for sorting out the difficult Latin clauses and finding not only the best English rendering but often offering valuable comments on issues we might have easily overlooked, belongs to Professor Paul B. Harvey, Jr. Although he joined our team in mid-course, his devotion to the task and his expertise made up for time lost.

The indices were compiled with the assistance of Mr. Balázs Nagy of Loránd Eötvös-University, Budapest (geographical names), and Dr. István Petrovics of Attila-József-University, Szeged (persons). Other colleagues and research assistants who helped in bibliography and related tasks are too numerous to be named. Our thanks go out to all of them. Special thanks are due to Romuald I. Lakowski, who took time off from his studies on Thomas More in order to help us prepare the computer-assisted camera-ready copies of this volume. He also contributed many good suggestions for typography and formating.

Michaelmas, 1991 *János M. Bak–Pál Engel–James Ross Sweeney*

HUNGARY
IN THE 15th CENTURY
0 50 100 km
HOLY ROMAN EMPIRE
AUSTRIA
STYRIA
MORAVIA
TRENCSÉN
ÁRVA
LIPTÓ
TURÓC
ZÓLYOM
NYITRA
BARS
HONT
NÓGRÁD
POZSONY
MOSON
SOPRON
GYŐR
KOMÁROM
ESZTERGOM
PILIS
PEST
VAS
VESZPRÉM
FEJÉR
ZALA
SOMOGY
TOLNA
KUNSÁG
VARASD
KŐRÖS
BARANYA
BODROG
CSONGRÁD
BÁCS
SLAVONIA
VERŐCE
POZSEGA
VALKÓ
SZERÉM
ZAGREB
CROATIA
DUBICA
ORBÁSZ
SZANA
BANATE OF SZREBERNIK
BANATE OF MACSÓ
BANATE OF JAJCA
BOSNIA
SERBIA
OTTOM
ADRIATIC SEA
Danube
Dráva
Sava
Duna
Buda
Pest
Óbuda
Esztergom
Visegrád
Pozsony
Zagreb
Pécs
Fehérvár
Veszprém
Kalocsa
Győr
Sopron
Trencsén
Nagyszombat
Nyitra
Komárom
Segnia (Zengg)
Tenen (Knin)
Vrana (Aurania)
Clissa
Jajce
Szrebernik
16°
18°
20°
48°
46°
44°

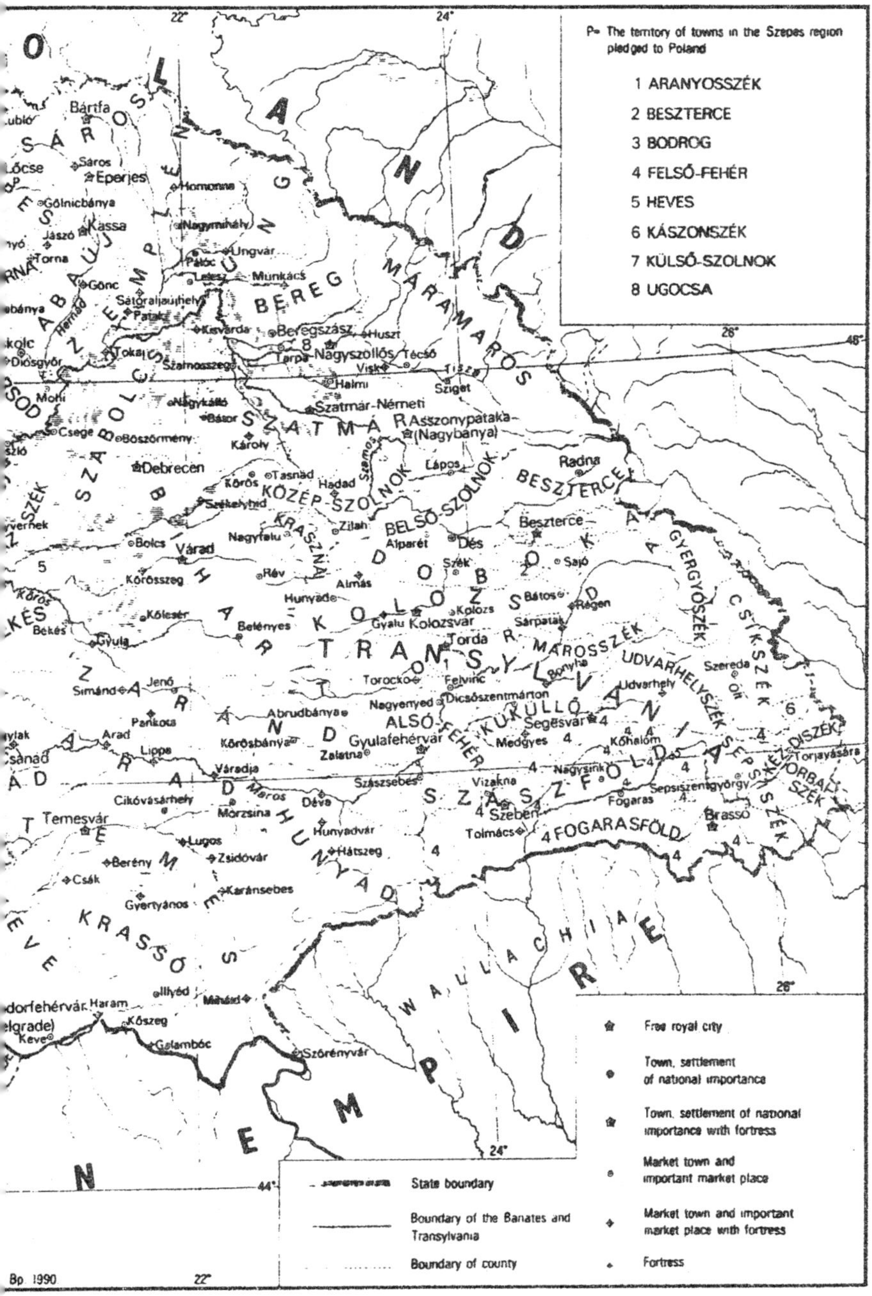

P= The territory of towns in the Szepes region pledged to Poland
1 ARANYOSSZÉK
2 BESZTERCE
3 BODROG
4 FELSŐ-FEHÉR
5 HEVES
6 KÁSZONSZÉK
7 KÜLSŐ-SZOLNOK
8 UGOCSA
POLAND
SÁROS
ZEMPLÉN
UNG
BEREG
MÁRAMAROS
ABAÚJ
SZABOLCS
SZATMÁR
KÖZÉP-SZOLNOK
BELSŐ-SZOLNOK
BESZTERCE
DOBOKA
KOLOZS
KRASZNA
BIHAR
ZARÁND
ARAD
CSANÁD
TEMES
KRASSÓ
HUNYAD
ALSÓ-FEHÉR
KÜKÜLLŐ
MAROSSZÉK
UDVARHELYSZÉK
CSIKSZÉK
GYERGYÓSZÉK
SEPSISZÉK
KÉZDISZÉK
ORBAISZÉK
SZÁSZFÖLD
FOGARASFÖLD
TRANSYLVANIA
WALLACHIA
OTTOMAN EMPIRE
Bártfa
Eperjes
Kassa
Homonna
Nagymihály
Ungvár
Munkács
Sátoraljaújhely
Beregszász
Huszt
Nagyszöllős
Técső
Sziget
Szatmár-Németi
Nagybánya
Debrecen
Várad
Kolozsvár
Torda
Beszterce
Dés
Radna
Gyulafehérvár
Segesvár
Szeben
Brassó
Fogaras
Déva
Temesvár
Lugos
Karánsebes
Arad
Gyula
Nándorfehérvár (Belgrade)
Szörényvár
Free royal city
Town, settlement of national importance
Town, settlement of national importance with fortress
Market town and important market place
Market town and important market place with fortress
Fortress
State boundary
Boundary of the Banates and Transylvania
Boundary of county
Bp 1990

LEGES HUNGARIAE
edendi operi praeest
Peter I. Hidas

Series I

DECRETA REGNI MEDIAEVALIS HUNGARIAE
A.D. 1000–1526

Tomus II

A.D. 1301–1457

critice recensuerunt et Anglice reddiderunt
János M. Bak, Pál Engel, James Ross Sweeney

Paul B. Harvey, Jr.
adjuvante

Salt Lake City
Apud Charles Schlacks, Jr.
MCMXCII

THE LAWS OF HUNGARY

editor-in-chief
Peter I. Hidas

Series I

THE LAWS OF THE MEDIEVAL KINGDOM OF HUNGARY
1000–1526

Volume 2

1301–1457

edited and translated by
János M. Bak, Pál Engel, James Ross Sweeney

in collaboration with
Paul B. Harvey, Jr.

Salt Lake City
Charles Schlacks, Jr., Publisher
1992

(c. 1320)

Vide praefatiunculam et notas infra paginas 155–57.

SECUNTUR TRACTATUS, QUANDO IUDICIA[1] PER HOMINES IUDICIS CURIE REGIE VEL DOMINI PALATINI VEL CONVENTUUM ET IUDICUM NOBILIUM[2] IUXTA HUIUS REGNI CONSUETUDINEM EXIGI SOLENT A CONVICTIS.

Iuxta quam partem est sciendum,[3] quod ante convalescentiam potentie serenissimi principis domini Karuli condam regis Hungarie felicis memorie in diversis partibus ipsius regni non modice insolentie discordie lites et guerre necnon actus potentiales exerceri dinoscebantur, ita videlicet, quod pauperes et inpotentes[4] per divites et potentes absque ulla misericordia opprimebantur, nullaque iustitia vel modica vigebat et regnabat,[5] ideo pretactus dominus rex Karolus prelatorum et regni sui baronum[6] salubri usus consilio super facto exactionis iudiciorum seu birsagiorum[7] talem statutum fecit seu decretum, litteris suis hoc corroborando:

I. Quod dicta iudicia per homines memoratorum iudicis curie seu regni palatini et comitum ac iudicum nobilium non aliter, nisi mediante homine regio sub testimonio alicuius capituli vel credibilis conventus[8] exigi possint a convictis, cuius quidem regalis statutionis hec est forma, quod quandocunque ipsorum iudiciorum exactores ad recipiendum iudicia per suos superiores destinantur, prius litteris regalibus receptis[9] debent transire ad ipsa loca testimonialia, receptisque et adductis secum regio homine et testimonio capituli vel conventus transire debent ad sedem iudiciariam illius comitatus, in quo exigi oporteret iudicia prenotata. Et ibi prius litteris regalibus et registro domini sui superioris,[10] utpote iudicis curie regie vel domini palatini vel comitis et iudicum nobilium, quis scilicet tunc talis exactor fuerit iudiciorum, perlectis et nobilibus illius comitatus in layca lingua reseratis[11] aliquem competentem terminum assignare debent sic notificando et promulgando, ut convicti in iudiciis ad nostram sedem[12] venientes se expedire niterentur iuxta continentiam registri prenotati. Qui si in terminis per eosdem iudiciorum exactores et regium ac capituli vel conventus homines ad id assignatis se expedire curaverint, extunc tales coram dicto regio et capituli hominibus retrahuntur de registro et recipiunt litteras expeditorias[13] exactoris iudiciorum supradictorum, easdemque litteras pro maiori cautela postmodum confirmant in capi-

(c. 1320)

For prefatory and explanatory notes, see below, pages 155–57.

WHAT FOLLOWS DEALS WITH HOW JUDGMENTS[1] (FINES) OUGHT TO BE EXACTED FROM THOSE CONVICTED ACCORDING TO THE CUSTOM OF THIS REALM BY THE MEN OF THE JUDGE ROYAL OR OF THE LORD PALATINE OR OF THE CONVENTS AND COUNTY MAGISTRATES.[2]

Be it known according to this division[3] that prior to the recovery of power by the most serene prince, lord Charles of happy memory, the late king of Hungary, innumerable feuds, wars and violent trespasses were committed in different parts of the kingdom, whereby the poor and the weak[4] were oppressed without any pity by the rich and powerful, and no justice or restraint flourished or prevailed.[5] Therefore, the said lord King Charles, with the beneficial advice of the prelates and barons of his realm,[6] issued this statute or decree concerning the procedure of exacting legal dues or fines,[7] and corroborated it by his letter, as follows:

1. That the said fines are not to be demanded from a convicted party by the men of the aforementioned judge royal, the palatine of the kingdom or county *ispánok* and magistrates in any other way, save with the assistance of the king's bailiff and with the testimony of some chapter or authenticating convent.[8] This royal ordinance should be carried out in this way: whenever collectors of fines are sent out by their superiors to receive fines, they shall go to these places of authentication after having obtained a royal mandate,[9] and then they should proceed accompanied by a royal bailiff and the witness of the chapter or convent to the seat of the court of that county in which the said fines are to be exacted. And there, after the royal mandate and the register[10] of their superior lord (that is, either the judge royal, the lord palatine or the *ispán* and the county magistrates, whichever of them ordered the fines to be collected) have been read and explained in the vernacular[11] to the nobles of that county, they shall assign a suitable time and make it known and promulgate it so that those convicted should come to our seat of justice,[12] and strive to acquit themselves of the fine according to the content of the said register. If the convicted persons take care to acquit themselves within the time assigned by the collectors of fines, the king's bailiff, and the man of the chapter or convent, then these persons should be struck from the register in front of the said men of the king and the chapter and they should receive letters of quittance[13] from the said collectors of fines. For greater surety they should have these letters confirmed afterwards by some chapter or

tulo vel conventu aliquali, plures autem nobiles pro maiori cautela non litteras dictorum exactorum sed in relatione regii hominis et testimonii capituli vel conventus litteras expeditorias eorundem capituli vel conventus recipere procurant pro ipsorum expeditione. Si vero nobiles vel cuiuscunque conditionis homines in iudiciis convicti in termino, ut premissum est, assignato ab eisdem iudiciorum exactoribus se expedire non curaverint, extunc iidem exactores cum predictis regio et capituli hominibus vel conventus transire debent ad possessiones vel loca habitationis hominum in iudiciis convictorum, et in fine ville eorum conscendentes in signum pacis et iustitie hastam cum suo ferro in terram figere[14] et tribus diebus facta legittima amonitione ibi expectare tenerentur solutioni et satisfactioni iudiciorum supradictorum, nil plus nisi victui necessaria recipientes. Et si talis convictus ibi se patienter expedierit, similiter de ipso registro retrahatur et littere expeditorie similiter emanentur, alioquin dictis tribus diebus transactis in rebus suis mobilibus et immobilibus sub federe impignorationis[15] per eosdem iudiciorum exactores inibi recipi debent, quantum equipolleret vel se extenderet ad qualitatem iudiciorum.

II. Secundo est notandum, quod si exactores iudiciorum domini palatini vel iudicis curie regie ad tales processus egrediuntur, tunc regium hominem et testimonium capituli vel conventus quo supra ac hominem comitis necnon unum vel duos ex quatuor iudicibus secum ducere debent pro testimoniis. Qui quidem exactores iudiciorum res pro iudiciis exactas inter se taliter dividere debent, quod primo decimam partem prefatis regio et capituli vel conventus hominibus simul, et tertiam partem comiti et iudicibus nobilium reddere, duas vero partes pro suo superiori debent reservare. Si vero exactores iudiciorum comitis et iudicum nobilium ad tales processus egrediuntur, non sic, sed tantummodo regium hominem et testimonium capituli vel conventus et secum ducere debent et decimam partem exactorum iudiciorum regio et capituli et conventus hominibus reddere, residuum vero inter se dividere debent, sicut est mos eorum.[16] Et tandem in fine, postquam omnia iudicia in tali comitatu egrediuntur et processus eorum rite terminantur, sepedictorum iudiciorum exactores ad ipsum capitulum vel conventum, cuius testimonium ad perficiendum exactionem duxerant,[17] redire et unicuique litteras expeditorias dare tenerentur et pro seipsis etiam recipere ac prenominatis comiti et quator iudicibus nobilium in relatione regii hominis et testimonii dicti capituli vel conventus similiter litteras expeditorias dare tenerentur sic alternatim pro cautela, prout hec et alia et levius lucidius et limpidius in statutis ipsius domini regis Karuli continentur, que quidem statuta in singulis comitatibus regni Hungarie in litteris ipsius domini Karuli conscripta habentur et conservantur.[18]

convent. If several nobles pay a fine, they should arrange to receive a letter of quittance, for greater surety, not from the said collectors, but—on the report of the king's bailiff and the witness of the chapter or convent—from the same chapter or convent for their quittance. If, however, nobles or men of whatever station convicted of a fine do not care to come to acquit themselves within the said time assigned by the collectors of fines, then these same collectors with the said men of the king and of the chapter or convent should go to the estates or places of residence of the men convicted of fines. When arriving at the edge of the village they shall thrust a spear with its head into the earth as a sign of peace and justice[14] and, having given legitimate warning, ought to await for three days in that place payment and satisfaction of the said fines, receiving nothing but the necessities of life. And if such a convicted man has submissively acquitted himself, his name is likewise to be stricken from the register and a letter of quittance is to be issued in the same way. Otherwise, after the said three days have passed, sufficient movable and immovable property ought to be taken as security[15] by the same collectors of fines, as is equivalent to, or amounts to, the sum total of the fines.

2. Secondly, it is to be noted that if the collectors of fines of the lord palatine or the judge royal go out to such proceedings, then they ought to take with them the king's bailiff and the witness of the chapter or convent (as above), as well as the *ispán*'s man and one or two of the county magistrates as witnesses. These collectors of fines ought to divide among themselves in this manner the property seized in judgment: to give first a tenth to the aforementioned king's bailiff and likewise to the man of the chapter or convent, and then one-third share to the *ispán* and the magistrates, while two shares shall be reserved for their lord. If, however, only the fine-collectors of the *ispán* and of the noble magistrates go out to such a proceeding, they shall not so divide, but—as they ought to take with them the king's bailiff and also the witness of the chapter or convent—they shall give a tenth to the men of the king and of the convent or chapter, and divide the rest among themselves as is their custom.[16] And finally at the end, when all fines are exacted in a county and all these procedures duly completed, the collectors of the oft-mentioned fines should return to the chapter or convent, the witness of which assisted them in accomplishing the collection, to give to each other, and receive for themselves, a letter of quittance; similarly, they should give letters of quittance mutually for surety to the aforementioned *ispán* and the four magistrates, on the report of the king's bailiff and the evidence of the said chapter or convent,[17] just as these and other things are more clearly, lucidly, and plainly contained in the statutes of the lord King Charles, which are kept and preserved in every county of the Kingdom of Hungary, written out in the edicts of lord Charles himself.[18]

10 Augusti 1324

Vide praefatiunculam et notas infra paginas 158–59.

Nos Karolus dei gratia rex Hungarie significamus, quibus expedit, presentium per te[norem] universis, quod prelati et universi nobiles regni nostri nobis [in] partibus Transilvanis[2] prope Cybinium in expeditione generali[1] existentibus ad nostram accedentes presentiam sua nobis conquestione significare curarunt, quod apud nonnullos iudices et comites parochiales in regno nostro et specialiter in comitatibus Wesprimiensi et Zaladiensi huiusmodi consuetudo, imo potius corruptela in regnicolarum grave dispendium et iacturam iam inolevisset, ut nisi iurans vel prestans sacramentum,[3] similiter et sui compurgatores vel codepositores iuramenti per uniformam verborum prolationem ut preiurans,[4] et eadem verba et eosdem singulos articulos in receptione iuramenti[5] iuxta formam contestate litis propositos singillatim resummendo iuraverint, extunc iurans cum suis codepositoribus iuramenti tanquam periurii reputantur et tamquam succumbentes in causa pro convictis habentur, nec etiam iurantes, si in iurando verba iuramenti contingenter variaverint vel si verba singula et singulos articulos[6] in receptione iuramenti propositos singillatim resummere nequiverint, ad resummendum et reiterandum ipsa verba et eosdem articulos amplius admittuntur, et sic plurimi causedicorum, alii in personis, alii possessionibus et nonnulli bonis omnibus extitissent hactenus contra iustitiam indebite condempnati. Per eosdem itaque prelatos et nobiles et specialiter pro parte venerabilis patris domini Herrici, dei gratia episcopi Wesprimiensis, aule domine r[egi]ne, consortis nostre karissime cancellarii, dilecti et fidelis nostri[7] nobis fuit humiliter suplicatum, ut super hoc iusto eis ac debito statuti moderamine dignaremur de benignitate [regia] providere. Nos itaque, qui ex susscepti regiminis [debito subditorum] nostrorum gravamina sublevare, eosque sub iuris et iustitie regula gubernare debemus, attendente[s, quod] regnicole nostri[8] et specialiter populi ecclesie et episcopatus Wesprimiensis pretextu huiusmodi abusive consuetudinis atque corruptele indebite et calumpniose opprimuntur, de prelatorum et [bar]onum nostrorum consilio et consensu penitus abolentes consuetudinem huiusmodi provida deliberatione duximus statuendum, ut iurantes seu deponentes iuramentum, tam actor, quam reus,[9] cum suis codepositoribus iuramenti in verborum succincta et compendiosa prolatione sua deponant iuramenta sub hac infrascripta forma exemplari, videlicet:

10 August 1324

For prefatory and explanatory notes, see below, pages 158–59.

We, Charles, by the grace of God, king of Hungary, make known to all to whom it may concern through the contents of these presents that the prelates and all nobles of our realm, who approached our presence while we were encamped on a general campaign[1] in Transylvania[2] near Nagyszeben, reported to us, complaining that among many judges and county *ispánok* of our kingdom, especially in the counties of Veszprém and Zala, such a custom or rather such an abuse had now become established, to the grievous loss and detriment of the people, so that if someone swearing or taking an oath,[3] as well as his oath-helpers or those swearing with him, should not swear by uttering words identical to those read to him at the taking of the oath[4] and did not repeat the very same words and the same individual items one by one in accordance with the subject matter of the litigation as established at the admission of the oath,[5] then the oath-taker and his oath-helpers would be considered to be perjurers and to have failed the oath and lost the case. Nor are the oath-takers permitted to repeat and state again the very words and the same items, if, in swearing the oath, they contaminated the oath by varying the wording or if they were unable to repeat word for word the language and specific items[6] prescribed at the admission to the oath. Thus, many litigants have hitherto been convicted unfairly and contrary to justice, some in their person, some in their estates, and not a few in all of their goods. Therefore, these same prelates and nobles and especially the venerable father Lord Henry, by the grace of God bishop of Veszprém, chancellor of the court of the Lady Queen, our dearest consort,[7] and our well-loved and faithful subject, besought us humbly that we should deign to make just and proper provision from royal benevolence, concerning these matters. And so we, who have undertaken the governance, are obligated to relieve the complaints of our subjects and to govern them under the rule of law and justice, considering that the inhabitants of the realm[8] and especially the people of the church and bishopric of Veszprém are improperly and scandalously oppressed on the pretext of this type of abusive custom, with the advice and consent of the prelates and our barons, we have decided, after careful deliberation, to abolish this sort of practice, and we decree that those swearing or taking an oath, plaintiff as well as defendant,[9] together with their oath-helpers, should take their oaths by a brief and concise speaking of words, according to the model form written below:

Petrus actor iurans contra Martinum reum dicat per hec verba: Ego Petrus iuro in animam meam, ut sic me deus adiuvet, quod Martinus in hiis, que super eum requisivi in iudicio, culpabilis mihi est, seu reus alias tenetur mihi in pecunia quam ab ipso petivi in iudicio Et similiter iuratur in ceteris casibus.

Item Martinus reus iurans contra Petrum actorem dicat per hec verba: Ego Martinus iuro in animam meam, ut sic me deus adiuvet, quod in hiis, que Petrus requisivit super me in iudicio, innocens sum et immunis, alias non teneor sibi in aliqua pecunie quantitate. Et similiter in omnibus casibus deponitur iuramentum.

Hoc expresso, quod si verba iuramenti non possent per uniformam verborum prolationem ad iuramentum proferri, saltem per alia quecunque verba eundem dumtaxat sensum importantia proferantur, et si in prolatione eorundem verborum deficerent vel in proferendo variaverint, ea resummendi et reiterandi semel, secundo et tertio liberam habeant facultatem. Unde palatino, iudici curie nostre, comitibus et universis iudicibus et iustitiariis in regno nostro nunc et pro tempore constitutis, quacunque dignitate, honore, nomine et titulo prefulgentibus, quibus presentes ostenduntur, regio edicto firmiter damus in mandatis, quatenus regnicolas nostros et specialiter universos populos ecclesie et epscopatus Wesprimiensis, tam in Wesprimiensi et Zaladiensi, quam in aliis comitatibus constitutos, cuiusvis status et conditionis ex[istant, contra] formam presentis edicti et statuti nostri in depositione et exactione iuramenti non debeant in aliquo aliquatenus aggravare, sed presens edictum et statutum-------[sub] pena capi[tis] et [sui hono]ris privatione debeant inviolabiliter observare. Quicunque autem secus facere presumpserit, regiam indignationem se n[overit incur]surum. [Datum-------] in festo sancti Laurentii martyris, anno domini M^o^CCC^o^ vicesimo quarto.

Peter, the plaintiff, testifying against Martin the defendant, should say these words: I, Peter, swear on my soul, so help me God, that in these things of which I have accused him at law Martin has offended against me, or, alternately, the defendant owes me money which I sought from him at law. And let a similar oath be sworn in other cases.

Then, Martin, the defendant, testifying against Peter, the plaintiff, should say these words: I, Martin, swear on my soul, so help me God, that I am innocent and guiltless of these things of which Peter has accused me at law, or, alternately, I do not owe him any amount of money. And the oath is to be similarly sworn in all cases.

Let it be stated that if they are unable to speak the words of the oath word for word by an identical recital of words, at least the important items should be stated in other words, provided that the sense is the same, and if anyone should fail in the recital of words or should mix them up in quoting, he should have the unimpeded opportunity of at once reiterating and repeating them a second and a third time. Therefore, to the palatine, our judge royal, to the *ispánok* and to all the judges and justices of our kingdom, who currently and for the moment hold office of whatever dignity, honor, name, and title they might have, to whom these presents are shown, we firmly command by royal edict that they shall not in any way oppress the inhabitants of the realm of whatever station or condition and especially the people dependent on the church and bishopric of Veszprém residing in the counties Veszprém and Zala or elsewhere, contravening the prescriptions of our present edict and statute concerning the taking and receiving of oaths, but they are bound to observe unchanged the present edict and statute . . . under the threat of capital punishment and the deprivation of their honor. Moreover, whoever would dare to contravene this edict should know that he will incur royal displeasure upon himself. Given . . . on the feast of St. Lawrence, the martyr, the year of Our Lord one thousand three hundred and twenty-four.

31 Octobris 1328

Vide praefatiunculam et notas infra paginas 160–61.

[C]arolus dei gratia Hungarie, Dalmatie, Croatie, Rame, Servie, Gallitie, Lodomerie, Comanie Bulgarieque rex, princeps Sallernitanus et honoris Montis Sancti Angeli dominus[1]. Omnibus Christi fidelibus presentibus pariter et futuris presentium notitiam habituris salutem in omnium salvatore. Ad petitiones fidelium tanto benignius regia debet condescendere celsitudo, quando id petitur, per quod regno prospicitur et corone. Proinde ad universorum notitiam harum serie volumus pervenire, quod quia nobiles de comitatu Scepesiensi[2] fideles nostri suo et omnium hominum cuiusvis status in eodem comitatu existentium nomine ad nostram accedentes presentiam nostre maiestati declararunt, ut inter ipsos talis calumpniosa consuetudo ymo potius quedam corruptela haberetur, ut cum quilibet alterum in causam coram quovis iudice attraxerit et quamvis suam litem per plurimos articulos et verborum multiplicationem contra eum proposuerit, tandem si cuiusquam partium litigantium iuramentum deponere adiudicatum extiterit ipsi plurimi et multiplicati articuli in iudicio propositi in depositione seu serie iuramenti parti iuramentum deponere debenti omnino seriatim comprehendere et repetere committerentur, in qua siquidem huius modi iuramenti plurimis articulis in lite propositis multiplicati depositione fere omnes convincerentur,[3] petentes a nostra celsitudine humiliter supplicando, ut quandam formam moderatam iuramenti perpetuo stabilem sub verborum collecta et succincta prolatione ipsorum multiplicatorum sensum articulorum plene comprehendentium regia auctoritate statueremus, ne amplius per huius modi calumpniosam consuetudinem aliquibus periculum possit in depositione iuramenti evenire.

Nos igitur ex regia pietate de qua debet nasci iustitia singularis et subiectorum onera sublevari, petitioni dictorum fidelium nobilium aures benignas inclinantes et eam—quia iusta et legitima erat—diligenter ad effectum perducere cupientes una cum prelatis et baronibus regni nostri nobiscum in partibus Transsilvanis cum valido exercitu existentibus decernentes cunctis iuramentum deponere debentibus hanc specificam et exemplarem formam despositionis iuramenti perpetuo observandam duximus statuendam.

Quod si Paulus agens contra Nicolaum defendentem iurare debebit qualiscunque sit sua actio et per quemcunque iudicem regni nostri existat iudicata iuret in hec verba dicens: Deus me ita adiuvet, quod

31 October 1328

For prefatory and explanatory notes, see below, pages 160–61.

Charles, by the grace of God, king of Hungary, Dalmatia, Croatia, Rama, Serbia, Galicia, Lodomeria, Cumania, and Bulgaria, prince of Salerno, and lord of the Honor of Monte Sant'Angelo,[1] to all the faithful of Christ, present as well as future, to whose notice these presents may come, greetings in the Savior of all. The royal eminence ought to respond to the petitions of his faithful subjects all the more kindly when the kingdom and the crown profit by what is requested. Therefore, we wish to notify everyone by these words that our faithful subjects, the nobles of the county of Szepes,[2] approached our presence in their own name and in that of all men of whatever station in the county. They declared to our majesty that among them such a scandalous practice or rather such a corrupt procedure existed that when someone hauled another before a judge in a lawsuit and laid out his charge against him openly and in many particulars and a great number of words, then, when finally an oath was judged to be taken by one of the litigant parties, these several and numerous items presented in the trial have to be completely understood and sequentially repeated when taking or speaking the oath by the party who has to take the oath. The result is that nearly everyone is convicted when the swearing of oaths is complicated by numerous items presented in a lawsuit.[3] They, humbly beseeching our eminence, requested that we establish for all time by royal authority a simplified form of oath of a succinct and brief utterance fully containing the sense of these multiple items, lest by this kind of scandalous practice people taking the oath be exposed to further dangers.

We, therefore, from royal compassion, from which particular justice in particular instances ought to arise and which ought to relieve the burdens of the subjects, incline benign ears to the petition of the said faithful nobles; and, since that petition was just and legitimate, we, sincerely desiring to fulfill it, decided, together with the prelates and barons of our kingdom who accompany us with a strong army in Transylvania, to decree for perpetual observance that all those who have to swear an oath should follow this specific and exemplary form of taking the oath.

That if Paul, suing Nicholas, the defendant, must swear an oath, whatever his suit may be and by whichever judge of our realm the oath is granted, he should swear in these words, saying: So help me God,

Nicolaus in his omnibus, que contra ipsum in iudicio proposui, mihi reus est vel tanta quantitate pecunie sue tali re tenetur.

Consequenter quidem quilibet de coniuratoribus suis dicat: Deus me ita adiuvet, quod Nicolaus in his omnibus, que Petrus[4] in iudicio contra ipsum proposuit, reus est vel tanta quantitate pecunie seu tali re sibi tenetur.

Item e converso si Nicolaus defendens contra Petrum agentem seu actorem iurare debebit iuret isto modo dicens: Deus me ita adiuvet, quod in omnibus per Petrum in iudicio contra me obiectis inculpabilis sum vel nulla quantitate pecunie seu re teneor sibi aut tanta pecunia seu tali re teneor sibi.

Consequenter autem quilibet de suis coniuratoribus dicat: Deus me ita adiuvet, quod Nicolaus in his omnibus, que Paulus in iudicio contra ipsum proposuit inculpabilis est vel sibi in nulla quantitate pecunie seu re tenetur aut tanta pecunia tenetur.

Hoc specialiter declarato, quod si quis iurans vel aliquis de suis coniuratoribus linguam habens impeditam etiam prescriptam moderatam formam depositionis iuramenti per uniformem verborum prolationem dicere non posset, sed per alia verba eundem sensum compleverit, pro iurato habeatur vel si prima vice quisquam iurans vel eius coniurator suum iuramentum premisso modo deponere nequiverit, secunda vice et tertia non tamen pluries repetendi suum iuramentum liberam habeat facultatem.

Super eo quoque ipsis nobilibus nobis querelantibus, ut ipsorum iobagiones[5] ad nostram seu palatini vel comitis parochialis aut iudicum nobilium presentiam citarentur, statuimus committentes, ut quilibet iobagiones habentes in omnibus causis exceptis causis furti, latrocinii vel violentie seu incendii contra quospiam ipsi iidem suos iobagiones debeant et possint iudicare et nullus valeat eos ad alterius iudicis presentiam evocare[6]; qui tamen ex parte iobagionum suorum si cuiusquam in reddenda iustitia negligentes extiterint, non sui iobagiones, sed ipsi idem ad presentiam ordinarii iudicis sui evocentur eo facto[7].

In cuius rei memoriam firmitatemque perpetuam presentes concessimus litteras nostras privilegiales novi et autentici sigilli nostri duplicis munimine roboratas. Datum per manus discreti viri magistri Andree prepositi ecclesie Albensis aule nostre vicecancellarii dilecti et fidelis nostri anno Domini M°CCC° vicesimo octavo pridie Kalendas Novembris, regni nostri anno similiter XX° octavo venerabilibus in Christo patribus et dominis fratre Ladizlao Colocensi archiepiscopo et aule nostre cancellario, Mesko Nitriensi, Benedicto Chanadiensi, Nicolao Iauriensi, Georgio Sirmiensi, Ladizlao Quinqueecclesiensi, Iwanka Waradiensi, fratre Petro Boznensi, Laurentio Waciensi, Andrea

that in all these things which I have affirmed against him at law, Nicholas is an offender against me, or owes me such and such an amount of money or such and such an item.

Subsequently anyone from among his oath-helpers should say: So help me God that in all these things which Peter[4] has affirmed against him at law Nicholas is the offender, or owes him such and such an amount of money or such and such an item.

Then, on the other hand, if Nicholas, the defendant, must swear against Peter, who sues him as plaintiff, he should swear in this manner, saying: So help me God that in all these things which Peter cited against me at law I am faultless, or I owe him no amount of money, or owe only so much money, or such and such an item.

Subsequently anyone from among his oath-helpers should say: So help me God that in all these things which Paul cited against him at law, Nicholas is faultless, or he owes him no amount of money, or nothing, or owes only so much money.

Let it be explicitly stated that if anyone who takes an oath or any of his oath-helpers is hindered in his speech and is not able to say even the aforesaid reduced form of the deposition of the oath by uttering the selfsame words but has fulfilled the same meaning by other words, he is to be held to have sworn the oath, or if the first time anyone swearing or his oath-helper was not able to take the oath in the aforesaid manner, he should have leave to repeat his oath a second and a third time, but not more.

Concerning that other matter about which these nobles also complained to us, namely, that their tenant peasants[5] were being summoned to our presence or to that of the palatine or of the *ispán* of the county or of the noble magistrates, we have decided to establish that all those having tenant peasants should themselves be allowed and obligated to judge their tenants in all cases except cases of theft, robbery, assault or arson committed against anyone, and no one shall have the right to summon them before another judge.[6] However, anyone who should be negligent in rendering justice in regard to his tenant peasants, he himself and not his peasants is to be summoned about this to the presence of his justice ordinary.[7]

For the firm and perpetual memory of which we have granted our present letter of privilege validated by the affixing of our new and authentic double seal. Given by the hand of the prudent master Andrew, provost of the church of Székesfehérvár, vicechancellor of our court, our beloved and faithful subject, in the year of the Lord one thousand three hundred twenty-eight, the day before the Kalends of November, in our regnal year likewise the twenty-eighth, when the following venerable fathers in Christ and lords felicitously governed the churches of God: friar Ladislas archbishop of Kalocsa and chancellor of our court, the bishops Meskó of Nyitra, Benedict of Csanád, Nicholas of

Transsilvano, Henrico Wesprimiensi, Chanadino Agriensi, et Ladizlao Zagrabiensi episcopis ecclesias Dei feliciter gubernantibus, magnificis viris Iohanne palatino et comite Simigiensi, Demetrio magistro tawarnicorum nostrorum, Thoma woiwoda Transsilvano, Mykch bano totius Sclavonie, Paulo iudice curie nostre, Dyonisio dapiferorum, Stephano agasonum nostrorum magistris, magistro Willermo comite Scepesiensi, Nicolao comite Posoniensi et aliis quam pluribus regni nostri comitatus tenentibus et honores.[8]

Győr, George of Szerém, Ladislas of Pécs, Ivánka of Várad, friar Peter of Bosnia, Lawrence of Vác, Andrew of Transylvania, Henry of Veszprém, Csanád of Eger, and Ladislas of Zagreb, and when the honorable lords John, count palatine and *ispán* of Somogy, Demetrius Master of our Treasury, Thomas voivode of Transylvania, Mikcs ban of all Slavonia, Paul our judge royal, Denis the steward, Stephen Master of our Horse, master William *ispán* of Szepes, Nicholas *ispán* of Pozsony and many others holding counties and honors in our kingdom.[8]

11 Decembris 1351

Vide praefatiunculam et notas infra paginas 162–68.

Lodouicus dei gratia Hungarie, Dalmatie, Croatie, Rame, Seruie, Gallicie, Lodomerie, Comanie, Bulgarieque rex, princeps Salernitanus et honoris montis Sancti Angeli dominus,[1] omnibus Christi fidelibus presentibus pariter et futuris presentium notitiam habituris salutem in eo, qui regibus dat feliciter regnare et victoriose triumphare. Tronus et potentia regalis dignitatis tunc dinosscitur roborari, cum subditorum quieti et tranquilitati provida circumspectione providetur, ipsisque digno remunerationis bravio in libertatibus largiendis, ymo etiam per alios reges pia consideratione institutis confovendis necnon confirmandis liberaliter respondetur. Nam observantia fidei, sui trahens originem, debitum rationis native legibus, stabilis perseverat,[2] cum benivolentia principis in suos ostensa regnicolas sic semper coalesscit in subditos, ut nisi vite suffocetur igniculus in corpore, vigor fidei non lentesscit. Eapropter ad universorum notitiam harum serie volumus pervenire, quod baronum necnon procerum et nobilium regni nostri cetus et universitatis ydemptitas[3] nostrum regium conspectum adeundo, fidelitatibus suis et fidelium servitiorum preclaris meritis in cunctis nostris et regni nostri negotiis prosperis et adversis cum sumpme fidelitatis studio et votiva diligentia nostre maiestati exhibitis et inpensis declaratis et nostram in memoriam revocatis, exhibuerunt nobis quasdam litteras privilegiales illustrissimi principis domini Andree, tertii Bele regis filii, olym incliti regis Hungarie, avi et predecessoris nostri pie recordationis aurea bulla sua roboratas, libertates ipsorum per sanctissimum Stephanum Hungarice gentis regem et apostolum,[4] ut predicte littere declarabant, ipsis institutas innovantes et confirmantes tenoris subsequentis, supplicantes unanimiter et conformiter nostre humiliter maiestati, ut ipsas acceptantes, ratificantes et approbantes presentibus de verbo ad verbum transsumpmi faciendo simul cum omnibus libertatibus eorum in eisdem expressis, excepto solummodo uno articulo in subsequentibus declarando, confirmare et easdem libertates in dictis litteris expressas ex regie benignitatis clementia auctoritate regia innovando ipsos in eisdem perempnaliter fruituros et gavisuros litteris nostris privilegialibus mediantibus stabilire dignaremur. Quarum tenor talis est:

11 December 1351

For prefatory and explanatory notes, see below, pages 162–68.

Louis, by the grace of God king of Hungary, Croatia, Rama, Serbia, Galicia, Lodomeria, Cumania, and Bulgaria, prince of Salerno and lord of the honor of Monte Sant'Angelo,[1] to all of Christ's faithful, both present and future, to whose notice these presents may come, greetings in Him who grants to kings a felicitous reign, and triumphant victory. The throne and power of the royal majesty are recognized as strong when the royal majesty maintains by provident foresight the peace and tranquility of its subjects and when those subjects are granted, as a deserved reward, expanded liberties, as well as the acknowledgment and confirmation of privileges given them with dutiful consideration by previous kings. For the preservation of loyalty, drawing on its own origin as something arising from the innate laws of reason, remains steadfast and thus always becomes firmly established among subjects when the prince exhibits benevolence toward his own gentlemen of the realm, with the result that the strength of loyalty does not weaken unless the flame of life is extinguished in the body.[2] Therefore, we wish to bring to the notice of all by these presents that the community and total university of the barons, nobles, and lords of our kingdom[3] appeared in our royal presence, where they demonstrated and recalled to our memory their loyalty, the burdens they had undertaken, and the outstanding merits of their steadfast services carried out with consummate zeal, loyalty, and devoted attention to our royal majesty in all our affairs and in those of the kingdom, in good times and bad. They showed us a certain charter of privilege from the most illustrious prince Andrew, son of king Béla III, once renowned king of Hungary, our ancestor and predecessor of revered memory. This charter, containing the matters set out below, is validated by his golden bull and renews and confirms the liberties granted to them, according to the said charter, by St. Stephen, king and apostle of the Hungarian people.[4] They humbly, with one voice and one wish, besought our majesty that we deign to affirm the charter by accepting, ratifying, and approving it, and causing it to be transcribed word for word together with all their liberties contained therein (with the exception of only one article, as stated below); and by renewing those same liberties contained in the said charter, we confirm in accordance with the clemency of royal benevolence and through our royal authority, by means of our own charter of privilege, their right to hold and enjoy those liberties in the future in perpetuity. The content of that charter is this:

(Decretum a. 1222, Aurea Bulla nominatum.)

Nos igitur petitioni dictorum baronum, procerum et nobilium regni nostri aures exaudibiles regio cum favore inclinantes, consideratis et in memoriam revocatis fidelibus obsequiis et sincerissimis complacentiis eorundem, quibus in cunctis nostris et regni nostri negotiis prosperis pariter et adversis, specialiter vero in sumpmenda vindicta innoxii sanguinis olym domini Andree, Jerusalem et Sycilie regis, fratris nostri karissimi beate recordationis, cuius dire necis acerbitas fere totius orbis fines seu plagas propulsavit,[5] ad dictum regnum Sycilie nobiscum proficisscendo, inopinatis fortune casibus et variis personarum periculis sumpma fidelitate fulti intrepide se submittendo nostre maiestati studuerunt complacere et se reddere utique gratiosos et acceptos, volentes voto ipsorum gratiose occurrere et eorum beneplacitum adimplere, ut ipsos ad similia fidelitatis opera exercenda devota mente incitemus, predictas litteras ipsius domini Andree regis, avi et predecessoris nostri karissimi aurea bulla sua roboratas, omni penitus suspicione carentes de verbo ad verbum presentibus insertas acceptantes, ratificantes et approbantes, simul cum omnibus libertatibus in eisdem expressis, excepto solummodo uno articulo modo prenotato de eodem privilegio excluso, eo videlicet, quod nobiles homines sine herede decedentes possint et queant ecclesiis vel aliis, quibus volunt, in vita et in morte dare vel legare, possessiones eorum vendere vel alienare, ymo ad ista facienda nullam penitus habeant facultatem, sed in fratres, proximos et generationes ipsorum possessiones eorundem de iure et legitime, pure et simpliciter absque contradictione aliquali devolvantur,[6] ut tenor continet privilegii bullati domini Andree regis supradicti, confirmantes et easdem libertates de beneplacita voluntate serenissime principisse domine Elyzabeth, eadem gratia regine Hungarie, genitricis nostre karissime[7] ac de consilio eorundem baronum nostrorum ex regie benignitatis clementia innovando ipsos in eisdem perempnaliter commisimus fruituros et gavisuros. In super pro tranquiliori statu et pacifico comodo eorundem regnicolarum nostrorum, de voluntate eiusdem genitricis nostre et consilio eorundem baronum nostrorum, ipsis ex solita liberalitate huiusmodi libertates infrascriptas superaddendo duximus concedendas:

I. Quod si prelati vel aliqui viri ecclesiastici contra nobiles regni nostri in aliqua causa in presentia alicuius iudicis regni nostri processerint et litem habuerint, tunc pro causa, pro qua agitur, lite pendente interdictum in eos ponere vel contra ipsos sententiam excommunicationis non possint promulgare, sicut hactenus usi sunt et consueti, absque scitu et notitia regie maiestatis.[8] Et si iidem viri ecclesiastici seu prelati tramite iuris observato in alicuius regii iudicis

(Decree of 1222, the Golden Bull of Andrew II)

We, therefore, having listened with royal favor to the petition of the said barons, lords, and nobles of our kingdom, having considered and recalled to our memory their faithful obedience and most sincere good will with which they were eager to please our majesty and endear, and in general recommend themselves to us in all our affairs and those of the kingdom, in good times and bad, particularly in avenging the innocent blood of the late lord Andrew, king of Jerusalem and Sicily, our dearest brother of blessed memory, the bitterness of whose savage murder filled the lands and territories of almost the entire world, by setting out with us to the said kingdom of Sicily and facing intrepidly the unforeseen circumstances of fate and all kinds of personal danger.[5] We wish to concur favorably with their request and to fulfill their wishes, in order to encourage them to engage with dedicated mind in similar works of faithful service. We accept, approve, and confirm the above-mentioned letter of the lord king Andrew II, our dearest ancestor and predecessor, validated with his golden bull, untouched by any doubt and, transcribed word for word, inserted in this charter with all the liberties contained in it, with the sole exception of the above-mentioned one paragraph to be excluded from this privilege, namely, that contrary to the clause according to which "noble men, dying without heirs should be able and allowed in life and death to give, grant, sell, or alienate their estates to churches or to others whom they wish," they should in fact have no right at all to do so, but the property of these same nobles should descend to brothers, collateral relatives, and clansmen by right and according to law, pure and simple, without anyone's objection;[6] with the gracious consent of the most serene princess, the lady Elizabeth, by the same grace, queen of Hungary, our dear mother,[7] and in accordance with the counsel of our barons, we confirm the same liberties in the words of the above-mentioned bull of privilege issued by lord king Andrew, and we renew them out of our royal benevolence and order that they shall be held and enjoyed by them in perpetuity for the future. Furthermore, on behalf of a more serene condition and peaceful situation for these same men, our gentlemen of the realm, and in accordance with the wish of our mother and the counsel of these same men, our barons, we, following our usual generosity, have thought it best to concede liberties of the following sort, by adding what is written below:

1. That if prelates or any clergy proceed against nobles of our kingdom in any suit and litigate in the court of any judge of our kingdom, then, in the matter of the lawsuit, while the case is pending, they are not allowed to impose an interdict upon the laymen or pronounce a sentence of excommunication against them, as has been the usage and custom until now, without the royal majesty's knowledge and notice.[8] And if the same clergy or prelates should be lawfully, with full process of law, condemned by any judge, then they should fall

presentia de iure convicti fuerint, tunc in eiusdem gravaminis penam, quo eorum adversarios intendebant honorare seu aggravare, incidant eo facto.

II. Nec pro funere hominum per aliquem vel aliquos interemptorum archydiaconi mala consuetudine, sicut usi sunt, unam marcam exigere valeant atque possint.[9]

III. Minuti etiam conventus ab emanatione litterarum suarum super perpetuatione possessionum conficiendarum cessent et eorum sigilla omni careant firmitate.[10]

IV. Lucrum vero camere, prout tempore incliti principis domini Karoli olym regis Hungarie, genitoris nostri Karissimi pie memorie de quolibet integro fundo curie tres grossi solvebantur,[11] sic et nunc cum tribus grossis in nostra camera cudendis, quorum grossorum unus sex denarios camere nostri in valore et quantitate sex latorum Wyennensium valeat, et ipsorum grossorum quatuordecim unum fertonem[12] faciant, persolvatur. Superfluos autem denarios, videlicet dicarum redemptionem[13] et victualia recipere non valeant.

V. Villicos et servientes in propriis eorum possessionibus commorantes[14] ac servos ipsius lucri camere dicatores dicare et super ipsos lucrum camere exigere non possint, et generaliter dicendo nichil plus quam tres grossos recipere valeant et extorquere.

VI. Preterea ab omnibus jobagionibus nostris aratoribus et vineas habentibus in quibuslibet villis liberis ac etiam vduarnicalibus villis[16] quocunque nomine vocitatis ac reginalibus constitutis, exceptis civitatibus muratis, nonam partem omnium frugum suarum et vinorum ipsorum exigi faciemus[15] et domina regina exigi faciet; ac predicti barones et nobiles similiter ab omnibus aratoribus jobagionibus et vineas habentibus in quibuslibet possessionibus ipsorum existentibus nonam partem omnium frugum suarum et vinorum suorum eorum usibus exigant et recipiant. Prelati quoque et viri ecclesiastici jobagiones habentes primo decimas et posthec similiter nonam partem omnium frugum suarum et vinorum ipsorum exigant.[17] Et si qui in exactione predicta secus fecerint, nos in talium rebellium et presentem nostram statutionem alternantium possessionibus pro usu nostro ipsam nonam partem ipsarum frugum et vini exigi faciemus sine diminutione et relaxatione aliquali, ut per hoc honor noster augeatur et ipsi regnicole nostri nobis fidelius possint famulari.[18]

VII. De possessionibus etiam a nobis et nostris successoribus inveniendis iuxta earum quantitatem, videlicet de possessione proventus decem marcarum facienti vicecancellarius noster unam marcam et scriptor unum fertonem, et de maioribus possessionibus proventus viginti marcarum facientibus duas marcas et scriptor similiter unum fertonem recipere possint et habere, et sic consequenter iuxta excresscentiam possessionum de novo inveniendarum.[19]

VIII. Tributa etiam iniusta super terris siccis[20] et fluviis ab infra descendentibus et supra euntibus non exigantur, nisi in pontibus et

immediately under the penalty for the same trespass as that which they intended to impose and inflict upon their opponents.

2. Archdeacons cannot and must not exact, as they used to by evil custom, one mark for the funeral of men murdered by one person or by many.[9]

3. Small convents must cease from issuing letters of confirmation on inheritance of property, and their seals shall be without any authority.[10]

4. The chamber's profit is now to be paid with three groats[11] to be minted in our Chamber, just as in the time of the famous lord prince Charles, late king of Hungary, our dearest father of sacred memory, when three groats were paid for a whole plot; and of these groats one must be worth six pennies of our Chamber in the value and quantity of six broad Viennese ones, and fourteen of them count for one *ferto*.[12] However, no additional pennies or victuals viz. as fee for the taxation,[13] are to be exacted.

5. Tax-collectors should not assess reeves and servitors living on their own property or their bondsmen, nor exact the chamber's profit from them;[14] and generally speaking, they shall not receive and exact more than three groats.

6. Furthermore, we and the lady queen will cause the ninth part of all their crops and vines to be exacted from all our tenant peasants holding ploughlands and vineyards in any free village of ours of whatever kind,[15] and also in the *udvarnok* villages by whatever name they are known,[16] and the villages of the queen, with the exception of walled cities; and similarly the said barons and nobles should exact and take for their own use the ninth part of all their crops and vines from all tenant peasants holding ploughlands and vineyards on any of their estates.[17] And also prelates and clergy having tenant peasants should exact first the tithes and after that similarly the ninth part of all their own crops and vines.[18] And if anyone should act differently as to the above exactions, we shall cause that on the estates of such a recalcitrant person who violates our present order, the ninth part of his fruits and vines be exacted for our own use without any allowance and dispensation, so that, in this way, our honor might be increased and our gentlemen of the realm might serve us more loyally.

7. Our vice-chancellor should receive and have his fee from properties that can be donated by us and our successors, according to their size, namely from a property bringing a revenue of ten marks, one mark, and the scribe should receive one *ferto*; from larger properties bringing a revenue of twenty marks, two marks, and likewise one *ferto* for the scribe, and so on, according to the increase of revenue from properties found to be free for donation in the future.[19]

8. No unlawful tolls, moreover, must be levied on dry land[20] and on rivers on those ascending or descending; only those who cross by bridge or in ferries must pay, for we have realized that nobles and

navigiis ab ultra transeuntibus persolvantur, cum in eisdem nobiles et ignobiles regni nostri multo et nimium percepimus agravari.

IX. Ceterum si quis nobilis ordine iudiciario in facto potentiali succubitus duelli,[21] in pena calumpnie,[22] astationis falsi termini et exhibitionis falsarum litterarum[23] ac sententie capitalis pro quocunque facto[24] in presentia palatini et iudicis curie nostre aut alterius cuiuscunque iudicis presentia convictus fuerit, iudex illius cause talem convictum recaptivet et tribus diebus causa reformationis pacis inter partes fiende et ordinande detineat, et si concordare nequirent, tunc in manus sui adversarii ad infligendam sibi penam iuxta regni consuetudinem et de iure debitam assignet.[25] Et si tali convicto pars adversa mortem vel aliam penam consuetudinis regni de iure debendam infligerit vel fecerit, tunc a iudice et parte adversa sine receptione alicuius pecunie vel gravaminis possessionis sue erit expeditus.

X. Filiique, fratres, proximi, sorores et uxores pro excessu talis pereuntis hominis non debeant agravari, sed in possessionibus, domibus et bonis ipsorum quieti et pacifici permaneant. Si autem cum parte adversa homo premisso modo convictus posset concordare, iudex non ultra, nisi quinquaginta marcas,[26] dando sibi terminum debitum ad easdem persolvendas, recipere possit; et si dato sibi termino solvere non curaret, de possessione sua, exspirato ipso termino, recepto homine regio et testimonio alicuius capituli vel credibilis conventus portionem vel portiones ipsas quinquaginta marcas valentem vel valentes possit occupare[27] tamdiu possidendam vel possidendas, donec per hos, quorum redemptioni eadem vel eedem magis convenire dinoscuntur,[28] pro ipsis quinquaginta marcis redimantur.

XI. Ad eorundem etiam nobilium petitionem annuimus, ut universi veri nobiles intra terminos regni nostri constituti, etiam in tenutis ducalibus sub inclusione terminorum ipsius regni nostri existentes sub una et eadem libertate gratulentur.[29]

XII. Lucrum etiam camere nostre nobiles inter fluvios Draue et Zaue ac de Posoga, necnon de Walko cum aliis veris nobilibus regni nostri unanimiter solvere teneantur, nec ratione collecte marturinarum Banzolosmaia vocatarum[30] amodo et in posterum molestentur, sed ab omni exactione aliarum quarumlibet collectarum hactenus persolvi consuetarum exempti penitus, tamquam ceteri regni nostri nobiles aliarum partium, immunes habeantur.

XIII. Si vero alique minere auri vel argenti, cupri, ferri vel alie fodine in possessionibus nobilium invenirentur, absque competenti concambio non auferantur, sed pro talibus possessionibus mineras auri in se germinantibus, si regie placuerit voluntati, equales possessiones conferat nobilibus prenotatis. Alioquin, si ipsas possessiones minerosas

nonnobles of our kingdom are greatly, indeed, too much oppressed by these tolls.

9. Furthermore, if any noble is condemned in a process of law by the palatine or the judge royal or any other judge, for defeat in judicial combat in cases of violent trespass,[21] frivolous prosecution,[22] false court appearance,[23] or proffering forged documents, or for any other capital offense,[24] the judge of such a case must seize such a condemned man and hold him for three days to allow peace to be restored and ordered between the parties; and if they do not reach agreement, then he must hand over the condemned man into the hands of his adversary who may inflict on him the penalty according to the custom of the realm and as required by law.[25] And if the plaintiff causes the death of the condemned party or inflicts any other penalty customary in the kingdom and required by law, then the latter shall be released without any payment or attachment of his property by the judge and the plaintiff.

10. Sons and brothers, relatives, sisters and wives should not be made liable for the crime of such an executed man, but should remain safe and undisturbed in their estates, houses, and property. Moreover, if a man condemned in the above manner is able to come to an agreement with his opposing party, the judge may take no more than fifty marks,[26] and has to grant him a reasonable date for completing payment; and if he does not pay up by the date given to him, the judge may on the expiration of that date, with the assistance of a royal bailiff and the witness of any authenticating chapter or convent, take possession of a portion or portions worth fifty marks from his property,[27] until it is or they are redeemed for that fifty marks by those who are known to be most entitled to redemption.[28]

11. We grant the petition of these same nobles, that all true nobles established within the borders of our kingdom, including also those living on ducal territory within the borders of our kingdom, should enjoy one and the same liberty.[29]

12. Nobles between the Drava and Sava Rivers and of the counties Pozsega as well as Valkó are required to pay our chamber's profit in the same way as other true nobles of our kingdom; they should not henceforth be disturbed by reason of the collection of the *mardurina*, called *bán-zsolozsmája*;[30] rather they should be held exempt from every exaction of any other tax customarily paid until now, just as the other nobles of our kingdom from other parts.

13. If deposits of gold, silver, copper, iron, or any other metal should be found on the estates of nobles, the deposits must not be confiscated without proper exchange; however, if it pleases the king, property of equal value should be conferred on the said nobles for those properties yielding gold. Otherwise, if the royal majesty does not wish to acquire the estates rich in minerals by exchange, then he should

regia maiestas pro concambio habere nollet, extunc ius regale seu urburas iuri regio pertinentes percipi suo nomine faciat, easdem possessiones ipsis nobilibus cum ceteris quibuslibet suis utilitatibus, proventibus et iuribus relinquendo, prout etiam idem dominus Karolus rex, genitor noster karissimus ipsis regnicolis annuerat litterarum suarum per vigorem.[31]

XIV. Si autem alicui possessionem vel possessiones contulerimus, ille possessionem vel possessiones eidem collatas pro se recapiat et non nomine nostro, sed nomine ipsorum proprio cum contradictoribus in statutione dicte possessionis apparentibus trahat litem, ita, quod nomen nostrum ipsi litigionarie questioni non immissceant, nec procuratorias litteras ad executionem talium causarum a nobis recipere possint seu inpetrare.[32]

XV. Nobiles etiam ad loca tributorum ire non compellantur, sed per portus, quos voluerint, libero transitu absque aliquali inpedimento potiantur.

XVI. Nec etiam jobagiones aliquorum regnicolarum nostrorum, ad regiam vel reginalem celsitudinem pertinentes, vel ad ecclesiarum prelatos aut potentes regni nostri attinentes,[33] absque voluntaria permissione dominorum eorundem jobagionum potenter abducantur.[34]

XVII. Denique istam consuetudinem, quod dum nobiles regni nostri ad conducendum uxores eorum accedunt et more solito cum eorum uxoribus ad propria redeunt, in pontibus et tributis una marca exigitur, duximus cassandam et anichilandam.

XVIII. Nichilominus etiam in civitatibus et liberis villis regalibus et reginalibus, prelatorum et baronum ac aliorum nobilium tenutis et possessionibus jobagiones regnicolarum nostrorum pro pristinis factis non possint inpediri, prohiberi seu arestari in rebus et personis, sed si iidem vulnera, lesiones, mortem, incendia et alia consimilia enormia perpetrarent manifeste, extunc ex parte eorundem iudicium et iustitia inpendatur, et quilibet querelantes in propriorum dominorum suorum presentia iudicium et iustitiam prosequantur congruentem.[35]

XIX. Porro pro excessibus patris filius nec in persona, nec in possessionibus, nec in rebus condempnetur.[36]

XX. Episcopi quoque, capitula, abbates, conventus, prepositi et cetere possessionate ecclesiastice persone cum tribus litteris inquisitoriis, nisi regia maiestas destinatis probis viris, quos maluerit, experiatur et informetur inter nobiles et ecclesias super possessionibus acquirendis, possessionem nec requirere nec retinere possint, nisi cum litteris privilegialibus regiis vel reginalibus, aut iudicum vices gerentium regie maiestatis.[37]

XXI. Homines autem capitulorum seu conventuum, qui ex mandato regio pro testimonio ducuntur, non possint esse alii, nisi hii, qui dignitates habent in eadem ecclesia. Et si ipsius capituli vel conventus testimonium in equo suo proprio ductus fuerit, tunc per diem

cause the royal dues or the royal portions of the *urbura* to be collected in his name, but leave the estates with all their other easements, revenues, and rights in the hands of the same nobles, just as the lord king Charles, our most dear father, approved for his gentlemen of the realm by force of his charter.[31]

14. He, on whom we have conferred any estate or estates, must occupy the estate or estates conferred on him in his own name and conduct litigation in his own name and not in ours against anyone disputing his right to the said possession, so that our name will not be mixed in any legally contested matter, nor may they acquire or receive letters of advocacy from us to conduct such cases.[32]

15. Nobles cannot be compelled to pass by places of toll-collection, but they may cross at any ford they wish free from hindrance.

16. Tenant peasants of any of our gentlemen of the realm or belonging to the king's or queen's majesty or to prelates of churches or magnates of our kingdom may not be removed by force without the voluntary permission of the lords of these same tenant peasants.[33]

17. Finally, we wish to declare null and void that custom by which one mark is exacted at bridges and tolls from nobles on their way to marry their wives and returning home with their wives.

18. Tenant peasants of our gentlemen of the realm cannot in any way be taken, seized, or arrested in their goods or persons in cities and free villages of the king or the queen, on holdings and estates of prelates, barons, or other nobles for previous misdeeds,[34] but if they have manifestly committed assault, injury, murder, arson, and other similar crimes, then justice and judgment should be meted out on their account, and any plaintiffs should seek justice and appropriate sentence from their lords.[35]

19. Furthermore, a son should not be condemned in person, property, or chattels for the crimes of his father.[36]

20. Bishops, chapters, abbots, convents, provosts, and other propertied ecclesiastics with three letters of inquiry may not acquire or hold property unless the royal majesty receives, concerning the properties to be acquired, proof on inquiry by trusted men selected by the royal majesty from the nobles and clergy, and unless letters of privilege from the king or queen or judges acting on behalf of the royal majesty are granted.[37]

21. The men of chapters or convents who are called upon as witnesses by royal order may not be other than those who hold offices in that same church. If a witness goes forth from his chapter or convent on his own horse, then he should be given two groats per day; if he is

duos grossos, si vero in equo ipsius nobilis ducetur, tunc per diem unum grossum ipsi idem nobilis dare teneatur.[38]

XXII. Homo autem regius, qui ducitur ad citandum vel ad inquisitionem faciendam, non possit esse aliunde, nisi de eodem comitatu vel districtu, in quo est ille, qui citatur vel contra quem fit inquisitio; et capitulorum testimonium de propinquioribus capitulis adducatur ad citandum aut ad inquirendum.

XXIII. Et inquisitiones non possint fieri per alium modum, nisi mediantibus litteris regalibus vel palatini aut iudicis curie regie, et congregentur nobiles illius comitatus vel districtus in unum et ab eis inquiratur manifeste.[39]

XXIV. Causantes etiam in quacunque maxima et ardua causa concordare voluerint, iudex prohibere non possit, et de iudicio pacis ab ipsis non plus, quam tres marcas exigere valeat quoquomodo.[40]

XXV. Universe etiam cause in facto possessionum mote et movende in tertio termino absque dilatione et prorogatione aliquali terminentur.[41]

Et ut presentis nostre confirmationis, innovationis, constitutionis et libertatum largitionis ac concessionis series robur optineat perpetue firmitatis, nec ullo unquam tempore per nos et nostros successores in aliqua sui parte quomodolibet valeat in irritum revocari, presentes concessimus litteras nostras privilegiales pendentis et autentici sigilli nostri dupplicis munimine roboratas.

Datum per manus venerabilis in Christo patris domini Nicolai, eadem et apostolice sedis gratia episcopi Zagrabiensis, aule nostre vicecancellarii, dilecti et fidelis nostri, anno domini M^{mo} CCC^{mo} quinquagesimo primo, tertio ydus Decembris, regni autem nostri anno decimo. Venerabilibus in Christo patribus et dominis Nicolao Strigoniensi locique eiusdem comite perpetuo et Dominico Spalatensi archiepiscopis, fratre Dyonisio archielecto Colocensi, Nicolao Agriensi, Demetrio Waradiensi, Andrea Transiluano, Colomano Jauriensi, Nicolao Quinqueecclesiensi, Mychaele Waciensi, Johanne Wesprimiensi, Thoma Chanadiensi, fratribus Thoma Syrimiensi, Peregrino Boznensi, Stephano Nitriensi et Blasio Tyniniensi episcopis, ecclesias dei feliciter gubernantibus. Magnificis baronibus Nicolao palatino et iudice Comanorum, Nicolao filio Laurentii woyuoda Transiluano, Olyuerio magistro tauarnicorum nostrorum et iudice curie domine regine genitricis nostre karissime, comite[42] Thoma iudice curie nostre, Stephano totius Sclauonie et Croatie, Dominico de Machou et Nicolao de Zeurino banis, Paulo magistro tauarnicorum reginalium, Bartholomeo pincernarum et Leukus dapiferorum, Dyonisio agazonum ac Theuteus ianitorum nostrorum, necnon Johanne filio eiusdem Olyuerii dapiferorum reginalium magistris, Symone filio Mauricii comite Posoniensi et aliis quampluribus regni nostri comitatus tenentibus et honores.[43]

taken on the horse of a noble, then he should receive from that noble one groat per day.[38]

22. The royal bailiff, who is called to summon or to make an inquest, cannot be from anywhere other than the same county or district where that man lives who is summoned or against whom the inquest is conducted; evidence from chapters must be sought from the nearest chapter for a summons or to an inquest.[39]

23. And inquests cannot be conducted in any other way except by means of a letter of the king or of the palatine or of the judge royal, and the nobles of that county or district must be gathered together and the inquest must be publicly conducted among them.

24. When litigants in any major and difficult case wish to settle, the judge cannot prevent them, and he may in no way exact from them more than three marks as the fine of peace.[40]

25. All suits that have been brought and will be brought in matters of property must be completed at the third term without any delay or prorogation.[41]

And in order that the contents of our present confirmation, renewal, ordinance, and magnanimous grant and permission of these liberties should acquire the force of everlasting validity and that no part of it should ever be rescinded by us or our successors, we have issued this charter of privilege of ours validated by our authentic, pendant double seal.

Given by the hand of the reverend father in Christ, lord Nicholas, by His grace and that of the apostolic see bishop of Zagreb, vice-chancellor of our court, our beloved and faithful subject, in the year of the Lord one thousand three hundred and fifty-one, three days before the Ides of December, the tenth year of our reign, when the reverend fathers in Christ and lords Nicholas, archbishop of Esztergom and perpetual *ispán* of the same place, Dominic, archbishop of Spalato, friar Dennis, archbishop-elect of Kalocsa, the bishops Nicholas of Zagreb, Demetrius of Várad, Andrew of Transylvania, Coloman of Győr, Nicholas of Pécs, Michael of Vác, John of Veszprém, Thomas of Csanád, friar Thomas of Szerém, friar Peregrinus of Bosnia, friar Stephen of Nyitra, and Blaise of Knin were felicitously governing the churches of God, and when the honorable barons Nicholas, palatine and judge of the Cumans, Nicholas, son of Lawrence, voivode of Transylvania, Oliver, our Master of the Treasury and judge of the court of our beloved mother the lady queen, count[42] Thomas, the judge royal, Stephen, ban of all Slavonia and Croatia, Dominic, ban of Macsó, Nicholas, ban of Severin, Paul, Master of the queen's Treasury, Bartholomew, our butler, Lőkös our steward, Dennis our Master of the Horse, Töttös, Master of our Doorkeepers, John, son of the said Oliver, steward of the queen, Simon, son of Maurice, *ispán* of Pozsony, and many others held counties and other offices in our realm.[43]

22 Iunii 1384

Vide praefatiunculam et notas infra paginas 169–70.

Maria dei gratia Hungarie, Dalmatie, Croatie, Rame, Servie, Gallicie, Lodomerie, Comanie Bulgarieque regina,[1] princeps Salernitana et honoris montis sancti Angeli domina[2] omnibus Christi fidelibus, tam presentibus, quam futuris, presentium notitiam habituris salutem in omnium salvatore.

Ea, que rei publice seu communis boni grata comoda respiciunt, tenemur aspicere consideratione gratiosa, quia tronus excellentie regalis culminis tanto solidatur felicius, quanto potestas principantis suos subiectos optate pacis presidio duxerit confovendos. Proinde ad universorum notitiam harum serie volumus pervenire, quod serenissimo principe domino Lodouico, eadem dei gratia inclito rege Hungarie, Polonie, Dalmatie etc. genitore nostro carissimo laudande recordationis volente domino celi, cuius nutu omnia reguntur et disponuntur, absque prole masculina de medio sublato,[3] nobisque iure successorio et ordine geniture solium et coronam dicti regni Hungarie ac sceptra regiminis ipsius genitoris nostri feliciter adeptis,[4] baronum necnon procerum et nobilium regni nostri cetus et universitatis idemptitas[5] missis ad nos et inclitam principem dominam Elizabeth, eadem dei gratia reginam Hungarie, Polonie, Dalmatie etc. genitricem nostram carissimam eorum nuntiis,[6] nobilibus scilicet viris Paulo litterato de Poduersya et Dyonisio filio Dominici de Oztopan,[7] exhibuerunt nobis quasdam litteras privilegiales memorati genitoris nostri priori suo sigillo autentico in partibus Vzure casualiter deperdito[8] consignatas, litteras privilegiales illustrissimi principis domini Andree, tertii Bele regis filii, olim incliti regis Hungarie, avi et predecessoris nostri pie recordationis aurea bulla sua roboratas super libertatibus ipsorum baronum, necnon procerum et nobilium regni nostri confectas in se confirmative continentes, tenoris et continentie per omnia infrascripte, supplicantes nostre serenitati precibus humilimis et devotis, ut memoratas litteras privilegiales ipsius genitoris nostri de verbo ad verbum inseri et transscribi faciendo simulcum libertatum articulis, tam per ipsum dominum Andream regem, quam etiam genitorem nostrum ipsis datis et concessis, et in tenoribus earundem expressis acceptare, approbare, ratificare et innovative nostro dignaremur privilegio perpetuo confirmare. Quarum tenor talis est:

22 June 1384

For prefatory and explanatory notes, see below, pages 169–70.

Mary, by the grace of God queen[1] of Hungary, Dalmatia, Croatia, Rama, Serbia, Galicia, Lodomeria, Cumania and Bulgaria, princess of Salerno, and lady of the Honor of Monte Sant'Angelo,[2] to all Christ's faithful, present and future, to whose notice these presents may come, greetings in the Savior of all.

We are obligated to look with favorable consideration on those aspects of the common good or commonwealth which are regarded as pleasing and suitable, since the throne, which is the pinnacle of royal excellence, is more happily strengthened the more the power of the ruler with the bulwark of desired peace will have considered that her subjects should be duly favored. Therefore, by these presents we wish to bring to everyone's attention that when the most serene prince, the lord Louis, by the same grace of God renowned king of Hungary, Poland, Dalmatia, etc., our dearest father of praiseworthy memory, was carried off from among us without male issue through the will of the Lord of heaven by whose decision all things are ruled and arranged,[3] and we, by hereditary right and by order of birth, happily acquired the throne and crown of the said kingdom of Hungary and the sceptre of governance from our said father,[4] then the assemblage and unified community[5] of barons as well as lords and nobles of our realm sent to us and to the renowned princess, the lady Elizabeth, by the same grace queen of Hungary, Poland, Dalmatia, etc., our dearest mother, their envoys,[6] namely the noble men, the learned Paul of Podversia and Denis, son of Dominic of Osztopán,[7] and showed us a certain charter of privilege of our said parent, signed with his first authentic seal (accidentally lost in the province of Ozora)[8] and containing in a manner of confirmation letters of privilege validated with his golden bull by the most illustrious prince lord Andrew, son of King Béla III, renowned former king of Hungary, our ancestor and predecessor of blessed memory, about the liberties of the same barons, lords, and nobles of our kingdom, in the words and contents written below. (These envoys) begged our serenity with most humble and devout requests that we should cause the said charter of privilege of our father to be inserted and transcribed word for word together with the articles of liberty granted and conceded them both by lord Andrew and our father and that we should through our own action, deign to accept, approve, ratify, and confirm by renewing the exact contents of that charter in a perpetual privilege. The contents of which is this:

(Decretum 11 Decembris 1351)

Nos itaque premissis supplicationibus memoratorum baronum, procerum et nobilium regni per dictos eorum nuntios nobis porrectis favorabiliter exauditis, memoratas litteras privilegiales paternas presentibus de verbo ad verbum insertas quoad omnes earum continentias et clausulas acceptamus, approbamus, ratificamus et nostro pro predictis baronibus, proceribus et nobilibus regni nostri privilegio innovantes perpetuo confirmamus.

In cuius rei memoriam firmitatemque perpetuam presentes concessimus litteras nostras privilegiales pendentis et autentici sigilli nostri dupplicis munimine roboratas. Datum per manus reverendissimi in Christo patris et domini, domini Demetrii, divina miseratione tituli Sanctorum Quatuor Coronatorum sacrosancte Romane ecclesie presbyteri cardinalis ac sancte Strigoniensis Ecclesie gubernatoris perpetui locique eiusdem comitis similiter perpetui et aule nostre fidelis cancellarii, anno domini $M^{o}CCC^{mo}$ LXXX^{mo} quarto, decimo kalendas mensis Julii, regni autem nostri anno tertio. Reverendis et venerabilibus in Christo patribus eodem domino Demetrio dicte sancte Strigoniensis ecclesie gubernatore perpetuo, Lodouico Colocensi, Petro Jadrensi, Vgulino Spalatensi et Petro Ragusiensi archiepiscopis, Emerico Agriensis, Paulo Zagrabiensis, Goblino Transsiluanensis, Valentino Quinqueecclesiensis decretorum doctore, Johanne Waradiensis, Guillermo Jauriensis, Benedicto Wesprimiensis, Johanne Chanadiensis, Georgio Boznensis, Petro Wacyensis, Johanne Syrimiensis, fratre Dominico Nitriensis, Paulo Tininiensis, Demetrio Nonensis, Grisogono Traguriensis, Matheo Sibinicensis, Beneuenuto Pharensis, Jacobo Makarensis, Michaele Scardonensis et Thoma Seniensis ecclesiarum episcopis, ecclesias Dei feliciter gubernantibus, Corbauiensi sede vacante. Magnificis viris Nicolao da Gara, regni nostri palatino et iudicie Comanorum, Ladislao woyuoda Transsiluano et comite de Zolnuk, comite[9] Nicolao de Zeech iudice curie nostre, Stephano de Lindua totius regni Sclauonie, Stephano filio Philpus de Machow, Templino de Sancto Georgio Dalmatie et Croatie banis, Nicolao dicto Zambo[10] tauarnicorum, Blasio dicto Forgach pincernarum, Nicolao filio Nicolai de Telegd ianitorum, Ladislao filio Nicolai de Wesen dapiferorum, Stephano filio condam domini Dyonisii woyuode agazonum nostrorum magistris, predicto Nicolao dicto Zambo comite Posoniensi aliisque quampluribus regni nostri comitatus tenentibus et honores.[11]

(Decree of 11 December 1351)

And thus, having listened with favor to the supplications of the said barons, lords, and nobles of the realm which were presented to us by their said envoys, we accept, approve, and ratify the said paternal letter of privilege with all its contents and clauses, inserting it word for word into the present charter, and we, in accordance with our right, renew and confirm it in perpetuity for the said barons, lords, and nobles of our kingdom.

In memory of this deed and for the sake of its perpetual legal force, we have granted in person our charter of privilege validated by our pendant and authentic double seal. Given by the hand of the most reverend lord and father in Christ, lord Demetrius, by divine mercy cardinal priest of the Holy Roman Church of the title of SS Quattro Coronati, and perpetual governor of the church of Esztergom, likewise perpetual *ispán* of that place and faithful chancellor of our court, in the year of the lord one thousand three hundred and eighty-four, the tenth day before the Kalends of the month of July, in the third year of our reign, when the following reverend and venerable fathers in Christ governed the churches of God felicitously: the same lord Demetrius, perpetual governor of the said holy church of Esztergom, and when archbishops Louis of Kalocsa, Peter of Zara, Hugolino of Spalato, and Peter of Ragusa, bishops Emeric of Eger, Paul of Zagreb, Gobelinus of Transylvania, doctor of canon law Valentine of Pécs, John of Várad, Guillaume of Győr, Benedict of Veszprém, John of Csanád, George of Bosnia, Peter of Vác, John of Szerém, Friar Dominic of Nyitra, Paul of Knin, Demetrius of Nona, Chrysogonus of Traù, Matthew of Sebenico, Benvenuto of Hvar, James of Makarska, Michael of Scardona, and Thomas of Zengg governed the churches of God felicitously, the see of Korbava being vacant; and when the honorable lords Nicholas of Gara was palatine of our realm and judge of the Cumans, Ladislas voivode of Transylvania and *ispán* of Szolnok, count[9] Nicholas of Szécs judge royal, Stephen of Lindva ban of all Slavonia, Stephen son of Phillip ban of Macsó, Templinus of Szentgyörgy ban of Croatia and Dalmatia, Nicholas called Zámbó[10] Master of the Treasury, Blaise Forgács, butler, Nicholas son of Nicholas of Telegd, Master of the Doorkeepers, Ladislas, son of Nicholas of Veseny, the steward, Stephen son of the late lord voivode Denis, Master of our Horse, the aforementioned Nicholas Zámbó, *ispán* of Pozsony, and many others holding counties and honors in our kingdom.[11]

14 Novembris 1385

Vide praefatiunculam et notas infra paginas 171–72.

Nos Maria dei gratia regina Hungariae, Dalmatiae, Croatie, etc. notum facimus universis, quibus incumbit, per presentes, quod cum nos sana et matura unacum prelatis et baronibus ac regni nostri proceribus deliberatione prehabita pro bono communi utilitateque eiusdem regni nostri, presertim pro reformandis deformatis remeliorandisque et discutiendis ac rectificandis universis et singulis ipsius regni nostri factis, cuiusvismodi existant, et generaliter sedandis et extirpandis omnibus maleficiorum generibus post felicem obitum olym excelsi principis domini Ludouici regis Hungariae, genitoris nostri carissmi, cuius memoria in benedictione est, hincinde inter ipsos nobiles et nostros regnicolas cuiusvis preeminentie existant, qualitercumque, quandocumque et quomodocumque subortis et alternatim pullulatis, annuente divine maiestatis clementia congregationem generalem Bude, octavo die festi Omnium sanctorum iam preteriti[1] celebrassemus, sic videlicet, ut de singulis ipsius regni nostri comitatibus singuli quatuor potiores nobiles ad diem et locum predictos convenire debuissent, demum ipso termino feliciter adveniente ipsisque nobilibus universaliter in locum predictum iuxta nostre celsitudinis decretum convenientibus cetus et universitas eorundem per certos et fidedignos ambasiatores ipsorum[2] maiestati nostre patefecerunt querulose, quomodo ipsi in illis omnibus libertatibus, inmunitatibus libertatumque prerogativis, quas eisdem sancti et alii reges Hungarie beatarum recordationum[3] ex bonarum et efficassimarum ipsorum litterarum vigoribus limitando concessissent, et quas idem olym genitor noster tandemque nos roborasse, approbasse at confirmasse perhibemur,[4] prorsus et in toto non haberentur, et in eisdem ipsi imminenti tempore non conservarentur, supplicantes iidem ambasiatores suis et dictorum universorum fidelium dicti regni nostri Hungarie nobilium in personis maiestati nostre subiective, ut ipsos in omnibus illarum libertatum prerogativis, quas eisdem dicti olym sancti et alii reges Hungarie concessisse dinoscuntur, et que per eundem olym patrem nostrum demumque per nos roborate et confirmate esse perhibentur, omni novitate exclusa dignaremur invariabiliter conservare. Nos igitur illam inviolabilem fidelitatis constantiam in acie nostre mentis revolventes,[5] qua iidem fideles dicti regni nostri nobiles a temporibus dictorum sanctorum et aliorum regum usque modo in tuitione et protectione huius nostri regni Hungarie, omniumque iuri sacre corone nostre regie subiectorum, specialiter autem in tuta conservatione confiniorum,

14 November 1385

For prefatory and explanatory notes, see below, pages 171–72.

Mary, by the grace of God, queen of Hungary, Dalmatia, Croatia, etc., make known to all to whom it may concern by these presents that when after sound and mature deliberation with the prelates, barons, and lords of our realm, for the common good and welfare of the same kingdom, for reforming in particular what was deformed and for improving, repairing, and rectifying all matters, of whatever sort they might be, of that very kingdom of ours and generally to pacify and to eradicate all kinds of crimes which have arisen or otherwise flourished in any way, time, or manner, among these same nobles and our subjects of whatever privilege, following the untroubled death of the late eminent prince, the lord Louis, king of Hungary, our dearest father of blessed memory, we, with the help of the gentle favor of the divine majesty, held a general assembly in Buda on the eighth day of the recent feast of All Saints,[1] in such a way that from each and every county of our kingdom four of the richer nobles were obliged to come for the said day to the said place, and when finally the appointed date happily arrived and all the nobles were all together in the said place in accord with the decree of our eminence, the entire assembly and community disclosed through selected and trustworthy envoys[2] in a complaint to our majesty how they were nowadays deprived of the full enjoyment of all the liberties, immunities, and privileges of freedom, which the holy and other kings of Hungary of blessed memory[3] had granted them by defining these in their good and most efficacious charters, which earlier our father and, recently, we ourselves have validated, approved, and confirmed,[4] but which in the present time are not being completely observed; these same envoys and the loyal nobles of our kingdom of Hungary humbly requested our majesty in person that we deign to preserve them in the enjoyment of all the privileges of liberty which the said holy and other kings of Hungary are acknowledged to have granted them and which are proven to have been validated and confirmed by our father and finally by us, as well, unchanged, without any innovations whatsoever. We, therefore, keeping steadfastly in mind[5] that unsullied constancy of loyalty with which these same loyal nobles of our said kingdom from the times of the holy and other kings up to the present have fearlessly taken care to render and show themselves faithful in the preservation and protection of this, our kingdom of Hungary and of all those subject to the jurisdiction of our royal Holy Crown, particularly in the safe preservation of the

limitum et terminorum eiusdem regni nostri Hungarie[6] promptos se intrepide reddere studuerunt fideles et exhibuerunt, per que huius regni gubernacula feliciter possidemus, eorundem nobilium regni nostri fidelium supplicationem veram, ymmo toti regno nostro proficuam fore agnosscentes, premisseque libertati ipsorum in toto vel in parte derogari nolentes, eisdem nobilibus regni nostri et cuilibet eorum harum serie firma et bona nostra fide mediante promittimus, spondemus et ex certa nostre maiestatis scientia[7] pollicemur, ut ipsos amodo in antea in omnibus illis libertatibus, immunitatibus et libertatum prerogativis, que eisdem per ipsos sanctos et alios Hungarie regni reges, nostros videlicet divos predecessores donate et concesse per nosque roborate existunt et confirmate, ut iidem ad tuitionem ipsius regni nostri Hungarie ipsamque eorum fidelitatem diuturnam inviolabiliter observandam ferventius animentur, tenebimus et conservabimus perpetuo et irrevocabiliter permansuros, fruituros et gavisuros; et in huius rei evidens testimonium ipsis fidelibus nobilibus regni nostri presentes duximus concedendas. Datum Bude, septimo die congregationis nostre predicte, anno domini millesimo trecentesimo octuagesimo quinto.

borders, frontiers, and boundaries of that kingdom of Hungary of ours,[6] on account of which we happily hold the governance of the realm, recognize that the requests of these faithful nobles of our kingdom are genuine and, moreover, beneficial to our whole realm, and, not wanting them to lack the aforementioned liberties in whole or even in part, promise, vow, and pledge in accordance with our specific understanding of our royal majesty[7] to these nobles of the kingdom, each one of them, in good and firm faith by the words of these presents that we will hold and preserve them henceforth as formerly, in perpetuity, and irrevocably, in all the liberties, immunities, and privileges of freedom which were granted and conceded to them by the saintly and other kings of Hungary, namely our holy predecessors, and which are now validated and confirmed by us, to abide in, use, and enjoy these, so that these same nobles might be most fervently moved to observe their long-held faith for the defense of our Hungarian kingdom; in manifest testimony of which we have caused the present charter to be granted to the same faithful nobles of our kingdom. Given at Buda on the seventh day of our said assembly, in year of the Lord one thousand three hundred and eighty-five.

(1386, post 27 Augusti)

Vide praefatiunculam et notas infra paginas 173–75.

Ad perpetuam rei memoriam. Noverit presens etas et futura posteritas, quod nos prelati, barones, proceres et universi regni nobiles pacis comoda provide attendentes et contentionum discrimina, que in ipso regno, proch dolor, acciderunt seu emerserunt, cogitantes et nostros animos ad concordie semitas convertentes, ut in pacis tranquilitate coli possit congruentius et salubrius actio pacis,[1] in Albam Regalem, in qua iuxta privilegiatam libertatem regni a sanctis regibus et eorum successoribus concessam in arduis negotiis tractandis et ordinandis solitum est regnicolis convenire,[2] facta generali proclamatione per omnes comitatus regni Hungarie die octavo festi beati regis Stephani[3] universaliter congregati prestito iuramento capite eiusdem sancti regis altari superposito cum sumpma reverentia manualiter tacto,[4] super eo, quod comodum rei publice et utilitatem regni ac sacre corone communem contra quoslibet vovebimus, etiamsi regia maiestas contra id facere vellet, sibi contradicemus ac prohibebimus eandem cum efectu,[5] contraque extraneam potentiam nos omnimode resistendo oponemus pro defensione regni et suarum tenutarum et confiniorum, necnon etiam contra quemlibet potentem internos insultantem et actus potentiarios exercentem et contra presentis pacis ordinationem rumpentem totis viribus insurgemus, pro reformatione et bono statu regni fecimus, ordinavimus et promulgavimus unionem et pacis reformationem, prout in capitulis et articulis infrascriptis lucide continentur, perpetue et inviolabiliter duraturam.

I. Item primo, si alique novitates[6] vel motiones dificiles in regno emergi contingerint, tunc regia maiestas prelatis et baronibus regni ad tractandum et consiliandum de potioribus nobilibus regni adiungat et assumpmat ad ea recuperanda.[7]

II. Item duos honores baronatus[8] una persona obtinere seu tenere non possit, et quod ecclesiastice persone seculares honores nullo modo obtinere possint, et e converso seculares persone ecclesiasticos honores quacunque occasione pretensa tenere vel usurpare non possint, maxime sedibus et dignitatibus vacantibus.

III. Item prelati et barones pro consiliariis deputati iurabunt, quod in consiliis exhibendis et dandis non solum regie maiestatis aut eorum vel suorum propriam querent utilitatem, sed communem utilitatem regni et sacre corone regie, et e converso ipsa regia celsitudo promittet bona fide consilia ipsa inviolabiliter sequi et observare; et si quipiam ex

(1386, after 27 August)

For prefatory and explanatory notes, see below, pages 173–75.

For the perpetual memory of this matter: let the present age and future posterity know that we, the prelates, barons, lords, and all the nobles of the kingdom, properly and carefully contemplating the advantages of peace, and the causes of the strife, which, alas, has occurred or arisen in this kingdom, considered and turned our minds to paths of agreement, so that the works of peace may be more appropriately and more profitably cultivated in the calm of peace.[1] We, after a general proclamation was made in all the counties of the kingdom of Hungary, have assembled together on the eighth day of the feast of the holy king Stephen,[2] in Székesfehérvár—where according to the privileged liberty of the kingdom granted by the holy kings and their successors, it is customary for the gentlemen of the realm to assemble to treat and arrange urgent affairs[3]—and swore an oath on the head of the same holy king[4] that had been placed on the altar and touched with our hands in the greatest reverence, that we shall undertake to protect the welfare of the commonwealth and the common good of the kingdom and the Holy Crown against anyone. We shall oppose and actively prohibit even if the royal majesty wishes to act in opposition[5] and shall also oppose any outside power with utmost resistance for the defense of the realm, its boundaries, and dependencies. Furthermore, we shall rise in all our strength against any powerful man committing attacks and violent trespasses, and disturbing the ordinance of the present peace; and acting in support of the restoration and good order of the kingdom, we have established and proclaimed a union and the restoration of peace to last perpetually and inviolably, as is clearly contained in the chapters and articles written below.

1. Then, first, if any novelties[6] or troublesome events chance to arise in the kingdom, then the royal majesty should augment the prelates and barons of the kingdom by having some of the more powerful nobles join them in discussing and taking counsel about restoring order.[7]

2. Then, one person may not obtain or hold two baronial offices,[8] and ecclesiastical persons may in no way receive secular offices, and, in turn, secular persons may not hold or usurp ecclesiastical prebends, especially vacant sees and dignities, on any pretense.

3. Then, prelates and barons chosen as counsellors will swear that in offering and giving advice they will seek not only what is advantageous for the royal majesty, themselves, and others, but rather the common advantage of the kingdom and the royal Holy Crown, and,

huiusmodi consiliariis regie serenitati falsum et communi bono contrarium suaserint consilium, extunc rescita huius veritate de medio huiusmodi consiliariorum tamquam falsi turpiter eiciantur nunquam ad eadem prebenda admittendi.

IV. Item regia serenitas promittet suo iuramento, quod omnem rancorem, invidiam, contemptum et iniuriam, [que] contra quoscunque et cuiusvis conditionis homines ex quibuscunque actenus habuisset causis, ex cordibus suis prorsus evellendo relaxabit, nec ipsis seu alicui eorundem palam vel latenter per se vel alios ratione previa quovis tempore quidquam inputabit, similiter et reginalis maiestas.[9]

V. Item quod tezaurum domus regie tam in reliquiis, quam in omnibus aliis tempore proxime rixe et pugne per Johannem banum Machouiensem[10] et fratres suos ac Johannem priorem Auranie[11] et ad eosdem pertinentes contra condam Nicolaum de Gara palatinum[13] et suos fratres, fautores et adherentes receptum idem Johannes banus et prior ac eorum fratres mediante ipsorum iuramento,[12] prout plenius possunt, recuperare procurent et domui regie restituere.

VI. Item omnes captivos, quos idem banus et prior Auranie ac fratres eorum et ad eosdem pertinentes pro nunc in ipsorum captivate habent et conservant, libere abire permittant, et nec ipsos vel ad eosdem pertinentes in possessionibus vel aliis bonis ipsorum inpediant et occupata eisdem remittant.

VII. Item idem banus et prior et eorum fratres omnia castra, civitates et fortalitia, opida, villas et possessiones et quevis iura regalia vel reginalia necnon ceterorum nobilium, que pro nunc occupata tenent, libere illis, ad quos pertinent, remittant sine mora.

VIII. Item quia premissa rixa non in contemptum vel iniuriam reginalis maiestatis, sed propter antiquas inimicitias inter predictas partes ortas et habitas commissa et facta extitit,[14] ideo ipse domine regine predictis Johanni bano, Johanni priori Aurane ac suis proximis adherentibus, familiaribus et sequacibus eorundem, quod si forte contra honorem regalem seu reginalem commissum extitisset, ut status regni in melius reformetur, radicitus de ipsarum cordibus evellendo, literis etiam ipsarum et aliis ad hec necessarie occurrentibus remediis confirmando,[15] ipsos in curiam reginalem benigne recipiant ipsosque secundum decentiam status et conditionis eorum regalibus honoribus honorando et sublimando, prout et ceteros nobiles ac barones regni regalis maiestas consuevit, condecenter in consiliis et aliis honorare atque sublimare dignentur.

conversely, the royal eminence will promise to follow and to observe inviolably the same advice in good faith; and if anyone from among these counsellors should give the royal serenity false advice contrary to the common good, then when the truth of this has been found out, he should be dishonorably expelled from their midst as a false counsellor, never to be admitted to these offices again.

4. Then, the royal serenity shall promise on oath to discard all rancour, envy, contempt, and harm which up to this point she might have held against any men of any estate for whatever reason by directly erasing it from her heart, nor will she bring any charges against them or against their people, publicly or privately, by herself or by others, at any time or for whatever previous reason; and the same shall hold true for her majesty the queen mother.[9]

5. Then, John, ban of Macsó[10] and John, the prior of Vrana[11] and their brothers should make sure to return and restore to the royal palace, under their own oath,[12] as fully as they are able, the treasures of the royal palace, both the relics and all the other things, taken away during the time of the recent strife and struggle of ban John, prior John of Vrana, their brothers and dependents with the late Nicholas of Gara, count palatine,[13] and his brothers, followers, and adherents.

6. Then, this same ban and the prior of Vrana, their brothers and dependents should permit all captives whom they now hold and keep in their custody to leave freely, and neither should they hold back possessions or other goods of the captives and their dependents, but should return to them all things they had seized.

7. Then, the same ban and the prior and their brothers should return freely without delay to those to whom they belong all the castles, cities and fortifications, towns, villages and estates, and the usurped royal rights of whatever sort, and those of the queen or other nobles, which they currently occupy.

8. Then, since the aforementioned strife arose not for the contempt or injury of the queen's majesty, but was induced and carried on because of ancient enmities among the aforementioned parties,[14] the same ladies, the queens, in order that the state of the kingdom may be restored for the better, should entirely root out from their hearts anything that the aforementioned ban John and prior John of Vrana, their close relatives, retainers, and followers, may have by chance committed against the royal honor or that of the queen; and they should confirm this by their letters and other necessary and pertinent remedies,[15] and they should kindly receive these men at the queen's court and should deign to honor and promote them appropriately in council and otherwise by honoring and promoting them to royal honors, which are in accordance with the preeminence of their station and birth, just as the royal majesty is wont to do with other barons and nobles of the kingdom.

IX. Et ut omnino radicitus et expressa denotatione via odiis malitiis, partialitatibus ac scandalis precludatur et in regno pacis commoda reform[entur, si] predicte domine regine et earum heredes vel soboles ab eisdem procreate aliquam vindictam, afflictionem vel perturbationem aut quomodocunque animi motionem super facto pugne superius expresse facerent vel fieri permittent, vel ad hoc consensum prebebunt ad suggestionem quorumcunque, ita quod si contingerit ipsarum maiestatem aliquorum suggestionibus et inductionibus incitari vel aliqua occasione commoveri, tunc omnes prelati, barones ac universi regni nobiles talem partem nullo modo fovere, ymo expresse contradicere et se retrahere tenebuntur. Nullus etiam omnino hominum super eodem facto ac interfectionibus hominum quorumcunque in ipsa pugna illatis et quibuscunque eventibus ibi accidentibus signanter autem heredes, consanguinei, affines, amici et quilibet attinentes illarum personarum, que ibi occubuerunt vel quomodocunque offense vel dampnificate extiterunt, verbo vel [facto] ---[16]

9. And in order that the road to hatred, ill will, partiality, and scandal be completely and expressly barred, and the advantages of peace in the kingdom be restored, then if the aforesaid ladies, the queens, and their heirs, and the offspring born to them should cause or permit any revenge, trouble, or disorder, or let a climate of enmity emerge because of the above-mentioned struggle, or consent to any suggestion by anyone so that the suggestions and intentions would incite or move their majesties to some incident, all the prelates, barons, and all noblemen of the kingdom will be bound in no way to support such a posture, but rather to speak up strongly against it and take no part in it. None of the people involved in this action, or the killing of any man in the said struggles and the events connected with them, particularly the heirs, relatives, kinsmen, friends, and others of their adherents who lost their lives there or suffered injury by word or action. . . .[16]

(October, 1397)

Vide praefatiunculam et notas infra paginas 176–83.

Nos Sigismundus dei gratia rex Hungarie, Dalmatie, Croatie etc. marchyoque Brandenburgensis etc. memorie commendante te[nore pre]sentium significamus quibus expedit universis, quod cum per insultus et potentiam Turcorum et aliorum scismaticorum ----[1] hominum in quibusdam annorum curriculis iam retrolapsis usque presens tempus in confiniis regni nostri Hungarie pridem plurime devastationes, spoliationes et concremationes possessionum, hominum utriusqe sexus, virorum scilicet et mulierum [su]bductiones, alia etiam enormia intollerabilia, per que facta nostra et omnium regnicolarum nostrorum potentia dimi[nuta es]se videbatur, creberrime commissa fuissent et committerentur de presenti, eapropter de bono et tranquillo statu ac restauratione confiniorum dicti regni nostri volentes contemplari, tam pretextu premissorum, quam etiam pro aliis factis et arduis negotiis ipsius regni nostri et sacre regie nostre corone universos prelatos et viros ecclesiasticos e[minenti] dignitate prefulgentes ac barones nostros, item de quibusvis comitatibus regni nostri singulos quatuor probos et nobiles viros plena potestate ceterorum consociorum ipsorum fungentes[2] ad festum presens beati Mychaelis archangeli[3] pro congregatione et consilio generali in premissis facienda huc in Temeswar litteris nostris mediantibus [convenir]e mandassemus, demum eisdem in locum et terminum prenotatos pariter accersitis et convenientibus annotati barones et nobiles regni nostri super omnibus premissis diligenti tractatu, sano consilio et matura deliberatione inter se prehabitis taliter inter se duxerunt disponendum et ordinandum:[4]

I. Ut annuatim in festo sancti regis Stepha[ni], nisi arduo negotio ingruente vel infirmitate fuerimus prohibiti, Albe teneamur solempnizare. Et si nos interesse non poterimus, palatinus procul dubio ibi erit pro nobis, ut vice nostra causas audiat et quemlibet presentibus partibus iudicet, et omnes servientes, qui voluerint, libere illuc conveniant.[5]

II. Et quod nec nos, nec posteri nostri in aliquo tempore servientes capiamus vel destruant favore alicuius potentis, nisi primo citati fuerint et ordine iudiciario convicti.[6]

III. Super predia servientum, nec domos nec villas descendimus, nisi vocati. Super populos etiam ecclesiarum ipsorum nullam penitus collectam faciemus.[7]

IV. Comites parochiani predia servientum non discutiant, nisi causa monetarum. Comites curie parochiani nullum penitus discutiant, nisi populos

(October 1397)

For prefatory and explanatory notes, see below, pages 176–83.

We, Sigismund, by the grace of God, king of Hungary, Dalmatia, Croatia, etc., and margrave of Brandenburg, etc., wishing that it be remembered, make known by these presents to all to whom it may concern that during the past few years to this very day the Turks and other wicked[1] schismatics by their attacks and violent actions have destroyed, looted, and burnt down many estates and have carried away people of both sexes, males and females, and have frequently perpetrated and are still committing terrible and intolerable deeds in the border regions of our kingdom of Hungary, by which our strength and that of all of our gentlemen of the realm appear to have declined; therefore, willing to provide for the proper and peaceful condition and restoration of the border regions of our said kingdom, we have—both for reasons already stated and also for other actions and urgent matters concerning our kingdom and our royal Holy Crown—bid by our letters all the prelates and others holding major ecclesiastical dignities, the barons, and four honest noblemen from each county of our kingdom with full powers from their fellow noblemen to assemble[2] on the present feast of St. Michael the Archangel,[3] at a diet and general discussion about the said matters to be held here in Temesvár; and the said barons and nobles of our kingdom, after being called to the said place and at the said time, and having here assembled, have decided after diligent discussion and mature deliberation of the above-mentioned matters, to issue the following orders:[4]

1. That we are bound to celebrate the feast of Saint Stephen annually in Székesfehérvár unless we should be beset by some urgent matter or prevented by illness. And if we cannot be present, the palatine will definitely be there for us, and shall hear and judge cases in our place, if all parties are present, and all the *servientes* who wish shall freely assemble there.[5]

2. And that neither we nor our successors should at any time seize or cause the ruin of any *serviens* for the benefit of some magnate, unless they first be summoned and duly sentenced by judicial process.[6]

3. We shall not exact hospitality in the houses or villages of the *servientes*, unless we have been called (there). We shall not collect any taxes at all from people attached to their churches.[7]

4. The *ispánok* of counties shall not render judicial sentences concerning the estates of the *servientes* except in cases pertaining to coinage. The *ispánok* of castles shall render judicial sentences on no one except those

sui castri. Fures et latrones bylokii regales discutiant, ad pedes tamen ipsius comitis.[8]

V. = 1222: VI.

VI. Si autem rex extra regnum exercitum ducere voluerit, servientes cum ipso ire non teneantur, nisi pro pecunia ipsius, et post reversionem iudicium exercitus super eos non recipiet. Item si extra regnum cum exercitu ierimus, omnes, qui comitatus habent vel pecuniam nostram, nobiscum ire teneantur.[9] Tempore autem maxime necessitatis huius regni Hungarie, dum scilicet extranea potentia paganorum scilicet et aliarum nationum metas et confinia eiusdem regni hostiliter subintrare conaretur, baro etiam in metis et confiniis dicti regni nostri honorem a nobis tenens[10] huiusmodi potentie resistere nequiret, tunc universi regnicole una nobiscum adversus iam dictorum potentiam more exercituantium, specialiter autem barones honorem a nostra maiestate possidentes personaliter et quolibet tempore unanimiter insurgere, aut si nos in dicto regno nostro aliis negotiis regni nostri occupati non essemus, tunc cum domino palatino regni nostri ad metas et confinia eiusdem regni nostri taliter exercituare,[11] ut nobiles, quotquot fuerint fratres in numero absque ulla divisione simul coniuncti et in una curia residentes,[12] unum ex ipsis mittere, ceteri vero divisionaliter ab invicem sequestrati, singuli singulariter exercituare teneantur. Si autem quispiam ipsorum possessionatorum hominum infirmitate inhibitus exercituare nequiret, tunc homines suos more exercituantium disponendo faciat exercituare. Minores autem nobiles jobagionibus orbati et privati, si evidenter eorum egritudinis causam declarare valebunt, expediti habeantur. Si vero quemquam possessionatorum hominum ab ipso exercitu abesse contingeret vel quispiam ipsorum in ipsum proficissci recusaret, tunc prout numerus et quantitas jobagionum ipsorum affuerit, videlicet in tantis florenis auri per centum denarios novos[13] conputatis, quantos jobagiones habuerint, cetere autem nobiles persone jobagionibus carentes in singulis tribus marcis denariorum convincantur[14] eo facto. Hoc non pretermisso, ut quivis baronum et nobilium regni nostri possessionatus secundum exigentiam status et possibilitatem virium ipsorum, scilicet de quibus vis viginti jobagionibus unum pharetrarium more exercituancium promptuare et in ipsum exercitum durante duntaxat presenti guerra paganorum secum ducere et exercituare facere teneatur.[15] Preteritis autem guerris presentibus [ge]neratio exercituantium regnicolarum universorum pristinam libertatem temporibus aliorum regum, nostrorum scilicet predecessorum assuetam viceversa optinebit.[16] Nichilominus exercituantes in itinere ipsius exercitus tam in eundo, quam etiam in redeundo in expensis ipsorum propriis procedendo ab omnibus spoliis, rapinis et receptionibus victualium inhibiti sint et prohibiti, si vero quemquam exercituantium secus in hiis facere contingeret, extunc idem absque prorogatione aliquali in facto potentie convincatur eo facto.

attached to their castles. Thieves and robbers shall be judged by royal judges, but only in the presence of the *ispán*.[8]

5. = 1222:6.

6. If the king, however, wishes to lead an army outside the kingdom, the *servientes* shall not be obligated to accompany him unless it be at his expense, and, after his return, he shall not permit judgment against them concerning the campaign. If we lead an army beyond the realm, all those who hold counties or receive money from us are bound to accompany us.[9] However, in time of great need of this kingdom of Hungary, namely when foreign forces, such as those of the pagans or other nations, are planning to attack the borders and frontiers of this same kingdom, and the baron who holds an honor[10] from us at the border and frontier fortresses of this our aforementioned kingdom cannot withstand such a force, then all the gentlemen of the realm must rise together with us in soldierly fashion against the aforesaid force, particularly all those barons in person who at that time hold honors from us; or if we are engaged in other matters of our realm, then they must go to war together with the count palatine of our kingdom[11] to the borders and frontiers of the same kingdom in such a way that those noble families in which however many brothers live together in one residence in an undivided household,[12] should send one, while those others, who have already divided their estates, are all obligated to go to war in person. And if any one of the landowning men is stricken by illness and cannot go to war, then he must send his people equipped as soldiers to fight. If lesser noblemen, lacking or having no tenant peasants, can unequivocally prove their illness, they may be excused. But if any of the landowning men should fail to join the levy, then he who is reluctant to go to war is to be convicted to pay in accordance with the number and quantity of his tenant peasants, namely, as many golden florins, counted in 100 new pennies,[13] as he has tenant peasants; other noblemen, lacking tenant peasants, are to be convicted to three marks of pennies each.[14] In addition to this, we order that all landowners among the barons and noblemen of our realm must equip and lead to war in accordance with the requirements of their station and the ability of their power from every twenty peasant tenants one archer in soldierly fashion and to make them fight during the present war with the heathen.[15] However, once the present war is over, the entire cohort of the gentlemen of the realm who have been to war will regain their ancient liberties which were customary in the reign of our predecessors.[16] Those on their way to the army and back are obligated to live on their own expenses; any kind of looting, robbery, and seizing of foodstuff is prohibited; if someone acts otherwise, he will be forthwith convicted of violent trespass in accordance with what he has done.

VII. Palatinus omnes homines regni nostri indifferenter discutiat. Iudices vicarios non habeant,[17] nisi unum in curia sua.

VIII. = 1222:IX

IX. = 1222:X

X. = 1222:XII

XI. = 1222:XIII

XII. Palatinus autem, iudex curie, bani et comites regios honores p[ossidentes, si se] iuxta honoris eorum qualitatem non habuerint vel distruxerint populos castri eorum, nobiles etiam et [al]terius cuiusvis status homines, convicti super hoc coram omni regno dignitate sua turpiter spolientur cum restitutione ablatorum.[18]

XIII. = 1222:XV.

XIV. = 1222:XVI.

XV. = 1222:XVII.

XVI. = 1222:XVIII.[19]

XVII. = 1222:XIX.

XVIII. = 1222:XXI.

XIX. = 12222:XXI.

XX. = 1222:XXIII.

XXI. = 1222:XXIV.

XXII. = 1222:XXV.

XXIII. = 1222:XXVI.

XXIV. = 1222:XXIX.

XXV. = 1222:XXX.

XXVI. = 1351:I.

XXVII. = 1351:II.

XXVIII = 1351:III.

XXIX. = 1351:IV.

XXX. = 1351:V.

XXXI. = 1351:VI.

XXXII. Item tam nos vel ----- [quam] etiam prelati, barones et nobiles et possessionati homines aquas piscinosas habentes tertiam partem omnium piscium ipsorum piscandorum in aquis fluentibus, in lacubus autem vulgo mo[char] seu morotua vocitatis[20] mediam partem quorumlibet piscium annuis piscationibus recipi faciemus et iidem [domini] prenotati recipere debeant, ut per hoc honor noster augeatur et ipsi regnicole nobis fidelius possint famulari.[21]

XXXIII. = 1351:VII.

XXXIV. = 1351:IX.

XXXV. = 1351:X.

XXXVI. Item supplicatum extitit nostre serenitati per regnicolas regni nostri universos, ut cunctos nobiles et quosvis possessionatos regni nostri Sclauonie, necnon comitatuum de Posega et de Valko homines in solutionibus lucri camere nostre seu mardurinarum nostrarum in eisdem libertatibus, in quibus iidem regnicole nostri Hungarie forent constituti, relinquere dignaremur.[22]

7. The count palatine shall judge without differentiation all the men of our realm. He shall have no deputy judge except one at his own court.[17]

8. = 1222:9.

9. = 1222:10.

10. = 1222:12.

11. = 1222:13.

12. If the count palatine, the judge royal, the bans, or any *ispán* holding royal honors does not honorably conduct himself according to the character of his office or brings ruin to those attached to his castle or to nobles or others of any estate, and if this is proven, he shall make good the damage and be dishonorably deprived of his office in front of the whole kingdom.[18]

13. = 1222:15.

14. = 1222:16.

15. = 1222:17.

16. = 1222:18.[19]

17. = 1222:19.

18. = 1222:21.

19. = 1222:22.

20. = 1222:23.

21. = 1222:24.

22. = 1222:25.

23. = 1222:26.

24. = 1222:29.

25. = 1222:30.

26. = 1351:1.

27. = 1351:2.

28. = 1351:3.

29. = 1351:4.

30. = 1351:5.

31. = 1351:6.

32. Then, we (. . .) as well as the prelates, barons, nobles and other landowners who own fishing waters shall ensure that we receive, and the same (lords) are entitled to receive, at the annual fishing one third of any kind of fish caught from running waters and half of the fish from lakes commonly called *mocsár* or *morotva*[20] so that our honor be increased and our gentlemen of the realm be able to serve us more faithfully.[21]

33. = 1351:7.

34. = 1351:9.

35. = 1351:10.

36. Then, all gentlemen of the our realm asked our majesty to deign to preserve all the noblemen and other landowners of Slavonia and of the counties Pozsega and Valkó in the same privileges concerning the payment of the chamber's profit and of the *mardurina* which were granted the gentlemen of the realm of our Hungary.[22]

XXXVII. = 1351:XIII.
XXVIII. = 1351:XIV.
XXXIX. = 1351:XVII.
XL. = 1351:XVIII.
XLI. = 1351:XIX.
XLII. = 1351:XX.
XLIII. = 1351:XXI.
XLIV. = 1351:XII.[23]
XLV. = 1351:XXIII.
XLVI. = 1351:XXIV.
XLVII. = 1351:XXV.

XLVIII. Preterea eisdem regnicolis necnon ad eorundem instantiam annuimus, ut omnes et quoslibet homines nostros alienigenas et advenas de dicto regno nostro emittimus et emitti faciemus[24] preter hos, videlicet magnificum virum dominum Stiborium wayuodam[25] ac venerabiles patres dominos Eberhardum[26] Zagrabiensis et Maternum[27] Transsilvanensis ecclesiarum episcopos, et quod nos ac prenotati episcopi et wayuoda nostri nostros et eorundem familiares alienigenas et advenas de cunctis nostris et eorundem castris, tenutis et possessionibus usque ad octavas festi Nativitatis domini nunc venturi[28] excipiemus, transmittemus et transmitti faciemus per dominos episcopos et w[ayuo]dam prenotatos. Nec amodo et deinceps plures homines advenas, secularies videlicet et ecclesiasticos ad honores seculares et beneficia ecclesiastica promovebimus nec predictis auctoritatem promovendi committimus, in cunctis etiam castris, tenutis et possessionibus infra ambitum dicti regni nostri habitis homines Vngaric[e nati]onis locabimus et deputari faciemus per iam dictos.

XLIX. Ceterum ordinatum etiam extitit et dispositum per antefatos barones et regnicolas universos, ut omnia castra, tenute, civitates et possessiones, que vel quas quibusdam eo tempore, quo iidem adversus nos animo indurato et manu poten[ti insur]rexissent, pre timore insurrectionis eorundem tradidissemus et donassemus, simil cum talibus donationibus, quas hiis, qui inter nostram serenitatem et predictos rebellizantes in nos pro pace facienda tunc laborassent aut pacem fecissent, contulissemus et tradidissemus pre timore prenotato, [merito] et iusto modo aufferre v[aleamus] ab eisdem. Donationes autem universas, quas hiis, qui nostre serenitati fideles famulatus inpendissent, et qui in nostris servitiis neci traditi et dimembrati fuissent aut suorum filiorum et proximorum ipsorum necem ac sanguinis eorundem effusionem passi essent, fecissemus, ratificabimus et confirm[abimus litter]arum nostrarum per vigorem, et quod cuncta castra, tenutas ac possessiones quaslibet, quas et que vendidissemus aut inpignorassemus, ab hiis, quibus ipsas et eadem vendidissemus aut inpignorassemus, sine omni pecuniaria solutione recipere et in ius ac proprietatem sacre corone nostre regie [ad manus nostras] applicandi habeamus auctoritatem.[30]

37. = 1351:13.
38. = 1351:14.
39. = 1351:17.
40. = 1351:18.
41. = 1351:19.
42. = 1351:20.
43. = 1351:21.
44. = 1351:22.[23]
45. = 1351:23.
46. = 1351:24.
47. = 1351:25.

48. Furthermore, on the request of our gentlemen of the realm, we agree to dismiss and cause to be dismissed all foreigners and newcomers from our kingdom,[24] except the following ones: the honorable voivode Stibor[25] and the reverend lords Eberhard, bishop of Zagreb,[26] and Maternus, bishop of Transylvania;[27] and we promise that we and the above-mentioned bishops and the voivode will expel and send away, and that we shall cause the aforesaid bishops and the voivode to send away all of our and their retainers who are foreigners or newcomers from our and from their castles, holdings, and estates by the eighth day of the coming feast of Christmas;[28] and henceforth we shall appoint no foreigners, be they laymen or clergy, to secular offices or ecclesiastical benefices, and we shall not grant liberty to do so to the above-mentioned officeholders either. We shall place only Hungarians in all castles, holdings, and estates on the territory of our kingdom and shall cause the aforesaid officeholders do the same.

49. In addition, the above-mentioned barons and gentlemen of the realm, all together have decided and ordered that we shall be able to revindicate justly all those castles, holdings, towns, and estates which we have given and granted to certain persons out of fear of their rebellion in the time when they obstinately had risen against us with mighty force, as well as the grants which we made because of the said fear to those who at that time exerted themselves to make peace or arranged the peace between our majesty and the rebels.[29] All other grants, however, which we have given those who had served our majesty faithfully and who were killed or maimed in our service or who suffered the shedding of blood of their sons or kinsmen, we shall uphold and confirm with the authority of our charter. Also, we shall have the authority to recover all castles, holdings, and other estates which we have sold or mortgaged, without paying any compensation to those whom we have sold or pledged them and to return them to the right and possession of the Holy Crown.[30]

L. Item si qui ex prelatis seu viris ecclesiasticis, baronibus et eorundem baronum filiis ac magnatibus contra quoscunque in quibusvis factis et causis, in facto potentie, delationis falsarum litterarum, calumpnie et astationis falsi termini[31] annotatis gravaminibus in presentia q[uorundam iu]dicum convincerentur, hos non protegemus, sed ad satisfaciendum eorum adversariis eosdem per dominum palatinum astringi faciemus.

LI. Nichilominus si quipiam terminos eorum iuramenti,[32] duelli, communis inquisitionis[33] et proprie obligationis[34] deputatos obmiserint, eisdem amplius alter terminus pro exse[cutione -----m][35]inime debeat deputari, sed secundum dignitatem talis cause iudex ordinarius procedere debeat.

LII. Nobiles etiam regni nostri et aliorum quorumvis jobagiones pro nullis factis regni nostri amplius dicari faciemus, sed eosdem in eisdem libertatibus, quibus iidem temporibus regum predecessorum [nostrorum sunt gavisi], frui et gratulari committemus.[37]

LIII. Hoc declarato etiam, quod si aliquis aliquas novitates,[38] scilicet facta potentiaria, spoliationes, derobationes et illegitimas possessionum occupationes ac alia consimilia cuipiam fecerit aut irrogasset, tunc vicecomes et iudices nobilium rescita prius de hiis omnimoda v[eritate, non obst]antibus litteris nostris regalibus gratiosis quibuscunque, ex parte talis sine omni dilatione satisfactionis complementum parti lese impendant.[39] Et si qua partium in huiusmodi inpensione iudicii non contentaretur, tunc discussio eiusdem iudicii inpensionis in nostram ac prelatorum et regni nostri baronum [presentiam tran]smitti debeat,[40] ubi nos et iidem prelati ac barones partibus ambabus, non obstantibus quibusvis litteris nostris prorogatoriis absque omni dilatione iudicium exhibere teneantur.

LIV. Hoc etiam non pretermisso, quod filias quorumvis regnicolarum nostrorum in possessionibus et hereditatibus patris sui infra quintam lineam generationis eiusdem in heredes masculos non procreabimus.[41]

LV. Item si aliquis in gravaminibus aliqorum iudiciorum in processu alicuius cause in presentia cuiusvis iudicis convictus fuerit, tunc iudex ipsius cause ante decisionem eiusdem pro ipsis iudiciis neminem captivare vel in rebus dampnificare presumpmat, demptis talibus personis, que ibidem in ipsius iudicis presentia in factis potentie, calumpnie, delationis falsarum litterarum et astationis falsi termini[42] convincerentur.

LVI. Item si aliquis quempiam nota infidelitatis denigraverit, talem una cum baronibus et regni nostri nobilibus iudicabimus et simul sententiabimus.[43]

LVII. Preterea beneficia ecclesiastica bullati[44] acceptare non valeant, nisi illi, quibus per patronos ipsarum ecclesiarum ipse ecclesie conferuntur.

50. Then, if any prelate or other ecclesiastic, baron, baron's son, or any magnate is convicted of violent trespass, proffering false documents, frivolous prosecution, or false court appearance[31] against anyone in any case by any judge, we will not protect him but will force him through the count palatine to give satisfaction to his adversaries.

51. Nevertheless, if anyone misses the date set for taking an oath,[32] for a judicial combat, for a common inquest,[33] or for paying a debt,[34] he ought not be granted another date for settlement of the matter,[35] but the judge ordinary of the case[36] shall proceed according to the merit of the case.

52. We shall not impose taxes for any matter of this kingdom on the nobles of the kingdom and on the tenant peasants of others, but shall let them enjoy the same liberty which they had during the reign of our predecessors.[37]

53. We also proclaim that if someone should commit any novelties,[38] that is, violent trespass, looting, robbery, illegal seizure of estates, or other similar acts against anyone, then the *alispán* and the noble magistrate, after having established the truth of the matter, should give adequate satisfaction without delay, to the aggrieved party,[39] regardless of any kind of royal letter of pardon. Should one of the parties not be satisfied with the judgment, then the suit ought to be transferred to us and to the prelates and barons,[40] where we and the same prelates and barons shall be obligated to do justice for both parties without any delay, regardless of any letter of prorogation issued by us.

54. It should also be mentioned that we will not grant boys' rights in the estates or in the heritage of their fathers the daughters of any gentleman of the realm within the fifth degree of the same clan.[41]

55. Then, if in any trial before any judge someone will have been condemned to pay a fine, the judge of the case should not dare to take into custody that person or have his goods harmed in order to obtain the fines before the end of the trial, except those who have been convicted in the same court by the same judge of violent trespass, frivolous prosecution, proffering false documents, or false court appearance.[42]

56. If anyone will be denounced by someone for high treason, we shall judge him and pass sentence only together with the barons and nobles of our kingdom.[43]

57. Moreover, *bullati* should not be allowed to receive ecclesiastical benefices[44] except those which are granted by the patrons of the churches themselves.

LVIII. Nobiles etiam ad loca tributorum ire non compellantur, sed per portus, quos voluerint, libero transitu absque aliquali inpedimento potiantur.[45] Littere autem nostre gratiose quibusvis mercatoribus in eo, ut iidem in locis tributorum regnicolarum nostrorum tributa non solverent, date per amplius non dentur,[46] et quod si aliquis tributum in possessione sua sine consensu nostro institueret, tunc talis possessio simul cum ipso tributo devolvatur et applicetur iuri nostro regio ipso facto. Universi autem prelati, barones, nobiles et alterius cuiusvis status homines tributa habentes litteralia eorum instrumenta vel alia iura, quibus ipsa tributa instituta aut donata sunt, in octavis festi beati Georgii martiris nunc venturi[47] coram nostra maiestate ac prelatis et baronibus nostris exhibere et declarare teneantur. Qui vero nulla iura super eorum tributis nec per attestationem hominum suorum conprovincialium ac aliam declarationem assignare et declarare possunt, amplius inibi tributum non exigatur.

LIX. Item victualia, munera et alia consimilia quorumvis possessionatorum hominum de u[na posse]ssione ipsorum ad aliam aut alia loca deferenda sine tributaria solutione dimittantur.[48]

LX. Ceterum fratrum aut parentum et consanguineorum interficientium possessiones non extraneis et aliis, nisi lesis per regiam maiestatem perpetuo conferantur.

LXI. Comes etiam Crisiensis et Zagrabiensis comitatuum sigillum suum, quo [ipse in suo offi]cio fungitur, ipsemet servare non possit, nisi talis notarius, cui nobiles eorundem comitatuum ipsum assignabunt, neque idem comes absque interessentia iudicum nobilium in aliqua causa iudicium et deliberationem faciendi habeat auctoritatem.[49]

LXII. Item pro causis regnicolarum nostrorum universis a[udiendis, discutiendi]s[50] et iudicandis ad octavas maiores,[51] in quibus ipse cause vertuntur, tres vel quatuor ex prelatis et baronibus nostris transmittere teneamur.[52] Evocatorias autem litteras, quas cancellarii nostri sub hac forma verborum, videlicet ubi tunc deo duce fuerimus constituti novis modis inv[entis-----am]plius minime dare teneantur.[53] Illi autem, qui nostram specialem in presentiam super quibusvis causis evocabuntur, easdem causas per neminem alium preterquam prelatos et barones nostros iudicari faciemus et super tali adiudicatione littere nostre sub nostro sigillo regio conficiantu[r.[54] --- citation]es, evocationes et proclamationes quelibet non ad quindenas alicuius termini, sed ad octavas fieri procurentur.[55]

LXIII. Extitit etiam per barones et nobiles regni nostri antedictos ordinatum, ut universi viri ecclesiastici mediam partem omnium proventuum ipsorum pro tuitione confiniorum dicti [regni nostri durante] dumtaxat guerra presenti paganorum prescriptorum dare deberent et aministrare teneantur, et quod nullus regnicolarum nostrorum mediam partem decimarum quarumvis a jobagionibus

58. Nobles cannot be compelled to pass by places of toll-collection, but they may cross at any ford they wish free from hindrance.[45] We shall no longer issue letters of permission, which we used to give certain merchants exempting them from tolls of our gentlemen of the realm.[46] And if someone sets up a toll on his own estate without our approval, the toll and the estate will escheat to the royal right and into the possession of our royal majesty. All prelates, barons, nobles, and others of any estate and condition, moreover, who own tolls are obligated to show and to produce for our majesty, our prelates, and barons the letters and titles by which their tolls were established and granted by the eighth day of the coming feast of St. George the Martyr.[47] Those who are not able to produce a title to their toll, by either the testimony of the people from their county or other evidence, will no longer be allowed to collect that toll.

59. Then, any landowner who carries his foodstuff, presents, or other similar things from one of his estates to another should be allowed to pass without paying toll.[48]

60. Further, the royal majesty should not grant the estates of those who kill their brothers, parents, or kinsmen to strangers or to others, but only to the aggrieved persons in perpetuity.

61. The seals used in official acts of the *ispánok* of Körös and Zagreb counties should not be kept by the *ispánok* themselves but by the notary to whom the nobles of those counties entrust it; and without the presence of the noble magistrate, the *ispánok* are not allowed to pass judgment or to pronounce sentence in any case.[49]

62. Then, we commit ourselves to delegate three or four of our barons and prelates for hearing, trying, and settling[50] the various cases of our gentlemen of the realm to the major octaves[51] at which these cases are treated.[52] Letters of summons, moreover, issued by our chancellors with the clause "wherever we will stay by God's will" should henceforth never be issued.[53] Those who in specific cases are to be summoned to our special presence should be judged by no one else but our prelates and barons, and the letters of judgment should be issued under our own seal.[54] (. . .) summons and proclamations must not be issued for the fifteenth day of a certain date but only to an octave.[55]

63. The above-mentioned barons and nobles of our kingdom have also ordered that all clergy give and render half of their income for the defense of the frontiers, but only during the above-mentioned war against the pagans; and our gentlemen of the realm should give half of the tithe from their tenant peasants not to the clergy but should deliver it to those who will be selected by our majesty, together with the barons

eorum provenientium ipsis viris ecclesiasticis, sed talibus, quos pro ipsis mediis fructibus et prov[entibus colligendis ac] aministrandis nos una cum baronibus et nobilibus regni nostri eligemus, dare teneatur, sic videlicet, quod tales proventus non ad alia aliqua facta, nisi pro tuitione regni nostri prenotata exponantur, nec etiam tales deputatos homines ad id astringemus, ut iidem ad ali[qua alia facta dictos provent]us darent vel aministrarent.[56]

LXIV. Item pretextu premissorum antedicti viri ecclesiastici cuipiam regnicolarum nostrorum interdictum aut excommunicationem iniungere vel domino apostolico querulari non audeant modo aliquali, si vero quispiam ipsorum secus in hiis facere attemptaret, extunc idem v[igore -------al]iarum litterarum nostrarum patentium sub nostro ac baronum nostrorum sigillis sigillatarum convincatur ipso facto.[57]

LXV. Preterea quia in litteris privilegialibus condam dicti domini Lodouici regis felicis recordationis confirmationis inter alia in eisdem expressa id, ut decime argento non re[dimantur, sed si]cut terra profert et germinaret,[58] persolverentur, cernebatur haberi, ideo per barones et nobiles regni nostri prenotatos propter facta paganorum prescriptorum unanimi voluntate sanccitum extitit pariter et ordinatum, ut usque tempus prefixum universi proventus ecclesiasticarum personarum, qui acten[us cum frugibus re]cipi consueverunt, cum denariis recipi et aministrari possint, preteritaque ipsa guerra aministratio proventuum iam dictarum ecclesiasticarum personarum secundum pristinam libertatem in ipsis litteris dicti domini Lodouici regis confirmationis conscriptam fieri procuretur.

LXVI. Item decimatores virorum ecclesiasticorum ad dica[ndos homine]s non ipsimet, sed cum uno iudice nobilium accedendo quosvis homines decimandos, prout iidem quantitatem rerum eorum dicandarum fide eorum mediante astrinxerint, dicare teneantur, et quod iidem decimatores nobiles pauperes jobagionibus carentes, famulos ignobiles et jobagi[ones quosli]bet[59] bladis et vinis deficientes dicare non presumpmant.

LXVII. Item iidem viri ecclesiastici tam super regales et reginales, quam etiam baronum et nobilium sacerdotes preter consuetas collectas taxare non audeant;[60] et quod quivis archidiaconorum ad singulos sacerdotes et ecclesiarum rectores solum cum quat[uor equ]is semel in anno descendere possit.[61]

LXVIII. Interea homines ignobiles habita licentia et iusto terragio ipsorum persoluto usque quindecim dies omnibus debitoribus suis satisfaciendo et transactis ipsis quindecim diebus seque de omnibus expurgati, quo maluerint, transseundi liberam habeant [auct]oritatem: et si per quempiam non dimitterentur, tunc dominus talium hominum ignobilium, ad quem scilicet illi transsire voluerint, assumpto secum uno ex iudicibus nobilium tales vel eundem hominem ignobilem ad se et

and nobles of our kingdom, to collect and deliver the half of the ecclesiastical revenues and incomes, and these revenues should not be used for any other purpose but for the defense of our kingdom, and we should not force those appointed men to give or to use the said incomes for any other purpose.[56]

64. Then, none of those said clergy may dare to punish any gentleman of the realm for acting in accord with the aforementioned measure by interdict or by excommunication, or to lodge any complaint against them with the Apostolic Father; and if someone dares to act otherwise, that person should stand immediately convicted by the authority of our (. . .) letters patent sealed by our and by our barons' seals.[57]

65. Moreover, although the confirming letter of privilege issued by the late King Louis of blessed memory states among other matters that the tithe should not be commuted to money but should be rendered as the earth brings it forth,[58] the barons and nobles of our kingdom, pressed by the attacks of the above-mentioned heathens have unanimously decided and ordered that until the above date all the dues to the clergy which at present are usually collected in kind should be collected and delivered in money, but after the end of the present war the dues to the aforesaid ecclesiastics should be rendered according to the ancient privileges contained in King Louis' letter of confirmation.

66. Then, the tithing-men of the clergy should not go alone to assess the tithe but with the noble magistrate and should assess the tithe according to the tithe-payers' sworn declaration regarding their titheable goods; and the tithing-men should not dare to tithe poor nobles without tenant peasants, non-noble servants,[59] and such tenant peasants as have no wine and grain.

67. Then, these same clergy should not levy more taxes than the usual ones on the priests of the king, the queen, or of barons and nobles;[60] and the archdeacon is allowed to visit each priest and head of parish church only once a year accompanied by only four horses.[61]

68. Non-noblemen, once they have received leave, paid their just rent, and have satisfied all their creditors within fifteen days, are to be allowed to go freely wherever they wish after the fifteenth day when they have absolutely cleared themselves. And if someone is not allowed to go, then his noble master, namely to whom he wants to go, shall have unconditional right to lead and take him to his own estate with the assistance of a noble magistrate.[62]

suam possessionem modo premisso absolutam deducendi et asportandi habeat facultat[em.]

LXIX. Universique notarii, tam nostri, quam etiam domini palatini et iudicis curie nostre, necnon banorum et wayuode nostrorum in redemptionibus litterarum quarumvis earum redemptiones non aliter, nisi prout tempore dicti condam domini Lodouici regis fuit constitutum,[63] habere possint, de litteris scilicet sententialibus quib[usvi]s octo florenos auri per centum denarios novos numerando recipere valeant.

LXX. Postremo vero dicatores florenorum et viginti unius denariorum novorum per nos ac prelatos et barones nostros pridem intra ambitum regni nostri constituti in octavis festi Epiphaniarum domini similiter nunc affuturi, coram nobis comparere teneantur rationem expositionis ipsius taxe assignaturi efficacem.[64]

69. All notaries, ours or those of the count palatine, the judge royal, the bans, and the voivode should receive no other fees for the redemption of charters than those which were established in the reign of the late King Louis,[63] namely, eight golden florins counted in one hundred new pennies for any kind of letter of judgment.

70. Finally, the assessors of the one florin and twenty-one new pennies, whom we, our prelates, and our barons appointed some time ago for the territory of our kingdom, are obligated to present themselves and to give an account of the collected taxes on the eighth day of the coming feast of Epiphany.[64]

6 Aprili 1404

Vide praefatiunculam et notas infra paginas 184–85.

Deliberatio domini regis et baronum.

Nos Sigismundus dei gr[atia] rex Hungarie, Dalmatie, Croatie etc. marchioque Brandemburgensis, sacri Romani imperii vicarius generalis et regni Bohemie gubernator universis et singulis presentes inspectu[ris] et presertim, presentium serie volumus fieri manifestum, quomodo nonnulli, ymmo quamplures regnicole nostri, ecclesiastici videlicet et seculares creberrimis vicibus tribulationes, vexationes, dampna, nocumenta, iurium et iurisditionum ipsorum altercationes ac violationes ipsis per bullatos[1] hactenus irrogatas et illata fuisse ac irrogari de presenti lamentabilibus vocibus et turbatis animis nobis propalarunt, adeo insuper se per censuras ecclesiasticas, utputa citationes extra regnum, excommunicationes, interdicta, monitiones, pecuniarum, rer[um et b]onorum exinde exactiones, extorsiones et pactationes gravatos, impeditos et molestatos acclamarunt, quod, nisi superinde eis remedium relevationis et liberationis a[d]hiberetur oportunum, ad ingentem exinanitionem rerum et bonorum, necnon status, libertatis et iurisditionis eorundem exterminium eos oporteret devenire, supplicantes nostro culmini humiliter et devote, ut eis et eorum statui totiusque regni nostri utilitati et comodo regali presidio et defensionis auxilio succurrere dignaremur. Nos itaque, qui cunctorum et precipue nobis subiectorum incomodis subvenire et calamitates, quibus gravantur, reprimere tenemur, eisque toto nostro posse et voluntate ob[vi]are, auditis premissis lamentabilibus querelis et experientia nonnullis temporibus super eis recepta, oppressiones nichilominus et huiusmodi tribulationes, hucusque presertim hiis proximis disturbiorum et regni nostri motionum temporibus[2] per bullatos[3] ac alios auctoritate sedis apostolice, quam ad nostri honoris, status et gradus deiectionem, regni nostri et corone in alium translationem, ac alias ad nostri totalem depositionem laborasse et adhuc sentimus indefesse laborare, nobis et regnicolis nostris illatas et irrogatas animo iam ulterius tollerare non v[a]lentes patienti, attendentes potissime nefarium illi obedientie debitum debere reddere, qui subditorum utilitati et paci repugnans eos dolosis machinationibus et latentibus insidiis afficere et publicis nocumentis non desinit lacessere, omnium prelatorum, baronum, procerum, militum, nobilium et universitatum ditionis sacre corone regie Hungarie atque nostro consilio et matura deliberatione diutius prehabitis eorumque utilitate, intentione, ymmo petitione ad hoc circa nos laborantibus, presentium

6 April 1404

For prefatory and explanatory notes, see below, pages 184–85.

Decision of the lord king and the barons.

We, Sigismund, by the grace of God king of Hungary, Dalmatia, Croatia, etc., margrave of Brandenburg, vicar general of the Holy Roman Empire, and regent of Bohemia, wish that each and every person who will see these presents be informed by these words that some or indeeed many of our gentlemen of the realm, both clerical and lay, have revealed to us with lamenting words and perturbed souls that on many occasions they have suffered persecutions, insults and damages, challenges, and infringements to their rights and jurisdiction from papal collectors;[1] furthermore, they have complained of ecclesiastic punishments, notably of being summoned abroad, of excommunications, prohibitions, warnings, as well as of exaction, extortion, and forced sale of their money, goods, and chattels, which burden, obstruct, and worry them to such an extent that without timely help to protect and to relieve them they could not avoid the considerable destruction of their goods and chattels and the annihilation of their station, liberty, and rights; therefore, they have respectfully and with reverence requested our eminence that, with the bulwark and protection of the crown, we deign to come to their aid, their station, and the best interests and advantage of our entire kingdom. Hence, we, who are obligated to assist everyone, above all our aggrieved subjects, to confront and obviate the annoyances by which they are beleaguered with all our might and ability, having heard these sorrowful complaints, and having, in addition, personal experience on several occasions, no longer intend to tolerate these injuries and insults which befell us and our gentlemen of the realm, particularly during the recent disturbances and commotions in the kingdom,[2] when clerics with papal letters[3] and others empowered by the Apostolic See—which, as we know, has been assiduously attempting to destroy our honor, estate, and status, and to transfer our kingdom and crown to someone else, and also otherwise totally to depose us—for we regard it as particularly nefarious to show obedience to him who, attacking the welfare and peace of subjects, never ceases to mislead them with sly practices and hidden stratagems and to trouble them with open injuries. Therefore, we with our council and as a consequence of extensive and mature deliberation with all the prelates, barons, magnates, knights, nobles, and communities subject to the Holy Crown of Hungary, and considering their welfare, intention, and even explicit petition in this

serie auctoritate eiusdem sacre corone et de plenitudine regie potestatis volumus, pronunctiamus, sanctimus, decernimus et declaramus, quemadmodum pridem factum et dispositum fuisse recolimus,[4] ut nullus bullatus auctoritate videlicet apostolica vel alia quavis preterquam nostra, sine nostro speciali consensu et assensu beneficia ecclesiastica curata vel non curata, cuiuscunque valoris existant, olim, uti percepimus, vigore litterarum apostolicarum vel legatorum eius seu aliorum quorumcunque prelatorum acceptari et assequi solita acceptare, assequi et etiam tempore disturbiorum proxime preteritorum regni nostri assecuta et obtenta possidere, retinere et habere, durantibus instantibus dissensionum regni nostri temporibus et presenti decreto nostro immutato vel ir[re]vocato per expres[su]m, nec aliquis prelatorum eorundem et virorum ecclesiasticorum, cuiuscunque s[t]atus, ordinis, gradus, conditionis vel preeminentie existat, preter nobiles seculares ius patronatus[5] eligendi et presentandi habentes, beneficia qualiacunque vel quomodocunque vacantia vel vacatura cuiquam providere et de eis disponere in toto vel in parte preter nostram maiestatem, cuius dispositioni, collationi et provisioni ea pleno iure reservamus, nullas quoque litteras apostolicas et rescripta, cuiuscunque tenoris seu legatorum, cardinalium, auditorum ac iudicum, officialium et executorum quorumcunque, sive in Romana curia, sive extra eandem, cuiuscunque tenoris, roboris, firmitatis et comminationis existant, tam in causis beneficialibus, quam in aliis quibuscunque causis litigiosis, criminalibus vel prophanis[6] emanatas vel obtenta valeat atque possit, auctoritate regia supradicta irritum decernentes et inane, si contra hec per quempiam scienter vel ignoranter contigerit attemptari, contradictores denique et huic decreto repugnare attemptantes crimen lese maiestatis incurrere et irremissibiliter volumus condigna ultione puniri. Quocirca vobis universis et singulis prelatis, abbatibus, prepositis, prioribus, gwardianis, capitulis, ecclesiarum parochialium et capellarum rectoribus, aliis etiam cunctis viris ecclesiasticis, cuiuscunque status, conditionis et dignitatis existant, firmo regio sub edicto necnon sub pena capitis et privationis beneficiorum et rerum singulorum precipiendo mandamus, quatenus amodo deinceps nullas huiusmodi litteras apostolicas, legatorum, cardinalium, auditorum et aliorum quorumvis iudicum et officialium curie Romane, necnon cit[ati]ones, inhibitiones, rescripta, executiones et processus, cuiuscunque tenoris existant, tam in causis beneficialibus, quam in foro contentioso, sive in dicta Romana curia, sive extra per quoscunque iudices principales et executores emanatas et obtenta recipere, publicare et executioni demandare quovismodo presumatis sine nostro consensu et licentia speciali, et aliud sub pena premissa facere non ausuri. Presentes etiam volumus in locis et ad id aptis publice facere proclamari. Datum Posonii, dominico die in octava Pasche, anno domini millesimo quadringentesimo quarto.

matter, do by the authority of the aforementioned Holy Crown and by the plenitude of our royal power, will pronounce, establish, decide, and decree—through these presents, what we remember having recently enacted[4] and decided—that no clergy with apostolic authority or any other authority except our own be allowed to accept or to obtain ecclesiastical benefices, with or without the cure of souls, of whatever value they may be, which—as we understand—have been accepted and obtained through apostolic letters or those of papal legates or of other prelates, or to hold, retain, and keep those received during the recent disturbances in the kingdom, without our specific consent and permission, until the explicit modification or withdrawal of the present decree; nor is any one of the said prelates and clergy of whatever station, order, rank, condition, or standing, except for the lay nobles who have by reason of patronage[5] the right of selection and presentation, allowed to appoint someone to any kind of benefice, in whatever way vacant now or in the future, or to dispose of a benefice in whole or in part, except our majesty for whom we reserve these with the full right of disposal, collation, and provision. No one is allowed and enabled to receive, promulgate, and act upon apostolic letters and rescripts of whatever content, whether those of legates or cardinals, auditors, and judges, officials, and agents of anyone with whatever purport, force, validity, or sanction, issued or received from the Roman Curia or outside of it, regarding benefices as well as other lawsuits of any sort, criminal or profane,[6] which we declare null and void by our aforesaid royal authority; and if anyone attempts deliberately or through ignorance to act against these commands, he who contravenes them or dares to contest them, commits the crime of lèse majesté, and we will punish him with deserved revenge.

Therefore, we order each and every one of you, prelates, abbots, provosts, priors, wardens, chapters, rectors of parish churches and chapels, and all other clergy of whatever station, rank, and dignity, by our strict royal edict and under capital penalty and the loss of benefice and goods, that henceforth in the future you must not receive, promulgate, and act upon any kind of letter from the Apostolic See, from legates, cardinals, auditors, and magistrates or any other judge or official of the Roman Curia, nor any citation, prohibition, rescript, order, and legal writ of whatever purport they may have both in cases concerning benefices or other lawsuits, issued by or received from the said Roman Curia or outside of it, by any higher judge or agent without our specific consent and permission, and you will not dare to act otherwise subject to the above mentioned penalty.[7] We want these presents to be proclaimed publicly in places suitable for that purpose.

Given at Pozsony on the eighth day of Easter in the year of the Lord one thousand, four hundred and four.

21 Decembris 1404

Vide praefatiunculam et notas infra paginas 186–87.

Nos Sigismundus dei gratia rex Hungarie, Dalmatie, Croatie etc. marchioque Brandenburgensis etc. sacri Romani imperii vicarius generalis et regni Bohemie gubernator memorie commendamus per presentes, quod quemadmodum nobis alias extra regnum nostrum in partibus Bohemie pro sacri Romani imperii honore et iure nostri patrimonii pro posse insudantibus et laborantibus,[1] quidam prelati, magnates proceresque et nobiles regni nostri malo freti consilio, ymmo rebellionis calcaneo ducti et in reprobum sensum dati, ingrati et immemores beneficiorum a celsitudine nostra receptorum in crimine lese nostre maiestatis simul conspirantes nos verum regem et dominum Hungarie dyademate et solio ipsius regni nostri, cui iam deo propitio fere sedecim annis feliciter regnavimus, privare et destituere, aliumque eis ignotum regem, utputa Ladislaum filium condam Karuli de Duracio[2] eligendo in dictum regnum nostrum introducere satagebant, tandemque asistente nobis divini remedii adiutorio, nonnullorumque fidelium baronum et procerum nostrorum interveniente subsidio gubernacula dicti regni nostri votive readipisscentibus plerosque ex dictis infidelibus nostris iuxta demeritorum suorum exigentiam digna correctionis linea feriri alios quoque castris, tenutis, districtibus, civitatibus, opidis, possessionibus et cunctorum bonorum maneriebus privari disponentes et destitui, huiusmodi castra, tenutas, districtus, civitates, opida, possessiones et cunctorum bonorum maneries, tamquam per notam infidelitatis huiusmodi rebellionis ad manus nostras regias devoluta et redactas de dictisque manibus nostris regiis nonnullis predictis fidelibus baronibus, proceribus et nobilibus nostris partem nostram animo constanti et fidelitate firma tenentibus, foventibus et magnificantibus iuxta laudabilium servitiorum ipsorum merita vigore certarum litterarum nostrarum exinde confectarum iure perennali dedisse, donasse, contulisse et distribuisse perhibemur et recordamur; ita nunc nonnulli forent incole regni nostri, quorum, ut premittitur, possessiones et iura possessionaria per maiestatem modo premisso pretactis nostris fidelibus donate et distributa existunt, qui hiis tribus modis infrascriptis lamentabilibus querelis nostram infestant maiestatem:

Primo, qualiter nonnulli essent ex ipsis, quorum licet iura possessionaria propter notam infidelitatis ipsorum dictis nostris fidelibus in evum contulerimus, tamen tandem moti regia pietate, qua delinquentibus veniam solemus impertiri, ipsis capitibusque,

21 December 1404

For prefatory and explanatory notes, see below, pages 186–87.

We Sigismund, by the grace of God king of Hungary, Dalmatia, and Croatia, margrave of Brandenburg, etc., vicar general of the Holy Roman Empire, and regent of the kingdom of Bohemia, wish to be remembered by the words of these presents that during the time when we were exerting ourselves and working to the best of our ability for the honor of the Holy Roman Empire and our hereditary rights outside the kingdom in the regions of Bohemia,[1] certain prelates, magnates, lords, and nobles of our kingdom, relying on evil counsel or even led by rebellious intent and imbued with ill will, ungrateful to us, and unmindful of the benefits they have received from our majesty, conspired to commit high treason by attempting to deprive us and eject us, true king and lord of Hungary, from the crown and throne of the same kingdom, over which we had been, by God's permission, reigning for almost sixteen years now, by electing another person, not known to them personally, namely Ladislas, son of the late Charles of Durazzo, as king, and bringing him into the said kingdom of ours.[2] Finally, when with the help of divine assistance and the aid of some faithful barons and lords of ours we regained, according to our wishes, the governance of our said kingdom, we caused suitable punishments to be meted out according to their misdeeds to several of the said traitors against us and ordered that others be deprived of and expelled from their castles, tenancies, districts, cities, towns, estates, and all kinds of possessions. We have been reminded and remember that we gave, granted, transferred, and distributed in perpetuity these castles, tenancies, districts, cities, towns, estates, and other kinds of possessions, as having fallen and devolved to our royal hands by the deed of high treason of the said rebels, by our royal hands through certain charters of ours written in this matter to several of our said faithful barons, lords, and nobles, according to the merit of their praiseworthy service, who stood by us with steady heart and firm fidelity, supported us, and augmented our honor. Now then, there are several such people in our kingdom, whose estates and property rights, as mentioned before, have been distributed by our majesty among our said followers in the aforesaid manner, who now besiege our majesty with sorrowful complaints on the three following counts:

First, that there are among them such persons whose property rights, owing to their high treason, we have granted in eternity to our said followers, but to whose heads, estates, and all goods and chattels

possessionibus ac rebus et bonis ipsorum universis gratiam fecissemus specialem.

Secundo autem quibusdam ex ipsis, licet iura ipsorum possessionaria per eandem notam infidelitatis aliis fidelibus nostris donaverimus, tamen ipsi iuxta gratiam per nos ac domino Johanni archyepiscopo Strigoniensi, necnon utrique Nicolao alias vayuodis nostris Transsilvanensibus factam[3] a quibusvis malorum generibus, necnon actibus potentiariis et iniuriis cuipiam inferendis supersedissent prorsus et cessassent, nec unquam post predictam gratiam nobis aut cuipiam regnicolarum nostrorum, adherendo nostris rebellibus et emulis, aliquam iniuriam, dampna, nocumenta insolentiasque et obprobria intulissent.

Tertio autem essent tales, quorum similiter iura possessionaria pro premissa nota infidelitatis aliis nostris fidelibus certarum litterarum nostrarum donationalium vigore contulissemus, qui nunquam et maxime in hiis proxime elapsis disturbiorum temporibus aliquid noxii criminis infidelitatis aut alicuius contagionis infidelitatis notam in se continentis contra nostram maiestatem et sacrum nostrum regium dyadema aut alios quoscunque fideles nostros palam vel oculte perpetrassent et commisissent, propter que ipsi huiusmodi eorum possessionibus et iuribus possessionariis non essent digne et merito privandi et destituendi, supplicantes nostro culmini vocibus gemebundis, ut ipsis circa premissa de remedio providere dignaremur opportuno.

Nos itaque, qui ex suscepti regii regiminis officio causas quorumlibet oppressorum et querulantium animo metiri debemus iustitia requirente, auditis et sane intellectis propositionibus premissis, unacum fidelibus prelatis, baronibus et proceribus nostris maturo exinde prehabito et digesto consilio circa premissos articulos, obiectiones et querelas per memoratos querulantes modo superius specificato coram nobis ac ipsis prelatis et baronibus nostris propositos et declaratas, unacum eisdem sanximus, decrevimus et instituimus super hiisque statutum fecimus:

I. Ut hii omnes et singuli regnicole nostri, quorum, uti superius expressatum est, iura possessionaria aliis fidelibus nostris pretextu premisse note infidelitatis contulisse dinoscimur, hos nostros fideles, apud quos dicta iura possessionaria existunt, in domibus eorum propriis, aut alias, ubi reperiri poterint, mediantibus hominibus nostris regiis et testimoniis aliquorum credibilium capitulorum vel conventuum contra se ipsos personaliter vel per procuratorem nostre maiestatis personalem, ubi pro tunc deo duce unacum eisdem prelatis, baronibus et proceribus nostris fuerimus constituti,[4] evocent in presentiam, merum, plenum et condignum iudicium finemque decisivum recepturos causa in premissa.[5]

II. Adveniente autem ipso termino ipsis partibus coram nobis pro habendo in eorum causa moderativo iudicio comparentibus, si et in

we have later granted the same special pardon moved by royal grace we are accustomed to grant trespassers.

Second, some of them, although we have granted their property rights, because of the same charge of high treason, to other followers of ours, had—according to the pardon granted by us to the lord John, archbishop of Esztergom, as well as the two Nicholases, our former voivodes of Transylvania[3]—completely avoided and ceased to commit any kind of misdeed, act of violent trespass and harmful action against anybody, nor caused after that pardon any injury, damage, harmful insolence, or abuse against us or any of our gentlemen of the realm by joining our enemies or rivals.

Third, there are also those whose property rights we have granted by the force of specific charters, similarly for the said act of high treason, to other followers of ours, but who had never, particularly not in these recently past times of troubles, committed or perpetrated anything punishable by the charge of high treason or were involved in any other criminal complicity, publicly or secretly against our majesty, the Holy Crown, or any of our followers; hence, it would be neither right nor proper to deprive them of their estates and property rights and to expel them; they beseeched our eminence with lamentations that we deign to provide suitable remedy for the matters said before.

We, therefore, who by our received office of governance ought to weigh at all times the case of any oppressed and complaining person, having, as justice demands, heard and sufficiently pondered the aforesaid matters, have, after having taken and accepted due counsel with our faithful prelates, barons, and lords, together with them decided, decreed, and ruled regarding the above listed articles, objections, and complaints of the aforementioned complainants which were presented and enunciated in our presence together with the same prelates and barons, in the way described above have issued the following statutes :

1. That those of our gentlemen of the realm, individually and collectively, whose property rights we, as described above, are known to have granted by reason of the said act of high treason to other followers of ours, should summon those followers of ours who now hold these said property rights, from their own houses or from wherever they can find them, through our royal bailiffs and the witness of any chapter or convent of authentication, personally or through their lawyer to the personal presence of our majesty, wherever we, with God's guidance, shall be, together with our prelates, barons, and lords,[4] so that they might receive a true, complete, and appropriate judgment and final conclusion for the said matter.[5]

2. When, then, at the appointed time, these parties appear before us, in order to receive exemplary judgment in their case, if they will have unanimously and by common will submitted and committed

quantum ipse partes unanimi et concordi voluntate se ipsas in eorum causa attestationi seu testimonio aliquorum fidedignorum proborum et nobilium virorum, qui fideles fuerunt a principio et sunt nostre maiestati, sponte submiserint aut compromiserint, extunc ibidem ipsa compromissio ipsis partibus per nos ac ipsos barones nostros admittatur et consentiatur; inter ipsasque partes iuxta formam huiusmodi compromissionis aut attestationis iudicium et iustitia exhibeatur indilate, prout conveniens fuerit et iuri videbitur expedire.

III. In casu vero, quo partes pretacte in huiusmodi testium electione discordes fuerint, tunc nos prelatos, barones aut tales nobiles illius comitatus, in quo ipse possessiones donate et collate existunt, qui nobis fideles fuere, vel si in ipso comitatu tot et tanti nobis fideles in numero pro tunc non fuissent, quorum testimonium super hiis sufficiens esset et acceptandum, tunc alios nostros fideles alterius comitatus ipsis possessionibus collatis propinquiores de fidelitate vel infidelitate partis, que inculpatur, per certas nostras litteras requirere et ab ipsis exinde meram certitudinem recipere et experiri tenemur, ut recepta rei veritate inter ipsas partes finem facere valeamus indilatum.

Ad conclusionem autem horum articulorum:

IV. Primo quicunque regnicolarum nostrorum, quorum iura possessionaria modo antelato cuipiam fidelium nostrorum sunt collata, se annotatam gratiam per nos ipsis domino archyepiscopo et wayvodis factam per evidens documentum aut alia credibilia testimonia veraciter observasse comprobare poterunt, tales rursus in plenum dominium universorum iurium ipsorum possessionariorum debent esse in continenti restituendi. Illis vero nostris fidelibus, apud quos ipsa iura possessionaria extiterint, loco eorundem alias possessiones dare non tenebimur. Illi autem fideles nostri, qui possessiones aliquorum infidelium nostrorum notoriorum a nobis impetrarunt, et se ipsos ipsi infideles ab ipsa nota infidelitatis expurgare non valerent, allegantes solum sibi ipsis capitibus, possessionibus et bonis eorum post ipsam donationem nostram per nostram maiestatem gratiam fore factam, in pleno dominio ipsarum possessionum ipsis donatarum in evum debeant remanere, nec unquam ipsas possessiones ab eisdem nostris fidelibus modo qualicumque absque bona eorum annuentia et voluntate aufferre valeamus, nec ipsis infidelibus nostris ipsa gratia nostra, quoad rehabitionem ipsarum possessionum eorum possit in aliquo suffragari, quoniam volumus huiusmodi donationem nostram semper et ubique in sui roboris firmitate inviolabiliter permanere.

V. Item quicunque fidelium nostrorum alias possessiones nostrorum infidelium a culmine nostro modo qualicumque obtinuerit vel impetraverit, se ipsumque in dominium huiusmodi possessionum per nos sibi donatarum tepiditate aut aliqua alia inertia ductus infra tempus legittimum, utputa infra anni revolutionem per nostrum et capituli aut conventus homines, prout moris est, statui non fecerit,[6] talis vigores litterarum suarum donationalium perdiderit, ipseque

themselves to the testimony and declaration of certain trustworthy and honest noblemen who have been faithful to our majesty from the beginning by their own free will, then and there an agreement among the parties themselves shall be admitted and consented to by us and our barons. The judgment among the parties themselves, according to the wording of such an agreement or declaration shall constitute immediate justice and shall be expedited to the extent that it is convenient and congrues with law.

3. In the case, however, that the said parties will not have been able to agree in the selection of such witnesses, we are obligated to inquire through specific letters of ours and to find out the truth from the prelates, barons, or other nobles who have been our followers in that county where these estates are granted and donated, or if in that county we should not have at the time an adequate number of followers whose testimony would be sufficient and admissible in this matter, then from other followers of ours in another county closest to the transferred estates, regarding the faithfulness or unfaithfulness of the accused party; so that, having ascertained the truth in the matter, we should be able to pass final decision between the same parties.

In conclusion of these points we have decreed:

4. First, that any gentleman of our realm whose property rights have been in the above-mentioned manner transferred to any one of our followers, but who can prove by appropriate record or other trustworthy testimony that he truly observed the said pardon granted by us to the lord archbishop and the voyvodes, should immediately receive again full dominion of all his property rights; and we are not held to give to those followers of ours in whose hands these property rights have been any other estate in their stead.

Those followers of ours, however, who had asked from us the estates of such traitors who could not clear themselves from the charge of high treason, but merely maintain that our majesty had granted pardon to their lives, estates, and goods after the said donation, should be left for ever in the full dominion of the estates granted to them. We shall have no right to take away these estates from these our followers under any pretext without their free consent and will, and our pardon for those traitors should have no value whatsoever for the recovery of these estates, because we wish that these grants of ours should remain always and everywhere in full and inviolable force.

5. Then, if any of our followers who had requested or obtained from our eminence in whatever way an estate of the traitors, but because of laxity or laziness of some sort did not arrange to take *seisin* of such an estate within the statutory period, namely one year, by a bailiff of ours or of a chapter or a convent, as is usual,[6] should lose the force of such a charter of donation, and the estates should immediately fall to our royal hands straightaway, or, in such a case, they should be

possessiones rursus ad manus nostras regias sunt devolvende eo facto, aut hiis regnicolis nostris, quibus capitibus et possessionibus gratiam fecissemus, in eo casu debent esse utique restituende. Illorum autem infidelium possessiones, quorum solum capitibus et non possessionibus gratiam fecisse perhibemur, nobis remaneant, aut si cuicunque ipsas maluerimus donare, id in nostra constat et constare poterit voluntate. Qui vero modo et consuetudine observatis se vigore donationis nostre regie in dominium possessionum sibi datarum infra tempus legittimum per nostrum et capituli aut conventus homines introduci ac per ipsos homines fassionem debitam coram dicto capitulo aut conventu, prout moris est, fieri procuravit, occurrentibusque interim et imminentibus sibi aliquibus impedimentis aut obstaculis eorundem capituli et conventus, vel ipsi capitulum et conventus ipsas litteras statutorias ob contradictionem, inhibitionem aut aliam potentiariam resistentiam aut amore seu formidine dictorum nostrorum infidelium vel fratrum eorundem, aut aliis causis ex premissis extradare et emanari facere recusassent, tunc ex eo non debet perdere vigores littere sue donationalis, dummodo de re legittime doceat et super hiis perhibeat testimonium veritatis.

VI. Preterea quicumque fidelium nostrorum in dominium possessionum ob notam infidelitatis alicuius per nos sibi donatarum infra anni revolutionem aut hucusque ob metum et potentiam sui adversarii vel de nostra commissione seu mandato aut prorogatione se statui facere nequivisset et in dominium earundem legittime introire, et id rite et legittime cum sufficienti testimonio posset comprobare, similiter nolumus, ut ex eo perdat vigores suarum litterarum donationalium.

VII. Volumus etiam et presentis scripti nostri patrocinio stabilimus, ut hii omnes et singuli nostri fideles, qui de possessionibus eorum per nostram maiestatem eis pretextu aliquorum infidelitatis donatis vigore gratie nostre per nos ipsis infidelibus facte aut per ipsos infideles aut alios quoscunque potentialiter exclusi essent, vel qui, ut premisimus, ob metum dictorum adversariorum eorum hucusque dictas possessiones intrare nequivissent, rursus in dominium plenum earundem per comites parochiales illorum comitatuum, in quibus ipse possessiones existunt, modis omnibus restituantur et introducantur.

VIII. Volumus etiam, ut numerus eorundem fidelium nostrorum augeatur et via recludatur delinquentium, sanximus, ut quicumque regnicolarum nostrorum quibusvis nostris infidelibus facto, consilio aut subsidio expensarumque largitione subvenisse aut ipsis hospitalitatem prebuisse comprobari poterunt, hii omnes similiter perdant iura ipsorum possessionaria universa, harum nostrarum vigore et testimonio litterarum.[7]

Datum in Zolyo, in festo beati Thome apostoli, anno domini millesimo quadringentesimo quarto.

restored to those of our gentlemen of the realm to whom we had granted pardon for their lives and estates. However, the estates of those traitors whom we had granted pardon for their heads only but not for their properties, we shall retain ourselves or have and shall have the liberty to grant to whomever we prefer. The donation charters of those, however, who kept the law and custom and had taken *seisin* through a bailiff of ours and of a chapter or convent, of the dominion of the estates granted them, and made, as is usual, the proper declaration through those men before the chapter or convent, but in the meantime this chapter or convent denied them or refused to issue the letters of *seisin* because of some obtacles or difficulties having emerged before them or the chapter or convent, or because of some problem or violent resistance, or owing to favor or fear from the said traitors or their kinsfolk or for any other specific cause, should not for this reason lose their validity, provided that the grantees legally document these things and present truthful testimony concerning them.

6. Furthermore, if any of our followers was unable because of fear or the violence of his opponent or because of a command, mandate, or extension of ours to take *seisin* within a year of the dominion of the estates granted him by us owing to the high treason of someone, and is able to prove this properly and legally with sufficient witnesses, we are thus unwilling that his charter of donation should lose its force.

7. We also wish and establish by the protection of these presents that all and every one of our followers who have been violently barred by the traitors or by anyone else from their estates, granted them by our majesty on the basis of some act of treason, or those, who, as said before, were not able to enter into possession of the estates owing to fear of their said adversaries, should be by all means restored to and granted full dominion of these by the *ispán* of those counties in which these estates are located.

8. We also wish that the number of our followers may increase and the road for the evildoers be barred; therefore, we have decreed that any of our gentlemen of the realm who can be proven to have abetted by deed, counsel, assistance, or contribution of expenses any of the traitors or to have offered them hospitality should, by the force and witness of these presents, likewise lose all their property rights.[7]

Given in Zólyom, on the feast day of St. Thomas, the Apostle, in the year of the Lord one thousand, four hundred and four.

15 Aprili 1405

Vide praefatiunculam et notas infra paginas 188–93.

Sigismundus dei gratia Hungarie, Dalmatie, Croatie, Rame, Seruie, Gallicie, Lodomerie, Comanie Bulgarieque rex, marchioque Brandemburgensis ac sacri Romani imperii archicamerarius, necnon Bohemie et Lucemburgensis heres, universis Christi fidelibus tam presentibus, quam futuris, presentium notitiam habituris salutem in omnium salvatore. Sceptrigera regalis dignitatis altitudo eo vigilantiori cura subditorum suorum conservationem ac tranquillitatem exquirit, quo felicitatem publicam in sui augmentum et gloriam, calamitatem vero in sui cernit detrimentum et ignominiam redundare. Neque enim princeps esse potest inglorius, qui de subiectorum pace et securitate semper cogitat, neque non ignavus, qui futuris malis et periculis non previdet, quando potest. Hinc est, quod convocatis ex omnibus regni nostri comitatibus ac districtibus civitatum, opidorum et liberarum villarum regie iurisditioni pertinentium nunciis et legatis,[1] auditis et diligenter intellectis eorum et cuiuslibet ipsorum petitionibus, requisitionibus, informationibus, opinionibus et querelis, de prelatorum, baronum et potiorum regni nostri procerum, ipsorum etiam legatorum consilio, matura quoque superinde deliberatione prehabita pro bono et pacifico statu evidentique utilitate totius regni nostri quasdam civitates murorum ambitu cingendas,[2] quasdam liberas villas seu opida civitatis honore sublimandas, quasdam consuetudines, que potius abusiones videbantur, abolendas, quasdam moderandas, quasdam in melius reformandas, quedam etiam de novo statuenda decrevimus, sanximus et ordinavimus, prout infra.

Ad quam rem una potissimum consideratio mentem nostram induxit, quod retroactis temporibus, prout in cronicis legitur Hungarorum,[3] hoc regnum nostrum variis sepe afflictionibus interdum per Bissenos, aliquando per Tartaros, nonnunquam per alios paganos, novissime vero per Turcos irrogatis solummodo ob muratarum civitatum seu aliarum munitionum carentiam et defectum, cum homines, ubi se et bona sua recludere seu reducere possent, loca fortia non haberent, quin ymo cuncta exposita predis hostium in propatulo subiacerent, miserabiles desolationes, tristissimas populorum abductiones et generaliter innumerabilia, que horror est referri, et inestimabilia pertulit detrimenta.

I. Primo namque quorundam subditorum nostrorum precibus inclinati libertates infradeclarandas statuimus, quod in omnibus civitatibus, opidis, castris et villis, et generaliter ubicunque intra regni

15 April 1405

For prefatory and explanatory notes, see below, pages 188–93.

Sigismund, by the grace of God, king of Hungary, Dalmatia, Croatia, Rama, Serbia, Galicia, Lodomeria, Cumania, and Bulgaria, margrave of Brandenburg, archchamberlain of the Holy Roman Empire, heir of Bohemia and Luxemburg, to all Christ's faithful, present and future to whose notice these presents may come, greetings in the Savior of all.

The more the sceptre-bearing eminence of royal dignity perceives that happiness of the subjects serves the growth and glory of the kingdom, while their misery causes its detriment and bad reputation, the more he desires to maintain by vigilant care their sustenance and peace. For no prince can be inglorious who constantly contemplates the peace and safety of his subjects, and none worthy who does not forestall future dangers and disasters when he can. That is why, after having called together the emissaries and delegates of cities, towns, and free villages under royal jurisdiction, from every county and district of our realm,[1] and having listened to and understood well all their petitions, requests, presentations, views, and complaints, we have decided, ordered, and commanded for the good and peaceful state and the manifest advantage of our entire kingdom, with the counsel of the prelates, barons, and the greater lords of our kingdom as well as of the delegates, having held mature deliberations in these matters, that certain cities be surrounded by protective walls,[2] certain free villages and towns be raised to the status of cities, certain customs, which appear rather to be abuses, be abolished, others changed, others improved, and some newly established.

One major consideration led us to these decisions, namely that this kingdom in times past, as one can read in the chronicles of the Hungarians,[3] had to endure deplorable destruction, sorrowful abduction of people, and in general innumerable and inestimable damages horrible to relate, from different and frequent attacks, once by the Pechenegs, once by the Mongols, or other pagans, and more recently by the Turks, only because, owing to the lack of walled cities and other fortifications, there were no fortified places in which people with their goods could have found refuge and shelter, but were instead completely exposed unprotected, easy prey to the enemy.

1. First, moved by the requests of some of our subjects, we establish the following liberties: that in all cities, towns, castles and villages, be they ours or others', and in general everywhere in the realm,

weights, scales, ells, and the measures of wine, grain, and everything measurable and weighable shall be weighed and measured according to the measures of our city of Buda,[4] with the exception of the measure of the tithes and of the tribute of the mountains commonly called *hegyvám*, in German, *Pergrecht*,[5] as well as the income, rent, land, and revenue of priests and ecclesiastical persons which we wish to remain in their present state, quality, quantity, and value. Moreover, if anyone dares to act otherwise, he shall be punished by the loss of the thing so weighed or measured, losing the entire item subject to weight or measure even if only a part was weighed and measured incorrectly.

2. We have also decided that foreign merchants should not be permitted in any city to cut cloth and sell it by the ell, or moreover, to sell less than six bolts at once at any time, not even during fairs,[6] provided that these merchants are known to have six or more pieces of cloth. If they have fewer than six bolts, they should be allowed and permitted to sell or exchange these bolts individually. If there is an attempt to act otherwise, the pieces of cloth sold, transferred, or exchanged in contravention of this ordinance of ours, as well as the money that may have been paid for them, should be confiscated.

3. We have decreed, furthermore, that no notary public dare to intervene in any way or act as an advocate in cases between two laymen, either before an ecclesiastical or a lay judge;[7] and no outside testimony shall be introduced into cases of burghers, nor should noblemen or clergy be able to institute inquisitions againt them.[8]

4. Furthermore, each and every citizen, settler or inhabitant of any of our cities or free villages attached to one of the major cities[9] is permitted to appeal any sentence passed by the judges and burghers to our Master of the Treasury or to the judges of that city in accordance with the laws of which his city or free village makes use. Nor has the case to be carried further to the bench of other judges from the judgment or sentence of those to whom the appeal was made, but is to be completed and closed before them.[10]

5. In addition: since the palatine, the county *ispánok*, and others holding the honor and office of baronage, who by ancient custom of our kingdom, observed both by the holy kings, our predecessors, and ourselves, judged, sentenced, punished, or proscribed at palatinal meetings and general law-courts any thief, robber, or other criminal proscribed and extradited[11] there, and also noblemen, by special royal grace granted to them, have had the full authority to judge as criminals and punish those culprits whom they had caught in misdeeds and crimes on their estates,[12] we have thought best to establish by the present statute that henceforth, for the keeping of the peace, the more

nostri ambitum, tam in nostris, quam aliorum, quorumcunque sint, libra, statera, ulna, mensura vini, frugum et generaliter omnes res mensurabiles et ponderabiles ponderentur et mensurentur secundum mensuram civitatis nostre Budensis,[4] demptis tantummodo mensuris decimarum et montium tributis vulgo heguam, in Teutonico pergreht,[5] ac lucris, censibus, feudis et redditibus presbiterorum et virorum ecclesiasticorum, quos in suis statu et iustitia, quantitate et valore volumus permanere. Si quis autem contrarium facere presumpserit, incidet in penam amissionis rei ponderate vel mensurate, perdendo pro parte ponderata vel mensurata totam rem ponderandam vel mensurandam.

II. Sanximus preterea mercatoribus forensibus in civitatibus quibuslibet pannos incidere et ad ulnam vendere, ymmo nec pauciores sex staminibus simul vendere ullo tempore, etiam diebus nundinarum non licere, dummodo iidem mercatores sex pannos vel plures habere dinoscantur.[6] Si vero pauciores sex haberent, eosdem integros vendere vel commutare valeant atque possint. Quod si secus attemptatum fuerit, perdantur quelibet stamina contra huiusmodi ordinationem nostram vendita, alienata vel commutata, necnon pecunia, si qua forte soluta fuisset pro eisdem.

III. Decrevimus insuper, quod nullus publicus notarius in causis, que inter duos laicos vertuntur, sive coram iudice ecclesiastico, sive seculari procurare audeat vel ullatenus advocare,[7] sed nec extraneum testimonium inter cives locum habeat, nec nobiles seu viri ecclesiastici inquisitiones possint facere contra eos.[8]

IV. Porro omnibus et singulis civibus, hospitibus et populis quarumcunque[9] civitatum nostrarum et liberarum villarum alicui ex principalioribus civitatibus annexarum a quacunque sententia per eorum iudices et cives lata ad magistrum tauarnicorum nostrorum vel ad iudicium illius civitatis, cuius libertate talis civitas vel villa libera fungitur, liceat appellare, nec ab illorum, ad quos appellatum fuerit, iudicatu vel sententia sit ulterius in aliorum iudicum presentiam procedendum, sed ipsa causa debeat coram eisdem finaliter terminari.[10]

V. Ad hec, quemadmodum ex antiqua regni nostri consuetudine per divos reges predecessores nostros et nos hactenus observata palatinus, comites parochiales aliique honorem seu dignitatem baronatus tenentes in congregationibus ac generalibus iudiciis quoslibet fures, latrones ac alios malefactores inibi proscriptos et extradatos[11] iudicare, condempnare, punire seu proscribere consueverunt, et insuper veluti nobiles ex speciali gratia regia ipsis concedi consueta in eorum possessionibus etiam malefactores, quos in maleficiis et culpis deprehendunt, condempnare penaliter ac punire facultatem liberam habuerunt,[12] ita et nos in presenti sanxione duximus statuendum, quod de cetero pro conservanda pace proque civitatum et villarum uberiori

tranquillitate, pro viarum securitate, pro itinerantium comodo, et ut malefactoribus delinquendi materia subtrahatur, omnes et singule civitates ac libere ville seu iudices et iurati earundem huiusmodi malefactores, qui in eorum tenutis maleficia perpetrassent, quemadmodum et nobiles ex gratia et donatione regia facere possent, condempnandi et debitis puniendi suppliciis plenam et liberam habeant facultatem, salvo si ipsi rei et suppliciis digni a regia maiestate obtinuissent gratiam superinde. Sin autem palatinus, comites et aliqui honorem baronatus habentes, necnon civitatum rectores huiusmodi malefactores extradatos comprehendere et punire non possent, sed nichilominus eos culpabiles iudicando proscriberent, eo casu teneantur illi, qui proscriptionem fecerint, tales malefactores proscriptos cunctis iudicibus et iustitiariis regni nostri et etiam omnibus civitatibus denunciare et per eorum litteras maleficii eorundem seriem continentes manifestare. Qui iudices et iustitiarii ac etiam civitatum rectores, postquam huiusmodi littere ad manus eorum pervenerint, ipsos malefactores, si in eorum tenutis et districtibus invenerint, possint et valeant, ymmo teneantur et debeant arestare, captivare, punire et iuxta eorum demerita dignis affligere suppliciis et tormentis, salvo semper, si a regia maiestate venie gratiam impetrassent. Quod si quis iudicum, iustitiariorum vel rectorum predictorum ipsos malefactores, cum in manus ipsorum inciderint, punire contempserit, sciat se procul dubio indignationem maiestatis nostre gravissimam incursurum et a nostra serenitate iuxta qualitatem excessus exinde dependentis irremissibiliter puniendum. Nullus etiam omnino presumpmat eosdem malefactores fovere, protegere vel aliqualiter defensare sub pena superius annotata.

VI. Sanximus preterea, ut amodo in antea cives, hospites seu jobagiones nostri regales de nostris civitatibus, possessionibus, opidis et liberis villis castrorumque nostrorum tenutis in ecclesiarum, nobilium et alterius preeminentie hominum possessiones, et e converso earundem ecclesiarum, necnon nobilium et alterius preeminentie hominum jobagiones in prefatas nostras possessiones castrorumque nostrorum tenutas et generaliter quilibet libere conditionis homines de possessionibus nobilium in ecclesiarum possessiones et de ecclesiarum possessionibus in nobilium possessiones temporibus semper successivis universis et perpetuis liberam, tutam et omnimodam manendi causa se transferendi habeant facultatem harum nostrarum litterarum per vigorem.

His moderaminum limitationibus clare presentibus expressatis, ut quicunque et quorumcunque jobagionum dominus aliqua birsagia sua, quibus jobagio suus aliquo tempore fuisset convictus, infra unius mensis spatium non exegisset super eundem, extunc birsagia talia super eundem jobagionem suum dicto mense elapso recipere et eundem jobagionem retinere non valeat, sed idem jobagio, quo maluerit, modo

prosperous calm of the cities and villages, the safety of the roads, and the comfort of travellers as well as for the repression of the delinquency of evildoers, each and every city and free village or their judges and jurors should also have the full and complete right to condemn and duly punish those criminals who commit crimes in their territories—just as the nobles are also allowed to do by special royal grace and grant—excepting when the culprits or those worthy of punishment have received in this matter pardon from the royal majesty forgiving them their deeds.

If, however, the palatine, the *ispánok* and others holding the honor of baronage, or the magistrates of the cities were not able to capture and punish such outlawed criminals but nevertheless judge them guilty and proscribe as such, in that case those who have issued the proscription should denounce these proscribed criminals to all judges and justices of our realm and also announce this proscription to all the cities in a letter containing a description of the crimes.

Judges and justices, as well as the magistrates of the cities, once they have received such a letter, should have the right and power, nay, the duty to arrest, capture, punish, and mete out punishment and torture to these criminals, according to their misdeeds if they find them in their territories and regions, excepting always if they have received pardon by the grace of the royal majesty.

Whoever of the said judges, justices, and magistrates may fail to punish such criminals when they fall into his hands should know that he will beyond doubt call upon himself the most grave disapproval of our majesty and that he shall be pitilessly punished by our majesty according to the nature of his trespass. Also let no one dare to support, protect, or in any way defend these criminals under threat of the punishment noted above.

6. We have decreed furthermore that just as in the past, so for all times in the future our royal burghers, settlers, and tenant peasants should have the liberty, generally and in eternity, to move freely, safely, and in any manner from our cities, estates, towns, free villages, and appurtenances of our castles to the estates of churches, nobles, and people of other eminent condition and take residence there; so too may the tenant peasants of churches and nobles as well as of people of other eminent condition move to our said estates and the appurtenances of our castles, and in general people of free condition from nobles' estates to lands of the church and from ecclesiastical lands to estates of nobles.

With the following moderating limitation expressed in these presents, that if a lord of any tenant peasant has not collected from his tenant peasant any fine to which his tenant peasant was at any time condemned within a month, he should not have the right to collect such a fine after the lapse of the said month, nor to restrict such a tenant peasant, but the said tenant peasant should settle where he prefers,

prehabito indempnis moraturus accedat.[13] Jobagiones autem ultra Draue fluvium residentes huius libertatis privilegio gaudere nolumus, sed potius in suis antiquis consuetudinibus decrevimus permanere.[14]

VII. Decernimus insuper et ordinamus, quod nullus ex prelatis, baronibus, proceribus, nobilibus aut alterius cuiuscunque dignitatis, ordinis, status et conditionis hominibus, regnicolis et subditis nostris occasione debiti, delicti, culpe aut maleficii unius persone seu hominis, cuiuscunque status et conditionis existat, audeat vel presumat civitatem, opidum vel villam, ubi talis debitor, delinquens, culpabilis aut maleficus residere consuevit, seu cives, opidanos vel villanos arestare, detinere vel modo aliquo impedire; sed si quis contra talem quidquam actionis habet vel habuerit, id in presentia iudicis sui ordinarii exequatur, prout retroactis temporibus fieri in talibus secundum regni nostri iustitiam consuevit, ita quod innoxii pro nocentibus nullo modo aggraventur.[15]

VIII. Statuimus etiam et ordinamus, quod quemadmodum antiqua regni nostri habet consuetudo, ut si cuiquam in villa vel possessione alicuius domini terrestris, cuiuscunque status et conditionis, tam ecclesiasticus, quam secularis existat, aliqualis inferretur iniuria, dampnum vel offensa, talis lesus seu dampnum passus primo ad dominum seu iudicem illius possessionis accedendo iustitiam postulare teneatur,[16] et si talis dominus vel iudex sibi iustitiam facere contempserit, ad comitem provincialem valeat appellare, et si comes etiam in reddenda iustitia tepidus fuerit vel remissus, ad nostram regiam maiestatem possit etiam appellare, ita nunc quoque volumus, ut si alicui persone regnicole[17] vel extranee in aliqua civitatum, opidorum et villarum liberarum nostrarum per aliquem, cuiusvis status existat et conditionis, aliqualis iniuria, offensa vel dampnum fuerint irrogate vel illata, tunc talis lesus seu dampnum passus primo coram iudice illius civitatis suam debeat prosequi iustitiam. Et si iudex et iurati illius civitatis iustitiam sibi debitam facere recusaverint vel exhibere distulerint, tunc ipse lesus vel dampnum passus ad magistrum tauarnicorum nostrorum suam causam attrahere valeat atque possit. Deinde si etiam ipse magister tauarnicorum nostrorum super huiusmodi querela iustitiam ministrare contempserit, tunc liceat annotato leso vel dampnum passo ipsius magistri tauarnicorum iudicio dimisso suam causam in nostre maiestatis presentiam attrahere,[18] nosque, uti ex regiminis nostri regalis officio tenemur, unicuique ministrabimus iustitie complementum. Quod si quispiam lesus vel dampnum passus hoc ordine non servato auctoritate propria se presumpserit vindicare et sibi satisfactionem recipere, talis transgressor huius nostri decreti in facto potentie convincatur, cum neminem liceat nulla postulata iustitia propria se auctoritate vindicare.

IX. Decrevimus etiam, quod in quibuscunque causis et processibus, de quibus iudices causarum quarumcunque nonam et decimam ab illa

unharmed in the way described before.[13] We do not grant the privilege of this kind of liberty to the tenant peasants beyond the River Drava, but rather decree that they remain in their old customs.[14]

7. We have decreed and ordered, furthermore, that no prelate, baron, lord, noble, gentleman of the realm, or any one of whatever rank, order, station, or condition or any of our subjects may dare or attempt in any way to arrest, capture, or harass any citizen, townsman, or villager or any city, town, or village where such a debtor, delinquent, criminal, or malefactor used to reside, because of debt, delict, crime, or misdeed of a person or man of whatever station or condition, but whoever has or will have any case against such a person should sue him before his justice ordinary, as has usually been done in the past according to the laws of our kingdom, so that the innocent shall in no way suffer for the guilty.[15]

8. We have also established and ordered, just as ancient custom of our realm demands, that if anyone of whatever station and condition, be he clergy or layman, suffers some injury, damage, or harm in the village or estate of a landowner, that such a damaged or wronged person must first turn to the lord or judge of that estate and demand justice;[16] and if such a lord or judge refuses to grant him justice, he should be able to appeal to the *ispán* of the county; and if the *ispán* is slow or negligent in granting justice, he should be allowed to appeal also to our royal majesty.

Thus we now also wish that if any person, resident[17] or foreigner, has suffered or incurred any injury, harm, or damage by anyone of whatever station or condition in one of our cities, towns, or free villages, then such an person wronged or suffering injury or loss should pursue his claim to justice first before the judge of that city. And if the judge and jurors of that city refuse or delay granting him due justice, then the person wronged or suffering injury or loss should be allowed and should be able to carry his case to the presence of our Master of the Treasury. If, thereafter, even the Master fails to administer justice concerning the complaint, then the said person wronged or suffering injury or loss should have leave to bring his suit, bypassing the jurisdiction of the Master of the Treasury, to the presence of our majesty, and we shall render full justice to all as we are held to do in accordance with the obligations of our royal office.[18] If, however, some person wronged or suffering injury or loss not following this order, presumes to avenge himself and secure satisfaction on his own behalf, then such a transgressor of our present decree shall be convicted of violent trespass because no one is allowed to avenge himself on his own authority without requesting proper justice.

9. We have also decreed that in the future in all those cases and lawsuits in which the judges of the case used to receive a ninth and

parte, que causam obtinet, recipere consueverunt, de cetero non ab ipsa parte, que causam obtinet, sed ab illa, que in ipsa causa convincetur, recipere debeant iudices illius cause et extorquere, cum non sit equum, ut qui iustus est, pro iniustis puniatur et in rebus dampnificetur.[19]

X. Statuimus etiam, ut quilibet civis et inhabitator quarumlibet civitatum nostrarum amodo et in antea ad collectas nostras regales et contributiones pro rata, non obstantibus quibuscunque libertatibus ipsis hactenus datis et in posterum per nos et nostros successores concedendis, quas quoad premissa ipsis non volumus ullatenus suffragari, solvere et cum illis nostris civibus contribuere teneantur. Si vero per nos vel nostros successores aliquos cives nostros libertare et exemptos facere contingeret, tunc et in eo casu nos et nostri successores predicti, quicquam ipsi cives libertati ad collectas solvere deberent, id de communitatis computo defalcando ad nostram tenemur et debebunt recipere rationem.

XI. Item licet cives nostri Budenses inter ceteras eorum libertates tali libertate per nostros predecessores ipsis largita et concessa ac per nos confirmata freti et usi hucusque dinoscuntur, utputa quod omnes et singuli tam regnicole, quam extranei mercatores universas et quaslibet res mercimoniales ac bona venalia et commutabilia tam ascendendo, quam descendendo in ipsorum civium Budensium medio deponere ac depositas inibi vendere et commutare abindeque nullatenus alias abducere, neque deportati facere debuissent et fuissent assueti;[20] tamen, quia nunc facta generali congregatione quarumlibet civitatum, opidorum ac liberarum villarum nostrarum regalium, habito superinde consilio visum et consultum extitit, ut pro ampliori fructuositate et uberiori statu, comodo et communi bono regni et regnicolarum ac precipue civium et mercatorum nostrorum, ne propter utilitatem et augmentum unius civitatis tota regni nostri communitas dampnum et incomodum suscipiat et nocivum recipiat detrimentum, omnes et singuli mercatores nostri, videlicet regnicole de regno nostro exeuntes et in regno nostro commorantes universas et quaslibet ipsorum res mercimoniales et bona venalia seu commutabilia per totum regnum nostrum et extra ipsum regnum quocunque, quotiescunque et quandocunque voluerint, liberam, meram, plenam et securam deducendi, deferendi, pellendi, reducendi, deponendi ac depositas vendendi, commutandi ac abinde deferendi et deduci faciendi ac cum eisdem iuxta eorum voluntatis libitum disponendi habeant facultatem, non obstantibus quibuscunque libertatibus et privilegiis dictis civibus nostris Budensibus super premissa rerum depositione quomodolibet datis et concessis, quas et que quoad premissa ex certa scientia revocamus, exceptis extraneis, qui teneantur in premissis antiquam consuetudinem observare.[21]

XII. Insuper omnes et singuli cives civitatum, quas de novo creavimus, quibuscunque aliarum civitatum constituimus libertatem, si

tenth from the winning party, the judges of the case should receive and collect not from the party that has won the case, but from the party that was convicted in that case,[19] for it is not equitable that the just should be punished for the unjust and be fined.

10. We have also decided that, henceforth, regardless of any privilege which had been granted them in the past or will be granted them in the future by us and by our successors, of which they are not allowed to avail themselves in these matters, all burghers and inhabitants of any of our cities are to be obligated without distinction to pay their portion of our royal dues and taxes. And if we or our successors happen to exempt and excuse one of our burghers, in that case we and our successors are obligated and will be bound to deduct that amount by which the exempted burghers would have contributed to the taxes from the accounts of the community and credit it to our account.

11. Furthermore, although it is well known that the burghers of Buda up to now have held and enjoyed among other rights that privilege which was granted them by our predecessors and had been confirmed by us, namely that customarily each and every merchant, including residents and foreigners, whether coming or going, must unload all wares to be sold or traded in the presence of the burghers of Buda, and to sell or exchange those unloaded wares there, and was not allowed to transport them anywhere else;[20] nevertheless, in the common assembly held recently with all our cities, towns, and free villages, after deliberation on this subject, for the increase of the income of our country, its inhabitants, and especially of the burghers and merchants, for the improvement of their condition, and for the public good, lest because of the profit and growth of one city the whole community of our country suffers loss, damage, and injury, we found it right and so we decided that each and every one of our merchants, that is, the residents of our kingdom, may carry, transport, drive, bring back, and unload all and any kind of merchandise for sale or exchange when leaving the country or when staying here, wherever, whenever and as often as desired, across the country or anywhere outside of it, completely unobstructed and absolutely safely, and may sell, trade, transport, carry away, and handle freely the unloaded wares at their pleasure, regardless of the aforementioned liberties and privileges of the said burghers of Buda granted and permitted them concerning the unloading of wares, which we explicitly repeal regarding the said matter, excepting foreign merchants who are held and obligated to observe the old custom concerning this matter.[21]

12. Moreover, whenever burghers of those cities which we have recently founded and provided with the privileges of other cities do not

de iudicatu et sententia iudicum et iuratorum suorum noluerint contentari, ad illam civitatem, cuius libertate funguntur, aut ad magistrum tauarnicorum nostrorum valeant appellare; ita tamen, quod postquam magistrum tauarnicorum elegerint, ad iudices et iuratos recurrere non valeant, nec e contra ad nullum ulterius, nisi si opus fuerit, ad presentiam nostram personalem appellatio possit fieri quovis modo.[22]

XIII. Sanximus nichilominus statuentes, ut cives et hospites nostri quarumlibet civitatum nostrarum regalium intra ambitum et climata regni nostri existentium dona seu munera ipsorum in novo quolibet anno pretextu strennarum regie maiestati debita sic et eo modo nostre maiestati dare et solvere, quemadmodum noviter convenimus cum eisdem, et in quarumlibet civitatum, opidorum et liberarum villarum nostrarum litteris per nos ipsis concessis, inter alias eorum libertates clare exprimuntur, debebunt et tenebuntur.[23] Preterea magistro ianitorum nostrorum tempore in prefixo non plus, quam sex florenos dare et cum eisdem nostris muneribus annis singulis solvere teneantur. Dum autem ubi et quando nostram vel reginalem claritatem in aliquam civitatum, opidorum et liberarum villarum regni nostri intrare contigerit, extunc cives et hospites loci illius, in quem ingressum fecerimus, nostre aut reginali maiestati victualia oportuna ad unum prandium et unam cenam, si prandium et cenam ibidem habere voluerimus, aut prandium vel cenam tantummodo, si nisi semel nos ibidem comestionem habere contigerit, habundanter dare et amministrare teneantur.[24] Magistro vero agazonum civitates, per quas nostram seu reginalem maiestatem transire contigerit, illius scilicet civitatis artifices cuiuslibet generis, utputa omnes pellifices unum pellicium, omnes frenatores unum frenum et sic de singulis una vice dumtaxat in anno, quandocunque nos inde transire contingat, et non aliter, dare et enceniare teneantur, demptis tantummodo civitatibus, que ad premissa ex antiqua consuetudine nullatenus obligantur. Ceteris vero officialibus, tam nostris, quam reginalibus, videlicet pincernarum et dapiferorum magistris, dispensatori, hostiariis, cocis et aliis quibuscunque nichil penitus dare seu solvere teneantur.

XIV. Disposuimus etiam de modo ac consuetudine ab antiquo solitis observari, quod prelati et quipiam viri ecclesiastici causas aliquas inter regnicolas nostros motas amodoque et in antea qualitercunque, quomodocunque et ubicunque movendas et suscitatas, utputa iudicium seculare concernentes iudicare et diffinire minime valeant neque possint, et e converso barones, comites provinciarum et alii regni nostri nobiles civesque et hospites causas aliquas, lites seu questiones, forum videlicet ecclesiasticum tangentes discutere et iudicare non debeant, neque presumant. Et si inter ipsos viros ecclesiasticos ab una, parte vero ex altera iudices seculares pretaxatos super aliquibus causis in eorum presentia vertentibus circa ipsarum causarum iudicium, cuius

want to agree to the judgments or decisions of their judges and jurors, they can appeal to that city by the laws of which they live or to our Master of the Treasury. However, if they appeal to the Master of the Treasury, they are not allowed in any way to return to their judges and jurors or to appeal to any other authority, except to make an appeal to our personal presence, should this become necessary.[22]

13. In addition we have decreed the rule that the burghers and settlers of our royal cities within the territory and boundaries of our kingdom will be obliged to grant and deliver those gifts and donations, called New Year's presents, which they owe our majesty in that form and way as we have recently agreed to with them and as it is distinctly expressed together with other privileges of theirs in the charters we gave our cities, towns, and free villages.[23] Moreover, they must give six florins and not more to the Master of our Doorkeepers at the fixed time annually, which they must pay together with the presents due to us. If and when their majesties the king and the queen happen to visit any of the cities, towns, and free villages of our kingdom, the burghers and settlers of that place which they visit must deliver and serve food sufficient for a midday meal and for an evening meal if they are to take the meals there or a luncheon or a supper in the case that they happen to take only one meal there.[24] To the Master of our Horse, those cities or rather each craftsman of the mentioned city which we or her majesty the queen might pass through, except those which by right of ancient practice are not obligated to render these duties, is bound to give and deliver one product of his craft, namely, every furrier a furcoat, every saddler a bridle-bit, and so forth, but only once a year whenever we should pass through those cities. To our other office-holders or those of the queen, namely the masters of the cupbearers and the butlers, the stewards, doorkeepers, cooks, and others, or to anyone else, they do not have to give and pay anything.

14. Observing the customs and practices of old, we also order that no prelate or clergy should judge or pass final sentence in suits among inhabitants of our country opened or started or to be opened or started in any way and anywhere, insofar as these pertain to secular courts; and vice versa, barons, county *ispánok*, and other nobles of our country, as well as burghers and settlers, should not and ought not treat and judge cases, lawsuits, and questions which belong to ecclesiastical courts. And if disagreement or argument arises between the clergy on the one hand and the aforesaid secular judges on the other concerning which court has jurisdicion in a certain case, then the parties are obliged to transfer that contested case or those contested cases to the

videlicet ipsorum iudicio pertineant, discordia seu disceptatio aliqualis extiterit suborta, extunc partes eedem causam seu causas huiusmodi litigiosas in specialem nostram presentiam, ubi deo duce pro tunc fuerimus constituti, cum prelatis et baronibus nostris[25] dirimendas transmittere teneantur, ubi decernentes sanctiemus, ad cuius partis iudicium seu forum spectare debeant et pertinere cause prenotate.

XV. Insuper, quemadmodum et ab antiquo iuxta statuta regia aurum, argentum, cuprum et alia metalla de regno nostro educi prohibita existunt[26] ita inter alias constitutiones civitatibus, opidis et liberis villis ad presens editas sanximus et statuimus, ut in qualibet civitatum, opidorum et liberarum villarum duo iurati cives ad id idonei per iudicem et cives eligantur, qui quibuslibet ligationibus et obstructionibus ballarum, vasorum et aliorum ponderum ligandorum interesse et easdem conspicere debeant, sine quibus civibus ad id deputatis nulli mercatores, institores ac alii quicunque commutatores ipsorum ballas ac alia pondera ligare aut concludere presumant, quas quidem ballas et pondera iidem duo cives eorum sigillorum appositione consignare debeant et munire; et si contrafactum fuerit, extunc ipse balle vel mercimonia non inspecte nec sigillata, ut premittitur, totaliter amittantur et fisco nostro regali penitus applicentur. Quibus quidem ballis aut aliis quibusvis ponderibus sic ligatis et consignatis ad locaque tricesimarum nostrarum deductis et portatis, si et in casu, quo nostri tricesimatores aut eorundem officiales talibus sigillationibus fidem nollent adhibere,[27] sed huiusmodi ballas pretenderent disligare, extunc, si currus, in quibus balle et pondera deferuntur, magni onerati, in vulgo masa dicti[28] extiterint, unam marcam auri vel sexaginta quatuor florenos aut monetam eiusdem valoris, si vero currus, medius, modicus seu parvus foret, tunc mediam marcam aut florenos vel monetam equivalentes[29] ad temonem ipsius currus apponendo, easdem ballas et pondera disligare et conspicere valeat atque possit. Et si in huiusmodi ballis seu ponderibus aurum, argentum vel alie res prohibite non reperirentur, extunc tricesimator amittat marcam seu pecuniam appositam, que domino earundem rerum seu mercatori debeant remanere. Si vero aurum, argentum vel alique res prohibite reperte fuerint in ipso curru et invente, tunc non solum eedem res prohibite, sed etiam alie universe et bona quevis in ipso curru et balla existentes et habita simul cum marca seu pecuniis huiusmodi per ipsos tricesimatores aut eorum officiales auferantur et recipiantur.

XVI. Statuimus etiam et ex deliberatione decrevimus, ut nullus omnino mercatorum, alterius etiam cuiusvis regni nostri status, conditionis et preeminentie hominum res mercimoniales ac bona quevis venalia et commutabilia forensium ac extraneorum sub nomine rerum et mercantiarum propriarum, prout in talibus astutia aliquorum hactenus facere consuevit, acceptare, recipere, tenere, conservare, vendere, commutare seu etiam modo quovis expedire, societatesque

court of our special personal presence, wherever we, by God's guidance, happen to be staying at that time, and we will decide with the prelates and barons[25] by judgment which of the parties has the right to hold the court and to which court the said cases belong.

15. Furthermore, since exporting gold, silver, copper, and other ores from the country had been prohibited as of old,[26] we order and decree among the other decisions now issued for cities, towns, and free villages that in every city, town, and free village the judges and burghers are to elect two burghers suitable for this task as jurors whose duty will be to be present at the packing and wrapping up of crates of goods, vessels, and other packaged goods, and to examine them, and no merchant, dealer, or trader may dare to pack and wrap up his crates of goods and other bales without the presence of the jurors delegated to oversee the packing; and these packs and loads must be marked and certified by the seals of those two burghers.[27] Anyone who may act contrariwise will lose all the bales and goods which were not searched and sealed in the aforesaid manner, and these all will go to our royal treasury. And when the packs and other kinds of loads wrapped and sealed in this way have been carried and delivered to our customs post, in the case that our customs collectors or their officials do not accept the seals, but wish to open these bales, if these bales and loads were transported on large carts, commonly known as *mázsa*,[28] then, after depositing on the pole of the cart one golden mark or sixty-four florins, or money of the same value,[29] or if the cart is medium or moderate-sized or a small one, then half a mark or florins or money of the same value, the officials are allowed to open and to search the packs and bales. If they find in these packs and bale neither gold, silver, nor any other prohibited merchandise, the customs collector will lose the deposited mark or money, which goes to the owner of the goods or to the merchant. But if they find or detect gold or silver or any other prohibited merchandise on the cart, not only that merchandise which is under prohibition, but all the other goods and chattels on that cart along with the said mark or money must be confiscated and kept by the customs collectors or their officials.

16. We have decided and after due deliberation have decreed that no merchant or any other inhabitant of our kingdom of whatever station, rank, and condition may dare in any way to accept, receive, or keep, retain, sell, exchange, or dispose of wares or any kind of goods for sale or exchange owned by strangers or foreign merchants pretending that they were his own goods and wares, as had been cunningly done in the past, or to establish, create, set up, organize, and make partnership

cum ipsis forensibus contrahere, facere, stabilire, ordinare et firmare ratione atque causa, ut sub colore huiusmodi societatis premissa libere exerceant dictoque nostro decreto contrafaciant, ullatenus audeat atque possit[30]; contrarium vero facientes rerum omnium et bonorum sub huiusmodi cautulosa collusione in nostri presentis edicti contemptum in regnum nostrum apportatarum, venditarum et vendendarum, commutatarum et commutandarum irremissibilem perditionem et fisco nostro regio applicationem personasque ipsas penam arbitrariam nostre maiestatis incurrere volumus eo facto, totiens quotiens in contrarium premissorum per quempiam contrafactum fuerit, seu etiam attemptatum.

XVII. Preterea quia noviter certis iustis et rationabilibus causis moti pro rei publice utilitate totiusque regni conservatione, pro qua etiam retroactis temporibus predecessores nostri Hungarie reges multa statuta multasque consuetudines inducere curaverunt, unacum predictis prelatis, baronibus ac regni nostri potioribus proceribus decrevimus, ut universi mercatores, negotiatores et alii, cuiuscunque status et conditionis homines extra regni nostri limites mercimonia seu res mercimoniales et venales deferentes et exportantes tricesimam partem,[31] quemadmodum de illis, que introducuntur in regnum, solvere et amministrare teneantur, idcirco in premissi decreti nostri noviter instituti aliqualem alleviationem et etiam recompensam sanximus et ex liberalitate regia concessimus, quod huiusmodi mercatores ac negotiatores et alii prenominati per quecunque loca tributorum seu teloniorum nostrorum regalium[32] cum personis, equis, curribus ac quibuscunque eorum mercimoniis ac rebus et bonis universis libere et expedite, sine aliquali solutione tributaria transire valeant, totiens quotiens eis fuerit opportunum, mandantes tributariis nostris quibuslibet, tam presentibus, quam futuris, quatenus huiusmodi personas sub pena indignationis nostre gravissime contra formam premisse libertatis nullatenus impedire, neque ab eis tributum aliquod petere et exigere audeant.

XVIII. Ceterum cum in omnibus regnis reges quadam prerogativa precipua monetam tam auream, quam argenteam cudi facere liberam habeant facultatem, inhonestum satis et detestabile videretur, quod pecunia cusa per cudentis ditionem cursum et expositionem debitam non haberet, sed multo detestabilius, si circumcideretur vel eligeretur aut modo aliquo vitiaretur. Cupientes igitur hiis enormibus casibus salubribus remediis obviare, requisito super eo prelatorum, baronum procerumque nostrorum, necnon universorum civium civitatum regalium presentialiter constitutorum consilio, pro utilitate totius regni pariter et augmento proque iustitie splendore conservando ordinavimus et etiam statuimus, quod nullus omnino hominum, cuiuscunque status et conditionis existat, audeat vel presumat pecuniam nostram regalem sive auream, sive argenteam, dummodo iusta et recta sit, reicere vel

with foreigners in order that under the cover of this sort of partnership he may freely do these things in contravention of our said decree.[30] We order that those who act or even attempt to act contrariwise shall each and every time pitilessly lose forthwith in favor of our royal treasury the goods and items sold or to be sold, exchanged or to be exchanged, which they have brought into our kingdom in contempt of this decree by clever collusion and shall also receive a penalty regarding their persons to be decreed at our pleasure.

17. Furthermore, having been guided by definite just and reasonable principles for the common good and the survival of the whole kingdom in favor of which our predecessors, the kings of Hungary, have taken care to decree many laws and introduce many customs, we have recently decided, together with the prelates, barons, and distinguished lords of our kingdom, that every merchant, trader, and any other person of whatever station or condition who takes and exports goods and wares or things for sale beyond the borders of our kingdom will have to pay and render the thirtieth thereof,[31] just as he has to do for the things imported into the kingdom. We have ordered and by royal generosity we have allowed for the extenuation and compensation of our recently decreed and aforementioned order, that those merchants and traders and others mentioned above may cross the borders of the kingdom in person with their horses, carts, and all kinds of goods and items any of the royal tolls or tribute posts[32] without paying tolls, freely and unobstructedly, as many times as they wish to. We order all our present and future toll collectors that they dare not under penalty of our most serious displeasure, by contravening the abovementioned privilege, obstruct these persons under any circumstances by demanding or collecting from them any tribute.

18. Moreover, because the kings of all countries by the right of certain paramount privileges have the power to cause gold or silver money to be minted, it seems to be a very dishonest and accursed thing that coined money should not properly circulate and be used in the whole territory of its issuer, and it is even more accursed when it is chipped, shaved, or defaced in any way. Therefore, wishing to forestall by suitable means these enormities, after having consulted in this matter with the prelates, barons, and lords as well as with the burghers of royal cities who appeared in person, we have decided and ordered the following, for the profit and growth of our kingdom and the maintenance of the splendor of justice, that no one of any station and condition may dare or attempt to decline or to refuse in any way our gold or silver money, provided that it is legitimate and true, nor to chip the coins,

aliquatenus refutare, item nec circumcidere, graves a levibus secernere vel aliquo artificio seu ingenio vitiare. Contrarium quidem attemptare presumentes hoc modo debeant puniri, videlicet ille vel illi, qui pecuniam eandem recipere recusaverint, cadant in penam amissionis pecunie, que sibi deberetur, vel rei, pro qua pecuniam solvere tenentur, ita quod iudex et iurati illius loci illam pecuniam vel rem habeant et debitor a creditore suo ac emptor a venditore proinde liber sit et absolutus, ac si eidem dictam pecuniam persolvisset; ille vero vel illi, qui regiam pecuniam circumcidere, diminuere, eligere vel vitiare presumpserint, ut prefertur, tamquam falsarii et malefactores non tantum in rebus, sed etiam in personis iuxta regni nostri consuetudinem antiquam puniantur; quod si facere ipsi iudices et iurati, in quorum manus tales transgressores inciderint, rennuerint et eos impune abire permiserint, pro pecunia vel re relaxata in tanta quantitate pecunie vel valore ipsius rei fisco regio subiaceant condempnati; pro falsariis vero dismissis in illam penam incidant sive pecuniariam, sive personalem, quam nostra maiestas eis duxerit imponendam et etiam infligendam.[33]

XIX. Verum ut ipsa pecunia nostra in sua rectitudine conservetur, nullusque presumpmat ipsam decidere vel vitiare, sanximus etiam, quod in qualibet nostra civitate sit cambsor regius, qui solus cambiendi et commutandi pecuniam, videlicet pro florenis aureis monetam et pro moneta florenos aureos habeat facultatem; interdicentes universis et singulis regnicolis nostris et etiam extraneis, cuiuscunque status et conditionis existant, ut de cetero cambire seu commutationem aliquam de pecunia et florenis aureis pro pecunia facere non valeant, neque possint sub pena amissionis ipsius pecunie cambse vel cambiende, que eidem cambsori regio nomine fisci nostri debeat apportari.[34]

XX. Demum cum predecessores nostri Hungarie reges probabili sanctione statuerint, ut intra limites regni nostri Hungarie nulli sales expeditionem seu cursum habere deberent, nisi tantummodo sales, qui in ipso regno nostro effodiuntur,[35] nostra quoque maiestas considerans hanc sanctionem fore iustissimam et honestam, cum quodammodo pars sit magna dementie, id, quod de suo quispiam habere potest, ab alio mutuare, similiter statuit sanctiendum, habito tamen prius superinde nostrorum prelatorum, baronum ac procerum consilio nostro et deliberatione prematura, quatenus de cetero nullus omnino hominum, cuiuscunque status, dignitatis et conditionis existat, sive regnicola, sive advena, audeat vel presumat sales alicuiusmodi, preterquam solummodo sales nostros regales in regno effossos intra regnum nostrum inducere, deferre, vendere, emere, distrahere, consumere vel aliqualiter habere sub pena inferius annotata, videlicet, quod si apud quospiam, cuiusvis status et conditionis existant, reperti fuerint huiusmodi sales in regno nostro non effossi, ille vel illi, apud quos reperti fuerint, primo

separate the lighter ones from the heavier ones, or deface them through any art or cunning. Whoever would dare attempt to do anything against this order must be punished in the following way: he or those who are unwilling to accept our money will as a penalty lose the money that is owed them or those goods for which they have to pay, so that the money or goods should go to the judge and jurors of that place, and the debtor towards his creditor or the buyer towards the seller will be free and quit, as if he had paid the said money; and those who dare chip or shave or deface the royal money, will be punished as if counterfeiters and criminals, not only in their goods but also in their persons, according to long-established custom of our kingdom. Judges and jurors who hesitate to keep the aforesaid rules if these offenders fall in their hands, and let them go unpunished, will be charged for the loss of money and goods with the same amount of money or the value of the goods in favor of the royal treasury, and for the release of the forgers will suffer such personal or financial punishment as our majesty will find proper to inflict and to impose.[33]

19. In order to keep the true value of our money and prevent anyone from damaging or defacing it, we have also decreed that in each of our cities there should be a royal money-changer who alone will be empowered to change and exchange money, namely, to exchange gold florins for minted coins and minted coins for gold florins, and we prohibit each and every one of our inhabitants as well as foreigners of any station or condition to be able and empowered to change and exchange money and gold florins for minted coins; otherwise, they will be punished by the loss of the money exchanged or to be exchanged which must be handed over to the royal money-changer in favor of our royal treasury.[34]

20. Finally, since our predecessors, the kings of Hungary, ordered by proper decision that, within the borders of our kingdom, no other salts besides the ones mined in the kingdom shall be used and circulated[35] and this ordinance has been also seen very just and proper by our majesty, for it is surely foolish to borrow things which one can get from one's own, therefore we similarly have decreed an order, but only after consulting with our prelates, barons, and lords, and after mature deliberation, that no one of any station and condition, be he inhabitant or newcomer, may dare or attempt to bring into our kingdom to transport, carry, sell, buy, distribute, consume, or obtain in any way salts other than our royal salts, mined in the kingdom under pain of the following punishment: if such salts not mined in our kingdom are found on anyone of any station or condition, then first he or those on whom these are found shall lose these salts immediately and suffer the consequences; and if someone before being caught has already sold the salt, he shall have to return the money, and the salts and money are to

perdant et amittant ipso facto protinus ipsos sales. Si vero quispiam venumdaverit, antequam apud eum reperiantur, tunc ad restitutionem pecunie irremissibiliter teneatur, quos sales vel quam pecuniam camerarius regius nomine fisci regalis indilate auferat et exigat ab eisdem.

XXI. Denique pro communi bono et totius utilitate regni providere volentes, ne aurum et argentum, quod in ipso regno effoditur, extra regnum per quempiam deferatur, nisi prius conversum fuerit in monetam, hoc etiam salubri remedio duximus statuendum, videlicet ut nemo montanus cuiquam hominum, cuiusvis status et conditionis existat, aurum vel argentum publice vel secrete vendere, nemoque omnino montanus, cuiusvis etiam status et conditionis existat, a montano seu laboratore emere audeat vel presumat, sed omne et totum aurum, argentum, quod et quantum ubique per regni nostri climata effoditur et etiam invenitur, debeat sine aliquali diminutione camare regalis monete tam auree, quam argentee presentari vendendum camarario regio pro pretio et pretiis hactenus limitatis.[36] Item nec ab aliqua alia persona causa mercationis seu venditionis publice vel secrete emi aut vendi liceat aurum vel argentum, etiamsi de alienis partibus ipsum aurum et argentum ad hoc regnum portaretur, sed semper quicunque venditor illud debeat camarario regie monete presidenti vendere et nulli alteri; ipseque camararius dare sibi pretium non secundum estimationem montanorum, sed prout in loco, ubi tunc fiet venditio, teneatur. Pro usu vero proprio, videlicet pro vasis aureis et argenteis, balteis et aliis ad cultum vel ornatum spectantibus laborandis unusquisque vendendi et emendi liberam habeat facultatem. Si quis autem forte contrarium facere presumpserit, et venditor aurum vel argentum et emptor pecuniam amittat protinus ipso facto, quod aurum vel argentum, queve pecunia fisco nostro regio pro medietate et pro reliqua medietate accusanti, si quis accusator extiterit, applicetur. Ob hoc etenim nolumus, quod quispiam audeat vel presumpmat acum seu lapidem illum, in quo auri vel argenti qualitas dinoscitur, habere,[37] item neque testam seu intimam pro argenti fusione et finantia tenere, exceptis dumtaxat aurifabris; insuper nec separandi cum aqua aurum ab argento artem exercere, nisi ille vel illi, quibus huiusmodi officia duxerimus specialiter committenda.

In quorum omnium et singulorum testimonium firmitatemque perpetuam presentes litteras nostras privilegiales pendentis et autentici novi sigilli nostri duplicis munimine iussimus roborari. Datum per manus reverendissimi in Christo patris et domini domini Eberhardi, premissa dei et apostolice sedis gratia episcopi Zagrabiensis, aule nostre regie sumpmi cancellarii, dilecti nostri et fidelis, anno domini millesimo quadringentesimo quinto, decimo septimo Kalendas mensis Maii, regni autem nostri anno decimo septimo. Venerabilibus in Christo

to be taken away and collected immediately by the royal chamberlain in the name of the royal treasury.

21. And then, since we wish to provide for the public good and for the profit of the entire realm and to prevent anyone from taking out of the kingdom gold or silver mined in the kingdom without first exchanging it for money, we consider it a good preventative measure to decree that none of the miners may dare or attempt to sell gold or silver openly or secretly to persons of any station and condition nor by any means may a miner of any station and condition, dare to buy gold or silver from another miner or mine worker; but all the gold and silver, as much as is found and mined anywhere within the territory of our kingdom, has to be delivered up without any lessening to the royal Chamber of the gold and silver coins, to be sold to the royal chamberlain at the previously determined prices.[36] Likewise, gold or silver may not be bought or sold openly or secretly from or to any other person for the purpose of selling and buying, not even gold and silver brought into this kingdom from abroad, but if someone wants to sell gold or silver, he must give it to the royal chamberlain presiding over the mint and to no one else, and the same chamberlain must set the price not according to the estimation of the miners but according to the current market price. However, for personal use, such as making golden or silver vessels, strapping for sabres, or other articles of luxury or religious use, everyone is allowed to sell or buy freely. If someone dares act contrariwise, both the seller of gold or silver and the buyer will lose his money without further ado so that one half of the gold or silver and of the money concerned will go to our royal treasury and the other half to the accuser if there is one. For the very same reason, we prohibit that anyone except a goldsmith may keep in his possession *acus*, or that stone by which the quality of gold or silver can be assayed,[37] or utensils or instruments suitable for casting or alloying silver; in addition, no one shall practice the craft of separating gold from silver by water unless entrusted by us with this task.

In witness of all this, in parts and in general and for its everlasting validity we have ordered that our present charter be confirmed with our new double authentic seal pendant. Given by the hand of the most reverend father in Christ, lord Eberhard, by the grace of God and the apostolic see bishop of Zagreb, archchancellor of our court, our beloved faithful servant, in the year of the Lord one thousand, four hundred and five, the seventeenth day before the Kalends of May, in the seventeenth year of our reign, during the time, when the following reverend fathers

patribus et dominis Valentino tituli sancte Sabine sacrosancte Romane ecclesie presbitero cardinali et ecclesie Quinqueecclesiensis gubernatore, Johanne Strigoniensi, Colocensi sede vacante, Andrea Spalatensi et altero Andrea Ragusiensi archiepiscopis, Luca Waradiensis, Stephano Transsiluanensis, eodem domino Eberhardo Zagrabiensis, Agriensi sede vacante, Johanne Boznensis, Wesprimiensi sede vacante, Johanne Jauriensis, Nicolao Waciensis, Petro Nitriensis, fratre Dosa electo Chanadiensis ecclesiarum episcopis, ecclesias dei feliciter gubernantibus, Syrimiensi, Traguriensi, Scardonensi, Tininiensi, Nonensi, Sibinicensi, Corbawiensi et Segniensi sedibus vacantibus; necnon magnificis viris Nicolao de Gara, regni nostri Hungarie palatino, Johanne et Jacobo wayuodis nostris Transsiluanensibus, comite Frank filio condam Konye bani, iudice curie nostre, Paulo Bisseno et altero Paulo de Pech Dalmatie et Croatie predictorum ac totius Sclauonie, Johanne de Maroth Machouiensi banis, honore banatus Zewriniensis vacante, Nicolao Treutul de Newna tauarnicorum et comite de Posega, Simone filio dicti condam Konye bani ianitorum, Martino Ders dapiferorum, Laurentio de Tary pincernarum, Petro Cheh agazonum nostrorum magistris, Smylone de Wethaw comite Posoniensi aliisque quampluribus regni nostri comitatus tenentibus et honores.[38]

in Christ and lords bishops governed felicitously the churches of God: Valentinus, cardinal priest of the holy Roman church with the title of St. Sabina, governor of the church of Pécs, archbishops John of Esztergom, the see of Kalocsa being vacant, Andrew of Spalato and the other Andrew of Ragusa, bishops Lucas of Várad, Stephen of Transylvania, the same Eberhard of Zagreb, the see of Eger being vacant, John of Bosnia, the see of Veszprém being vacant, John of Győr, Nicholas of Vác, Peter of Nyitra, brother Dózsa bishop-elect of Csanád and the sees of Szerém, Scardona, Knin, Nona, Sebenico, Corbava, and Zengg being vacant; and when the honorable lords Nicholas of Gara, palatine of our kingdom of Hungary, John and James our voivodes of Transylvania, count Frank, son of the late ban Kónya, judge royal, Paul of Bessenye and the other Paul, of Pécs, bans of the said Dalmatia and Crotaia as well as of all of Slavonia, John of Marót, ban of Macsó, the banate of Severin being vacant; Nicholas Treutel of Nevna, Master of our Treasury and *ispán* of Pozsega, Simon, son of the said late ban Kónya, Master of the Doorkeepers, Martin Ders, Master of the Table, Lawrence of Tary, Master of the Cupbearers, Peter Cseh, Master of the Horse, Smilo of Wettau *ispán* of Pozsony, and many others held comital and other offices of our realm.[38]

31 Augusti 1405

Vide praefatiunculam et notas infra paginas 194–96.

Sigismundus Dei gratia Hungarie, Dalmatie, Croatie, Rame, Servie, Galitie, Lodomerie, Comanie Bulgarieque rex, marchio Brandenburgensis, sacri Romani imperii archicamararius, necnon Bohemie et Lucenburgensis heres. Omnibus Christi fidelibus presentibus pariter et futuris presentium notitiam habituris salutem in eo, qui dat principibus feliciter gubernare et virtuose triumphare. Inter ceteras animi nostri sollicitudines una est nobis cura precipua, ut quotiens gravioribus sumus ab agendis expediti ad ea etiam, que commissorum imperio nostro subditorum utilitatem commoditatemque concernunt, pia dispositione operam impendamus. Est enim subditorum tranquilitas gloria regnantis et ubi aliquid a principe modeste sancte ac prudenter pro communi utilitate decernitur, eius profectu diligentie sollicitudo magnopere collaudatur. Proinde in archano nostri pectoris perspicaci consideratione pensantes multa incommoda multaque dampna ex diversis consuetudinibus et sepe contrariis in regno nostro vigentibus nostris regnicolis evenire, celebrato prelatorum, baronum procerumque nostrorum conventu, de ipsorum consilio, auctoritate et consensu maturaque discussione prehabita, pro totius regni bono, utilitate profectu et augmento has leges, sive constitutiones ex auctoritate regia duximus salubriter statuendas, quas ab omnibus et singulis regnicolis nostris, tam ecclesiasticis, quam secularibus nemine excluso volumus et precipimus plene, integre et inviolabiliter observari.[1]

I. Primitus et primarie una cum eisdem prelatis, baronibus potioribusque regni nostri proceribus sanccientes et stabilientes statuimus et statutum fecimus hoc modo et ordine isto: quod prelati, barones, nobiles et alterius status condicionis et dignitatis homines in regno nostro ad instar exercituantium procedentes aut aliquibus ipsorum negotiis seu causis versus nostram maiestatem, aut cum ea, vel alias ubicunque et in quibuscumque partibus regni nostri progredientes, fidelibus regnicolis nostris quibuscunque dampna, spolia, iniurias, lesiones, aut aliqua malorum genera contra deum et eius iustitiam absque iuris tramite facere et inferre nullatenus presumant.[2] Et si quipiam contra huiusmodi nostra statuta quicquam genus malificii perpetraverit exindeque nostre maiestati, aut alii iudici ordinario per quempiam querimonia porrecta extiterit et conquerens in huius modi suam querimoniam evidenti documento comprobare valuerit, extunc dictorum factorum potentiariorum perpetratores in facto potentie eo facto convincatur. Lesis autem et dampnum passis nos, aut idem iudex

31 August 1405

For prefatory and explanatory notes, see below, pages 194–96.

Sigismund, by the grace of God king of Hungary, Dalmatia, Croatia, Rama, Serbia, Galicia, Lodomeria, Cumania and Bulgaria, margrave of Brandenburg, archchamberlain of the Holy Roman Empire, and heir of Bohemia and Luxemburg to all of Christ's faithful, present as well as future, to whose notice these presents may come, greetings in Him, who grants the princes felicitous reign and triumphant victory. Among the various cares of our soul one specific concern is that, whenever we are free of more grave duties, we should also labor with dutiful regard for the profit and comfort of those committed to our governance. For the peace of his subjects is the ruler's glory, and when the prince arranges something for the common good by moderate, devoted, and wise action, success is the highest praise for his solicitous diligence. Therefore, contemplating with acute awareness in the depth of our heart that much harm and many disadvantages are caused to our gentlemen of the realm by the different and frequently conflicting customs prevailing in our kingdom, having held an assembly with our prelates, barons, and lords, with their counsel, authority, and consent, after mature deliberation, we have decided to issue by royal authority for the good, profit, advancement, and growth of the whole realm the following salubrious laws or constitutions which we wish and order to be observed wholly, totally, and unchanged[1] by each and every one of our gentlemen of the realm, clerical as well as secular, no one excepted.

1. To begin with and first, we have ordered and issued, by deciding and establishing together with the same prelates, barons, and major lords of our kingdom, the following statutes in this manner and order: that when prelates, barons, nobles, and other men in our kingdom of whatever station, dignity, and condition set out for a military campaign, or travel to or with our majesty on any of their business or lawsuit, or otherwise, anywhere and in any part of our kingdom, they should not act contrary to the path of right and inflict on any of our loyal gentlemen subjects harm, damages, injuries, wounds, or any other kinds of crimes against God and His justice.[2] And if anyone commits any kind of crime in defiance of this statute, and someone complains in this matter to us or to one of the justices ordinary, and such a plaintiff is able to prove his complaint with manifest evidence, then the perpetrators of the stated violent trespasses should be for that reason convicted of violent trespass. And we or these justices ordinary will without delay grant and are obligated to grant complete satisfaction to

ordinarius indilate, summarie et de plano ac sine strepitu et figura iudicii[3] exhibebimus et exhibere teneatur satisfactionem.

II. Porro nullus omnino hominum cuiuscumque preeminentie dignitatis et condicionis existant in nostris regalibus, reginalibus, seu ecclesiarum, vel nobilium possessionibus pignora, seu vadia[4] pro quibuscunque factis aliquorum regnicolarum, seu plebicolarum nostrorum,[5] scilicet at aliorum quorumcumque eorum auctoritate mediante auferre, aut recipi facere valeant neque possint. Horum contrarium facientes in facto potentie convincantur.

III. Preterea nullus omnino iudicum et iustitiariorum, aut alii quipiam procerum regni nostri mutilationes, seu dimembrationes quibusvis plebicolis et regnicolis nostris facere presumat neque valeat, nisi hii solummodo, quibus per nos potestas nostra regia rite fuerit attributa.[6] Contrarium facientes penam premissi facti potentie incursuri eo facto.

IV. Decrevimus etiam, quod prelati, palatinus regni nostri, iudex curie nostre, magister tawarnicorum nostrorum et alii barones, nec non comites parochiales et generaliter quivis iudices et iustitiarii regni nostri ecclesiastici et seculares proceres et nobiles, castellani et civitatenses per climata regni nostri spolia, derobationes rerum et bonorum ablationes, sanguinis effusiones et alia actuum potentiariorum genera nostris fidelibus regnicolis, cuiusvis status et condicionis existant, facere, inferre et committere nullatenus audeant.[7]

V. Sanximus nihilominus, ut castellani et officiales nostri regales in nostris regiis propriis possessionibus, districtibus et tenutis iudicesque et iurati cives nostri regales in eorum medio, item prelati, barones, nobiles et alterius dignitatis homines possessiones habentes in eorum propriis possessionibus res et bona fidelium incolarum, seu plebicolarum nostrorum, quovis quesito colore, aut causa arestare vel prohiberi facere non sint ausi modo aliquali, nisi in possessionibus aliorum, vel loco communi,[8] prout regni nostri consuetudo id requirit. Et volumus hos omnes tales, qui in contrarium huiusmodi nostri decreti contraire, quod non credimus, presumpserint, facto potentie subiacere.

VI. Statuimus preterea, ut universe annone, nec non vina, blada, panni et aliorum bonorum, seu victualium genera et alie res venales, cuiuscunque speciei vel maneriei existant, illis et eisdem iustis, equis et veris cubulis, ponderibus, mensuris et ulnis in universis nostris, scilicet et aliorum quorumlibet regnicolarum nostrorum civitatibus, oppidis et villis mensurari, vendi, seu venditioni exponi, nec non emi, aut commutari et solvi ac aministrari debeant, qui et que in civitate nostra Budensi ab antiquo inventi sunt et stabilita[9] habentur de presenti. Contrarium facientes penam ablationum huiusmodi suarum rerum venalium patiantur ipso facto.

VII. Computationem autem, seu numerationem florenorum in regno nostro currentium hoc modo duximus limitandum, quod omnibus

the injured and wronged party summarily and publicly, without further litigation and legal process.[3]

2. Further, absolutely no one, whatever high rank or condition he may have, should have the right and liberty to exact or to take a pledge or a security on his own authority for any deed[4] from any of our gentleman subjects or common folk or other subject of ours[5] on the estates of the king, the queen, the churches, or the nobles. Those acting contrariwise must be convicted of violent trespass.

3. Moreover, absolutely no judge, justice, or any other lord of our kingdom may dare or presume to maim or dismember any of our gentleman subjects or common folk excepting those to whom this privilege has been legally granted by us.[6] Those acting contrariwise will incur for that reason the penalty for violent trespass.

4. We have also decreed that the prelates, the count palatine of our kingdom, our judge royal, our Master of the Treasury, and other barons, as well as *ispánok* of the counties, and in general all judges and justices of our kingdom, both clerical and secular, lords and nobles, castellans and burghers, should not dare to inflict or to commit at all any damage, theft of goods, robbery of chattels, shedding of blood, or any other kind of violent trespass in any part of the realm against any of our loyal gentlemen of whatever station or rank they might be.[7]

5. We decree as well that our castellans and royal officials in our royal estates, districts, and holdings, as well as our royal urban judges and jurors in their jurisdictions, and likewise the prelates, barons, nobles, and propertied men of other rank in their own estates, must not presume to distrain upon or garnish the goods and chattels of our loyal tenants and other common folk, under any pretended reason or cause, on their own estates but only on the estates of others or at public places,[8] as the custom of our realm demands. And we wish that all who are of the sort who would dare to act in defiance (that we do not believe) of this our decree be subject to the charge of violent trespass.

6. We have decreed further that all sorts of grain, wine, cereal, cloth, other goods and victuals, or wares for sale of whatever kind and type must be measured, sold, offered for sale, bought or exchanged, paid for, and handled in all of our cities, towns, and villages as well in those of the gentlemen of the realm with the same true, just, and correct bushels, weights, rods, and ells which have been established of old in our city of Buda[9] and are confirmed herewith. Those acting contrariwise should suffer for their action the penalty of confiscation of their merchandise.

7. We intend to regulate the counting or calculating of the florins current in our kingdom in the following manner: that by entirely

numeris dictorum florenorum minoribus in nonnullis regni nostri partibus, uti agnovimus, abusive adinventis, prorsus abolitis in quarumlibet rerum et bonorum emptionibus et venditionibus alter numerus ipsorum florenorum non dicatur, nec computetur, nisi florenus aureus veri, boni et iusti ponderis, vel alter florenus per centum novos denarios computatus.[10] Huiusmodi nostri statuti transgressores bonorum et rerum ipsorum venalium et emptionalium ablationes patiantur indilate.

VIII. Interea quidem non improvide, sed deliberata mente presenti nostro decreto seriosius duximus stabiliendum, quod nullus omnino hominum incolarum scilicet aut extraneorum, mercatorum aut commutatorum sales extraneos, seu regnorum alienorum in regnum nostrum venundationis, aut alia quadam de causa importare, aut eis uti, vel in quibusvis partibus regni nostri cum eis procedere quovis modo audeat vel presumat. Nam ubicunque et in quorumcunque possessionibus ipsi sales extranei venditi, vel vendendi, emptive aut emendi per quospiam reperiri poterunt, volumus, ut dominus terre aut possessionum illarum, in quibus dicti sales, ut premittitur, reperti fuerint, ab eorum venditoribus emptoribusve et commutatoribus auferre teneatur, vel si forsan favore, aut pretio allectus, seu circumventus dictos sales auferre renueret, extunc similiter volumus, ut huiusmodi possessiones nobilium, in quibus, uti premisimus, memorati sales reperientur, per comites nostros, tam provinciales, quam parochiales pro nostra utique occupari debeant maiestate.[11]

IX. Insuper edicimus statuendo cunctis fidelibus regnicolis nostris, ut amodo imposterum et peramplius ac in antea nullus eorum et nullo penitus dempto quospiam infideles nostros, aut proscriptos, vel alia quavis labe, seu nota crimineque, aut contagio scrupuli offuscatos et denigratos palam, vel occulte, publice seu manifeste, directe, vel indirecte apud se retinere, conservare, aut ipsis favorem auxilium et hospitalitatem prebere, vel largiri presumat quovis temporum in eventu.[12] Quoniam contrarium facientes illa et eadem pena, qua huiusmodi nostri infideles proscripti, aut alia nota denigrati forent cruciandi, feriri debeant et puniri incompassibiliter ipso facto.

X. Stabilimus denique, ut si aliqui ex nostris regnicolis, cuiuscunque status et dignitatis existant, quicquam iuris seu questionis contra et adversus villanos seu rusticos prelatorum, baronum, nobilium, aut alterius status hominum habent vel habuerint, id primitus et primarie in presentia ipsorum dominorum terrestrium legitime prosequi debeant.[13] Et si domini ipsorum villanorum seu rusticorum iustitiam facere denegarent, aut in reddenda eadem essent remissi, extunc huiusmodi domini terrestres pretextu abnegate ipsius iustitie in presentiam comitis provincialis, vel vicecomitis eiusdem, aut iudicum nobilium illius comitatus, in quo ipsa iustitia esset abnegata, legitime evocentur. Qui quidem comes parochialis, vicecomes et iudices

abolishing the counting of the said florins for lesser value, which, we have heard, has become an abuse in several regions of our kingdom, (we order that) when buying and selling of any goods or wares the florin must not be assessed or counted in any other way but as one gold florin of true, good, and just weight, or as the other florin, which is counted for 100 new pennies.[10] Trespassers against this ordinance of ours will suffer immediately the confiscation of their goods to be bought or sold.

8. Moreover, we deem it to be established by the present decree, not heedlessly but by considered forethought, that absolutely no one, resident or foreigner, merchant or trader, should dare to import for sale or for any other reason or use or to transport in any part of the realm foreign salt, that is, salt of another country. If anyone finds such foreign salt anywhere, on anyone's estates, sold or for sale, bought or about to be bought, the lord of that land or estate on which the said salt, as mentioned above, is found, is obligated to take it away from its seller, buyer, or trader; and if perhaps, as a favor or having been bribed or deceived, he fails to confiscate the said salt, we order that the estates of such a noble on the estates of whom, as mentioned above, the said salt was found, be seized for our majesty everywhere by our *ispánok*, of counties as well as of districts.[11]

9. Furthermore, we decree by ordering all of our loyal gentlemen of the realm that henceforth and in the future, just as before, none of them, without exception, should dare any time to keep with him, protect, grant, or bestow aid and hospitality overtly or covertly, publicly or secretly, directly or indirectly, any traitor against us, or any proscribed criminal or other men tainted or soiled by the stain of infamy, crime, or suspicion.[12] Those acting contrariwise will be for their action punished and penalized without pity with that selfsame penalty which such proscribed traitors and others blemished by crime would have to suffer.

10. Further, we declare that if any of our gentlemen subjects, of whatever station or dignity he may be, has or will have a case or a lawsuit against villagers or peasants of the prelates, barons, nobles, or men of any other estate, he ought first and foremost to prosecute them before the court of their lords.[13] And if the lords of these villagers or peasants should refuse to administer justice or are lax in doing so, then that lord for having failed to do justice should be legally summoned to the court of the *ispán*, or *alispán*, or noble magistrates of that county where justice was refused. These *ispánok* and *alispánok* and noble magistrates of the county are in turn obligated under the penalty of losing their office and our pleasure to pass summary sentence, justice,

nobilium sub privationis honorum ipsorum et nostre indignationis penis iudicium et iustitiam ac omnis iuris complementum ex parte ipsorum indilate absque strepitu et figura iudicii summarie et de plano,[14] favore etiam odio et amore quibusvis relegatis debebunt et tenebuntur exhibere.

XI. Sicque decrevimus, ut quicunque regnicolarum nostrorum, similiter cuiuscunque dignitatis vel ordinis existerent, adversus cives nostros regales quicquam actionis habent, vel habuerint, id ipsi in presentia iudicum et iuratorum civium nostrorum regalium, ubi et in quo loco ipsi cives nostri inculparentur, aut officialium seu iudicum, quibus regia maiestas gubernationem, officiolatum, seu iudicatum nostrarum regalium civitatum duxisset committendum, rite et legitime prosequantur, qui ex parte ipsorum iudicium et iustitiam exhibere teneantur. Et si ipsi iudices et iurati cives nostri regales, aut alii officiales seu iudices nostri prenotati inibi deputati, in faciendis quibuspiam iudicio et iustitia extiterint remissi, extunc huiusmodi nostri iudices et iurati cives, vel alii officiales seu iudices ad exhibendam ipsam iustitiam per magistrum tavarnicorum nostrorum auctoritate nostra regia astringantur et compellantur. In casu vero, quo ipsis querulantes de iudicio ipsorum iudicum et iuratorum civium contentari noluerint, tunc in huiusmodi eorum agendis ad presentiam magistri tavarnicorum nostrorum secundum antiquam consuetudinem possint appellare, qui ipsi in eorum iudicium et iustitie complementum exhibere et ipsum suum iudicium per annotatos iudices et iuratos cives nostros efficaciter tenebitur facere observari. Et si memorati querulantes tam de ipsorum iudicis et iuratorum civium quam dicti magistri thavarnicorum nostrorum iudicio contenti non fuerint, tunc huiusmodi causas ipsorum coram nostra maiestate more alias consueto prosequi valebunt, quibus nos iudicium et iustitiam faciemus, prout expostulat ordo iuris.[15]

XII. = 15 Apr. 1405: XIV.

XIII. Specifice nichilominus digna premeditatione annuentes statuimus, ut universi regnicole persone, ecclesiastice videlicet et seculares, cuiuscunque dignitatis et preeminentie existant, qui in faciebus possessionum ipsorum mineras auri vel argenti, aut alterius cuiuscunque metalli ad nos et ad camaram nostram regiam de iure et consuetudine pertinentes amodo in antea invenire et reperire possent, non obstante, si regiam gratiam in eo non haberent, ut maiestas regia huiusmodi possessiones ipsorum mineras supradictas habentes in concambium aliorum iurium regalium ab ipsis auferre non valeret, possessiones easdem ab ipsis absque eorum spontanea et libera voluntate de plenitudine nostre regie potestatis et presenti nostra gratia speciali per nos ipsis regaliter attributa non auferemus nec ipsas ab eisdem alienabimus contra formam presentis nostre gratie supradicte. Sed tamen volumus, ut rectam et equalem medietatem urburarum

and all matters related to judgment in regard to these plaintiffs, immediately and publicly, without any further legal procedure,[14] and without favor or hatred or preference towards anyone.

11. We have likewise decided that if any of our gentlemen subjects, similarly of whatever dignity or station, has or will have a legal case against our royal burghers, then he should sue them legally and properly before our royal burgher judges and jurors, where and in which place these burghers of ours are accused, or before those officials or judges to whom the royal majesty deemed right to entrust the governance and jurisdiction of our royal cities, who, in turn, are obligated to render justice and judgment in their regard. And if those royal burgher judges, and jurors of ours or the said officials and judges in charge of the place are remiss in rendering justice and judgment, then these burgher judges and jurors, or royal officials and judges, should be forced and compelled to administer justice through the Master of the Treasury by our royal authority. In cases where the plaintiffs are unwilling to acquiesce in the judgment of these burgher judges and jurors, that in such cases they are free, according to ancient custom, to appeal to the court of the Master of our Treasury, who is obligated to pass judgment and to do justice in their case and to assure that that judgment be properly observed by the said burgher justices and jurors of ours. And if the aforesaid plaintiffs are not content with the judgment of either their burgher judges and citizen jurors or of our said Master of the Treasury, then they should have leave to bring such a case before our majesty in the usual way, and we shall do justice as the order of law demands.[15]

12. = 15 April 1405: 14.

13. We specifically decree, moreover, after suitable deliberation, that if any gentleman of the realm, clerical or lay person of whatever dignity or eminence, who anywhere on his estate may in the future find and discover ores of gold or silver, or of any other metal, belonging by right and custom to us and our royal chamber, we shall not take away those estates from them, according to the present special grace royally given them by the fullness of our royal power, and not remove these from them against this aforementioned grant of ours without their free and spontaneous agreement, regardless of the lack of such a royal grant which would imply that the royal majesty has no right to take away by exchange for other royal rights these estates containing the aforesaid minerals. We order, rather, that these ecclesiastics and nobles transfer and render to our royal fisc the true and equal half of the mining dues (*urbura*) that usually accrue from these mines.[16] And

mineris de eisdem provenire solitarum iidem viri ecclesiastici et nobiles nostro fisco regio assignent et aministrari faciant, aliam vero medietatem eorundem ex presenti nostro indulto pro se ipsis valeant reservare.[16] Nec iidem viri ecclesiastici, nobiles ac laboratores minerarum predictarum aliquod aurum et argentum ex ipsis mineris provenientia extra regnum nostrum deferre, aut aliis quibusvis hominum personis venditioni exponere debeant. Sed huiusmodi aurum et argentum, sicut de aliis mineris et montanis nostris ad camaram nostram vendere est consuetum, ad vendendum in camaram nostre maiestatis teneantur apportare et exponere huiusmodi venditioni.[17] In casu vero, quo iidem nobiles, vel viri ecclesiastici nec non laboratores predicti huiusmodi auro et argento cyphos, coclearia, aut alia clenodia, sive argenteria, neve aurea pro usu ipsorum reservando preparari facere, aut ipsum aurum et argentum in specie erga se ipsos pro usu et commodo suis retinere maluerint, in h[is eisd]em plene libertatis concessimus et harum serie concedimus facultatem. Horum autem contrarium facientes et huiusmodi nostri decreti transgressores huiusmodi gratia nostra regia per nos ipsis quoad presens circa conservationem, gubernationem, adeptionem et limitationem iam dictorum metallorum, minerarum urbararum modo, quo supra regaliter indulta et attributa destituantur illico et priventur ipso facto.

XIV. = 15 Apr. 1405: VI.[18]

XV. Preterea quicunque, vel quorumcunque iobagionum dominus collectam, seu dationem aliquam super suum imposuerit iobagionem termino unius mensis ad hoc sibi assignato dationem eandem expirato ipso termino unius mensis infra quindecim dies super eundem recipere protelasset, extunc ipse dationem huiusmodi sic protelatam super eundem iobagionem suum ipsis quindecim diebus expiratis, extorquere et iobagionem eundem retinere non queat, neque possit. Sed idem iobagio superius limpide nominatus, quo voluerit quitus et pacificus libere moraturus discedat.

XVI. Ceterum si alicuius terre dominus suum iobagionem, aut aliquem de villa ante tempus licentie receptionis eiusdem in facto aliquo non inculpaverit et calumpniatus non extiterit, extunc ipse iobagionem talem post tempus receptionis ipsius sue licentie calumpnia quavis relegata liberum a se abire permittendo, in nullo queat dampnificare, aut disturbare presentis scripti et decreti nostri patrocinio mediante.

Et ut huiusmodi sanxionis nostre decretum salvum semper habeatur et solidum, volumus et presentibus firmissimo edicto precipimus et mandamus universis et singulis comitibus vel vicecomitibus et iudicibus nobilium illorum comitatuum, in quibus in eventu temporis pretitulata disceptatio fuerit fortasse exorta, ut ipsi nostros regios et earundem ecclesiarum nec non baronum, nobilium et alterius status ac preeminentie homines castellanos, officiales, iudices et villicos ipsarumque ecclesiarum rectores nec non nobiles et alterius

these ecclesiastics, nobles, and the miners of the said mines are not permitted to export from the realm or to offer for sale to any person any of the gold and silver from these mines. But they ought to offer for sale and present to the chamber of our majesty such gold and silver, just as such minerals are customarily sold from our mines to our chamber.[17] If, however, these nobles, ecclesiastics, or the said miners prefer to have cups, spoons, other jewels, or silverware made for their own use from such gold and silver, or to keep the same gold and silver for their own use and comfort, we herewith grant them leave and liberty to do so. From those, in turn, who act contrariwise and transgress this decree of ours, this royal grant given and permitted to them regally, regarding the keeping, administering, acquiring, and handling of the aforesaid metals and mining revenues (*urbura*), as described above, should be right away revoked for such an action.

14. = 15 April 1405: 6.[18]

15. Furthermore, any lord of any tenant peasant who has imposed any fines or dues on his tenant peasant with the term of one month assigned to this for him and has delayed collecting his dues from them within fifteen days after the elapse of the said term of one month cannot nor will be able in any way to exact the due delayed in this way from his tenant peasant after the expiration of fifteen days. But the said tenant peasant, in the way clearly noted above, may depart, as he wishes, freely in peace.

16. Furthermore, if the lord of any land has not accused or charged his tenant peasant or any villager with any trespass before the time of granting his leave, then after the time of receiving leave, he must permit such a tenant peasant to leave by abandoning any charges and in no way harm or impede him under the protection of the present charter and decree.

And so that the decree of our sanction should always be held safe and strong, we wish and we command, enjoining by the firmest possible royal edict and order, each and every *ispán*, *alispán*, and noble magistrate in those counties, in which at any future time disagreement may arise on the above, that they always compel, force, coerce, and obligate our royal castellans, officials, judges, and reeves, as well as those of churches, nobles, and men of other status or rank, and also the

regni nostri status homines ac officiales eorundem ad premissi nostri decreti regalis observationem cum eorum dampnis et gravaminibus compellant semper et coerceant, teneant ac astringant mera nostra regia auctoritate per nos eis attributa mediante.[19]

In cuius rei memoriam firmitatemque perpetuam presentes concessimus litteras nostras privilegiales pendentis et autentici novi nostri sigilli dupplicis munimine roboratas. Datum per manus reverendi in Christo patris domini Eberhardi dei et apostolice sedis gratia episcopi Zagrabiensis, aule nostre regie supremi cancellarii, fidelis nostri dilecti anno domini millesimo quadringentesimo quinto secundo Kalendas Septembris, regni autem nostri anno decimo septimo. Venerabilibus in Christo patribus et dominis Valentino tituli sancte Sabine sacrosancte Romane ecclesie presbytero cardinali et ecclesie Quinqueecclesiensis gubernatore, Iohanne Strigoniensi, Collocensi sede vacante, Andrea Spalatensi, et altero Andrea Ragusyensi archiepiscopis, Luca Waradiensis, Stephano Transsilvanensis, eodem domino Eberhardo Zagrabiensis, Agriensi sede vacante, Iohanne Boznensis, Wesprimiensi sede vacante, Iohanne Iauriensis, Thoma electo Segniensis, Wacyensi sede vacante, fratribus Hykone Nitriensis et Dosa Chanadiensis electis ecclesiarum episcopis, ecclesias Dei feliciter gubernantibus, Syrmiensi, Macarensi, Traguriensi, Scardonensi, Iadriensi, Tynyniensi, Nonensi, Sibinicensi, Maccharensi, Farensi et Corbaviensi sedibus vacantibus, nec non magnificis viris Nicolao de Gara, dicti regni nostri Hungarie palatino, Iohanne filio Henrici et Iacobo Lachk waywodis nostris Transsilvanis, comite Frank filio condam Konye bani, iudice curie nostre, Paulo Bisseno et altero Paulo de Peech Dalmatie et Croatie predictorum ac totius regni nostri Sclavonie, Iohanne de Maroth Machoviensi banis, honore banatus Zewriniensis vacante, Nicolao Trewtel de Neuna tavarnicorum et comite de Posega, magistratu ianitorum nostrorum vacante, Martino Ders dapiferorum, Laurentio de Taar pincernarum, Petro Cheh agazonum nostrorum magistris, Sylstrangh comite Posoniensi aliisque quam pluribus regni nostri comitatus tenentibus et honores.[20]

rectors of those churches, nobles, and men or officials of our kingdom of any other status to observe our preceding royal decree under fines and penalties issued against them, by the means of our royal authority granted them by the present writing.[19]

In the remembrance and perpetual force of this matter we have granted our charter of privilege validated by affixing our new authentic double seal pendant. Given by the hand of the reverend father in Christ, lord Eberhard, by the grace of God and the Apostolic See bishop of Zagreb, archchancellor of our royal court, our beloved and faithful servant, in the year of the Lord one thousand, four hundred and four, two days before the Kalends of September, in our seventeenth regnal year. When the following venerable fathers in Christ and lords governed the churches of God felicitously: Valentinus, cardinal priest of the holy Roman church with the title of St Sabina, governor of the church of Pécs, archbishops John of Esztergom, the see of Kalocsa being vacant, Andrew of Spalato and the other Andrew of Ragusa, bishops Luke of Várad, Stephen of Transylvania, the same Eberhard of Zagreb, the see of Eger being vacant, John of Bosnia, the see of Veszprém being vacant, John of Győr, Thomas bishop-elect of Zengg, the see of Vác being vacant, brothers Hinkó and Dózsa bishops-elect of Nyitra and Csanád and the sees of Szerém, Makarska, Traù, Scardona, Zara, Knin, Nona, Sebenico, Maccaro, Hvar and Corbavia being vacant; and when the honorable lords Nicholas of Gara, palatine of our kingdom of Hungary, John son of Henry and James Lack our voivodes of Transylvania, count Frank, son of the late ban Kónya, judge royal, Paul Besenyő and the other Paul, of Pécs, bans of the said Dalmatia and Croatia as well as of all of Slavonia, John of Marót ban of Macsó, the banate of Severin being vacant, Nicholas Treutel of Nevna, Master of our Treasury and *ispán* of Pozsega, the office of the Master of our Doorkeepers being vacant, Martin Ders, Master of the Stewards, Lawrence of Tar, Master of the Cupbearers, Peter Cseh, Master of the Horse, Silstrang *ispán* of Pozsony, and many others held comital and other offices of our kingdom.[20]

1411, ante 18 Martii

Vide praefatiunculam et notas infra paginam 197.

Sigismundus dei gratia Romanorum rex semper augustus ac Hungarie etc. rex fidelibus nostris universis dictatoribus et exactoribus tam lucri camare nostre regalis,[1] quam decimarum archyepiscopalium vel episcopalium in quibuscunque comitatibus dicti regni nostri Hungarie constitutis vel quocunque temporum in eventu constituendis, presentes inspecturis salutem et gratiam. Cum nos pridem unacum prelatis et baronibus nostris ad instantiam et querimoniam nonnullorum regnicolarum nostrorum contra et adversum vos nostre maiestati porrectam super dicatione et exactione dictorum lucri camare nostre, necnon decimarum huiusmodi decretum perpetuo duraturum per vosque firmiter observandum duxerimus institutendum:

I. Quod dicatores seu exactores dicti lucri camare nostre tempore importationis et solutionis pecuniarum per eos dicatarum ab unoquoque vilico ipsas importante seu solvente nil plus, neque pintam vini vel valorem eiusdem, nec quidquam aliud quodcunque preterquam duos denarios pro tempore currentes pro redemptione dicarum,[2] prout id solitum extitit tempore illustrissimi principis condam domini Lodouici similiter regis Hungarie, patris et soceri nostri charissimi, recipere possint atque valeant.

II. Item decrevimus, ut iidem dicatores in huiusmodi dicatione ipsorum unam portam integram, per quam currus intrare et exire potest, si etiam curia in eadem plures habitarent domestici, quam unus, in triginta denariis novis,[3] et unam valvam seu parvam portam vulgo werecke dictam non magis, nisi in quindecim novis denariis seu pro media porta, ubi vero aliquem jobagionem seu incolam se a solutione dicti lucri camere nostre fraudulose precavere satagentem ab anteriori parte curie sue parvam portam seu hostium, retro vero magnam portam habere conspexerint, huiusmodi curiam similiter in una porta dicare teneantur.[4]

III. Item statuimus, ut prefati dicatores antedicti lucri camare nostre regalis tempore dicationis huiusmodi villicos et operarios, necnon tales familiares, qui de curia dominorum suorum victibus et amictibus sustentantur,[5] et hoc domini ipsorum ad suam humanitatem[6] dumtaxat, villici autem vel officiales eorundem dominis absentibus fide mediante dicere presumpserint, quod ita sit, dicare non presumant.

IV. Item sanximus, ut elapso termino solutionis prescripti lucri camare nostre regalis illud, quod in eo remaneret insolutum, idem comes lucri camare nostre, vel sui officiales sed exactores propria

1411, before 18 March

For prefatory and explanatory notes, see below, page 197.

Sigismund, by the grace of God, ever august king of the Romans, king of Hungary etc., to all our loyal men who have been or in the future will be appointed in any county to assess and collect both the chamber's profit, as well as the archiepiscopal and episcopal tithes,[1] and who will read these presents, greetings and grace. Because of the request and complaint of several gentlemen of the realm submitted to our majesty against and about you in matters of the assessment and exaction of our chamber's profit and of the tithes, we, together with our prelates and barons, have recently decided to order you to observe firmly this following everlasting edict:

1. That the officials who assess and collect the said profit of our chamber must not take more than two of the currently circulating pennies as a fee from the reeves for the quittance, not even a pint of wine or the value of the same, nor anything else on the occasion of the delivery and payment[2] of the money they had imposed, just as was the custom during the reign of the most glorious prince lord Louis, likewise king of Hungary, our renowned father and father-in-law.

2. Then, we have decreed, that the officials who assess the taxes should in their assessments impose thirty new pennies[3] for a whole gate through which a cart can leave and enter, even if more than one peasant lives on the plot, and no more than fifteen pennies for a hinged door, namely for a small gate commonly known as *verőcze*, just as for a half gate; but where they notice that the tenant peasant or other inhabitant who, by fraudulent stratagem, in order to avoid the chamber's profit has a small gate or door at the front of his plot and a big one at the rear, then for this plot they must impose as much as for a whole gate.[4]

3. Then, we have established that the said officials who assess the said profit of our royal chamber should not dare to impose a tax on reeves, on day laborers, and on those servants whom their lord provides with food and clothing on his demesne farm,[5] if their lord declares on his word,[6] or, in his absence, his reeves or officials claim under oath that this is so.

4. Then, we have decided that, after the date of payment of our aforementioned royal chamber's profit, neither the counts of the chamber's profit, nor their officials nor the collectors of taxes should

eorum auctoritate exigere et extorquere, aut pro eo pignus recipere nequaquam presumant, nisi auxilio comitis vel vicecomitis et iudicum nobilium huiusmodi comitatuum, in quibus lucrum camare nostre exigitur prenotatum.

V. Item, disponimus etiam, ut dicatores decimarum capetias seu acervos frugum secundum proprias eorum considerationes et estimationes dicare non presumant, sed domesticus ille, cuius fruges dicantur, super hoc iuramento solito, tacto crucis dominice signo prestito fateri teneatur, quot et quantas illo anno capetias habuisset, et super hoc predicti dicatores contentari tenentur.[7] De dica vero decimationum nullus denarius exigatur.

VI. Volumus nihilominus, quod decimator decimas non solutas vigore seu subsidio comitis vel vicecomitis parochialis exigere et extorquere non possit, nisi per censuram ecclesiasticam, canonica tamen ammonitione precedente. In casu vero, ipsi dicatores et exactores tam prescripti lucri camare nostre, quam etiam decimarum iam dictarum contra premissum nostrum decretum in aliquo ultra modum iam limitatum facere vel procedere attemptarent, extunc idem comes parochialis ac iudices nobilium cum nobilibus illius comitatus, in quo hoc agitur, admittere non debeant et consentire.[8]

Et ut ipsum nostrum decretum vim perpetue firmitatis roburque perhempnale ac debitum effectum semper futuris temporibus optineat, volumus omnino et eisdem vestris fidelitatibus firmissimo nostro regio sub edicto districte precepimus et mandamus, quatenus premissum nostrum generale decretum dum ad possessiones, necnon bona et iura possessionaria honorabilis capituli ecclesie Sancti Martini in dictis comitatibus habitas et existentia dictum lucrum camere nostre, necnon decimas prenotatas dicaturi accesseritis et profecti fueritis, firmiter et in solidum inconcusseque ac inviolabiliter quoad omnes suas clausulas, continentias et articulos observantes populos et jobagiones in quibuscunque possessionibus eorum commorantes, tam ratione dicti lucri camare nostre, quam etiam decimarum predictarum iuxta modum s[uper]ius in decreto limitatum et non ultra dicare debeatis. Aliud contra formam premissi generalis nostri decreti facere nullatenus presumpmatis gratie nostre sub obtentu. Presentes quoque solito sigillo nostro fecimus consignari, quam post earum lecturam semper reddi iubemus presentanti. Datum Cassouie, refia quarta proxima ante dominicam Letare, anno domini M^{mo} quadringentesimo undecimo.

presume under any circumstance by virtue of their office to collect, extort, or take a pledge for the payment of the outstanding amount, unless with the help of the *ispán*, or the *alispán*, and the noble magistrates of that county where our said chamber's profit has been imposed.

5. We have also ordered that the tithing-men dare not tithe the shocks, namely, the heaps of grain, by using only their own discretion and estimation, but that the peasant to whom the grain belongs should, besides swearing the usual oath (touching the sign of the Lord's cross), testify to the number and size of his shocks in that year, and the said tithing-men must be satisfied with that.[7] Not a single penny shall be demanded for the tithing.

6. We also desire that the tithing-man be not allowed to collect or to extort the unpaid tithes with the help and power of the county's *ispán* or *alispán*, but only by way of ecclesiastical punishment preceded by canonical warning. Should those who assess and collect both our said chamber's profit and the aforesaid tithe dare act and proceed in any way against our aforementioned decree exceeding the established quantities, then the county's *ispán* and the noble magistrates, together with the nobles of that county in which this occurs, must not let it happen or condone it.[8]

And in order that henceforth the aforementioned decree should always have the validity of perpetual strength, everlasting force, and the required effect, we order and altogether command and bid your collective loyalty with our strictest royal decree, that when you go and travel to the estates or rights of the honorable lord Peter of Perény, former *ispán* of the Székely and George son of Peter of Dob,[9] located or lying in whichever county, to assess our said chamber's profit and the tithe, you must keep the aforementioned general decree, each of its clauses, contents, and articles firmly, totally, unalterably, and unchanged. And you must also assess the people and the tenant peasants wherever they might live on their estates for the chamber's profit and the tithes in the amount and not more than has been laid down in this aforestated decree. Do not dare to act in any way in contravention of this general decree of ours. We have also ordered that these presents, sealed with our privy seal, should be returned to the bearer, after having been read. Given in Kassa on Palm Sunday in the year of the Lord one thousand, four hundred and eleven.

23 Iulii 1421

Vide praefatiunculam et notas infra paginam 198.

Nos Sigismundus dei gratia Romanorum rex semper augustus ac Hungarie, Bohemie, Dalmatie, Croatie etc. rex memorie commendamus tenore presentium significantes quibus expedit universis, quod nobis Posonii unacum prelatis et baronibus proceribusque dicti regni nostri Hungarie in sede nostra iudiciaria sedentibus[1] nonnulli proceres et nobiles ipsius regni nostri Hungarie nostre maiestatis consurgendo in conspectum humiliter curarunt significare, quomodo comites vel vicecomites nostri in plerisque comitatibus prescripti regni nostri Hungarie constituti ipsos contra se super diversis causarum articulis ad sedem iudiciariam eiusdem comitatus, quem pro honore tenerent, in causam convenirent, propter quod ipsi in eorum iuribus fuissent defraudati adeo et in tantum, ut per predictos comites vel vicecomites in eorum rebus dampnificati extitissent et spoliarentur. Supplicaverunt itaque hiis dictis nostre claritati, ut eis circa hoc regale remedium opportunum dignaremur adhibere. Verum cum via iuris et iustitie exigente, dicti etiam regni nostri Hungarie consuetudine dictante, nullus iudicum et iustitiariorum prescripti regni nostri Hungarie in una et eadem causa iudex et actor esse potest,[2] ideo nolentes prescriptos regni nostri proceres et nobiles per predictos comites et vicecomites sic de facili et indebite opprimi et in eorum iuribus ac rebus dampnificari, matura deliberatione prehabita duximus statuendum, quod amodo inposterum nullus comitum vel vicecomitum cuiuscunque comitatus aliquem ex nostris regnicolis contra se pretextu alicuius facti ad sedem iudiciariam comitatus illius, in quo pro honore essent constituti vel constituerentur, contra se per modum citationis vel aliter in causam convenire et cum eis in lite procedere valeant atque possint, sed si quid actionis ipsi comites vel vicecomites adversus aliquos regni nostri Hungarie regnicolas aut aliquem eorum habent vel habere pretendunt, id in curia nostre serenitatis coram nostra speciali presentia aut palatinali sive iudicis curie nostre ad instar aliorum causantium requirere exequique debeant et teneantur.[3]

Quocirca vobis prescriptis regni nostri Hungarie universis comitibus vel vicecomitibus presentibus et futuris presentium notitiam habituris firmo nostro regio damus sub edicto, quatenus amodo inposterum contra formam prescripte nostre gratie dictis nostris regnicolis modo previo facte in nullis causis et causarum articulis contra vos ipsos in dicta sede vestra iudiciaria in causam convenire, eosque

23 July 1421

For prefatory and explanatory notes, see below, page 198.

We, Sigismund, by the grace of God always august king of the Romans, and king of Hungary, Bohemia, Dalmatia, Croatia, &c., wish to have remembered through the words of these presents by all to whom it may concern that, when we were sitting on our seat of judgment at Pozsony with the prelates, barons, and lords of our said kingdom of Hungary in attendance,[1] several lords and nobles of this our kingdom of Hungary, rose up in the presence of our majesty and humbly undertook to inform us that in many counties of our aforesaid kingdom of Hungary our *ispánok* and *alispánok* conduct trials concerning various cases of law against themselves at the court of that county the honor of which they hold, and that because of this the lords and nobles have been defrauded of their rights to such an extent and manner that they had suffered losses and had been despoiled by the said *ispánok* and *alispánok*. And so, after relating these things, they requested from our highness that we deign to extend to them appropriate royal remedy against these procedures. Truly, because the way of law and justice so directs and the custom of our said kingdom of Hungary so prescribes, no judge or justice of our said kingdom of Hungary may be judge and advocate in one and the same case,[2] the said lords and nobles of our kingdom do not wish to be readily and unduly oppressed, nor to be harmed in their rights and goods by the said *ispánok* and *alispánok*; hence we, after mature deliberation, order it decreed that from now on into the future no *ispán* or *alispán* of any county is permitted or enabled to conduct trials by means of citation or otherwise against any one of our gentlemen of the realm in a case against himself by any allegation at the court of that county to the honor of which he has been or will be appointed or to proceed against them in a dispute; but, if the *ispánok* or *alispánok* should have or allege to have any kind of case against any one or more gentlemen of the realm in our kingdom of Hungary, they are obligated and required to sue and to proceed in the court of our highness at the court of the special royal presence, or that of the palatine, or of our judge royal, just like other litigants.[3]

Therefore we order you, the said *ispánok* and *alispánok* of our kingdom of Hungary, present and future, who will take notice of these presents, by our firm royal edict that from now into the future you should not presume in any way to summon our said gentlemen of the realm contrary to the intent of our previously noted royal grant in any case or article of a case against yourselves to a hearing at your said

vexare et impedire nullatenus presumpmatis nec sitis ausi modo aliquali, sed si quid actionis contra eos habetis, vel habere pretenditis, in dicta curia nostre serenitatis ad instar aliorum iuridice exequi debeatis.[4] Presentes etiam post earum lecturam semper reddi edicimus presentanti.[5]

Datum in dicto Posonio, feria quarta proxima ante festum beati Jacobi apostoli, anno domini millesimo quadringentesimo vigesimo primo, regnorum nostrorum anno Hungarie etc. XXXquinto, Romanorum undecimo et Bohemie primo.

county court, nor to dare to vex or to harrass them in any manner, if you have or allege to have any suit against them, you must pursu to judgment in the said court of our serenity in the same way as others.[4] We also decree that this charter be always returned to bearer after its being read.[5]

Given at the said Pozsony, on the Thursday before the feast of James the Apostle, in the year of the Lord one thousand four hund and twenty-one, the thirty-fifth year of our reign in Hungary &c., eleventh as king of the Romans, and the first in Bohemia.

17 Martii 1427 (a)

Vide praefatiunculam et notas infra paginas 199–200.

Nos Sigismundus dei gratia Romanorum rex semper augustus ac Hungarie, Bohemie, Dalmatie, Croatie etc. rex memorie commendamus tenore presentium significantes, quibus expedit universis, quod nos frequentibus querelis regnicolarum nostrorum, tam ecclesiasticorum, quam secularium super illationibus violentiarum, dampnorum et multarum incomoditatum per nostros ac prelatorum et baronum, militum et nobilium regni nostri familiares exercitualiter proficiscentes in possessionibus nostris et eorundem tempore expeditionum exercitualium perpetratis assidue propulsati,[1] cupientes super hiis de remedio condigno providere, una cum eisdem prelatis et baronibus nostris mature deliberantes de eorundem beneplacito et consilio ordinavimus, statuimus ac presenti decreto sancimus:

I. Ut quicunque exercituantium victualia et res necessarias, quibus carere non possunt, videlicet panes, vinum, pabulum, fenum, ova, caseum, blada, pisces, legumina, ancas, pullos, porcellos, agnellos, butirum, carnes et similia minora violenter aut pretio non soluto, seu non plene soluto abstulerint aut aliter in hiis dampna intulerint, requisitique non satisfecerint, contra illos homines dampnificati seu eorum domini debeant convocare duos iudices nobilium illius comitatus, in quo dampnum fieri contingit, et coram illis homines dampnificati simul cum eorum villico deponere debent iuramentum de quantitate dampni illati, ipsique iudices nobilium similiter ad eorum iuramentum, quod prestiterunt tempore electionis eorum in iudices,[2] debent dare litteras eorum testimoniales dictis dampnificatis sub sigillis comitis illius comitatus et ipsorum iudicum nobilium, hominesque dampnificati cum eisdem litteris accedentes ad iudices regni in curiam regiam tempore, quo in aliqua die octavarum[3] fit iudicium regni, ubi iidem iudices regni predictis litteris testimonialibus plenam fidem adhibere et dampnificatis super dampno principali in dictis litteris testimonialibus contento, necnon super omnibus expensis, laboribus et fatigiis in requisitione dictorum dampnorum factis et fiendis conscientioso moderamine prehabito litteras sententiales et perceptorias[4] comiti illius comitatus, in quo exercituantes predicti, qui dampnum intulerunt, existunt, sub certo autentico sigillo[5] dare debeant, vigore quarum dictus comes indilatam et plenam satisfactionem tam super dampno principali, quam super dictis expensis, fatigiis et laboribus iuxta moderamen dictorum iudicum cum rebus promptis et pecuniis aut occupatione possessionum et non cum estimatione exhibere teneatur.[6]

17 March 1427 (a)

For prefatory and explanatory notes, see below, pages 199–200.

We Sigismund, by the grace of God ever august king of the Romans and king of Hungary, Bohemia, Dalmatia, Croatia, etc., wish to be remembered by notifying all to whom it may concern through the words of these presents that, induced by the complaints of our gentlemen of the realm, both clerical and lay, about the violent acts, damages, and many kinds of impositions committed by the armed retainers mobilized for campaigns by us, the prelates, barons, knights, and nobles of the kingdom on our estates and theirs while they go to war,[1] and wishing to remedy these by suitable means, after mature deliberation with the same prelates and barons and following their pleasure and counsel, we have ordained, established, and decreed the following.

1. If any soldier takes by force or without payment or without full payment or causes any kind of damage in victuals and other necessities without which one cannot live, such as bread, wine, fodder, hay, eggs, cheese, grain, fish, vegetables, geese, poultry, piglets, lambs, butter, meat, and similar things of lesser value, and does not offer satisfaction to the one demanding payment, then against him the persons who have suffered loss or their lords ought to call upon two noble magistrates of that county in which the damage was done and the plaintiffs shall swear, publicly together with their reeve, an oath on the amount of the damage incurred. The noble magistrates, according to the oath that they swore at their election to the office,[2] ought to give the said plaintiffs a letter of evidence under their own and of the county *ispán*'s seals, and then these plaintiffs ought to appear with this letter before the judges of the royal court when on an octavial term[3] royal court is held. At that place and time the judges must give full credence to the said letter of evidence, and after conscientious examination issue a letter of judgment and order[4] on the damage contained in the said letter of evidence as well as on the expenses, exertions, and labors spent and to be spent by the plaintiffs for the recovery of their losses, under their distinct authentic seal,[5] addressed to the *ispán* of that county where the soldiers who had caused the damages are to be found. On the strength of this letter, the *ispán* is obligated to secure immediate and full satisfaction not only for the main damage but also for the aforementioned expenses, exertions, and labors according to the decision of the said judges, in kind or in money or by seizing of estates, but not in the amount of the estimated value.[6]

II. Item quicunque res maiores, videlicet equos, boves, vestes, porcos, lardos et alias res maiores, quibus sine necessitate carere possent, abstulerint, seu domos, cellaria et scrinia rusticorum confregerint, aut vina receperint, currus oneran[tes] ac alia similia dampna maiora intulerint, omnes tales per dampnificatos seu eorum dominos ad curiam regiam ad certas octavas in presentiam alicuius iudicum curie evocentur. Qui si ad ipsas octavas venire contempserint vel neglexerint, in ipso primo termino tamquam culpabiles reputentur et sententientur, per hoc tamen factum potentie et occupationis possessionum non incurrant, sed dampnum, quod contra eos propositum fuerit, quater appreciare et persolvere dampnificatis ipsis per iustitiarios regni predictos compellantur.[7] Si vero ad ipsas octavas venerint seu per procuratorem legitimum comparuerint, extunc dampno confesso similiter sententialiter condempnentur et ad satisfactionem compellantur, dampno vero negato iudices predicti mediantibus eorum litteris debent remittere dampnificatos ad inquisitionem comitatus, in quo dampna sunt illata, ubi exactis attestatoriis iuramentis corporalibus[8] super eorum fassione constiterit dampnum illatum, illatores huiusmodi supradictis penis condempnentur et satisfacere modo premisso compellantur.

III. Quicunque autem maiora facinora et delicta commiserint, videlicet interfectiones hominum, oppressiones et raptus mulierum et virginum, effractiones ecclesiarum et vasorum sacrorum ac domorum nobilium, tales tribus inquisitionibus[9] per illos, quibus iniuria huiusmodi fuerit illata, fieri procuratis, erga domos dominorum eorum ad certas octavas in curiam regiam debeant evocari rationem premissorum reddituri. Qui si comparuerint et se in talismodi illatis iniuriis innocentes fore allegaverint, tunc probatio ipsarum illatarum iniuriarum ad attestationem nobilium illius comitatus, in quo hoc patratum fuerit, committatur. Ubi autem in octava predicta non comparerent, extunc in sententia capitali eo facto convincantur;[10] et si tales convicti reperti non fuerint vel reperiri non possent, extunc prefatus dominus eorum homagia ipsorum[11] persolvat et de dampnis et iniuriis illatis lesis satisfacere teneatur.

IV. Item in omnibus premissis ubicunque illatores dampnorum et facinorum predictorum per passos iniuriam et dampnum eo, quod tales forte impossessionati vel ignoti, aut nimis remoti extiterint, ad evocandum inveniri non possent, sufficiat huiusmodi evocationem fieri circa habitationem baronis vel domini eorum, sub cuius nomine et banderio in huiusmodi exercitu procedebant,[12] et idem dominus evocationem eandem ad notitiam suorum famulorum deducat.

V. Item si aliquis ex baronibus extiterit presens cum suis gentibus in exercitu[13] et eidem contra suos familiares de aliquo dampno illato conquestum fuerit, de quo satisfacere non curaverit, extunc de eis dampnificati eorum dampna super ipsum baronem satisfacere non curantem requirendi et recuperandi habeant facultatem.

2. Then, those who will have taken major things, such as horses, cattle, clothes, pigs, bacon, and other valuable items without which one can survive, or who destroy the houses, cellars, and barns of the peasants or seize all their wine or loaded carts or cause similar major damage, should be cited by the plaintiffs or their lords to the royal court at an octavial session to the bench of a judge. Those who neglect or avoid appearing at that octave are to be judged at that first term as guilty and to be sentenced. Whereas they should not incur the punishment of confiscation of their estates for this violent trespass, they should nonetheless be forced by the said royal justices to repay these damaged persons four times the estimated value of the damage which was charged against them.[7] If, however, they appear personally or through legal counsel at that octavial court and admit the damage, they should also be duly sentenced and compelled to repair the damage. However, if they deny the damage, the said judges ought to send the plaintiffs with their letters to the county where the damage occurred, and there, when the damage inflicted has been testified to by statements sworn on corporeal oath,[8] the accused must be condemned to the aforesaid punishment and must repair the damages in the said manner.

3. Those, however, who have committed major crimes and delicts, such as the killing of people, maltreatment or rape of women and virgins, robbery of churches or of houses of nobles, or theft of sacred vessels, are to be summoned from the houses of the plaintiff's lords to an octavial session at the royal court after a threefold inquiry[9] by those who have suffered such damage in order to respond to the complaints. If they appear and claim to be innocent of the harm caused, then the proof of these inflicted damages ought to be requested from the nobles of that county where the damage was committed. If, however, they do not appear at the said octave, they should incur capital sentence for that reason.[10] If these culprits have not been or cannot be found, then the said lords of theirs have to pay their composition[11] and make satisfaction for the damages and injuries caused by them.

4. Then, whenever regarding the aforesaid matters those who have suffered the damages and injuries cannot find those who caused the damages or inflicted the injuries in order to summon them, either because of being unpropertied or unknown or living too far away, it will suffice to deliver such a summons to the residence of that baron or lord under whose banner and name they serve in the army,[12] and that lord has to bring the summons to the notice of his retainers.

5. Then, if any baron who is among his men under arms[13] and does not take care that satisfaction be given by a retainer of his when he is requested to do so by someone who had suffered damage, then these damaged parties should have the right to demand and claim their damages from that very baron who failed to satisfy them.

VI. Item exercituantes tempore estivo et alio, quo in campo stare possunt, teneant campestres descensus; gramina tamen atque ligna silvatica ignibus apta, similiter tempore iemali hospitia, sive iidem multi, sive pauci procedant, eisdem prohiberi et denegari non debent, et in istis exercituantes predicti a nemine debeant inquietari impediri atque molestari. Casu autem, quo in aliquo locorum gramina pastui iumentorum exercituantium necessaria non invenirentur, sed tantummodo prata et fenilia ad domos rusticorum reservata et custodita, tunc in illis iumenta exercituantium depasci possent et enutriri, antequam forent falcata et simul congregata. Postquam autem falcata fuerint, non recipiantur vi neque gratis, sed nisi pecunia condigna valoris eiusdem.

VII. Preterea pro avena vel ordeo aut siligine tempore caristie pro cubulo Budensi[14] solvantur denarii triginta unus, tempore autem fertilitatis solvantur viginti quinque.

Item pro feno pro uno equo per diem unum et noctem solvatur unus [denariu]s, et non tamen substernatur fenum, sed quantum equo petitur, tantum detur.

Item pro pane, quantum potest conpetere et sufficere duabus personis pro uno prandio, solvatur denarius unus.

Item--- ante adventum exercituantium communiter tabernarii---[15]

Item pro anca una solvantur denarii quinque.

Item pro pullo antiquo solvantur denarii tres, pro iuveni duo.

Pro porce[llo sol]vantur denarii quinque et demum pro agnello solvantur denarii octo.

Item pisces, legumina, carnes mactate, caseum, butirum et similia, de quibus non potest haberi ratio singularis, emantur et solvantur pretio competenti, considerata tamen temporis et loci qualitate.

Item ova pro denario octo.

Item si qui voluerint emere boves, porcos maiores, lardos, non emant aliter, quam cum bona voluntate vendentis et solvant secundum quod poterunt de pretio concordare.

VIII. Item videtur, quod in omnibus locis, in quibus sal regium potest sufficienter haberi, sit prohibitum vendi vel emi sal extraneum. Si quis contra fecerit, venditor prima vice repertus per camerarium regium toto sale privetur, secundo vero sale simul cum curru et animalibus ipsum currum vehentibus destituatur; tertio vero vel pluries personaliter detineatur et pena condigna, sicut cum camerario ipso concordare poterit, puniatur. Emptor sal amittat et insuper pretium, quod pro sale dederat, camerario regio secundario persolvat.[16]

IX. Item, quod de sale regio tamdiu, quousque ducitur sub nomine regio, nullus audeat exigere tributum in terra aut in aqua, nisi qui possent probare se in hoc ius habere speciale. Similiter fiat de sale dato exercituantibus,[17] donec eorum nominibus ducitur et venditur.

6. During summer or such time when they can stay in the open, the army should camp in the fields, but they, be they many or few, ought not to be denied straw and firewood from the forest nor housing in wintertime, and in these matters the soldiers should be neither molested nor harassed or hindered. Where there is not enough pasture for the beasts of the army beyond those meadows and pastures which are necessary and reserved for the peasant households, then the animals of the army should graze and feed only before the meadows are mown and the hay gathered. After the mowing, no hay must be taken by force or without payment, but only for the proper price according to its value.

7. Furthermore: for oats, rye, and barley, for a *cubulus* of Buda[14] in lean years 31 pennies are to be paid; in fertile years, 25 pennies.

Then, for hay for a horse for a day and a night, one penny, but the hay should not be strewn under the horse; only as much hay should be given as the horse needs.
Then, for bread, sufficient for two people to eat for one meal, one penny is due.
Then, . . . before the army's arrival, tavernkeepers . . .[15]
For a goose, 5 pennies are to be paid.
For an old hen, 3 pennies are due; for a young chicken, 2 pennies.
For a piglet, 5 pennies, and furthermore, for a lamb, 8 pennies are to be paid.
Then, fish, vegetables, cut meat, cheese, butter, and suchlike which cannot be listed singularly, should be bought and paid for at a suitable price, always considering the conditions of time and place.
Then, for a penny, eight eggs.
Then, if anyone wishes to buy cattle, fat pigs, or bacon, he should not do so without the good will of the seller and should pay the price agreed to.

8. Then, it seems best that in places where a sufficient amount of royal salt can be acquired, the buying and selling of foreign salt be prohibited. If someone acts against this, the seller at first offense should be deprived by the royal chamberlain of all the salt, at the second time also of the cart and the animal drawing the cart, at the third time or thereafter, he should be personally arrested and punished by suitable punishment according to his bargain with the chamberlain. The buyer should lose the salt and in addition should pay as much to the royal chamberlain as he paid for the salt.[16]

9. Then, no one should dare to demand toll for the king's salt wherever it is shipped in the king's name, on water or land, unless he can prove that he has a special right to do so. The same should hold for the salt of the soldiers[17] as long as it is transported or sold in their

Postquam autem huiusmodi sal sive de camera regia, sive ab exercituantibus ad mercaturam devenerit, mercatores ipsi videntur teneri ad tributum. Quicunque autem tributariorum de huiusmodi sale regio vel exercituantium tributum exegerit, et camerarius regius domino illius tributarii intimaverit, teneatur idem dominus dictum tributarium assignare dicto camerario ad satisfactionem ipsi camerario iuxta eius voluntatem adstringendum presentium litterarum nostrarum privilegialium testimonio mediante.

Datum Brassouie, feria secunda proxima post dominicam Reminiscere, anno domini millesimo quadringentesimo vigesimo septimo, regnorum nostrorum anno Hungarie etc. XL, Romanorum XVII et Bohemie septimo.

name. Once, however, such salt of either the royal chamber or soldiers passes into the hands of a merchant, the merchants are cons ered liable for the toll on it. Wherever a toll-collector demands toll such royal or military salt, and the chamberlain reports this to master of the toll-collector, the master of the said toll has to hand o that toll-collector to the chamberlain in order to satisfy tl chamberlain, according to his demands, by the force of this, our pres letter of privilege.

Given at Brassó, on Monday following the Sunday Remembrance, in the year of the Lord one thousand, four hund twenty-seven, in the fourtieth year of our reign in Hungary etc., seventeenth as king of the Romans, and the seventh year of our rei in Bohemia.

17 Martii 1427 (b)

Vide praefatiunculam et notas infra paginas 201–02.

Sigismundus dei gratia Romanorum rex semper augustus ac Hungarie, Bohemie, Dalmatie, Croatie, Rame, Servie, Galicie, Lodomerie, Comanie Bulgarieque rex, marchio Brandemburgensis et Lucemburgensis heres necnon Barbara d[ei] gratia regnorum predictorum regina[1] omnibus Christi fidelibus presentibus pariter et futuris presens scriptum inspecturis salutem in omnium salvatore. Cum inter ceteras animi nostri curas, quibus ad profectum regnorum nostrorum utilitatemque nobis subiectorum meditatione continua distrahimur, mente volveremus quemadmodum et ipsorum regnorum nostrorum expeditionibus et diversis statibus eorundem subditorum nostrorum in cusione, cursu et consuetudine monete tam auree quam argentee utiliorem et fructuosiorem dispositionem ederemus, habito cum prelatis et baronibus nostris, quorum sigilla una cum nostris pro maiori evidentia consensus eorundem presentibus sunt appensa,[2] maturo superinde consilio, provida deliberatione precedente ordinationes, statuta, edictalia scripta infra contenta decrevimus, sanximus et decernimus tam effectui mancipanda quam futuris temporibus continue firmitate servanda.

I. Ordinavimus itaque statuimus, sanximus et conclusimus monetam auream nostre maiestatis in eisdem qualitate, quantitate et gradibus auri, quibus hucusque cusa est et nunc cuditur, de cetero cudi et remanere, monetam vero argenteam maiorem a modo in antea cudi et fabricari de argento finissimo in tanta quantitate, quod de una marca puri argenti exeant denarii sexcenti, quorum centum currant pro floreno auri. Minores vero denarii vulgariter filler vocati camare nostre regie hactenus cusi—quousque durabunt—remaneant et currant nec cudantur de cetero plures de istis vel alii fillerii, nisi tandem tum per nos ac prelatos et barones nostros predictos pro nostra et regni nostri utilitate de cusione minoris nostre monete aliud cogitatum extiterit et provisum.[3]

II. Quocirca ex vigore presentis decreti et sanxionis nostre maiestatis de prelatorum et baronum nostrorum predictorum unanimi voluntate, consensu et ordinatione firmissimo sub precepto per universos comitatus et provincias ac loca dicti regni nostri insinuari, publicari et proclamari mandamus, ut omnes regnicole[4] et alii quivis homines in regno nostro commorantes falsos denarios minores seu fillerios, quorum admixtione vera moneta camare nostre regie hactenus

17 March 1427 (b)

For prefatory and explanatory notes, see below, pages 201–02.

Sigismund, by the grace of God ever august king of the Romans, king of Hungary, Bohemia, Dalmatia, Croatia, Rama, Serbia, Galicia, Lodomeria, Cumania, and Bulgaria, margrave of Brandenburg and heir of Luxembourg, as well as Barbara, by the grace of God queen of the above kingdoms,[1] to all Christ's faithful, present and future, who will read these presents, greetings in the Savior of all. When, among other concerns of our mind with which we are occupied in steady contemplation of the improvement of our kingdoms and the advantage of our subjects, we turn our thoughts to the question of how we could issue a more useful and fruitful regimen regarding the minting, circulation, and usage of money, both gold and silver, for the enterprises of our kingdoms as well as for the diverse status of our subjects in them, after having held mature counsel with our prelates and barons, whose seals are appended along with ours for greater evidence of their consent to these presents,[2] we have decreed, ordered, and established, after having considered the preceding consultations, that the ordinations, statutes, and edicts set out below should be immediately observed and kept with perpetual force in the future.

1. We have therefore ordained, determined, ordered, and decided that the gold coinage of our majesty should be minted and should remain further in the same quality, quantity, and fineness of gold in which it has been minted until now and is still being minted; and the larger silver coinage should be minted and produced henceforth from the finest silver in such quantity that six hundred pennies should be minted from a mark of pure silver, and one hundred of these should equal one gold florin. The smaller pennies of our royal chamber, commonly called *fillér*, thus far minted should remain in circulation as long as they last, but neither more nor different *fillérek* must be minted, unless we and our said prelates and barons will have considered and decided otherwise in regard to the minting of our smaller money for our profit and for that of our kingdom.[3]

2. Therefore, by the power of the present decree and order of our majesty following the unanimous will, consent, and command of our said prelates and barons, we order by most strict ordinance that it be made known, published, and proclaimed in all counties, provinces, and places of our said kingdom that all residents[4] and any others sojourning in our kingdom are required, by the next coming feast of St. James the Apostle,[5] to discard, destroy, and abolish forged small pennies or

extitit et nunc est depravata, usque ad festum sancti Jacobi apostoli proxime venturum[5] prorsus abicere, anichilare et abolire teneantur, nullatenus de cetero eosdem apud se detinere presumendo. Volentes et eodem edicto committentes, ut infra ipsum terminum iudices presidentes et rectores curie, nundinarum et fororum[6] omnes falsos obulos seu fillerios[7] necnon officiales nostri regales ad id deputandi in locis et foris suarum iurisdictionum diligenter requiri ac inventos incidi et destrui facere te[neantur] sicque incisos et destructos eis, apud quos inventi fuerint, nec hoc cupiditati imputetur, restitui faciant et resignari. Lapso autem huiusmodi termino festi sancti Jacobi apostoli, si quis cum moneta omnino falsa segregata videlicet a moneta vera camare nostre regalis ad numerum adminus duodecim denariorum se extendentem fuerit deprehensus, talis pena delatoris false monete puniatur.[8] Quicumque vero falsam monetam intermixtam bone monete camare regie usque ad decimum, puta inter centum fillerios decem falsos aut in centum florenis verorum denariorum decem florenos falsorum, deferre comperti fuerint, tales in personis detineri ac pena falsificantium monetam puniri debeant prenotata. Denarii vero falsi sic inventi modo premisso aboleantur. Moneta autem falsa infra pretaxatum numerum, ratione cuius scilicet delator persone aut rerum subire non merebatur penam, similiter ab eisdem iudicibus et presidentibus nundinarum, fororum et civitatum ac officialibus nostris requiratur, incidatur et aboleatur.

III. Statuimus insuper et sanximus, quod quicumque homines regnicole vel forenses—cuiuscumque status et conditionis existant—in tantam malitiam suam temeritatem extenderint, quod predictam monetam nostram novam argenteam vel aliam quamlibet contra veteres et varias nostre maiestatis ac dictorum prelatorum et baronum nostrorum ordinationes et inhibitiones radere vel quomodolibet incidendo minorare aut rasam vel minutam defferre seu cum tali quovismodo mercari vel negotiari presumpserint, pena falsorum denariorum plectantur prenotata eandemque penam subire volentes et decernentes omnes segregatores, exponderatores et electores graviorum denariorum a levioribus huiusmodique ingenio cursum et valorem dicte monete nostre vilificare satagentes.

IV. Item statuimus, ordinavimus pro statutoque et sanxione irrevocabili habere volumus et reliquimus, ut marca puri argenti Budensis ponderis valeat quingentos et quinquaginta denarios monete maioris supradicte, quorum scilicet centum currant pro floreno auri.[9]

V. Preterea statuimus, sanximus et ordinavimus, quod nemo in mercaturis, emptionibus, venditionibus et commutationibus presumat procedere et negotiari cum auro vel argento non monetato, sed totum aurum et argentum comportetur ad camaram monete nostre regalis

filléreket, and no one should dare to keep any of them for himself, since mixing them has caused and is still causing the devaluation of the true money of our royal chamber. We also wish and command by the same edict that within this time limit the presiding judges and the supervisors of the towns, markets, and fairs,[6] as well as our royal officials appointed to this in the places and areas of their jurisdiction are required to have all forged *obuli* or *filléreket*[7] diligently searched out and to cut up and destroy those found; and in addition, they must see to it, lest they be accused of cupidity, that the cut up, and destroyed coins be restored and returned to those in whose possession they were found. After the expiration of this time limit of the feast of St. James the Apostle, anyone who is caught at all with forged money set aside from the true money of our royal chamber in the amount of at least twelve pennies, will be punished with the penalty of a counterfeiter of forged money. Whoever is found guilty of mixing forged money with good money of our royal chamber up to one tenth, that is, ten forged *filléreket* among one hundred, or ten florins of forged pennies among one hundred florins of true pennies, must be detained in person and punished with the penalty for forgers of money as noted above.[8] Forged pennies found in the above manner must be destroyed. Forged money of less than the above quantity, for which the culprit does not merit undergoing the penalty of person or property, must similarly be confiscated, cut up and destroyed by the said judges and supervisors of markets, fairs, and towns or by our officials.

3. We have laid down and ordered furthermore that any residents or foreigners, of whatever station or condition, who would extend their boldness to such evil that they dare to clip or diminish by cutting our said new silver or any other money, have in their hands clipped or diminished money, or conduct commerce or business with such, contrary to old and various orders and prohibitions of our majesty and of our said prelates and barons, should be punished with the penalty noted above of counterfeit pennies; and we wish and decree that all those who separate, weigh out, and select heavier pennies from lighter ones and by this cunning attempt to reduce the circulation and to cheapen the value of our said money should suffer the same penalty.

4. Then, we have laid down and ordered and we wish and leave it to be held by irrevocable statute and order that a mark of pure silver of Buda weight should be worth five hundred and fifty pennies of the larger money mentioned above, namely that of which one hundred equals a gold florin.[9]

5. Furthermore, we have laid down, decreed, and ordered that in commerce, buying, selling, and exchange no one should dare to proceed or to negotiate with gold or silver that is not coined, but should bring all gold and silver to the chamber of our royal mint where it must be sold

vendaturque ibi pretio suo modo premisso limittato.[10] Mercantie vero quelibet exerceantur et fiant cum moneta regali vel commutationibus aliarum rerum preter aurum et argentum. Si quis autem contrarium fecerit, emptor tam aurum et argentum non monetatum modo premisso in huiusmodi negotiationibus expositum quam alia cuncta bona sua tunc secum habita et reperta, venditor vero rem venalem pro huiusmodi auro et argento non monetato expositam amittat ipso facto.

VI. Ad hec unanimi consensu et voluntate prelatorum et baronum predictorum sanximus et statuendo commisimus perpetue firmiter observanda, ut nullus omnino hominum regnicola vel forensis—cuiuscumque status et conditionis existat—aurum et argentum necnon pecuniam auream et argenteam de regnis nostris corone nostre Hungarie suppositis sub pena capitis ac perditionis omnium bonorum suorum mobilium et inmobilium ubilibet habitorum audeat exportare ultra rationabiles et condecentes expensas considerata dignitate et conditione personarum, prelatis tamen et baronibus ac nobilib[us et] ceteris regnicolis nostris secundum cuiuslibet conditionis facultatem pro clenodiis et l[ab]oribus propriis aurum et argentum emenda ac ubi maluerint purgari, fabricari et laborari faciendi [libe]ra facultate remanente vigore et testimonio presentium literarum nostrarum privilegialium mediante.

Datum Brassovie feria secunda proxima post dominicam Reminiscere anno domini M^{mo} CCCC^{mo} XX^{mo} VII^{mo}, regno[rum] nostrum anno Hungarie etc. XL^{mo}, Romanorum XVII^{mo} et Bohemie septimo.

for the price fixed in the preceding manner.[10] All business affairs must be conducted and take place with royal money or by the exchange of other goods besides gold and silver. If anyone should do otherwise, the buyer should lose the uncoined gold and silver mentioned above used in any such business, as well as all other goods in his possession and found with him, and the seller should for the same reason lose the goods exposed for sale for uncoined gold and silver in the same way.

6. With the unanimous consent of the said prelates and barons and their agreement to all this, we have ordered and committed it to be laid down firmly so that it be observed perpetually that no resident or foreigner at all—whatever station and condition he might be—should dare to export gold and silver as well as gold and silver money from our kingdoms subject to our crown of Hungary, beyond reasonable and proper expenses appropriate to the dignity and worth of the person, under the capital penalty and the loss of all his movable and immovable goods held anywhere; however, for our prelates, barons, nobles, and other gentlemen of the realm, according to the means of their respective stations, the free allowance should remain valid by the force and witness of our present privilege to cause gold and silver to be used for their own jewels and works (of art) or, if they prefer, to purify, fabricate, and work with gold and silver.

Given at Brassó on Monday following the Sunday of Remembrance, in the year of the Lord one thousand, four hundred and twenty-seven, the fortieth year of our reign in Hungary, etc., the seventeenth as king of the Romans, and the seventh in Bohemia.

8 Martii 1435

Vide praefatiunculam et notas infra paginas 203–07.

Sigismundus divina favente clementia Romanorum imperator semper augustus ac Hungarie, Bohemie, Dalmatie, Croatie, Rame, Seruie, Gallicie, Lodomerie, Cumanie Bulgarieque rex universis Christi fidelibus, presentibus pariter et futuris, presentium notitiam habituris salutem in omnium salvatore. Inter cuncta, que pro subiectorum salute conservanda nostre meditationis perpendit acumen, ad ea presertim cordis nostri curas innata nobis inclinatione nature solemus divertere, quibus humane temeritatis audacia effrenata nonnunquam iuncta potentie reprimatur et iuris integritas abutentium prevaricatione depravata nunc apertiori priorum consuetudinum declaratione, nunc novarum utili constitutione legum principantis providentia reformetur. Proinde ad universorum, tam presentium quam futurorum notitiam volumus pervenire, quod cum nos pro imperialis fastigii honore finaliter adipiscendo post electionem nostram in regem Romanorum factam et prime corone regie Romane Aquisgrani susceptionem novissime sacri Romani imperii principibus electoribus nobis consulentibus in partes Lombardie descendentes in civitate Mediolani secundam coronam regiam Romanam recepissemus, et demum in urbem Romanam profecti fuissemus infulasque nostras imperiales de manibus sanctissimi domini nostri domini Eugenii pape quarti cum debita solemnitate suscepissemus et deinde nonnullis partibus Italie et Germanie perlustratis rebusque tam sancte Romane ecclesie, quam nostris imperialibus nobis interim occurrentibus votive dispositis exonerati,[1] tandem in peculiare regnum nostrum Hungarie medio tempore presentia nostra regali viduatum iniuriisque et dampnificationibus potentialibus in suo statu et sue quietis ac pacis amenitate disturbatum regressi in hac civitate nostra Posoniensi primam residentiam personalem fixissemus ac unacum fidelibus nostris, prelatis videlicet et baronibus eiusdem regni nostri ad nostram maiestatem confluentibus certam conventionem nobilium de singulis ipsius regni nostri comitatibus convocari fecissemus, tandem ipsorum congregatione adunata de eorundem prelatorum et baronum nostrorum necnon nobilium regni nostri totum corpus eiusdem regni cum plena facultate absentium representantium[2] unanimi consilio, deliberatione et consensu pro debita, ordinata et conformi iustitie amministratione incolis eiusdem regni equaliter omnibus de cetero exhibenda, necnon quieto et tranquillo statu eorundem regnicolarum infrascriptas constitutiones, statuta et leges in perpetuum duraturas et inviolabiliter

8 March 1435

For prefatory and explanatory notes, see below, pages 203–07.

Sigismund, with the aid of divine mercy ever august emperor of the Romans and king of Hungary, Bohemia, Dalmatia, Croatia, Serbia, Rama, Galicia, Lodomeria, Cumania, and Bulgaria to all of Christ's faithful, present as well as future, who will have notice of these presents, greetings in the Savior of all. Among all the matters which our attentive mind contemplates concerning the preservation of the welfare of our subjects, we are accustomed, by innate inclination of our nature, to turn our heart's attention particularly toward those things, with which the prince's foresight may restrain by a clearer definition of ancient custom as well as by the useful creation of new laws, the unbridled recklessness of human rashness not infrequently coupled with acts of violence, and may restore the integrity of justice, debased by the devious actions of abusers. Therefore, we wish herewith to notify all, both present and future, that recently, after we had been elected and made king of the Romans, and received the first Roman royal crown in Aachen, we then, with the advice of the electors of the Holy Roman Empire, went to Lombardy, in order to obtain the supreme imperial dignity, and received in Milan the second royal crown of the Roman Empire. Next, we visited the city of Rome and there received the imperial symbols with the usual solemnity from the hands of our most holy lord, lord pope Eugene IV, then visited many regions of Italy and Germany, setting aside, at our discretion matters we encountered on our way regarding both the holy Roman Church as well as our empire.[1] Returning finally to our very own Hungarian kingdom, which had been deprived of our royal presence and was disturbed in her state and enjoyment of peace and tranquillity by unjust and harmful violence, we established our first personal residence in our city of Pozsony, whence we summoned to our majesty, together with our loyal subjects, namely, the prelates and barons of this kingdom of ours, a special assembly of the nobles from every county of our kingdom. Finally, after they have gathered together, we have decided, determined, declared, decreed, and confirmed with the unanimous counsel, deliberation, and consent of these prelates and barons and nobles of ours, representing the whole body of our kingdom with full powers of those absent,[2] in the interest of a proper, well-ordered and just administration of justice, which shall be rendered equally to every inhabitant of this kingdom and also for the peace and tranquillity of the

observandas disposuimus, decrevimus et duximus ordinandas, declarandas et firmandas.

I. Primo quidem, ut omnis scrupulosa suspicio, que contra iudices et iustitiarios ipsius regni nostri de favore vel odio aut quoquomodo concipi posset, de cordibus quorumlibet penitus removeatur et tollatur, statuimus, ut semper successivis temporibus omnes et singuli iudices et iustitiarii dicti regni nostri, tam ecclesiastici, quam seculares, qui videlicet in palatinum, iudicem curie regie, magistrum tauarnicorum regalium, cancellarium aut vicecancellarium regalem, in prothonotarios seu vicesgerentes iudicum pretactorum ac etiam assessores[3] eorundem in iudicio, in wayuodam partium Transsiluanarum, comitem Siculorum, banum regnorum Dalmatie et Croatie, banum Sclauonie, banum Machouiensem ac in comites quorumlibet comitatuum et iudices nobilium eligentur et assumentur, eorundemque in iudicatu vicesgerentes substituti et assessores tempore receptionis eorundem ad huiusmodi honores et officia, amministrationis iudicii et iustitie in manibus nostris regiis vel deputatorum a nobis iuramentum prestare teneantur per formam verborum infrascriptam, videlicet sic: Ego T. iuro per deum et per gloriosam dei genitricem virginem Mariam, per omnes sanctos et electos dei, quod omnibus et singulis coram me causantibus absque cuiusvis persone, divitis scilicet et pauperis acceptione omnibusque prece, premio, favore, amore et odio postpositis et remotis, prout scilicet secundum deum et iustitiam faciendum cognovero, iustum et verum iudicium et iustitiam faciam meo pro posse. Sic me deus adiuvet et beata virgo Maria et hoc lignum vivifice crucis domini nostri Jhesu Christi.[4]

II. Iudices autem nobilium in quolibet comitatu eligantur et preficiantur ex nobilibus potioribus et bene possessionatis illius comitatus communiter omnibus nobilibus eiusdem comitatus concorditer visi et merito acceptandi, et ipsi electi teneantur non refutare, sed suscipere officium iudicatus sub pena viginti quinque marcarum per ipsam communitatem, si secus fecerint, irremissibiliter exigendarum, exceptis tamen officiolatus et honores regios, reginales, prelatorum, baronum vel aliorum tenentibus vel stipendia ratione exercituandi habentibus vel aliis rationabilibus ex causis in ipso comitatu continuam residentiam non facientibus, et huiusmodi officium ad minus per annum exercere, habendo sigillum cognoscibile ad dandum cum sigillis aliorum iudicum nobilium et comitis vel vicecomitis litteras fidedignas. Si vero elapso anno voluerint, habeant recusandi facultatem. Quod si resignaverint aut per communitatem nobilium comprovincialium remoti seu mutati fuerint, ante annum quintum futurum ad idem officium assumendum inviti non coartentur.[5] De birsagiis autem sedium parochialium ad portionem iudiciariam cedentibus comes parochialis et iudices nobilium equam inter se divisionem facere teneantur in duas partes.

same inhabitants, the following decrees, statutes, and laws to last forever and to be obeyed without fail.

1. Namely, first of all, in order to destroy and remove entirely all disquieting suspicion from everyone's heart which may arise against the judges and administrators of justice of this kingdom of ours because of favor or hatred or any other reason, we have decided that henceforth for all times in our said kingdom each and every one of the judges and administrators of justice, both ecclesiastical and secular, namely those who may be elected and appointed as palatines, judges royal, Masters of the royal Treasury, royal chancellors, vicechancellors, and the protonotaries and deputies of the said judges and the assessors of their courts, voivoides of Transylvania, *ispánok* of the Székely, bans of the Dalmatian and Croatian kingdoms, the bans of Slavonia and Macsó, also the *ispánok* and noble magistrates of any county, together with their deputies at court who are to be appointed to substitute for them, and the assessors of the county court,[3] should at the time of their installation into these legal and jurisdictional honors and offices swear an oath into our royal hands or into that of our appointed deputies in the following words, namely: I, T., swear to God and to the Holy Mother of God, Virgin Mary, to all the saints and God's chosen ones that I will pass just and true judgment and do justice to the utmost of my ability, leaving aside and discarding any kind of request, reward, favor, love, or hatred, as I understand that according to God justice is to be done, to each litigant appearing before me, each and every one of them, without regard to person, not discerning between rich or poor. So help me God and the blessed Virgin Mary and this wood of the life-giving cross of our Lord, Jesus Christ.[4]

2. Noble magistrates of every county must be elected and appointed from the richer and wealthier noblemen whom all the nobles of that county by common consent regard and consider suitable for that office, and those elected must not refuse the magistracy but must accept it under the penalty of 25 marks which must be pitilessly collected by the county community from those who act contrariwise, except those who are placed by the king, the queen, prelates, or barons or others into honors or offices or who receive payment as soldiers or who for other proper reason do not live permanently in the county; and those elected are bound to hold this office for at least a year and to have seals which are easily recognizable, so that they will be able to issue trustworthy documents together with the seals of other noble magistrates and *ispánok* and *alispánok.* After one year they are free to refuse the office. If they resign or are removed from office or are replaced by the community of the county's nobles, they are not to be forced against their will to accept the same office before the fifth following year.[5] From the fines levied at the court of the county magistrates, the portion due to the judges must be divided in two equal parts between the *ispán* and the noble magistrates.

III. Verum quia frequenti querela regnicolarum nostrorum ymmo quadam palpabili experientia teste nostra percepit celsitudo per nonnullas novas possessionum occupationes et potentiariorum actuum illationes[6] eosdem regnicolas, inferiores videlicet a potentioribus multipliciter opprimi et gravari, ideo volentes insolentiis et novis attemptationibus per remedia opportuna viam precludere statuimus et ordinavimus, quod quandocunque et ubicunque fuerint facte nove possessionarie aut terrarum occupationes, potentialiter vadiationes seu rerum et bonorum ablationes, succisiones silvarum, interemptiones, vulnerationes et verberationes hominum, domorum et possessionum invasiones et depredationes ac alii similes novi actus potentiarii maiores, extunc lesi, dampnum et iniuriam passi impetratis litteris nostris regalibus querimonialibus et preceptoriis[7] comites parochiales et iudices nobilium comitatus illius, in quo facta huiusmodi patrata extiterint, accedant et requirant. Qui quidem comites et iudices nobilium cum testimonio capituli vel conventus illi comitatui deservire soliti a vicinis et commetaneis ac nobilibus comprovincialibus sub certis penis in huiusmodi litteris nostris regalibus declarandis in sedem eorum iudiciariam per modum proclamate congregationis[8] partibus quoque litem habentibus convocatis ad fidem eorum deo debitam fidelitatemque nobis et sacre corone observandam tactis sanctorum reliquiis prestitam super huiusmodi novis occupationibus possessionariis et aliis actibus potentiariis plenam et indilatam requirant veritatem, qua requisita et inventa possessiones occupatas auctoritate eis in hac parte attributa mediante restatuant eisdem, a quibus fuerant indebite occupate, ipsosque in dominio earundem protegant et conservent, alia vero bona et vadia potentialiter ablata absque defectu reddant et restitui faciant.

IV. Super facto autem potentie in talibus commisse partes utrasque discussionem et sententiam finalem recepturas ad certum terminum mediantibus eorum et dicti capituli vel conventus litteris seriem totius facti exprimentibus ac propria et possessionum factum huiusmodi attestantium nomina continentibus[9] in personalem presentiam nostram regiam aut palatinalem seu iudicis curie nostre transmittant, ubi absque ulterioris termini et litigionarii processus observatione et continuatione, etiam partis non venientis absentia non obstante, nos vel iudex alius, ad quem causa transmissa fuerit, iuramentum capitis[10] decernendo tandem finalem sententiam proferemus et proferre tenebitur. Partes tamen litigantes, quandocunque voluerint, absque requisitione iudicis et onere solutionis birsagiorum liberam concordandi habeant facultatem, quemadmodum antiqua et laudabilis regni nostri consuetudo huiusmodi concordiam in quibuscunque factis potentialibus et aliis libere fiendam dictat et consentit.[11]

V. Ne autem barones, iudices et alii honores regios et officiolatus a regia maiestate tenentes seu comites parochiales honori et iudicatui ipsorum subiectos, quibus ipsi etiam ab aliis iustitiam tenentur

3. As our majesty perceives from the repeated complaints of the gentlemen of the realm and also from personal experience that the more powerful gentlemen of the realm oppress and harm the less powerful in many ways by new seizures of estates and acts of violent trespass,[6] wishing to hinder by suitable means these unusual acts and new atrocities, we establish and order that wherever and whenever anyone commits new seizures of estates or lands, takes a security by violence, robs goods and chattels, cuts down forests, beats, wounds or kills men, breaks into houses and estates and pillages them, or commits other similar new acts of violent trespass, then the aggrieved, damaged and injured parties should, after having acquired our royal letter of complaint and command,[7] go to the *ispánok* and noble magistrates of that county where these acts were committed and call upon them. These *ispánok* and noble magistrates should then establish the full and complete truth about these new seizures of estates and acts of violent trespass with the testimony of that chapter or convent that usually acts in the county, summoning the neighbors, abutters and other fellow nobles from the county in form of an extraordinary county assembly,[8] under the penalty specified in our royal letter on this matter, to their county court together with the parties of litigation under their oath sworn by touching the relics of saints, on their faith in God and their fidelty to us and to the Holy Crown. Then, having inquired and established the truth, they should by their authority in this matter restore the occupied estates to those from whom they were illegally taken away, and defend and save them in these possessions, and completely restore and enforce the return of other violently abducted things and securities.

4. In order that they should have a trial and final judgment on the violent trespass in these cases, both parties are to be sent to our personal presence or to that of the count palatine or our judge royal by a set date with their letter and that of a chapter or convent describing the course of all the facts together with the names and the names of the estates of those who testify in this matter,[9] and we or any other judge to whom the suit will have been entrusted shall and must pronounce final sentence without setting any further term or process of trial or extension, regardless of the absence of a party not appearing, by granting capital oath.[10] The parties of the suit, however, should have leave to settle without the intervention of a judge or the payment of any fine whenever they wish, for the ancient and laudable custom of our kingdom prescribes and allows free settlement to be made in such cases of violent trespass and others.[11]

5. Moreover, so that neither barons or judges or others who have been royal office-holders and those who have been appointed to honors by the king or the county *ispánok*, moved by greed or ill will, at any

ministrare, per se ipsos quavis cupiditate vel propria voluntate allecti aliqua occasione indebite gravent, opprimant seu dampnificent, aut per eorum vicesgerentes talia fieri permittant, statuimus, ut a talibus lesi, dampnificati et iniuriati impetratis litteris nostris ipsorum querelam continentibus preceptoriisque, modo pretacto coram iudicibus nobilium ac testimonio capituli vel conventus eiusdem comitatus per modum similis proclamate congregationis veritatem inquiri facere et sua dampna ac gravamina comprobare valeant, et per ipsos iudices nobilium unacum nobilibus comprovincialibus comitatus eiusdem iudicium et iustitia ex parte huiusmodi officialium impendatur, aut nostre maiestati seu iudicibus et iustitiariis curie nostre prenotatis modo prescripto per litteras ipsorum iudicum nobilium seu capituli et conventus seriem totius facti continentes causa discutienda ad certum terminum transportetur, ubi huiusmodi causa modo premisso sine dilatione terminetur. Si vero iidem barones seu officiales regales aut comites debitum moderamen sui officii in tantum excesserint, ut ex parte totius communitatis officiolatui suo subiecte generalis vociferatio querulosa contra eos emerserit, extunc nos ad fidelem et litteratoriam assertionem iudicum comprovinicialiumque nobilium et capituli aut conventus comprovincialis personaliter vel per idoneum hominem ad hoc specialiter deputatum volumus et tenebimur ex parte talium condignam iustitiam ministrare.[12]

VI. Statuimus itaque et ad reprimendum potentiariorum actuum effrenatum abusum presenti ordinatione sancimus, quod si qui castellanorum aut ceterorum officialium nostrorum, aut reginalium, necnon prelatorum ac baronum et nobilium ac regnicolarum nostrorum de castris, officiolatibus et cum potentiis dominorum suorum, a quibus huiusmodi castra, possessiones et officiolatus pro honore obtinent, aliquos actus potentiarios, dampnificationes, iniurias et quecunque mala perpetraverint et commiserint, talium domini, qui eisdem huiusmodi castra, officiolatus et honores contulerunt, super omnibus dampnis et nocumentis per se et de suis bonis plenam satisfactionem exhibere sint obligati et teneantur effective, se ipsos in huiusmodi actibus potentiariis per suos castellanos seu officiales perpetratis inscios, innocentes et immunes fore debito iuramento purgaturi, suum autem dampnum in huiusmodi satisfactione pretacta perceptum, si voluerint, a suis familiaribus, castellanis seu officialibus, qui ipsi satisfactioni causam dederant, per ablationes rerum et bonorum ipsorum ac possessionum occupationes seu rebus et bonis ac possessionibus minus sufficientibus personarum eorum detentionem et in captivitatem redactionem et conservationem usque ad recuperationem damnorum suorum predictorum fiendam, non obstante nobilitatis, libere conditionis et alterius cuiuslibet dignitatis privilegio,

occasion unjustly burden, oppress or damage those people who are subject to their honor and jurisdiction and to whom they are bound to render justice against others, or let their deputies act in such a way, we have decided that those injured, damaged, or aggrieved persons who have suffered unjustly shall be able to find truth and prove their damages and injuries before a similar extraordinary assembly, with the testimony of the county's noble magistrate and a chapter or convent, by obtaining our letter of command which contains their complaints presented in the way mentioned above. And the noble magistrates, together with the noblemen of the same county, must carry out the law and render justice vis-à-vis these office-holders, or, following the way mentioned above, the noble magistrate or the convent or chapter must send a letter by a fixed date containing all the facts of the case to our majesty or to the judges and administrators of justice of our court so that it can be tried there, so that the case can be settled finally and without delay in the aforesaid manner. And if these barons or royal office-holders or *ispánok* exceed the power given them by their office to such an extent that against them the whole community of their subjects lodges a general complaint, then we in person, by appointing a suitable man to this particular task, will and must, based on a true written statement by the noble magistrates, the nobles of the same county, and by the chapter and convent, render justice to the community as they deserve.[12]

6. We have decided and, in order to repress the unrestrained offense of violent trespass, command in our present decree that if castellans or officers appointed to castles by us, the queen, the prelates, barons, nobles, or our gentlemen of the realm commit violent trespass, cause damage, act against the law, or carry out other evil deeds from the castle and with the power of their masters who have granted them these castles, estates, offices, or honors, then their masters who had given them the castles, offices, or honors are obligated and bound personally and from their own properties, to give full satisfaction for all damage and injury and must clear themselves by a proper oath that they were not privy to, nor involved in, and are innocent of the acts of violent trespass committed by their castellans or officers; and if the masters wish, they are allowed to make their retainers, castellans, and officers who caused the need for satisfaction compensate for the damage which the masters suffered in giving such satisfaction by taking away their goods and chattels and seizing their estates and, if these goods, chattels, and estates are not sufficient, by arresting them in person and taking and holding them captive until all the said damages are repaid, regardless of nobility, free station, or privilege of any other status whatever, but not exceeding the amount of the damages arising out of the said payment.[13]

liberam habeant facultatem, quantitatem tamen sui dampni in solutione huiusmodi percepti non excedendo.

VII. Ut autem officiales et comites nostri pretacti nobiles et incolas regni nostri sub suo honore et iudicatu constitutos indebitis birsagiorum exactionibus gravandi occasionem non habeant, antiquam in hac parte consuetudinem regni nostri imitando declaramus, quod nullus iudicum secularium iudicia seu birsagia extorquere possit, nisi tempore congregationis palatinalis vel alterius per regiam maiestatem ad congregationes generales celebrandas deputati in singulis comitatibus celebrande secundum consuetudinem ab antiquo observatam, exceptis casibus infrascriptis, quibus etiam extra tempus dictarum congregationum generalium birsagia exigi debite possint.

Primo videlicet propter violentam retentionem aut dampnificationem jobagionum petita licentia, iusto terragio deposito aliisque suis debitis persolutis ad alterius possessionem se transferre volentium, quo casu comes parochialis cum suis iudicibus nobilium, absque quibus nullum in talibus processum facere debet, ab hiis, qui in hoc casu culpabiles legittime inventi fuerint, iudicium seu birsagium trium marcarum toties quoties et quandocunque culpabiles inventi fuerint, ~~sine expectatione extorquere potest~~, jobagionem retentum seu dampnificatum cum omnibus bonis suis, dampnis etiam recuperatis liberum abire permitti faciendo.

Item si quis jobagionem alterius non petita nec obtenta licentia, vel petita sed non obtenta ante dies quindecim huiusmodi petite licentie potentialiter abduxerit, talis pro abductione violenta jobagionis huiusmodi birsagium trium marcarum solvet et eundem jobagionem cum aliis tribus marcis birsagialibus per comitem parochialem cum iudicibus nobilium restituere compellatur. Si vero jobagio aliquis non obtenta licentia sed furtive ad possessionem alterius recesserit et idem, ad cuius possessionem accesserit, requisitus reddere recusaverit, extunc ad restitutionem ipsius jobagionis fugitivi comes parochialis talem cum birsagio trium marcarum compellere debeat et teneatur.[14]

Item violator sedis iudiciarie birsagium viginti quinque marcarum persolvat.

Item quicunque furem vel latronem aut aliquem publicum malefactorem captivaverit et eum de captivitate sua voluntarie abire permiserit, solvere debet comiti parochiali homagium malefactoris prenotati.[15]

Item ubicunque lucrum camere tempore debito solutum non fuerit, comes parochialis cum iudicibus nobilium de qualibet villa non persolvente post emanationem litterarum birsagialium per iudices nobilium contra tales dari solitarum exigere debeat ipsum lucrum camere cum birsagio trium marcarum.[16]

Consimiliter quia certa scientia meminimus nostrorum predecessorum litteris et per nostram maiestatem frequentius litteratorie ex

7. In order that our said officers and said *ispánok* have no opportunity to burden the nobles and the inhabitants of our kingdom living under their administration and jurisdiction by arbitrary fines, we, following in this the ancient custom of our kingdom, declare that no penalties or fines are to be exacted by any secular judge at any other time but at an assembly held according to long-established custom by the count palatine or by someone appointed by the royal majesty to hold general assemblies, except in the following cases when penalties can be collected at times other than at the general assembly:

First, to wit, for the forced retention and harm caused to tenant peasants, who after having paid the just rent and all their debts, requested leave to move to someone else's estate, the county's *ispán* with the noble magistrates (without whom he must not act in such cases) is allowed to exact the penalty or fine of 3 marks without delay at any time and as often as he finds him guilty from whomever they find guilty of this according to the law, in order to let the tenant peasant who was restrained and defrauded leave freely with all his goods and with his losses recompensed.

Then, anyone who abducts by violence someone else's tenant peasant who has neither requested nor obtained leave or has requested 15 days in advance but did not obtain it, shall pay the penalty of 3 marks for this violent abduction of the tenant and shall be forced by the county's *ispán* and the noble magistrates by the penalty of another 3 marks to return the same tenant peasant. If, however, any tenant peasant secretly escapes to someone else's estate without having obtained leave to move, and he to whose estate the tenant moved refuses to return him having been called upon to do so, then the county's *ispán* must and is bound to force him to return the tenant by a fine of 3 marks.[14]

Then, for contempt of court the penalty is 25 marks.

Then, anyone who will have captured a thief, a robber, or any other common criminal and then deliberately releases him must pay the criminal's composition to the county's *ispán*.[15]

Then, if the chamber's profit is not paid by the appointed date, then after the usual letter of fines is issued by the noble magistrate to the offenders, the county *ispán* with the noble magistrate is to collect the chamber's profit together with the fine of 3 marks to be paid by the village which has not paid the tax.[16]

Similarly, since we specifically recall edicts of our predecessors and also several writings of our majesty established the custom and made it

laudabili consuetudine regni nostri precipi solitum esse et usitatum fore decimas ecclesiarum de singulis villis decimas persolvere post interdictum ecclesiasticum certo consueto tempore observari commissum recusantibus per comites parochiales aut vices suas gerentes exigi debere cum singulis tribus marcis, ideo presentis ordinationis et statuti vigore eandem consuetudinem ratam habentes, innovantes et imitantes committimus, quod post interdictum ecclesiasticum in singulis diocesibus et locis temporibus hucusque solitis impositum de singulis villis, que per unius mensis spatium huiusmodi interdictum ecclesiasticum animo indurato tollerando easdem decimas persolvere recusaverint seu non curaverint, mox elapso ipsius mensis spatio comites vel vicecomites parochiales per decimatores requisiti decimas easdem cum singulis tribus marcis birsagialibus pro se indilate exigendis eis, quibus solvi debent, absque dilatione et defectu persolvi facere teneantur.[17]

Item quandocunque nobiles alicuius comitatus vigore litterarum regalium per modum proclamate congregationis sub pena trium marcarum in eisdem litteris regalibus expressa convocati fuerint, quicunque ad illam congregationem non venerint, nisi egritudine, senio, viduitate, orphaneitate, paupertatis impotentia, absentia remota vel eorum arduis negotiis rationabiliter se excusare potuerint, comes parochialis et iudices nobilium predictas tres marcas in dictis litteris nostris expressas indilate exigere possunt.

Item palatinus et iudex curie et ceteri iudices ordinarii ecclesiastici et seculares universa iudicia in causis coram eis vertentibus aggregata statim ipsis causis finitis ac per sententiam finalem conclusis primo parti adverse de sua portione satisfactionem impendere teneantur et ad partem suam iudiciariam cedentia exigendi liberam habent facultatem.[18]

VIII. Item statuimus, quod ad faciendas statutiones, inquisitiones et evocationes et alios quoslibet processus cum hominibus et testimoniis capitularibus et conventualibus fieri solitos, que communiter fidedignitates vocantur, de capitulis et conventibus persone seu homines simplices non mittantur, sed de ipsis capitulis canonici ad minus aut persone in beneficiis vel officiis constitute, de conventibus vero monachi conventuales sacerdotes destinentur.[19] Qui quidem pro huiusmodi testimoniis capitularibus et conventualibus deputati, priusquam ad faciendas aliquas possessionarias statutiones, metarum reambulationes, revisiones possessionarias et communes inquisitiones transmittantur et procedant, iurare teneantur, ut in eisdem factis fideliter et recte procedent et veram relationem seu fassionem facient. Homines etiam regii in premissis procedentes tempore reversionis eorum ac fassionis seu relationis coram ipsis capitulis et conventibus faciende simile iuramentum prestare teneantur. Quicunque autem contra suum iuramentum falsum processum vel falsam relationem fecisse repertus

usual, that according to the honorable custom of our kingdom, *ispánok* of counties or their deputies collected the ecclesiastical tithe with the penalty of 3 marks each from villages which were reluctant to pay after the lapse of the specific and customary time following the church ban, we, therefore, approving, renewing, and following this practice, command by the force of these presents that after the imposition of the ban at times usual for the individual dioceses and places, the county *ispánok* or their *alispánok* are bound to make each village which has stubbornly suffered the ban for a month and still refuses or neglects to pay the tithe, pay this tithe on the request of the tithing-men after the lapse of a month immediatly, without delay and in full, to whomever it has to be paid, along with a fine of 3 marks each for the officers themselves.[17]

Then, when the nobles of any county are summoned to an extraordinary county assembly by royal mandate in which it is stated that they are under the penalty of 3 marks, the county's *ispán* and the noble magistrates have the right to collect without delay the said 3 marks specified in our letter from those who do not come to that assembly unless their absence is caused by illness, old age, widowhood, orphanhood, or by disability of poverty, or if they can excuse themselves reasonably on account of urgent matters.

Then, the palatine, the judge royal, and every common judge ordinary, both ecclesiastical and secular, have the right immediately after finishing a case and passing final judgment in all cases tried in the courts to give first of all satisfaction to the opposing party from his portion and also to collect the judicial fines due to him.[18]

8. Then, we have decided that in cases of *seisin*, inquest, summons, and other judicial procedures which are usually done with the participation of the men and the testimony of chapters and convents, commonly known as cases of authentication, the chapters and convents should appoint no common or simple members but from the chapters only canons, or at least such who hold ecclesiastical prebends or offices, and from the convents only monks who are consecrated priests.[19] The persons appointed to such testimonies by chapters or convents should, before they are sent to assist and to act at *seisins*, inspections of boundaries, examination of estates, or common inquests, take an oath that they will proceed faithfully and justly and will give true report or evidence in the matter. And the king's bailiff who proceeds in the aforementioned cases also must take an oath upon returning and before giving evidence or making a public report to the chapter or convent. Whoever is found to have proceeded unfaithfully and to have made a false report against his oath should be punished as a forger and

extiterit, talis tamquam falsarius et periurus pena amissionis beneficii sui, si quod habuerit, puniatur, et insuper, sive beneficiatus, sive non beneficiatus existat, perpetuis carceribus mancipetur; homo vero regius, si in premissis possessionariis statutionibus, metarum reambulationibus ac revisionibus sinistre vel false processerit, in facto periurii, pena capitis ac amissione omnium bonorum suorum convincatur. Quicunque vero nobilis per alium seu alios quoscunque mediantibus nostris regiis aut aliis consuetis litteris nomen suum continentibus pro homine regio coram testimonio alicuius capituli vel conventus requisitus onus huiusmodi processus assumere et exequi recusaverit, in birsagio consueto trium marcarum per comitem parochialem indilate exigendo convincatur eo facto.

IX. Statutiones autem possessionarie, metarum reambulationes et revisiones aliter fieri non debeant, nisi vicinis et commetaneis huiusmodi possessionum inibi legittime convocatis, et ut fraus et dolus in talibus melius evitentur, nomina singulorum vicinorum et commetaneorum tempore premissorum processuum illuc presentialiter convenientium in litteris capitularibus et conventualibus superinde emanandis seriatim conscribantur.[20]

X. Et ut materia discordie super facto redemptionis litterarum capitularium et conventualium, necnon super satisfactione viarum seu laborum testimoniis capitularibus et conventualibus fienda hactenus sepius suboriri consueta de cetero cesset et succidatur, presenti ordinatione antiquam tamen et laudabilem consuetudinem imitantes statuimus, ut in omnibus locis, tam capitularibus, quam conventualibus pro qualibet littera evocatoria per se, videlicet evocatoria prima, secunda et tertia in capitulo aut conventu simul cum eorum notario et scriptore pro redemptione littere recipiantur seu solvantur[21] singuli denarii viginti quatuor maioris monete.[22]
Item pro qualibet littera proclamatoria denarii centum.
Item pro qualibet littera procuratoria denarii viginti quatuor.
Item pro qualibet littera prohibitoria, protestatoria et aliis similibus, si patenter emanantur, denarii viginti quatuor, si vero clause, denarii duodecim.
Item pro qualibet littera fassionali emanata privilegialiter denarii centum, patenter vero denarii viginti quatuor, clause autem denarii duodecim. Item pro qualibet littera inquisitoria sive patenta, sive clause denarii viginti quatuor.
Item de paribus antiquarum litterarum in conservatoriis requisitarum custodi seu requisitori per se denarii centum et pro redemptione littere requisite, si non habuerit multum de scriptura et patenter confecta fuerit, denarii viginti quatuor, si vero labor scribendi fuerit magnus et littera privilegialiter confecta, denarii centum.
Item de simplicibus transcriptis seu transcriptionalibus litteris patenter emanatis, ubi labor scribendi magnus non fuerit, denarii viginti

perjurer by losing his prebend if he has any, and in addition, whether he has a prebend or not, by being incarcerated forever. If the king's bailiff proceeds illegally and unfaithfully in the said cases of *seisins*, examination or inspection of boundaries, then he will be convicted of perjury and of capital punishment, losing all his properties. Any nobleman, asked to be the king's bailiff accompanying the witness of a chapter or convent by one or more persons with our royal mandate containing his name or with any other customary type of letter, who refuses to accept and to bear the burden of proceeding and acting in this manner, is therefore under penalty of the usual 3 marks which is to be collected by the county's *ispán* without delay.

9. *Seisins* of estates, examinations and inspections of boundaries ought not be done except with the neighbors and abutters legally summoned there, and to prevent fraud and cheating in such cases, the names of the neighbors and the abutters who were present at the time of the said proceeding must be fully included in the reports issued by chapters and convents.[20]

10. And in order that the causes for disagreement, which until now frequently arose regarding the charges for redeeming letters issued by chapters or convents, as well as for travel expenses so that the trouble of the witnesses of the chapters or convents should cease to exist in the future and be eliminated, we order by the present ordinance, following old and, indeed, honorable custom,[21] that in all places of authentication, both chapters and convents, for each letter of summons, that is the first, second, and third, 24 pennies of the larger coin[22] are to be paid and rendered to the convent or chapter, together with their notary and scribe, for redemption of the letter.
Then, for any letter of final summons, 100 pennies.
Then, for any letter of advocacy, 24 pennies.
Then, for any letter of prohibition, protest, or similar document, if issued as letters patent, 24 pennies, if close, 12 pennies.

Then, for any letter of record, if issued as privilege, 100 pennies, if letters patent, 24 pennies, if close, 12 pennies.
Then, for any letter of inquest, whether patent or close, 24 pennies.

Then, for copies of ancient deeds retrieved from the archives, 100 pennies for the guardian or the retriever and for the redemption of the retrieved charter; if there was not too much writing and it was issued as letters patent, 24 pennies;but if the task of copying is extensive and it was issued as a privilege, then 100 pennies.
Then, for simple transcripts or for transcripts issued as letters patent

quatuor, ubi autem littera fuerit prolixa aut privilegialiter emanata, denarii centum.
Item de littera statutoria, in qua contradictio facta fuerit, denarii viginti quatuor, de litteris vero statutionalibus perpetuis, in quibus contradictio facta non fuerit, recipiatur redemptio litterarum secundum quantitatem possessionis et numerum sessionum modo subscripto, videlicet de sessione una, duabus aut tribus vel quatuor in toto denarii centum, ubi autem fuerint ultra quatuor sessiones usque ad decem, pro qualibet sessione denarii triginta tres, ubi vero fuerint ultra decem usque viginti, de qualibet sessione denarii viginti quatuor; ubi autem fuerint ultra viginti usque centum, de qualibet sessione denarii duodecim; si vero fuerint ultra centum usquequaque, de qualibet sessione denarii octo.
Item de litteris reambulatoriis metalibus, in quibus contradictio et evocatio facta non fuerit, denarii viginti quatuor; in reambulationibus autem metalibus, in quibus simplex consignatio vel cum hominibus regiis de curia regia transmissis similis consignatio vel finalis metarum erectio cum iuramento super terram[23] in forma iudiciaria aut partibus concordantibus facta fuerit, pro redemptione littere denarii quadringenti. Ubi autem partibus in huiusmodi reambulationibus et demonstrationibus metalibus discordantibus causa ad curiam regiam reducta fuerit, tunc pro redemptione talium litterarum denarii ducenti.
Item de communi inquisitione ordine iudiciario commissa denarii centum.
Item de revisione possessionarie occupationis denarii centum.
Item de occupationibus possessionum hominum in sententia capitali convictorum et rerum ablationibus iudiciaria commissione mediante fiendis de rebus ablatis ex antiqua consuetudine capitulum habebit decimam partem; pro redemptione autem littere denarii centum.
Item de estimationibus possessionariis iudiciaria commissione fiendis denarii centum.
Item de possessionariis divisionibus de singulis possessionibus divisis singuli denarii centum.
Item de expeditoria iuramentali denarii viginti quatuor.
Item de expeditoria iuramentali continente nomina coniuratorum denarii centum.
Item de solutionibus pecunialibus coram capitulis vel conventibus, vel eorum testimoniis fieri solitis capitulum seu conventus decimam et nonam partes exigere non possint, nisi quando propter discordiam partium in eorum sacristiis seu conservatoriis huiusmodi pecunie reposite fuerint; de talibus nempe de iure decimam et nonam recipere possint, ad illius tamen partis rationem, que causam dederit pecuniam huiusmodi in conservatoriis reponendi.

Personis autem testimonialibus capitulorum et conventuum pro singulis diebus, quibus in itinere fidedignitatis processerint, solvantur singuli duodecim denarii maiores, sive in propriis equis, sive in equis

for which the the task of copying is not great, 24 pennies, but where the writing was long and was issued as a privilege, 100 pennies.
Then, for letters of *seisin* when contradiction was made, 24 pennies, and for letters of *seisin* in perpetual possession without contradiction, a redemption of the letter is to be paid according to the size of the property and the number of plots in the following manner: namely, for one, two, three, or four plots, 100 pennies; where there will be more than four plots but fewer than ten, for each plot 33 pennies; where there will be more than ten but fewer than twenty, for every plot, 24 pennies; where there will be more than twenty plots up to a hundred, for each plot 12 pennies; and where there will be any number of plots above a hundred, 8 pennies for each plot.
Then, for letters of inspection of boundaries, when no contradiction or summoning will be made, 24 pennies; but in the case of inspection of boundaries with simple conscription, or when similarly a simple conscription and final designation of boundaries is made with a royal bailiff sent from the court and an oath is sworn on the soil[23] in proper legal form or with the consent of the parties, for the redemption of the letter 400 pennies. Where, however, the case is sent to the royal court because the parties do not agree in such an inspection of boundaries, for the redemption of such letters, 200 pennies.
Then, for common inquests by judicial procedure, 100 pennies.

Then, for the inspection of seizure of estates, 100 pennies.
Then, for seizing the properties of men sentenced to capital punishment and the confiscation of their chattels on court order, the chapter receives according to ancient custom the tenth of things taken away; and for redemption of the letter, 100 pennies.
Then, for estimations of estates on court order, 100 pennies.

Then, for the divisions of estates, 100 pennies from each divided estate.

Then, for proof of an oath, 24 pennies.
Then, for proof of an oath containing the names of the oath-helpers, 100 pennies.
Then, from amounts paid in the presence, or with the testimony of chapters or convents, the chapter or convent has no right to take a tenth or ninth unless when such an amount is deposited in their sacristy or safekeeping because of a disagreement between the parties; from those payments they can rightfully receive a tenth and ninth at the expense of that party which caused that the amount had to be deposited in this way.

The men of the chapters and convents taken as witnesses should receive for every day which they spend on the business of authentication, 12 larger pennies, whether they ride their own horses

causantium ambulent et ducantur; ita tamen, quod in victualibus et expensis causantium et ipsos ad facta sua conducentium simul cum equis et familiaribus eorum de domo iterum in domum semper duci debeant et reduci.

XI. Preterea ex quo in iudiciis in curia nostra regia fieri consuetis coram iudicibus ordinariis eiusdem curie ac eorum notariis supratactis littere et redemptiones earum necessario occurrunt, ideo ad tollendam cuiuslibet altercationis occasionem, que inter ipsos notarios et causantes emergi possent, antiquam consuetudinem redemptionis litterarum earundem modo subscripto duximus similiter declarandam,[24] videlicet quod in ipsa curia nostra notariis ipsius curie iudiciarie de una littera prorogatoria communi solvantur denarii duodecim;
de littera iudicali seu birsagiali similiter denarii duodecim;
de simplici littera inquisitoria similiter denarii duodecim;
de secunda evocatoria denarii viginti quatuor;
de tertia evocatoria denarii centum;
de proclamatoria denarii centum;
de littera iuramentali tertio vel sexto se alicui adiudicata denarii viginti quatuor;
de eo, qui iurabit duodecimo vel vigesimo quinto aut quinquagesimo se, denarii centum;
de communi inquisitione denarii centum;
de littera duellari denarii ducenti;
de iuramentali super caput denarii ducenti;
de prima instrumentali exhibitione denarii viginti quatuor; de secundaria et tertiaria instrumentali exhibitione cum gravamine assumpta similiter denarii viginti quatuor;
de prorogatoria respondenti cum tribus marcis denarii viginti quatuor;

de littera procuratoria patenti denarii viginti quatuor;
de littera fassionali communi denarii viginti quatuor;
de aliis litteris generalibus, videlicet prohibitoriis et similibus denarii viginti quatuor;
de prohibitoria facie ad faciem denarii centum;
de littera sententionali facti potentialis conservatori sigilli floreni decem per centum, scriptori autem denarii ducenti;
de litteris statutoriis et reambulatoriis simplicibus denarii viginti quatuor;
de litteris autem adiudicatoriis reobtentionis possessionum seu aliarum rerum iuxta quantitatem possessionis seu rei reobtente habita concordia inter causantes et prothonotarios fiat solutio.

XII. In cancellaria autem nostra regia quoad redemptiones litterarum iuridicarum et consuetarum servetur antiqua consuetudo eiusdem cancellarie; similiter de donationibus et confirmatoriis pensata quantitate rei donate vel confirmate erit concordandum cum cancellario modo hactenus observato.[25]

or are taken and led on the horses of the parties; thus, they and their horses and servants are to be taken from and led home on the victuals and expenses of those in whose case they were summoned.

11. Besides, because the issuance of letters and their redemption frequently occur in course of normal trials in our royal court by the judges ordinary and their aforementioned notaries, in order to prevent occasions in which argument can arise between the notary and the litigants, we regarded it advisable to declare the old custom of the redemption of these letters in the following way,[24] namely, that for letters of prorogation, 12 pennies must be paid to the notary of the court of judgment;
for a letter of judgment or fine, also 12 pennies;
for an ordinary letter of inquest, also 12 pennies;
for a second letter of summons, 24 pennies;
for a third letter of summons, 100 pennies;
for a letter of final summons, 100 pennies;
for a letter on oaths taken, if the oath is granted to be sworn with two to five oath-helpers, 24 pennies;
from him who swears with twelve, twenty-five, or fifty oath-helpers, including himself, 100 pennies;
for a common inquest, 100 pennies;
for a letter on judicial combat, 200 pennies;
for a letter on capital oath, 200 pennies;
for the first presentation of legal instruments, 24 pennies;
for second or third presentations of legal instruments under specific penalty, similarly 24 pennies;
for letters of prorogation on summons to respond at 3 marks fine, 24 pennies;
for letters patent of advocacy, 24 pennies;
for a common letter of record, 24 pennies;
for other common letters, such as those of protest and similar ones, 24 pennies;
for a letter of protest face-to-face, 100 pennies;
for a letter of sentence in cases of violent trespass, to the keeper of the seal, 10 florins with 100 pennies each, and to the scribe, 200 pennies;
for a letter of *seisin* into estates and simple inspection of boundaries, 24 pennies;
for a letter of sentence on the recovery of an estate or other things, the fee should be decided by agreement between the litigants and the protonotaries according to the size of the recovered estate or chattels.

12. Regarding fees for the redemption of customary letters of sentence in our chancellery, the old custom of the chancellery is to be retained; and similarly in regard to letters of donation and confirmation, agreement is to be made with the chancellor according to the size of the granted or confirmed estate in the manner hitherto followed.[25]

Quia vero in omnibus premissis redemptionibus litterarum et aliis quibuscunque solutionibus ac birsagiorum exactionibus de numero et quantitate denariorum pro tempore currentium sepenumero mentio facta est, gratia removendi dubii presentium serie declaramus, ut denarii tales intelligantur, quorum singuli centum unum florenum auri valeant et representent. Et si denarios minores pro aliquo tempore cursum habere contigerit, ad eandem rationem cum ampliori et equivalenti numero suppleantur.[26]

XIII. Item de arestationibus mercatorum et aliorum hincinde proficiscentium, que pro debitis et aliis excessibus propriis aut alienis in possessionibus seu locis communibus[27] tam per ecclesiasticos, quam seculares, nobiles et ignobiles satis frequenter fieri solent, in quibus etiam hactenus nonnulla impedimenta et dampna ac iniurie per extraconsuetudinarias huiusmodi arestationes commissa sunt et patrata, eandem antiquam regni nostri consuetudinem approbantes declaramus, quod nullus arestare volens in suis propriis aut fratrum suorum condivisionalium possessionibus, terris aut officiolatibus pro quacunque causa arestationem aliquam facere possit, alioquin pro indebito aresto in pena trium marcarum convincatur et arestum huiusmodi indebite factum cum altero birsagio trium marcarum relaxare et liberum permittere per comitem parochialem compellatur. Cum autem in loco communi[28] quispiam arestationem facere voluerit, iudex ipsius loci communis eandem arestationem coram se sic et non aliter fieri patiatur et acceptet, si videlicet arestans prius se a domino vel villico possessionis, in qua arestatus residentiam habuit, iustitiam postulasse et huiusmodi iustitiam aut sibi temerarie denegatam aut finaliter exhibitam fore et satisfactionem debitam non impensam extitisse litteris comitis vel vicecomitis parochialis aut iudicum nobilium vel aliis credibilibus poterit comprobare. Dum autem hec premissa modo pretacto evidenter potuerit comprobare, extunc dominus vel iudex aut villicus ipsius loci seu possessionis communis arestum retinere et inter partes more in talibus consueto iudicium et iustitiam faciendo super debitis aut aliis excessibus vel rebus coram eo rationabiliter obtentis debite satisfactionis complementum de rebus et bonis iudicialiter condempnati aut rebus et bonis ipsius minus sufficientibus per detentionem personalem impendere teneatur.

XIV. In casu enim, quo ipse iudex aresti pro favore aut timore cuiuscunque vel ex qualibet alia causa rationem non habente arestum coram eo legittime factum seu fiendum retinere iudiciumque et iustitiam ac satisfactionis complementum modo superius descripto exhibere recusaverit, extunc ipse arestatori, cuius adversarium liberum abire permiserit, pro dampno, quod per huiusmodi arestum requirere et mediante iustitia obtinere poterat, et pro toto interesse teneatur et existat obligatus, nisi arestandus vel arestandi tantam potentiam et vim habuerint, propter quam dominus seu iudex loci communis eis

And because in all the cases of the abovementioned redemption of letters and of other payments and exaction of fines frequent reference was made to the number and quantity of pennies presently circulating, in order to remove any doubt, we declare in these presents that such pennies are meant of which 100 are equal and worth one golden florin; and if at any time smaller pennies happen to appear in circulation, then they will have to be augmented proportionately, with higher numbers of equal value.[26]

13. Then, considering the all too frequently occurring uncustomary arrests of merchants and of other travellers for debts and other offences of theirs or of others,[27] by clergy and laymen, nobles and nonnobles, on their own property or that of others or in public places, by which hitherto much harassment, damage, and injury has been done and inflicted in the course of these sorts of irregular arrests, we declare, sanctioning the ancient custom of our kingdom, that anyone who intends to arrest someone is not allowed to make the arrest for any reason on the persons's own or his co-proprietor brothers' estates, land, or official tenancy; otherwise, he must pay for unfair arrest a penalty of 3 marks, and the county's *ispán* must force him to end the imprisonment and to release his prisoner with another penalty of 3 marks. If, moreover, someone wants to make an arrest in a public place,[28] then the judge of that very place should permit and allow the arrest in his presence only if the arrester can prove with a letter of either the county *ispán* or *alispán* or of the noble magistrates or some other authentic proof that he has already sought justice from the lord or the reeve of the estate where the arrested person lives, but he was recklessly refused, or if he was given final judgment that was not satisfactory and complete, and not otherwise. Once he has clearly proven the said facts in the aforementioned way, then the lord or the judge or reeve of that public place or estate has to keep the arrested person in custody and, by administering the law and justice among the parties in the customary way, give satisfaction for debts or other offences or things proven at his bench from the judicially-seized goods and chattels of the convicted person or, if his goods and chattels are insufficient, by detaining him in person.

14. In a case, however, in which the judge of the arrest, because of fear or favor or for any other unwarranted reason, would hesitate to confirm the arrest which was or is going to be legally accomplished in his presence or would hesitate to mete out justice and judgment and give satisfaction in the manner described above, then he should be altogether liable and indebted to the arrester whose adversary he permitted to go free, for the damage which would have been sued for by the arrest, unless the person or persons who are to be arrested has such power and might that the lord or judge of the place cannot resist or

resistere et eos retinere non valebit, aut alia potentia superveniens arestatos contra voluntatem iudicis aresti violenter abduxerit; quo casu eveniente ad sui excusationem super eo, quantocius poterit, suis vicinis et commetaneis publice protestetur.[29]

XV. Volumus autem, quod in nostris et reginalibus liberis civitatibus, opidis, villis et possessionibus mediantibus eorum iudicibus, officialibus et presidentibus quibuscunque per cives, mercatores, hospites et incolas earundem pro suis debitis, rebus et acquisitionibus quibuscunque arestationes huiusmodi modo suprascripto et sub penis antedictis per magistrum tauarnicorum aut alios eorum superiores indilate exigendis fieri nullatenus debeant neque possint, sed in locis communibus et coram iudice communi, cum necesse fuerit, fiant arestationes per eosdem modo superius declarato.

XVI. Iudex autem communis arestationes huiusmodi coram eo debite et legittime factas discernens et iudicans pro suo labore et honore, si fuerit iudex per dominum possessionis constitutus aut dominus ipsemet, quadraginta denarios, si vero villicus,[30] duodecem denarios ab homine iudicialiter condempnato pro se exigendi habeat facultatem.

XVII. Porro equitatem et iuris observantiam, quam inter regnicolas nostros vigere peroptamus, a nostra regia maiestate exordium habere demonstrare volentes presenti decreto stabilimus, quod in quocunque comitatu aliqua iura per defectum seminis quorumcunque decedentium devoluta fuerint, et de huiusmodi possessionibus manifeste non constat, an ad ius regium pertineant vel aliquos fratres generationales seu heredes feminei sexus[31] concernant, sed inter ista duo, videlicet ius regium et ius aliorum, scilicet generationalium vel femineum dubium intervenerit, extunc homo communis nobilis et idoneus in quolibet comitatu ad id per comitem parochialem cum iudicibus nobilium et aliis nobilibus comprovincialibus in unum locum congregatis, non tamen ex baronibus, nec de potentioribus, sed de mediocribus nobilibus electus huiusmodi iura devoluta et dubiosa, et etiam alia similia, si qua contigerint, tamdiu conservet et manuteneat[32] absque damnificatione qualibet, excepto solum, quod de proventibus consuetis huiusmodi possessionum, donec in manibus suis remanebunt, expensas moderatas capere et facere possit, de quibus tandem rationem reddere valeat et teneatur, quousque huiusmodi devolutio iurium sine herede decedentium in sede iudiciaria curie nostre regie publicata fuerit, ipsaque publicatione facta quiscunque easdem possessiones et iura sibi pertinere allegaverit, in certis octavis sequentibus quantocius rationabiliter poterit, iura sua producendo easdem ad se pertinere comprobet; quod si facere poterit, iudices curie regie eidem statui mandent et faciant cum effectu. Si vero in probatione defecerit, iuri regio relinquantur; et si qui ulterius ad easdem ius habere speraverint, eas de manibus regiis legittime requirant.

arrest him or if the arrested person manages to escape from the custody with the help of external power and against the will of the judge; in such a circumstance, the judge ought to protest in his own behalf publicly as soon as possible in the presence of his neighbors and abutters.[29]

15. We also wish that the burghers, merchants, settlers, and other inhabitants of the free cities, towns, villlages, and the estates of the king and the queen should not and must not make such arrests in the abovementioned way through their judges, officials, or magistrates on behalf of debts, properties, and other claims under the abovementioned penalties to be collected without delay by the Master of the Treasury or by their other superiors; if it is necessary to make arrests, they should be made in the same abovementioned way in a public place by a public judge.

16. The judge who acts and passes judgment regarding an arrest made properly and legally in his presence has the right to exact for himself, if appointed by the lord of the estate or if he is the lord himself, for his trouble and office, 40 pennies; if he is the reeve of the community,[30] 12 pennies from the legally convicted person.

17. Furthermore, as we greatly desire that justice and observance of the law flourish among the gentlemen of the realm and because we want to prove that these qualities have their origin in our majesty, we establish by our present decree that if in any county the rights of a deceased person escheat because of the extinction of the line and it is not clear whether such a property falls under royal right or belongs to the kinsmen or to the heirs in the female line[31] and there is doubt regarding these two, namely the right of the king and that of others, that is, of kinsmen and of female heirs, then those escheated and doubtful rights and any other rights which might occur in these cases must be looked after and held in trust until the devolution of the rights of such an heirless deceased owner is announced by the judicial bench in our royal court, by a suitable lesser nobleman, elected in each county by the county's *ispán*, the noble magistrates, and other nobles gathered together in a meeting from among the middle-ranking nobles and not the barons or major lords,[32] without causing any damage, except that he is allowed to make and to spend moderate expenses from the usual income of these properties for which he must and is obliged to give account afterwards; and if after the announcement anyone should claim these estates and rights, he should go as soon as possible to one of the upcoming octavial courts in order to prove that he has right to these; and if he can do so, then the judges of the royal court should order and carry out *seisin* of the estate. If however, evidence fails him, the estates and rights shall remain under royal right and whoever wants to submit claims later will have to seek his rights at law from the hands of the king.

XVIII. Ubi autem uxores vel filie huiusmodi hominum absque heredibus masculinis decedentium in talibus possessionibus et iuribus remanserint, extunc possessiones eedem et iura a manibus earum occupari et aufferri non debeant, priusquam de earum iuribus, videlicet an hereditarie et perpetuo ad ius femineum pertineant, aut ne, veritas inquiratur. Quod si repertum fuerit eadem iura iuri femineo non competere, extunc dictis uxoribus talium decedentium, antequam de dominio dictarum possessionum excludantur, per regiam maiestatem vel alios, ad quos reperte fuerint esse devolute, de earum dotibus[33] et iuribus plena satisfactio impendatur. Filiabus vero usque tempus maritationis earum domus paterna cum quarta parte possessionum paternarum pro quarta filiali[34] secundum consuetudinem regni nostri sequestretur et possidenda relinquantur. Postquam vero maritate et traducte fuerint, de earum iure quartalitio pecuniaria solutione mediante satisfiat. Ubi autem aliqua ex ipsis filiabus homini impossessionato maritata fuerit, dictante eadem regni nostri consuetudine in perpetuo iure et dominio huiusmodi quarte filialis possessionarie succedere debet et remanere, ita tamen, si ipsa de voluntate et consensu fratrum seu consanguineorum suorum, in quos post ipsius matrimonium huiusmodi iura sua quartalitia reverti et redundare deberent, homini, ut prefertur, impossessionato nupserit. Alioquin sive de domo paternali, sive de curiis et servitiis baronum seu maiorum nobilium,[35] dictis suis fratribus seu consanguineis aut parentibus irrequisitis et nolentibus seu non consentientibus id fecerit, ius suum quartalitium non cum possessione, sed cum satisfactione pecuniaria requirendi habebit facultatem.

XIX. Adiicientes statutis superioribus, quod nullus comes, banus, wayuoda seu alius officialis regius cuiuscunque denominationis et dignitatis existat, ecclesias episcopales, archiepiscopales, abbatiales, prepositales et alias quascunque regio iure patronatus disponendas, earundemque tenutas, pertinentias, decimas et possessiones intra terminos et limites sui honoris seu officiolatus absque speciali mandato regio occupare aut se de eisdem partialiter vel totaliter ingerere presumat.[36]

XX. Verum quia ex inmoderata et superflua exactione tributaria per longiturni temporis abusum et inadvertentiam ac neglectum dispositionis superinde necessarie multa gravamina, dampna et incomoda regnicolis nostris et extraneis hominibus cum eorum rebus et mercibus in regno nostro hincinde proficiscentibus per tributarios, tam nostros regales et reginales, quam aliorum propria cupiditate nullo ad dei timorem aut equitatem habito respectu allectos illata fore hactenus ferventiorique aviditate dietenus irrogari experientia teste nostra cognovit celsitudo, ideo presenti sanctione decernimus, quod in singulis comitatibus regni nostri tempore celebrationis generalium congregationum palatinalium per palatinos pro tempore constitutos vel alios ex

18. Where, however, wives or daughters of men dying without male heirs are left in the estates and rights of such a man, these estates and rights ought not to be seized and taken from their hands until the truth is established about their rights, namely,whether those rights belong by heredity in perpetuity to the female heirs or not. If it is found that these rights do not belong to the female line, then, before the wife of such a deceased man is excluded from the dominion of the abovementioned estate, she is to be given full satisfaction for her dowry[33] and other rights by the royal majesty or by those to whom the rights devolved. For the daughters, however, the paternal house and a quarter of the property are to be set aside as filial quarter and kept in her possession until the time of her marriage, following the customs of our country.[34] After the daughter has been given away and married, she should be given satisfaction by way of a monetary payment for her rights to the filial quarter. When, moreover, one of these daughters marries a man without property, then she should enter into the possession of the filial quarter according to the same customs of our country and keep it in perpetuity, provided that she married the abovementioned man without property with the knowledge and permission of her brothers and of those kinsmen of hers to whom these rights and the filial quarter would devolve after her marriage. Otherwise, if she marries either from the paternal home or from the court and service of a baron or a major noble,[35] without the knowledge and permission or without asking the consent of her brothers, kinsmen or her parents, she can demand her filial quarter not in land, but as a monetary satisfaction.

19. In addition to the preceding decisions we order that no *ispán*, ban, voivode,or other royal official of whatever title or position should dare to seize the churches of bishops, archbishops, abbots, or provosts or any other churches under royal right of patronage or their lands, appurtenances, tithes, and estates within the confines of their power and authority without special permission of the king, nor should they dare to enter partly or entirely into these rights.[36]

20. Then, because our eminence knows from experience that our toll collectors and those of the queen and of others, spurred by their own greed, not fearing God or respecting the law, owing to long-lasting abuse and carelessness as well as to neglect of necessary measures, have been able to cause a great deal of trouble, damage, and loss to our people and to foreigners travelling to and fro in our country with their merchandise and goods, by taking excessive and unnecessary tolls, we decree by our present statute that in every county of our kingdom sworn judges of the general assembly should ascertain at a general assembly held by the palatine currently serving or by someone appointed by the king the number and places of true tolls usually

regia deputatione celebrandarum inquirantur a iuratis assessoribus huiusmodi congregationum numerus et loca verorum tributorum in ipso comitatu exigi solitorum et a dominis seu possessoribus eorundem tributorum petantur exhiberi littere primarie institutionis tributorum eorundem, in quibus si inventa fuerit quantitas solvendi tributi de singulis rebus solvi consueti, talis solutio moderetur et reducatur ad rationem presentis monete taliter, quod tributariis seu tributa habentibus eorum iusti proventus non decrescant, nec e contrario solutionis modus onus in tributa solvere debentium supercrescat.[37]

XXI. Ubicunque autem huiusmodi littere primarie institutionis tributorum reperiri et exhiberi non poterunt, aut reperte forsitan et exhibite quantitatem solvendi tributi non expresserint, tunc a predictis iuratis assessoribus dicte congregationis similiter inquiratur et resciatur quantitas solutionis tributorum in quibusvis tributis ipsius comitatus de singulis rebus tributari solitis tempore antiquiori, quod humana memoria comprehendere potest, fieri consuete et retrahatur ad consuetudinem antiquam compensata qualitate, quantum iustius fieri poterit, pecunie tunc currentis, semper absque dampno et detrimento tributa exigere et solvere debentium, equitate videlicet utriusque partis semper salva. Similiter inquiratur, discutiatur et moderetur, que et ubi sint false vie et indirecte quorumlibet tributorum, et quantum longe vel prope huiusmodi vias falsas singuli tributarii obsidendi ac itinerantes in eisdem prohibendi vel impediendi iustam et consuetudinariam habuerint et habere debeant facultatem. Vias autem novas in locis, quibus vie ab olim nunquam esse consueverunt, nemo pro communi et universali transitu itinerantium in detrimentum et dampnum tributorum vicinorum in faciebus suarum terrarum adinvenire presumat, alioquin de huiusmodi viis noviter adinventis in predictis congregationibus generalibus iuxta affirmationem iuratorum assessorum huiusmodi congregationum decernatur, an pro falsis viis reputande sint vel aliter restringende et moderande. Habentes insuper et exigentes tributa ratione pontis vel navium pontes huiusmodi aut naves sub debita reformatione semper studeant conservare taliter, quod viatores et tributa solventes absque impedimento per pontes et naves eorum transitum liberum et non impeditum facere possint; id vero facere negligentes penis et gravaminibus opportunis ad debitam reformationem et conservationem suorum pontium et navium in dictis congregationibus promulgandis per comites eorum parochiales astringantur toties, quoties eorum negligentia exigente fuerit opportunum.[38]

XXII. Postremo antiquam regni nostri consuetudinem presenti edicto confirmantes prelatorum, baronum et nobilium regni nostri approbante conventu stabilimus et ordinamus, quod nullus prelatorum, baronum, nobilium et regnicolarum nostrorum cuiuscunque status, dignitatis et conditionis existat, quoscunque infideles manifestos nostros et corone nostre ac regni nostri, necnon publicos fures, latrones ac

collected in that county and request the lords or owners of those tolls to present the letters about the initial establishment of the same tolls, and if in the letter the amount of the toll which is normally to be paid for each ware is given clearly, then the amount is to be adjusted and reduced to the presently circulating money, so that neither the just income of the collectors or owners of the toll be diminished nor the burden of those who pay the toll be increased.[37]

21. Where, however, the letters about the first establishment of the tolls cannot be found and presented, or the found and presented letter perhaps does not state the amount of the toll to be paid, in that case, the said sworn judges of the aforementioned assembly are similarly to inquire and to ascertain the amount of tolls collected, and usually paid, in the past at the various tolling places in the county for certain goods subject to tolls, as far as the memory of men can recall, and adjust value of the toll to the value of the currently circulating money in the most just way without causing any loss or disadvantage to the collectors or to the payers of tolls and saving the rights of both sides. They are also bound to investigate, examine, and restrict those illegal routes and detours which are used to evade the tolls; they are also to decide how far from or close to these illegal routes the toll collectors should have and ought to have customary and just right to prohibit or hinder travellers from using these roads. Where, moreover, roads have never been established, no one may dare to create new ones across his fields for the common and general crossing of travellers, to the loss and damage to the nearby tolls; otherwise these newly created routes are to be judged by the community during the aforementioned assembly according to the reports of the sworn judges whether they are to be considered as illegal routes or to what extent their use is to be reduced or restricted. Those, moreover, who collect tolls for bridges and ferries must always take diligent care to keep the bridges and ferries in good repair so that the travellers and toll-payers can cross by these bridges and ferries freely and unimpeded without any hindrance; those who neglect to do so should be forced by suitable penalties and fines issued by the county's *ispán* announced at the abovementioned assembly, as often as the negligence of the toll-collectors makes it appropriate, to make the necessary repairs and maintenance on their bridges and ferries.[38]

22. Finally, confirming by our present charter the old custom of our kingdom, we generally establish and order, with the approval of the prelates, barons, and nobles of our kingdom, that none of the prelates, barons, nobles, or any of our gentlemen of the realm of whatever station, rank, or condition dare to receive, entertain, or keep in his castles, houses, estates, and properties or give help, hospitality, or

malefactores presertim in congregationibus generalibus proscriptos in suis castris, domibus, bonis et possessionibus retinere, hospitare et conservare aut eis auxilium, hospitalitatem et favorem impendere presumat sub pena consimilis infidelitatis et furum ac latronum hospitalitatis, excepto, quod fures, latrones et alios malefactores in congregationibus generalibus proscriptos, demptis infidelibus, barones et castellani nostri in confiniis regni castra et fortalitia ac officiolatus et honores pro defensione confiniorum tenentes usque tempus acquirende gratie poterunt in huiusmodi castris et fortalitiis metalibus receptare et retinere.[39]

In cuius rei memoriam firmitatemque perpetuam presentes concessimus litteras nostras privilegiales pendentis autentici sigilli nostri novi dupplicis, quo pro nunc uti rex Hungarie utimur, munimine roboratas. Datum per manus venerabilis domini Mathie de Gathalowcz, prepositi ecclesie Quinqueecclesiensis, aule nostre sumpmi cancellarii, fidelis nostri dilecti, anno domini millesimo quadringentesimo tricesimo quinto, octavo idus Martii, regnorum nostrorum anno Hungarie etc. quadragesimo octavo, Romanorum vigesimo quinto, Bohemie quintodecimo, imperii vero secundo. Venerabilibus in Christo patribus dominis Georgio Strigoniensi, Johanne Colocensis et Bachiensis canonice unitarum, Duymo Spalatensi archiepiscopis, Jadrensi sede vacante, Petro de Rozgon Agriensis, Waradiensi sede vacante, Georgio Lepes Transsiluanensis, Zagrabiensi sede vacante, Henrico Quinqueecclesiensis, Simone de antedicta Rozgon Wesprimiensis, Clemente Jauriensis, Waciensi sede vacante, Georgio Nitriensis, Chanadiensi sede vacante, Jacobo Sirimiensis, Joseph Boznensis, Johanne Tininiensis, Vito Corbauiensis, Johanne de Domnis Segniensis ecclesiarum episcopis ecclesias dei feliciter gubernantibus, Sibinicensi, Nonensi, Scardonensi, Traguriensi, Makarensi et Pharensi sedibus vacantibus. Item magnificis Mathyus de Palocz predicti regni nostri Hungarie palatino, spectabili et magnifico Hermanno Cilie et Zagorie comite, socero nostro carissimo, totius regni nostri Sclauonie bano, comite Stephano de Bathor iudice curie nostre, Ladislao de Chaak wayuoda nostro Transsiluanensi, Johanne et Stephano de Wegle, Segnie et Modrussie comitibus, regnorum nostrorum Dalmatie et Croatie predictorum, Desew et Ladislao de Gara Machouiensibus, Nicolao de Radwycz crucifero ordinis Prutenorum Zewriniensi banis, Johanne de sepedicta Rozgon tauarnicorum, Emerico filio Nicolai wayuode de Marczali ianitorum, Johanne et Stephano de Peren dapiferorum, Paulo et Johanne Komploth de Nana pincernarum, Laurentio de Hedrehwar agazonum nostrorum magistris ac Stephano et Georgio de antelata Rozgon comitibus nostris Posoniensibus aliisque quampluribus regni nostri comitatus tenentibus et honores.[40]

favor to those who are manifestly disloyal to us, our crown, and our kingdom, likewise to common thieves, robbers, and criminals, particularly to those who have been proscribed in general assemblies, under the penalty of the same treason as that of receiving thieves and robbers, except those barons and castellans of ours who hold castles and fortifications or offices and honors in the frontier regions for the defense of these borders, who are allowed to receive and keep thieves, robbers, and other criminals who were proscribed in a general assembly, but not traitors, in the castles and border fortresses until such time as they receive pardon.[39]

In memory and in perpetual validity of which we have issued our present letters of privilege confirmed with our new authentic double seal pendant that we now use as king of Hungary. Given in the city of Pozsony, by the hand of the reverend lord Matthew of Gathalóc, provost of the Church of Pécs, Archchancellor of our court, and our beloved faithful servant, in the year of the Lord one thousand, four hundred and thirty-five, on the eighth of March, in the forty-eighth year of our reign as king of Hungary etc., the twenty-fifth as king of the Romans, the fifteenth as that of Bohemia, and the second as emperor; when the following reverend fathers in Christ governed the churches of God felicitously: archbishops George of Esztergom, John of the canonically united sees Kalocsa and Bács, and Duim of Spalato; bishops Peter of Rozgony of Eger, the Várad see being vacant, George Lépes of Transylvania, the see of Zagreb being vacant, Henry of Pécs, Simon also of Rozgony of Veszprém, Clement of Győr, the see of Vác being vacant, George of Nyitra, the see of Csanád being vacant, James of Szerém, Joseph of Bosnia, John of Knin, Vid of Corbava, John de Dominis of Zengg, the sees of Sebenico, Nona, Scardona, Traù, Makarska and Hvar being vacant; further, when the honorable lord Matthew of Palócz held the palatinate of our said kingdom of Hungary, the respectable and honorable Hermann, count of Cilli and Zagorje, our beloved father-in-law was ban of all Slavonia, count Stephen of Bátor, judge royal, Ladislas of Csák, our voivode of Transylvania, John and Stephen, counts of Veglia, Sengg and Modrus bans of our said kingdoms of Dalmatia and Croatia, Desiderius and Ladislas of Gara ban of Macsó, Nicholas of Radwicz from the Prussian Order of Crusaders ban of Severin, John of the oftmentioned Rozgony was Master of the Treasury, Emeric, son of voiovode Nicholas of Marczal Master of the Doorkeepers, John and Stephen of Pereny Masters of the Stewards, Paul and John Kompolt of Nana Masters of the Cupbearers, Lawrence of Hédervár Master of the Horse, and Stephen and George of the said Rozgony *ispánok* of Pozsony, and many others held honors and comital offices of our realm.[40]

12 Martii 1435

Vide praefatiunculam et notas infra paginas 208–09.

Nos Sigismundus dei gratia Romanorum imperator semper augustus ac Hungarie, Bohemie, Dalmatie, Croatie etc. rex, notum facimus tenore presentium significantes, quibus incumbit universis, quod nos, cuius regie celsitudinis providentia subditorum suorum et terrarum ac regnorum sue ditionis tuitioni et illese conservationi nedum introrsus, verum potius ab extraneis invasoribus officio sue dignitatis exigente se obligatam profitetur, volentes fines regni nostri predicti a partibus Bohemie et Morauie, a quibus propter ingruentiam presentis temporis ab aliquibus elapsis annis hucusque frequentiores ferventioresque ipsum regnum pertulit hostilitates,[1] vi nostra regia reddere securiores, onus infrascriptum sponte, ymmo ex debito regali in nostras regias curas et expeditiones duximus assumendum:

I. Videlicet, ut civitates et castra subscripta: civitatem et castrum Posoniense, civitates Tirnauiensem et Zakolcza, castrum Trinchiniense et alia castra ac munitiones et fortalitia in confinio Morauie et iuxta fluvium Wag situatas, quemadmodum tam in ipso ex parte Bohemie, quam in aliis omnibus confiniis et metis regni nostri[2] ex quacunque parte apud nostras regias manus habita et in futurum quovis eventu et casu eisdem nostris manibus applicari contingentia nostris sumptibus regalibus contra gwerram Bohemorum et alias undecunque emergentes muniemus et tutabimus sufficientibus gentibus, armis et victualibus, aliisque necessariis, tam pro conservatione et defensione castrorum ac munitionum in se, quam ad tenendos campos et defendenda circumiacentia campestria contra quosvis insultus hostiles occurrentes. Si autem tanta potentia inimicorum irrepserit, quod maior foret viribus gentium nostrarum imperialium, nec ab invasione finium regni arceri et prohiberi per easdem gentes nostras imperiales posse verisimiliter videretur, extunc prelati deputati pro defensione illarum partium cum suis banderiis et viribus iuxta dispositionem de ipsis factam et observari consuetam,[3] necnon comites singulorum comitatuum pro earundem partium vel aliarum gwerras habere contingentium defensione modo simili deputatorum sub banderio regali cum baronibus, proceribus et nobilibus dictorum comitatuum et eorum gentibus per modum generalis expeditionis exercitualis viribus coniunctis et adunatis succurrere debebunt ad repellendos insultus hostiles supradictos.

II. Conclusum est insuper et statutum per nostram maiestatem cum prelatis, baronibus et regnicolis nostris prenotatis, quod tempore

12 March 1435

For prefatory and explanatory notes, see below, pages 208–09.

We, Sigismund, by the grace of God ever august emperor of the Romans and king of Hungary, Bohemia, Dalmatia, Croatia etc. notify by these presents all to whom it may concern that we, who profess to be bound by the duty of our royal eminence to protect and, safely maintain the subjects, territories, and countries of our dominion not only internally but even more against foreign invaders, wish to make more secure the borders of our said kingdom with our royal might from the direction of Bohemia and Moravia, whence, because of the present circumstances, this country has been exposed for several years to ever more frequent and violent attacks,[1] have decided, of our own accord and in keeping with our royal obligation, to assume the following burden as part of our royal care and concern.

1. Namely, that we will support at our royal expense against Bohemian or any other kind of attack and provide with sufficient men, arms, foodstuff, and everything else which is necessary for the maintenance and protection of the castles and fortifications and for campaigns to secure the neighboring fields and, defend the surrounding regions against any sort of hostile attacks the following cities and castles: city and castle of Pozsony, the cities of Nagyszombat and Szakolca, castle Trencsén, and those other castles, fortresses, and fortifications which are on the border towards Moravia, on the banks of the river Vág, and also those which are there towards Bohemia, and those situated on any of the borders and borderlands of our country on either side,[2] both those in our possession now and those which may fall into our hands under whatever circumstance. If, however, enemies should invade our country in strength that is greater than that of our imperial forces, and we with these imperial troops of ours would not appear to be able to hold them back and to prevent them from overrunning our borders, then those prelates who have been ordered to protect this frontier region with their *banderia* and soldiers according to the arrangements made and customarily observed in this matter,[3] as well as the *ispánok* of those counties which were designated in the same way to defend that frontier region or to repel any attack together with the said counties' barons, lords, and nobles, and their men, will be obligated to relieve us with joined and united forces under the royal banner, according to the rules of the general levy, in order to repel the said hostile attacks.

2. Our majesty, together with our abovementioned prelates, barons, and gentlemen of the realm, has furthermore decided and

universalis exercitus generaliter proclamati singuli barones, proceres et nobiles possessionati secundum quantitatem dominiorum ipsorum, videlicet de singulis triginta tribus jobagionibus proprias sessiones et terras more aliorum jobagionum in possessionibus, quibus resident, habentibus, ac census, collectas, munera et alia servitia dominorum cum aliis jobagionibus supportantibus unum, de centum vero tres[4] et sic consequenter de aliis, quotquot habuerint, de singulis centum singulos tres pharetrarios equestres, ad minus videlicet arcus, pharetras, gladios et biccellos habentes et ad bellandum aptos et utiles ipsimet personaliter antecedendo ad quoslibet exercitus regni generales conducere teneantur. Hii vero, qui minus quam triginta tres habent jobagiones, suos jobagiones, quos habuerint, cum jobagionibus aliorum taliter coniungere et connumerare teneantur, quod semper de triginta tribus jobagionibus quorumcunque unus pharetrarius modo premisso armatus et dispositus ad exercitus generales transmittatur. Ceteri denique nobiles jobagionibus carentes singuli singulariter propriis in personis, hii videlicet, qui dominos habere dinoscuntur, sub quorum nominibus et expensis exercituare solent, cum eorum dominis ac gentibus seu banderiis,[5] alii autem huiusmodi dominos non habentes, de propriis ipsorum possessionibus, domibus et expensis cum eorum comite parochiali, illis tantum exceptis, quos decrepite etatis, viduitatis aut orphaneitatis et alterius consimilis impotentie causa necessaria videtur excusare, similiter pro sua facultate condecenter armati et dispositi exercitualiter proficisci teneantur. Ubi autem duo vel plures fratres indivisi et in uno victu manentes extiterint, uno eorum ad huiusmodi generales exercitus proficiscente alius vel alii remanere debent excusati.[6] Illi vero, qui propriis in personis sub banderio et stipendio regali vel baronum procedere habebunt, preter et ultra gentes suas de honoribus aut stipendiis regalibus vel baronum secum servientes et exercituare debentes nichilominus pretactum numerum exercituantium de suis propriis possessionibus cum comite suo parochiali seu comitibus illius seu illorum comitatuum, in quo vel in quibus possessiones sue existunt, expediant et transmittant ad illas partes in pro illo tempore, quibus iidem comites parochiales singulorum comitatuum debebunt exercituare.

III. Preterea prelati, barones et nobiles regni nostri castra, fortalitia et munitiones habentes eorum castellanos seu alios nobiles pro custodia huiusmodi fortalitiorum necessarios, similiter ipsi barones, nobiles et maiores persone seculares coram coniugibus et domesticis suis personas nobiles pro magistris curie et alias ad conservandum honorem curiarum suarum deputandi et relinquendi habeant facultatem, moderate tamen et tantummodo inevitabiliter necessarias personas in huiusmodi servitiis occupando et relinquendo.[7]

IV. Et propterea commissum est, quod in quolibet comitatu universitas nobilium eiusdem comitatus conveniendo certum ex eis

established that when a general levy is announced, each baron, lord, and propertied nobleman is obligated to appear in person and to lead with him to the general royal army a certain number of soldiers in relation to the size of his property, namely, for every thirty-three tenant peasants who have a plot and land in peasant tenancy in the village where they live, pay rent, taxes, and dues, and render other seigneurial services, together with the other tenants, one soldier; hence, for every 100 tenant peasants, three mounted archers,[4] and, in the same way, for each additional 100 tenant peasants whom they have, three additional equestrians who will at least have bows, quivers, sabres and daggers, and are fit and able to fight. Those, however, who have fewer than thirty-three tenant peasants, must jointly count their tenants with other tenant peasants, so that for every thirty-three tenant peasants they always send one mounted archer, armed and prepared in the abovementioned manner to the general levy. Those, however, who have no tenant peasants have to go to war in person; those among them who have masters under whose name and at whose expense they customarily go to war should serve with their masters' men and *banderia*;[5] others who have no such masters must proceed to the army from their own properties and houses at their own expense, with their county's *ispán*, likewise properly armed and equipped according to their means, except those who are excused from service because of old age, widowhood, being orphaned, or owing to some other disability. Where two or more brothers live on undivided family property within the same household, only one of them has to go to war during such a general levy, while the other or the others are excused and may stay at home.[6] Those, however, who serve under the banner and on the payroll of the king or of the barons, nevertheless, must also send and dispatch, besides their own men serving and fighting with them from their royal or baronial offices and stipends, soldiers armed and equipped in the abovementioned manner from their own properties and with that county *ispán* or with those county *ispánok* where their estates lie to that region and for that time where and when the county *ispánok* of the counties in question are to be deployed.

3. Furthermore, those prelates, barons, and nobles of our realm who own castles, fortresses, or fortifications should be free to command and leave behind castellans or other noblemen needed for the protection of these types of strongholds; likewise barons, nobles, and other major secular lords may leave with their spouses and households noble persons and others as stewards of their household for the preservation of the honor of their court, but only in reasonable measure and only as many persons as are unavoidably necessary to stay home and perform these services.[7]

4. It has been ordered, therefore, that in each county the community of nobles should assemble and elect one person from the

eligere debeant de mediocri statu nobilium, non ex potentioribus, qui cum iudicibus nobilium illius comitatus numerum jobagionum quorumlibet regalium, reginalium et baronum ac nobilium in ipso comitatu possessiones habentium tempore proclamationis exercitus generalis fideliter computet, dicet, conscribi faciat et registrari, par seu copiam huiusmodi registri tradendo comiti suo parochiali.[8]

V. Item quod quilibet tam in generali exercitu regnicolarum, quam ad stipendia exercituare debens die et termino expeditioni exercituali, cui interesse debebit, assignatis absque omni crastinatione in loco deputato cum omni gente sua, cum qua ad exercitum ire tenetur, constituatur. Quicumque autem ad huiusmodi generales exercitus proficisci debentes tempore proclamationis et instaurationis eorundem contumaciter ire et proficisci neglexerint, aut multum tarde terminum et locum universalis conventionis ipsius exercitus prenotatos studiose pretermittendo, ceteris exercituantibus fatigatis aut dispersis seu conflictu bellicoso iam commisso et habito supervenerint, aut tempore debito venientes et comparentes tandem ante debitam et finalem expeditionem belli occasione qualibet conficta, non habita nostra vel capitaneorum ipsius exercitus licentia, de eodem exercitu temerarie recesserint, tales expediti minime reputentur, sed eorum possessiones pro huiusmodi non venientia vel tarditate aut temerario discessu occupentur; et de huiusmodi possessionibus occupatis per nostram maiestatem de consilio prelatorum et baronum nostrorum, quid agendum sit, deliberetur.[9]

VI. Item quod exercituantes tempore estivo in villis et segetibus descensus facere non debeant, sed in campis vacuis, in quibus segetes pedibus equorum non conculcent neque destruant, nullaque dampna et nocumenta inferre presumant, nichil omnino preter herbas non falcatas, ligna et aquam absque debito pretio capientes seu auferentes. Pretia vero victualium cuiuslibet generis, tam pro hominibus, quam equis necessariorum in quolibet comitatu ante adventum exercituantium per communitatem nobilium eiusdem comitatus secundum fertiliorem vel infertilem eventum temporis et anni limitentur, moderentur et taliter ordinentur, ut intuitu ipsorum exercituantium pretia victualium in nullo excrescant ultra cursum priorem et communem in foris communibus usitatum, prout cupiditate hominum fieri consuevit.[10]

VII. Si qui vero contra premissam ordinationem in villis et aliis locis modo pretacto prohibitis descensus facere aut victualia cuiuscunque maneriei absque pretio ordinato auferendo dampna irrogare presumpserint, extunc homines dampnificati, sive nobiles sint, sive ignobiles, ad presentiam comitis parochialis et iudicum nobilium comitatus illius, in quo huiusmodi descensus et dampna facta et illata extiterint, accedendo super quantitate damnorum, que sibi illata fore conquesti fuerint, si nobiles, per se, si vero ignobiles fuerint, cum suo villico et duobus vicinis suis domui sue ex utraque parte proxime

middle rank landowners, and not from the mighty ones, who, when a general levy is announced, together with the noble magistrates of the county, will count, declare, register, and hold a true list, compiled of all the tenant peasants of the king, the queen, the barons, and nobles who have estates in that county and shall hand to the *ispán* of the county the duplicate or the copy of it.[8]

5. Then, that both those who have to go to war with the general levy of the gentlemen of the realm and those who serve for pay must present themselves together with all the men whom they are obligated to lead to the army, without delay at the designated place, on that day and date for which the campaign was announced. Moreover, anyone who should appear at such a general levy, but obstinately refuses to go and appear at the time for which the campaign is called and summoned, or, deliberately ignoring the time and place for assembling, comes and appears too late, when the other warriors have already been exhausted or have been scattered or the combat has already been held and fought, or though having presented himself and arrived on time impudently leaves the army before the proper and final settlement of the battle on any pretext, without our permission or that of the commanders of the army, is in no way to be considered as free from his obligation, but because of his absence, delay, or impudent desertion his estates are to be seized, and our majesty will consult with the prelates and barons concerning what should be done with the estates of such a person.[9]

6. Then, that in summer time soldiers are not to quarter themselves in villages or on sown land, but in empty fields, where the horses will not trample down or spoil the crop; they should not cause any damage or loss, and they are not allowed to take or collect anything without paying its due price, except for uncut grass, wood, and water. In every county the community of nobles of that county ought to fix, prescribe, and determine the price of all the foodstuff needed by the soldiers and the horses before the army's arrival, according to the fertility or infertility of the year and the season, so that upon the arrival of the army the prices of foodstuff should not rise above the previous general price asked at the public market, as usually happens because of people's greed.[10]

7. If anyone dares to billet in villages or other prohibited places or dares to take any kind of food without paying the established price, against the aforementioned ordinance, then the wronged persons, be they nobles or not, ought to go to the court of the county *ispán* and noble magistrates of that county where that kind of billeting or damage happened or was inflicted, and swear an oath on the amount of damage done which they claim to have suffered; noblemen swear by themselves, nonnobles with their village reeve and with two next-door neighbors from either side of their house. The *ispánok* and the noble

coniunctis iuramentum prestent, ipsique comes et iudices nobilium super huiusmodi dampno et iuramento ipsi conquerenti litteras eorum testimoniales tradant, vigore quarum, quamprimum ad curiam regiam in presentiam iudicum et iustitiariorum ipsam curiam iudicantium accesserit, mox absque ulteriori probatione et litium protractione eisdem conquerentibus et dampnificatis iuxta contenta litterarum predictorum comitis et iudicum nobilium illius videlicet comitatus, in quo huiusmodi dampna per quoscumque exercituantes illata fuere, quibus quidem litteris absque ulterioris probationis, requisitione ex vigore presentis constitutionis plena fides adhibeatur, ex parte cuiuslibet dampna inferentis omnimoda satisfactio dampnorum necnon expensarum pro ipsis dampnis requirendis factarum sententialiter fieri decernatur, et cum executione debita finaliter et effective per sententiam iudiciariam, quam palatinus aut iudex curie pro tempore constitutus vel eorum vicesgerentes et sigilliferi litteratorie dare et proferre teneantur, comitibus vel vicecomitibus et iudicibus nobilium illorum comitatuum, in quibus ipsi exercituantes, qui premissa dampna irrogasse modo antelato comprobati fuerint, possessiones et bona habere dinoscuntur, per huiusmodi litteras sententiales scribatur et demandetur, quatenus ipsi mox receptis dictis litteris sententialibus huiusmodi lesis et dampnum passis ex parte ipsorum dampna inferentium per ablationes rerum et bonorum eorundem, et si necesse fuerit, possessionum occupationes, super omnibus in huiusmodi litteris sententialibus contentis coram testimonio alicuius capituli vel conventus omnimodam et indilatam satisfactionem teneantur exhibere.[11]

VIII. Quicunque autem ex huiusmodi exercituantibus potentiarias seu voluntarias succensiones et combustiones aut depredationes villarum et possessionum, effractiones ecclesiarum, nobilium et virorum ecclesiasticorum propriarum curiarum et domorum invasiones et depredationes, mulierum vel virginum spoliationes, raptus et dehonestationes, hominum interfectiones, verberationes et vulnerationes et alios similes maiores et enormes actus potentiarios committere presumpserint, extunc contra tales premisso modo et ordine in illis comitatibus, in quibus huiusmodi facta potentiaria patrata fuerint, inquisita et comperta veritate in facto potentie convincantur, et ex parte eorum indilata satisfactio modo superius declarato per sententiam iudicariam impendenda declaretur et demandetur, ac per comites parochiales et iudices nobilium ipsius delinquentis et in facto potentie convicti ad executionem earundem sententiarum per occupationes possessionum, rerum et bonorum ablationes et alia in talibus fieri solita per palatinum aut iudicem curie finaliter et effective procedi litteratorie committatur et demandetur.

In cuius rei memoriam firmitatemque perpetuam presentes concessimus litteras nostras pendentis et autentici sigilli nostri novi dupplicis, quo ut rex Hungarie utimur, munimine roboratas. Datum Posonii, in festo beati Gregorii pape, anno domini millesimo quadringentesimo tricesimo quinto, regnorum nostrorum anno Hungarie etc. quadragesimo octavo, Romanorum vigesimo quinto, Bohemie quintodecimo, imperii vero secundo.

magistrates ought to issue a letter of evidence on the damage and on the oath to the claimant, by the authority of which, as soon as the plaintiff arrives at the royal court, at the bench of the judges and justices sitting there, then without further inquiry or litigation on the case, on the basis of the abovementioned letter of the *ispán* and the noble magistrates of that county where the damage had been inflicted by a soldier—since that letter, by authority of the present law, is granted full credit without requiring further proof—full satisfaction must be given in regard to the damages done by anyone to the wronged person as well as for the expenses incurred while claiming the damage in a final and valid judgment, which must be issued and given by the count palatine or the judge royal, or by their deputies and the keepers of their seals in writing. By this letter of judgment the *ispánok, alispánok,* and noble magistrates of those counties where estates and estates of those soldiers lie who have been proven guilty in the abovementioned way of committing the said damages are to be informed and commanded that after having read the said letter of judgment they ought to confiscate the soldiers' goods and chattels and, should it be necessary, seize their estates in the presence of witnesses from a chapter or convent and give full satisfaction without delay to the wronged and damaged party, in accordance with all the items of the letter.[11]

8. Those soldiers, however, who violently and deliberately set fire to, burn down, or loot villages and estates, attack churches, invade, and loot residences and houses of nobles and clergy, rob, violate, and rape women and virgins, kill, beat or injure people, or commit any other similar atrocious violent act, ought to be, after proper inquiry and the establishment of the truth, indicted of violent trespass in the counties where they have committed these violent acts in the abovementioned way and manner, and immediate satisfaction must be given. The count palatine or the judge royal should require in writing the county *ispánok* and the noble magistrates to ensure complete and effective judgment on the person found guilty and convicted of violent trespass by seizing his estates, confiscating his goods and chattels, and other things customary in such cases.

For the eternal memory and force of which we have issued these presents and validated it with our new, authentic double seal pendant which we use as king of Hungary. Given at Pozsony on the feast of St Gregory the pope, in the year of the Lord one thousand, four hundred thirty-five, in our forty-eighth regnal year in Hungary, etc., the twenty-fifth as king of the Romans, the fifteenth in Bohemia and as emperor the second.

29 Maii 1439

Vide praefatiunculam et notas infra paginas 210–15.

Nos Albertus dei gratia Romanorum rex semper augustus ac Hungarie, Bohemie, Dalmatie, Croatie etc. rex et dux Austrie etc.[1] memorie commendamus tenore presentium significantes quibus expedit universis, quod excellentissimo principe domino Sigismundo, Romanorum imperatore ac prefati regni Hungarie etc. rege, patre nostro carissimo laudande memorie tempore noviter preterito deo celi, cuius nutui humana fragilitas nequit obviare, volente viam universe carnis ingrediente nobisque divina favente clementia in regimen et solium ipsius regni Hungarie votive succedentibus prelatorum et baronum necnon procerum et nobilium regni nostri cetus et universitatis idemptitas[2] nostrum regium conspectum adeundo et libertates ipsius regni nostri, quibus ipsi prelati, barones et nobiles eorumque predecessores temporibus divorum regum, presertimque condam serenissimi principis domini Lodouici regis felicis recordii, predecessoris nostri[3] freti fuere et gavisi, in quampluribus suis articulis diminutas esse recitantes et nostram regiam serenitatem super reformatione status dicti regni nostri precibus et instantia propulsantes infrascriptos articulos et in eis contenta nostris litteris inseri et conscribi facere, approbare et in eisdem se per nos illibate conservari humillime supplicarunt; nosque promisimus, ymmo promittimus bona fide, quod articulos infrascriptos tenere et adimplere volumus et debemus.

I. Primo quod antiquas leges et consuetudines huius regni et libertates regnicolarum ecclesiasticorum et secularium cuiuslibet status ad priorem suum modum et statum, quantum de iure et cum honore eorundemque prelatorum et baronum ac regni nobilium consilio et auxilio possumus, reducemus, reintegrabimus et reformabimus, et de cetero in eisdem manutenebimus et conservabimus.

II. Insuper quod regia maiestas palatinum regni antiqua consuetudine ipsius regni requirente[4] eo, quod idem palatinus ex parte regnicolarum regie serenitati, et ex parte ipsius regie serenitatis regnicolis iudicium et iustitiam facere potest et tenetur, ex consilio prelatorum ac baronum et regni nobilium pari voluntate eligat.

III. Item quod regia dignitas pro tuitione regni et confiniorum ipsius conservatione hominibus suis exercituantibus de stipendio regali

29 May 1439

For prefatory and explanatory notes, see below, pages 210–15.

We, Albert, by the grace of God ever august king of the Romans, and king of Hungary, Bohemia, Dalmatia, Croatia, etc. and Duke of Austria etc.,[1] entrust to memory notifying through these presents all to whom it may concern, that when in time recently past, by the will of the God of heaven, whose command human frailty cannot resist, the most excellent prince lord Sigismund, emperor of the Romans and king of the said kingdom of Hungary etc., our most dear father of blessed memory, went the way of all flesh, and we, favored by divine grace, according to our prayer, succeeded to the governance and the throne of the same kingdom of Hungary, then the body and unified community[2] of prelates, barons, lords, and nobles of our realm approached our royal presence and told us that those liberties of the same kingdom of ours, which these prelates, barons, and nobles and their ancestors relied upon and cherished in the time of the holy kings, and especially under the late most serene lord King Louis of blessed memory, our predecessor,[3] were infringed upon in many respects, and they urged and most humbly entreated our royal serenity with urgent requests to reform the state of the said realm of ours, and to have the following articles and what is contained in them inserted and written down in a charter of ours, approved and to keep them in these said liberties. And so we promised; furthermore, we promise in good faith that we desire and feel obligated to maintain and fulfill the following articles.

1. First, that we shall restore, renew, and reform the ancient laws and customs of this kingdom and the liberties of the gentlemen of the realm both ecclesiastical and secular, of whatever station, to their prior form and station and, henceforth, preserve and maintain them in these as far as we shall be able to do so by law, in honor and according to the aid and counsel of the same prelates, barons, and nobles of the kingdom.

2. Furthermore, that the royal majesty shall choose a palatine of the kingdom, with the unanimous counsel of the prelates, barons, and nobles of the realm as required by ancient custom of the same kingdom,[4] because the palatine is empowered and required to render judgment and justice to the royal majesty on behalf of the gentlemen of the realm, and to the gentlemen of the realm on behalf of the royal majesty.

3. Then, that the royal eminence shall make provision from the royal income for his soldiers for the safety of the kingdom and the

dispositiones faciat, sic quod regnicolas ipsi stipendiati exercituantes non predentur. Exercitus vero generalis regnicolis tamdiu, donec huiusmodi stipendiati exercituantes adversariis resistere poterunt, non proclametur.[5] Ubi autem ipsi exercituantes regnicolas predati fuerint, tunc tales pronunccientur ad instar aliorum patratorum actuum potentiariorum. Dum vero necessitate urgente exercitum generalem proclamari contigerit, tunc nobiles regni ultra metas et confinia regni ex quacunque parte eiusdem regni inviti more exercituantium non ducantur antiqua eorum libertate[6] requirente.

IV. Item quod novitates et nocive consuetudines introducte aboleantur et destruantur.

V. Item alienigenis et forensibus hominibus, cuiuscunque nationis et linguagii existant, officia in ipso regno nostro non committemus, nec castra, fortalitia, metas, possessiones, honores, prelaturas, baronias, comitatus vel quascunque ecclesiasticas vel seculares dignitates ad tempus vel imperpetuum extraneis vel forensibus, nisi hominibus Hungaris conferemus, quodque prelati et barones homines extraneos et forenses non conservent.[7]

VI. Item de tricesimis, lucro camare, montanis, urburis, cusionibus monetarum, camaris salium eorundemque comitibus, necnon mardurinis, quinquagesimis[8] et quibuscunque officiolatibus[9] in arendam vel amministrative seu aliter quovis modo similiter hominibus idoneis, corone Hungarie suppositis et non extraneis[10] liberam disponendi facultatem more consueto habeamus.

VII. Item lucrum camare in regno Hungarie, quinquagesimam in partibus Transsiluanensibus ac mardurinas in regno Sclauonie exigi consuetas exigi more alias ab antiquo consueto faciemus, reducendo ad statum tempore prefati condam domini Lodouici regis observatum.[11]

VIII. Item prelati et barones duas dignitates, honores, baronias, scilicet seculares et ecclesiasticas simul tenere non valeant,[12] nec homo secularis, sive vir ecclesiasticus dignitates ecclesiasticas occupative servare possit.

IX. Item nullus mercatorum forensium et extraneorum, cuiuscunque nationis existat, ad mercandum seu forizandum in medium regni, sed ad loca tempore pretacti condam domini regis Lodouici ad forizandum ac emendum et cambiendum deputata negotiationes suas peracturus more consueto accedat.[13]

X. Item quod monetam auri et argenti in valore et cursu, quibus pro nunc existit, sine consilio prelatorum, baronum et regni nobilium non immutabimus, sed cudantur obuli in eadem lega, qua ipsi maiores denarii cuduntur, quorum obulorum duo unum integrum denarium valeant;[14] et quod penes dominum archiepiscopum Strigoniensem et magistrum tauarnicorum unus fidelis et idoneus vir in probatorem huiusmodi cusionis monete, auri scilicet et argenti deputetur.[15]

preservation of its borders, so that the paid soldiers will not pillage the inhabitants. A general levy of the gentlemen of the realm ought not be proclaimed, as long as these paid soldiers are able to resist the enemy.[5] When, however, the soldiers plunder the gentlemen of the realm, such men should be sentenced like other perpetrators of violent trespass. When it happens by urgent necessity that a general levy is proclaimed, the nobles of the kingdom, from whatever part of the kingdom they may come, should not be led on campaign beyond the borders and confines of the kingdom, as their ancient liberty[6] requires.

4. Then, that novelties and harmful customs that were introduced should be abolished and eliminated.

5. Then, we shall not entrust offices in our kingdom to aliens and foreign men, of whatever nation and language they might be; nor shall we confer castles, fortifications, borderlands, estates, honors, prelacies, baronies, counties, or any ecclesiastical or secular dignities temporarily or in perpetuity on strangers or foreigners, only on Hungarians; and that prelates and barons should not keep strangers or foreigners in their service.[7]

6. Then, regarding the thirtieths, the chamber's profit, mines, mining dues, the minting of coins, chambers of salt and their counts, as well as the *mardurina*, the fiftieths,[8] and other offices,[9] we should have the right of free disposition to grant these in farm, administration or in any other way, by approved custom, to suitable men subject to the Crown of Hungary, and not to strangers.[10]

7. Then, we shall cause the chamber's profit, usual in the kingdom of Hungary, the fiftieth, usual in Transylvania and the *mardurina*, usual in the kingdom of Slavonia, to be collected as of old according to ancient custom, reducing these to the status observed in the time of the aforesaid late King Louis.[11]

8. Then, prelates and barons should not be permitted to hold two dignities, honors, or baronies, at the same time,[12] whether secular or ecclesiastical, nor are secular or ecclesiastical men permitted to hold ecclesiastical dignities by way of occupation.

9. Then, no foreign or outside merchant, of whatever nation he may be, should go to transact business, market, or trade in the middle of the kingdom, but should do so by approved custom at the places that were designated for trade or buying and exchange in the time of the aforementioned lord King Louis.[13]

10. Then, that we shall not change the presently existing value and duration of validity of the gold and silver coinage without the counsel of the prelates, barons and nobles of the kingdom; but halfpennies should be struck in the same alloy as that of the large pennies, in which two halfpennies should equal one whole penny;[14] and that one faithful and suitable man should be assigned to the lord archbishop of Esztergom and the Master of the Treasury as inspector of the minting of coinage—that is, of gold and silver.[15]

XI. Item monete et pecunie extranee atque sales forenses in regnum non inducantur et nec acceptentur;[16] et de hoc fiat provisio celerius, quantum potest.

XII. Item quod dispositio pro serenissima principe domina Elizabeth regina et eius status honoris conservatione, ex quo est heres huius regni,[17] fiat ubicunque vult in regno, sic tamen, quod ipsa domina regina honores et officiolatus suos non extraneis et alienigenis, sed incolis huius regni, quibuscunque maluerit, conferendi et collatos, dum sibi placuerit, ab eis secundum suum arbitrium habeat facultatem auferendi.

XIII. Item dum in exercitibus et pugnis seu quibuscunque rixis cum inimicis regni committendis Hungaros aliquos de hostibus captivare vel aliquid aliud lucrari contigerit, tunc ipsi Hungari huiusmodi captivos et lucrum, exceptis notabilibus personis vel capitaneis ipsorum exercituum inimicorum regie maiestati in captivos pertinentibus, quos nos ab ipsis captivantibus pro donis condignis recipere valeamus, pro se retinendi vel vendendi aut ecclesiis perpetue servitutis iugo tradendi et donandi habeant potestatem.

XIV. Item quod in defensionibus et conservationibus metarum et confiniorum huius regni consiliis regnicolarum utemur.[18]

XV. Item honores seculares absque quolibet consilio[19] hominibus istius regni Hungarie et non advenis liberum arbitrium conferendi et ab eisdem auferendi habeamus.

XVI. Item possessiones et iura possessionaria non forensibus, sed bene meritis incolis tamen regni et corone Hungarie subiectis iuxta eorum merita et obsequia et non pro pecunia conferemus.[20] Perpetuas vero venditiones vel impignorationes iurium regalium et corone nec cum consilio, neque sine consilio quorumcunque faciemus.

XVII. Item quod proscriptiones seu dispositiones super metis et graniciebus inter Hungariam et Austriam prius facte in suo robore perdurent. De metis vero et graniciebus inter Hungariam et Morauiam quitquid de consilio eorundem prelatorum, baronum et regni nobilium de iure facere debemus, libenter faciemus.[21]

XVIII. Item quod in possessionibus et bonis nobilium et ecclesiarum seu quarumcunque secularium et ecclesiasticarum personarum violentas exactiones victualium, procurationes hospitalitatum et alias quascunque aggravationes preter voluntatem invitantium non faciemus nec fieri permittemus, nec in domibus et locis prelatorum, baronum et in aliarum quarumcunque secularium et ecclesiasticarum personarum pro tractatibus habendis et aliis quibuscunque negotiis disponendis ipsis invitis morabimur aut eos expensis, victualibus, curruum et sarcinarum vecturis, nunciorum et familiarium ac quorumcunque ad nos

11. Then, foreign coinage, money, and salt from abroad must not be brought into the kingdom and should not be accepted;[16] and let this be attended to as quickly as possible.

12. Then, that provision for the most serene princess lady Queen Elizabeth and for the preservation of the honor of her station, whence she is the heir of this kingdom, should be made wherever she wishes in the kingdom;[17] with this exception, that the lady queen should not have the power of conferring her own honors and offices on strangers and foreigners, but only on inhabitants of this kingdom, whomever she prefers, and of removing these from them according to her own will.

13. Then, if, while engaged in wars and battles or any other conflicts with enemies of the kingdom, Hungarians happen to capture any of the enemy or anything else of value, then those Hungarians should have the right to retain their captives or plunder for themselves, or to sell or to give or donate to churches into the yoke of perpetual servitude, except for notable people or commanders among the captives who are enemies of the royal majesty, whom we should have the right to acquire from their captors in return for suitable gifts.

14. Then, that regarding the defense and preservation of the borders and boundaries of this kingdom, we shall take counsel with the gentlemen of the realm.[18]

15. Then, we should have the right freely without any counsel[19] to confer secular honors on, and to remove them from men of this kingdom of Hungary, and not on newcomers.

16. Then, we shall not confer estates and proprietary rights on foreigners, but on deserving inhabitants of the kingdom and subjects of the crown of Hungary according to their merits and services and not for money.[20] We also shall not sell in perpetuity nor shall we mortgage the rights of the king and the crown, either with or without the counsel of anyone.

17. Then, that decisions and arrangements made earlier on the borders and boundaries between Hungary and Austria should remain in force. Regarding the boundaries between Hungary and Moravia, we shall gladly do whatever we ought legally to do, according to the counsel of the prelates, barons, and nobles of the realm.[21]

18. Then, that we shall neither make nor permit to be made forced exactions of supplies, demands for hospitality, or any other oppressions in the estates and goods of nobles and churches or any secular or ecclesiastical person, against their will; nor shall we remain uninvited, against their will, in the houses or places of prelates, barons, or any other secular or ecclesiastical persons for the purpose of holding meetings or conducting other business; nor shall we oppress them with expenses, provisions, the supply of carts, the transporting of baggage, or the requirements of messengers, retainers, or others belonging to us

pertinentium procurationibus ultra eorum spontaneam voluntatem in aliquo gravabimus, sicut abusive et contra eorum voluntatem ab aliquo tempore retroacto fieri erat inchoatum.[22]

XIX. Item ecclesie et ecclesiastice persone a taxis non diu abusive introductis libere et absolute relinquantur, servitia tamen exercitualia more alias consueto facere teneantur.[23]

XX. Item quod de maritatione filiarum nostrarum agemus cum consilio prelatorum et baronum ac nobilium regni nostri Hungarie, necnon cognatorum et proximorum atque subditorum regnorum et ducatuum nostrorum.[24]

XXI. Item quod ecclesiastica beneficia vacatura non faciemus neque permittemus per seculares occupari personas.

XXII. Item quod habitationem nostram hic in Hungaria more aliorum regum faciemus et continuabimus.

XXIII. Item quod procuratores nostre regie et reginalis maiestatum in sede iudiciaria una cum iudicantibus sedere non possint, sed inter causantes tempore, quo videlicet causa ipsarum regie et reginalis maiestatum agitur, stare debeant.[25] Litteras etiam per causidicos in ipsa sede exhibendas per se non conspiciant, nec tractent suis manibus, nisi magistri iudicantes.[26]

XXIV. Item in facto possessionum per regiam aut reginalem maiestatem aut eorum procuratores a talibus, qui perprius in dominio earum extiterunt, recaptivandarum et iuri regio[27] acquirendarum, quas regalis seu reginalis maiestates iure mediante vigore huiusmodi recaptivationis sibi appropriare non possent, contra tales, qui sic indebite et absque iure impediti et expensis fatigati fuerint, ipse maiestates in estimatione[28] talium possessionum ad instar aliorum similia facientium regnicolarum convincantur. Et similiter, si quipiam aliqua iura possessionaria nomine iuris regii pro se impetrarent et eadem ipsi iuri regio pertinere comprobare non valerent, in estimatione eorundem, si vero tales impetrantes ante decisionem cause in facto huiusmodi iurium impetratorum mote se de dominio ipsorum iurium ac de proventuum eorum perceptione occupative seu alio quovis modo intromitterent, nec tandem iuridice sibi appropriare possent, contra partem lesam seu litigantem et expensis fatigatam in facto potentie, prout ordo iuris requirit, convincantur.

XXV. Item iuxta requisitionem regnicolarum nostrorum nos unacum eisdem operabimus, quod despotus Rascie et comes Cilie[29] ceterique magnates, dominia, videlicet possessiones, castra, fortalitia, civitates, opida et alia bona in hoc regno Hungarie habentes et tenentes huiusmodi castra, fortalitia, opida civitates et possessiones non advenis et forensibus, sed Hungaris hominibus pro honore dare debeant.

in any way beyond their free will, as had become the abusive usage, against their will, for some time.[22]

19. Then, churches and ecclesiastical persons are to be freed and absolutely relieved from taxes abusively introduced not long ago, but, nevertheless, they are required to perform military service as was customary of old.[23]

20. Then, that concerning the marriage of our daughters, we shall act with the counsel of the prelates, barons, and nobles of our kingdom of Hungary, as well as of our relatives, kinsfolk, and the subjects of our kingdoms and duchies.[24]

21. Then, that we shall not keep ecclesiastical benefices vacant or permit them to be occupied by secular persons.

22. Then, that we shall take up residence and maintain it here in Hungary as other kings have done.

23. Then, that at such times when a case of the royal majesties is being heard, the advocates of the majesties of the king and queen cannot sit on the judicial bench with those judging, but must stand among those pleading cases.[25] They should not look at records presented to the bench by the opposing parties, nor should they take them in their hands; only the judging masters[26] may do that.

24. Then, in cases of such estates which are disputed by the king's or queen's majesty or their advocates in order to recover them for the royal right[27] from such men who previously had dominion in them, if the king's or queen's majesty cannot appropriate for themselves through legal process by way of this action of recovery, their majesties should be convicted, just as any other gentlemen of the realm doing the same things in the estimated value[28] of these estates in favor of those who have thus been harassed and burdened with expenses unwarrantedly and unlawfully. And similarly, those who may request for themselves any proprietary rights under the title of royal right and are not able to prove that it belongs to royal right should be convicted in its estimated value in the same way; and if such claimants enter into the dominion of these rights or the income from them by occupation or any other way before the case regarding these requests has been decided, and then they can not appropriate them legally for themselves, they should be convicted of violent trespass against the injured or litigant party burdened with expenses, as the order of law requires.

25. Then, according to the request of the gentlemen of the realm, we shall strive together with them that the despot of Serbia and the count of Cilli[29] and other magnates (namely, those lords who have and hold possessions, such as estates, castles, fortifications, cities, towns, and other properties in this kingdom of Hungary) should not give such castles, fortifications, towns, cities, and estates as honors to newcomers and foreigners, but to Hungarians.

XXVI. Item honores et officia nostra illis regnicolis nostris Hungaris, quibus voluerimus, more ab antiquo consueto iuxta huius regni nostri Hungarie consuetudinem conferemus.[30]

XXVII. Item quod nullus nobilium regni pro quibuscunque factis per quemcunque preter talem, contra quem sententia capitalis iuridice lata fuerit, possit detineri seu quoquomodo captivari.[31]

XXVIII. Item quod nobiles tam jobagiones habentes, quam non habentes decimas dare non teneantur antiqua eorum libertate requirente.[32]

XXIX. Verum quia frequenti querela regnicolarum nostrorum, ymmo quadam palpabili experientia teste nostra percepit celsitudo per nonnullas novas possessionum occupationes et potentiariorum actuum illationes eosdem regnicolas, inferiores videlicet a potentioribus multipliciter opprimi et gravari, ideo volentes insolentiis et novis attemptationibus per remedia opportuna viam precludere statuimus et ordinavimus, sicuti etiam in decreto maiori antefati condam domini Sigismundi imperatoris alias Posonii de unanimi prelatorum et baronum ac potiorum huius regni nostri nobilium consilio assensuque et voluntate edito aperte continetur,[33] quod quandocunque et ubicunque fuerint facte nove possessionarie aut terrarum occupationes, potentiarie vadiationes seu rerum et bonorum ablationes, succisiones silvarum, interemptiones, vulnerationes et verberationes hominum, domorum et possessionum invasiones et depredationes ac alii similes novi actus potentiarii maiores, extunc lesi et dampnum et iniuriam passi impetratis litteris nostris regalibus querimonialibus et preceptoriis, comites parochiales et iudices nobilium comitatus illius, in quo facta huiusmodi patrata extiterint, accedant et requirant. Qui quidem comites et iudices nobilium cum testimonio capituli vel conventus illi comitatui deservire soliti a vicinis et commetaneis ac nobilibus comprovincialibus sub certis penis in huiusmodi nostris litteris regalibus declarandis in sedem eorum iudiciariam per modum proclamate congregationis partibusque litem habentibus convocatis ad fidem eorum deo debitam fidelitatemque nobis et sacre corone observandam tactis sanctorum reliquiis prestitam super huiusmodi novis occupationibus possessionariis et aliis actibus potentiariis plenam et indilatam requirant veritatem, qua requisita et inventa possessiones occupatas auctoritate in hac parte eis attributa mediante restatuant eisdem, a quibus fuerant indebite occupate, ipsosque in dominio earundem protegant et conservent, alia vero bona et vadia potentialiter ablata absque defectu reddant et restitui faciant. Super facto autem potentie in talibus commisse partes utrasque discussionem et sententiam finalem recepturas ad certum terminum mediantibus eorum et dicti capituli vel conventus litteris seriem totius facti exprimentibus ac propria et possessionum factum huiusmodi attestantium nomina continentibus in personalem presentiam nostram regiam aut palatinalem seu iudicis curie nostre transmittant, ubi absque ulterioris termini et litigionarii processus observatione et continuatione, etiam partis non venientis absentia non obstante, nos vel iudex alius, ad quem causa transmissa fuerit, iuramentum capitis decernendo tandem finalem sententiam proferemus et

26. Then, we shall maintain the custom of conferring our honors and offices in the usual way, according to the ancient customs of our kingdom of Hungary, on those of our Hungarian gentlemen of the realm whom we wish.[30]

27. Then, that no nobleman of the kingdom can be detained or held captive in any way by anyone for any deed excepting those against whom a capital sentence has been passed by law.[31]

28. Then, that nobles, having tenants or not, must not be required to pay tithes, in accordance with their ancient liberties.[32]

29. As our majesty perceives from the repeated complaints of the gentlemen of the realm and also from personal experience that the more powerful gentlemen of the realm oppress and harm the less powerful in many ways by new seizures of estates and acts of violent trespass, wishing to hinder by suitable means these unusual acts and new atrocities, we establish and order, just as is also clearly contained in the *decretum maius* previously published by the said former lord Emperor Sigismund in Pozsony with the unanimous counsel, will and assent of the prelates, barons, and greater nobles of our kingdom,[33] that wherever and whenever anyone commits new seizures of estates or lands, takes a security by violence, robs goods and chattels, cuts down forests, beats, wounds or kills men, breaks into houses and estates and pillages them, or commits other similar new acts of violent tresspass, then the aggrieved, damaged, and injured parties should, after having acquired our royal letter of complaint and command, go to the *ispánok* and noble magistrates of that county where these acts were committed and call upon them. These *ispánok* and noble magistrates should then establish the full and complete truth about these new seizures of estates and acts of violent trespass with the testimony of that chapter or convent that usually acts in the county, summoning the neighbors, abutters, and other fellow nobles from the county in form of an extraordinary county assembly, under the penalty specified in our royal letter on this matter, to their county court, together with the parties of litigation, under their oath sworn by touching the relics of saints, on their faith in God and their fidelity to us and to the Holy Crown. Then, having inquired and established the truth, they should by their authority in this matter restore the occupied estates to those from whom they were illegally taken away, and defend and save them in these possessions, and completely restore and enforce the return of other violently abducted things and securities. In order that they should have a trial and final judgment on the violent trespass in these cases, both parties are to be sent to our personal presence or to that of the count palatine or to our judge royal by a set date with their letter and that of a chapter or convent describing the course of all the facts, together with the names and the names of the estates of those who testify in this matter, and we or any other judge to whom the suit will have been entrusted shall and must pronounce final sentence without setting any further term or process of trial

proferre tenebitur. Quicunque autem huiusmodi attestationem vicinorum et commetaneorum ac aliorum nobilium comprovincialium fieri de dampnisque et ablatis lesis et dampnificatis satisfactionem impendi non permitteret eisdem omnino resistendo, extunc talis in illo termino, ad quem factum seu causa huiusmodi per comitem ac capitulum seu conventum rescribetur, in facto potentie convictus pronuncietur seu decernatur eo facto. Volumus etiam et presentibus decernimus, ut talismodi premissorum executio seu causa per modum proclamate congregationis[34] exinde mota sive vertens nec nostris regalibus seu reginalibus, neque prelatorum seu baronum quorumcunque, etiam confinia regni nostri tenentium litteris, nec videlicet ratione exercitualis expeditionis, neque conservationis castri cuiuscunque possit quoquomodo prorogari, sed eadem causa in uno termino ad hoc deputato finaliter concludatur.

XXX. Item quod quilibet patrator novorum actuum potentiariorum, qui coram regia maiestate aut palatino seu iudice curie nostre regie per querulantes personaliter reperietur, in continenti sine ulla prorogatione ullaque cautela adinventa super omnibus sibi obiciendis ipsi querulanti debeat respondere, alioquin contra tales tamquam absentes ipsa congregatio generalis detur.[35] Partes tamen litigantes, quandocunque voluerint, absque requisitione iudicis et onere solutionis birsagiorum liberam concordandi habeant facultatem, quemadmodum antiqua et laudabilis regni nostri consuetudo huiusmodi concordiam in quibuscunque factis potentialibus et aliis libere fiendam dictat et consentit.[36]

XXXI. Redemptiones autem litterarum et adductiones testimoniorum capitularium seu conventualium, et qualiter aut quomodo false vie tributorum custodiantur, in eodem statu, quo in ipso decreto domini Sigismundi imperatoris et regis continentur,[37] relinquantur.

XXXII. Item alia facta potentiaria minora, pro quibus videlicet proclamata congregatio non datur, in tribus terminis seu octavis finaliter in iudicio concludantur, sic videlicet, quod duas evocationes precedentes trina forensis proclamatio subsequatur.[38] In factis autem seu acquisitionibus quarumcunque possessionum similiter duabus evocationibus et trina forensi proclamatione precedentibus pars adversa respondere teneatur, tali modo, quod si aliqua litteralia instrumenta apud se habere asseruerit, tunc semel sine onere, binis autem vicibus cum oneribus iudiciorum absque confidentia ulterioris prorogationis exhibere teneatur; aut si ad primum terminum exhibitionis non venerit, tunc etiam duo termini, et si ad secundum non venerit, tunc unus terminus compleatur, causaque in facto possessionario mota finem sortiatur effectivum. Si vero pars adversa sua litteralia instrumenta apud manus alienas habere asseruerit, tunc eidem pro requisitione huiusmodi suorum litteralium instrumentorum unus annus assignetur,

or extension, regardless of the absence of a party not appearing, by granting capital oath. If anyone does by outright obstruction not permit that evidence of this kind be given by neighbors and abutters or other fellow nobles concerning losses and outrages committed and that satisfaction for losses inflicted be paid, then such a man, in that term to which a deed or case of this kind is assigned by the *ispán* or chapter or convent, shall be pronounced and regarded as convicted by that fact in the deed of violent trespass. We wish also and we decree by the present statute that the conclusion of the aforesaid matters or a suit of this kind initiated or heard at an extraordinary county assembly[34] cannot be delayed for any reason, not even by a charter of our royal self or of the queen or of any prelate or baron or of those barons guarding the borders of the kingdom, or by reason of a military campaign, or of the defense of any castle; the case must be concluded finally in the one term appointed to it.

30. Then, that any perpetrator of recent acts of violent trespass, who, when personally confronted by the plaintiffs in front of the royal majesty or the palatine or our judge royal, must reply substantively, without any delay or frivolous evasion to all matters brought against him by the plaintiff; otherwise, a general assembly must be granted[35] against such men even if they are absent. The parties of the suit, however, should have leave to settle without the intervention of a judge or the payment of any fine whenever they wish, for the ancient and laudable custom of our kingdom prescribes and allows free settlement to be made in such cases of violent trespass and others.[36]

31. Payments for letters, arrangements for the testimony of chapters or convents and how or in what way the illegal roads avoiding customs should be guarded, should be left in the same state as they are contained in the same decree of the lord Emperor and King Sigismund.[37]

32. Then, other minor cases of trespass, namely those for which an extraordinary county assembly is not granted, must be concluded in three terms or octavial courts by judgment; thus, namely, that a threefold proclamation at market days must follow the two prior summons.[38] In matters regarding estates or their acquisition, the opposing party must be required to reply after two summons and a threefold proclamation in the same way, in such a manner, that if the said party claims to have any written instruments with him, then he must show them at the first term without, or at the second time with, the burden of a fine without expectation of further delay; or if the said party does not come to the first term to present them, then two more terms, and if he does not come to the second, then one more term must be granted, and the case moved in the matter of possession must be brought to an effective end. However, if the opposing party asserts that he has his written instruments in the hands of someone else, then one

ut contra adversarium in facto ipsorum instrumentorum terminus compleatur sic, quod elapso ipso anno in primo termino iuridice assignato dicta instrumenta sua exhibeat, vel si exhibere nollet aut non posset, tunc absque ulteriori prorogatione ipsa causa similiter finem sortiatur effectivum. Si vero in acquisitione alicuius possessionis tres vel quatuor aut quinque sive plures persone, unius tamen et eiusdem generationis[39] in causam fuerint attracte, non obstante absentia et non venientia unius vel duorum aut plurium, aut si ex ipsis unus vel duo aut plures in exercitu aut in conservatione confiniorum seu castri vel aliis quibuscunque servitiis regalibus fuerint constituti, tunc ratione horum causa in facto talis possessionis mota nullatenus prorogari possit, sed in eadem causa cum uno vel pluribus eorundem in propriis residentibus termini legitimi simul compleantur. Ubi autem omnes huiusmodi in causam attractos nullo penitus eorum in propriis remanente in notabilibus regni vel regiis servitiis occupari contigerit, extunc causa ipsa dempto facto proclamate congregationis generalis ad ulteriorem terminum more alias consueto poterit prorogari.

XXXIII. Item quecunque persona ecclesiastica aliquem nobilem in presentiam cuiuscunque iudicis ordinarii citaverit vel evocaverit, et si idem nobilis contra ipsam personam ecclesiasticam ordine iudiciario in sententia convictus fuerit, tunc gravamina maiora incurrere non possit idem nobilis, nisi homagium suum, scilicet emendam capitis sui precise eodem modo, sicuti ipsa ecclesiastica persona,[40] et de dampnis tam ex parte ecclesiasticarum, quam secularium personarum iudex dampnum patienti satisfactionem impendere teneatur.

XXXIV. Item decrevimus, prout etiam per certos predecessores nostros reges decretum fuisse intelleximus,[41] quod pro funeribus hominum per aliquem vel aliquos interemptorum archidiaconi seu plebani parochiani, prout hucusque de mala consuetudine fuit observatum, nullam solutionem pecuniariam recipere valeant sive possint.

Nos itaque huiusmodi petitionibus ipsorum prelatorum, baronum, nobilium et regnicolarum nostrorum aures exaudibiles regio cum favore inclinantes[42] suprascriptos articulos quoad omnes suas continentias et clausulas mera nostra auctoritate et potestatis plenitudine ex certaque nostre maiestatis scientia,[43] necnon de consensu et beneplacito prefate domine Elizabeth regine, consortis nostre predilecte presentibus nostris litteris inseri fecimus, ipsos prelatos, barones, nobiles et regnicolas nostros premissis libertatibus in eisdem articulis superius expressis perhenniter fruituros et gavisuros committendo. Addicimus preterea ac nostro et pretacte domine regine, consortis nostre nominibus spondemus, quod memoratos regnicolas nostros et totum regnum nostrum in quibuscunque eorum necessitatibus non deseremus, sed fideliter et toto posse nostro pariter cum eisdem ipsum regnum ac

year must be granted to him for the recovery of such written instruments of his, so that the term may be completed against the adversary in the matters of the instruments; thus, when the year granted has elapsed, he must show his said instruments in the first judicial term, and if he is unwilling or unable to show them, then without further delay the case must be brought to an effective end in the same way. However, in the acquisition of any estate, if three, four, five, or more persons of one and the same clan[39] have been summoned to the case, notwithstanding the absence or non-arrival of one, two, or more, or if one, two, or more of them are serving in the army or in the guard of the borders or of a castle or in any other royal service, then, for this reason, by no means should the case initiated in such a matter of a possession be postponed, but judicial terms must be similarly completed in the same case with one or more of those who reside at home. However, where it happens that all such men summoned to a case are occupied in the royal service or affairs of the realm with none of them remaining at home, then, unless the case pertains to an extraordinary general asembly, it can be delayed to a later term as is the usual custom.

33. Then, if any ecclesiastical person should cite and summon any noble to the presence of any justice ordinary, and, if that noble should be convicted with a sentence against that ecclesiastical person by the order of law, then that noble cannot incur greater penalties than his composition, namely the price of his head in precisely the same manner as the ecclesiastical person,[40] and the judge is required to order compensation for the losses as much on behalf of ecclesiastical persons as of secular ones.

34. Then, just as we understand that some of the kings preceding us also decreed,[41] we have decreed that no archdeacon or parish priest may or should take any payment in money for the funerals of men killed by a person or persons, as has become usual until now by evil custom.

Having turned our listening ears[42] with royal favor to these petitions of our prelates, barons, nobles, and gentlemen of the realm, we have caused, therefore, the above articles in regard to all their contents and clauses to be inserted in our present charter entirely by our own complete authority and fullness of power in accordance with our specific understanding of our royal majesty,[43] as well as with the assent and approval of the said Lady Queen Elizabeth, our beloved consort, and shall permit our prelates, barons, nobles, and gentlemen of the realm to enjoy and to cherish eternally the aforementioned liberties described in those same preceding articles. Furthermore, we add and promise in our name and in that of the said lady queen, our consort, that we shall not abandon our said gentlemen of the realm and our entire kingdom in any of their exigencies, but we shall defend this

preassertos omnes regnicolas nostros ab omnibus emulis defensabimus ac in cunctis, tam premissis, quam etiam in aliis singulis bonis et laudabilibus ac iustis antiquis consuetudinibus eorum et regni nostri Hungarie predicti inviolabiliter semper et ubique tenebimus et conservabimus effective.

Quicunque autem hominum, cuiuscunque status et conditionis existant, hec ipsa, que in superioribus continentur, quavis illicita occasione impugnare molirentur, contra omnes et quoslibet tales ad eorum proterviam domandam et compescendam pariter cum eisdem regnicolis nostris, prout et ipsi omnes universaliter id ipsum se facturos spoponderunt, operabimur toto posse, presentium litterarum nostrarum, quibus secretum sigillum nostrum, quo ut rex Hungarie utimur,[44] appensum est, vigore et testimonio mediante. Datum Bude, feria sexta proxima ante festum sancte Trinitatis, anno domini millesimo quadringentesimo tricesimo nono.

realm and its inhabitants, together with them, faithfully and with all our might against all enemies; and we shall keep and preserve them effectively and inviolably, always and everywhere, in all the aforesaid and other good, praiseworthy and just ancient customs of theirs and of our said kingdom of Hungary.

If any man, moreover, of whatever station and condition he may be, dares to attack those things which are included in the above by any illicit act, we shall act with all our might against any and all such men, together with our gentlemen of the realm, as they have conjointly agreed to do, to restrain and harness their insolence, by the force and testimony of these presents to which our privy seal that we use as king of Hungary[44] is appended. Given at Buda, on the Friday before the feast of the Holy Trinity in the year of the Lord one thousand, four hundred and thirty-nine.

20 Iulii 1440

Vide praefatiunculam et notas infra paginas 216–18.

Wladislaus dei gratia Hungarie, Polonie, Dalmatie, Croatie, Rame, Seruie, Galitie, Lodomerie, Comanie, Bulgarieque rex etc., Lithwanieque princeps supremus et heres Russcie[1] ad perpetuam rei memoriam. Preesse feliciter et pro[desse] salubriter auctore domino cunctis nostris subditis cupientes, quamvis omnium opiffice largiente ampla undique manus nostra concluserit et sibi commissa regat dominia, quibus intrinseca principatus sublimitate de [---extrinsec]us oblata regnorum fastigia minime nos appetere opus esset, vocati tamen novissime et assumpti dispositione, ut creditur, superna ad huius regni circumquaque emulorum atriti insultibus gubernacula, eam in primordio operam accuratius agere instituimus, illamque diligentiam primitialiter pro subiectorum utilitate et eque bono statu apud eos gerentes decrevimus, per quam et eorum desiderio propensius satisfiat et commoditas profutura uberius subsequatur, ut eo facto illic amplior nostre solertie benivolentia appareat, ubi multo desiderio expectati intensiore studio inviti ex debito cogimur, sicut pro p------[2] inter subditos penitus volentes discrimina conculcare, fovere iustitiam et impunitam licentiam delinquentium obvio remedio refrenare. Sane cum nuper post obitum condam serenissimi principis domini Alberti Romanorum ac Hungarie etc. regis[3] per universitatem dominorum prelatorum et baronum, comitum, militum, procerum et nobilium huius regni sibi, secundum quod eiusdem regni undique emulorum vicinato turbati exposceret necessitas,[4] de novi regis confestino presidio providere cupientium efficaci vocatione et electione ad suscipienda huius regni gubernacula primum invitati et demum multa instantia etiam perducti fuissemus, tam[en, quia tempore inter]medio corona illa, [cum] qua reges Hungarie perprius coronari soliti fuere, per dominam Elizabeth reginam, prefati condam Alberti regis relictam de castro Wissegradiensi propter multum incautam conservationem eiusdem clandestine sublata fuerit,[5] tamen nunc ipsi prelati, barones, comites, milites, proceres et nobiles eiusdem regni in multitudine tam maxima, quantam precedentium regum coronationis tempore in memoria hominum non comprehendit, ad nos congregati, profitentes denuo se rectores idoneos festina gubernatione carere non posse iteratoque electionem nostram pretactam uno animo approbantes et confirmantes consequ[enterque]---[6] alia corona beatissimi regis Stephani, apostoli et patroni huius regni in theca reliquiarum capitis eiusdem alta veneratione conservata, eque

20 July 1440

For prefatory and explanatory notes, see below, pages 216–18.

Wladislas, by the grace of God king of Hungary, Poland, Dalmatia, Croatia, Rama, Serbia, Galicia, Lodomeria, Cumania, Bulgaria, etc., grand prince of Lithuania and heir of Russia,[1] for the perpetual memory of this matter. Since it is our wish to preside happily over and to bring healthy prosperity to all our subjects with God's guidance, although, because of the intrinsic majesty of our lordship, we had no need to strive for the heights of rulership offered from without since our hands enclosed and ruled dominions far and wide, bestowed by the Maker of all; nonetheless, having been recently called by a command from on high, so we trust, to the governance of this kingdom which has been worn down by attacks of enemies on all sides, we have decided and chosen as our first and foremost task to exert ourselves for the advantage of our subjects and for conditions equally favorable to all of them, by which both their desires would be more fully satisfied and future benefits would accrue more fruitfully, so that, in that fashion, the benevolence of our care would be more apparent there where the strong desire for us and the great zeal exerted for our invitation obligates us as if we were indebted, desiring. . .[2] to eliminate thoroughly conflicts among the subjects, to foster justice, and to restrain the unbridled licence of lawless men by readily available remedy. Recently, after the death of the former most serene prince lord Albert, king of the Romans and of Hungary etc.,[3] when we had been first invited and then by many entreaties convinced to undertake the governance of this kingdom, because necessity implored it from a neighbor of this kingdom troubled by enemies on all sides,[4] we were brought with great urgency by the effective summons and election of the lord prelates and barons, counts, knights, lords, and nobles of this kingdom assembled to provide for the urgent protection of a new king. However, because meanwhile that crown, with which the kings of Hungary have been accustomed to be crowned previously, was secretly taken from the castle of Visegrád by the lady Queen Elizabeth, widow of the said former King Albert, owing to the very careless watch on it,[5] nonetheless, now the prelates, barons, counts, knights, lords, and nobles of the kingdom, having been assembled in our presence in greater numbers than the memory of men records for the coronation of any previous king, stated again that they could not be suitable guardians if they lacked auspicious rule and approved anew and confirmed unanimously our aforesaid election and consequently. . .[6]

egregii operis et pretiosa solempniter coronari fecerunt ipsoque sacro dyademate insigniri, omne robur et omnem efficaciam ipsius prioris corone hac vice et etiam in perpetuum, si ea recuperari non poterit,[7] in hanc modernam transfundendo, committendoque nobis in decreto omnem regie potestatis plenitudinem et artem principatus dirigendam. Quibus in dei nomine feliciter peractis subsequenter ipsa universitas regni nostri prehabitis inter se communiter m[ul]tis [tractatibus supplicantes] sibi de [gener]ali dispositione, per quam et nociva reformentur et utilia conserventur, indebiteque commissa emendentur, per nos provideri, exhibuerunt et obtulerunt nostre celsitudini quendam libellum[8] in sui contenti tenore per eos, ut dicebant, diligenter masticatum, certos articulos constitutionum et dispositionum ex litteris condam Andree filii tertii Bele regis[9] et Lodouici[10] dominorum Hungarie regum predecessorum nostrorum, item ex quibusdam aliis litteris olim prelatorum, ecclesiasticorum et nobilium regni tempore coronationis condam alterius Andree regis Hungarie dicti de Venetiis emanatis[11] extractos et exceptos in se continentem, supplican[tes celsitudini nostre una]nimiter et humiliter, ut ex quo eedem constitutiones modo, prout in ipso libello seu registro continentur, eorum bono statui convenientes fore atque ad utilitatem eorum et totius regni conducere posse viderentur, easdem quoad omnem continentiam innovantes confirmare dignaremur. Cuius quidem libelli sed et constitutionum pretactarum tenor sequitur et est talis:

LIBERTATES ET CONSTITUTIONES REGNI HUNGARIE EX LITTERIS ANDREE REGIS, FILII TERTII BELE REGIS EXTRACTE:[12]

CONSTITUTIONES PER PRELATOS ET BARONES AC NOBILES REGNI HUNGARIE TEMPORE CORONATIONIS ANDREE REGIS DICTI DE VENETIIS FACTE SECUNTUR IN HUNC MODUM:[13]

SECUNTUR NUNC LIBERTATES ET ORDINATIONES REGNO HUNGARIE DATE ET CONCESSE ULTRA LIBERTATES, QUAS CONDAM DOMINUS REX ANDREAS, FILIUS TERTII BELE REGIS DEDIT ET CONCESSIT PREDICTO REGNO, QUAS ETIAM IPSE DOMINUS LODOUICUS REX CONFIRMAVIT. TENOR AUTEM DICTE CONFIRMATIONIS IPSIUS LODOUICI REGIS SEQUITUR PER OMNIA IN HEC VERBA:[14]

Nos igitur humillimis et devotis pretacte universitatis regnicolarum nostrorum supplicationibus instantius propulsati, quia ex eorundem assertionibus manifestis constitutiones, libertates et ordinationes superius specificatas veterum provida dispositione

with another crown, equally precious and of equally remarkable work, of the most blessed King Stephen, apostle and patron of this kingdom, preserved with great veneration on the reliquary of his head, have caused us to be solemnly crowned and to be honored with that sacred diadem, while transferring all the force and all the efficacy of the previous crown to this new one as a substitute—and if that cannot be recovered, in perpetuity[7]—and committing to us in a decree complete royal power and the means to govern the polity. When these things had been done felicitously in the name of God, the community of our kingdom held extensive common discussions among themselves and requested us to provide for them a general decision by which harmful things can be altered, useful features preserved, and unlawfully committed deeds corrected. Then they have shown and offered to our highness a certain booklet;[8] they had, as they said, diligently chewed over the text of this which contained certain articles of the constitutions and dispositions from charters of the former king Andrew, son of King Béla III,[9] and of Louis,[10] our predecessors as lord kings of Hungary, also extracts and excerpts from certain other charters of former prelates, ecclesiastics, and nobles of the kingdom originating from the time of the coronation of the former other Andrew, called the Venetian.[11] They begged our eminence unanimously and humbly that we deign to confirm by renewing the contents of these constitutions as they are comprised in this booklet or register, which seem to be useful for their good state and which could lead to their greater utility and that of the entire kingdom. And the content of this booklet and also of the abovementioned constitutions follows here and runs thus:

THE LIBERTIES AND CONSTITUTIONS OF THE KINGDOM OF HUNGARY TAKEN FROM THE CHARTERS OF KING ANDREW, SON OF KING BÉLA III: [12]

THE CONSTITUTIONS MADE BY THE PRELATES AND BARONS AND NOBLES OF THE KINGDOM OF HUNGARY AT THE TIME OF THE CORONATION OF KING ANDREW, CALLED THE VENETIAN, FOLLOW IN THIS WAY:[13]

THERE FOLLOW NOW THE LIBERTIES AND ORDINANCES GIVEN AND CONCEDED TO THE KINGDOM OF HUNGARY BEYOND THOSE LIBERTIES WHICH THE FORMER LORD KING ANDREW, SON OF KING BÉLA III, GAVE AND CONCEDED TO THE AFORESAID KINGDOM, WHICH THE LORD KING LOUIS HIMSELF HAS CONFIRMED. THE TEXT OF THE SAID CONFIRMATION IN ALL THINGS BY KING LOUIS FOLLOWS IN THESE WORDS:[14]

We, therefore, strongly urged by the most humble and devoted pleas of the said community of our gentlemen of the realm, since from their manifest claims we recognized that the constitutions, liberties, and ordinances specified above founded by the provident disposition of

conditas ad utilitatem et bonum statum ipsorum cooperari posse verisimiliter cognovimus, libenter eorum voto admissionem concessimus pretactasque seu supranotatas constitutiones, libertates et ordinationes eo sensu, prout ad utilitatem rei publice christiane proficiunt, quoad omnes ipsarum continentias, clausulas et articulos, precipue vero intentionem supradicti Lodouici regis, quantum ad articulos per eum moderatos et mutatos acceptamus, aprobamus, ratificamus easque nichilominus ex certa nostra scientia[15] huic regno nostro innovantes perpetuo vallituras confirmamus, et decernentes et committentes per hec scripta, ut huiusmodi constitutiones, libertates et ordinationes tam per modernos et futuros prelatos, quorum interest et intererit, quam etiam universos barones, iudices, milites et proceres amodo in posterum successivis semper temporibus universis inviolabiliter observentur et exsecutioni debite demandentur. Quas et nos per omnia observare et immutabiliter observari debere statuimus variatione sine omni; quodque ultra hec premissa ad dictorum regnicolarum nostrorum instantiam eis nunc ex novo annuimus et declaramus:

I. Ut nullus virorum nobilium regni huius possessiones habentium vel non habentium decimas dare teneatur, prout etiam itidem in decreto supranominati Alberti regis[16] perhibetur contineri, sed quilibet talium nobilium, dum eis per maiestatem regiam precipitur, contra emulos huius regni dimicando huiusmodi decimarum debita sanguinis sui effusione et virili defensione recompensare teneatur.[17]

II. Statuimus preterea et presenti decreto stabilimus, ut si aliquem ex baronibus aut nobilibus huius regni nostri Hungarie possessiones et bona aliorum baronum seu nobilium aut etiam ecclesiarum pro pignore vel qualitercunque occupata detinentem et possidentem temporis per successum infidelitatis notam contra coronam eiusdem regni incurrere contigerit, extunc illi, quos perpetuitas huiusmodi possessionum et bonorum inpignoratorum vel ocupatorum concernit, fideles existendo propter delictum eiusdem infidelis huiusmodi iure perpetuitatis eorum non priventur, sed semper talismodi ius perpetuitatis ipsorum salvum permaneat, idemque, dum eis placuerit, prosequi valeant atque possint, consuetudine horum in contrarium hucusque tempta non obstante; quam scilicet et singula preteritis hactenus temporibus secundum eandem consuetudinem et in premissorum contrarium acta, facta iudicataque atque gesta revocamus et revocata esse committimus per hec scripta.[18]

III. Ceterum decernimus, ut dum et quandocunque per affutura tempora aliquem rusticum seu jobagionem baronis vel nobilis cum presbitero seu clerico quocunque rixare vel contendere, aut inter eos vituperia et minas simpliciter vel etiam subsecutis verberibus in thabernis vel aliis locis suspectis sive dampnorum illatione[s] vel in factis profanis suboriri contigerit, extunc talis presb[iter] vel cl[ericu]s

the ancients are most likely to be able to contribute to the utility and good state of the same community, have freely acceded to their prayer and approve the said abovementioned constitutions, liberties, and ordinances with the purpose that they might enhance the well-being of the Christian commonwealth; we approve all their contents, clauses, articles, and especially the intention of the abovementioned King Louis inasmuch as we accept the articles changed and altered by him, and we ratify and confirm them as valid for this kingdom, as well as renew them in accordance with our specific understanding of our royal majesty,[15] by decreeing and committing through these presents that these constitutions, liberties, and ordinances must be inviolably observed and duly implemented by present and future prelates, whom it concerns and will concern, and also by all barons, judges, knights, and lords in posterity in all succeeding times forever. And we also decree that they be observed in all things just as we shall be required to observe them immutably without any change; in addition to the aforesaid we promise anew and declare at the request of our said gentlemen of the realm:

1. That no nobleman of this kingdom, whether holding estates or not, should be required to pay tithes, just as is also demonstrated to be contained in the decree of the abovenamed King Albert,[16] but any noble, when he is directed by the royal majesty, is required to pay the debts of such tithes by fighting against the enemies of this kingdom with the spilling of his blood and with manly defense.[17]

2. In addition, we order and establish by the present decree that if it happens that any baron or noble of our kingdom of Hungary, while holding the estates and goods of other barons or nobles or of churches in security or in any other way, should in the course of time be convicted of an act of treason against the crown of this kingdom, then those to whom the perpetual right of such mortgaged estates or pledged goods pertains should, if they are faithful subjects of ours, not be deprived by the crime of this traitor of their heritage, but such a right of perpetuity must always remain intact, and they should have the right and the means to enforce it, as long as it pleases them, notwithstanding that usage which has been recently introduced against these customs; for we revoke and order to be held revoked herewith that usage and all and every act that has been undertaken, judged, or performed in previous times according to that usage and in infringement of the above.[18]

3. We further decree that while and whenever in future it happens that any peasant or tenant of a baron or noble fights or brawls with any priest or cleric, or that there arise among themselves insults and threats or also subsequent brawls in taverns or other places of ill-repute or the inflicting of damages or profane deeds, the priest or cleric may not charge and summon the peasant or tenant to a spiritual court

[rusticum] seu jobagionem in sedem spiritualem non aliter, nisi prius petita [iustitia] a domino talis rustici citare et in causam convenire possit; sed petita prius iustitia huiusmodi, si tandem de iudicio domini eiusdem rustici contentari noluerit, vel si ipse dominus talis rustici sibi iustitiam facere recusaverit, ipsum rusticum in presentiam episcopi vel vicarii dyocesiani liberam citandi habeat facultatem.[19]

IV. Postremo per nos ac universitatem pretactorum regnicolarum nostrorum conclusum vetusta consuetudine exigente declaramus, ut nullus omnino hominum indigenarum vel forensium cuius[cunque nationis et conditionis existat], sine licentia nostra aut successorum nostrorum regum Hungarie aliquas bullas vel scripta papales vel concilii aut delegatorum ab eis sive factum beneficiorum, sive penarum aut litium quarumcunque exprimant, ad hoc regnum nostrum et intra eius limites inportare aut se de quocunque beneficio vigore earundem intromittere vel etiam quemcunque regnicolarum nostrorum citare seu extra regnum in causam atrahere presumat.[20] Si quis autem huiusmodi bullas vel rescripta inportaverit vel inportatas exsecutioni nobis inconsultis demandare presu[mpserit, ----- su]perinde observata puniatur. Illud tamen quibuslibet indulgemus, ut in lite seu causa quacunque forum spirituale concernenti in hoc regno nostro et in presentia iudicum ordinariorum eiusdem mota et ventillata, finita huiusmodi lite seu causa liberam ad curiam appostolicam vel concillium appellandi habeant facultatem.[21]

Ut autem premissarum constitutionum et confirmationis series robur obtineat perpetue firmitatis, presentes concessimus litteras nostras privilegiales. In cuius rei memoriam firmitatemque perpetuam presentes concessimus litteras sigilli nostri, [quo ut rex Hungarie] utimur, appensione munitas. Datum in Albaregali in festo beati Elie prophete, anno domini millesimo quadringentesimo quadragesimo.[22]

unless justice has first been sought from the lord of such a peasant, and not otherwise. But if justice was first sought in this way, if in the end he is not satisfied with the judgment of the lord of that peasant, or if the lord of such a peasant declines to render justice to him, then he should be free to summon that peasant into the presence of the bishop or the vicar of the diocese.[19]

4. Finally we declare, on the decision of ours and the community of our said gentlemen of the realm, in conformity with ancient custom, that no man, native or foreign of whatever nation or condition he may be, may presume without our licence or that of our successors as kings of Hungary to bring into our kingdom or within its borders any bulls or letters issued by popes, councils, or their delegates regarding benefices, penalties, or cases of any kind or to interfere with any prebend on their authority or to summon any one of our people[20] or to prosecute him in a case outside the kingdom. If anyone brings in bulls or rescripts of this kind or presumes to recommend their importation for implementation without consulting us, let him be punished for what he has done. However, we grant this indulgence to anyone that in any trial or case in our realm pertaining to a court spiritual and moved and argued in the presence of a justice ordinary, when ~~a trial~~ or case of this sort has been finished, he may have leave to appeal to the apostolic court or to the council.[21]

In order that the contents of the preceding constitutions and confirmations may hold the force of perpetual validity, we have granted these presents. For the memory of which and for its perpetual validity, we concede that these presents be fortified by appending our seal which we use as king of Hungary. Given in Székesfehérvár on the feast of the blessed prophet Elijah, in the year of the Lord one thousand, four hundred and forty.[22]

(Martius 1443)

Vide praefatiunculam et notas infra paginas 219–20.

Wladislaus dei gratia Hungarie, Polonie, Dalmatie, Cruatie etc. rex, Lythwanieque princeps supremus et heres Russie ad futuram memoriam. Cum a primevo ingressu nostro in hoc regnum avidi semper et sumpme diligentes fuerimus ad ea exercenda precipue, per que attriti regni eiusdem incomoda potuissent conpetentius celeriusque submoveri, preter multos in id factum quesitos attemptatosque modos novissime vocatis ad hunc locum in presentiam nostram magnificis fidelibus nostris Nicolao de Wylak et Johanne de Hunyad, partium nostrarum wayvadis Transsilwanarum,[1] festinam pro eorundem adventu prelatorum et baronum, millitum ac procerum regni huius convocationem fieri iussimus eo animo eoque propensito, ut adhibenda eiusdem regni necessitatibus opportuna proviso ampliori deinceps mora et negligentia non traheretur, sed ut de prefatorum wayvadarum nostrorum consilio, communi tandem omnium aliorum baronum nostrorum et procerum pretactorum deliberatione subsequente concluderetur tempestius, quomodo, quo denique ordine horrenda regni huius, tum ex paganorum, tum christianorum insultantium parte hactenus perlata turbatio reici fugarique posset atque tolli. Ob quam rem venientibus iuxta vocationem nostram pretactam diebus hiis in hunc locum memoratis wayvadis nostris concurrentibusque nichilominus ad istam previa ratione promulgatam congregationem multis aliis baronibus, spiritualibus et secularibus, sed et pluribus militibus et proceribus huius regni nostri,[2] copiosos ad rem pretactam cum eisdem tractatus transsegimus, finaliterque in nomine domini, cuius nutu reguntur universa et diriguntur, ad certas regno eidem nostro et eorundem iudicio utiles conclusiones devenimus, quarum ordo et tenor sequitur in hunc modum:

I. Primo et principaliter, ut in estate proxime affutura pro regni huius defensione et reparando statu notabilis armorum exercitus instauretur, pro eiusque institutione et instauratione opportuna per totum regnum nostrum generaliter pecunialis contributio fieri debeat sub modis et ordine ac conditionibus et penis, qui seu que in aliis litteris nostris ad singulos comitatus regni nostri transsmissis distincte notificate sunt et expressate.[3]

II. Sed ut tam in huiusmodi exercituali progressu, quam in aliis agendis sive contra emulos paganos, sive alios quoscunque nocivos regni hostes et oppressores instaurandis eo liberius quietiusque et diligentius procedatur, quo citius a singulorum cordibus alterni odii et

(March 1443)

For prefatory and explanatory notes, see below, pages 219–20.

Wladislas by the grace of God king of Hungary, Poland, Dalmatia, Croatia, etc., grand prince of Lithuania, and heir of Russia, for future memory. Because ever since our first entry into this kingdom we have always been most eager and diligent in pursuing, in particular, those things by which the troubles of this weakened kingdom could be more suitably and more quickly removed, after having attempted several measures, consequently, having first summoned just recently our distinguished loyal subjects Nicholas of Ujlak and John Hunyadi, voivodes of our Transylvanian regions,[1] to this place into our presence, we have ordered that an urgent assembly be held on the occasion of their arrival by the prelates and barons, knights, and lords of this kingdom with that thought and intention in mind that proper provision for the necessities of this kingdom should not be retarded by further delay and negligence, but that we should decide swiftly with the counsel of our aforementioned voivodes and then with the subsequent deliberation of all our other said barons and lords in what way and in which order the terrible disturbances of this kingdom from the attacks of both pagans and Christians hitherto endured should be resisted, held off, and stopped. For this reason after our said voivodes have come according to our said summons at this time to this place and when many other barons, spiritual and secular, as well as many knights and lords of our kingdom have come together to an assembly proclaimed for the above reason,[2] we accomplished much in treating of the said business with them, and finally in the name of the Lord, by whose will all things are ruled and governed, we arrived at certain decisions useful in our judgment and theirs for that kingdom of ours, the order and content of which follow in this manner:

1. First and principally, that in the coming summer for the defense and recovery of the state of this kingdom a great military army must be established, and for its proper institution and establishment a financial contribution must be levied generally throughout our whole kingdom in the form and order and under the conditions and penalties which have been clearly promulgated and described in our other letters sent to all the counties of our kingdom.[3]

2. But in order that both the campaign of this army and other actions against pagan enemies or any other vicious fiends and other oppressors of the kingdom might be done more boldly, smoothly, and efficiently, so as to eliminate more quickly reasons for mutual hatred,

oppressionis seu dampnificationis materia secludatur, conclusum est et determinatum, ut quicunque inter nostros fideles hiis disturbiorum temporibus sua propria presumptione, demptis donationibus per infidelitatis notam factis, alterius fidelis nostri bona occupavit et illicite detinet, talis coram testimonio capituli vel conventus, ut hactenus moris fuit, per litteras nostras regias ad instantiam querulantium modo premisso et dampnificatorum emanandas quanto citius ammoneatur, ut hinc ad infra quindecimum diem festi beati Georgii martiris proxime affuturi[4] singula huiusmodi bona modo, quo pretangitur, usurpata illis, a quibus illicite ac propria auctoritate occupata sunt, restituere et remittere teneatur dilatione et difficultate sine omni; quatenus in progressu exercitus prenotati, ubi pro defensione fidei expediendaque de inimicis crucis Christi ultione sincere fidelium certabit devotio, nullus talis appareat, qui suis notoriis criminibus ab omnipotenti deo oppressorum contra se precibus provocato iram potius, quam adiutorium mereatur.[5] Qui si fecerit, bene quidem, alioquin quilibet talis alienorum bonorum occupator ad instantiam huiusmodi oppressi vel oppressorum presenti insinuatione vim evocationis peremptorie ex nunc prout ex tunc obtinente hic Bude coram iudicibus deputandis octavo die festi Penthecostes[6] proxime affuturi per se vel procuratorem tanquam legitime et peremtorie, ut pretangitur, evocatus absque spe ulterioris termini obtinendi comparere teneatur rationem detentionis huiusmodi occupatorum bonorum redditurus efficacem. Quo quidem adveniente termino, ipsisque partibus iuxta formam premissorum comparentibus, si ex efficacibus documentis ibidem iudicialiter compertum fuerit ipsum, qui ratione occupationis quorumcunque bonorum accusatus fuerit, ad eadem bona, que detinet, efficax ius habuisse et habere liciteque eadem per ipsum detineri, extunc talis in iure suo illese relinquatur. Ubi autem illicite occupasse et detinere compertus fuerit et ammonitus modo premisso ipsa restituere noluerit, extunc mox sine omni ampliori exceptione aut dilatione sententie capitali, pene facti potentialis subiciatur et ipsorum bonorum detentorum possessione privetur indilate, bonaque ipsa illi, ad quem pertinent, adiudicentur sententialiter et restituantur. Nec autem in premisso casu cuipiam dictarum partium amplior ad comparendum et respondendum terminus assignari valeat; quin ymo communi deliberatione statutum est, ut prefatus terminus nec per ingressum in exercitum et neque quocunque alio modo aut ---[7] prolongari valleat, sed quod in absentia alicuius dictarum partium non venientis ad partis comparentis instantiam iudex prefatus dispositionem et determinationem prefatam nichilominus prosequatur, effec----- sententieque modo premisso late et diffinite extiterunt, illi duo capitanei nostri, qui pro defensione eius partis regni nostri, ex qua antefata lis orta fuerit,[8] subscripto ordine deputabuntur ------[9] reum et condempnatum in premissis iuxta requisitionem antelati iudicis facere debeant omni favore procul moto.[10]

oppression, and harm from the hearts of all men, it has been concluded and determined that any one of our loyal subjects who in these times of troubles by his own audacity has occupied and illegally keeps the goods of another loyal subject of ours, with the exception of grants made on the basis of high treason, must be warned as soon as possible with the testimony of a chapter or convent, as has been the usual custom, by means of our royal charters to be issued upon the request of those complaining and who suffered damage in the said manner, from now until the fifteenth day of the next feast of Saint George the Martyr,[4] that he is required to restore and to return without any delay or hindrance all the goods wrongfully acquired in the abovementioned way to those from whom they were taken illegally, while acting solely on his own authority. Moreover, where the devoted faithful will fight sincerely to defend the faith and to exact vengeance from the enemies of the cross of Christ, no such man may take part in the campaign of the said army, who by his notorious crimes would more deserve anger than help from almighty God moved by the prayers of the oppressed against him.[5] If he does make restitution, all is well; otherwise any such usurper of the goods of others is required, in accord with the present notice, on the complaint, new or outstanding, of the oppressed person or persons to appear, in person or through an advocate without the hope of obtaining a further term on the eighth day of the next feast of Pentecost[6] here at Buda in front of judges to be appointed, in order to render an acceptable reason for holding the usurped goods. If the man accused of usurping properties, when the term opens and the parties appear according to the said form, is found from proper records by law to have and to have had, proper rights to those properties which he holds and that they are legally held by him, then such a man should be left unmolested in his right. However, if he is found to have usurped and holds something illegally and after being warned in the said manner is unwilling to restore it, then at once without any further excuse or delay he will be subject to capital punishment, the penalty for an act of violent trespass, and will be deprived at once of the continued possession of the properties usurped, and the properties themselves will be adjudicated at law and restored to whomever they belong. In the aforesaid case none of the said parties should be granted a further term for appearing and answering; and, furthermore, it has been decided by common deliberation that the said term cannot be prorogued by joining the army or by any other means . . .,[7] but in the absence of any on the request of the party present, the said judge must make the said decision and disposition. Once a sentence has been given and pronounced in the said way, then those two captains of ours, who are responsible for the defense of that part of our kingdom in which the preceding case arose,[8] will be appointed by the following procedure, in order to enforce . . .[9] the culprit and the condemned in the foregoing according to the requirement of the said judge unmoved by any favor.[10]

III. Quia autem usque ad hoc tempus maxima causa huiusmodi oppressionum et occupationis bonorum alienorum ex eo accidisse creditur, quod littere et mandata nostra regia, que ex iusta causa vel ad instantiam aliquorum vel querimoniam iuridice actenus exire et emanare contingit, per aliquot barones, dignitarios et officales nostros regales, seu ipsorum vicesgerentes plerumque levipense et inexecuta mansserunt, idcirco prefatorum prelatorum, baronum, militum et procerum regni nostri nunc in antefata congregatione existentium communi deliberatione et ordinatione commissum est et statutum, ut hinc in posterum quilibet regnicolarum nostrorum, cuiuscunque dignitatis aut conditionis existat, litteras et mandata nostra regia, dummodo ex iusta causa et iuridice exeant et emanent, prout aliorum regum predecessorum nostrorum temporibus solitum fuit, sine omni repugnantia sub pena infrascripta observare et exequi toto posse teneatur. Quicunque autem id facere contempnerent, nisi celeriter per nunccium fidedignum aut litteras efficaces se super non observatione huiusmodi mandatorum in presentia nostra ac prelatorum et baronum nostrorum aput nos pro tempore presentium se excuset, si fuerit simplex nobilis aut vicesgerens baronis aut dignitarii, seu comitis alicuius, possessiones seu bona ac res eiusdem mox ad mandatum nostrum occupentur, de eisdemque domini ipsorum[11] lesis et iniuratis, si ad quantitatem dampnorum se extenderint, digne satisfactionis dupplum impendant, cuius una pars in sortem dampnatorum, altera vero pro iniuriis illatis cedat. Si vero possessiones eiusdem rei ad valorem dampnorum pretactorum se non extenderint, tunc eiusdem rei persona ad manus iniuriati et dampnificati assignetur. Vel ubi autem idem dominus suus, cuius scilicet familiaris ipse reus extiterit, id facere non valeret aut ob favorem eiusdem recusaret, extunc statim excuset se efficaciter per suas litteras, quod huiusmodi dampnificatio non fuit cum voluntate sua, coopereturque omni posse pro persone talis dampnifficatoris et dampnati reis condempnatoris detentione, ac quod amplius talem nocivum hominem et sub suo nomine et in eius familiaritate non conservet; ab honoreque seu officiolatu suo in continenti per dominum suum deponatur, licet ad talem honorem sine gratia nostra de cetero venire deputatis valeat.[12]

IV. Si vero prelatus aliquis aut baro sive dignitarius aut comes seu alter officialis regalis mandatorum nostrorum notorius contemptor aut transgressor extiterit, extunc super eo nicholominus, sicuti habuimus et habemus, ita efficacius ex deliberatione prefata de cetero habeamus potestatem eundemque a sua dignitate vel baronia, honore seu officiolatu sine omni eiusdem contradictione amovere, stetque in arbitrio et voluntate nostra, quo ordine eum corripere volumus et punire.

3. Since hitherto the most important cases of oppression and usurpation of properties of others seem to have happened because our royal letters and mandates, which until now were issued and sent out by law for a just reason or at the instance or complaint of someone, have been taken lightly or remained unexecuted by certain barons, dignitaries, and royal officials of ours, or by their deputies, therefore it has been decreed and ordered by common deliberation and decision of the said prelates, barons, knights, and lords of our kingdom now gathered in the above mentioned assembly that from now on into the future anyone of our gentlemen of the realm, of whatever dignity and condition he may be, should be required to observe and to follow with all his ability without any reluctance, under the penalties written below, our royal letters and mandates, insofar as they are issued and sent out for just reasons and by law, just as was customary in the times of the other kings, our predecessors. Any man who is found to be in contempt of this, be he a simple noble or a deputy of a baron or office-holder of any *ispán*, his estates or properties and possessions should be occupied on our order, and from these their lords[11] should pay double the proper amount of compensation for damages and injuries if they suffice for the amount of losses, and one part should go to the share of the damaged party and the other for the injuries sustained, unless he quickly excuses himself by a suitable messenger or the proper letter regarding his contempt of such an order of ours in our presence and in that of our prelates and barons who accompany us at that time. If, however, his estates do not cover the value of the aforementioned losses, then his person must be given over into the hands of those injured and robbed. If, however, his lord, namely whose retainer the accused is, is not able to do this or refuses for favor of him, then at once he must properly excuse himself through his letter, stating that the loss caused was not at his will and he will do his best to arrest the person of such an evil-doer who scorns the one who suffered the loss, and that he would not keep any longer such a harmful man under his name and in his retinue; and he should be immediately deposed from his honor or office that he holds, by his lord, even if he would be eligible to receive such an honor without our grace.[12]

4. If any prelate, baron, dignitary, *ispán*, or other royal official happens to be notoriously in contempt or in transgression of our orders, then, regarding this person, just as we used to have and still have, the more effectively we should now have, based on the above deliberation, the power to remove this man from his dignity or barony or honor without any objection from him, and it should be acording to our judgment and will in what way we wish to seize and punish him.

V. Preterea ut eo citius cuiuslibet oppressionis et dampnificationis inter subditos nostros occasio adimatur, conclusum est et determinatum, quod omnia fortalitia[13]-------atum, munitiones ecclesiarum seu monasteriorum aut aliorum locorum quorumcunque, que sub nostra obedientia hiis disturbiorum temporibus absque utilitate et defensione regni aut necessitate notabili regnicolarum nostrorum erecta facteque et constructe sunt, de quibus inter fideles nostros spolia, dampna seu nocumenta committuntur, et que tantas pertinentias aut proventus consuetos, ut de eisdem tueri possent, non habentes de bonis aliorum regnicolarum nostrorum conservantur, hinc infra quindecimum diem festi beati Georgii martiris proxime affuturi[14] deleantur et distrahantur, possessionesque talium huismodi spolia de ispo fortalitio committentium pro nostra maiestate per banum aut comitem seu capitaneum occupentur, quibus occupatis prius lesis et dampnificatis in eisdem possessionibus satisfactione inpensa, relique ad nostrum mandatum conserventur.

VI. Item quod partes illas, puta versus Cassouienses, Sczepusienses, Zolienses, Trinchinienses, Zaladienses et Castriferrei, in quibus videlicet certorum forensium insultus[15] pullulat, confestim per opportunos modos mittantur et preficiantur duo et duo capitanei cum dispositione decreti, qui ab ipsorum insultantium hostium infestationibus regnicolas nostros in partibus illis, ad quas singuli eorum missi fuerint, toto posse liberare defensareque tenantur, ac etiam inter regnicolas nostros alterna spolia mutuasque dampnificationes agere non permittant, ymo lesis et dampnificatis iustitiam et satisfactionem durante ipsorum officio facere studiosius curent, sententiasque et mandata nostra regalia seu iudicum per nos previa ratione deputandorum fideliter et sine favore aut odio quorumcunque observari compellant et suo modo exequantur. In casu autem, quod ipsi capitanei nostri ad hec omnia facienda vel aliqua gravamina ex eis peragenda potentes cum suis armatis gentibus aut sufficientes non essent, extunc nos ac subscripti prefati barones, milites et proceres[16] seu hii, quos ex eisdem ipsi requisierint, ipsos sine dilatione, totiens quotiens necessarium fuerit, adiuvare, singuli etiam regnicole nostri sub ipsorum capitaneatu existentes in eorum succursum mox, postquam hoc commiserint, insurgere sub pena occupationis possessionum ipsorum debeant et teneantur.

VII. Item quod iidem capitanei de cetero super bonis nostrorum fidelium per quempiam census vulgo hold[17] inponere aut inpositos exigere non permittant, quodque de illis dampnis et iniuriis, quos et que regnicole nostri, partem scilicet nostram facientes sibi ipsis mutuo inter se hucusque intullerint irrogaverintque et fecerint, eisdem, quibus huiusmodi dampnificationes et iniurie illate existunt, libera plenaque iuxta consuetudinem huius regni iuridice requirendi concedatur et remaneat facultas et iustitia ex parte talium damnatorum cuipiam non denegetur.

5. Furthermore, in order that the cause of any oppression or damage among our subjects might be more quickly removed, it has been agreed to and decided that all fortifications. . .,[13] defenses of churches and monasteries or of any other places under our obedience which were built, made, and constructed in these times of troubles and do not serve the defense of the kingdom or important needs of our people, or which, lacking such appurtenances or regular revenues from which they can be kept, are maintained from the properties of other subjects of ours, must be destroyed and demolished between now and the fifteenth day of the next feast of St. George the martyr,[14] and the estates of those who committed the said plunderings from these fortifications ought to be seized for our majesty by a ban or *ispán* or captain, and after these properties have first been seized and compensation has been made for damages and losses in the estates of others, the remainder must be kept for our disposal.

6. Then, that two captains each should be sent and placed in charge by suitable means ordered by a decree immediately to those regions, namely to those of Kassa, Szepes, Zólyom, Trencsén, Zala, and Vas, in which the attacks of certain foreigners[15] are increasing. They will be required to free and to defend with all their might our gentlemen of realm against the insults of the attacks of those enemies in those regions to which each of them was sent, and that they shall not permit further plundering and mutual harm to be done among our gentlemen of realm, but rather that they should take care zealously to render justice and compensation for damages and losses during their term of office, and that they should compel the observance and the fulfilment in the prescribed way of the sentences and orders of our royal selves or of judges to be appointed by us on the above grounds faithfully and without favor or hatred of anyone. However, in case our captains are not powerful enough or have sufficient armed men to do all these things or to rectify other complaints rising from these, then they can ask us and the said barons, knights, and lords undersigned,[16] and then we and the said barons, knights, and lords written below or those whom they would ask among them must and are required to assist without delay, as often as is necessary, as well as all our gentlmen of the realm living under their captaincy after they have been asked, under the penalty of the confiscation of their estates.

7. Then, that these captains must not permit any man to impose or to demand in the future the rents commonly called *hold*[17] on the properties of our loyal subjects, and those who suffer such damages and wrongs, should be granted free and full faculty and the right to proceed legally according to the custom of this kingdom against those who cause, conjure up or do such damages and wrongs among our gentlemen of realm, namely those belonging to our party, mutually among themselves, and justice against such evil-doers must not be denied to any man.

VIII. Insuper ex quo nos unicuique regnicolarum nostrorum, quantum in nobis fuerit, suum ius ministrare et illesum relinquere parati sumus, propterea ut et nos iuribus nostris regalibus ex parte ipsorum regnicolarum nostrorum fraudari non videamur, conclusum est et determinatum ---[18]

8. Furthermore, just as we are prepared to administer his own law to every one of our gentlemen of realm as far as it is up to us and to leave him unmolested, therefore, so that we ourselves should not appear to be defrauded of our royal rights by those same gentlemen of our realm, it has been decided and determined. . .[18]

18 Aprili 1444

Vide praefatiunculam et notas infra paginas 221–24.

Nos Wladislaus dei gratia Hungarie, Polonie, Dalmatie, Croatie etc. rex Lithwanieque princeps supremus et heres Russie ad universorum notitiam harum serie volumus pervenire, quod quamvis hoc preterito tempore, quo pravis pravorum ausibus multa variaque in regno isto nocumenta viguere, sepius quesita sit via, per quam eiuscemodi nociturnitatibus, turbinibus quoque, sed et tot periculis, tot denique dissensionibus et malorum generibus, que pululasse obtigisse et efluxisse iam sub oculis visa sunt,[1] continuatio et occasio clauderetur; quia tamen effrene mentis dissoluta manus cohiberi non facile patitur, quanto mollius incautiusque parabatur reprimi, tanto diuturnior malis peiora iungens perdurabit. Nunc autem, cum in dies magis magisque huius regni turbatio succresceret, visum est communi omnium voto eo celeriori remedio occurrere, quo et amarior tot malorum dilatio sentiretur. Ob hoc post novissimum reditum nostrum ab expeditione exercituali, quam adversus paganos Turcos felicibus divino munimine potiti triumphis transegimus,[2] generali convocatione promulgata convenit prelatorum, baronum, militum et regnicolarum nostrorum in hunc locum multitudo tam magna, quam maior vix umquam in simili congregatione visa fuit, quibus per hos plures iam dies in tractatibus mutuis residentibus, tandem domino volente una nobiscum pro reintegranda pace et concordia mutua agendaque tutela regni huius ad infrascriptos articulos firmissime sub penis infrascriptis observandos devenerunt.

I. Primo, ut recto ordine a capite inceptum videatur, statutum est, ut pro ampliori et validiori potentia et facultate nostra ad nostros regendos quilibet prelatorum, baronum, nobilium et regni procerum nunc hic presentium et etiam absentium, qui scilicet sub nomine et obedientia nostris se hucusque gesserunt et gerent, obligent se nobis per eorum proprias litteras sigillis eorum, quibus utuntur, appensis pro fidelitate observanda, et quod nobis viventibus nullum alium pro rege Hungarie preter nos habebunt et nominabunt, nobisque in omnem eventum assistent et adherebunt.[3] Qui vero pro aliquo fratre suo nunc absente responderet, talis frater absens infra unum terminum sibi per nos deputandum teneatur advenire modo simili nobis se obligaturus.

II. Item, sicut predecessores nostri reges Hungarie habuerunt, conclusum est, ut imposterum omnimodam facultatem auferendi omnes

18 April 1444

For prefatory and explanatory notes, see below, pages 221–24.

We, Wladislas, by the grace of God king of Hungary, Poland, Dalmatia, Croatia, etc., grand prince of Lithuania and heir of Russia, wish to bring to the knowledge of all by these words that even though in this time just past, when, owing to the distorted daring of the depraved, many, and varied harmful things thrived in this kingdom, means have frequently been sought by which the continuance and opportunity for harm, turmoil, numerous dangers, and as many dissensions and kinds of evils, which our eyes have seen to grow, spread and overflow,[1] can be stopped; because a dissolute hand led by an unrestrained mind does not easily tolerate being restrained, and the more gently and carelessly repression is pursued, the longer will the worsening evil last. Now, therefore, since every day upheaval in this kingdom grows more and more, day by day, it seems that the more bitterly felt the spread of evil is, the quicker will a remedy be sought by the common assent of all. Hence, after our recent return from a military campaign, which we conducted against the heathen Turks with happy victories granted by divine help,[2] when a general assembly was called, a greater multitude of our prelates, barons, knights, and gentlemen of the realm came together than had ever been seen in such an assembly. After having held mutual discussions through these many days, they finally, by the Lord's will, agreed as one with us that for the sake of restoring peace and mutual concord as well as for the safety of this kingdom, the articles written below should be kept most firmly under the penalties written below.

1. First, so that things might be undertaken in a proper manner starting at the beginning, it has been decided that in the interest of our fuller and stronger power and capacity to rule our subjects, any one of the prelates, barons, nobles, and lords of the kingdom here present now and also those absent—namely those who so far have acted and act subject to our name and obedience—should promise us by their own charters with their seals, which they use, appended as proof of fidelity, that as long as we live they will have and name no one else except us as king of Hungary, and that they will assist and stand by us in every event.[3] In the case of those who promise on behalf of an absent brother, the absent brother is required to come to us within the term determined for him by us in order to bind himself to us in a similar manner.

2. Then, it has been resolved that henceforth we have, just as the kings of Hungary our predecessors had, every right to withdraw all our

honores et officiolatus nostros habeamus, toties quoties et quandocunque voluerimus, et illis, quibus maluerimus, regnicolis tantum et non alienigenis, conferre valeamus,[4] omnisque dignitarius et officialis huiusmodi honores, dignitates et officiolatus suos, puta palatinus palatinatum, wayuoda wayuodatum, banus banatum, cancellarius cancellariatum, comites comitatus et quoslibet alios honores et officiolatus ad statim ad manus nostras regias resignet per nos hiis, quibus voluerimus, distribuendos. Preterea ordinatum est, ut camare salium nostrorum regalium, tam in partibus Transsiluanensibus, quam Maramorosiensibus sicuti alii officiolatus ad manus nostras regias remittantur disponende per nos de eisdem illis, quibus voluerimus.

III. Item, quia lucrum camare de dicto regno nostro Hungarie, proventus mardurinarum de regno nostro Sclauonie et proventus quinquagesimales de partibus nostris Transsiluanensibus[5] communi omnium regnicolarum nostrorum contributione pro sustentatione curie regie ac defensione regni agenda instituti et dispositi fuerant, et nec ab aliquo regum, predecessorum scilicet nostrorum iidem proventus a corona regia in toto vel in parte alienari debere potuissent, idcirco conclusum est, ut huiusmodi proventus alienati rursum ad coronam regni reintegrentur,[6] et non obstante exemptione qualicunque aut remissione eorundem per quemcunque regum facta, de omnium possessionibus, puta tam nostris regalibus et reginalibus, quam ecclesiasticorum prelatorum baronum et procerum regni ac aliorum possessionatorum hominum exsolvantur integre et sine defectu.

IV. Item de camaris salium tam Transsiluanarum, quam Maramorosiensium partium, de fodinis et montanis urburarum,[7] de proventibus tricesimalibus,[8] civitatum ac Comanorum, Philisteorum[9] et Judeorum[10] conclusum est, ut quia neque nos, neque nostri predecessores reges cuiquam relaxare perpetue, aut pro pignore locare, seu quomodolibet aliter a corona alienare potuimus et potuerunt, ideo debeant corone reappropriari et in manibus nostris resignari.[11]

V. Item conclusum est, quod omnes et singuli ex prelatis, baronibus ac nobilibus regni nostri universas possessiones et bona ac proventus decimales et alios, que minusiuste et illicite ex eis aliquis tenet seu occupavit et usurpavit hiis disturbiorum temporibus ab hiis, qui nobis fideles fuerunt et partem seu adherentiam nostram tenuerunt, eisdem fidelibus nostris remittere et resignare teneantur; et etiam illa, que nos illicite et minus iuste cuipiam donavimus, remittantur, ac etiam illis, qui usque in presentem diem venerunt ad fidelitatem nobis, bona eorum, etiamsi cuipiam per nos donata fuissent, restituantur, et nos contentemus illos, cui ipsa donaveramus, exnunc vel quocunque modo, aut promittamus, quod successive de hiis, que devolventur ad coronam, eos contentabimus.[12]

honors and offices, as often and whenever we wish, and of conferring them on whomever we prefer, provided they are residents of the kingdom and not aliens.[4] And every dignitary and official must immediately resign his honors, dignities, and offices, as, for example, the palatine the palatinate, the voivode the voivodeship, the ban the banate, the chancellor the chancellery, the *ispánok* the counties, and any other honors and offices into our royal hands for distribution by us to whomever we prefer. It was also ordained that the chambers of our royal salts, both in Transylvania and in Máramaros, must be surrendered into our royal hands as with the other offices, for distribution by us to whomever we wish.

3. Then, because the chamber's profit of our said kingdom of Hungary, the revenues of the *mardurina* of our kingdom of Slavonia, and the fiftieth revenues of our Transylvanian regions[5] were instituted and allocated by the common contribution of all our gentlemen of the realm for the sustenance of the royal court and for the defense of the kingdom, and these revenues could not be alienated from the royal crown in whole or in part by any of the kings, our predecessors, therefore, it has been resolved that such alienated revenues must be returned to the crown of the kingdom,[6] and, notwithstanding any reduction granted them by any of the kings, they must be paid from all estates, both those of the king and the queen as well as those of ecclesiastics, prelates, barons and lords of the kingdom and other men of property without fail and in entirety.

4. Then, it has been resolved that the chamber of the salt-works of Transylvania and in Máramaros, dues of mines and mining,[7] and the revenues of the thirtieth,[8] the cities, the Cumans, the Philistines,[9] and the Jews[10] must be returned to the crown and resigned into our hands because we cannot, nor could the kings our predecessors, cede these in perpetuity to any man, or use them as collateral, or in any way alienate them from the crown.[11]

5. Then, it has been resolved that each and every prelate, baron, and noble of our kingdom is required to return and to hand over to our loyal subjects all estates and goods as well as revenues from tithes and other sources, which any of them holds by defective right and illicitly, or in these times of troubles has occupied and usurped from those who were faithful to us and held fast to our cause or adherence; and also those things, which we gave illicitly and by defective right to anyone, must be returned; and the properties of those who up to the present day have come to pledge fidelity to us must be restored, even if they have been given by us to someone else, and we shall compensate those, to whom we had given those things, now or in any other way, and we promise that we shall compensate them in due course from those properties which devolve to the crown.[12]

VI. Item quod illi etiam omnes, qui ex parte alia nobis adversa infra festum Penthecostes proxime venturum[13] nobis ad fidelitatem venerint, tales etiam sub pretacta conclusione quoad restitutionem bonorum ipsorum contineantur, sed contententur, ut supra. Qui autem usque ad terminum pretactum nobis ad fidelitatem venire non curaverint, tales in perpetua nota infidelitatis remaneant[14] et bona ipsorum hiis, quibus voluerimus, conferre valeamus, nec amplius iidem ad gratiam admittantur.

VII. Item, quia ex variatione monete notabilia, ymmo indicibilia regno huic detrimenta provenisse visa sunt, idcirco ad obviandum huiusmodi periculis statutum est, ut nullus ex prelatis et baronibus aut regnicolis nostris monetam quamcunque cudat, nec cudere vel cudi facere presumpmat et valeat, sed solum nos in locis seu cameris, ubi ab antiquo moneta cudi solita fuit, ipsam monetam cudi faciamus, nec nos habeamus facultatem indulgendi cuipiam ipsam cusionem monete sub qualicunque colore, et quod lega ipsius monete, in qua cudi inchoabitur, non possit per nos immutari absque voluntate et scitu regnicolarum nostrorum.[15] Contra premissa autem faciens notam infidelitatis seu falsarii incurrat.

VIII. Item moneta talis cudatur, ut centum denarii et ducenti obuli dentur et cambiantur pro uno floreno auri sub pena premissa.[16]

IX. Item de factis potentiariis conclusum est, quod nos ab illo, cui officia maiora vel minora, puta sive palatinatum sive banatum, vel iudicatum curie aut comitatum contulimus vel contulerimus, talem obligationem recipiamus, quod nec ipse solus iniurias, dampna et nocumenta aut occupationes bonorum faciat, nec fieri per quempiam sub suo officiolatu et honore consentiat seu permittat, nec in hac parte alicui faveat. Quod si talis dignitarius vel comes huiusmodi facta illicita perpetrasse vel aliis in faciendo consensisse aut favorem impendisse vel patrantes non emendasse compertus fuerit, extunc talis mox ipso honore privetur et privatus intelligatur, nec amplius ad tale officium recipi aut promoveri valeat. In iudiciis autem, que wayuoda, banus vel aliquis comes in sua provincia fecerit, cum transmitti in curiam nostram petuntur, teneatur semper defferre appellationi seu transmissioni in curiam nostram regiam, et talis causa in curiam nostram deducta in primo termino, ad quem devenerit, terminetur et ipse wayuoda sive banus vel comes tandem adiudicationem curie nostre exequi teneatur.[17] Quod si idem wayuoda, banus aut comes in dispositione pretacta non perstiterit, aut contra premissa cuipiam favorem exhibuisse visus et compertus fuerit, extunc ultra premissam privationem honoris sui in facto potentie sit convictus; et quod lesis et dampnificatis de propriis eorum bonis satisfactio impendatur. Premissa tamen libertatibus antiquis ecclesiarum non obsistant.[18]

6. Then, that all those who, from the other party opposing us, come to our fidelity before the next feast of Pentecost,[13] shall also be included in the aforesaid resolution in regard to the restoration of properties, and shall be compensated, as above. Those, however, who do not care to come to pledge fidelity to us by the aforesaid date should be treated as perpetual traitors,[14] and we shall have the right to confer their possessions on whomever we wish, nor may they be admitted to grace again.

7. Then, owing to the variation of coinage, considerable—nay, indescribable—harm appears to have been caused to this kingdom. Therefore, to preclude such dangers, it has been ordered that no prelate or baron or any of our gentlemen of the realm may mint or presume or attempt to mint or cause to be minted any money, but we alone may cause money to be minted in places or in chambers where of old money has been customarily minted, nor shall we be able to grant the right to mint money by any means to anyone; and that the alloy of the money, once it has begun to be minted, cannot be changed by us without the will and knowledge of our gentlemen of the realm.[15] Anybody acting against the foregoing will incur the charge of high treason or forgery.

8. Then, money should be minted so that 100 pennies and 200 half-pennies should be given and changed for one gold florin under the above penalty.[16]

9. Then, concerning acts of violent trespass, it has been resolved that we should take such a pledge from all those on whom we have conferred or will confer major or minor offices, be it the palatinate or banate, royal judgeship or the office of *ispán*, that neither they themselves will cause injuries, losses, harm, or occupation of goods, nor will they consent or permit such to be done by anyone subject to their office or honor, nor will they favor anyone in this respect. If such a dignitary or *ispán* is found to have perpetrated such illicit deeds or to have consented to or favored others doing them or not to have punished those committing such deeds, then he shall be deprived of his honor and considered as such, and he is not again to be received or promoted to such an office. Furthermore, when a transfer to our court is sought in the case of trials which a voivode, ban, or any *ispán* may hold in his presence, the latter are required to refer the appeal or transfer to our royal court, and such a case brought to our court must be completed in the first term in which it comes, and then the voivode, ban, or *ispán* is required to implement the judgment of our court.[17] If that voivode, ban, or *ispán* does not abide by the aforesaid decision or he is seen or found to have shown favor to someone contrary to the foregoing, then in addition to the abovementioned deprivation of his honor he should be convicted of violent trespass, and compensation must be given to the damaged and injured party from his own goods. Nevertheless, the foregoing provisions should not restrict the ancient liberties of churches.[18]

X. Item in quolibet comitatu eligantur per communitatem quatuor probi homines ex nobilibus illius comitatus penes comitem et iudices nobilium,[19] qui cum comite ac ipsis iudicibus nobilium et communitate querulantibus iudicium ministrent et dent litteras opportunas. Si qui autem ex ipsis electis actus potentiarios commiserint, tales iudicio comitis et iudicum nobilium ac communitatis subiaceant.

XI. Item iudicia in facto possessionum fiant iuxta consuetudinem regni.[20]

XII. Item omnia fortalitia et castella in parte nostra, ex quibus spolia, nocumenta, exactiones censuum vulgo hold dictorum,[21] furta et alia maleficia commissa sunt, de novo erecta distrahantur et aboleantur.

XIII. Item omnia iudicia et sententie in disturbiis preter illa, que, ubi partes presentes fuere, habita sunt, revocentur et revocata intelligantur.[22]

XIV. Item omnes statutiones de bonis aliorum facte, quarum donationes supra revocate sunt,[23] vigoribus careant, demptis tamen illis, quarum donationes licite per nos de propriis nostris vel devolutis facte sunt.

XV. Item quod nullus ex baronibus aut nobilibus secularibus ecclesias episcopales vel abbatias aut prepposituras seu alias quascunque amplius occupatas teneat, et nec imposterum titulo gubernationis[24] aut iure patronatus vel alio quocunque colore se de huiusmodi ecclesiis intromittat, salvo qui ex fundatione ius patronatus habent.

XVI. Item quod illi, qui pecunias taxe anni preteriti recollectas habuerunt et pro se retinuerunt, ipsas pecunias reddant sub penis pretactis.[25]

XVII. Item quod in progressu regali nostro vel exercituali, vel ad curiam nostram vel ad alia quecunque loca nullus baronum vel aliorum in villis aut opidis, in quibus descensus facient, dampna aliqua inferat, nec in domibus nobilium descendat. Quodsi quicunque huiusmodi dampna intulerint et descensum fecerint, tales mox una evocatoria evocentur in curiam nostram ad proximam octavam,[26] et sive compareat evocatus, sive non, in eodem termino causa sententialiter terminetur.[27]

XVIII. Item de restitutionibus jobagionum sine licentia recedentium teneatur antiqua consuetudo et pena.[28]

XIX. Item quicunque aliis de parte nostra intulerint dampna extra servitia nostra vel regni nostri in domo persistendo,[29] coram iudicibus prefatis iuxta consuetudinem regni per dampnificatos in causam attrahi valeant et per eosdem iudices iuxta iudicata ad satisfationem compellantur.

10. Then, in every county, four trustworthy men must be elected by the community from the nobles of that county to join the *ispán* and the magistrates,[19] who with the *ispán* and the magistrates and the community will render judgment to plaintiffs and will issue the appropriate documents. If anyone of those elected commits acts of violent trespass, he should be subject to the judgment of the *ispán*, the magistrates, and the community.

11. Then, trials concerning estates must be conducted according to the custom of the kingdom.[20]

12. Then, all fortifications and castles newly constructed in our domain from which plunderings, destruction, exactions of the rents commonly called *hold*,[21] thefts, and other evil deeds were committed must be razed and destroyed.

13. Then, all judgments and sentences which were passed during these troubles are revoked and held as revoked, except those which were passed in the presence of the litigants.[22]

14. Then, all measures taken concerning the goods of those whose donations were revoked above[23] shall be null and void, except for those whose grant was legitimately made by us from our own properties or those devolved to us.

15. Then, that no baron or secular noble may occupy any longer episcopal churches, abbacies, or priories, or any other churches, nor henceforth may he interfere with such churches by a claim to secular protection[24] or right of patronage or any other title, except those who from the foundation have the right of patronage.

16. Then, that those who had money collected for the tax of the last year and have retained it for themselves must return the money under the abovementioned penalties.[25]

17. Then, that no baron or any other person should cause any damage in the villages or towns where he takes lodgings during our royal travels or military campaigns or on his way to our court or elsewhere, nor should he billet in the houses of nobles. If, however, anyone does inflict such losses and exacts hospitality, he should be summoned with one summons to our court for the next octavial term,[26] and, whether the person summoned appears or not, the case must be concluded with a sentence in the same term.[27]

18. Then, concerning the recovery of tenants absconding without licence, the ancient custom and punishment must be followed.[28]

19. Then, those not in our service, nor that of our kingdom, who remained at home, but inflicted damages to others who are on our side,[29] may be prosecuted by the damaged party before the aforementioned judges, according to the custom of the kingdom, and should be compelled by the same judges to give satisfaction in accordance with the judgment.

XX. Item quicunque hiis disturbiorum temporibus possessiones aliorum indebite occupaverunt, usque festum Penthecostes proxime venturum easdem remittant et absque subterfugio resignent. Quod si non fecerint, evocentur ad proximam octavam, et sive compareant, sive non, sententia finalis in eadem octava terminetur. De factis autem potentiariis post pridiernum nostrum decretum commissis modo simili usque dictum festum Penthecostes lesis et dampnificatis satisfactio impendatur. Quod si qui non fecerint, similiter ad proximam octavam evocentur et in eadem octava causa sententialiter terminetur.

XXI. Item redemptiones litterarum et solutiones testimoniorum capituli vel conventus fiant secundum decretum condam domini imperatoris.[30]

XXII. Item quod tributa omnia, que tam per condam dominum Albertum regem predecessorem nostrum, quam per nostram maiestatem donata essent, revocentur et revocata habeantur.[31]

XXIII. Item quod comes parochialis in possessionibus nobilium non descendat, et si descenderit, dampna non inferat; quod si fecerit, in facto potentie convincatur, demptis solummodo antiquis consuetudinibus et exactionibus birsagiorum.

XXIV. Item quicunque prelatorum, baronum et regni nobilium in presentia nostre maiestatis personali aut palatini seu iudicis curie nostre durante presenti congregatione repertus et per quemcunque citatus fuerit, teneatur super patratis post decretum anni iam elapsi[32] respondere ad obiecta. Quodsi presumptione ductus comparere rennuerit, extunc mox contra talem sententia detur et emanetur.

XXV. Item quicunque prelatorum, baronum et regni nobilium aut aliorum possessionatorum hominum occupationes possessionum aut spoliationes, sive nobilium captivationes aut interemptiones, sed et alia similia facta amodo deinceps perpetraverint, tales per hominem nostrum regium presente testimonio capituli vel conventus ad primam octavam cum insinuatione evocentur; ipsique patratores huiusmodi actuum potentiariorum ad ipsam octavam venire teneantur; et ipsis partibus comparentibus fiat iudicium partes inter easdem, causaque huiusmodi nec ab eadem octava per litteras regias aut per alium quemcunque modum ulterius differatur. Si vero evocatus non comparuerit, non obstante ipsius absentia, sententia capitalis cum amissione bonorum suorum contra talem pronuncietur et emanetur; sententiamque ipsam exequantur tandem presentibus hominibus nostris et capitularibus seu conventualibus, si necesse fuerit, comites parochiales et alii premisso modo deputati sine omni negligentia.[33]

XXVI. Item quod universe cause, que in ultima octava tempore predicti condam Alberti regis habite erant et vertebantur, in eodem statu, in quo tunc existebant, in octavis festi beati Jacobi apostoli proxime venturi[34] inchoventur et verti debeant iuxta antiquam consuetudinem regni.

20. Then, any men who in these times of troubles have occupied the estates of others improperly must remit and resign them without subterfuge before the next feast of Pentecost. If they do not do this, they must be summoned to the next octave, and, whether they appear or not, a final sentence must be given in that octave. Concerning acts of violent trespass committed after our previous decree, compensation for damages and losses must similarly be paid before the said feast of Pentecost. Culprits who fail do so must be summoned similarly to the next octave, and the case must be terminated with a sentence in the same octave.

21. Then, fees for charters and payments for testimonies of a chapter or convent should be paid according to the decree of the late lord emperor.[30]

22. Then, that all tolls, which were granted by the late lord king Albert, our predecessor, and by our majesty, are revoked and must be kept revoked.[31]

23. Then, that no *ispán* of a county should sojourn on the estates of nobles, but if he does, he should not cause harm; if he does so, he must be convicted of an act of violent trespass unless there exists some ancient custom or he is collecting fines.

24. Then, if any prelate, baron, or noble of the kingdom, who in the personal presence of our majesty or of the palatine or of our judge royal during the present assembly has been identified and accused by someone, he is required to reply to the accusations on what was done after last year's decree.[32] If, guided by presumption, he refuses to appear, then a sentence against such a man must be given and pronounced.

25. Then, if any prelate, baron, or noble of the kingdom or any other men of property who henceforth in the future should occupy or plunder estates, or capture and kill nobles, or commit other similar deeds, must be summoned by final summons through our royal bailiff in the presence of a witness from a chapter or convent to the first octave; these perpetrators of acts of violent trespass are required to come personally to that octave; and when the parties have appeared, a trial should be conducted, and such a case may not be prorogued beyond that octave by royal letters or any other means. If the man summoned does not appear, notwithstanding his absence, a capital sentence with the loss of his goods must be passed and pronounced against him; our bailiffs and the men of the chapter or convent, or, if necessary, the *ispán* of the county and others deputed in the aforesaid manner must execute that sentence without any negligence.[33]

26. Then, that all cases which were conducted and treated in the last octave in the time of the said late King Albert must be resumed at whatever stage they were then and continued in the next octave of the feast of St. James the Apostle,[34] according to the ancient custom of the realm.

XXVII. Item quod tempore istorum disturbiorum quecunque littere sub quacunque forma verborum sub sigillis capitulorum vel conventuum illorum, qui per manus potentum tenti fuissent, emanate extitissent, tales cassate et vigoribus cariture habeantur.[35]

XXVIII. Item quod nullus omnino hominum gentes forenses et extraneas ad hoc regnum nostrum causa inferendi malum inducat sub pena amissionis capitis et omnium bonorum suorum.[36]

XXIX. Item quod nullus prelatorum, baronum et regni procerum preter consensum nostrum cum quibuscunque hominibus nobis et regno nostro adversantibus treugas inire presumpmat.[37]

XXX. Item quod quicunque in premissis non prestiterit et monitus per litteras nostras se non emendaverit, talis pro ipso facto in pena facti potentialis convincatur. Et quod quicunque mandatis nostris regiis, licitis tamen et iustis, non paruerit et monitus se non excusaverit, in simili pena convincatur ipso facto.

XXXI. Ut autem iidem nostri fideles subnominati exinde primum a nobis certitudinem sumpmant, presentium tenore et vigore in verbo nostro regio iureiurando promittimus, nos ea omnia, que in prescriptis articulis notificata et declarata sunt, ex nostri parte irrefragabiliter observare velle et tenere per aliosque, qui forsitan in hac parte rebelles comperti fuerint, cum adiutorio, consilio et assistentia ipsorum infranominatorum fidelium nostrorum teneri facere et observari, et quod ad inferendas penas pretactas singulis talibus, qui hiis premissis repugnare presumpserint, toto posse cum eisdem nostris fidelibus intendemus, et si opportunum fuerit, procedemus, in omnem eventum eis in hac parte indivisibiliter assistemus faciemusque et exequemur etiam alia omnia, que nobis cum eorum consilio in hac re et circa eam incubuerint facienda.

In quorum omnium premissorum testimonium presentes concessimus litteras sigilli nostri, quo uti rex Hungarie utimur, appensione munitas. Datum Bude, decimo octavo die mensis Aprilis, que est sabbatum proximum post festum Pasce domini, anno eiusdem millesimo quadringentesimo quadragesimo quarto.

XXXII. Intelligatur etiam conclusum in premissis, quod nec perpetuitates, nec beneficia, nec officolatus, sed neque castellanatus alienigenis conferamus, ymmo et collata talibus ab eisdem auferamus, excepto episcopatu Transsiluanensi per nos domino Matheo Polono[38] collato. Hec dispositio facta est per prelatos, barones, milites, proceres et nobiles infrascriptos suis et communitatis totius regni Hungarie predicti nominibus et personis non obstante, si perprius in quocunque decreto huius contrarium fuisset. Datum ut supra.

Et nos Simon de Rozgon episcopus Agriensis, regie maiestatis sumpmus cancellarius, Johannes Waradiensis, Mathias Wesprimiensis, Petrus Chanadiensis, alter Petrus Waciensis et Demetrius Tininiensis

27. Then, that any charters issued in whatever form of words in these times of troubles under the seals of any chapter or convent, which was in the hands of some powerful man, must be regarded as cancelled and without force.[35]

28. Then, that no man may bring in any foreigners or strangers to our kingdom in order to inflict evil under the penalty of the loss of his head and all of his goods.[36]

29. Then, that no prelate, baron, or lord of the kingdom may presume to make treaties without our knowledge with anyone who is an enemy of ours and of our kingdom.[37]

30. Then, that anyone who does not obey the foregoing and does not mend his ways after having been warned by our letters will be convicted for this action of an act of violent trespass. And he who does not follow our legitimate and just royal orders and, after having been warned, does not excuse himself will also be convicted of the same penalty for his failure.

31. In order that our loyal subjects named below might be confident in us, we promise by the words and force of these presents and swear by our royal word, that we will observe unswervingly on our part and to make others, who perhaps have been found rebels in this matter, observe all those things which were announced and set out in the foregoing articles and to cause them to be held and observed with the help, counsel, and assistance of our loyal subjects named below, and that we intend to inflict the aforementioned penalties on all those who presume to reject these foregoing with all our power, together with our faithful servants. And, if it is suitable, we shall proceed in any event to assist, achieve, and fulfill together with them all other things which are incumbent on us and related to this matter with their counsel.

In witness of all the foregoing we have granted the present charter validated by the appending of our seal, which we use as king of Hungary. Given at Buda, on the eighteenth day of the month of April, which is the next Saturday after the feast of Easter, one thousand, four hundred and forty four.

32. It is also understood to be included in the preceding that we shall not confer donations in perpetuity, benefices, offices, or castellanies on foreigners, and shall even remove those conferred on such men from them, with the exception of the bishopric of Transylvania conferred by us on the lord Matthew the Pole.[38] This decision has been passed by the prelates, barons, knights, lords, and nobles written below in their own names and that of the said community of the whole kingdom of Hungary, notwithstanding if earlier there was something contrary to this in any decree. Given as above.

And we Simon of Rozgony, bishop of Eger and archchancellor of the royal majesty, bishops John of Várad, Matthias of Veszprém, Peter of Csanád, the other Peter of Vác and Demetrius of Knin, George,

ecclesiarum episcopi, Georgius despotus Rascie, Laurentius de Hedrehwara regni Hungarie palatinus, Nicolaus de Wylak et Johannes de Hwnyad wayuode Transsiluanenses, Michael Jakch de Kwsal alias similiter wayuoda Transsiluanensis, Georgius de Rozgon iudex curie domini regis et comes Posoniensis, Ffranko comes Cetine, regni Sclauonie banus, Emericus de Hedrehwara banus Machouiensis, Stephanus de Bathor alias similiter iudex curie regie, Ladislaus de Palowcz magister curie domini regis, Emericus, Ladislaus, et Stephanus de Pelsewcz, Johannes de Peren comes de Vgocha, Simon de dicta Palowcz magister agazonum regalium, Michael Orzaag de Gwth sumpmus thezaurarius domini regis, Paulus filius bani de Alsolindwa, Henricus filius wayuode de Thamasy comes de Posega, Johannes senior de Peren, Simon Zudar de Olnod magister pincernarum regalium, Johannes Orzaag de Gwth predicta magister thauarnicorum regalium, Stephanus de Homonna, Ladislaus de Zechen comes Neugradiensis, Johannes Kompolth de Nana, Ladislaus filius wayuode de Lewa, Johannes de Korogh, Stephanus et Detricus Poharnok de Berzeuicze comites Hewesienses, Nicolaus et Paulus de Peren, Ladislaus Rykalff comes Liptouiensis, Silvester de Thorna, Georgius filius Lorandi de Serke, Ladislaus de Nazpal, Nicolaus et Dominicus de Kyswarda, Akus de Chap, Ladislaus de Naghmihal, Paulus et Philipus de Zekchew, Ladislaus iunior et Petrus Jakch de Kusal, Ladislaus Pethew de Gerse comes Zaladiensis, uterque Johannes Fforgacz dicti de Gymes, Rupertus de Thar, Paulus de Hedrehwara, Emericus filius Johannis et Ders filius bani de Zerdahel, Nicolaus Anthimi de Thapson, Nicolaus filius Lorandi de Berzencze, Nicolaus de Beltevk, Ffrank de antefata Gwth, Gregorius Bado et Pangracius de Dengeleg vicewayuode Transsiluanenses, Johannes de Somos, Michael de Beel, alter Michael de Cyl, Ladislaus de Zenthmihal, Georgius Orros, Demetrius de Pam, Ladislaus de Thold, Petrus Zopa, alter Petrus Thwz de Lak, Michael Etre, Nicolaus filius Draag, Ladislaus Tythews de Bathmonostra, Ladislaus de Zeche, Andreas de Anual, Thomas Zyrke, Sandrinus de Helemba, Simon de BodogAzzonfalwa, Michael Poharnok, Georgius de Sebes, Johannes de Zana, alter Johannes de Solyag, Michael de Izmen, Path de Gywla, Michael Pooch, Johannes de Kallo, Nicolaus de Zakal, Petrus de Ugra, Nicolaus Sobonya, Andreas de Kozar, Ladislaus de Maroth pridem banus Machouiensis, Raphael Herczeg electus ecclesie Boznensis, Michael abbas Simigiensis, Clemens de Thapan, Sebastianus de Zend, Nicolaus de Zenthmihal, Michael de Philpes, Brictius de Gych, Nicolaus Nyakathlan de Thytews, Georgius Orros de Seryen, Johannes et Thomas filii Ipoliti de Gywrke, Petrus de Tetetlen, Stephanus Danch de Maczadonya, Georgius de Maryas, Thomas Chirke de Poly, Gywla de Ratold, Georgius de ZenthJanus, Bernardus de Dengeleg, Johannes de Apay, Nicolaus Kwn de Kessenew, Johannes de Scepus, Ladislaus de Myske, Stephanus de Bayon, Nicolaus de

despot of Serbia, Lawrence of Hédervár, palatine of the kingdom of Hungary, Nicholas of Újlak and John Hunyadi, voivodes of Transylvania, Michael Jakcs of Kusaly, former voivode of Transylvania, George of Rozgony, judge royal and *ispán* of Pozsony, Franko count of Cetina, ban of the kingdom of Slavonia, Emerich of Hédervár, ban of Macsó, Stephen of Bátor, former judge royal, Ladislas of Pálóc, Master of the Royal Court, Emerich, Ladislas and Stephen of Pelsőc, John of Perény, *ispán* of Ugocsa, Simon of the said Pálóc, Master of the Royal Horse, Michael Ország of Gút, chief treasurer of the lord king, Paul, son of the ban of Alsólendva, Henry, son of the voivode, of Tamási, *ispán* of Pozsega, the elder John of Perény, Simon Cudar of Ónod, Master of the Cupbearers, John Ország of the said Gút, Master of the Royal Treasury, Stephen of Homonna, Ladislas of Szécsény, *ispán* of Nógrád, John Kompolt of Nána, Ladislas, son of the voivode, of Léva, John of Kórógy, Stephen and Detricus Pohárnok of Berzevice, *ispánok* of Heves, Nicholas and Paul of Perény, Ladislas Rikalf, *ispán* of Liptó, Sylvester of Torna, George son of Roland of Serke, Ladislas of Necpá, Nicholas and Dominic of Kisvárda, Akusius of Csap, Ladislas of Nagymihály, Paul and Philip of Szekcső, Ladislas jr. and Peter Jakcs of Kusaly, Ladislas Pető of Gerse, *ispán* of Zala, both Johns Forgács of Gimes, Rupert of Tar, Paul of Hédervár, Emerich, son of John and Ders son of the ban, of Szerdahely, Nicholas Antimus of Tapsony, Nicholas son of Roland of Berzence, Nicholas of Béltek, Frank of the aforementioned Gút, George Bodó and Pancrace of Dengeleg, vice-voivodes of Transylvania, John of Somos, Michael of Bóly, the other Michael of Cil, Ladislas of Szentmihály, George Orros, Demetrius of Pány, Ladislas of Told, Peter Zopa, the other Peter Tuz of Lak, Michael Ettre, Nicholas Drágfi, Ladislas Töttös of Bátmonostora, Ladislas of Szöcsény, Andrew of Hanva, Thomas Csirke, Sandrinus of Helemba, Simon of Boldogasszonyfalva, Michael Pohárnok, George of Sebes, John of Zana, the other John of Sólyag, Michael of Izmény, Pat of Gyula, Michael Pócs, John of Kálló, Nicholas of Szakoly, Peter of Ugra, Nicholas Szobonya, Andrew of Kozár, Ladislas of Marót, former ban of Macsó, Raphael Herceg, bishop-elect of Bosnia, Michael, abbot of Somogyvár, Clement Tapán, Sebastian of Szend, Nicholas of Szentmihály, Michael of Fülpös, Brictius of Gic, Nicholas Nyakatlan of Töttös, George Orros of Serjé, John and Thomas, sons of Hyppolit of Györke, Peter of Tetétlen, Stephen Dancs of Macedónia, George Máriási, Thomas Csirke of Pólyi, Gyula of Rátót, George of Szentjános, Bernard of Dengeleg, John of Apagy, Nicholas Kun of Besenyő, John of Szepes, Ladislas of Miske, Stephen of Bajon, Nicholas of Osgyán, Peter

Ozdyan, Petrus de Pap, Johannes de Ina, Ladislaus filius Mathei de Menche, Johannes de Chaan, Colomanus de Dewregd, Paulus Paznan, Daniel de Kustan, Ladislaus de Paka, Ladislaus de Tetetlen, Ladislaus de Horth, Georgius de Rohman, Petrus de Hangon, Stephanus de Janusy, Michael Barowcz de Wislas, Martinus prepositus de Posega, Michael de Gench, Johannes filius Stephani de Zenthmihal, Georgius de Rathan, Nicolaus de Zombor, Gregorius Josa de Galya, Ladislaus de Chepon, Georgius de Gergellaka, Ladislaus de Somos, Ladislaus de Rohman, Ladislaus de Zelemyr, Gaspar de Were, Simon de Hutichyna et Mathias de Klisich de regno Croatie, Demetrius de Thapaz, Georgius de Megyurechya, Egidius de Peder, Johannes de Zytha, Ladislaus litteratus de Pethke, Albertus litteratus de Zenthmarthon, Johannes de Bakta, Sandrinus de Kewde, Mathias de eadem, Stephanus de Dombo, Andreas de Stanch, Sebastianus de Kolyn, Ladislaus Gagan de Gywrky, Ladislaus Hernad de Hernadfalwa, Michael de Monak, Matheus de Tofev, Nicolaus de Alak, Jacobus de Pelys, Andreas de Lukafalwa, Petrus Fanch de Gordwa, Laurentius de Keer, Jacobus de Leztemeer, Vincentius de Ruzka, Ladislaus de Irsa, Stephanus de Laczk, Ladislaus filius Abrahe de Gerla, Nicolaus filius Petri de Zenthlelek, Dionisius de Zeech, Blasius de Bewren, Ladislaus de Myske, Elias de Kecczer, Nicolaus Warias, Georgius Orzag de Gwth, Marcus de Nadan, Ladislaus de Monostor, Georgius de Wiccza, Gaspar et Georgius de Hathna, Benedictus de Lykwa, Bartholomeus abbas de Borsmonostra, Georgius prepositus Scepesiensis, Stephanus filius Georgii de Telekes, Michael Aztalnok de Herman, Benedictus de Zempes, Sigismundus de Chap, Benedictus de Bewken, Laurentius de Cheged, Ladislaus de Bolyan, Petrus de Kemend, Petrus de Berenthe, Benedictus de Wamos, Ladislaus de Nytazeg, Georgius de Domanhyda, Johannes de Lyzka, Jacobus de Rypak, Oswaldus Feyer, Jacobus de Chepen, Dionisius de Wag, Johannes Bak de Berend, Valentinus de Magofalva, Blasius de Dobo, Martinus de Pethenye, Johannes filius Viti de Mohora, Johannes de Kalna, Laurentius de Kallo, Paulus de Zerdahel, Georgius de Bathor, Johannes de Wask, Clemens de Kesy, Andreas de Jakabfalwa, Johannes Kewtheu de Kewthewgyan, Andreas de Kohar, Ladislaus de Wesen, Petrus de Basky, Zorardus de Zenthersebeth et Ladislaus de Thapalowcz,[39] ceterique proceres et regni nobiles in presenti congregatione constituti fatemur omnia et singula superius descripta quoad omnes eorum articulos de nostro communi consilio, deliberatione et assensu acta et conclusa fuisse et esse, et propter hoc ea omnia, que superius describuntur, promittimus bona fide inviolabiliter observare et per alios, qui hiis premissis in parte vel in toto contraire vellent, omni modo et via opportunis totis viribus observari facere, presentium, quibus iuxta sigillum regale sigilla nostra appensa sunt, testimonio mediante. Datum ut supra.[40]

of Papi, John of *Ina*, Ladislas son of Matthew of *Menche*, John of Csány, Coloman of Dörögd, Paul Pázmány, Daniel of Kustán, Ladislas of Paka, Ladislas of Tetétlen, Ladislas of Hort, George of Rohmány, Peter of Hangony, Stephen of Jánosi, Michael Barocz of Vizslás, provost Martin of Pozsega, Michael of Gencs, John, son of Stephen, of Szentmihály, George of Ráton, Nicholas of Zombor, Gregory Józsa of Gallya, Ladislas of Csépán, George of Gergelylaka, Ladislas of Somos, Ladislas of Rohmány, Ladislas of Zelemér, Caspar of Vere, Simon of Hutichyna and Matthias of Klišić from the kingdom of Croatia, Demetrius of Tapász, George of Megyericse, Giles of Peder, John of *Zytha*, the learned Ladislas of Petke, the learned Albert of Szentmárton, John of Bakta, Sandrinus of Réde, Matthias from the same place, Stephen of Dombó, Andrew of Sztáncs, Sebastian of Kolyn, Ladislas Gógán of Gywrky, Ladislas Hernád of Hernádfalva, Michael of Monok, Matthew of Tófő, Nicholas of Alag, James of Pilis, Andrew of Lukafalva, Peter Fancs of Gordova, Lawrence of Kér, James of Lesztemér, Vincent of Ruszka, Ladislas of Irsa, Stephen of Laczk, Ladislas, son of Abraham, of Gerla, Nicholas, son of Peter, of Szentlélek, Dennis of Zech, Blaise of Berény, Ladislas of Miske, Elias of Keczer, Nicholas Varjas, George Ország of Gút, Mark of Nadány, Ladislas of Monostor, George of Vica, Caspar and George of Hatna, Benedict of Likva, Bartholomew, abbot of Borsmonostor, George, provost of Szepes, Stephen, son of George of Telekes, Michael Asztalnok of Hermán, Benedict of Zempes, Sigismund of Csap, Benedict of Bökény, Lawrence of Csegöd, Ladislas of Polyán, Peter of Kemend, Peter of Berente, Benedict of Vámos, Ladislas of Nyitraszeg, George of Dománhida, John of Liszka, James of Ripak, Oswald Fejér, James of Chepen, Dennis of Vág, John Bak of Berend, Valentine de Makófalva, Blaise of Dobó, Martin of Petenye, John, son of Vitus of Mohora, John of Kálna, Lawrence of Kálló, Paul of Szerdahely, George of Bátor, John Vaski, Clement of Keszi, Andrew of Jakabfalva, John Köte of Kötegyán, Andrew of Kohár, Ladislas of Vezseny, Peter of Bask, Zoárd of Szenterzsébet, Ladislas of Tapalóc,[39] and the other lords and nobles of the kingdom constituted in the present assembly acknowledge all things described above as far as all their articles have been and are made and concluded from our common council, deliberation and assent, and because of this we promise to observe inviolably in good faith all things, which are described above, and to cause them to be observed by others, who might wish to act against the preceding articles in part or in whole, in every way and by the way of all appropriate force, by witness of those present, whose seals are appended next to our royal seal.[40] Given as above.

7 Maii 1445

Vide praefatiunculam et notas infra paginas 225–28.

Nos universi prelati, barones, milites, nobiles ac civitatenses regnicoleque regni Hungarie in presenti generali congregatione Pestiensi pro reformanda pace et reipublice utilitate eiusdem regni insimul congregati presentium serie ad universorum volumus notitiam devenire, quod cum occulto dei iudicio regnum hoc Hungarie, quod Christi fidelium propugnaculum existit,[1] ex sui intrinseca divisione et guerrarum intestina concitatione hiis temporibus cepisset fluctuare et in casus periculosissimos proh dolor devenire, ita quod patrimonium Jesu Christi, ecclesie videlicet et ecclesiarum prelati ac barones unacum nobilibus utriusque sexus et incolis ipsius regni nostri per paganos aliasque circumadiacentium regionum nationes, sed et per intraneos inquietos malefactores in omnium facultatum suarum invasione et vastatione, prede continue, incendiorum et aliorum maleficiorum universorum commissione tantam passi fuere oppressionem et dampnificationem, quod nisi altissimi dei gratia celeris provisionis remedio humanis etiam sollicitationibus occurrentibus fuerit opportune provisum, regnum hoc ad extremam devenire cernebatur periclitationem, maxime considerato casu illo magis periculosiori, qui dei ex permissione regie maiestati anno proxime elapso ex causa fidei et Christiane defensionis cum regnicolis contra paganos Turcos, videlicet istius regni nostri atrocissimos et infestissimos emulos usque ad fines regni Bulgarie penes Nigrum Mare proficiscenti et conflictum cum paganis ipsis facienti taliter acciderit,[2] quod usque ad septimum mensem conflictus sui nulla de eius reditu haberi potuit certitudo. Ne tamen per huiusmodi divisionem nostram et intestinam guerram maiora pericula et graviora mala nobis et ipsi regno per eiusdem anichilationem subsequi contingat, inter nos variis hincinde habitis tractatibus respectibusque et difficultatibus ad talem devenimus concordie unionem, quod si supradicta regia maiestas usque octavum diem festi sancte Trinitatis proxime venturum[3] non redierit, aut de vita sua per nostrum nuncium ea de causa nunc ad Poloniam transmissum plena et indubitata certitudo reportata non fuerit, extunc omnes universaliter illustrissimum principem dominum Ladislaum natum condam domini nostri Alberti regis Hungarie, si et in casu, quo nobis eundem cum sacra regni huius corona restituere et in medium nostri dominus rex Romanorum, in cuius manibus ad presens consistunt, dare voluerit dederitque et de facto assignaverit,[4] in verum et legittimum regem Hungarie et dominum nostrum assumemus et pro rege

7 May 1445

For prefatory and explanatory notes, see below, pages 225–28.

We, all the prelates, barons, knights, nobles, townsmen, and gentlemen of the realm of the kingdom of Hungary gathered in the present general assembly at Pest for the restoration of peace and the profit of the commonwealth of the same kingdom, wish to make known to all, that by the inscrutable judgment of God this kingdom of Hungary, which is the bulwark of Christ's faithful,[1] owing to internal division and the passions of internecine war, began in these times to be shaken and has, alas, fallen into a most perilous state, so that the patrimony of Jesus Christ, namely, the churches and the prelates of the churches, as well as the barons, nobles of either sex, and the inhabitants of our kingdom have suffered so many invasions and devastations, continual plunderings in every possible way, losses by arson, and many other kinds of evils not only from pagans and other nations of surrounding regions but also from lawless native evil-doers, that unless swift remedy is provided by the grace of God most high and also by concurrent human effort, this kingdom may very well fall into final decline. Above all, this very dangerous situation has been considered, that by the permission of God last year, the royal majesty, for the cause of the faith and the defense of Christians with the gentlemen of the realm set out for the borders of the kingdom of Bulgaria as far as the Black Sea against the pagan Turks, these most violent and outrageous enemies of this kingdom of ours, and seven months after the battle with the pagans took place[2] it has not been possible to receive certain knowledge of his return. To avoid that, through this dissension and internecine war of ours, greater dangers and worse evils come upon us and the kingdom, leading to its extinction, we have reached among ourselves through various discussions, considerations, against all obstacles such an agreement of concord that, if the aforesaid royal majesty will not have returned before the eighth day after the next feast of the Holy Trinity,[3] or full and certain knowledge of his life is not brought by our messenger sent now to Poland concerning this matter, then we all together will accept the most illustrious prince lord Ladislas, born of our late lord Albert, king of Hungary, as the true and legitimate king of Hungary and our lord, and we shall consider and hold him as king for the future while life is granted to him, provided and if the lord king of the Romans, in whose hands he is at present, is willing to hand over and will hand over and in fact entrusts him to us and restores him to our midst, together with the Holy Crown of this kingdom.[4] In the

habebimus et tenebimus vita semper sibi comite in futurum. Casu autem, quo eorundem restitutio et in medium nostri assignatio nobis fuerit recusata, in nullo sibi, scilicet Ladislao principi volumus esse obligati; quin ymo huius regni moderno statu et necessitate requirentibus providebimus de rege et principe, cuius sub regimine ipsum regnum a suis periculis et oppressionibus valeat opportune liberari et in statu tranquillo et pacifico permanere. Et ut huiusmodi dissensionis et divisionis nostre multiplicata materia sopiatur, malaque predicta in antea non committantur et pax pristina reformetur, subscriptas dispositiones effective observandas in hac generali nostra congregatione duximus proinde ordinandas.

I. Primo dispositum est, quod omnes occupationes castrorum possessionumque et terrarum, generaliterque aliorum quorumlibet iurium et bonorum, sive vigore donationum per regiam vel reginalem maiestates, vel propria temeritate seu expugnatione per quoscunque, Hungaros scilicet, Bohemos, Polonos, Thewtunicos seu cuiuscunque alterius linguagii homines quorumcunque a tempore inceptionis presentium guerrarum facte usque ad octavum diem dicti festi sancte Trinitatis[5] hiis, apud quos tempore inceptionis huiusmodi guerrarum eedem extiterunt, sub pena perpetue infidelitatis remittantur;[6] et signanter hii, qui in presenti congregatione sunt presentes, promittant se velle remittere et presenti ordinationi parere et obedire effective, ut sic inter eos mutuus amor et fraternalis dilectio odio et rancore exclusis vigeat et permanere dinoscatur.

II. Item quod omnes donationes post mortem dicti condam comini Alberti regis de possessionibus regalibus et ad regium ius spectantibus per regiam vel reginalem maiestates facte[7] firmari vel infirmari differantur usque ad tempus coronationis regis.

III. Item de actibus potentiariis hiis temporibus disturbiorum perpetratis iudicium similiter ad illud tempus differatur, exceptis dumtaxat interemptionibus hominum, possessionum occupationibus, litteralium instrumentorum ablationibus ac virginum et honestarum dominarum dehonestationibus, de quibus iudicium et iustitia petentibus ministretur per iudicem competentem.[8]

IV. Item omnia fortalitia in ipso disturbio erecta usque ad octavum diem prefati festi sancte Trinitatis[9] per eos, qui ea erexerunt vel nunc possident, sub pena infidelitatis deponantur; in partibus tamen regni Sclauonie penes fluvium Zawa et Transsiluanis ac Posega[10] fortalitia propter metum Turcorum facta, si que ex eis deponi debeant, relinquantur voluntati nobilium partium earundem et deponenda sub predictis penis deponantur, exceptis quinque castris, videlicet castro Palatha Nicolai wayuode in comitatu Albensi[11] ac Werewcze Emerici filii wayuode de Marczali in regno Sclauonie,[12] necnon Wamus Emerici de Pelsewcz in comitatu de Borsod, item Nana Johannis de Kompolth in Hewesiensi[13] et Pelsewcz Nicolai et Stephani de eadem Pelsewcz in

case of refusal of his being returned and entrusted to our midst, we wish not to be obligated to him, namely Prince Ladislas, in any way; moreover, we shall provide such a king and prince for the requirements of the present state and needs of this kingdom under whose rule the kingdom can suitably be freed from its dangers and oppressions and remain in a peaceful and tranquil condition. And in order that the manifold cause of our dissension and division may be removed and that the said evils may not be committed henceforth, but the earlier peace be restored, we in this general assembly of ours have formulated the decisions written below to be observed effectively and ordained henceforward.

1. First, it has been decided that all occupations of castles, estates, and lands, and generally of any other rights and goods, whether by a grant from the king's or the queen's majesty, or by his own boldness and violence by anyone, whether Hungarian, Czech, Pole, German, or one of any other language, perpetrated from the time of the beginning of the present wars up to the eighth day after the said feast of the Holy Trinity,[5] must be handed over to those whose they were at the time of the beginning of the wars, under penalty of perpetual treason;[6] and, in particular, those who are present at this assembly must promise to be willing to hand them over and thus effectively fulfill and obey the present command, so that mutual love and affection can flourish and be sustained among them, eliminating hatred and rancor.

2. Then, that the confirmation or cancellation of all grants made after the death of the said late lord King Albert by the king's or the queen's majesty[7] from the royal estates or from those pertaining to royal right must be delayed until the time of the coronation of a king.

3. Then, similarly, trials regarding acts of violent trespass perpetrated in these times of troubles must be deferred to that time, with the exception, of course, of killing of men, occupation of estates, theft of written instruments, and rape of virgins and honest matrons, concerning which, trial and justice must be administered to those seeking it by an appropriate judge.[8]

4. Then, all fortifications built in these troubles must be demolished by the eighth day after the said feast of the Holy Trinity[9] by those who built them or now hold them, under penalty of treason. However, the fortifications built for fear of the Turks in the regions of the kingdom of Slavonia along the Sava River, in Transylvania, and in Pozsega,[10] if they are among those which must be demolished, may be left by the will of the nobles of those same regions while those that must be demolished should be demolished under the aforesaid penalties, except for five castles, namely Palota of the voivode Nicholas in Co. Fehér,[11] Verőce of Emerich of Marczal, son of the voivode in the kingdom of Slavonia,[12] Vámos of Emerich of Pelsőc in Co. Borsod, Nána of John of

Gewmeriensi comitatibus existentibus[14] et de eorundem propriis domibus fabricatis, que castra ipsis dominis unanimi et pari consensu tenere et habere permisimus atque relinquimus. Ita tamen, quod ipsa castra de propriis proventibus conserventur et ceteris nulla spolia, dampnificationes seu quascunque molestias de eisdem inferant, neque ad labores huiusmodi castrorum aliorum jobagiones, ecclesiasticorum virorum videlicet aut nobilium, seu aliorum possessionatorum hominum compellant. Qui si contrarium fecerint, ad primas octavas cum insinuatione evocentur et contra eosdem in eisdem octavis sententia capitalis facti potentialis decernatur et castra ipsa distrahantur sub pena predicta.[15]

V. Item qui contumacia ducti predicta fortalitia deponenda infra prefixum tempus non deposuerint, procedatur contra ipsos tanquam contra infideles regni, pro quorum rebellione conterenda ex ista parte Ticie et Transdanubium dominus Nicolaus wayuoda cum ceteris dominis et nobilibus ac civitatensibus partibus in eisdem existentibus, ex alia autem parte Ticie dominus Johannes wayuoda et versus Cassouiam domini Georgius de Rozgon, Johannes Giskra comes de Saros et Emericus de Pelsewcz cum Cassouiensibus et aliis civitatensibus, in terra autem Mathie domini Michael Orzag et Pangracius similiter cum dominis et nobilibus ac civitatensibus earundem partium sunt electi et deputati;[16] ita tamen, quod si illi domini electi alicuius favore allecti premissa non facerent, tunc tales electi in premissa pena convincatur.

VI. Item omnes cause litigiose a tempore decreti anno proxime preterito facti[17] tam finaliter terminate, quam etiam pendentes vigorose permaneant et prosequantur in suo cursu, omnesque et singule cause ad octavas festi beati Jacobi apostoli proxime venturi[18] prorogentur.

VII. Item, quod hii, qui pecunias regni pro tutela et defensione eiusdem annis proxime preteritis contra Turcos dispositas levarunt et nulla servitia exinde pro utilitate ipsius regni impenderent sibipsis easdem usurpando, in pena facti potentialis et amissione omnium bonorum et possessionum suarum convicti permaneant.[19] Stipendiarii vero ipso anno preterito exercituantes de dampnis, nocumentis et malorum perpetrationibus in eorum processibus per eos commissis per hos, quibus eadem intulerunt, iudicialiter conveniri valeant compellanturque iidem ad satisfactionem per iudicem suum.[20]

VIII. Item cusiones monetarum exnunc cassari debeant in omni loco usque ad regis voluntatem sub pena communi regni ab antiquo statuta et decreta.[21]

IX. Item de cusionibus monetarum prescriptarum, sed et aliis quibusvis proventibus regalibus, in quibuscunque rebus consistant, qui de salariis et provisionibus baronibus, capitaneis atque gentibus ad tuitionem et defensionem regni et confiniorum deputatis resultabunt,[22] quispiam hominum, cuiuscunque status et dignitatis existat, se quomodolibet intromittere non presumat, sed talismodi proventus fisco regio reserventur et amministrentur.

Kompolt in Co. Heves,[13] and Nicholas of Pelsőc and Stephen of Pelsőc in Co. Gömör,[14] built by these same lords around their own homes, which castles we permit and grant leave to these lords to hold and to keep by unanimous and equal consent. However, these castles must be maintained from their own revenues without being used for despoiling or causing damages or any other molestations to others and without compelling tenants of others, namely of clergy, or nobles, or other men of property, to work for these castles. Whoever acts contrary to this must be summoned by final summons to the first octavial court, and a capital sentence must be passed against them in the same octave, and their castles must be razed under the aforesaid penalty.[15]

5. Then, those who, guided by obstinacy, do not demolish the aforesaid condemned fortifications within the set time must be prosecuted as traitors against the kingdom. To quell their rebellion on this side of the Tisza and in Transdanubia, the lord voivode Nicholas with the other lords, nobles, and townsmen living in those parts, on the other side of the Tisza the lord voivode John, and towards Kassa the lords George of Rozgony, John Giskra *ispán* of Sáros, and Emerich of Pelsőc, with the citizens of Kassa and other towns, in the land of Mátyusföld the lords Michael Ország and Pancrace,[16] similarly with the lords, nobles, and townsmen of these regions have been elected and appointed in such a way that if these elected lords do not carry out the foregoing, having chosen to favor anyone, then such elected men must be convicted of the foregoing penalty.

6. Then, all court cases from the time of the decree made in the year just past[17] either finally terminated or still pending should remain open and be prosecuted in due course, and each and every case should be delayed until the octave of the next feast of St. James the Apostle.[18]

7. Then, that those who in the years just past had collected the revenues of the kingdom intended for its safety and defense against the Turks and have rendered no services from them for the benefit of the kingdom but usurped them for themselves must remain convicted of the penalty of an act of violent trespass and the confiscation of all their goods and estates.[19] The paid soldiers of the same past year ought to be summoned judicially, concerning damages, harm, and evil perpetrated during their campaign, by those whom they harmed and be compelled by their judge to pay compensation.[20]

8. Then, the minting of coinage must cease from now on in every place until the king orders otherwise under the penalty of the country established and decreed of old.[21]

9. Then, no one, of whatever station and dignity he might be, may presume to interfere in any way with the minting of the said coinage or with any other royal revenue of whatever form which remains after paying the salaries and provisions due to barons, captains, and their men for the safety and defense of the realm and its borders,[22] but such revenues ought to be reserved for and administered by the royal fisc.

X. Item si qui absque iudicio in captivitatem devenissent per Hungaros, Thewtunicos sive Bohemos ex quacunque parte, et in eadem captivate pro eliberatione ipsorum castra, civitates, possessiones aut alia bona qualiacunque, sive etiam obsides dedissent aut conventionem pecuniariam fecissent, sin etiam si aliqui amici et fratres pro eisdem captivis fideiussores extitissent et pro eadem fideiussoria cautione castra et possessiones ipsorum pro eisdem assignassent fide aut litteris obligatoriis, aut qualicunque forma seu colore mediante se ad hec obligassent, absque omni solutione remittere debeant et teneantur, excepto eo casu, quo si quipiam causa fraternitatis aut amicitie pro sui capitis seu possessionum redemptione quibuscunque pecuniam propriam sponte accomodassent seu mutuassent, quod mutuum creditoribus eorundem omnino refundere teneantur.

XI. Item quod nullus hominum, cuiuscunque status et dignitatis existat, in antea possessionum occupationes, spolia, vastationes et quascunque alias oppressiones per se vel per alium facere audeat sub pena potentiarii actus, amissionis scilicet capitis et bonorum; super quo querulanti fiat debita amministratio et executio iustitie per iudicem in primis occurrentibus octavis, et propter nullam causam prorogari valeat, quin in eisdem primis octavis leso iustitia impendatur et sententia capitalis emanetur.[23]

XII. Item quicunque post emanationem litterarum prelatorum et baronum pridem Albaregali[24] de et super conventione eorundem et regnicolarum in presentem congregationem factam spolia, vastationes et quorumcunque malorum perpetrationes commiserunt, ad primas octavas cum ammonitione et insinuatione evocentur et in eisdem octavis sententialiter causa terminetur. Qui autem de huiusmodi spolio et malorum perpetrationibus convicti extiterint, pena infidelitatis, ut littere convocationis pretacte continebant, innodentur et puniantur.[25]

XIII. Item quod si imperator Turcorum venturus est, ut famatur,[26] extunc teneantur omnes et singuli totius regni possessionati homines et cuncti civitatenses in propriis personis exercitualiter procedere contra ipsum iuxta antiquam consuetudinem et libertatem regni Hungarie.[27]

XIV. Item omnes episcopatus, abbatie et cetera beneficia ecclesiastica vacantia manibus laycalibus et quibusvis aliis iniustis detentoribus inde exclusis conferantur personis idoneis et benemeritis dilatione sine ulteriori, non tamen alienigenis, sed tantum[28] regnicolis. Et quod omnes decime et alii proventus ecclesiastici solvantur et restituantur prelatis et personis ecclesiasticis, quibus alias de iure solvi consueverunt; hoc expresso, quod ipse abbatie et quecunque alie prelature religiose professis suorum ordinum et non aliis conferri debeant.[29]

10. Then, if anyone who has without trial fallen into captivity of Hungarians, Germans, or Czechs belonging to either side, and while in captivity for the sake of liberating himself has given away castles, towns, estates, or any other goods, even if they have given hostages or made agreements to pay, and even if any of their friends or kinsmen have acted as guarantors for these captives and have transferred on their behalf by trust or letters of obligation as guarantees of bonds any castles or estates, or have obligated themselves in any way or form whatsoever, are and ought to be released without any payment, except in that case in which someone has pledged his own money or taken a loan from anyone of his own free will for the sake of kinship or friendship for the redemption of his own head or estates, because then he is required to repay the loan to his creditors without fail.

11. Then, that no one, of whatever station or dignity he might be, should dare himself or through others to carry out henceforth occupations, plunderings, wastings of estates, or any other attacks under the penalty of an act of violent trespass, namely the loss of his head and goods. In such cases the justice due to the plaintiff should be administered and done by a judge in the first octave that occurs and may not be delayed for any reason, but recompense for the damage must be rendered in the first octave and a capital sentence passed.[23]

12. Then, anyone who commits plunderings, wastings, and any other evil deeds after the issue of the charter of the prelates and barons at their and the gentlemen's of the realm recent meeting at Székesfehérvár,[24] regarding the present assembly, must be warned and cited with terminal summons to the first octave, and the case must be terminated with a sentence in the same octave. Those who are convicted of such plunder and perpetration of evil must be held and punished by the penalty of treason, as contained in the charter of the said assembly.[25]

13. Then, that if the emperor of the Turks is about to invade, as is rumored,[26] then each and every man of property of the whole realm and all the townsmen are required in person to set out on campaign against him according to the ancient custom and liberty of the kingdom of Hungary.[27]

14. Then, all vacant bishoprics, abbacies, and other ecclesiastical benefices must be released from lay hands and other illegal usurpers and conferred on suitable and meritorious persons without further delay, not on aliens, however, but only on inhabitants of the kingdom.[28] And that all tithes and other ecclesiastical revenues should be paid and restored to prelates and ecclesiastical persons, to whom they are usually required to be paid by right, but with this specific provision, that abbacies and any other monastic prelacies should be conferred on those professed in their own orders and not on others.[29]

XV. Item quod disponatur unum sigillum, in quo sit signetum crucis, sicuti signetum regni Hungarie,[30] et illud sigillum servetur in civitate Budensi, ut querulantes habeant sub illo sigillo litteras querimoniales, et procedatur iustitia secundum quod decet usque coronationem regis.

XVI. Item quod nullus presbiterorum regularium vel secularium atque clericorum sive laicorum huius regni per viam simplicis querele in quibuscunque causis ad curiam Romanam ex regnicolis quempiam citare et vexare presumat, sed prius hic in regno coram iudicibus eorum ordinariis, videlicet coram episcopo loci illius, in cuius dyocesi moram trahit, et ab episcopo ad suum metropolitanum trahere possit in causam.[31]

XVII. Item quod omnia tributa et theolonia tam terrestria, quam navalia a tempore decessus et mortis condam bone memorie domini Alberti regis Hungarie ex cuiuscunque et qualicunque donatione vel commissione erecta, instituta et acquisita deleantur et deponantur, et de cetero ab exactionibus eorundem omnes et quilibet prorsus et per omnia sub penis et notis prenotatis cessent et abstineant, cessareque et abstinere debeant et teneantur.[32]

XVIII. Item quod omnes mercatores et negotiatores tam intranei, quam extranei seu forenses libere tute pacificeque et secure per queque et universa loca et civitates regni iuxta antiquam consuetudinem cum suis rebus et mercimoniis hincinde procedere valeant omnium et singulorum cuiuscunque gradus, officii et dignitatis atque conditionis hominum absque impedimento, invasione et dampnificatione, iustis tamen tricesimis et tributis suis in antiquis et consuetis locis semper persolutis.[33]

XIX. Item quod quicunque hominum, cuiuscunque conditionis et status existat, post emanationem litterarum convocationalium prelatorum et baronum pridem in Albaregali congregatorum ad sua fortalitia atque castra homines advenas seu forenses, cuiuscunque linguagii existant, introduxisset et assumpsisset, per eosque spolia, vastationes, invasiones et rapinas fecisset et commisisset, ac faceret et committeret in futurum, sententiam capitalem et amissionem omnium bonorum suorum, sed et notam perpetue infidelitatis, prout in premissis litteris in Albaregali, ut predicitur, emanatis continetur, incurrat.[34]

XX. Item quod quilibet exercituans aut viator in possessionibus aliorum quorumcunque pro se aut pro equis suis victualia pro pretio condigno ad arbitrium vendentium limitato emere debeat. Alioquin, si in huiusmodi victualium aut quarumcunque aliarum rerum receptione violentiam fecerit aut fieri permiserit, in facto actus potentialis eo facto convincatur fiatque super eo iudicium et ministratio iustitie in primis occurrentibus octavis passo dampnum querulanti.[35]

XXI. Item quod tam prelati, quam barones regni nostri, qui ex dispositione et antiqua consuetudine tempore generalis exercitus[36]

15. Then, that a single seal be cut, on which there should be the sign of the cross, as the sign of the kingdom of Hungary,[30] and that seal be kept in the city of Buda so that plaintiffs may have letters of complaint under that seal and that justice may proceed suitably until the coronation of the king.

16. Then, that no regular or secular priest or cleric or layman of this kingdom may presume to harass or to summon to the Roman curia by way of a simple complaint in any case any gentleman of the realm, but in the first instance the case should be brought to the court of his justice ordinary here in the kingdom, that is, before the bishop of that place in the diocese of which he resides, and from the bishop to the metropolitan.[31]

17. Then, that all tolls and customs established both on land and water, instituted and acquired by anyone or in any kind of grant or commission since the time of the passing and death of the late lord King Albert of Hungary of good memory, must be abolished and cancelled, and henceforth everyone should cease and desist, and is obliged and compelled to cease and desist from exacting them in any way under the said charges and penalties.[32]

18. Then, that all merchants and traders, both native and alien or foreign, should be able to proceed freely, safely, peacefully, and securely to and from each and every place and city of the kingdom with their goods and merchandise without obstruction, harm, or damage from anyone of any rank, office, dignity, or condition, according to ancient custom, so long as they always pay their thirtieths and customs duties in the ancient and customary locations.[33]

19. Then, that anyone, of whatever condition and station he might be, who, after the issue of the call to the assembly of the prelates and barons recently gathered in Székesfehérvár, introduced and admitted to his fortifications and castles alien or foreign men of whatever language and caused and committed plunderings, devastations, invasions, and robberies with them, or causes and commits these in the future, incurs a capital sentence and the loss of all his goods, as well as the charge of perpetual treason, just as is contained in the said charter promulgated in Székesfehérvár, as was mentioned before.[34]

20. Then, that any soldier or traveller should be able to buy supplies for himself and for his horses at a just price set by the decision of those selling. Otherwise, if he causes or permits the causing of violence in taking such supplies or any other goods, he shall be convicted immediately of an act of violent trespass, and a trial and administration of justice should be instituted against him at the complaint of the harmed party in the first occurring octave.[35]

21. Then, that the prelates and barons of our kingdom, who by arrangement and ancient custom usually supply *banderia* at the time of

banderia levare consueti sunt, cum eorum banderiis tempore huiusmodi exercitus prompti esse debeant et parati, ut et alii regnicole eo diligentiori advertentia se ad exercituandum promptos habeant et conservent.

XXII. Item quod quilibet possessionatorum hominum jobagiones suos iusto terragio deposito et aliis debitis iustis persolutis ad aliorum possessiones recedere volentes semper dimittere teneatur sub pena alias in decreto condam domini Sigismundi imperatoris Romanorum ac huius regni Hungarie etc. regis desuper edito contenta. Et consimiliter de restitutionibus jobagionum violenter abductorum teneantur modus et pena in eodem decreto contenti.[37]

XXIII. Item quod ministratio iudicii et iustitie de occupationibus possessionum tempore huius disturbii, hominum interemptionibus et virginum ac honestarum dominarum deflorationibus ac litteralium instrumentorum ablationibus, prout superius in quodam articulo continetur, intelligatur in primis occurrentibus octavis, ut de novis actibus potentiariis sententialiter fieri debendis.[38]

Ut autem hec omnia et quevis premissorum singula debitam efficaciam et robur obtineant firmitatis ab omnibusque et singulis effective observentur, nos prelati, barones, nobiles proceres, civitatenses et incole regni huius Hungarie predicti singuli singulariter et universi universaliter promittimus fide nostra christiana mediante inviolabiliter observare et toto posse nostro facere observari, harum litterarum nostrarum, quibus uniuscuiusque sigilla nostrum appendi fecimus, vigore et testimonio mediante.[39]

Datum et actum in civitate Pesthiensi secundo die festi Ascensionis domini, que fuit septima Maii, anno eiusdem millesimo quadringentesimo quadragesimo quinto.

a general levy,[36] must be prompt and prepared with their *banderia* at the time of such a levy, so that the other gentlemen of the realm might prepare and keep themselves more ready with diligent attention for campaigning.

22. Then, that any man of property is at all times obliged to dismiss his tenant peasants after a just payment of rent and of other just debts when they wish to leave for the estate of others under the penalty contained in the decree of the late lord Sigismund, emperor of the Romans, king of this kingdom of Hungary, etc., on this matter. And similarly they are required by the means and penalty contained in that decree to return tenants violently abducted.[37]

23. Then, that the administration in the first occurring octave of law and justice concerning occupation of estates, killing of men, rape of virgins and honest matrons, and theft of written instruments in these times of troubles, as contained in the article above, must be understood so that final sentences have to be passed just as for acts of new violent trespass.[38]

In order that all these things and any of the foregoing receive the required efficacy and force of validity and be observed effectively by each and every person, we the prelates, barons, nobles, lords, townsmen, and inhabitants of this said kingdom of Hungary singly and together universally promise by our Christian faith to observe inviolably and to cause to be observed with all our might, by means of the strength and testimony of these our letters, to which we have caused the seals of every one of us to be appended.[39]

Given and enacted in the city of Pest on the second day of the feast of the Ascension of the Lord, which was the seventh day of May, in the year one thousand, four hundred and forty-five.

13 Junii 1446

Vide praefatiunculam et notas infra paginas 229–30.

Nos Johannes de Hwnyad pro illustrissimo infante Ladislao nato condam Alberti regis electo regni Hungarie gubernator generalis et waywoda Transsiluanus[1] notum facimus presentium tenore quibus incumbit universis, quod cum universitate dominorum prelatorum, baronum et nobilium ac aliorum singulorum possessionatorum hominum huius regni Hungarie iuxta dispositionem et ordinationem eorundem nuper in civitate Albaregali factam[2] in hanc presentem sollennem congregationem amplissime coadunata eas res modosque, quibus divina gratia suffragante tot diebus totque annorum curiculis alternis insidiis et mutuis persecutionibus acerrime contra sese fine dato pacem reformare et caritativi sibinvicem commorari possent, avidissime exquirere cepissent, tandem post multos habitos labores partibus ad tam salubre necessariumque opus non sine divine miserationis gratia inter se unitis pari consensu ad articulos infrascriptos observandos concordarunt. Quorum tenor verbalis hic est:

I. Primo, quod eligent et deputabunt unum gubernatorem.

II. Secundo, quod universi prelati, barones et quivis alii castra, castella, fortalitia, civitates, opida, possessiones et queque iura possessionaria, necnon episcopatus, abbatias, prepossituras decimasque et quevis beneficia ac iura ecclesiastica per ipsos hiis gwerrarum temporibus occupatas et usurpata remittent et resignabunt.[3] Civitates etiam, quas hactenus capitanei tenuissent, pristino earum statui, dispositioni, custodieque et conservationi earum proprie remittent, ipsique capitanei excipient manus et gentes ac familiares eorum de eisdem; quique ex huiusmodi occupatoribus ac capitaneis in hac congregatione presentes forent, interim non recedent de eadem, donec huiusmodi remissionem et resignationem efficient suo modo.[4] Quodque universa castra, castella, fortalitia hiis disturbiorum temporibus erecta durante presenti congregatione diruantur et deleantur, demptis hiis, que in confinibus pro defensione regni sunt erecta et etiam, que in preterita Pestiensi congregatione[5] certis personis indulta fuere et concessa, ac que universitas comitatuum, in quo eadem erecta sunt, pro sui defensione stare censuerit et voluerit; nec interim hii, qui huiusmodi fortalitia erexerunt vel pre manibus habent, qui scilicet hic presentes forent, recedent, donec eadem deponi facient et delere.[6]

13 June 1446

For prefatory and explanatory notes, see below, pages 229–30.

We, János Hunyadi, regent-general of the kingdom of Hungary and voivode of Transylvania, on behalf of the most illustrious heir-elect Ladislas, born of the late King Albert,[1] notify all to whom it may concern, by the contents of these presents, that when the community of lord prelates, barons, nobles, and other individuals who are property-owners of this kingdom of Hungary were all brought together into this present solemn assembly, according to the decisions and orders of the same men recently passed in the city of Székesfehérvár,[2] they had most avidly taken up the enquiry into the ways and means by which, with the assistance of divine grace, they might be able to restore peace and maintain charity among themselves, by ending so many days and so many cycles of years of attacks most bitterly prosecuted mutually against one another. Finally, after much labour at such salubrious and necessary work, not without the divine grace of compassion and united among themselves in common agreement, they agreed to observe the articles written below. The verbal form of these is this:

1. First, that they will elect and appoint a regent.

2. Second, that all prelates, barons, and others who seized and usurped castles, residences, fortifications, cities, towns, estates, and any property rights, and also bishoprics, abbacies, priories, tithes, and any benefices or ecclesiastical rights during these times of wars will hand these over and resign them.[3] They will also return the cities, which the captains had held until now, to their former conditions, that is, to their own government, custody, and maintenance, and the captains will remove their troops, men, and retainers from them; any of these usurpers or captains who are present at this assembly must not leave it until they have carried out such a surrender and resignation.[4] And that all castles, residences, and fortifications built during these times of troubles must be demolished and razed while the present assembly lasts, with the exception of those which were built on the borders for the defense of the kingdom, those granted and conceded to certain persons in the previous assembly at Pest,[5] or those which the community of the counties in which they were built chooses and wishes to keep for their defense, and those who built or now hold fortifications of this kind, namely, those of them who are present here, must not leave until they arrange that they be demolished and razed.[6]

III. Tertio, quod omnes domini barones honores et officiolatus eorum, quos habent, in presenti congregatione deponent, manibusque et dispositioni ac distributioni aliorum dominorum prelatorum, baronum et regnicolarum libere et sine contradictione committent et assignabunt.

IV. Quarto, quod universa alia, que in hac conventione pro pace, utilitate et comodo regni statuentur, concludentur et disponentur, firmiter observabunt in eisdemque persistent, ac eis obedient et parebunt.

V. Quinto, quod omnes tractatus, confederationes et vincula inter quoscumque prelatos, barones et regnicolas in alterutrum et mutuo fide mediante vel aliter quomodocunque facte et ordinate, que scilicet utilitatem regni et reipublice impedirent, casse, annullate et inanes habeantur, et quod ipsi domini prelati et barones in omnibus pro utilitate regni regnicolis assistent et contra omnes statuta et ordinationes regni infringentes insurgent toto iuxta posse.

Quibus quidem articulis modo premisso inventis et confectis ad contentaque eorundem observanda singulis singulariter, tam scilicet maioribus, quam minoribus in forma ad hec ordinata iuratis[7] unanimi et pari omnium voto et consensu nos licet inmeritos ad onus huiusmodi gubernationis elegerunt, idem humeris nostris imposuerunt exercendum.[8] Cumque quamvis inviti iuramento tamen modo quo supra prestito astricti effugere non valentes iuxta vires nostras paratum serviendi animum obtulissemus, sicut ipsis dominis prelatis et baronibus placuit, voluimus, ut limitatam habuissemus viam et modum, quibus et officium gubernationis huiusmodi et debitum eiusdem regnique huius tuitionem exerceremus et etiam non excederemus modum, quo vel in minimo contra prefatum iuramentum laxasse manum cerneremur. Eapropter iidem domini prelati, barones et nobiles universi post maturam eorum superinde factam deliberationem articulos infrascriptos limitationem petitam in se continentes nobis presentarunt hanc seriem verbalem continentes:

VI. Gubernator eligendus habebit tantam auctoritatem, quam haberet regia maiestas, dempto quod donationes perpetuales possessionum facere non possit ultra limitationem infrascriptam, nec etiam quempiam sine scitu consilioque et requisitione regnicolarum nota infidelitatis proscribere, nec etiam infidelibus ratione transgressionis statuti in presenti congregatione fiendi notam infidelitatis incurrentibus aliisque quibuscumque infidelibus similiter sine requisitione prelatorum, baronum et regnicolarum gratiam facere queat, sed nec archiepiscopatus, episcopatus et abbatias maiores absque scitu, voluntate, consensu et collaudatione consiliariorum suorum conferre valeat.

VII. Item gubernator manebit, ubicunque voluerit, in castris, civitatibus et opidis regalibus aut reginalibus, omniaque castra,

3. Third, that all the lord barons should lay down their honors and offices, whatever they hold, and commit and assign them freely and without objection, in the present assembly into the hands of the other lord prelates, barons, and gentlemen of the realm for their decision and distribution.

4. Fourth, that in all respects they will firmly observe, adhere, and obey what will be decided, concluded, and ordered in this assembly for the peace, order, and advantage of the kingdom.

5. Fifth, that all treaties, confederations, and ties among any prelates, barons, and gentlemen of the realm on either side made and arranged in any way by mutual oath or otherwise, namely those which might be against the interests of the kingdom, must be considered cancelled, annulled and void, and that the lord prelates and barons will assist the gentlemen of the realm in all things for the order of the kingdom and rise up with all their might against all those infringing the statutes and laws of the kingdom.

When these articles were devised and composed in the manner stated above, and when all in attendance, both those of greater as well as those of lesser rank, swore individually in the form prescribed for such matters,[7] to observe the contents of these articles, they then, by unanimous vote and common agreement, elected us, although unmerited, to the burden of government and upon our shoulders the exercise of this burden.[8] Since we, although unwilling, were bound by oath in the manner described above and unable to flee, have turned our soul, according to our strength, toward service, as it pleased the same lord prelates and barons, we wish to limit the ways and means by which we exercise this office of regency and the protection of this realm, and we shall not exceed the means nor shall we be deemed to have in the least relaxed our hand contrary to the aforesaid oath. Therefore, the same lord prelates, barons, and all the nobles after their mature deliberation hereon have presented to us the articles written below containing the limitation sought in them in the following words:

6. The regent to be elected will have such authority as the royal majesty would have, except that he should not be able to make perpetual grants of estates beyond the limitation written below, or to proscribe any man by the charge of treason without the knowledge, counsel, and request of the gentlemen of the realm, nor should he be able to grant pardon to traitors incurring the charge of treason by reason of transgression of a statute made in the present assembly or to any other traitors without the request of the prelates, barons, and gentlemen of the realm, and neither may he confer archbishoprics, bishoprics, and the greater abbacies without the knowledge, will, agreement, and approval of his councillors.

7. Then, the regent may stay wherever he wishes in castles, cities, and towns belonging to the king and queen, and all castles, cities,

civitates, opida et queque tenuta regales aut reginales sibi, dum et quandocunque ac quotienscumque voluerit, liberum prestent ingressum;[9] stabuntque cum eodem tempore celebrationis iudicii octavarum duo prelati ecclesiastici et alii duo barones seculares una cum palatino et iudice curie ac sex nobiles ad id deputandi. Medio autem tempore unus prelatus et unus baro et duo nobiles manebunt cum eodem, cum quibus querelas et necessitates audiet regnicolarum, quorumque consilio eisdem faciet relationem.[10] Ultra autem hos consiliarios de prelatis, baronibus, militibus et nobilibus huius regni incolis tot et tantos, quot et quanti sibi necessarii fore videbuntur, poterit penes se conservare consiliumque requirere ab eisdem.

VIII. Item de proventibus regalibus, quibus ipse gubernator ac sui consiliarii utantur, et de dispositione ipsis fienda committitur iudicio dominorum prelatorum et baronum, quibus de qualitate proventuum regalium plenior constat certitudo.

IX. Item gubernator ipse proficisci debebit et exercituari, dum necesse fuerit, exigente magnitudine rei per se contra hostes.

X. Item ipse dominus gubernator hiis, qui fideliter sacre regni corone servierint, de illis possessionibus, que deinceps ad sacram coronam pure legittimeque sine cuiuspiam alterius iure per defectum seminis, item propter delationem falsarum litterarum, propter cusionem falsarum monetarum et fabricationem falsi sigilli, necnon propter inductionem extranee potentie in hoc regnum ac positionem ignis in eodem fuerint devolute, in quibus scilicet possessionibus triginta due sessiones et non plures fuerint vel fieri poterint, et etiam in quibus infra eundem numerum triginta duarum sessionum fuerint vel fieri poterint, facere valeat donationes. Si vero civitates, opida et possessiones ultra numerum prescriptarum triginta duarum sessionum etiam prescriptis modis ad sacram coronam fuerint devolute, illas partiri seu dividere in triginta duas sessiones non valeat et sub nomine triginta duarum sessionum de illis facere cuipiam donationem, sed huiusmodi omnes civitates, opida et possessiones indivise ipsi sacre corone reserventur.[11]

XI. Item dominus gubernator, si cui donationem premisso modo semel fecerit, amplius eidem donare non valeat. Et cum donationes castrorum, civitatum, opidorum ac possessionum et similium ad ius regium dumtaxat spectare dinoscantur, igitur ipse dominus gubernator quibuscunque donationes premisso modo fecerit, illi tempore suo teneantur accedere ad dominum regem pro earum confirmatione obtinenda.

XII. Item possessiones illorum, quorum propter delationem falsarum litterarum aut cusionem falsarum monetarum vel alio quovis modo superius expressato ad coronam fuerint devolute, quousque illi per iudices suos competentes iudicialiter secundum antiquam et approbatam regni consuetudinem sententiati fuerint, occupare et donationem de eis facere non valeat quovismodo.[12]

towns, and royal estates belonging to the king or the queen will offer him free entry while and whenever and as often as he wishes;[9] and two ecclesiastical prelates and two other secular barons, together with the count palatine and the judge royal and six appointed nobles, should accompany him at the time of holding octavial court. At other times, one prelate, one baron, and two nobles should stay with him, with whom he will hear the complaints and cases of the people, and with whose counsel he will issue legal instruments.[10] Over and above these councillors, he should have the right to keep with him and include in his council such and so many prelates, barons, knights, and nobles of this realm, which and as many he finds necessary.

8. Then, the decision regarding what part of the royal revenues the regent and his council should use and have assigned to them should be entrusted to those prelates and barons who have more definite knowledge of the nature of the royal revenues.

9. Then, the regent should himself set out and fight against enemies, if it appears necessary, according to the seriousness of the matter.

10. Then, the lord regent should be able to make grants to those who faithfully serve the Holy Crown of the kingdom from those estates which henceforth devolve to the Holy Crown clearly and legitimately owing to the lack of an heir, because of proffering false documents, minting counterfeit money or the making of false seals, or because of the introduction of a foreign power into this kingdom or committing arson, if no one has a right in them and these estates have and can have no more than thirty-two plots, and also those estates in which there are and can be less than the said number of thirty-two plots. If cities, towns, and estates with more than the said number of thirty-two plots also devolve to the Holy Crown in the foregoing manner, he should not be able to cut or divide them into portions of thirty-two plots and make grants from them under the heading of thirty-two plots, but all such cities, towns, and estates must be reserved undivided to the same Holy Crown.[11]

11. Then, the lord regent may not grant anything further to the same man whom he once granted something in the aforementioned manner. And, since grants of castles, cities, towns, estates, and similar possessions are known to belong to the royal right, the lord regent may make grants to anyone in the preceding manner, but they should come at the proper time to the lord king to receive confirmation of them.

12. Then, those estates which devolve to the crown because of their owners' proffering of false documents, minting of counterfeit money, or any other reason expressed above should not be seized and given away unless the accused have been judged at law by the appropriate judges according to ancient and approved custom of the kingdom.[12]

XIII. Item valeat in absentia consiliariorum facere relationem et expeditionem in occurrentibus causis, que si iudiciarie fuerint, et huiusmodi relatio inventa fuerit contra ius consuetudinarium, huiusmodi relatio et expeditio per iudices ordinarios regni valeat emendari, prout temporibus regum fieri consueverit.

XIV. Item ut si quid de proventibus regalibus ab expeditionibus regni remanserit, valeat dominus gubernator castra, civitates, opida et possessiones regias impignoratas nomine regio redimere de eisdem, et ea corone reappropriando domino regi reservare, quorum proventus similiter pro expeditione regni exponantur.

Nos igitur huiusmodi potestatis nostre gubernationis limitatione ab eisdem dominis prelatis, baronibus et nobilibus regni modo premisso articulata recepta, iuxta eandem obtulimus eisdem omnem diligentiam, sollicitudinem et curam nostram, facereque et exercere officium gubernationis huiusmodi melius, ut possumus, atque sicut iuramento modo quo supra promisimus, limitationem et articulos suprascriptos in nullo excedere velle. In quorum testimonium presentes litteras nostras eisdem dominis prelatis, baronibus et nobilibus regni universis sigillo nostro, quo ut waywoda Transsiluanensis utimur, inpendenti comunitas duximus concedendas. Datum in amplissima prelatorum, baronum et regnicolarum congregatione generali in campo Pestiensi celebrata, feria secunda infra octavas Penthecostes, qui fuit tredecima Junii, anno domini millesimo quadringentesimo quadragesimo sexto.

13. Then, in the absence of the councillors he may issue reports and mandates in cases coming before him, but, if they are legal matters and such a report is found to be against customary law, then the report and the document may be amended by the justices ordinary of the kingdom, as was customary in the times of the kings.

14. Then, that if anything remains from the royal revenues after covering the expenses of the kingdom, the lord regent may redeem with it mortgaged royal castles, cities, towns, and estates and preserve them for the lord king to be reappropriated to the crown, with their revenues being similarly utilized for the affairs of the kingdom.

We, therefore, having received this limitation on our power of regency from the lord prelates, barons, and nobles of the kingdom specified in the above manner, offer to them according to it our every diligence, solicitude, and care, and we promise to use and exercise the office of regent in this way as well as we are able, and as we have promised by our oath above, to wish in no way to exceed the limitation and the articles above. In witness of which we found it proper to grant the lord prelates, barons, and nobles of the kingdom these presents completed by appending our seal, which we use as voivode of Transylvania. Given at the fullest general assembly of prelates, barons, and gentlemen of the realm held on the field of Pest, on the Monday within the octave of Pentecost, which was the thirteenth of June, in the year of the Lord one thousand, four hundred and forty-six.

25 Martii 1447

Vide praefatiunculam et notas infra paginas 231–33.

Prelati, barones, nobiles et proceres regni Hungarie universi ad futuram rei memoriam. Quoniam in novissima nostra Pestiensi congregatione generali circa festum Penthecostes proxime elapsum celebrata[1] certos articulos, qui tunc magis necessarii et utiliores conductioni pacis fore videbantur, in formam decreti sub nostre universitatis et magnifici domini Johannis de Hwnyad gubernatoris sigillis redigi feceramus, alios vero certis ex causis suspendendo prorogaramus, ut maior circa illos et maturior fieret circumspectionis ruminatio; nunc itaque divino nutu tam super prescriptis prioribus articulis decretatis, quam etiam modernis in hac nostra conventione uno voto et voluntate convenimus et concordavimus, illosque articulos, tam scilicet prius decretatos, quam nunc moderatos in unum redigi et ordinari voluimus et volumus articulatim. Quorum quidem prius decretatorum articulorum primus is est, quod universi prelati . . .[2]

Aliorum vero articulorum in hac nostra conventione moderatorum et concordatorum primus articulus talis est:

I. Quod gubernator proventus regales percipiet et pro utilitate regni fideliter dispenset.

II. Item si gubernator de celebranda congregatione generali per aliquem comitatum requisitus fuerit, potestatem habebit huiusmodi congregationes generales celebrari facere per palatinum.

III. Item iuxta dispositionem in priori Pestiensi congregatione nostra factam omnes cause super actibus potentiariis in disturbiali tempore patratis ad tempus coronationis regis suspendantur,[3] demptis hiis, que emerserunt post congregationem certorum prelatorum et baronum anno tertio circa festum beate Dorothee virginis in Alba factam[4] inter homines utriusque partis commissi, super quibus actibus potentiariis iustitia expeti poterit et ministrari.

IV. Item honores comitatuum parochialium perpetualiter in antea non conferantur.[5]

V. Item nemo prelatorum, baronum et regnicolarum forenses et extraneos ad sua castra, fortalitia et tenutas in offensam quorumcunque inducere debeat sub pena infidelitatis.[6]

VI. Item nullus prelatorum vel quorumcunque hominum beneficia ecclesiastica et honores hominibus extraneis conferat, sed incolis huius regni tantum.[7]

VII. Item nullus baronum et regnicolarum fures, latrones, spoliatores aut quoscunque notorios malefactores apud se aut in suis

25 March 1447

For prefatory and explanatory notes, see below, pages 231–33.

All the prelates, barons, nobles, and lords of the kingdom of Hungary, so that this matter may be remembered in the future. In our last general assembly at Pest, around the past feast of Pentecost,[1] we caused certain articles, which now seem to be even more necessary and useful for the maintenance of peace, to be set out in the form of a decree under the seals of our community and of the excellent lord regent János Hunyadi, while we postponed certain others for definite reasons, namely, that there might be greater and more mature consideration applied to them. Now, therefore, by divine guidance we have met and agreed with one voice and one will to both the previously written and agreed upon articles as well as the ones now adopted in our assembly, and we wished and do wish to collect in one place and ordain point by point these articles, that is, the previously decreed and the now adopted ones. Of the articles previously decreed, this is the first, . . .[2]

The first article of the others adopted and agreed upon in our assembly is this:

1. That the regent should collect the royal revenues and dispense them faithfully for the needs of the realm.

2. Then, if the regent is requested by any county to hold a general assembly, he will have the right to have the palatine call such general assemblies.

3. Then, according to the decision made in our previous assembly at Pest, all cases concerning acts of violent trespass committed in the times of troubles should be suspended until the time of the coronation of the king,[3] save those committed by men of either party after the assembly of certain prelates and barons held in Székesfehérvár three years ago around the feast of St. Dorothy the Virgin;[4] for these acts of violent trespass justice may be sought and administered.

4. Then, the honor of county *ispán* may, henceforth, not be conferred perpetually.[5]

5. Then, none of the prelates, barons, or gentlemen of the realm is permitted to bring in foreigners and aliens to his castles, fortifications, and holdings in order to attack anyone, under penalty of treason.[6]

6. Then, no prelate or any other person may confer ecclesiastical benefices and honors on foreigners, but only on inhabitants of this kingdom.[7]

7. Then, no baron or gentleman of the realm may keep with him or protect in his castles, residences, estates, and holdings thieves, robbers,

castris, castellis, possessionibus et tenutis teneat aut conservet, alioquin nobiles comitatus illius, in quo huiusmodi malefactores per quempiam conservari reperti fuerint, universaliter in loco sedis iudiciarie congregati huiusmodi malefactores vel malefactorem esse promulgaverint et pronuncciaverint, litterasque eorum superinde sub sigillis comitis vel vicecomitis et iudicum nobilium emanari fecerint, mox gubernator vel ille, qui per universitatem nobilium ad id requisitus fuerit, universas possessiones huiusmodi malefactoris vel malefactorum conservatoris occupandi et tamdiu conservandi habeat facultatem, donec idem gratiam pro se poterit impetrare. Si autem malefactor ipse nobilis fuerit et possessionatus, per universitatem nobilium eiusdem comitatus modo prehabito promulgatus et proscriptus, similiter omnibus suis iuribus possessionariis usque ad gratiam impetrandam privetur per gubernatorem vel alium per universitatem nobilium ad id deputandum. Ipsum autem malefactorem, sive sit nobilis, sive ignobilis, universi cuiusvis status et conditionis homines spoliandi resque et bona eiusdem aufferendi tamquam proscripti hominis liberam habeant potestatem, nec unquam propter hoc iudicio debeant conveniri.

VIII. Item neque dominus gubernator, neque bani exercitum generalem promulgare debeant, nisi cum tanta et tam magna inimicorum multitudo supervenerit, ad cuius resistentiam ipse gubernator de proventibus regalibus ac banderia prelatorum et baronum ac cetere dispositiones et stipendia a viris ecclesiasticis more consueto debentia non sufficerent. Alias autem idem gubernator de proventibus regalibus ac banderiis prelatorum et baronum et ceteris dispositionibus exercituare teneatur. Nobiles etiam in exercitu generali non ulterius, nisi usque ad confinia regni vel metas transire teneantur more ab antiquo consueto.[8]

IX. Item persone laycales contra personas ecclesiasticas in facto potentie vel calumpnie[9] convicte non debeant pro ipso facto potentie vel calumpnie in pena vel sententia capitali ac amissione possessionum et bonorum aggravari, sed solummodo in eorum homagiis,[10] quemadmodum ipse persone ecclesiastice contra seculares convinci solent. Damnum tamen illatum ultra id debet refundi effective.

X. Item si aliquis regnicolarum contra dominum gubernatorem aut totum regnum in aliquo insurgeret, extunc ipse gubernator contra talem exercitum generalem aut tot comitatus, quot sibi sufficere videbuntur, insurgere faciet et promulgabit.

XI. Item constitutio capitaneatuum in congregatione priori Pestiensi facta est abolita.[11]

XII. Item littere annuales[12] ecclesiis et viris ecclesiasticis ulterius non dentur.

XIII. Item si littere et litteralia instrumenta alicuius per Turcos, Bohemos, Thewtunicos vel quoscunque alios hiis disturbiorum temporibus combuste vel ablata forent, et id cum vicinis et

plunderers, or any notorious criminals; otherwise the community of the nobles of that county in which such criminals have been found to be protected by anyone, assembled at the county's court, will denounce and declare him or them as a criminal or criminals and will issue a letter to be sent out under the seals of the *ispán* or the *alispán* and the noble magistrates. Whereupon the regent or someone who will have been requested for that task by the community of nobles will have the power of occupying all the estates of such a protector of a criminal or criminals and of keeping them until such time as he is able to ask for mercy for himself. If, however, the criminal denounced and proscribed in the said manner by the community of nobles in the same county is himself a noble and a man of property, he must similarly be deprived of all his estates by the regent or by someone else appointed to that task by the community of nobles until he asks for mercy. However, regarding the criminal himself, whether he is a noble or not, anyone of any station and condition should have the freedom to plunder his possessions and take his goods as those of a proscribed man, without ever being summoned to judgment for that.

8. Then, neither the lord regent nor the bans ought to raise a general levy, unless so many and such a great multitude of enemies invade, that the forces of regent himself from the royal revenues, with the *banderia* of the prelates and barons and other income and pay usually due from ecclesiastical persons are not sufficient to resist them. Otherwise the regent is required to campaign from the royal revenues, with the *banderia* of the prelates and barons and from other military revenues. Nobles, however, have to proceed with a general levy only to the borders of the realm and not farther, according to ancient custom.[8]

9. Then, laymen convicted of violent trespass or frivolous prosecution[9] against ecclesiastics must not be sentenced to a capital penalty or sentence or the loss of estates and goods for that crime of violence or frivolous prosecution, but only to the payment of their composition,[10] just as clergy themselves are customarily convicted in suits against laymen. However, the damage caused must be completely compensated for.

10. Then, if any gentleman of the realm rises up against the lord regent or the whole kingdom in any matter, then the regent will raise and call against the usurper a general levy or a levy from as many counties as he deems sufficient.

11. Then, the institution of captaincies established at the previous assembly at Pest is abolished.[11]

12. Then, annual letters[12] for churches and ecclesiastics may no longer be given.

13. Then, if the charters and written instruments of anyone are burnt or taken by Turks, Czechs, Germans, or by any others in these times of troubles, and he is able to prove this with his neighbors,

commetaneis suis ac nobilibus sui comitatus declarare posset, extunc talis suis iuribus possessionariis, in quorum dominio existeret vel tunc extitisset, non privetur, nisi si quis aliqua causa rationabili posset iuridice obtinere.

XIV. Item quod quatuor octave[13] continue celebrentur et nulla alia de causa prorogentur, nisi ratione exercitus generalis, nec etiam cuiuscunque cause propter conservationem castrorum aut confiniorum regni seu custodiam eorundem valeant prorogari.

XV. Item quicunque hominum ulterius interemptiones, vulnerationes, mutilationes, combustiones litterarum et ablationes earundem, invasiones domorum seu alia similia notabilia mala perpetraverint, aut post decretum Pestiense in anno proxime transacto editum perpetrassent, tales mediantibus litteris nostris aut domini gubernatoris vel palatinalibus seu iudicis curie regie ad primas octavas cum insinuatione evocentur,[14] in quibus sine omni dilatione iudicium inter partes ministretur.

XVI. Item quod statuta tam in Pestiensi predicta, quam Albensi civitatibus edita[15] in suis vigoribus permaneant, demptis hiis, que per modernas constitutiones immutabuntur.

XVII. Item nullus omnino prelatorum, baronum et regnicolarum pro quibuscunque debitis vel factis arestationes seu vagiationes facere debeat, qui si fecerint et ex huiusmodi vagia recipientibus quipiam interempti, lesi vel dampnificati fuerint, tales tanquam latrones censeantur, et nec propter hoc[16] per quempiam iudicum iudicialiter valeant condempnari.

XVIII. Item domus dominorum prelatorum et baronum ac nobilium et ecclesiarum in civitate Budensi habite dicari non debeant, sed hospites in eisdem domibus existentes iuxta eorum facultatem dicari possunt.

XIX. Item comites vel vicecomites nunquam aliquod vagium vel birsagium sine iudicibus nobilium per universitatem nobilium transmissis exigere possint. Qui si sine eisdem exigere voluerint, lesionem, interemptionem vel damnificationem et iniuriam, si quam ibidem passi fuerint, sufferant, nec unquam iudicio lesorem superinde valeant convenire.

XX. Item comites vel vicecomites et iudices nobilium birsagia non exigant, nisi in congregatione generali,[17] nec etiam alibi extra sedem eorum iudiciariam iudicium facere possint, sed nec nobiles sui comitatus vel jobagiones ipsorum eisdem comiti vel vicecomiti victualia dare teneantur.

XXI. Item omnia theolonia post obitum imperatoris facta et indulta aboleantur, sed et alia theolonia, que propter conservationem pontium fieri concessa sunt, si huiusmodi pontes bene non conservantur, similiter aboleantur. Insuper ut a clericis et ecclesiasticis viris ac peregrinis, necnon rebus et victualibus nobilium, que non mercandi causa deferuntur, nullum penitus tributum exigatur.[18]

abutters, and the nobles of his county, then such a man must not be deprived of the property rights which he holds and has held, unless someone else is able to obtain them through reasonable cause by law.

14. Then, that the four octaves[13] should be held without interruption and may be delayed for no other reason than that of a general levy, nor is the proroguing of cases of anyone permitted because of the guarding of castles or the borders of the realm.

15. Then, whoever commits or did commit killings, woundings, mutilations, burning and theft of charters, invasions of houses or other similar major crimes, after the publication of the decree enacted at Pest in the previous year must be cited by terminal summons[14] by way of our letter or that of the lord regent or of the palatine or of the judge royal to the first octave, at which session a judgment must be handed down to the parties without delay.

16. Then, that both the aforesaid statutes issued in Pest and those of Székesfehérvár[15] should remain valid, except for those which will be changed by new constitutions.

17. Then, no prelates, barons, or gentlemen of the realm at all are permitted to make arrests or take pledges for any debt or deed, and if they do this and are killed or maimed or harmed by anyone during such a pledge-taking, they should be treated as robbers, and nobody should be legally condemned for that[16] by any judge.

18. Then, the houses of the lord prelates, barons, nobles, and churches in the city of Buda must not be assessed for portal tax, but burghers living in these houses can be assessed according to their means.

19. Then, *ispánok* and *alispánok* should never exact any pledges or fines without the presence of noble magistrates delegated by the community of nobles. If they attempt to do so without these officers, let them suffer the injury, death, loss, or damage that they have sustained while doing so, nor should the person injuring them be ever prosecuted by judgment for it.

20. Then, *ispánok*, *alispánok*, and magistrates may not exact fines except in a general assembly[17] nor conduct a trial anywhere away from their court of law. The nobles of their county or their tenants are not required to give victuals to the *ispán* or *alispán*.

21. Then, all tolls established and tolerated after the death of the emperor are abolished; and other tolls which were permitted to be levied for the maintenance of bridges are similarly abolished if those bridges are not well maintained. Furthermore, no toll at all can be demanded from clerics, ecclesiastical men, or pilgrims, nor on the goods and victuals of nobles which are not carried for the sake of selling.[18]

XXII. Item si dominus alicuius tributi de eo, que sint false vie sui tributi, literatorie docere non poterit, extunc illud discernendum committitur iudicibus nobilium illius comitatus, in quo ipsum tributum existit.

XXIII. Item lucrum camare non prius, quam tempore ab antiquo solito dicari debeat,[19] et cum moneta currenti exigatur, nullusque cogatur cum florenis auri facere eiusdem solutionem.

XXIV. Item comites vel vicecomites et iudices nobilium aliique omnes iudices pro qualibet marca birsagiali centum denarios recipere teneantur.[20]

XXV. Item in capitulis et conventibus redemptiones litterarum solvantur et recipiantur iuxta dispositionem in decreto condam Sigismundi imperatoris expressam, et similiter solutiones viarum testimoniis capitularibus vel conventualibus fiende fiant iuxta eandem dispositionem, videlicet [= 8 Martii 1435: X].

Capitula autem et conventus in premissis contrarium facientes per regiam maiestatem aut gubernatorem consiliariosque deputatos sigillis priventur eo facto, nec unquam huiusmodi loca valeant sigillum habere ultra.

XXVI. Item nobiles vel ignobiles, qui ulterius castra, fortalitia seu domos dominorum suorum quomodocunque alteri tradiderint, infideles habeantur, idemque dominus, cuius sic castrum traditum fuerit, huiusmodi traditorem ubicunque capiendi habeat potestatem.

XXVII. Item si dominum regem quocunque tempore decedere contingat, extunc domini prelati et barones in electione novi regis inter se dispares esse non debent, sed de singulis comitatibus certos nobiles convocari facientes cum eisdem unanimiter faciant electionem.[21]

XXVIII. Item quod singulis annis ad festum Penthecostes omnes prelati, barones, magnates et nobiles regni, demptis nobilibus nullum jobagionem aut minus quam viginti jobagiones habentibus, in eodemque loco et die gubernator ipse officium sue gubernationis ceterique barones et consiliarii honores et officia ipsorum deponant[22] tractentque ibidem utiliter de factis regni.

XXIX. Item quod omnes fassiones per quoscunque in captivitate vel aliter invite et coacte facte similiter cum litteris superinde confectis casse habeantur.

XXX. Item de litteris statutoriis[23] resignatarum possessionum vel castrorum seu quorumcunque iurium possessionariorum hiis disturbiorum temporibus occupatorum capitulum vel conventus non plus quam unum florenum auri recipiat vel valorem floreni.

XXXI. Item si quis castra aut castella seu possessiones etc. resignatas iterum occuparet, penam infidelitatis incurrat et per suum iudicem superinde sententietur.

22. Then, if the owner of any toll is unable to give written proof of the existence of illegal roads circumventing his toll, then the matter must be submitted for decision to the noble magistrates of the county in which the toll is located.

23. Then, the chamber's profit may not be assessed any earlier than the time when it is usual as of old and should be paid in the usual currency; no one may be compelled to make payment of it in golden florins.[19]

24. Then, *ispánok* or *alispánok* and magistrates and all other judges are required to accept one hundred pennies for a mark of fine.[20]

25. Then, fees for letters may be paid and received in chapters and convents according to the disposition expressed in the decree of the late emperor Sigismund, and similarly payments for expenses of witnesses of chapters and convents may be made according to that ordinance, namely. . . (= 8 March 1435: 10).

Chapters and convents acting contrary to the aforesaid are to be immediately deprived of their seals by the royal majesty or the regent and his appointed councillors, nor may such places ever have a seal again.

26. Then, nobles or nonnobles who in future surrender castles, fortifications, or houses of their lords to another in any way at all must be considered traitors, and that lord whose castle was thus surrendered will have the power of capturing the traitor anywhere.

27. Then, if it should happen that the lord king dies at any time, then the lord prelates and barons must not be divided among themselves in the election of a new king, but by summoning specific nobles from every county should hold a unanimous election with them.[21]

28. Then, that every year at the feast of Pentecost, all prelates, barons, magnates, and nobles of the kingdom, except those nobles who have no tenant or fewer than twenty tenants, at the same place and day at which the regent himself must surrender the office of his regency and the rest of the barons and councillors their honors and offices,[22] shall have useful discussion about the affairs of the kingdom.

29. Then, that all declarations made by anyone in captivity or otherwise involuntarily or by coercion should be held void and so should any charter issued on the matter.

30. Then, a chapter or convent may not take more than one gold florin or the value of a florin for a letter of *seisin*[23] regarding estates or castles or any other property rights surrendered after they had been occupied in these times of troubles.

31. Then, if anyone reoccupies castles, residence, estates, and the like, which have been surrendered, he will incur the penalty of treason and will be sentenced for this by his own judge.

XXXII. Item cum partialitas sit mater discordie et guerrarum, ob hoc statuimus, ut nullus ex regnicolis nostris, cuiuscunque status existat, pro questu principis, cum principem pari voluntate electum habeamus, directe vel indirecte, palam vel occulte aliquibus forensibus principibus seu aliis cuisvis status hominibus preter voluntatem communitatis regnicolarum de medio eorundem se excipiendo adherere et partialitatem in hoc regno practicare seu facere quoquomodo presumat. Qui si, quod absit, presumpserit contra communitatem, nota perpetue infidelitatis eo ipso sit aggravatus, cui nec rex, nec gubernator preter scitum et voluntatem ipsius communitatis gratiam facere valeat atque possit.

XXXIII. Item quanta mala et discordie ex provisionibus ecclesiarum kathedralium collegiatarumque et aliarum dignitatum et beneficiorum ecclesiasticorum per sedem apostolicam preter presentationem nostram factis in hoc regno exorta fuerunt et sunt, peroptime claret. Proinde statuimus, ut nullus omnino clericorum seu religiosorum virorum absque presentatione et nominatione regis vel nostra aliquam ecclesiam kathedralem vel quodcunque beneficium ecclesiasticum sibi per sedem apostolicam conferri et se in eisdem confirmari facere, ac etiam aliquem regnicolarum ad curiam Romanam seu extra hoc regnum, nisi per viam appellationis citare audeat. Quoquomodo contrarium facientes infideles et exules regni habeantur.[24]

XXXIV. Item gubernator nulli sententionato aut proscripto seu alicui malefactori gratiam facere valeat, nisi prefixo termino in talibus consueto leso et parti adverse satisfactio impendatur. Quibus quidem sententiatis et aliis pretactis nullus hospitalitatem teneat aut eos defendat quoquomodo; qui si fecerint, similem notam maleficii incurrant eo facto.

XXXV. Item quia hactenus propter frequentem variationem et depravationem monetarum in exactione decimarum diverse controversie fieri consueverunt, ideo gratia removendi huiusmodi controversiarum statuimus, ut deinceps omnes decime tam vinorum, quam bladorum, que usque modo in pecunia secundum consuetudinem dyocesium uniuscuiusque archiepiscopatus et episcopatus solvi consueverunt, de rebus ipsis in specie eisdem dominis prelatis et hiis, quibus huiusmodi decime de iure vel consuetudine debentur, exsolvantur, videlicet quod de frugibus et bladis in campo in capetiis et manipulis congregatis sine fraude ac dampno aliquali in ipsis capetiis et manipulis decime ipse persolvantur. Pecora autem et cetera animalia per villanos vel alios quoscunque ad loca agrorum, in quibus huiusmodi decime iacuerint, infra tempus consuetum uniuscuiusque ville hactenus in talibus observatum nullatenus admittantur, alioquin hii, quibus huiusmodi dampna fuerint irrogata, eadem valeant iure mediante recuperare. Et cum plures esse perhibeantur dyoceses, in quibus

32. Then, since inequity is the mother of discord and wars, therefore we have ordered that no one from our subjects, of whatever station he might be, may presume in any way, in search for a prince—since we have a prince elected by common agreement—directly or indirectly, openly or secretly, to adhere to any foreign prince or anyone of any estate against the will of the community of the gentlemen of the realm in order to stir up or foster inequity in this kingdom. He who, God forbid, would act against the community will by that act incur the charge of perpetual treason, and neither the king nor the regent ought or can grant him pardon without the knowledge and will of the community.

33. Then, it is exceedingly clear how many evils and discords have arisen and are arising in this realm from provisions of cathedral and collegiate churches and other ecclesiastical dignities and prebends by the apostolic see without our presentation. Therefore we have ordered that without the king's or our presentation and nomination no cleric or monk should in any way dare to be assigned to any cathedral church or any other ecclesiastical benefice or to cause himself to be confirmed to them by the apostolic see, or to cite any gentleman of the realm to the Roman curia or outside the kingdom, except by the way of appeal. Those acting against this in any way will be regarded as traitors and exiled from the kingdom.[24]

34. Then, the regent may not grant pardon to any sentenced, proscribed, or other criminal, unless his injured and wronged adversary has received satisfaction within the term usual in such cases. No one may give hospitality to the sentenced or other aforementioned men or defend them in any way; whoever does so will incur a similar charge of criminality by that very deed.

35. Then, because up to this time, on account of the frequent variations and degradation of coinage, various controversies have commonly arisen in the collection of tithes, therefore, for the sake of removing disputes of this kind, we have ordered that all tithes both in wine and in grain, which have been customarily paid up till now in money according to the diocesan custom of every archbishopric or bishopric, should be paid from the goods themselves in kind to the lord prelates and to those to whom tithes of this kind must be paid by right or by custom, namely, so that the tithes should be paid from the fruits and grains of the field in stacks and sheaves gathered without any fraud or loss in these stacks and sheaves. Neither peasants nor anyone else may admit cattle and other animals to fields in which tithes of this kind lie before the customary time hitherto observed in each village in such matters; otherwise those, on whom losses are inflicted by such acts, may recover them by law. And since it is understood that there are several dioceses in which up to now the customary tithes have been

hactenus de pullis et ceteris animalibus, necnon rebus decime solvi fuerunt consuete in eisdem rebus, igitur decrevimus, ut et deinceps in illis dyocesibus et locis de prescriptis rebus in specie decime ipse persolvantur.[25]

XXXVI. Item nobiles tam jobagiones habentes, quam non habentes decimas et lucrum camere solvere non teneantur, prout ab antiquo fuit observatum.[26]

XXXVII. Item cusio monete reduci debeat ad priorem statum, prout decretatum et ordinatum per nos fuerat in novissima nostra congregatione Pestiensi, ita quod singuli ducenti denarii unum florenum auri valeant et representent, cuius scilicet monete tertia pars argentum existat, que nunquam immutari possit, nisi cum consensu totius communitatis; nullaque alia moneta intra ambitum regni cudi et etiam cursum habere possit, qua tum lucrum camere, quam etiam alii proventus ab antiquo in moneta parva solvi consueti solvantur.[27] Ad cuius quidem monete cusionem et intentamenta prudentes et experti ac fideles homines de civitatibus per totam communitatem regnicolarum eligi et deputari debeant, qui favore vel timore seu aliqua ambitiositate quorumcunque magnatum et potentum huiusmodi monetam vilificare, depravare et immutare nullatenus presumant. De quibus tempore suo tota communitas regnicolarum, vel hii, quos ipsa communitas ad id deputaverit, rationem recipere valeant atque possint. Ubi autem ipsi, qui ad huiusmodi cusionem monete fuerint deputati, contra premissa seu aliquod premissorum fecerint, extunc pena alias in talibus consueta irremissibiliter plectantur.

XXXVIII. Item nullus archiepiscoporum et episcoporum vel eorum vicariorum de iudicio seculari se intromittat, sed solum, quod ad forum ipsorum ecclesiasticorum spectat, contractet.[28]

XXXIX. Item gubernator ecclesias vacantes tempore debito cum consiliariis deputatis personis ydoneis iuxta traditam sibi potestatem conferat, ne eedem per longam vacationem ad irrecuperabile dampnum incidant et ruinam, et neque ipsas ecclesias vacantes per manus laycales faciat occupare, possessionesque et bona earundem detinere. Volumus autem, ut ecclesias religiosorum virorum vacantes et vacaturas ydoneis et religiosis viris habitum illius ordinis habentibus, cuius ipse ecclesie vacantes et vacature existunt seu extiterint, conferat atque donet.[29]

XL. Item in exercituali progressu spoliationes, rapine et exactiones victualium ac iniuste verberationes hominum non committantur. Nam si per quempiam huiusmodi spoliationes, rapine et verberationes hominum fuerint perpetrate, fiat contra eos evocatio cum insinuatione, quarum veritate comperta in primis octavis tales in facto potentie convincantur. Exactores vero victualium tam exercituando, quam etiam

paid from poultry, other animals, and goods, therefore we have decreed that in those dioceses and places tithes must be paid in kind from the abovementioned goods.[25]

36. Then, nobles, having tenants or not, are not required to pay tithes and the chamber's profit, just as has been observed from old.[26]

37. Then, the minting of coinage must be returned to its prior state, as in the decree and ordinance made by us in our last assembly at Pest, so that two hundred pennies will always be valued at and will be equal to one gold florin; the third part of this coin must be silver, and this can never be changed, except with the consent of the whole community; and no other coinage can be minted and have currency within the borders of the kingdom, except coins of small change with which both the chamber's profit and other revenues are customarily paid as in ancient times.[27] For the minting and maintenance of this coinage, prudent, expert, and faithful men must be chosen and appointed from the cities by the whole community of the gentlemen of the realm, who will never presume to make such coinage worthless, to devalue and to change it because of favor or fear or for seeking popularity with any magnate and powerful man. From these people the whole community of gentlemen of the realm, or those whom the community has appointed to that duty, should and must receive an account at the proper time. Where the men who are appointed to the minting of coinage act against the foregoing in general or particular, they will be irrevocably punished with the penalty customary in such cases.

38. Then, no archbishop, bishop, or his vicar may interfere with any secular trial, but may only conduct cases pertaining to their ecclesiastical courts.[28]

39. Then, the regent, with those appointed to his council, should confer vacant churches within the appropriate time on suitable persons according to the power invested in him, lest they fall into irrecoverable loss and ruin due to long vacancy, and he may not cause those vacant churches to be taken or their estates and goods to be occupied by lay hands. We also wish that he confer and give the churches of monastic orders that are or will become vacant to suitable regular clergy having the habit of that same order to which the vacant churches and those becoming vacant belong or will belong.[29]

40. Then, in the course of a general levy, no plundering, robbery and exaction of victuals, or unjust beating of people may be committed. If such plundering, robbery, and beatings of people is perpetrated by anyone, let him be finally summoned, and when the truth has been discovered, he should be convicted at the first octave of violent trespass. Those exacting victuals either for military use or for any other

alias quocunque proficiscendo, cuiuscunque status et preeminentie existant, similiter evocentur cum insinuatione; quorum veritate comperta tales condempnentur ad valorem victualium ablatorum ac expensas in prosecutione huiusmodi cause per actorem factas cum solius iuramento[30] recipiendas.

XLI. Item potentes vel magnates tam in progressu exercituali, quam alias per regnum hincinde peragrantes in domibus nobilium sive locupletum aut pauperum non descendant.

In quorum omnium et singulorum premissorum robur atque testimonium presentes litteras sigillo nostre universitatis fecimus communiri. Datum Bude, in festo Annunciationis virginis gloriose, anno domini millesimo quadringentesimo quadragesimo septimo.

campaign, of whatever station and eminence they are, must similarly be finally summoned; when the truth of the accusation has been found, they must be condemned for the value of the victuals taken and the expenses incurred in the prosecution of the case by the plaintiff on his oath alone.[30]

41. Then, henceforth powerful men or magnates travelling through the kingdom on a military expedition or otherwise must not exact hospitality from the houses of nobles, whether rich or poor.[31]

We have caused these presents to be fortified with the seal of our assembly[32] for the force and testimony of all the foregoing. Given at Buda, on the feast of the Annunciation of the Glorious Virgin, in the year of the Lord one thousand, four hundred and forty-seven.

29 Januarii 1453

Vide praefatiunculam et notas infra paginas 234–35.

Nos Ladislaus dei gratia Hungarie, Bohemie, Dalmatie, Croatie etc. rex, Austrieque et Stirie dux, necnon marchio Morauie[1] memorie commendamus per presentes, quod cum nobis novissime de manu, potestate et educatione domini Friderici imperatoris Romanorum exeuntibus prelati, barones et nobiles regni nostri Hungarie generali conventione primum nuper Vienne ad nos congregati, relictis omnibus dissensionibus nos verum et naturalem eorum regem et dominum devota fidelitatis oblatione concordi animo honorassent, recognovissent et suscepissent, consequenterque possessionem huius regni nobis grata oblatione reddentes invitassent nos et conduxissent in hanc civitatem nostram Posoniensem pro faciendis ordinationibus, que pro conservando statu et pace ipsius regni opportune videbantur,[2] tandem inter alia, que hincinde concorditer expedita sunt, prefati prelati, barones et nobiles universi exhibuerunt nobis concorditer et presentarunt articulos infrascriptos desiderantes et supplicantes, ut eos et in eis contenta rata habere, admittere et nos observaturos promittere dignaremur. Quorum quidem articulorum tenor sequitur in hec verba:

I. Primo dominus rex iurabit, quod regnum suum Hungarie cum suis regnicolis in omnibus et singulis iuribus, libertatibus et legibus ac approbatis consuetudinibus inviolabiliter conservabit, in quibus predecessores sui, puta dominus Sigismundus imperator avus et dominus Albertus pater sui idem regnum et eius regnicolas tenuerunt et conservaverunt, et quod metas regni Hungarie non alienabit, sed pro posse defendet et alienata recuperabit.[3]

II. E converso domini prelati, barones et nobiles ac proceres cetérique fideles regni sui Hungarie universi et singuli, sed et deputati nobiles hic Posonii existentes iuramentum prestare debeant et teneantur eidem domino nostro regi super observanda fidelitate et obedientia.

III. Preterea conclusum est, quod dominus noster rex extraneis dignitates ecclesiasticas et seculares ac honores, officiolatus vel perpetuitates conferre non debeat usque dietam Albaregalensem, quam idem dominus rex cum celebrare voluerit, quadraginta diebus prius litteris suis mediantibus ipsis regnicolis promulgare teneatur, ut ipsi in eadem dieta Albensi possint et valeant interesse;[4] et tandem ea, que in hac parte in ipsa congregatione prelatorum et baronum ac regnicolarum deliberata fuerint et conclusa, firmiter observabit.

29 January 1453

For prefatory and explanatory notes, see below, pages 234–35.

We, Ladislas, king by the grace of God of Hungary, Bohemia, Dalmatia, Croatia, etc., duke of Austria and Styria, and margrave of Moravia,[1] wish to be remembered through these presents that, after we had been released from the hand, custody, and upbringing of the lord Frederick, emperor of the Romans, the prelates, barons, and nobles of our kingdom of Hungary, recently gathered in a general assembly with us for the first time in Vienna, honored, recognized, and accepted us as their true and natural king and lord with an avowed offering of fidelity in a spirit of concord, having laid aside all dissension, and consequently, returned the state of this realm to us as a voluntary oblation, they invited and escorted us to this our city of Pozsony to make the arrangements which seemed proper for preserving the state and peace of the realm;[2] finally, among the other things done by agreement at this place, all the said prelates, barons, and nobles unanimously compiled and presented to us the articles written below, desiring and entreating us to deign to approve, accept, and promise to observe them. The content of these articles follows in these words:

1. First, the lord king will swear that he will preserve his kingdom of Hungary inviolably and its gentlemen of the realm in each and every one of the rights, liberties, laws, and approved customs in which his predecessors, namely his grandfather, the lord emperor Sigismund, and his father the lord Albert, held and kept the kingdom and its gentlemen of the realm, and that he will not alienate the borders of the realm of Hungary but will defend them with all his might and he will recover what had been alienated.[3]

2. In return, the lord prelates, barons, nobles, lords, and the other loyal subjects of his realm of Hungary, individually and collectively, and also the delegated nobles who are here at Pozsony must and are required to swear an oath to observe faith and obedience to our same lord king.

3. Furthermore, it has been resolved that our lord king must not confer ecclesiastical and secular honors, offices, or perpetutal donations on foreigners until the diet of Székesfehérvár, which the lord king must announce by means of his letters to the gentlemen of the realm forty days in advance of when he will wish to hold it, so that they could be able to and may take part in the same diet at Székesfehérvár;[4] and, finally, that he will observe firmly that which was deliberated and resolved in these matters in this assembly of prelates, barons, and gentlemen of the realm.

IV. Item dominus noster rex omnibus et singulis regnicolis ac aliis cuiusvis status et conditionis hominibus ad coronam regni Hungarie pertinentibus, hiis videlicet, et qui presentes sunt et absentes, super omnibus et cunctis offensis et excessibus, qualitercunque et quibuscunque modis contra suam regiam serenitatem et eius coronam a tempore obitus condam domini Alberti regis felicis recordationis usque ad presentem diem illatis et perpetratis plenam gratiam facere dignetur et modis omnibus indulgere. Ita tamen, quod neque in presenti, neque in posterum, quocunque temporum in processu idem dominus noster rex de eisdem reminisci velit, neque imputare, et neque possit modis quibuscunque, et super hiis litteras suas gratiosas singulis, qui maluerint, dare dignetur.[5]

V. Item quod idem dominus rex omnes donationes condam serenissime domine Elizabeth regine matris sue et etiam condam domini regis Polonie[6] pro quorumcunque parte et quibuscunque ac quavis ratione factas revocabit et cassabit et committet omnino viribus carituras, excepta dumtaxat per eandem dominam reginam ecclesie Albensi facta.

VI. Item quod omnia nova castella in hiis partibus superioribus erecta et habita a die presenti usque ad quindecim dies inmediate sequentes, in partibus autem inferioribus existentia usque ad octavum diem medie quadragesime,[7] demptis illis, que sunt erecta ex indulto regum aut sub sigillo communitatis regnicolarum, sub pena infidelitatis deponantur et deponi teneantur. Qui si fecerint, bene quidem, alioquin contra eos, qui non fecerint, detur sententia in Albaregali.[8]

VII. Item castra, castella, possessiones et portiones possessionarie ac terre et alia iura, ecclesiastica videlicet et secularia, [per] quoscunque absque rationabili causa occupata usque ad predictum diem medie quadragesime sub pena premissa remittantur per detentores eorum.[9]

VIII. Item quod donationes per dominum gubernatorem [iuxta] vigorem decreti facte in suis vigoribus confirmentur.

IX. Item quod insinuationes in suis vigoribus remaneant.

X. Item taxe inconsuete ulterius non fiant quovismodo aut quacunque ratione.

Nos [igi]tur acceptis articulis prenotatis maturaque super eis deliberatione prehabita eosdem admisimus atque super primo eorundem solito more regale corporaliter prestitimus iuramentum, quoad s[ecundum vero] e converso nos ab eis omnibus simile iuramentum suscepimus super fidelitate et obedientia nobis observari debenda, ceteros autem omnes descriptos articulos et singulum eorum invi[olabiliter ob]servare, complere et exequi promittimus et volumus cum effectu. In quorum omnium testimonium presentes litteras nostras eidem universitati prelatorum, baronum ac nobilium regni nostri Hungarie [duximus concedendas]. Datum Posonii, feria secunda proxima ante festum Purificationis beate Marie virginis, anno domini millesimo quadringentesimo quinquagesimo tertio, regni autem [nostri anno] tredecimo.

4. Then, our lord king should deign to grant full pardon and complete indulgence to each and every gentleman of the realm and others of any station and condition belonging to the crown of the realm of Hungary, namely both those who are present and those absent, regarding all and any crimes and excesses inflicted and perpetrated by any means and by anyone against his royal peace and his crown from the time of the death of the late lord King Albert of happy memory until now. This should be done so that neither in the present nor at any time in the future should our lord king wish or be able to remember these matters or blame anyone for them, and to those who so wish he should deign to grant particular letters of pardon.[5]

5. Then, that the lord king should revoke, declare void, and deprive of all validity all grants of his mother, the late most serene lady queen Elizabeth, and also those of the late lord king of Poland[6] made in favor of anyone, for whatever reason, except the one granted to the church of Székesfehérvár by the lady queen.

6. Then, that all new residences built and inhabited in these upper regions of the country ought and must be razed between the present day and fifteen days immediately following it, and those in the lower regions before the eighth day of the middle of Lent[7] under pain of treason, except those which were built by permission of kings or under the seal of the community of gentlemen of the realm. For those who do this, all is well; but against those who do not comply, sentence will be passed in Székesfehérvár.[8]

7. Then, castles, residences, estates, parts of a propertyright in land, and other rights, namely both ecclesiastical and secular, usurped by anyone without reasonable cause must be handed over by their occupiers before the said day of the middle of Lent under pain of the aforementioned punishment.[9]

8. Then, that grants made by the lord regent empowered by decree should be confirmed in their validity.[10]

9. Then, that terminal summons should retain their validity.[11]

10. Then, unusual taxes must no longer be levied in any way or for any reason.

We, therefore, having received the above articles, accepted them after mature deliberation, and on the first of them we have offered a corporal oath by the usual royal custom, and in regard to the second article we have in return received a similar oath from all of them on faith and obedience to be observed to us, and for each and every one of the remaining articles written above, we promise and we wish actively to observe, fulfill, and follow inviolably. In witness of all this we have commanded our present charter to be granted to the community of prelates, barons, and nobles of kingdom of Hungary.

Given at Pozsony, on the Monday before the feast of the Purification of the Blessed Virgin Mary, in the year of the Lord one thousand, four hundred and fifty-three, the thirteenth year of our reign.

25 Januarii 1454

Vide praefatiunculam et notas infra paginas 236–38.

Ladislaus dei gratia Hungarie, Bohemie, Dalmatie, Croatie etc. rex, Austrieque et Stirie dux, necnon marchio Morauie, fidelibus nostris universis prelatis, baronibus, nobilibus et alterius cuiusvis status et conditionis possessionatis hominibus in comitatu de Zabolch[1] constitutis et existentibus salutem et gratiam. Crebrarum a dudum invalescentium novitatum notabilium hominum fidedignorum huius regni nostri Hungarie pericula formidantium patefactione edocti sumus luculenter, quomodo perfidissimus imperator Turcorum potentissima paganorum coadunatione solito multiplicata in finale exterminium firma intentione machinatur hoc regnum nostrum Hungarie subintrare.[2] Proinde nos vigili advertentia in animo revolventes, ne velud olim hoc regnum nostrum Hungarie ex Tartarorum invasione improvisa advertentia regnicolarum in flebilem ruinam fuerat positum et in presentiarum inevitabili cursu dicti imperatoris Turcorum et campestri conflictu indispositos, quod deus avertat, nos contingat periclitari et totius huius regni machina sacra religione christiana imbuta penitus diruatur, quemadmodum etiam in proximis diebus evolutis exemplari intuitu civitati Constantinopolitane per eundem imperatorem Turcorum[3] illatum fore iam experti sumus manifeste; quapropter predicti fideles nostri prelati, barones, nobiles et proceres dicti regni nostri Hungarie unacum certis electis nobilibus hominibus singulorum comitatuum eiusdem regni nostri, quibus per alias litteras nostras nuper superinde dederamus in mandatis, in hac civitate nostra Budensi hiis diebus congregati super eo, qualiter huiusmodi imperatoris Turcorum invasio prestolanda valeret tutius evitari, uniformem habentes tractatum et deliberationem,[4] nos cum eisdem validam expeditionem exercitualem ad natalem patriam nostram altissimo propitio defendendam adversus paganorum insultus decrevimus instaurandam, presentibus litteris nostris sub certorum articulorum inclusionibus subnotandis vobis notificandam, videlicet:

I. Quod primo spectabilem et magnificum Johannem de Hwnyad, perpetuum comitem Bystriciensem[5] infra presentis anni integri revolutionem capitaneum generalem instituimus huiusmodi exercitus nostri instaurandi.[6]

II. Item disposuimus, quod e medio dictorum prelatorum, baronum, necnon etiam nobilium et procerum regni nostri certi eligantur, qui videre debeant, quot banderia nostra regalia de proventibus nostris regalibus poterunt elevari, qui et ulterius provideant, qualiter ipsi

25 January 1454

For prefatory and explanatory notes, see below, pages 236–38.

Ladislas, by the grace of God king of Hungary, Bohemia, Dalmatia, Croatia, &c., duke of Austria and Styria, and margrave of Moravia, grace and greetings to all our faithful prelates, barons, nobles, and landowning men of any other station and condition assembled and living in the county of Szabolcs.[1] We understand from news that has proved to be true, passed on to us by trustworthy noble men who fear for this our Hungarian kingdom, that the most perfidious emperor of the Turks is scheming to attack this our Hungarian kingdom with a very powerful force of pagans, far greater than expected, in order finally to extirpate it.[2] Hence we, searching in our mind for a way to guard against this, lest—as before, when this our realm of Hungary was brought to pitiful ruin by the unexpected invasion of the Tartars—the inappropriate response of the gentlemen of the realm and our unpreparedness to open battle against the said emperor of the Turks, may, God forbid, lead us into such danger that the edifice of this whole realm, deeply imbued with the holy Christian faith, may be destroyed, just as we are well aware that most recently has been done, as a warning example to us, to the city of Constantinople by the same emperor of the Turks,[3] called our said faithful prelates, barons, nobles, and lords of our said realm of Hungary along with certain elected nobles from every county of our kingdom, to whom we had recently given mandates by our letters, to gather in this our city of Buda during these days and hold common discussion and deliberation concerning that matter,[4] as to how such a threatened invasion by the emperor of the Turks could be more safely avoided. We, along with them, have decreed the launching of a major campaign to defend the land of our birth, with the help from up high, against the attacks of the pagans about which we notify you by our present charter, including certain articles in it, namely:

1. That first we appoint the notable and distinguished János Hunyadi, perpetual count of Beszterce,[5] as captain-general for one full year from now to raise our army.[6]

2. Then, we have decided that from the said prelates, barons, nobles, and lords of our realm certain men should be elected who should see how many of our royal *banderia* can be raised from our royal revenues and who should further attend to the manner in which our

proventus nostri regales in cameram nostram regalem aministrentur, et qualiter e camera iidem proventus dispensentur, quodque honores baroniarum tenentibus,[7] qui scilicet more alias consueto ipsorum banderia exercitualiter soliti fuerunt elevare, de eisdem proventibus nostris regalibus eorum stipendia extradentur, et cum eorum banderiis prompti sint exercituare.[8]

III. Item domini archiepiscopi, episcopi, prepositi et capitula ac abbates, et alii dignitates et honores ecclesiasticos maiores tenentes, quemadmodum tempore condam domini Sigismundi imperatoris et regis, avi nostri consueti fuerunt,[9] cum ipsorum banderiis ac numero lancearum exercituare teneantur, ita videlicet, quod quarumcunque ecclesiarum seu personarum ecclesiasticarum proventus per inimicos extitissent minorati, iuxta limitationem electorum hominum predictorum[10] etiam huiusmodi exercituatio earundem ecclesiarum sive personarum ecclesiasticarum cum tanto defectu minoretur. Quod etiam alie persone ecclesiastice dignitates et honores ecclesiasticos minores tenentes, quorum nomina eorum in registro nostro exercituationis scripta non existunt,[11] secundum conscientiosam limitationem electorum hominum predictorum iuxta quantitatem proventuum earundem personarum ecclesiasticarum exercituare teneantur.

IV. Item in quibuslibet comitatibus tot probi et fidedigni homines potiores per communitatem nobilium eorundem comitatuum eligantur, quot in eisdem comitatibus iudices nobilium habentur, qui unacum eisdem iudicibus nobilium comitatus, in quo connumeratio fieri debebit, prestitis iuramentis per eosdem connumeratisque portis jobagionalibus ad rationem et numerum lucri camere faciendum,[12] de centum portis jobagionalibus tam ecclesiasticarum, quam secularium personarum quatuor equites pharetrarios et duos pedites[13] similiter pharetras et clipeos ac cuspides habentes ad exercituandum hac vice tantum, et usque ad metas et terminos regni nostri Hungarie et non ulterius disponant.[14] Ac in quolibet comitatu per eandem universitatem nobilium e medio ipsorum unus idoneus conductor belli illius comitatus eligatur, qui cum eisdem hominibus exercituantibus connumeratis ad generalem capitaneum exercitus tempore debito teneantur accedere.[15] Universi etiam nobiles regni nostri jobagiones non habentes per singula capita aut cum dominis ipsorum iuxta limitationem electorum hominum teneantur exercituare. Et qui equester vel pedester proficisci debeant, vel qui propter paupertatem, senium vel infirmitatem exercituare non possunt, iidem electi homines discernant et disponant. Pro personis vero filiorum magnatum parvulorum homines armati, pro aliis vero pueris et orphanis iuxta ipsorum facultatem consimiliter homines exercituantes transmittantur.[16]

V. Universi autem magnates, barones, milites, nobiles et proceres dicti regni nostri, maiores scilicet et minores ab invicem divisi[17] per singula capita propria hac vice exercituare teneantur. In castris ex

royal revenues are to be administered in our royal Chamber, how the same revenues should be dispensed from the Chamber, and that stipends should be paid to those holding baronial honors,[7] that is, those who by approved custom usually raise their own *banderia* for campaign, and that they should be prompt in coming to campaign with their *banderia*.[8]

3. Then, the lord archbishops, bishops, provosts, chapters, abbots, and others holding the greater ecclesiastical dignities and honors are required to come on campaign with their *banderia* or a number of lances, just as they used to in the time of the late lord king and emperor Sigismund, our grandfather,[9] however, in such a manner that the contingents of churches and ecclesiastics whose revenues were diminished by the enemy shall be suitably reduced according to the estimation of the said elected men.[10] Also other clergy holding the smaller ecclesiastical dignities and honors, whose names are not recorded in our military register,[11] are required to participate in the campaign in accordance with the careful estimation by the said elected men according to the size of the revenues of these same clergy.

4. Then, in every county as many proven and trustworthy powerful men as there are magistrates should be elected by the community of nobles of that county, who, with the magistrates of the county in which a census must be taken, having sworn oaths after enumerating the tenant plots in the way as is done for the chamber's profit,[12] should send, for every one hundred tenant plot belonging to both clergy and laymen, four mounted archers and two foot-soldiers[13] similarly armed with bows, shields, and spears for a campaign at this time only and only as far as the borders and confines of our kingdom of Hungary.[14] In every county the community of nobles must elect from among themselves one suitable war-leader for that county who must go to the captain-general of the army with the enumerated fighting men at the required time.[15] All the nobles of our realm who do not have tenants are required to campaign singly or with their masters at the direction of the elected men. And the same elected men should decide and direct who should set out on horseback or on foot, or who cannot campaign because of poverty, age, or infirmity. Soldiers should be sent in place of the small children of the magnates, and similarly for other children and orphans, according to their capacity.[16]

5. Each and every magnate, baron, knight, noble, and lord of our said realm, both the greater and the lesser who hold separate properties,[17] must this time campaign in person. It should be sufficient for one

pluribus castellanis sufficiat unum remanere cum tot personis, quot pro conservatione talis castri sufficientes fore iudicaverint electi homines prenotati, alii personaliter debebunt exercituare.[18]

VI. Item in domibus notabilium nobilium unus nobilis pro provisore curie possit remanere, ita tamen, quod quicunque modo predicto remanserint, teneantur homines suos exercituantes connumeratos transmittere.[19] Ex nobilibus vero et aliis maioribus filios aut fratres indivisos habentibus[20] sufficiat unum ad exercitum proficisci antiqua consuetudine observata.

VII. Item quod jobagiones exercituantes[21] nobilium in pluribus comitatibus possessiones habentium electi homines connumeratores talium comitatuum erga et penes dominos ipsorum in illum comitatum, ubi tales domini eorum residentiam facerent personalem, transmittant. Qui quidem nobiles seu domini cum talibus hominibus eorum exercituantibus, si voluerint, sub banderio dominorum ipsorum accedant et proficiscantur, qui etiam rationem de numero et personis talium suorum exercituantium generali capitaneo dare ac de eisdem respondere tenebuntur.[22]

VIII. Item quilibet exercituans tam maior, quam minor teneatur in propriis expensis tam in eundo, stando et redeundo proficisci, nullusque audeat aliquas res vel victualia absque conpetenti solutione recipere. Si qui autem violenter in aliquibus locis aliquas res vel victualia receperint, ductor exercitus talis comitatus dampnificato ex parte dampnificantis teneatur impendere satisfactionem indilatam. Et si ipse dampnificans unde satisfaceret, non haberet, caput eiusdem in manus dampnificati debeat assignari[23] per ductorem belli comitatus prenotatum. Quod si ductor talis belli facere non posset propter persone talis dampnificantis maioritatem, aviset superinde capitaneum generalem, qui teneatur dampnificato satisfacere. Alioquin dampnum passus valeat dampna sua acquirere iure mediante secundum contenta decreti dominorum prelatorum et baronum.[24]

IX. Item omnes libere civitates tam nostre regales et reginales, quam dominorum despoti et comitis Cilie[25] ac aliorum magnatum, necnon totum regnum nostrum Sclauonie, de quibus lucrum camere nostre solvere non consuevissent,[26] modo premisso connumerari debeant, et similiter Philistei, Comani, Walahii et Tartarii[27] connumerati debeant exercituare.

X. Item omnes celebrationes octavarum et iudiciorum tam ecclesiastice, quam seculares usque descensum exercitus nostri in proximo consurgendi cessare debeant. Post descensum vero presentis exercitus, aut si huiusmodi exercitus levari non debuerit, omnes octave, signanter festi beati Georgii inmediate sequentis[28] usque finem celebrentur. Quodque jobagiones quorumcunque usque ad festum sancti Martini proxime affuturum nullo modo deducantur hincinde moraturi.[29]

of the castellans to remain in every castle with so many men as the aforesaid elected men will have judged sufficient to guard such a castle; the others must campaign in person.[18]

6. Then, in the houses of the greater nobles one nobleman may remain as the steward of the court with this proviso, that whoever remains for this reason is still required to send his enumerated men to camp.[19] It is sufficient for one to set out on campaign from among the nobles or other greater men who live together with adult sons or brothers,[20] in observance of ancient custom.

7. Then, armed tenants[21] of nobles holding estates in several counties should be sent by the men elected as enumerators of such counties to their lords in that county where such lords make their personal residence. Those nobles and lords may, if they wish, come and set out with these men under the banner of their masters, who then will be required to give account of the number and person of such men and answer for them to the captain-general.[22]

8. Then, every soldier, whether rich or poor, is required to travel at his own expense in going, in camp, and in returning, and none should dare to take any goods or victuals without adequate payment. If anyone should take violently any goods or victuals anywhere, the leader of the troops of that county must assure that compensation is given without delay to the plaintiff on behalf of the trespasser. And if the trespasser does not have the means to pay compensation, his head should be placed in the hands of the plaintiff[23] by the war-leader of that county. If that war-leader is unable to do so, because of the high status of the trespasser, he then should inform the captain-general, who must compensate the plaintiff. Otherwise the plaintiff may recoup his losses at law according to the contents of the decree of the lord prelates and barons.[24]

9. Then, all free cities belonging to the king and the queen, to the lord despot and to the count of Cille[25] or other magnates as well as the people of the entire realm of Slavonia, who do not customarily pay our chamber's profit,[26] must be enumerated in the aforesaid manner, and similarly Philistines, Cumans, Wallachs, and Tartars[27] must be also enumerated and join the campaign.

10. Then, all sessions of octavial and other courts, both ecclesiastical and secular, must be suspended until the disbanding of the army of this imminent campaign. After the disbanding of the present army—or if such an army need not be levied at all—all octavial sessions should be held until their business is completed, particularly the one at the feast of St. George now following.[28] No peasant tenant of anyone should be moved to a new home until the next feast of St. Martin.[29]

XI. Disposuimus insuper, quod quicunque tam prelatorum ac virorum ecclesiasticorum, quam baronum ac magnatum, necnon nobilium, possessionatorum hominum predictam dispositionem et ordinationem in toto vel in parte observare et adimplere nollent vel non curarent, extunc tales dicti electi connumeratores in [eo mox] admonere debeant, ut pro defectu huiusmodi non perfectionis dispositionis et ordinationis predictorum pro quolibet equite sedecim florenos auri et pro quolibet pedite decem florenos usque quintumdecimum diem diei amonitionis eorundem computandum dicto capitaneo nostro generali dare et solvere debeant et teneantur. Qui si non solverint, extunc ductor exercitus talis comitatus una cum electis hominibus et iudicibus nobilium ipsius comitatus, ubi talismodi dispositiones infringerentur seu non perficerentur, illas portiones possessionarias, de quibus ipse dispositiones perfecte non fuerint, occupare occupatasque tamdiu, donec per hos, quorum redemptioni eedem magis competunt, pro dictorum sumpma et quantitate florenorum redimantur, conservare valeant atque possint.[30]

XII. Quodque premissa dispositio exercitualis ad aliquam pecuniariam solutionem nullatenus et per nullum modum per quempiam convertatur. Quod si per aliquem factum fuerit, penam sententie capitalis incurrat ipso facto.[31]

XIII. Item exercituantes illi, qui scilicet de exercitu furtive recedunt, si nobiles fuerint, possessiones eorum amittant, si vero ignobiles, pene capitali subiaceant. Et similiter illi, qui a dominis ipsorum dispositionem habuerint vel pecuniam eorum levaverint, cum eisdemque proficisci noluerint, eandem sustineant penam capitalem.[32]

XIV. Preterea quia premissam dispositionem exercitualem contra antiquam consuetudinem et libertatem tam ecclesiasticarum personarum, quam etiam aliorum regnicolarum nostrorum, maiorum scilicet et minorum propter presentis validissimi belli apparatus dicti imperatoris Turcorum in huius regni invasionem, quod deus avertat, faciendam pro eiusdem regni, natalis scilicet solii nostri regii et patrie paterne defensione et conservatione inpresentiarum levare opportuit et promulgari, ideo nos et ipsi prelati, barones, ceteri nobiles et proceres dicti regni nostri spondemus et fide nostra christiana prestita etiam cum nostri et ipsorum prelatorum ac baronum sigillorum inpressionis roboratione promittimus et policemur, quod a modo et deinceps nullo unquam tempore talem inconsuetam exercituationem promulgabimus et faciemus, neque ipsi facient et promulgabunt, sed tam nos, quam ipsi prelati, barones et proceres regni nostri penes dictam antiquam consuetudinem exercituationis semper permanebimus et ipsi permanebunt.[33]

XV. Item pro compescendis quarumcunque nociturnitatum generibus disposuimus, ut pretacti electi homines in singulis comitatibus unacum iudicibus nobilium omnibus querulantibus super

11. We have further decided that anyone, whether prelate, clergy, baron, magnate, noble, or landed resident, who is unwilling or hesitant to observe and fulfill in whole or in part the said arrangement and order, then the said elected enumerators must quickly warn such men, that for the damage caused by failure to perform the said arrangement and order they must and are required to give and to pay to our said captain-general sixteen florins of gold for every horseman and ten florins for every foot-soldier by the fifteenth day of the warning. If they will not pay, the leader of the army of that county with the elected men and the magistrates of that county where such arrangements are infringed upon or not performed, can and should occupy appropriate parts of his possessions for which the arrangements were not met and keep them occupied until such time as they are redeemed by those who are more prepared to redeem them for the said amount and quantity of florins.[30]

12. And that the said military service may not be commuted to any monetary payment at any time and by any means by anyone. If that is done by anyone, he should immediately incur the penalty of capital sentence.[31]

13. Then, those soldiers who leave the army secretly, if they are nobles, should lose their estates; if they are nonnobles they should be subject to a capital penalty. And similarly those who make an arrangement for their lords or raise their money, if they are unwilling to set out with them, should sustain the same capital penalty.[32]

14. Furthermore, because the preparation of the very powerful machinery of war by the said emperor of the Turks for the invasion of this kingdom, God forbid, demanded that for this one time the aforesaid military arrangements be made and promulgated for defense and preservation of the kingdom, namely, of our royal throne and ancestral land, against ancient custom and the liberty of both ecclesiastics and our other gentlemen of the realm, the greater and the lesser alike, therefore, we and the prelates, barons, other nobles, and lords of our said realm vow, promise, and pledge with the offering of our Christian faith and also with the strength of the impression of our seals and those of the prelates and barons that never in any way or at any time will we or they promulgate and arrange such an unprecedented campaign, but both we and the prelates, barons, and lords of our realm will always persist in the said ancient custom of campaigning.[33]

15. Then, to repress any kind of harmful deeds we have ordered that the said elected men in every county with the magistrates must render justice and sentence to all plaintiffs regarding any acts of violent

quibuscunque factis potentiariis et etiam possessionum occupationibus ex parte in causam attractorum, habita prius superinde diligenti inquisitione compertaque sufficienti rei veritate, absque dilatione et terminorum protractione iudicium et iustitiam querulantibus teneantur exhibere, comesque parochialis iuxta huiusmodi iudicium modo premisso faciendum teneatur mox satisfactionem indilatam et plenariam ex parte huiusmodi in causam attractorum lesis ministrare. Quod si ipse comes parochialis ex quacunque causa facere nollet, extunc talis comes parochialis honore suo privetur, causaque huiusmodi modo pretacto adiudicata in curiam nostram regiam per eosdem iudices transmittatur, ubi in primis octavis celebrandis fine conclusivo absque ulla prorogatione ulteriori terminetur.[34] Ubi si ipsi comites vel vicecomites parochiales nobilibus et quibusvis possessionatis aut ignobilibus hominibus quevis facta potentiaria, iniurias, nocumenta et dampna quoquomodo fecerint vel ad se pertinentibus facere permiserint, tunc iidem electi homines et iudices nobilium talis comitatus ipsos comites et vicecomites premissa patrantes in eo, ut ipsi in prima die sedis iudiciarie super talismodi actibus potentiariis, dampnis atque iniuriis lesis et dampnificatis omnimodam impendere debeant satisfactionem, amoneant. Qui si id facere recusaverint, tunc ipsi electi et iudices nobilium seriem huiusmodi non satisfactionis in litteris eorum conscribi facere et ad primas octavas tunc celebrandas transmittere, iudexque ordinarius octavis in eisdem contra tales comites et vicecomites litteras sententionales lesis et dampnificatis dare et easdem executioni demandare debeant et teneantur.[35]

Quocirca fidelitati vestre precipimus et mandamus, quatenus mox postquam pretacti homines electi dicti comitatus Zabolcz hic Bude inpresentiarum constituti hinc vestri in medium cum presentibus revertentur et prevenerint, ad locum vestre sedis iudiciarie universaliter congregati iuxta contenta dispositionum nostrarum unacum dictis prelatis, baronibus et electis hominibus per vos deputatis ceterisque nobilibus et proceribus dicti regni nostri in superioribus articulatim conscriptarum vos cum celeritate more exercituantium tam expedite disponatis et apromptuetis, ut dum et quamprimum annotatus comes Johannes generalis capitaneus exercitus nostri prenotati vobis scripserit, in continenti cum apparatu exercituali fulciti, previo ductore belli ipsius comitatus vestri modo pretacto vestri de medio eligendo ad loca, que idem capitaneus noster generalis duxerit notificanda, ad resistendum predictorum inimicorum nostrorum insultibus proficisci valeatis. Aliud sub penis predictis et nostre indignationis facere non ausuri in premissis.

Datum Bude, in festo Conversionis beati Pauli apostoli, anno domini millesimo quadringentesimo quinquagesimo quarto.

Ad relationem dominorum prelatorum et baronum cons[iliariorum][36]

trespass and occupations of estates on behalf of the damaged party, after having held proper enquiry and sufficiently established the truth in the case without delay and protraction of terms. The *ispán* of the county is required to exact at once full and undelayed compensation for losses, according to such a judgment made in the said manner on behalf of the damaged party.[34] If the *ispán* of the county is unwilling to do so for any reason, then such an *ispán* should be deprived of his office and the case decided in the said manner should be sent to our royal court by the magistrates, where it will be brought to a conclusive end in the first octave held without any further prorogation. If *ispánok* or *alispánok* of counties commit or allow the commission of acts of violent trespass, injuries, harm, and damage of any kind by nobles, gentlemen of the realm, or nonnobles, then the same elected men and the magistrates of such a county should warn the *ispánok* and the *alispánok* committing the aforesaid that they must pay compensation for such acts of violent trespass, losses, injuries, and damages caused in any way on the first day of the county court's session. If they refuse to do this, then the elected men and the magistrates must and are required to have the facts of such noncompensation written down in their letter and to send it to the first octave held, and the justice ordinary ought and will in that octavial court grant a letter of sentence for the damages and losses against such *ispánok* and *alispánok* and will order its execution.[35]

Therefore, we have ordered and mandated your fidelities that after your said elected men of the said county of Szabolcs at present here at Buda return and arrive home with the present charter, you should assemble at the seat of the county court, and, according to the contents of our arrangements written in the above articles issued together with the said prelates, barons, and elected men chosen by you along with the other nobles and lords of our said realm, you must arrange and make ready quickly in the customary way of campaigning, so that when and as soon as the said Count János, the captain-general of our said army, writes to you, you will be able to set out equipped for war, with the war-leader of your county previously elected in the said manner from your midst, to the place which our captain-general will designate, to resist the attacks of our said enemies. Do not dare to act otherwise under the said penalties and the risk of our indignation.

Given at Buda, on the feast of the Conversion of St. Paul the Apostle, in the year of the Lord one thousand, four hundred and fifty-four.

On the instruction of the lord prelates and barons of the council.[36]

APPENDICES

APPENDICES

2 Februarii 1342

Vide praefatiunculam et notas infra paginas 239–44.

Nos Karolus dei gratia rex Hungarie memorie commendantes tenore presentium quibus expedit universis significamus, quod nos prelatorum et baronum regni nostri voto unanimi et de consilio eorundem, considerata sagaci industria magistri Endre Chempeliny,[1] comitatus camerarum nostrarum[2] de Syrmia et de Quinqueecclesiis cum omnibus comitatibus, districtibus, civitatibus, villis et opidis, qui et que ab antiquo ad easdem cameras dinosscuntur pertinuisse, scilicet cum comitatibus Syrmiensi, Bachyensi, de Wolkow et de Bodrugh, item de Baranya, Symigiensi, Tholnensi et Zaladiensi[3] eidem magistro Endre pro mille et quingentis marcis,[5] partim in florensis seu aureis denariis camere nostre Bude cusis et cudendis,[6] partim vero in integris camere nostre monetis[7] annorum preteriti, tertii, quarti et presentis,[8] per totum nostrum uniformiter discurrendis et per preteriti anni modum tam per ipsum, quam per alios regni nostri camerarios ampliandis, nobis in terminis infrascriptis persolvendis, anno domini millesimo CCC^{mo} XL^{mo} secundo a data presentium per anni circulum simulcum decimis archyepiscopalibus[4] dedimus iterato et locavimus ad exercendum, procurandum et tenendum isto modo:

I. Quod idem magister Endre faciet fabricari integros denarios camere nostre argenteos vere combustionis tertie, ad modum et formam ac valitudinem denariorum annorum preteriti, tertii et quarti, eosdem ampliando in vera et recta combustione tertia, ex quibus de una marca fini argenti duodecim pense incidentur,[9] et octo pense ex eisem et non plures unam marcam ponderis Budensis in statera ponderabunt[10] et current pro marca fini argenti in montanis.[11]

II. Qui quidem denarii nostri integri cambientur per hunc modum: quod ipse comes camere vel sui officiales in singulis foris civitatum et liberarum villarum nostrarum regalium et reginalium ac quorumlibet aliorum presentibus hominibus archyepiscopi Strigoniensis,[12] magistri tawarnicorum[13] et comitis parochyalis ac uno iudice nobilium, sub testimonio alicius capituli[14] in eisdem foris ipsos denarios camere ampliandos et multiplicandos publice super tabula sua exponere debeant et tres ex eisdem denariis pro quatuor latis Wyenensibus vel aliis camere nostre monetis quinti anni iam abolitis aut etiam in aliis precedentibus annis fabricatis, combustionem Wyenensium habentibus cambientur,[15] et sex ex eisdem tam denariis novis, quam annorum preteriti, tertii et quarti camere monetis, quia ipsos annorum preteriti,

2 February 1342
Cameral Contract

For prefatory and explanatory notes, see below, pages 239–44.

We, Charles, by the grace of God king of Hungary, make known to all to whom it may concern by entrusting it to memory through the contents of these presents that having carefully considered the keen diligence of master Andrew of Csempelény[1] with the unanimous agreement and counsel of the prelates and barons of our realm, we have granted and farmed to the same master Andrew the office of count of our chambers[2] of Szerém and of Pécs, with all the counties, districts, cities, villages, and towns which are known to have belonged to these same chambers from ancient times, that is, with the counties Szerém, Bács, Valkó, Bodrog, as well as Baranya, Somogy, Tolna, and Zala,[3] together with the archiepiscopal tithes[4] to handle, manage, and hold in the one thousand, three hundred and forty-second year of our Lord from the date of the present time for a whole year for one thousand and five hundred marks[5] to be paid out to us at the following terms, partly in florins, namely, gold pennies of our chamber, minted or to be minted in our mint at Buda,[6] partly in full weight money[7] of the past four years[8] and of the present year that are to be circulated in our entire (realm) just as they were circulated by him, as well as by other cameral counts of our realm in the past year, in the following way:

1. That the said Andrew will cause to be made at our chamber full-weight silver pennies of exactly a third firing in the manner, form, and validity of pennies of the past four years, issuing them in a just and right third firing, so that twelve *pensae* must be cut from one mark of fine silver;[9] eight *pensae* of them and not more will weigh on the scale one mark of the weight of Buda[10] and should circulate in the value of a mark of fine silver at the mining towns.[11]

2. These full-weight pennies shall be issued for exchange in the following manner: the count of the chamber himself or his officials in the various market places of the cities and free villages of our domains and the queen's domains and those of any others, in the presence of the men of the archbishop of Esztergom,[12] of the Master of the Treasury,[13] and of the *ispán* of the county, as well as one noble magistrate and the witness of a chapter,[14] must set out publicly, on their own table in these same marketplaces, the coins of our chamber to be circulated and exchanged, and three of these same pennies shall be exchanged for four broad Viennese pennies or for other monies of our chamber of four years ago now recalled, or for money made in other preceding years similar to the Viennese firing.[15] And because we wish that these

tertii et quarti camere denarios in suo esse cursu et cambio remanere volumus, pro grosso,[16] et octo pense ac sedecim denarii pro marca pagamenti absque aliquali augmentatione ubique currant et solvantur.[17]

III. Si qui vero iam dictas monetas nostras annorum preteriti, tertii et quarti veras et etiam hoc anno pro earundem ampliatione in eodem valore fabricandas in numero augmentantes reperti fuerint, tamquam transgressores regalium nostrorum mandatorum et statuta camere infringentes in rebus et personis per ipsum comitem camerarum nostrarum puniantur nostra auctoritate mediante.

IV. Item si leviores denarii in istis presentibus, preteriti, tertii et quarti annorum camere monetis vel peioris combustionis plures quam octo pense et tres vel quatuor denarii marcam ponderantes apud quemcunque, sive in civitatibus, sive in aliis locis, seu etiam circa camerarios vel suos officiales, aut numerum marcarum augmentantes ubicunque invenirentur, tamquam falsarii nostra auctoritate puniantur.[18]

V. Propter quod volumus et committimus, ut in cunctis civitatibus et locis publicis statera cum suis ponderibus semper habeatur et servetur ad evitandum, quod mercatores vel alii forenses, aut etiam quicunque ex civibus et hospitibus iuxta abusivam eorum consuetudinem et fraudem graviores denarios ipsius monete camerarum nostrarum annorum presentis, preteriti, tertii et quarti non possint eligere vel diminuere per incisiones.[19]

VI. Istud tamen pro multiplicatione earundem monetarum camere nostre, maxime et specialissime cum ipso comite camerarum nostrarum iuxta suam spontaneam obligationem et nostram omnimodam intentionem volumus et committimus, ut in cunctis locis camerarum, in quibus monete camerarum cudi solent, nunc in principio ad minus mille marcas idem camerarius fabricari faciat cambio exponendas,[20] qui si facere neglexerit, tamquam nos seducens et regnicolas nostros decipiens remanebit.

VII. Item ordinavimus, quod abhinc unusquisque campsores denariorum, ut soliti fore dicuntur, per se servare cesset omnino et desistat.[21] Si enim aliquos ex eisdem campsoribus in detrimentum camerarum servare et habere ipse comes camerarum sciverit et in presentia hominum dominorum archyepiscopi Strigoniensis et magistri tawarnicorum triumque aliorum predictorum et unacum eisdem invenerit, nedum ipsi campsores, verum etiam ipsi domini eorum in ablatione rerum et bonorum ipsorum punientur et dehonestabuntur in personis.[22]

VIII. Item florenus seu aureus denarius camere pro nonaginta denariis integris camere nostre ampliandis semper absque augmentatione et refutatione ubique acceptetur et cambiatur.

pennies of the past four years retain their value and circulation, six of these new pennies, just like those of our chamber from the past four years, should count for a groat,[16] while eight *pensae* and sixteen pennies are to be circulated everywhere and accepted as tender without surcharge for a mark of payment.[17]

3. If anyone is discovered increasing the amount of our true money minted in the past four years and even of this year made and issued in the same value, namely, by increasing the number of coins minted from a mark, such a transgressor of our royal mandate and the statute of the chamber is to be punished by our authority in his goods and in his person by the count of our chambers.

4. Then, if, among the present money of our chamber or that of the past four years, lighter pennies or such pennies of less valuable firing of which more than eight *pensae* and three or four pennies weigh a mark are found in anyone's possession, whether in the cities or in any other place, or even among the chamberlains or their officials, or among those minting more money from a mark, then these are to be punished by our authority as counterfeiters.[18]

5. Therefore, we command and enjoin that a scale with weights be always kept and maintained in all cities and public places to prevent merchants or other traders, or anyone from among the citizens and burghers, from being able—following their abusive custom and fraud—to pick out the heavier pennies from the money of our chambers of the present year and each of the past four years or to reduce them by clipping.[19]

6. Moreover, particularly and expressly for the increase of these monies of our chamber we wish and mandate that in all the places of the chambers in which money is customarily minted, the count of the chamber, according to his voluntary obligation and our intended purpose, should as a start cause to be minted and distributed not less than a thousand marks.[20] If he neglects to do this, he will be condemned as deceiving us and cheating our subjects.

7. Then, we have ordered that, henceforth, everyone should cease and desist completely from keeping a private minter as some are said to be accustomed to do.[21] Indeed, if the count of the chamber finds out that someone keeps a minter to the detriment of our mint and establishes this in the presence of the men of the lord archbishop of Esztergom, of the Master of the Treasury, and the three aforesaid others, not only these minters but also their lords will be punished by the loss of their goods and chattels, as well as being personally dishonored.[22]

8. Then, the florin or golden penny of the chamber is to be always accepted and exchanged everywhere without surcharge or refusal for ninety full-weight pennies to be issued by our chamber.[23]

IX. Item una marca auri ponderis Budensis duodecim karatorum cambitur cum septem marcis ipsorum denariorum camere cum eodem pondere Budensi, levando in statera.[23]

X. Et nullus possit cambire aurum vel argentum cum pecunia numerata, sed debeat cambire in camera regali cum eisdem denariis camere ampliandis levando in statera.[25] Si qui autem secus fecisse vel facere reperti fuerint, pena condecenti tamquam transgressores regalis mandati et statuta camerarum infringentes puniantur.

XI. Ceterum statuimus, ut nullus omnino hominum cum aliquibus antiquis monetis aut auro vel argento, in specie et specialiter cum parvis et eciam mediocribus Wyenensibus, quorum omnimodam extirpationem volumus et commictimus, preterquam cum ipsis monetis camerarum nostrarum mercandi habeat facultatem, alioquin emptores et venditores suas res et bona perdent et dehonestabuntur in personis.[26]

XII. Preterea nullus mercator extraneus vel huius regni superveniens palam vel oculte in domibus aut camera suas res et bona, tam in pannis, quam in alii generis et speciei rebus, pro aliis monetis antiquis, cuiuslibet forme, auro vel argento, vendere aut commutare presumpmat, sed pro monetis camere predictis; de noticia tamen et ad scitum comitis camerarum aut predictorum hominum domini archyepiscopi et magistri tawarnicorum ac aliorum dum ad locum depositionis[27] ad vendendum vel commutandum devenerit, vendendi habeat facultatem. Si qui autem secus facientes et exercentes per ipsum comitem camerarum vel suos officiales reperti seu per eosdem deprehensi fuerint, res venditioni tam in pannis, quam in aliis rebus expositas et pro venditis rebus receptas perdant et puniantur in personis. Et nedum illi, qui per se et sua propria auctoritate contra ordinationem camerarum nostrarum et nostram voluntatem aurum vel argentum in specie, preterquam in aureis vel argenteis novis denariis exportantes inventi fuerint, ablatione eorundem et dehonestatione personarum suarum puniantur. Verum etiam et si sub sigillis vel signis camerariorum huiusmodi aurum vel argentum quoquam extra regnum deferendum fuerit inventum,[28] et si camerarii alios ad exportandum aurum vel argentum admiserint, iidem comites camerarum, quorum signa vel sigilla in ipso auro vel argento apposita invenientur, tamquam falsarii et transgressores regalium mandatorum puniantur.

XIII. Hoc tamen in presenti articulo specialiter expresso, quod comites camerarum nostrarum, sub quorum iurisditione montana habentur et existunt, pro comparando plumbo et aliis evidentibus necessariis camerarum et montanarum, sine quorum copia minere auri et argenti minime videntur posse procurari,[29] ad notitiam eorundem hominum domini archyepiscopi et aliorum, si tamen evidens necessitas id requirit, de auro vel argento tantum ad comparationem premissorum habebunt transmittendi facultatem.

9. Then, one mark of gold of the Buda weight of twelve carats is to be exchanged for seven marks of pennies of the chamber with the same Buda weight weighed on the scale.[24]

10. And no one may exchange gold and silver for counted money, but must exchange them for pennies issued by the royal chamber weighed on the scale.[25] If, however, anyone will be found to do or to have done otherwise, he is to be punished by a suitable penalty as transgressor of the royal mandate and infringer of the statute of the chamber.

11. We have decreed besides that no one at all should have the right to trade in any old money or unminted gold or silver, and particularly in the small or even medium Viennese ones which we wish and command to eradicate completely, but only in the money of our chamber; otherwise, buyers and sellers will lose their goods and chattels and will be personally dishonored.[26]

12. Henceforth, no foreign merchant or trader coming to this country should dare to sell overtly or covertly or to exchange his wares or goods, be it cloth or any other type and kind of merchandise, publicly or secretly, in houses or at the chamber, for old money of any form, or for gold and silver, but only for the said money of the chamber. Nevertheless, he should be allowed to sell when he comes to a place of staple,[27] for selling or trading with the knowledge and the advisement of the count of the chamber or the aforesaid men of the lord archbishop and of the Master of the Treasury and the others. However, if the count of the chamber or his officials find or apprehend any of the people acting or proceeding differently, these should lose the things set out for sale, cloth as well as other goods, and the price received for the goods sold, and they should be punished in person as well. And even more, not only those who are found exporting unminted gold or silver, other than the new gold and silver pennies, by their own authority against the ordinance of our chamber and our will, shall be punished by its confiscation and the dishonoring of their persons, but also, if gold or silver to be sent out of our kingdom is found with the seals or signs of the chamberlains,[28] and if the chamberlains allow gold or silver to be exported, the counts of the chamber whose seals or signs are found on this gold or silver must also be punished as counterfeiters and transgressors of the royal mandates.

13. Moreover, this is particularly emphasized in the present charter that the counts of our chamber under whose jurisdiction the mines lie, for the sake of procuring lead and other evident necessities of the chamber and the mines (without an abundance of which no gold and silver could be procured),[29] should have the power of transferring an amount of gold or silver with the knowledge of the men of the lord archbishop and the others, but only if it is obviously necessary.

XIV. Item sub cuiuscunque comitis camerarum comitatu vel in provinciis presens nostra moneta ex mala procuratione falsificata fuerit, et discurrere ac habundare ceperit, ipseque comes camerarum eandem falsam monetam captivare et anichilare non procuraverit, ipsi comiti camerarum sic imputabitur, ac si in locis camerarum suarum ipsa falsa moneta fuisset fabricata. Si autem ipse comes camerarum ad compesscendum eosdem falsarios de eorum malitiosis operibus propriam alicubi non habuerit facultatem, extunc idem camerarius sub testimoniis predictorum quinque hominum, veritate de eorundem falsariorum maleficiis indagata et recepta, eosdem falsarios nobis et nostris baronibus ac regno nominatim deberit declarare et nos pro extirpatione eorundem sollicite tenebitur incitare.

XV. Item quia volumus, ut presens moneta nostra tertie combustionis amplianda per totum regnum nostrum immutabiliter possit perpetuari et habundari, et ipsi denarii camere nostre annorum preteriti, tertii et quarti unacum eisdem novis pariter debeant discurrere et acceptari, statuentes ordinavimus et committimus, ut in quolibet comitatu de singulis portis, per quas currus cum feno vel frugibus honeratus intrare potest et exire, sive sub eadem porta seu curia portam habente tres vel quatuor, aut etiam plures existant homines residentes, sive solum unus commoretur in eadem, nisi in tantum sit egens et pauper, ut solvendi non habeat facultatem, quos videlicet prememorati quinque homines archyepiscopi et aliorum iuxta ipsorum conscientiam solvere posse cognoverint et commiserint, ac domini terre sibi solutionem facere posse vel non posse iuramento suo dixerint, exceptis servis et conditionariis nostrorum regalium et reginalium, ecclesiarum ac aliorum quorumlibet, necnon exercituantibus servientibus dominorum terre, quos ipsi iuramento eorum exceperint et iidem quinque homines, scilicet domini archyepiscopi et aliorum fore exercituantes investigando sciverint, et eciam exceptis ecclesiis, civitatibus vel aliis evidenti priivilegiata libertate fultis, facta dicatione infra quintumdecimum diem decem et octo denarios predicte camere nostre pro lucro camere ipsi comiti camerarum dare et solvere teneantur. Tali tamen expressione mediante, quod ubi et in quibus comitatibus aut regni nostri partibus porte tum ex consuetudine non habentur, tum etiam propter defectum lignorum fieri non potuerint, inibi et ipsi tales predictum lucrum camere, secundum quod in aliis temporibus, iuxta tamen dispositionem et conscientiosam ordinationem predictorum quinque hominum infra idem tempus solvere tenebuntur.

XVI. Civitates autem et alii regnicole nostri predictam evidentem libertatem habentes a solutione lucri camere taliter sint exempti, si tamen ipsas monetas camere nostre in tenutis ipsorum et inter eos ac iobagiones eorundem acceptari faciendo continuum cursum et cambium earundem voluerint facere et exercere; sin autem, non per nos, sed per se ipsos libertates eorum infringentur et sic ad solutionem eiusdem lucri

14. Then, if in the county or province of any count of the chamber our present money is by evil management forged and distributed and becomes abundant, and the count of the chamber has not taken care of seizing and destroying this same money, it will be deemed as though the false money had been made on the minting premises of this count of the chamber. However, if this same count of the chamber has not had sufficient force in any place to curb the forgers in their wicked works, then that chamberlain with the witness of the aforesaid five men, having investigated and learned the truth about the evil deeds of the counterfeiters, must denounce these very forgers by name to us, our barons, and our council, and urge us to root them out.

15. Then, since we wish that our present money of third firing issued in increased amount should remain unchangeably in circulation and be made abundant throughout our whole realm and that the pennies of our chamber of the last three years should be equally distributed and accepted with the new pennies, we have ordered and decreed by mandate that in every county from every gate through which a wagon loaded with hay or grain can enter or leave, whether behind this same gate or on a plot having a gate, three or four or even more men live, or if only one lives there,[30] eighteen pennies of our said chamber as the chamber's profit are to be rendered and paid on the fifteenth day after the assessment to the count of the chamber,[31] with the following exceptions: those who are so needy or poor that they cannot pay, what the aforementioned five men of the archbishop and the others on their conscience define and command to be able to pay, and the lords of the land swore on their oath whether they are able to pay or not; servants and *conditionarii* of the king, the queen, the churches or others;[32] the military *servitors* of the lords, whom they exempted on their oath, and the five men (namely the men of the lord archbishop and the others) found by investigation to be such soldiers; and also churches, cities, or others with explicit privileged liberty. Nevertheless, noting that such payment is to be halved there and in such counties or parts of our realm where gates are not customary, or where they cannot be built because of lack of wood; there and then such people are liable to pay the said chamber's profit just as in other times, at the same term according to the circumspect decision of the said five men.[33]

16. However, citizens and other subjects of ours having the aforesaid patent liberty shall remain exempt from the payment of the chamber's profit if they ensure the continuous circulation and exchange of these monies among them and the tenant peasants on their estates. Otherwise, their liberties are infringed upon not by us, but by themselves, and then they are just as liable as our other subjects for the

camere sicut alii regnicole nostri, sic et ipsi, dummodo hoc, ut ipsa moneta nostra per eos non fuerit acceptata, nec inter ipsos et ad eos pertinentes cambiri curata fuerit, ad relationem quinque hominum predictorum, videlicet domini archyepiscopi et magistri tawarnicorum ac comitis parochyalis, unius iudicis nobilium et alicuius capituli nobis pateat evidenter, tenebuntur.[34]

XVII. Ita tamen, quod quivis camerariorum ad singulos comitatus sue camere sufficientes denarios camere nostre pro multiplicatione dictorum modernorum denariorum nostrorum ad scitum et notitiam eorundem quinque hominum in tanta habundantia, quod ipse comitatus de ipsis contentetur, dare debeat cambio exponendos, qui si non faceret, aut ipsos nostros denarios in tam larga copia cambio exponere non curaret, illic et in illis comitatibus iura sua perdendo nec dicam faciendi, nec lucrum camere exigendi habeat facultatem.[35]

XVIII. Solventibus autem in quolibet comitatu unus locus communis et conveniens pro dicta solutione deputetur, et si qui presentes pre multitudine solventium aut aliquo impedimento alio prepediti die assignato solvere non possent, absque aliquo gravamine quatuor diebus continuis expectentur, nec infra ipsos quatuor dies integros, si solutionem fecerint, possint aggravari.

XIX. Hoc expresso, quod iidem comites camere ipsum lucrum camere ratione cambii signater impositum non aliter, videlicet cum Wyenensibus aut aliquibus antiquis denariis vel grossis per formam compositionis aut alicius alterius coloris cautela, nisi cum ipsis integris denariis camere nostre ampliandis exigere tenebuntur; et quod universos denarios antiquos aut Wyenenses grossos, tam Bohemicales, quam Racenses et alios, cuiuscunque forme existant,[36] exceptis solummodo presentibus integris denariis camere nostre perpetuo currere statutis comburrere et infundere ac in formam modernorum denariorum nostrorum redigi facere pro multiplicatione eorundem teneantur, conditione tali, quod si qui facta dicatione in termino assignato lucrum camere non persolverent, tunc iidem quinque homines ad possessionem, de qua ipsum lucrum camere non est persolutum, accedant, et tamdiu moram ibi faciant absque destructione et spoliatione possessionaria, in expensa moderata eiusdem possessionis, donec ipsum lucrum camere cum iudicio trium marcarum persolvatur.[37]

XX. Si vero populi vel domini villarum non solventium lucrum camere prenotate preterito termino solutionis dictis hominibus in officio camere procedentibus cum pecunia debita et iudicio ordinato extra villam obviarent placaturi, extunc ipsi executores negotiorum camere in talibus villis descensum facere non valeant aliqualem.

XXI. Comites autem parochiales et iudices nobilium favore vel pretio corruptos iustitiam camere celantes et homines de dicta solutione

payment of this chamber's profit, and so these people, provided that it be clearly evident to us from the report of the said five men, namely, the men of the lord archbishop, the Master of the Treasury, the *ispán* of the county, a noble magistrate and a man of a chapter, that our money was not accepted by them, nor was it arranged to be exchanged among them or by those belonging to them.[34]

17. Moreover, every chamberlain should dispatch for exchange in every county of his chamber sufficient pennies produced by our chamber for the multiplication of our said new pennies with the knowledge and acknowledgement of the five men in such abundance that the county is supplied by them to satisfaction. If he has not done this or does not take care to set out for exchange our new pennies in such an abundant amount, then in those counties he should lose his rights and shall not be able to demand the chamber's profit nor any other tax.[35]

18. In every county one common and convenient place is to be designated for those paying the said payment, and if those present are not able to pay on the day assigned because of the great number of taxpayers or some other impediment, they are to be awaited without penalty for four continuous days; nor may they be penalized if they make the payment within these four days.

19. It should also be noted that these same counts of the chamber are not allowed to collect the chamber's profit imposed exclusively for the purpose of exchange in any other way, that is, in Viennese or other old or large pennies by any kind of agreement or under any pretext, but only in the full-weight pennies of our chamber now issued, and that they are required to melt down and cast all old pennies or large Viennese, Bohemian, as well as Serbian ones, and others of any form,[36] save only the current whole pennies of our chamber which we have decreed to remain permanently in currency, and mint them into our new pennies for their increase; on such a condition that if anyone was not paying the chamber's profit after the assessment at the assigned term, then the same five men should move onto the property from which this chamber's profit was not paid and stay there without destruction or spoliation, at a moderate cost to the property, until the chamber's profit is paid together with a fine of three marks.[37]

20. However, if the people or the lords of the villages are remiss in paying the profit of the said chamber at the term of payment meet the said men acting in the business of the chamber outside the village with the money owed and the assessed fine ordered to be paid, then these agents of the business of the chamber should not have the right to move onto any property in such villages.

21. *Ispánok* of counties and noble magistrates who for favor or for a payment conceal and release men from the said payment in any way

deferendentes vel quoquo modo contra nostram ordinationem procedentes, dummodo contra ipsos hoc evidenter possit comprobari, penis non solventium decrevimus puniendos.

XXII. Et quia promisimus seriem omnium premissorum inviolabiliter observare, volumus, ut iidem comites camerarum nostrarum immutabiliter in premissis perseverent. E converso nec remedio aliquarum litterarum post emanationem presentium confectarum aut acquisita aliqua astutia quicquam immutare queant de singulis premissorum. Quia si qui contra hoc facere ex ipsis comitibus camerarum attemptarent, dictos quinque homines, sine quorum iuvamine lucrum camere exigendi nolumus eos habere facultatem, a societate ipsorum auctoritate presentium iubemus separari. Nam hanc dicam non pro exactione antiquarum monetarum aut Wyenensium, sed pro ampliatione monetarum camere nostre[38] perpetuo discurrere in toto regno nostro ordinatarum duximus disponendam.

XXIII. Item volumus, quod dicti comites camere nostre absque predictis quinque hominibus in negotiis camere exterioribus seu extraneis, videlicet in comitatibus fiendis et peragendis, utpote in dicationibus et exactionibus lucri camere nichil possint exercere. Si vero ausu temerario contra hoc procederent et in hoc malum aliquid paterentur, merito patientur et sustinebunt.

XXIV. Item si comitibus camere et suis sequacibus aut cum eo procedentibus violentiam quipiam inferrent manifeste, tales secundum qualitatem et quantitatem delicti puniantur.

XXV. Civitatenses vero sub comitatu et iurisditione eorundem comitatuum camere existentes iuxta presentem taxationem nostram et baronum nostrorum certam sumpmam pecunie de predictis monetis camere ampliandis similiter infra pretacti temporis spatium pro argento cambire vel finationem eiusdem monete camere in eisdem denariis camere ampliandis dare et solvere teneantur, videlicet Zalankemen ducentas et quadraginta marcas, item Zemlyn quindecim, item Zenthdemeter quinquaginta, item Engh sexaginta, item Noghaloz viginti quinque, item Eztyen triginta, item Segusd, Aranyas, Labaad et Chehy cum suis pertinentiis centum, item Peech quadraginta marcas[39] modo predicto cambire teneatur; ita videlicet, quod aut ipsi civitatenses receptis ipsis quantitatibus pecunie nove monete camere pro qualibet marca octo pensas in statera ponderanti unam marcam fini argenti, vel saltim nichil recipiendo combustionem seu finationem singularum marcarum ipsius monete, videlicet de singulis marcis super ipsos impositis singulas quatuor pensas predictarum monetarum, quarum octo pense marcam ponderant, dare debeant.[40] Si qua autem civitatum negligens fuerit in solvendo, predicti executores negotiorum camere in medio talis civitatis tamdiu permanebunt, quosque cum gravamine duodecim

against our ordinance should be punished with the penalty of those who do not pay if there is clear proof against them.

22. Since we have promised to observe inviolably all of the foregoing, we wish that these same counts of our chamber should also strictly adhere to these matters. And, conversely, neither by means of any charter issued after the present one, nor by some clever cunning should anyone dare to change anything of the foregoing. Thus if any one from among the counts of the chamber should attempt to act against this order, we command that the said five men, without whose assistance we do not wish the chamber's profit to be collected, should exclude him by the force of this letter from their midst, for we have commanded this tax to be collected not for levying old or Viennese monies but for the increase of the monies of our chamber[38] with coins which we intend to keep permanently circulating throughout the whole realm.

23. Then, we wish that the said counts of our chamber should not be able, without the said five men, to enter into foreign or outside business of the chamber, namely such matters that should be conducted and transacted in the counties, particularly in the assessment and levying of the chamber's profit. If they rashly attempt to proceed contrariwise and hence something evil occurs to them, they will deserve to endure and suffer it.

24. Then, anyone who attacks the count of the chamber, his company, or those traveling with him with manifest violence shall be punished according to the quality and quantity of the delict.

25. Burghers living in the cities located in counties of the counts of the chamber and under their jurisdiction are required, according to our and our barons' present assessment, to exchange a certain sum of money from the said money of the chamber issued for their increase within the said space of time for silver or to pay for the refining of this same money of the chamber issued for their increase in the pennies of the chamber. The following have to exchange in the aforesaid manner: Szalánkemén 240 marks, Zimony 15, Szentdemeter 50, Eng 60, Nagyolasz 25, Esztyán 30, Segesd, Aranyos, Labod, and Csehi with their appurtenances 100, and Pécs 40 marks[39] in such a way that these citizens either render one mark of fine silver after having received these quantities in the new money of the chamber for any mark weighing eight *pensae* by weight or, without accepting anything, pay for the refining or firing of that money, for every mark assessment four *pensae* of the said monies, of which eight *pensae* weigh a mark.[40] If, however, a city is negligent in paying, the said agents of the business of the chamber shall remain in such a city at the moderate expense of the city with the help of the judge and jurors of the same until the said payment with a fine of twelve marks is paid.

marcarum solutionem faciet prenotatam, in expensa tamen eiusdem civitatis moderata cum adiutorio iudicis et iuratorum eiusdem civitatis.

XXVI. Hoc declarato, quod quilibet nobilis super solutione lucri camere litteras expeditorias[41] a comite camerarum pro uno grosso redimere, licet plures habeat possessiones, teneatur.

XXVII. Item statuimus, quod in quibuslibet solitis locis camere in civitatibus debeat fieri domus regalis, ad quam omnes homines aurum et argentum ad vendendum, comburrendum et cambiendum defferre teneantur,[42] et si palam vel occulte alias comburrere, vendere vel commutare presumpserint et in hoc reperti fuerint, per eundem comitem camerarum omina bona sua presentibus supradictis testimoniis auferantur et insuper ut infideles puniantur.

XXVIII. Volumus etiam, ut nullus alias preterquam in domo regia aurum, quot karatorum fiat, probare debeat, sed camerarius debeat examinare in domo regia et ponere karatos et signo nostro regio inprimi faciat et consignari. Contra hoc autem presumpmentes per eundem comitem camerarum predicta pena iussimus puniendos.

XXIX. Ceterum statuimus, ut nullus mercator aut quilibet alter ultra duas marcas denariorum ad montana secum defferre presumpmat pro expensis. Si autem ipse comes camerarum vel sui officiales apud tales ultra duas marcas reperient in denariis, auferant bona sua universa et puniant eum in persona presentibus testimoniis supradictis.[43]

XXX. Et ut camerariorum nostrorum iustitia appareat in denariis fabricandis, statuimus, ut quidlibet eorum in ipsorum monetis signum habeat, per quod moneta per ipsum fabricata cognoscatur.[44]

XXXI. Ceterum volumus, ut ipse comes camerarum monetarios vel cusores denariorum ubique in civitatibus aut in villis invenire poterit et eosdem captivare voluerit, tunc iudex, iurati et universitas civitatis vel ville, in qua reperti fuerint, ad requisitionem ipsius comitis camere vel eius officialium ipsos monetarios captivare et ad manus comitis camerarum teneantur assignare. Si qui autem secus fecerint, eadem pena, qua monetarii contumaces sunt plectendi, puniantur.

XXXII. Item ipse comes camerarum nostrarum in civitatibus nostris, ubi monete nostre fabricantur, debet habere duo scrinia, in quorum uno ferramenta formalia sub sigillis hominum dominorum archyepiscopi et magistri tawarnicorum conserventur,[45] in altero vero virgule pro monetis fuse, absque monetis novis, sub sigillis tribus et clavibus tribus eorundem trium hominum, videlicet archyepiscopi et magistri tawarnicorum ac eiusdem camerarii debent conservari et semper in presentia hominum ipsorum archyepiscopi et magistri tawarnicorum apperiantur, nec possint aliquo ipsorum absente aperiri vel opera monetarum exerceri. Ita, quod si idem comes camerarum nostrarum ipsis duobus testibus absentibus vel aliquo ipsorum absente

26. It is also stated that every noble is required to procure a letter of quittance[41] for one large penny from the count of the chamber on payment of the chamber's profit even if he has several possessions.

27. Then, we have ordered that in the usual cameral locations in the cities a royal house should be established to which everyone must bring gold and silver for sale, refining, and exchange.[42] If any one dares publicly or privately to refine, sell, or exchange elsewhere and is discovered in this, all his goods are to be confiscated by the count of the chamber in the presence of the aforementioned witnesses, and he is also to be punished as a traitor.

28. We command that no one should test gold (for how many carats it contains) in any place except in a royal building, but the chamberlain should examine it in the royal house, and he should have the carats engraved and marked with our royal mark. We have ordered that those daring to act contrariwise are to be punished by the aforesaid penalty by the same count of the chamber.

29. Furthermore, we order that no merchant or any other person should dare to take with him to the mining areas more than two marks of pennies for expenses. If the count of the chamber or his officials should find on such a person more than two marks in pennies they should confiscate all his goods and punish him in person in the presence of the said witnesses.[43]

30. In order that the justness of our chamberlains in the minting of the pennies should be apparent, we have ordered that each of them should have a sign in his mint by which money made by him can be recognized.[44]

31. Furthermore, we wish that, should the count of the chamber find counterfeiters or makers of pennies in any city or village and attempt to capture them, the judge, jurors, and all the people of the city or village in which they were found be obligated, at the request of the count of the chamber or his official, to capture these minters and to surrender them into the hands of the count of the chamber. If, however, anyone does otherwise, he should be punished by the penalty for contumacious counterfeiting.

32. Then, in our cities where our money is made, the count of our chamber should have two chests. In one chest the iron tools for minting should be kept under the seal of the men of the lord archbishop and the Master of the Treasury,[45] in the other chest no new coins, but the cast rods for minting money should be kept under three seals and three keys of the same three men, namely the men of the archbishop, the Master of the Treasury, and the officer of the chamber, and they should always be opened in the presence of the men of the archbishop and of the Master of the Treasury; when any of them is absent the chest must not be opened nor money minted. If the count of our chamber, when these two witnesses are absent or when even one is absent, should break the

fractis clavibus et sigillis monetas faceret fabricari, per ipsum magistrum tawarnicorum tamquam falsarius puniatur, dummodo hoc iidem homines domini archyepiscopi et magistri tawarnicorum fateantur.

XXXIII. Specialiter dum funditur argentum, omnes personaliter interesse debeant et singulis septimanis ipsos novos denarios nostros ipsi homines domini archyepiscopi et magistri tawarnicorum in combustione quadraginta eorundem denariorum novorum debeant examinare, et sic iidem novi denarii cambio exponantur.[46]

XXXIV. Item cusores denariorum et fabricatores in eisdem nostris civitatibus commorantes, ne ipse comes camerarum nostrarum pro falsis monetis inculpetur, sub potestate et iurisditione eiusdem remanebunt. Ceterum antiqua libertate camerarum nostrarum requirente statuimus, ut omnes servientes et officiales ac monetarios ipse comes camere nostre et non alter debeat iudicare; et si ipse ex parte quorum iustitiam dare neglexerit, magister tawarnicorum nostrorum predictus iustitiam facere teneatur quibuscunque querulantibus de eisdem.

XXXV. Item pro ampliatione earundem monetarum camerarum nostrarum statuimus, ut universi ecclesiarum prelati decimas et debita ac quosvis reditus ac etiam cuncti regni nostri barones et nobiles aliique cuiusvis status homines ipsorum proventus universos, scilicet tributa, terragia et quasvis collectas a quibuscunque ipsorum debitoribus et jobagionibus, tributariis et officialibus cum ipsis monetis camere nostre aut florenis recipere et exigi facere teneantur, dummodo ipsi denarii camere nostre in tanta copia cudantur, ut omnes debitores sua debita cum ipsis denariis camere persolvendi habeant facultatem. Nos autem promittentes assumpmimus universas nostras collectas regales et reginales per totum regnum nostrum, specialiter tributa nostra et tricesimas nostras[47] exigi facere et recipere cum eisdem.

XXXVI. Item si qui contra ipsum comitem camerarum nostrarum ratione iniuriarum seu dampnorum aut nocumentorum personis camerariorum nostrorum in officio procedentibus illatorum ad nostram vel magistri tawarnicorum presentiam citati fuerint, in primo termino,[48] absque ulteriori dilatione, dante iustitia ipsa causa finaliter debeat terminari. Quicunque autem comitem camere nostre predictum ordine iudiciario in causam attraxerit, prelibatus magister tawarnicorum nostrorum ex parte eiusdem iustitiam faciet nostra auctoritate mediante.

XXXVII. Hoc etiam ordinavimus, ut de quibuslibet rebus et bonis ipsarum camerarum nostrarum ubicunque in terra et in aquis per earundem officiales deferendis nullum tributum exigatur.

XXXVIII. Preterea de qualibet marca unum pondus ad rationem denariorum ratione conservationis ferramentorum homini eiusdem archyepiscopi omni die operis,[49] et dimidius ferto[50] homini ipsius

seals and the lock and cause money to be minted, he should be punished as a counterfeiter by the Master of the Treasury if the men of the lord archbishop and the Master of the Treasury so testify.

33. Particularly, when silver is cast, all these people must be present in person, and every single week the men of the lord archbishop and of the Master of the Treasury should examine our new pennies by melting down forty of them before they are put out for exchange in the described way.[46]

34. Then, in order to avoid that the count of the chamber be accused because of counterfeit money, the minters and makers of pennies living in our said cities shall remain under his power and jurisdiction. Furthermore, as the ancient liberty of our chamberlains demands, only the count of the chamber and no other ought to judge all *servientes*, officials, and minters, and if he should neglect to render justice in regard to his men, our said Master of the Treasury is to give justice to any complainant.

35. Then, for the increase of the monies of our chamber we order that all prelates of churches be obligated to receive and to collect the tithes, debts, and any other payments, just as all barons and nobles of our realm and others of whatever estate, all revenues, namely tolls, rents, and whatever other taxes from their debtors, tenant peasants, toll collectors, and officials, in the money of our chamber or florins, as soon as pennies of our chamber are struck in such abundance that all debtors will be able to pay their debts with pennies of the chamber. In turn we promise and agree to receive and to collect all our royal taxes and those of the queen throughout our entire realm, particularly our tolls and our thirtieth,[47] in these same pennies.

36. Then, if anyone will be summoned to our presence or to that of the Master of the Treasury in any offense against the count of our chamber by reason of injury or damage or harm inflicted to the men of our chamber acting on business, the suit should be terminated without further delay at the first term,[48] as justice demands. If, however, the said count of our chamber should be sued at law by anyone, the said Master of the Treasury, by our authority, shall ensure justice on behalf of that person.

37. We have ordered also that no tolls are to be demanded for any goods or chattels of our chambers shipped anywhere by land or by water by the officials of the chamber.

38. Furthermore, one *pondus* reckoned in pennies is to be paid for every mark to the man of the archbishop at every day of work for the safeguarding of the minting tools,[49] and half a *ferto*[50] to the man of the

magistri tawarnicorum preter sumpmam conventionis nostre regalis persolvatur. Si vero ipse comes camere nostre quolibet die operis de singulis marcis cusis singula pondera denariorum et dictos dimidios fertones premisso modo persolvere recusaverit vel dilationem facere vellet, homines ipsius domini archyepiscopi et magistri tawarnicorum ferramenta formalia includendi habeant facultatem.

XXXIX. Item aule nostre vicecancellario idem comes camere nostre proventus ab antiquo consuetos, videlicet triginta marcas in terminis solutionum subscriptarum, salvis proventibus notariorum remanentibus, plene dare et solvere teneatur.

XL. Hoc etiam adiecto, quod iniurias et dampna officialibus camerarum per quoscunque irrogata prefatus magister tawarnicorum prosequatur et emendet. De falsariis autem et eorum fautoribus antiquam regni nostri consuetudinem volumus observari.[51]

XLI. Item statuimus, ut comites parochyales quorumlibet comitatuum non plus, quam tres marcas octo pensarum nove monete nostre a comitibus camerarum nostrarum petere vel recipere ratione fororum presumpmant.[52] Nobiles autem vel cuiusvis alterius status homines fora habentes pretextu fororum ipsorum ab eisdem camerariis quicquam petere vel recipere non presumpmant.

XLII. Volumus etiam quod tam magister tawarnicorum suos dimidios fertones, quam dominus archyepiscopus sua pondera quibuspiam vendere non possint et locare; quod si fecerint, hiis iuribus ipsorum priventur.[53]

XLIII. Preterea iidem archyepiscopus et magister tawarnicorum tales homines in prosequendis negotiorum camerarum transmittant, qui possessiones habeant, et si demerita eorum requirerent, perdere habeant.

XLIV. Item comites camerarum nostrarum, qui anno sequenti cameras nostras conducere voluerint, in die Strennarum venturo de predictis suis debitis rationem nobis personaliter reddendo conducant.

XLV. Item quia superius tetigimus,[54] ut prefati quinque homines executores negotiorum camere super civitates huic nostre ordinationi rebellantes lucrum camere in expensa moderata commorando, cum subsidio iudicum et iuratorum earumdem civitatum plene exigere cum gravamine iudicii duodecim marcarum et eisdem comitibus camerarum nostrarum plenarie persolvi facere teneantur, ideo volumus, ut si ipsi iudices et iurati presenti nostro mandato obedire recusarent, extunc ipsum lucrum camere non solutum plene et dictum iudicium duodecim marcarum cum dupplo persolvere teneantur.

XLVI. Exprimentes etiam, quod quecunque res et bona ratione non observationis aliquorum articulorum premissorum et transgressionis mandati nostri regalis seu violationis statuti camere a quibuscunque personis hominum et quibuscunque locis auferentur, in tres partes

Master of the Treasury, above the amount established in our royal contract. If the said count of our chamber should refuse to pay in the aforesaid manner or should wish to delay payment on any day of work the *pondera* of pennies or the said half *fertones* for every mark minted, the men of the said lord archbishop and of the Master of the Treasury shall have the right to lock up the minting tools.

39. Then, the same count of our chamber must pay in full the vicechancellor of our court the long-established customary revenue, namely, thirty marks at the dates of the payments written below, besides the revenue due to the notaries.

40. We also wish to add that the aforementioned Master of the Treasury should prosecute and amend injuries and losses inflicted by anyone on the officials of the chamber. Concerning counterfeiters and their protectors, we wish that the ancient custom of our kingdom be observed.[51]

41. Then, we have ordered that no *ispán* of any county should presume to demand or to collect from the counts of our chamber as market fee more than three marks of eight *pensae* each from our new money.[52] Nobles or other men of any estate holding market rights should not dare to demand or collect anything from these chamberlains.

42. We also command that neither the Master of the Treasury should be able to sell or to lease his half *fertones* to anyone, nor the lord archbishop his *pondera*; should they do so, they are to be deprived of their rights.[53]

43. Moreover, to attend to the business of the chamber the same archbishop and Master of the Treasury must send men who have possessions, so that if their tresspasses may warrant it, they could lose these.

44. Then, the counts of the chamber who wish to farm our chambers in the following year should farm them on New Year's Day, having given account of their debts to us personally.

45. Then, if—as we have touched on this above[54]—the said five men, agents of the chamber's business, who are required to stay at a moderate expense and collect with the help of the judge and the jurors the chamber's profit and twelve marks fine in cities that are reluctant to hand it over completely to the count of the said chamber, find that the judge and jurors refuse to obey this ordinance of ours, we command that they are held to render the chamber's profit in its entirety together with double the amount of the twelve marks fine.

46. We state also that all goods and chattels confiscated from anyone anywhere because of contempt for any of the said articles, for transgression of our royal mandate or violation of the statute of the chamber, ought to be divided into three equal parts, two of which should

debeant dividi coequales, quarum due partes ipsi comiti camerarum, tertia vero pars in manus predictorum hominum domini archyepiscopi et magistri tawarnicorum debeant provenire.

XLVII. Item de quibuslibet marcis pro lucro camere in quibuslibet comitatibus dicatis et exactis unum grossum seu unum pondus homini domni arhyepiscopi, alium vero grossum seu pondus homini magistri tawarnicorum dare et solvere tenebitur comes camerarum predictarum.[55]

XLVIII. Istud tamen expresse volumus, quod si ipse comes camerarum nostrarum ipsam monetam camere nostre in locis solitis camere cudendo habundanter fabricari non fecerit, et ipse solum ad dicam et exactionem lucri eiusdem camere se dissimulando commiserit, extunc ipse talis, tamquam nos seducens et regni nostri deceptor seu mendax contra nostram maiestatem convincatur.

XLIX. Ut autem idem comes camerarum memoratam sumpmam pecunie mille et quingentarum marcarum nobis facilius solvere possit, ordinantes decrevimus, ut in octavis festi Nativitatis beati Johannis Baptiste trecentas et septuaginta quinque marcas, item in octavis Nativitatis beate virginis similiter trecentas et septuaginta quinque marcas et modo simili trecentas et septuaginta quinque marcas in octavis festi beati Martini, residuas vero trecentas et septuaginta quinque marcas in octavis diei Strennarum nunc venturis ultimam solutionem faciendo, in terminis sese invicem subsequentibus nunc venturis,[56] hic in Wyssegrad cum monetis prenotatis modo premisso solvere nobis tenebitur. Penam duppli incurrat, si aliquem terminorum premissorum obmiserit insolutum.

Datum in Wyssegrad in festo Purificationis beate virginis, anno domini supradicto.

go to the same count of the chamber, the third to the hands of the said men of the lord archbishop and the Master of the Treasury.

47. The count of the said chamber will be required to render and pay from every mark collected as the chamber's profit in any county one large penny or one *pondus* to the man of the lord archbishop and another large penny or *pondus* to the man of the Master of the Treasury.[55]

48. However, we command expressly that if the count of our chamber does not cause money of our chamber to be made in the accustomed places of the chamber in abundance, and, by dissimulation, merely declares his intent to collect the chamber's profit, then such a man is to be punished as leading us astray, as a deceiver of our kingdom and a liar against our majesty.

49. In order that the count of the said chamber should be able to pay us more easily the sum of fifteen hundred marks, we have ordered and decreed that he should pay us at the octave of the feast of the nativity of the blessed John the Baptist three hundred and seventy-five marks and similarly three hundred and seventy-five marks on the octave of the feast of the Blessed Virgin, and in a similar manner three hundred and seventy-five marks in the octave of the feast of the Blessed Martin, making the last payment of the remaining three hundred and seventy-five marks at the octave of the New Year's Day at subsequent dates,[56] here in Visegrád in the said money and the said manner. If he omits any payment of the said terms he should incur a double penalty.

Given at Visegrád on the feast of the Purification of the Virgin in the above-mentioned year.

Propositiones
(1432/33)

Vide praefatiunculam et notas infra paginas 245–48.

CIRCA MODUM ET FORMAM DEFENSIONIS TOTIUS REGNI HUNGARIE CONTRA OMNES INIMICOS EX QUACUNQUE PARTE IPSUM REGNUM INSULTANTES NOTATA SUNT INFRASCRIPTA.

I. Quia ex regni Hungarie ab antiquo observata lege et consuetudine debitum fuit, ut ultra defensionem, quam rex et regina ac prelati ecclesiarum et viri ecclesiastici ipsius regni de regiis et reginalibus ac ecclesiarum proventibus pro conservatione regni eiusdem et confiniorum suorum ex omni parte facere tenentur, etiam universitas regnicolarum nobilium et possessionatorum pro huiusmodi defensione confiniorum regni contra omnes inimicos regnum ipsum insultantes in generali exercitu regni universaliter proficisci tenetur; item quia etiam rex Hungarie utitur ultra titulum regni Hungarie horum regnorum titulis, videlicet Dalmatie, Croatie, Rame, Seruie, Gallicie, Lodomerie, Cumanie et Bulgarie, que scilicet regna sunt ab antiquo eidem regno Hungarie incorporata,[1] et ad horum cuiuslibet conservationem et confiniorum defensionem per regem, reginam, prelatos, viros ecclesiasticos et communitatem nobilium et possessionatorum hominum necessario semper est intelligendum, videtur itaque regie maiestati, quod domini prelati et barones in unum locum et ad certum terminum facerent generalem convocationem et aliquos de quolibet comitatu totius regni advocarent, cum quibus habito tractatu declarent per expressum de locis et terminis per totum circuitum regni, usque quem scilicet locum et terminum, ac quamdiu pro regni defensione contra inimicos communitatis regnicolarum generalis exercitus deberet, sicut tenetur, ingruente necessitate proficisci atque stare.

II. Item quia precedentia gesta generalis exercitus communitatis regnicolarum manifestam prebuerint experientiam generalis utilitatis, qualis profectus provenerit ex generali exercitu regnicolarum circa defensionem et conservationem regni, cum alii ex eisdem plurimi aut paupertate aut senio aut alia impotentia constricti potius baculis, quam armis fulciti verius mendicitati, quam militie actu vacaverunt,[2] disponendum ergo esset et providendum, quod hi, qui irent pro defensione regni, non essent inermes, sed haberent saltem arcus et alia arma, quibus pro defensione regni ad offensam hostium se exponere possint. Videtur utilius, quod de quolibet comitatu mitterentur certo

Propositions of c. 1432/1433

For prefatory and explanatory notes, see below, pages 245–48.

THE FOLLOWING ARE TO BE NOTED ON THE MEANS AND METHODS OF DEFENDING THE WHOLE KINGDOM OF HUNGARY FROM ALL ENEMIES ATTACKING THAT KINGDOM FROM ANY DIRECTION.

1. Whereas it was due by law and custom observed since ancient times that beyond the defense forces, which the king, the queen, the prelates of churches, and the clergy of the kingdom are required to maintain from the king's and queen's revenues and from those of the churches for the preservation of this kingdom and its borders from any direction, the community of noble gentlemen of the realm and men of property is also required to set out together in general levy of the kingdom for the same defense of the borders of the realm against all enemies attacking this kingdom; and whereas besides the title of the kingdom of Hungary the king of Hungary also uses the titles of Dalmatia, Croatia, Rama, Serbia, Galicia, Lodomeria, Cumania, and Bulgaria, namely of those kingdoms which of old have been included in the kingdom of Hungary,[1] and the preservation of these and the defense of their borders by the king, queen, prelates, clergy, and the community of nobles and men of property must necessarily be also understood at all times, therefore, it appears to his royal majesty that the lords, prelates, and barons should summon a general assembly to one place and at a particular time and call men from every county of the whole kingdom and, after discussing the matter with them, should define expressly places and borders along the circumference of the whole kingdom, namely, those places and borders to which the general levy of the community of the gentleman of the realm has to go, and how long it has to stay there to defend the kingdom against enemies, when necessary.

2. Then, because past deeds of general levies of the community of the gentlemen of the realm offer clear proof of its overall usefulness, what benefit would arise from a general levy of gentlemen of the realm for the defense and preservation of the kingdom, if many of them, hindered by poverty, age, or other weaknesses, appear more on crutches rather than with arms, more like beggars than warriors?[2] Therefore, it should be arranged and provided that those who will set out to defend the kingdom ought not to be defenseless, but should at least have a bow and other arms with which they can withstand the attacks of enemies for the defense of the kingdom. It seems more useful

numero pharetrarii equestres secundum facultatem cuiuslibet comitatus, et ab huiusmodi pharetrariorum assignatione nullus nobilium se excusare et abstrahere possit, sed quilibet nobilis in illo comitatu, in quo possessionem habet, teneatur communiter cum communitate tale onus portare. Ita videlicet, quod videtur maiestati regie, ut in relevationem oneris pauperum, senum, orphanorum et viduarum nobilium ac possessionatorum[3] cuiuslibet comitatus ipsius regni, ut de quolibet comitatu certi numeri equestres pharetrarii bene valentes pro huiusmodi defensione confiniorum darentur et mitti deberent pro temporis necessitate; sic et ut pauperes nobiles, orphani et vidue non aggravarentur, ut per singula capita secundum regni consuetudinem proficiscerentur, sed ut computarentur tanti secundum eorum facultatem, quanti ex eis communi expensarum contributione unum hominem pharetrarium equestrem mittere possent. De nobilibus autem jobagiones habentibus fieret in quolibet comitatu per nobilium communitatem certa limitatio secundum facultatem eorundem, quanti homines mitti deberent ab eisdem, et sic hominibus, quos tam pauperes nobiles, quam etiam nobiles possessiones habentes dare debent, simul computatis videretur, quanti homines de quolibet comitatu ad huiusmodi exercitum mitti possint, et quod omnes tales ad exercitum ire debentes proficiscerentur sub conductu proprii comitis provincialis, sicuti fuit antiquitus consuetum, prout super hoc etiam capi potest exemplum et informatio de gestis specialiter regis Salamonis, Geysse ducis et de comite Vid Bachiensi et Jan comite Sproniensi, qui in expeditionibus eorundem regis et ducis contra Runos et Bissenos circa Nandoralbam cum Bachiensi et Sproniensi militarunt.[4]

III. Item videretur etiam disponendum sub gravibus penis, quod exercituantes, sive sint regis, sive regine, sive prelatorum vel baronum, aut generalis exercitus regni, dum et quandocunque ad exercitum se profecturos levabunt, neminem in suo transitu vel reditu deberent damnificare, quia sepe regnum ab huiusmodi exercituantibus plus offenditur et damnificatur, quam ab inimicis.[5]

IV. Item quod regia maiestas non nunciat eis talismodi dispositionem faciendum ex eo, quod aliquam novam dispositionem in eorum medium introduceret vel ipsos aggravaret, sed ideo, quia, ut apparet sue maiestati, ex tali dispositione multo maior utilitas et profectus regno Hungarie provenient, et quamvis isto modo numerus exercituantium esset minor, quam si tota communitas per singula capita insurgeret, tamen multo plures utilitates inde regno possunt provenire, et talismodi exercituatio non propter quascunque leves causas insurgere debeat, sed solummodo tunc, cum tam magna potentia inimicorum regnum Hungarie vellet invadere aut ei insultare, cui dominus rex cum suo exercitu proprio nequaquam resistere valeret.

V. Item quia communitas regni Hungarie solet allegare, quod dum in generali exercitu contra inimicorum insultus insurrexerit, non vult

that a definite number of mounted archers should be sent from every county according to the capacity of each county and that no noble should be able to excuse himself or to avoid sending archers, but every noble should bear the burden in common with the community of that county in which he holds property. It, therefore, seems clear to the royal majesty that in order to relieve the burden on the poor, the old, and the orphans and on widows of nobles and men of property[3] in every county of this kingdom, a definite number of mounted archers, well prepared for the defense of the borders, should be equipped and sent from every county in the time of necessity, in such a way that poor nobles, orphans, and widows should not be burdened by serving personally according to the custom of the realm, but it should be calculated how many of them are able by common contribution, according to their capacity, to send one man as a mounted archer. Concerning nobles having tenant peasants it should be exactly defined in every county by the community of nobles how many men should be sent, and thus having added the men sent by the poor and the propertied nobles, it should be clear how many men are to be sent to the army from every county altogether. These men, who are required to go to the army, should set out under the leadership of their own county's *ispán*, as was ancient custom, for which one may find example and guidance from the deeds particularly of king Solomon, duke Géza, Vid, *ispán* of Bács, and Jan, *ispán* of Sopron, who fought in the expeditions of that king and duke against the Greeks and Pechenegs around Belgrade with the troops of the counties of Bács and Sopron.[4]

3. Then, it also seems appropriate, and to be enforced by heavy penalties, that soldiers, whether they belong to the king, queen, prelates, barons, or, the general levy of the kingdom, as long as and whenever they are preparing themselves to set out for campaigning, cause no loss to anyone in marching to or from the army, for the kingdom is often harmed or injured more by its own soldiers than by enemies.[5]

4. Then, that his royal majesty sends the noble assemblies these propositions of future arrangements not in order to introduce some new arrangement to their midst or to burden them, but only because in the view of his majesty, greater advantage and profit will accrue to the kingdom of Hungary from such an arrangement. Although in this manner the number of soldiers may be less than if every member of the entire community rose up one by one, nevertheless, great profit can accrue to the kingdom, for such an army should not be raised for any trivial reason, but only if a very great force of enemies intends to invade or to attack the kingdom of Hungary and the lord king cannot resist it with his own army.

5. Then, because the community of the kingdom of Hungary usually insists that when it rises in a general levy against the attacks

amplius circa metas seu confinia regni stare, quam per quindecim dies, ideo videtur maiestati regie, ut si modo premisso per ipsam communitatem nobilium et possessionatorum hominum dicti equestres ex eorum medio pro exercitu generali fuerint deputati, contra quod tunc esset disponendum, quod huiusmodi equestres in metis illis, que iuxta pretacta scripta per communitatem nobilium declarabuntur seu limitabuntur, non tantummodo per dies quindecim contra inimicorum insultus stare deberent, sed tamdiu, quousque domino regi, si ipse in tali exercitu presens foret, vel capitaneis et ductoribus exercituum sua maiestate absente congruum et necessarium fore videtur, deberent permanere.[6] Et videtur maiestati regie, quod premissa, sicut scripta sunt, disponantur in alleviationem oneris pauperum nobilium, qui sunt impotentes ad exercituandum; teneantur secundum antiquam regni consuetudinem sic et taliter equis et armis decentibus apti et fulciti in exercitum acccedere aut suos mittere, ut non sint sic inerrnes, sicut preteritis temporibus fuerunt, quia aliter nihil boni eveniret ex talium exercituatione, sicut et alias de hoc sufficienter fuit expertum.

VI. Ut autem ad disponenda premissa consensu nobilium et possessionatorum hominum cuiuslibet comitatus accedente facilior et habilior modus habeatur, videtur, quod etiam pretacta ad quemlibet comitatum sint pro informatione in eodem existentium intimanda, ut in quolibet comitatu congregentur in unum propter habendam notitiam eis intimatorum et propter deliberare, si quid melius disponendum eis videbitur in premissis, ut cum sic deliberata eorum intentione aliquos ex eis instructos possint ad congregationem prelatorum et baronum destinare. Et ut premissa omnia ad notitiam communitatis cuiuslibet comitatus deduci possint, vult et mandat maiestas regia per vicecancellarium maioris sigilli sui regii ad quemlibet comitatum copiam huius regestri de verbo ad verbum scriptam pro informatione communitatis cuiuslibet comitatus destinare simul cum litteris eiusdem maiestatis tenorem littere sue hinc illac destinate[7] continentibus pro maiori certitudine voluntatis dicte maiestatis.

VII. Item videretur regie maiestati, quod si aliqui nobiles a rege vel regina, prelatis, baronibus, viris ecclesiasticis seu aliis quibuscunque essent stipendiati vel haberent officiolatus, tunc horum nullus propter servitia dominorum suorum ab exercituatione, quam ratione possessionum suarum facere debet, excusatus seu supportatus haberetur, sed pro se, ut disponeretur per communitatem comitatus, ratione possessionum suarum mittere teneretur, qui non secum, sed cum generali exercitu regnicolarum proficisceretur, ut sic quilibet ratione possessionum suarum cum communitate onus portaret.

VIII. Item videtur etiam disponendum, quantum pro una lancea et pharetrario equestri per regem, reginam, prelatos, barones et alios quoscunque exercituantibus stipendiariis solvi debeat, non tantum ad

of enemies it does not wish to remain at the frontiers or borders of the kingdom for longer than fifteen days, it seems right to his royal majesty that when the said mounted men have been dispatched for a general army from their midst in the above manner by the community of nobles and men of property, then these mounted men must remain against the attacks of enemies on those borders which will be declared or defined according to the aforementioned decision of the community of nobles, not for fifteen days only, but as long as it may seem necessary to the lord king, if he himself is present with the army, or in the absence of the majesty, to the captains and leaders of the armies.[6] And it seems proper to his royal majesty that the foregoing measures, as they are written, should be implemented in order to alleviate the burden on the poor nobles, who are unable to campaign; others should be required by ancient custom of the realm to go to the army or to send their men properly equipped and prepared with horses and arms so that they are not unarmed as they were in times past, because otherwise no good comes from an army of such men, as is well enough known from experience.

6. In order that the above should more easily and more conveniently receive the consent of the nobles and men of property of every county, it seems useful that the preceding should be sent to every county for the information of those living there, so that in every county they should be gathered together to receive notice of these matters communicated to them and to discuss, what seems to be the best arrangement for the foregoing, so that they can send suitable men with their decision to the assembly of prelates and barons. And in order that all the foregoing be brought to the notice of the community of every county, his royal majesty wishes and orders that the complete record word for word of this decision be sent for the information of the community of every county by the vice-chancellor under his greater royal seal, along with a letter containing the gist of his majesty's letter regarding this project[7] for greater certainty concerning the will of the same majesty.

7. Then, it seems good to his royal majesty that if any nobles are stipendiaries or hold offices from the king, the queen, the prelates, barons, ecclesiastics, or any others, then none of them may be held exempt or free because of service to his lords from military service, which he is required to perform owing to his property, but, according to his property subject to the decision of the community of the county, he must send someone in his stead, who will set out not with him, but with the general levy of the gentlemen of the realm, so that everyone will bear his burden, according to his holdings, along with the community.

8. Then, it also seems good that it be decided how much should be paid for one lance and one mounted archer by the king, the queen, the prelates, barons, and all others to the professional soldiers, and not the

dies, sed ad unam integram exercituationem, quia aliquando breviori tempore, et aliquando longiori poterit ipsa exercituatio expediri; et videtur, quod limitetur et taxetur huiusmodi pecunia pro lancea et pharetris ad unum florenum auri, ad quorum rationem solvatur cum moneta, quam pro eorum velle ex permissione regia prelati et barones locumtenentes maiestatis regie[8] et regnicole cudi facient, et quod nec dantes minus dare, nec etiam stipendiarii recipientes ad plus dandum teneantur, sicut etiam fuit factum per quondam comites Piponem et Dezpoth.[9]

IX. Et ut solutio nec solventi, nec recipienti cedere posset in damnum, sed esset in pretii moderamine equalitas utrique parti, videretur itaque disponendum et taxandum, ut venderentur et emerentur sales non eo modo, prout nunc fit, sed eo modo haberent pretium taxatum ad quodlibet sal, sicuti fuit tempore quondam domini regis Ludovici,[10] et videretur, quod sales ponderarent unum centenarium et statuerent pretium floreni auri, ut sic sciretur, quanto pretio emeretur centenarius salis et quanto libra una, ut tam lapides, quam etiam minuta salium haberent cursum in vendendo, et quod fieret talis limitatio, ut ultra expensas secture et etiam portature salium de camera ad cameram proventus regales in salibus non diminuerentur. In Polonia autem et per totam Alemaniam et Italiam ac in toto mundo sal venditur ad pondus et mensuram et sic ubilibet inter emendum et vendendum sal bona equalitas habetur, propter quod etiam regia maiestas desiderat disponi pro communi equitate, ut in regno Hungarie ad pondus et mensuram sal et minuta salium vendantur, si tamen eis videbitur.[11]

X. Item ordinaretur insuper, quod de salibus regalibus, qui de camera ad cameram portarentur, et etiam eorum conductoribus nullibi tributum reciperetur et contrafacientes subirent penam. Illi autem, que pro defensione regni et confiniorum ipsius de proventibus regalibus sunt disponenda, interim et hac vice disponant, prout ab ipsa maiestate regia per priora scripta habent in hoc datam eis facultatem.

XI. Videtur etiam necessario disponendum, quod omnes exercituantes generaliter et singulariter debeant et teneantur constitui die statuto et loco, in quo mandabitur eos debere, et quod hii, qui in die et loco statutis non constituerentur, subeant penam, quam vult regia maiestatis contra tales, quia sicut notum est, frequenter hi, qui prius venerant, fatigiis et tedio afficiuntur et usque dum ultimi adveniunt, in dissolutionem se converterunt.

XII. Item videtur etiam disponendum, quod nullus exercituantium de exercitu ante debitum ipsius tempus et sine licentia capitanei exercitus recedere presumeret, sub penis gravibus super hoc statutis et statuendis.

amount per day, but the one for an entire campaign, because one campaign may last a shorter time, another a longer time; and it seems right that this pay for lances and archers should be limited and prescribed as one gold florin, and that this amount should be paid in that money which at their wish by royal permission the prelates and barons, who are the vicars of of the royal majesty,[8] and the gentlemen of the realm will have minted, and that those paying must give no less and those paid must take no more than what is expected, just as was done by the late count Pipo and the despot.[9]

9. And in order that payment may cause no loss for either the payer or the receiver, but there should be equal moderation in the price on both sides, the following disposition and prescription seem equitable, that salt should not be sold and bought in the way it is now done, but the price should be set for any salt in the way it was in the time of the late lord king Louis;[10] and care shall be taken that one piece of salt should weigh one ton and its price be one gold florin, so that it be known what is the price of a ton of salt and what of one pound, so that both the blocks of rock salt and pieces of salt will have a value in selling. And there should be such a regulation that the royal revenues from salt should not be diminished beyond the expenses of cutting and of shipping the salt from chamber to chamber. In Poland, in all of Germany, in Italy, and indeed throughout the whole world, salt is sold by weight and quantity, and, consequently, there is fair exchange everywhere between salt for sale and salt bought; because this is so, the royal majesty also wishes to arrange, for the common good, that in the kingdom of Hungary blocks and pieces of salt should be sold by weight and quantity, but only if this seems right to them.[11]

10. Then, it should be further ordained that no toll may be exacted from the royal salt which is carried from chamber to chamber or from those carrying it; those acting otherwise will be subject to punishment. However, those means from the royal revenues which are to be assigned for the defense of the kingdom and its borders should be for the time being and this case disbursed in such way, as they are empowered by the royal majesty's earlier writings in this matter.

11. It also seems necessary to define that all soldiers together and singly must and are required to assemble at a set time and place which will be ordered for them, and that those who are not assembled at the arranged time and place must be subject to such punishment which the royal majesty desires for them, because it has been noted that frequently those who had come earlier, affected by weariness and tedium, begin to disperse by the time the last arrive.

12. Then, it also seems good to arrange that no man of the army should dare to leave the army before the set time and without leave from the commander of the army, subject to the heavy penalties that have been and are to be prescribed for this.

XIII. Et ut premissa sunt scripta et annotata super expeditionibus exercitualibus undecunque contra inimicos regni Hungarie insultantes futuris semper temporibus successivis pro defensione regni faciendis, verumtamen, quia inter respectum guerrarum Turcarum et Hwzitarum distincte et separatim fieri debent expeditiones exercituales, ideo hec, que sequuntur, maiestas regia duxit premissis addenda.

XIV. Item quia dominus rex est certificatus, quod oratores Huzitarum modis omnibus in sacro Basiliensi concilio existunt cum pleno mandato in materia fidei, qui uti spes firma habetur, suscepta a sacro concilio plena informatione dimissis erroribus ad obedientiam sancte matris ecclesie se reducent, et quia etiam ab ipso sacro concilio iam frequenter et litteris et nunctiis monita est ipsa maiestas, ut personaliter se ad ipsum concilium conferat, tum pro facto fidei, tum etiam reformatione morum et pace Christi fidelium,[12] quare ipsa maiestas attento, quod reditio Bohemorum Hwzitarum in facto temporalitatis sine ipsius principalitate debite et faciliter fieri non posset, cum et hoc idem scriptum est a concilio eius maiestati, attento etiam, quod temporale dominium Bohemorum concernit suam maiestatem, decrevit itaque sua maiestas negotiis imperialibus in Italia et specialiter cum Florentinis[13] ad statum votive dispositionis deductis citius, ut poterit, ad ipsum Basiliense concilium transire, ubi si ipsi Bohemi Hwzite ad obedientiam ecclesie et unitatem fidei reducti extiterint, sicut spes bona habetur de eisdem, extunc sine armis regnum Hungarie cum terris ab eisdem occupatis plenarie liberabitur ab Hwzitis, et ipsis reductis poterit concilium sub nomine passagii[14] a tota Christianitate de magna providentia providere, cum qua deo auxiliante sua maiestas personaliter proficiscendo poterit regnum Hungarie cum ceteris eidem annexis a Turcis penitus liberare et dominia sua dilatare atque ampliare. Si autem Hwzite in concilio reduci non poterint, extunc tota Christianitas providente ipso sacro concilio levabit manus suas in potentatu maximo contra ipsos Hwzytas, quo sic habito decrevit maiestas regia ipsa modis omnibus in Hungariam reverti personaliter et Tyrnauiam, Zakolcza ac alias terras et metas regni Hungarie ab ipsorum Hwzytarum manibus et potestate liberare.[15] Cum autem opportunum sit ante reversionem sue maiestatis in Hungariam per prelatos, barones et regnicolas sic disponere et providere de comitatibus, quorum nobiles et alii possessionati homines pro defensione regni ex parte Bohemie contra Hwzytas sunt deputati, sive per singula capita secundum antiquam consuetudinem regni veniant, sive de quolibet comitatu pharetrarii sub certo numero mittantur, ut omnes et singuli ad reditum ipsius maiestatis sue pro recuperatione civitatum, terrarum, metarum regni ab Hwzytis occupatarum sic promptos et dispositos se conservent, ut quamprimum moniti fuerint, statim possint ad exercituandum moveri et versus

13. All that which is written and noted above regards the deployment of armies for the defense of the kingdom against enemies of the kingdom of Hungary attacking from any direction at any time in the future; however, in the wars with the Turks and the Hussites, distinct and separate military campaigns have to be launched; therefore, his royal majesty has caused the following to be added to the above.

14. Then, since the lord king is certain that the Hussite delegates came to the holy council of Basle with full powers in all matters of faith, and, as he firmly hopes, will, after receiving full instruction from the holy council, renounce their errors and subject themselves again to the obedience of holy mother Church, and since the same majesty has been requested frequently by the same holy council in letters and by messengers that he personally should attend the same council, for the sake of the faith and also for the restoration of the morals and the peace of Christ's faithful,[12] wherefore, the same majesty, considering that the return of the Bohemian Hussites in secular matters cannot be suitably and easily accomplished without his leadership, which has been put in writing by the council to his royal majesty, and also considering that the temporal lordship of the Bohemians belongs to his majesty; therefore, his majesty has decided that, after having brought the imperial business in Italy and particularly with the Florentines[13] to such a conclusion as he desires, he will come as quickly as possible to the council at Basle, and, if the Bohemian Hussites there will have returned to the obedience of the Church and the unity of the faith, for which there is good hope, then the kingdom of Hungary together with the regions occupied by them will be fully freed from the Hussites without arms; and once they are reconciled, the council will be able to make provision under the name of *passagium*[14] for all Christianity with great foresight, and then his majesty may set out personally with the help of God and be able to free entirely the kingdom of Hungary and its attached regions from the Turks as well as to widen and enlarge his dominions. However, if the Hussites cannot be reconciled in the council, then by the decision of the holy council all Christianity will raise its hands with the greatest power against the Hussites; in this case his royal majesty has decided that he personally will by all means return to Hungary and free Nagyszombat, Szakolca, and other lands and border regions of the kingdom of Hungary from the hand and power of the Hussites.[15] It seems useful that before the return of his majesty to Hungary the prelates, barons, and gentlemen of the realm arrange and make provision for the counties whose nobles and other men of property have been appointed to defend that part of the kingdom facing Bohemia against the Hussites, that they should either come singly according to the ancient custom of the kingdom or that a particular number of archers should be sent from every county, so that all and every one of

Tyrnauiam proficisci, et ipsa maiestas in medium promptarum gentium exercituantium veniendo statim valeat agere pro rehabitione Tyrnauie et aliarum terrarum supradictarum, que quidem gentes non tantummodo quindecim diebus, prout consueverunt, sed usque necesse fuerit, debeant in agendis perseverare, quia si per totum ipsius recuperationis locorum pretactorum tempus remanere noluerint, utique et id, quod inceptum fuit pro recuperatione huiusmodi, transibit in vanum. Nec etiam ipsis aliter facientibus regia maiestas his personaliter vellet interesse, et qualitercunque hec disposita fuerint, certificetur superinde maiestas sua, pruisquam regnum Hungarie ingredietur.

XV. Disponatur etiam, quod rustici omnium et singularum villarum partium superiorum, de quibus saltem Hwzytis solvunt et ipsis obediunt, ut ad faciendos omnes labores, qui in recuperatione terrarum occupatarum fieri debent, illo tempore, quo super hoc eis iussum fuerit, venire teneantur et sint astricti, interim autem agant, ut melius poterint, pro bono et utilitate regni in offensionem Hwzytarum et recuperationem terrarum ab eisdem alienatarum et occupatarum.[16] Prefatus autem dominus rex et serenissima domina regina de proventibus suis levabunt potentiam suam in recuperationem premissorum, et etiam prelatorum potentiam, qui per prelatos, barones et regnicolas contra Hwzytas deputabuntur, illac accedere faciet, quam scilicet potentiam cum sua et dicte domine regine potentia retinebit et stare faciet ibidem pro defensione regni et in recuperationem locorum ab Hwzytis occupatorum per totum tempus recuperationis, prout fuerit opportunum. Et nichilominus iidem prelati, barones et regnicole disponant et provideant, qui ex prelatis et baronibus regni contra Thurcas versus Walachiam, Zewreniensem et illas partes Danubii ac versus Boznam teneantur pro defensione regni agere et invigilare.[17] Maiestas autem regia faciet etiam ad illas partes totum posse suum.

XVI. Item videretur maiestati regie, quod nobiles et possessionati homines cuiuslibet comitatus congregarentur sub certis gravaminibus et birsagiis, quemadmodum solitum est congregari, et quod in unum convenientes pariter condescenderent, et quilibet eorum absque quolibet timore libere secundum suum sensum dicerent suam opinionem singillatim ad singula, nec quisquam ditiorum vel potentiorum auderet quovis modo inferioribus vim adhibere aut minas imponere, ut non dicerent, quid sibi appareret, et hoc ordine observato requirerent quoslibet distinctim et seorsum per capita super sua opinione in premissis et opinionem cuiuslibet extensive perscriberent.[18] Hisque sic

them should be prepared and ready to recover the cities, lands, and borders of the kingdom occupied by the Hussites upon the return of his majesty, so that as soon as they are called upon, they should be able to march immediately and be deployed at Nagyszombat; and when his majesty arrives with his men ready for battle all should be able to act at once to recover Nagyszombat and the other abovementioned lands. The men must remain in action not for fifteen days only, as they have been accustomed, but as long as necessary, because if they do not wish to remain for the whole time required to recover the said lands, then what was begun for this recovery will be in vain. His majesty refuses personally to take part if this is done otherwise, and his majesty is to be informed about what has been arranged in this matter before he enters the kingdom of Hungary.

15. It should also be decided that the peasants of each and every village of the upper (i. e., northern) regions, at least those which pay tribute to the Hussites and obey them, be required and bound to come and to undertake everything which must be done to recover the occupied lands at the time they are ordered to act in this matter. In the meantime they should act as best they can for the good and utility of the kingdom in attacking the Hussites and recovering the lands occupied and alienated by them.[16] The said lord king and the most serene lady queen will raise their own force from their own revenues for the recovery of the above, and the king will also send there the force of the prelates, which will be raised by the prelates, barons, and landed residents against the Hussites, and he will keep this force with his own and that of the lady queen and have it remain there to defend the kingdom and to recover the places occupied by the Hussites throughout the whole time of the recovery, as seems suitable. In the meantime the same prelates, barons, and landed residents should decide and arrange which of the prelates and barons are required to move and be on guard for the defense of the kingdom against the Turks towards Wallachia, towards Severin and the Danubian region, and towards Bosnia.[17] His royal majesty will also do everything in his power for (the defense of) those regions.

16. Then, it seems good to his royal majesty that nobles and men of property of every county should be called together under definite penalties and fines, in the way they are customarily called together, and that those gathered should deliberate in equality, and every one of them, one by one, should give his opinion freely according to his feelings without fear, while none of the wealthier and more powerful persons should dare to use force or make threats in any way against his inferiors, so that they do not say what they find best; and by observing this rule they should call on everyone clearly and separately one by one for his opinion on the above and record in full everyone's opinion.[18]

peractis tandem a tota communitate nobilium divitum et pauperum, et non tantum a potentioribus et ditioribus eligerentur de quolibet comitatu certi nobiles et idonei viri, qui attentiorem haberent respectum et diligentiorem considerationem ad procurandas communitatis utilitates, quos de huiusmodi opinionibus et totali intentione eorum plene informatos ad prelatos et barones regni congregatos pro facienda in omnibus conclusione futuris semper temporibus observanda destinarent.

XVII. Videtur etiam, quod non essent admittendi quilibet nobiles alterius comitatus in medium congregatorum alicuius comitatus, nec daretur vox talibus in declaratione facienda, sed quod quilibet nobilis in suo comitatu, ubi habet domicilium, deberet dicere et suam proferre opinionem.

XVIII. Item omnia premissa circa defensionem regni descripta relinquuntur per maiestatem regiam arbitri et dispositioni prelatorum et baronum ac communitatis regni, ut quicquid pro meliori statu regni disponendum videbitur, statuant ordinent et disponant.

XIX. Licet in precedentibus sufficienter per maiestatem regiam sit tactum, quomodo sua maiestas vult per prelatos, barones et regnicolas per expressum declarare, usque quem locum et terminum communitas regnicolarum generalis exercitus ingruente necessitate teneatur proficisci et etiam quamdiu stare deberet in eodem, verumtamen, sicuti prius scriptum est, regna Dalmatie, Croatie, Rame, Seruie, Bozne, Gallicie, Lodomerie et Bulgarie dudum et etiam tempore serenissimi domini Ludouici regis recolende memorie ad coronam et regnum Hungarie pertinuerunt. Scit enim dominus Nicolaus de Gara palatinus et quamplures alii, quod terre et provincie, ut sunt Halomfeold, Hlewna, Berzezthel et alie, que nunc occupate tenentur per regem Bozne, et Boznenses ipsi predicto domini regi Ludouico tenebantur et possidebantur per banum regni Croatie.[19] Scit etiam idem dominus palatinus et quamplures alii, qualiter castrum Greben et alia castra ibi circumquaque existentia cum suis pertinentiis tempore dicti quondam domini regis Ludouici tenta fuerint per Hungaros.[20] Item sciunt, quod ecclesia Boznensis, cuius episcopus nunc in Dyako residet, est ultra Zavum, que similiter nunc cum suis terris a Boznensibus possidetur, et sciunt multi, quoniam Seruia sive Rascia, Bulgaria sive Walachia et specialiter partes Zewrenii tente et conservate fuerint per regem et coronam regni Hungarie.[21] His igitur respectibus maiestas regia per prelatos et barones ac regnicolas regni se vult declarare, utrum iidem dicant et velint esse dicta regna incorporata fuere regno Hungarie, intelligantque includi ac existere sub metis eiusdem. Que si sub metis regni Hungarie intelligunt et dicunt extitisse et debere esse, extunc petit sua maiestas, ut declarentur et exponantur, que loca per totum circuitum regni pro metis ipsius regni habeantur, et ad quem locum

After these matters have been accomplished, in every county certain nobles and suitable men should be elected from the whole community of nobles, both rich and poor, and not only from the more powerful and wealthier ones, such that would respect with care and studiously keep in mind what can be done for the common good; and they, fully informed of these opinions and all the intentions (of their county), should be sent to the prelates and barons of the kingdom to pass decision on everything that is to be done in all future times.

17. It also seems good that no nobles from another county should be admitted to the assembly of any county, nor should they be permitted to vote in arriving at a final decision, but every noble must speak in his own county, where he has his residence, and present his opinion there.

18. Then, everything set out above on the defense of the kingdom is left by his royal majesty to the decision and pleasure of the prelates, barons, and the community of the realm, so that they should establish, order, and decide whatever seems right to improve the state of the kingdom.

19. Although in the foregoing it was sufficiently treated by his royal majesty what his majesty wishes that the prelates, barons, and gentlemen of the realm should define regarding the place and the border to which the troops of the general levy of the gentlemen of the realm are required to set out and also how long they must remain there, nevertheless, as has been written earlier, the kingdoms of Dalmatia, Croatia, Rama, Serbia, Bosnia, Galicia, Lodomeria, and Bulgaria have been long since and also in the time of the most serene lord king Louis of venerated memory attached to the crown and kingdom of Hungary. For the lord palatine Nicholas of Gara and very many others know that that the lands and provinces, namely Hulm, Hlivno, Berzezthel, and others, which are now held occupied by the king of Bosnia and the Bosnians themselves, were subject to and held by the said lord king Louis through the ban of the kingdom of Croatia.[19] The same lord palatine and many others also know that castle Greben and other castles around there with their appurtenances were held by the Hungarians in the time of the late lord king Louis.[20] Then, they know that the Church of Bosnia, whose bishop now lives in Dyakus, extends beyond the River Sava, which similarly with its lands is in the possession of the Bosnians, and many know how long Serbia or Rascia, Bulgaria or Wallachia, and particularly the lands of Severin were held and retained by the king and crown of the kingdom of Hungary.[21] Regarding these things, therefore, his royal majesty wishes that the prelates, barons, and gentlemen of the realm announce, whether they declare and wish the said kingdoms to be incorporated into the kingdom of Hungary and whether they understand them to be included in and to be within its borders. If they understand them to be within the borders

communitas regnicolarum generalis exercitus pro recuperatione terrarum alienatarum proficisci debeat, ut dicta maiestas sua sciat, dum opus fuerit, ad que loca possit facere transire regnicolas suos, aut pro regni defensione, aut terrarum alienatarum recuperatione, nec sua maiestas et regna debent deficere in iis agendis cum ecclesiis regni. Considerat namque sua maiestas, quod regnum Hungarie cum regnis et terris eidem incorporatis est taliter et adeo amplum, potentissimum et copiosum gentibus, ut contra quoscunque inimicos ex quacunque parte regni existentes, si bene et ordinate gentes regni Hungarie dividantur, poterunt sufficientes gentes pro regni defensione et terrarum alienatarum recuperatione, hostiumque offensione deputari, et levari, sicut de huiusmodi defensione per maiestatem regiam in sequentibus, prout sibi apparuit, disposita poterint suscipere informationem, et in his petit et mandat regia maiestas per prelatos, barones et regnicolas suos, antequam regnum Hungarie ingrediatur, plenissime informari, quicquid ab eisdem fuerit circa hanc materiam dispositum, ordinatum, declaratum et conclusum, ut secundum ea sciat regia maiestas et possit se, sicut et intendit, conservare.

SEQUITUR DIVISIO

XX. Quemadmodum prelati et barones regni Hungarie iam plures concitaverunt et moverunt regnicolas contra Hwzitas, sic et nunc relinquitur per maiestatem regiam arbitrio eorundem prelatorum et baronum, ut in levatione regnicolarum contra Hwzytas faciant illud, quod eis videbitur faciendum. Quia tamen maiestas sua respectum et considerationem habet ad guerras, que tam ex parte Hwzytarum, quam Turcorum et aliunde habentur, et attento potissime, quod rex Bozne et Boznensis multis insolentiis et iniuriis affecerunt regnum et regnicolas Hungarie, ideo maiestas sua hoc respectu prelatos, barones et nobiles regni sui ordine subscripto divisit, si eis sic fiendum appareat, quorum una pars contra Turcos, alia contra Hwzytas, tertia contra Boznam continuum respectum pro regni defensione et hostium offensione habere teneantur, sicut hec divisio apparet in subscriptis.

XXI. Hec est dispositio contra Thurcos et eis colligatos ac adherentes:[22]

of the kingdom of Hungary and declare that they are and should be, then his majesty seeks that it be announced and defined which places around the whole kingdom should be held as the borders of the same kingdom, and to what place the troops of the general levy of the gentlemen of the realm have to set out to recover alienated lands, so that his said majesty may know to what points he can command his gentlemen of the realm, if necessary, to defend the kingdom or to recover alienated lands. Nor should his majesty and the kingdom, together with the churches of the realm, be deficient in their action. For his majesty considers the kingdom of Hungary with the kingdoms and lands included in it to be so wide, so very powerful, and so richly populated, that enough men can be enlisted and raised against any enemies from any border of the kingdom to defend the realm, to recover alienated lands and to attack the enemy, if the men of the kingdom of Hungary are well and properly distributed, so that they can take cognizance of the arrangements of defense, as it appears correct to his royal majesty in what follows. And, concerning this, his royal majesty seeks and orders to be informed as fully as possible by his prelates, barons, and gentlemen of the realm about what has been arranged, ordered, announced, and concluded on this matter by them before he enters the kingdom of Hungary, so that his royal majesty can rely upon these as it is his intention.

THE DIVISION FOLLOWS

20. Just as the prelates and barons of the kingdom of Hungary had raised and moved many people against the Hussites, it is now left by his royal majesty to the same prelates and barons to decide to do what seems to be best in raising the gentlemen of the realm against the Hussites. However, because his majesty considers and keeps in his mind that wars are fought both against the Hussites and the Turks as well as elsewhere, and is particularly concerned that the king of Bosnia and the Bosnians have afflicted on the kingdom and inhabitants of Hungary many insults and injuries; therefore, regarding this state of affairs his majesty has divided the prelates, barons, and nobles of the kingdom into the order given below, if it should please them that this should be done. One part of them is deployed to the defense of the kingdom and the attack of the enemies against the Turks, another part against the Hussites, and the third against Bosnia, as is apparent from the division below.

21. This is the arrangement against the Turks, their allies and followers:[22]

A parte Dalmatie seu maris et Croatie.

Banus Croatie	banderium
Ragusium	cum potentia
Comes Corbavie	banderium
Comes Cetine	banderium
Comes Segnie	banderium
Totum regnum Croatie et Walachi in eo existentes	cum potentiis eorum
Regale	banderium

Item versus fluvium Wn.

Banus Sclavonie	banderium
Domini de Blagay	banderium
Prior Aurane	banderium
Episcopus Zagrabiensis	banderium
Ladislaus Toth	equos centum

Item ad Wzura.

Despotus	cum quantis potest
Magister curie comes de Posega	equis centum
Episcopus Boznensis	equis centum
Petrus Cheh de Nema	equis C
Bani Machovienses	equis CCCC
Joannes filius Gregorii	banderium
Mathko nomine Zebernik	equites M
Joannes banus de Maroth	equites M
Episcopus Quinqueecclesiensis	banderium
Filii Bothos	equites C
Joannes de Gara	equites C
Henricus filius Waywode	equites C
Georgius filius Lorandi de Serke	equites C
Comitatus Zagrabiensis	Comitatus Crisiensis
Comitatus Warasdiensis	Comitatus de Werewcze
Comitatus de Posega	Comitatus Zewriniensis
Comitatus de Walko	Comitatus Bachiensis
Comitatus de Bodrogh	Comitatus de Baronya

On the Dalmatian [Adriatic] side, at the sea, in Croatia

Ban of Croatia	[one] *banderium*
Ragusa	with its forces
Count of Corbavia	[one] *banderium*
Count of Cetina	[one] *banderium*
Count of Segnia	[one] *banderium*
all the Kingdom of Croatia [and Slavonia] with the Wallachs living there	with all their forces
Royal *banderium*	[1000 horse]

Then, towards the River Una

Ban of Slavonia	[one] *banderium*
the lords of Blagaj	[one] *banderium*
Prior of Vrana	[one] *banderium*
Bishop of Zagreb	[one] *banderium*
Ladislas Tót	100 horse [one *banderium*]

Then, towards Ozora

The despot	with as many as he can [8000 horse]
Master of the Court, the *ispán* of Pozsega [i.e. Ladislas of Tamási]	100 horse
Bishop of Bosnia	100 horse
Peter Cseh of Nevna	100 horse
Bans of Macsó	400 horse
John, son of Gregory	[one] *banderium*
Matko for Sebernik	1000 horse
John of Marót, ban	1000 horse
Bishop of Pécs	[one] *banderium*
Sons of Botos	100 horse
John of Gara	100 horse [one *banderium*]
Henry, son of the voivode	100 horse
George, son of Roland of Serke	100 horse
[Bulgaria]	[4000 horse]
Co. Zagreb[23]	
Co. Varasd[23]	
Co. Pozsega	[300]
Co. Valkó	[200]
Co. Bodrog	[300]
[All the estates of Dalmatia, Croatia, Slavonia, likewise Bosnia and its parts, as well as the Duchy of St Sava send	9000 soldiers]
Co. Körös[23]	
Co. Verőce	[200]
Co. Szerém	[200]
Co. Bács	[500]
Co. Baranya	[500]

Comitatus Tholnensis	Comitatus Simigiensis
Comitatus Zaladiensis	

Si volunt isti contra Boznenses ordinari, facilius habebitur, si vero isti comitatus nollent adiuvare, manebunt priores cum eorum banderiis.

Versus Temeskeoz usque Zewrenium inclusive.

Archiepiscopus Colocensis	banderium
Episcopus Waradiensis	banderium
Episcopus Chanadiensis	banderium
Regia maiestas	banderium
Comitatus Themesiensis	Comitatus Chanadiensis
Comitatus Horodiensis	Comitatus de Sarand
Comitatus Chongradiensis	Comitatus Crasso
Comitatus de Kewe	Comitatus de Thorontal

Despotus cum quantis potest
Walachi, Sclavi et Iuanchi, Comani et Philistei.

Versus partes Transsyluanas.

Episcopus Transsyluaniensis	banderium
Waywoda Transsyluaniensis	banderia duo
Siculorum comes	banderia duo
Waywoda Moldavus contra Turcos et partes Transalpinas	cum tota potentia
Saxones, Siculi, nobiles Walachi partium Transsyluanarum	cum potentia
Comitatus Bihoriensis	Comitatus de Bekes
Comitatus Zathmariensis	Comitatus de Zabolch
Comitatus Maramarosiensis	Comitatus de Beregh
Comitatus de Wgocha	Comitatus de Krazna
Comitatus Zolnok mediocris	Comitatus Zolnok exterior
Regale	banderium

Et he tres partes tam scilicet versus Themeskewz quam versus partes Transalpinas respectum habent, mutuis semper respectibus contra Turcas ad loca, ad que necesse fuerit, iuvare poterunt et debent.

Co. Tolna	[200]
Co. Zala	[600]
Co. Somogy	[500]

If they want to be deployed against the Bosnians, that would be useful, but if these counties do not want to assist, the magnates will remain with their *banderia.*

Towards Temesköz including Severin

Archbishop of Kalocsa	[one] *banderium*
Bishop of Várad	[one] *banderium*
Bishop of Csanád	*banderium* [200 horse]
Royal majesty	*banderium* [1000 horse]
Co. Temes	[200]
Co. Arad	[200]
Co. Csongrád	[200]
Co. Keve	[100]
Co. Csanád	[300]
Co. Zaránd	[300]
Co. Krassó	[100]
Co. Torontál	[100]
The Despot with as many as he can[23]	
Wallachs, Slavs, "Iuanchi," Cumans and Jászok	[200]

Towards Transylvania

Bishop of Transylvania	[one] *Gauderium*
Voivode of Transylvania	two *banderia*
ispán of the Székely	two *banderia*
Voivode of Moldavia against the Turks and Wallachia	with all his might
Co. Bihar	[600]
Co. Szatmár	[200]
Co. Máramaros	[50]
Co. Ugocsa	[100]
Co. Middle-Szolnok	[with Szolnok Exterior, 400]
Co. Békés	[200]
Co. Szabolcs	[200]
Co. Bereg	[100]
Co. Kraszna	[100]
Co. Exterior Szolnok	[see above]
Royal	*banderium*
[Saxons and Székely]	[4000]
[The entire nobility of Transylvania]	[300]

And these three groups, namely both those toward Temesköz and toward Wallachia, should be able and obligated to go to the help of each other against the Turks, wherever need arises.

XXII. Pro custodia castri Posoniensis.[24]

Episcopus Wesprimiensis	lanceas L
Episcopus Jauriensis	lanceas L
Abbas Sancti Martini	lanceas XXV
Domini de Hederwara	lanceas XXV

per quartam partem toto anno pro custodia, et de residuo pro defensione castri et civitatis Posoniensis fiat dispositio comitibus Posoniensibus de proventibus regalibus.

Contra Hwzitas.

Archiepiscopus Strigoniensis	banderium
Episcopus Agriensis	banderium
Comitatus Soproniensis	Comitatus Castriferrei
Comitatus Wesprimiensis	Comitatus Albensis
Comitatus Jauriensis	Comitatus Strigoniensis
Comitatus Philisiensis	Comitatus Comaromiensis
Comitatus Mosoniensis	Comitatus Posoniensis
Comitatus Nittriensis	Comitatus Trinchiniensis
Comitatus de Thurocz	Comitatus de Arwa
Comitatus Lypthoviensis	Comitatus Zoliensis
Comitatus Scepusiensis	Comitatus de Saaros
Comitatus Zempliniensis	Comitatus Abawywariensis
Comitatus Borsodiensis	Comitatus de Tholna
Comitatus Geomeriensis	Comitatus Nogradiensis
Comitatus Hewesiensis	Comitatus Pesthiensis
Comitatus Zolnok exterior	Comitatus Hontensis
Comitatus Borsodiensis	Comitatus de Wngh
Et si deo placebit,	Archiepiscopus Strigoniensis
regia maiestas personaliter	Episcopus Agriensis

22. For guarding the castle at Pozsony[24]

Bishop of Veszprém	50 lances
Bishop of Győr	50 lances
Abbot of St Martin (of Pannonhalma)	25 lances
Lords of Hédervára	25 [100] lances,

for a quarter of the year for guard duty, and for the rest, the defense of castle and city Pozsony should be arranged by the *ispán* of Pozsony, from royal revenues.

Against the Hussites [on the German border, these serve:]

Archbishop of Esztergom	[two] *banderia*
Bishop of Eger	[two] *banderia*
Co. Sopron	[100]
Co. Veszprém	[100]
Co. Győr	[100]
Co. Pilis	[50]
Co. Moson	[25]
Co. Nyitra	[with Turóc, 600]
Co. Turóc	[see above]
Co. Liptó	[with Szepes, 200]
Co. Szepes	[see above]
Co. Zemplén	[with Borsod, 300]
Co. Borsod	[see above]
Co. Gömör	[with Heves, 400]
Co. Heves	[see above]
Co. Szolnok Exterior[23]	
Co. Borsod	[repetition]
Co. Vas	[with Fejér 100]
Co. Fejér	[see above]
Co. Esztergom	[with Komárom, 200]
Co. Komárom	[see above]
Co. Pozsony	[with Trencsén and Árva, 300]
Co. Trencsén	[see above]
Co. Árva	[see above]
Co. Zólyom	[with Sáros and Abaújvár, 600]
Co. Sáros	[see above]
Co. Abaújvár	[see above]
Co. Tolna	[with Nógrád and Pest, 100]
Co. Nógrád	[see above]
Co. Pest	[see above]
Co. Hont [and Bereg]	[300]
Co. Ung[23]	
And if pleases God, the royal majesty personally	[with 400 horse]
Archbishop of Esztergom	[repetition]
Bishop of Eger	[repetition]

Petrus Cheh
Comites de Bozyn
Wolfardus de Modor
Nicolaus filius Bani de Galgocz

Petrus et Joannes Forgach
Filii Noffry
Styborius
Michael Ernye
Stephanus Saffar
Magister tauernicorum
Emericus de Derenchen
Emericus de Palocz
Nicolaus de Kahmo
Henricus et Demetrius de Berzencze
Kwkalffus
Frank de Semse
Andreas de Budamer
Timoteus de Nesa
Ladislaus de Kanysa
Mathias de Hathwan

Comes de Sancto Georgio
Stybarius
Ladislaus de Zechen
Nicolaus filius Blasii de Gyarmath
Rubertus de Thar
Stephanus de Aran
Joannes filius Jacobi
Osualdus de Zelchen
Sebastianus de Degh
Domini de Pelsewcz
Joannes filius Emerici de Peren
Domini de Homonna
Paulus Kompolth
Joannes Zwdar

Simon Zwdar
Nicolaus et Georgius Soos
Georgius de Agaad
Frank de Zeech
Ladislaus Petheo
Eustachius et alii nobiles de Serk

XXIII. Item quamvis regia maiestas et regnum Hungarie a dictis partibus habent guerras, tamen quia nunc inter suam maiestatem et Florentinos sperat eadem maiestas, quod etiam Veneti per medium Florentinorum concordabunt cum sua maiestate, qua habita sperat sua maiestas, quod poterit nedum totam Turciam,[25] imo verius totam Italiam relinquere in bona pace et tranquillitate, et si habebitur concordia cum Venetis, he gentes, que contra ipsos sunt deputate,

Peter Cseh[23]	
Counts of Bazin[23]	
Wolfhard of Modor[23]	
Nicholas, son of the ban of Galgóc	[100]
Peter and John Forgács	[50]
The sons of Noffry	[50]
Zubor	[50]
Michael Ettre	[50]
Stephen Sáfár	[50]
Master of the Treasury [Peter of Berzevice]	[50]
Emeric of Derencsény	[50]
Emeric of Pálóc	[100]
Nicholas of Rihnó	[50]
Henry and Detricus of Berzevice	[50]
Rikalf of Tarkő[23]	
Frank of Semse[23]	
Andrew of Budamér[23]	
Timothy of Nézsa[23]	
Ladislas of Kanizsa[23]	
Matthias of Hatvan[23]	
Count of Szentgyörgy	[one *banderium*]
Stibor	[two *banderia*]
Ladislas of Szécsény	[100 horse]
Nicholas, son of Blaise of Gyarmat	[50]
Robert of Tar	[50]
Stephen of Arany	[50]
John Jakabfi	[100]
Oswald of Szelcsény	[50]
Sebastian of Dérg	[50]
the lords of Pelsőc	[200]
John, son of Emeric of Perény	[200]
The lords of Homonna	[200]
Paul Kompolt	[100]
John Cudar	[50, + Simon Cudar, 50]
Nicholas and George Sós	[50]
George of Agárd	[50]
Frank of Szécs	[100]
Ladislas Pető	[50]
Eustachius and other nobles of Serke	[50]

23. Then, while his royal majesty and the kingdom of Hungary are waging wars in the said areas, his majesty now has hopes for a concord between his majesty and the Florentines and trusts that the Venetians will also come to agreement with his majesty by the mediation of the Florentines. In this expectation his majesty is hopeful that he will be able to leave all Turkey[25] and even all of Italy in happy peace and quiet, and if agreement is made with the Venetians, those men who were deployed against the Venetians, will be free to turn against

poterunt libere se contra alios divertere. Si vero non concordaverint, tunc sua regia maiestas vult, ut omnes gentes, quibus per maiestatem suam scriptum est, intrent patriam Fori Julii, in quarum medium in ipsam patriam Fori Julii etiam maiestas sua personaliter proficiscitur ad gerenda bella contra Venetos.[26] Et si cum Turcis vel Hwzytis concordia habebitur et commode fieri poterit, tunc vult sua maiestas, quod etiam de illis partibus contra Turcas vel Hwzytas deputatis, quanto plures poterunt, tanto plures ipsam patriam Fori Julii intrent.

XXIV. Item de Hwzytis spes bona habetur, quod per sacrum concilium Basiliense ipsi Hwzyte in spiritualibus ad obedientim sancte ecclesie et in temporalibus ad obedientiam sue maiestatis reducentur. Quod si sic factum fuerit, sicut speratur, tunc et ille gentes contra Hwzytas deputate poterunt contra alios inimicos regis et regni se convertere. Habetur etiam tractatus super treugis ineundis cum Turcis, que si facte fuerint, non erit opus contra ipsos Turcas aliquam potentiam movere, et sic potentia illa que contra Turcas est deputata, poterit converti contra alios inimicos regnum Hungarie hostiliter invadere machinantes, et si cum quocunque ex predictis concordia habebitur, talis potentia, que deputate fuit contra talem, qui concordat, se poterit convertere ad partem cum sua maiestate et regno concordare nolentem. Casu autem, quo favente altissimo cum quolibet predictorum concordia fiet, sicut speratur, tunc, licet predicte gentes ad presens ab omni exercituatione penitus conquiescant et sint supportate, verumtamen utile est et valde necessarium, ut in omnem eventum regni pro futura defensione super exercituatione facienda nunc omnino dispositio fiat, ut tempore necessitatis occurrente nobiles quarumlibet partium et regnicole sciant, ad quas partes respectum habeant et se conservare debeant pro regni defensione facienda. Et petit atque mandat maiestas sua per prelatos et barones disponi, sicut et in precedentibus scriptum est, quantum dari debeat pro qualibet lancea ad rationem floreni auri, et quod etiam exercituantes tempore, quo se levant et in exercitum proficiscuntur, ac ab illo revertuntur, neminem ledere ac offendere et in suis bonis damnificare presumant, et quod tempore seu die constituto omnes exercituantes in loco deputato constitui teneantur. Disponant etiam, ut quamdiu necesse fuerit, in loco necessario debeant remanere et decernere penas contra hos, qui in aliquo premissorum contrarium facere presumpserint quovis modo.

others. However, if no agreement is made, then his royal majesty wishes all men to whom he has written to come to Friuli, where his majesty intends to join them personally to set out to campaign against the Venetians in the same land of Friuli.[26] And if an agreement can be made and suitably arranged with the Turks or the Hussites, then his majesty wishes that also those levied in the above regions against the Turks or the Hussites, the more the better, come also to Friuli.

24. Then, regarding the Hussites there is good reason for hope that the Hussites will be brought back in spiritual affairs to obedience to holy Church and in temporal affairs to obedience to his majesty by the holy council of Basle. If this can be so done, as there is hope, then the troops levied against the Hussites can turn against other enemies of the king and the kingdom. There are also talks on making a truce with the Turks, and if that can be done, there will be no need to move any forces against the Turks, and therefore that force which has been raised against the Turks can be turned against other enemies planning to invade the kingdom of Hungary by force, and if peace is reached with any of the above, the forces raised against the one which agreed to peace can be turned against those unwilling to make an agreement with his majesty and the kingdom. In the case that, by favor of the most high, agreement is reached with any of the above, which is to be hoped, then the said troops should at present refrain from all fighting and be excused. Nevertheless, it is useful and very necessary that plans should be made for mobilization for future defense of the kingdom for any event, so that in time of emergency the nobles and gentlemen of the realm of every region will know what parts they are responsible for and are to be prepared for in acting in the defense of the kingdom. And his majesty seeks and orders that it be arranged by the prelates and barons, as is written above, how much should be paid for every lance in terms of gold florins; and also that soldiers should not dare to harm or attack anyone or cause loss to his possessions when they are being raised and set out for the army or are returning from it; and that at the set time or day all soldiers must be ready in the proper place. They should also arrange that they must remain in the necessary place as long as is required and decide about the penalties of those who dare to act in any way against the above orders.

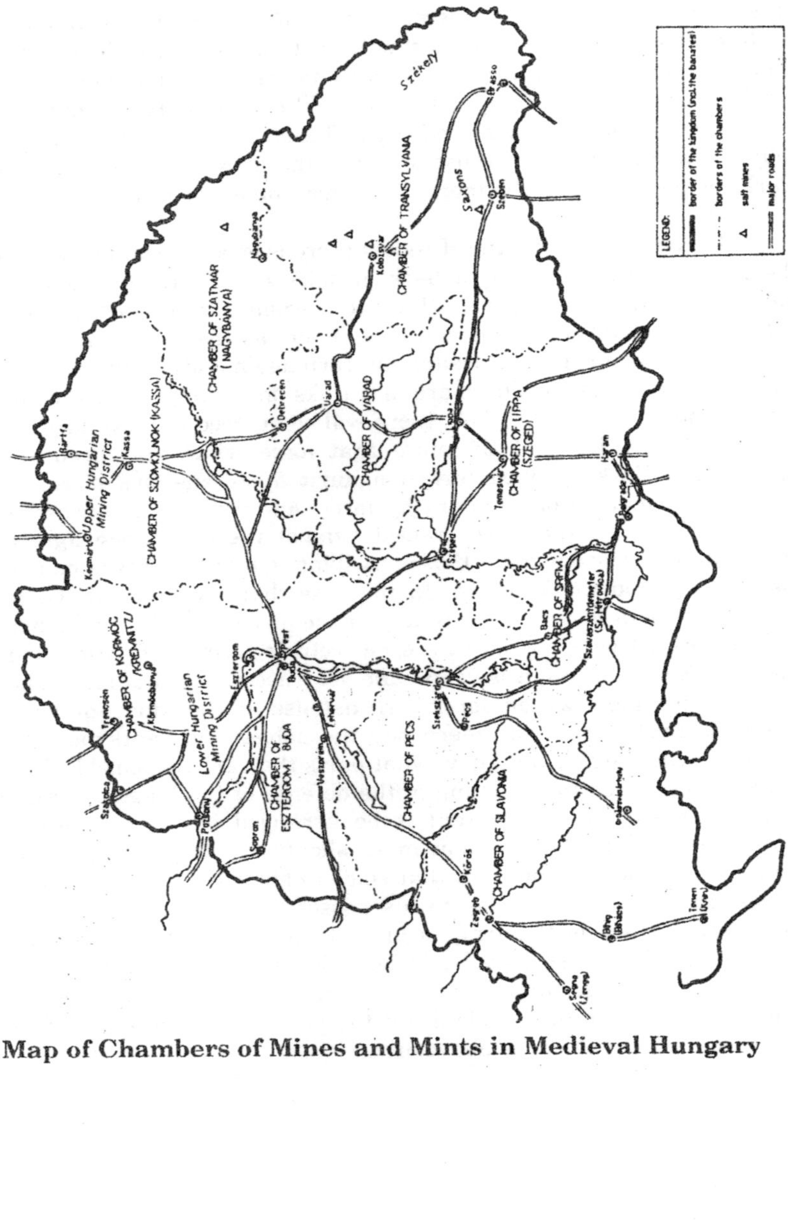

Map of Chambers of Mines and Mints in Medieval Hungary

Notes to (c. 1320)
pages 1–2.

Incipit: *Iuxta quam partem*

This first piece of evidence on the judicial reforms of King Charles I has survived in a mid-fifteenth-century *ars notaria*, probably compiled by John of Uzsa, Canon of Eger (Bónis, p. 247). It was issued, so its proem states, following the virtual civil war of the first decades of the fourteenth century and was in all likelihood part of a series of similar reforms. As the distribution of fines differs from those contained in Compilatio c. 1300:5 (*DRMH* 1:74) and references to its application can be found as early as 1326 and 1329 (Hajnik), it can safely be dated to the first or second decade of the century. Although the text identifies the measures as a *decretum seu statutum*, it was issued by the king and his council (not a diet) and came down to us in a formulary, comparable to the transmission of the Comp. c. 1300. We follow the decision of the editors of *DRH 1301–1457* in including it as the opening piece of the legislation of the Angevin kings.

MS.: (Ars Notaria) Österreichische Nationalbibliothek, Wien, Cod. 4276, ff. 104r–05r

EDD.: J. N. Kovachich, *Formulae solennes styli in cancellaria curiaque regum, foris minoribus ac locis credibiliis Regni Hungariae usati* (Pest: Trattner, 1799), pp. 2–3; Fejér, *Cod. dipl.* 7/1: 612–15 (dated 1316); *DRH 1301–1457*, pp. 73–75.

LIT.: Hajnik, *Bír. szerv.*, pp. 445–46; Gy. Gábor, *A megyei intézmény kialakulása és működése Nagy Lajos alatt* [Development and Functions of the County Under Louis the Great] (Bp.: Grill, 1908), pp. 173–75; L. Szilágyi, "III. Endre 1298. évi törvénye" [Andrew III's Law of 1298], *AUSBp, Sect. hist.* 1 (1957): 160–65; Gy. Bónis, "Uzsai János Ars Notariaja" [The Ars Notaria of J. of Uzsa], *Filológiai Közlöny* 7 (1961): 247.

1. After ordeals were abandoned in the mid-thirteenth century (see *DRMH* 1: 137, n. 3) the word *iudicium* usually meant fines, imposed on convicted offenders; see the Glossary.

2. On the judges (judge royal, count palatine, magistrate) and the places of authentication, see the Glossary.

3. The opening words both here and in art. 2 (*sciendum, notandum*), just as the title itself, are typical for formularies or textbooks (*artes notariae*) compiled for the use of notaries and other practicioners of law. On the role of these books in the training and practice of law in medieval Hungary, see Gy. Bónis, *Középkori jogunk elemei* [Elements of our medieval law] (Bp.: Közgazdasági K., 1972), pp. 141–62.

4. The words *pauperes et impotentes*, with biblical overtones (which in turn, go back, through Jerome's readings, to the political vocabulary of classical authors, such as Sallust and Tacitus), meant in the Middle Ages the lesser freemen, not the working poor or unarmed peasantry; see K. Bosl, "Potens und Pauper: Begriffsgeschichtliche Studien zur gesellschaftlichen Differenzierung im frühen Mittelalter," in *Festschrift für Otto Brunner* (Göttingen: Vandenhoek & Ruprecht, 1963), pp. 60–87.

5. At least since the death of King Andrew III, if not before, the country was exposed to open civil war between the supporters of the Angevin claimants to the throne and their opponents. Peace was not fully established before the death of King Charles' major adversary, Mathew Csák, lord of the northeastern parts of Hungary, on 18 March 1321. This date is, therefore, taken as a likely *terminus post quem* for this ordinance.

6. The wording suggests that this edict originated in the royal council. As we noted in the introduction, before the later fifteenth century no clear distinction can be made between *decreta* emanating from this body and from the diet of lords, nobles and clergy. King Charles seems to have held a few diets between his "election" in 1312 and ca. 1320, but no legislation has survived from these. No diet is known to have been called after 1320; see Kovachich, *Vestigia*, p. 182.

7. On *judicium*, see n. 1, above; the second word, *birsagium* is a Latinized form of the Hungarian *bírság*, also meaning "fine." The use of both words is merely a rhetorical repetition here.

8. On the *comes*, in Hungarian, *ispán* see the Glossary. On the office or commission of the royal bailiff (*homo regius*), see *ibid.*; also Hajnik, *Bír. szerv.*, pp. 160–63.; Eckhart, Glaubw. Orte, pp. 431–43.

9. Probably a letter of sentence (*litterae sententiales*), for which see the Glossary, is meant.

10. The two earliest registers of fines, which have survived from medieval Hungary are those of the judge royal from c. 1409; cf. Zs. O. 2, No. 7246.

11. Apparently such executionary procedures were opened in an assembly of nobles at the seat of the county, where the mandates were presented and translated into Hungarian (*layca lingua*) and a time period set for paying fines. No other details are known about these procedures.

12. Szilágyi (p. 161) suggested and the editors of *DRH 1301–1457* accepted that the words referring to the royal court here are out of place and rather the *sedes iudiciaria* of the county is meant. The mistake may have been that of the copyist of the formulary.

13. The document called *litterae expeditoriae* was issued for the quittance of many kinds of payments, see the Glossary; cf. also Eckhart, Glaubw. Orte, pp. 530–31.

14. Verbatim: "with its iron." Note the archaic symbolic action at the opening of the proceeding; cf. A. Alföldi, "*Hasta—Summa Imperii*: the spear as embodiment of sovereignty in Rome," *American Journal of Archaeology* 63 (1959) 1–27; and "Zum Speersymbol der Souveränität im Altertum," in *Festschrift Percy Ernst Schramm zu seinem siebzigsten Geburtstag von Schülern und Freunden zugeeignet*, P. Scheibert, C. P. Classen, eds. (Wiesbaden: Steiner, 1964) 1: 3–6. This peculiar use of the spear was noted by Jacob Grimm (*Deutsche Rechtsalterthümer* [Leipzig: Dieterich 1899, repr. Darmstadt: Wiss. Buchges. 1961], 1:120 in repr. 1:116), apparently as a symbolic action without West European parallels.

15. On security (*impignoratio*), see the Glossary. Usually cattle, or in case of higher fines, land was seized. Both could be redeemed by the convicted party or his kinsfolk; therefore, this temporary seizure was legally considered as a sort of pledge.

16. Cf. the differing arrangement for the division of fines in Comp. c. 1300: 5, *DRMH* 1:74. The text is unclear about the division when a tenth is given to the authentic witness; clearly one-third and two-thirds of the remaining amount is implied.

17. The formulary in which this text survived contains (as No.7) such a letter of quittance issued by a place of authentication for the collector of fines and notes that he should record exactly the sums collected; document No. 8 in the formulary is a certificate of the place of authentication about the proper exaction of fines (Kovachich, *Formulae*, pp. 5–6). On 16 May 1326 King Charles ordered certain chapters and convents to exact fines due to Count Palatine Philippe Drugeth in the manner prescribed in this decree and refers to this procedure as *consuetudo regni*; see I. Nagy, and Gy. Tasnádi Nagy, eds. *Anjoukori Okmánytár. Codex diplomaticus Hungariae Andegavensis* (Bp.: MTA, 1879–1920) [henceforth: *Cod. dipl. And.*] 2: 244–45.

18. None of the copies has survived, hence the other reforming statutes are unknown.

Notes to 10 August 1324
pages 3–4.

Incipit: *Quod prelati et universi*

This succinct mandate, issued on behalf of the bishop of Veszprém about the simplification of oath-taking, can be seen as an addition to the judicial reforms of Charles I. Even though issued only by the king in council and for a specific petitioner, the contents alter customary law and the text is styled *statutum* and *edictum*; hence, it is warranted to include it among the laws of the realm.

MS.: Original on parchment with remains of the great seal. Episcopal archives, Veszprém, No. 122

ED.: Hajnik, *Bír. szerv.* pp. 338–73, n. 55. *DRH 1301–1457*, pp. 77–80.

LIT.: Hajnik, *loc. cit.*

1. The general levy was called against the rebellious "Saxons" (privileged German settlers of Transylvania); it was, as usual, commanded by the king personally.

2. Medieval Hungarian texts usually speak of *partes Transylvanae*, i.e., Transylvanian parts of the kingdom, for the region between the forested mountains in the east of the Hungarian plain and the eastern and southern Carpathians was seen as enjoying only limited autonomy. We nevertheless translate the term simply as Transylvania.

3. Oaths remained the most significant formal proof even after the legal reforms of King Charles. However, they were now based on the written evidence presented in the early stages of the trial. The most usual way for a defendant of acquitting himself of a charge was to take the "purging" oath (*compurgatio*). Depending on the quantity and quality of evidence marshalled against the defendant, the judge decided whether a party was obliged to swear the oath alone or with a prescribed number of oath-helpers (*compurgatores*), who had to be "similar to him," that is of the same estate. Originally (up to the mid-fourteenth century) the oath-helpers were also supposed to be material witnesses who were in a position to prove the innocence of the defendant, later only their number and rank was relevant (see Hajnik, *Bír. szerv.*, pp. 317 ff.). In cases involving estates or other valuables, the number of oath-helpers was decided by the value of the case: the oath of a prelate or baron was worth 10 marks, that of a noble 5 marks, of a tenant a quarter mark.

4. The text of the oath that was to be repeated was read aloud by the man of the chapter or convent or by the king's bailiff, both also serving as witnesses to the procedure (see Hajnik, *ibid.*, p. 336). The necessity of precise pronunciation of oaths—and default for failure to use the exact wording—is typical of archaic legal proceedings. This practice remained in force for centuries and royal bailiffs were admonished to read the oath slowly, especially in cases involving extensive statements under oath (*ibid.* p. 339, n. 64; cf. *Tripartitum* Pars III, tit. 39). An exact parallel, for example, may be drawn with the *legis actiones* of early Roman law, wherein exact statement (and repetition) of the oaths, and so on, was required for proper procedure; Gaius *Institutiones* 4.11–12 (see, e.g., J. A. C. Thomas, *Textbook of Roman Law* [Amsterdam: North Holland], 1976, pp. 73f.). The repetition of a "failed" oath, as allowed by this law, seems to have been permitted only if the swearer did not move his hand from the altar (according to a decision of Voivode Thomas of 1342, see Fejér, *Cod. dipl.* 8/4:620), that is, in modern terms, "while still under oath."

5. Text, date and circumstances of the oath were decided by the judge; it was usual to swear the oath in the church of the chapter or convent of authentication, except the oath on the soil, which was to be sworn in a pit (grave) dug at the border of the disputed property, and the swearer had to speak the oath, dressed in burial cloths, with a clog of earth held above his head; the oath-helpers stood around the pit.

6. The text has *articuli*, but the term "articles" came to be used for "articles of law"; hence, we avoided it here.

7. On Henry, see the Index. The bishops of Veszprém held by ancient custom the office of chancellor of the queen. The tradition may have had its roots in the eleventh century when the queen's residence was in Veszprém; queens were also crowned by the bishops of the same see.

8. In this case the word *regnicola* (see the Glossary) is best translated in the more general sense, for the measures touch on the life of all subjects.

9. Though the oath was usually taken by the defendant, under certain circumstances the plaintiff, too, could prove his right by taking an oath "on the head" (*ad caput*) of his opponent, which, if performed successfully involved capital sentence (see the Glossary); hence the name. Oaths on the soil (see n. 5 above) (*super terram*) could also be taken by either party (see Hajnik, *ibid.*, pp. 314 ff.).

Notes to 31 October 1328
pages 5–7.

Incipit: *Ad petitiones fidelium*

This charter, issued in form of a privilege for the nobles of County Szepes repeats the essence of the decree of 10 August 1324, but adds to it an important paragraph about seigneurial jurisdiction. According to this, all tenant peasants and landless servitors are subject to the court of their lord, save in cases of major criminal delicts. In a charter of 17 January 1332 (OL Dl. 87019) King Charles referred to this—or an unknown, similar—decision as having been passed by the barons, prelates and nobles of the kingdom. This text is the first explicit mention of the seigneurial jurisdiction in a decree. It was unknown until published in *DRH 1301–1457*.

MS.: Original on parchment; only a yellowish-pink string, passed through four holes, remains of the pendant seal. OL Dl. 38882.

ED.: *DRH 1301–1457*, pp. 82–84.

1. The full royal style was used in those charters which were issued in the form of a privilege and corroborated with great seal of majesty. The "kingdoms" listed here were part of the royal style of the Árpádian rulers from c. 1270; with the exception of the first three they constituted claims of Hungarian rulers to lands south of the Sava and the lower Danube or east of the Carpathian Mountains. To these Charles I added in 1323 those of "Prince of Salerno" and "Lord of the Honor of Monte Sant'Angelo" which his successors continued to use until 1386. Both domains formed part of the kingdom of Sicily and were claimed by the Hungarian branch of the Angevin dynasty as their paternal inheritance. All the time, however, the honor (i.e., the barony) of Monte Sant'Angelo, situated on the Adriatic coast on the promontory of Gargano (some 175 km east-northeast of Naples), remained in the possession of the Durazzo line of the Angevins. (See E. G. Léonard, *Les Angevins de Naples* [Paris: Presses Universitaires de France, 1954], pp. 322, 376.)

2. It is not known why this edict was requested by and issued for the nobles of county Szepes (today part of Slovakia and Poland).

3. On the procedure of oath-taking, see the notes 3., 4., 5., and 9. to 10 August 1324, above.

4. In the second and third of these model oaths, the scribe has unconsciously substituted one model Christian name (Peter) for the correct model (Paul). In the last oath, the scribe used again the name with which he began. These model names are, of course, based on the names of the apostles; they were used by Christian legal authors to replace the pagan model names (Lucius Titius, Numerius Nigidius, etc.) used in Roman legal texts (e.g., Gaius, *Institutiones* 2.216, 3.167, 4.40–41).

5. For tenant peasant, *jobagio*, in Hungarian *jobbágy*—see the Glossary.

6. As early as the thirteenth century, all landowners had the right and duty of administering justice to their peasants, free or unfree. Seigneurial courts (*sedes dominalis* or *forum dominale*, Hung.: *úriszék*), consisting probably of tenant jurors, were presided over by the lord or his steward. Their jurisdiction was initially limited by royal privilege: cases involving bloodshed could be terminated only before a royal judge or county magistrate, thus criminals sentenced to death or mutilation had to be delivered to them by the seigneur. Since the early fourteenth century, however, some major lords were granted royal privilege to pronounce final judgment in all cases and set up gallows on their estates as symbols of their right to high justice, and by the mid-fifteenth century this privilege, often referred to a "free comity" (Hung.: *szabadispánság*) or *ius gladii* was exercized by all substantial landowners. In 1405 Sigismund granted the same right to royal cities (see below 15 April 1405:5). Cf. K. Szoika, *A földesúri bíráskodás az Árpádkori Magyarországon* [Seigneurial Jurisdiction in Árpádian Hungary] (Bp.: Faculty of Law, 1944) [German summary pp. 75–78].

7. Judicial practice was governed by the general principle that cases were to be prosecuted before the judge of the defendant. The term justice ordinary (*iudex ordinarius*) usually refers to those judges who were authorized to administer justice to free persons. See the Glossary and Hajnik, *Bír. szerv.* pp. 45–47.

8. The list of dignitaries, as a kind of dating clause (not as witnesses to the action), appears regularly in Hungarian charters of privilege between the mid-thirteenth and the early fifteenth century, see I. Szentpétery, *Magyar oklevéltan* [Hungarian Diplomatics] (Bp.: MTA, 1930), pp. 104f.. On the persons listed, see the Index.

Notes to 11 December 1351
pages 8–13.
Incipit: *Tronus et potentia*

This decree is the only piece of legislation issued from a diet under King Louis I. As contained in the proem, the king felt himself obliged to reward the great monetary and personal sacrifices of his nobles in the Sicilian wars with the confirmation of "their rights." The *decretum* contains in its first part the verbatim transcript of the Golden Bull of Andrew II of 1222 (from the 1318 transcript of the archbishop of Esztergom) with a significant change in regard to noble inheritance, where it restores the older tradition of unlimited claim by the clan. However, by re-issuing the privileges granted to the magnates of the thirteenth century (who were then alone called *nobiles*) and explicitly expanding them to the free soldiering elements in Transylvania, Slavonia, and Croatia, Louis in fact gave the entire Hungarian noblity a charter of liberty. The document was seen as such by contemporaries, and its renewal became an accepted tradition of later kings of Hungary.

The decree was passed in a diet of the nobility (clergy are not mentioned in the proem) that seems to have lasted several weeks: in a charter of 12 December 1351 the palatine speaks of a delay in a legal case "because of a royal meeting of the entire realm here in Buda for twenty-four days" (OL Dl. 4149). At least for the following year, the traditional judicial gathering on St. Stephen's Day, based on the renewed Golden Bull, was also reintroduced (cf. a charter of the same Palatine Nicholas Gilétfi of 24 August 1352, *Cod. dipl. And.* 5: 604). The importance of this charter of privilege for the lesser and moyenne nobility is suggested also by the fact that several original copies are known which were sent to the counties as a form of promulgation (see below, MSS).

MSS.: Eight originals are known: a copy for an unknown county (Co. Csanád?), Library of the MTA, 165:121, parchment, seal pedant lost; a copy for Co. Bereg, OL Dl. 4239/1, parchment with damaged double seal pedant; a copy for Co. Bihar, OL Dl. 41174, parchment with fragment of double pendant seal; a copy for Co. Körös OL Dl. 4239/4, parchment with damaged double pendant seal; a copy from the family archives of the Perényi (hereditary *ispánok* of Abaujvár, hence probably the copy for that county) OL Dl. 70630, parchment with double pendant seal; a copy from the *Archivum regnicolare,* OL Dl 4239/3, parchment with double pendant seal, waterdamaged; and a copy for Co. Sáros (later, as dorsal notes suggest, in Co. Szepes

and Turóc) OL Dl. 4239/2, parchment, without seal. Additionally, there are several transcripts: four copies of the transcript by Queen Mary in her decree of 22 June 1384 (see below, Notes to 1384); three copies of the transcript by King Matthias I in his coronation decree of 6 April 1464 (see *DRH 1458*, pp. 140–50); a transcript in privilegial form for Co. Pozsony, in the Slovak State Archives, Bratislava, Slovakia; a transcript in privilegial form for the city of Trencsén, in the City Archives Trenčin, Slovakia. (For detailed information on the manuscripts, see *DRH 1301–1457*, pp. 126–27.)

EDD.: *MTvt/CJH* 1: 170–81; Fejér, *Cod. dipl.* 9/2: 37–47; Marczali, *Enchiridion*, pp. 216–23; T. Smičiklas, *Codex diplomaticus regni Croatiae, Dalmatiae et Slavoniae* (Zagreb: Academia, 1904-) 12: 53–59; cf. also J. N. Kovachich, *Lectiones variantes decretorum comitialium inclyti regni Hungariae* (Pest: Trattner, 1816), pp. 47–55, 537–42.

LIT.: Gy. Bónis, *Hűbériség és rendiség a középkori magyar jogban* [Feudalism and Corporatism in Medieval Hungarian Law] (Kolozsvár: Erdélyi Tud. Intézet, s.d. [1947]) pp. 178–80; S. B. Vardy, G. Goldschmidt, L. S. Domonkos, eds. *Louis the Great, King of Hungary and Poland* (Boulder, Co.: East European Monographs, 1986), pp. 3–90 (the article on and the edition of the *decretum* of 1351, pp. 429–86 are obsolete).

1. On the Angevin royal style, see above, n. 1 to 31 October 1328. For Louis' interest in the vassal territories, see A. Huber, "Ludwig I. von Ungarn und die ungarischen Vasallenländer," *Archiv für österreichische Geschichte* 66 (1885): 1–44; G. McDaniel, "The House of Anjou and Serbia" in Vardy *et al.*, *Louis*, pp. 191–201.

2. The text as printed in *DRH 1301–1457* is translated. Editors have proposed a number of emendations (some of which were anticipated by medieval copyists): e.g., *debitam* for *debitum*, *naturae* for *nativae*. This translation follows one of the suggestions of Kovachich (*Lectiones* p. 538) in understanding *debitum* as a substantive in apposition to *originem*. The contorted and curious word order of this sentence may well be, as has been suggested, owed to the scribe's misunderstanding of what was dictated. In addition, no little confusion is owed to the author's patent attempt to compress several concepts, expressed (as throughout this preamble) in unusual terms, within one sentence; cf. the comments in *DRH 1301–1457*, p. 128, n. I–1.

3. Most frequently the term *cetus (coetus)* was used in the vague sense of "collectivity." It can be, and has been indeed, pointed out that the prelates are not explicitly mentioned in the text which seems to indicate that they did not take part in the assembly. Nevertheless they are listed in the eschatocol of the document in the way usual for charters of privilege.

4. The ascription of "ancient liberties" to the founder of the Christian kingdom was commonplace; the reference here is to the the Golden Bull, which also contains this claim, see *DRMH* 1: 34.

5. Andrew (b. 1327) was the second son of King Charles I of Hungary and a younger brother of Louis I. His father had married him to Joan, the grand-daughter and heiress of King Robert of Naples, in the obvious hope that Andrew would inherit the "Kingdoms of Jerusalem and Sicily" (that was the official name of the Kingdom of Naples). When in 1343 Joan I alone succeeded her grandfather and Andrew was merely given the simple title of Duke of Calabria, Louis was bitterly disappointed. In 1345 he managed to gain the consent of Pope Clement VI (as suzerain of Naples) to his brother's coronation, but before it could be performed, Andrew was murdered. Louis then declared himself heir of "King" Andrew and took revenge by conquering Naples in two major campaigns (1347–48, 1350). Having realized, however, that he would not be able to keep his conquest against both Joan and the papal court, he made a truce in 1352 and withdrew his armies, without ever formally renouncing his rights.

6. The inalienable status of most noble estates as defined here came to be called later aviticity (*aviticitas*, in Hungarian *ősiség*) and remained the law until 1848. It was based on the principle that the estate was the common inheritance of all those who descended, in the male line, from the ancestor (*avus*) who had acquired it (see the Glossary, s.v. "clan"). In the older literature the "law of aviticity" was held to have been "introduced" by Louis I. Today, actually ever since the seminal study of A. Murarik, *Az ősiség alapintézményeinek eredete* [Origins of the basic institutions of entail] (Bp.: Sárkány, 1938), this passage is seen rather as a reestablishment of an old custom rooted in the tribal traditions of pre-Christian times which had never disappeared. Even though suspended by Andrew II, this inheritance pattern became again the general rule under King Charles I, and Louis only sanctioned it. See E. Fügedi, "The *avus* in the Medieval Conceptual Framework of Kinship in Hungary," in Fügedi, *Kings*, ch. 4, pp. 137–42; J. M. Bak, "King Louis I and the Lesser Nobility," in Vardy, *et al.*, *Louis* pp. 67–80, with bibliography.

7. The dowager queen, Elizabeth, daughter of King Wladislas the Short of Poland and fourth wife of Charles I of Hungary, was considered co-regent of his son in an informal way and exerted a great influence on his policies until her death in 1380.

8. Similarly to other European laws of the fourteenth century, the article intends to limit the rights of ecclesiastics in secular courts. In the fourteenth century secular authorities increasingly viewed the imposition of ecclesiastical penalties, especially excommunication, by clerical litigants against their lay adversaries in a proceeding pending before a secular judge as an abuse of spiritual jurisdiction. For a recent discussion of these circumstances in France and England, particularly the development of the English writ of prohibition, see Elizabeth Vodola, *Excommunication in the Middle Ages* (Berkeley: Univ. of California Press, 1986) pp. 159–90. The Editors are pleased to thank Kenneth Pennington, Syracuse University, for this reference. Although this provision is the first to be included in a decretum of national validity, the measure was anticipated in a royal document applicable to Transylvania and pertaining exclusively to property disputes issued on 28 July 1344. This article has been, among others, adduced to

impugn an "anti-clerical" bias to the diet of 1351. We know that King Louis had already issued a mandate of this content, but that was meant only for Transylvania and only in matters of property; see Fejér, *Cod. dipl.* 9/1: 194.

9. This practice had already been prohibited in a papal letter by Pope Benedict XII, on the request of King Charles I (Theiner, *Vet. mon. hist.*, p. 607), but, judging from several later transcripts of the same (e.g., Knauz, *MES*, 3: 274; OL Dl. 5022) and from late fifteenth-century laws against it (Kovachich, *Supplementum*, 1: 277), without avail. Bónis assumed that the abuse goes back to some pre-Christian custom of composition, transferred in a "baptized" form to the archdeacon.

10. In the fourteenth century the reliability of minor convents as places of authentication came to be doubted, because it was assumed that they were easily influenced by outside parties. To limit their activity, this article cancelled one of their most important rights, the authentication of property transactions *in perpetuum*. This did not, apparently, solve the problem, for in 1353 King Louis ordered all convents and chapters to present their seals in Buda, perhaps for the purpose of granting full rights only to the major ones; see Eckhart, Glaubw. Orte, pp. 420–22; L. B. Kumorovitz, "Az authentikus pecsét" [The Authentic Seal], *Turul* 50 (1936): 62.

11. The groat (see the Glossary) of Charles and Louis had the value of 1/21 florin, so the chamber's profit (see Glossary) on one peasant holding amounted to 1/7 florin. Compared to other taxes it was not a heavy burden. In the early fifteenth century, 1/5 florin per plot was regarded the customary due. This direct tax is already mentioned in the same amount in the cameral contracts; see below, CC 1342:19, and *DRH 1301–1457*, pp. 119–20.)

12. For the *ferto*, a weight and a money of account, see the Glossary.

13. The word *redemptio*, usually meaning a fee for issuing documents, suggests that this measure referred to unlawfully demanded payments for letters of quittance.

14. For the reeve (*villicus*) see the Glossary. The propertied *servientes* here referred to, were, of course not those predecessors of the lesser nobility who were called *servientes regis* in the thirteenth century (see *DRMH* 1: 150) but most likely freeholders obliged to do perpetual military service under the banner of a secular or, more often, of an ecclesiastical lord. They were also subject to his jurisdiction but unlike unfree tenants they had their own court of justice. Their subordination was not of feudal character, for they possessed their estate (*predium*) by the same hereditary right as nobles did. On this account they were considered nobles themselves, but their status as *nobiles prediales* was lower than that of "true" nobles. Communities of *prediales* survived into the mid-nineteenh century. The interpretation of this passage was for a long time pivotal in the debate about the taxation of medieval nobility, see e.g., J. Illés, *Az Anjou-kori társadalom és az adózás* [Society and taxation in the Angevin era] (Bp.: Politzer, 1900), esp. pp. 51–55.

15. The payment called ninth is attested here for the first time. In fact it was the tenth part of the crop, namely, the ninth of what remained after rendering the tithe. (Hence, it was sometimes called "the second tithe".) Originally the ninth seems to have been the common tax on wine, later called *nona vinorum* or *tributum montis* (tax "of the hill," i.e., of the vineyards).

16. On the *udvarnokok*, see the Glossary. The villages inhabited by them (*ville udvornicales*) preserved their particular organization within the royal demesne until about 1400.

17. The purpose of this obligation on all landowners to exact uniform dues has been long debated. Present consensus holds that it was passed in defense of lesser landowners, who suffered from the labor shortage caused partly by the plague that had hit Hungary in the preceding years. They frequently lost their tenants to better-off nobles, who could afford to demand lower dues from those moving to their estates; see I. Bard "Louis I and the Serfs," in Vardy *et al., Louis*, pp. 81–90, briefly summarizing some of the relevant Hungarian literature. In a mandate of 1 August 1370 King Louis repeated his threat to collect the ninth for the fisc if not all landowners in Co. Győr exact the same dues; see Nagy, I. *et al.*, ed. *Hazai Okmánytár. Codex diplomaticus patrius*, 8 vols. (Győr–Bp.: MTA, 1865–1891) (henceforth *Cod. dipl. patr.*) 3: 189–90.

18. In spite of this decision, only a year later, in 1352, on the intervention of the popes the king ordered the tithe to be paid again in money. Even though only the edict to the estates of Transylvania has survived (see F. Zimmermann-C. Werner, *Urkundenbuch zur Geschichte der Deutschen in Siebenbürgen*. vol. 3 [Hermannstadt: Michaelis, 1882], pp. 88–90), one may presume that the regulation was general.

19. This regulation of fees for charters of donations differs from the earlier system as defined in Comp. c. 1300: 20 (*DRMH* 1: 77) by assigning 10 percent of the annual income to the vice-chancellor and a *ferto* (see the Glossary) to the scribe, which seems to be less than before. Cf. also the later regulation in 8 March 1435: 8.

20. The "dry tolls" seem to have been based on old custom, and the king saw himself forced to relent on this point; only a year later he granted the right to the nuns of Óbuda to levy such a toll, explicitly rescinding his law of 1351 (OL Dl. 4230 of 27 November 1352).

21. For the notion of "defeat in judicial combat," see the Glossary s.v. "combat."

22. For *calumnia* or "frivolous prosecution," see the Glossary.

23. For the delict of "false court appearance" *(astatio falsi termini)*, see the Glossary and Hajnik, *Bír. szerv.* p. 441.

24. On the meaning of "capital sentence," see the Glossary.

25. A capital sentence could be passed also in a civil process and the convicted was handed over to the winning party. This was usually followed by a contract allowing the convicted to redeem his head by paying his composition (see the Glossary), but up to the sixteenth century the execution of the sentenced was also permitted.

26. Fifty marks was the customary composition of a nobleman.

27. On this procedure of garnisheeing property, see above 1320, and also Comp.c.1300: 3 and 9 (*DRMH* 1: 73, 75).

28. The redemption of estates mortgaged or garnisheed pertained always to the next collaterals on the male line.

29. This sentence did not in 1351 have the far-reaching implications which later centuries, above all, Werbőczy (*Tripartitum* I,3) attached to it, namely that in Hungary all noblemen, from the owner of a single plot to the mightiest aristocrat, were equal (see Bak, in Vardy *et al., Louis*, pp. 71–72). Although in fact no legal division existed among "true" nobles, poor or rich, this article intended only to grant "true noble" status all the freemen in the "ducal" territories, i.e., Croatia, Slavonia, Dalmatia and perhaps also

Transylvania (for at that time all these were governed by the king's younger brother, Prince Stephen) and, apparently, also to the dependent nobles (*prediales*), see above, n. 14. On some of the implications of this decision, see below art. 12.

30. On the *mardurina (marturina)*, the general tax due from Slavonia and the neighbouring counties beyond the Drava see 1222:27 with n. 34 (*DRMH* 1:36, 101). The portion of the ban was called in Hungarian *zsolozsma* ("service," from the Slavonic *služba*) or *bánzsolozsmája* ("service to the ban") and was paid in kind, mostly in food and fodder (*victualia bani*) similar to royal *descensus* in Hungary proper. Even though abolished by the decree of 1351, the *mardurina* survived. It was so called as late as the fifteenth century and the peasants of Slavonia had to pay half the amount of what was exacted as the chamber's profit in the rest of the kingdom. The article is formulated rather equivocally, because it is believed that noble households were exempt from any taxation. It probably intended to stress that in collecting and paying the taxes from their estates the nobles of Slavonia were henceforth to enjoy the same standing as those living in Hungary proper (see art. 11, with n. 29, above).

31. Up to the early fourteenth century all mines were in royal hands. If mineral deposits were found on private estates, the king had the prerogative to acquire it by exchange of property. In order to make private landowners interested in opening up new deposits, Charles I allowed them in 1327 (see *DRH 1301–1457*, p. 80) to keep their property and to retain also one-third of the royal dues, the *urbura* (see the Glossary). It is believed that the expansion of precious metal mining in fourteenth-century Hungary was to a great extent due to this new arrangement; see B. Hóman, "La circolazione delle monete d'oro in Ungheria dal X al XIV secolo e la crisi europea dell'oro nel secolo XIV," *Rivista Italiana di Numismatica* 35 (1922): 109–56, here pp. 135 ff..

32. This article aims at eliminating the advantage of those grantees of royal favor who were permitted to entrust litigation, for example, in matters of "objection to *seisin*," to the king's advocate, who, of course, enjoyed considerable influence in the courts.

33. The traditional text is unclear and, according to I. Szabó (*Száz.* 88 [1954]: 525–26) an additional *etiam* ("also") is missing before the reference to the royal tenants. Bónis decided not to add a word but rather to solve the problem by punctuation, making the sentence an enumeration of different tenants, from those of the nobles through those of the royal couple to those of the prelates and magnates. Szabó may, however, be right in assuming that the words *prelati aut potentes* were added later to the decree and that is when the textual corruption crept in.

34. The prohibition of the violent removal of peasants from other landowners' estates may have become widespread because of the shortage of labor mentioned above (see n. 15, with the relevant literature).

35. This is not only a confirmation of the seigneurial jurisdiction of the nobility (see 31 October 1328, above) but according to the detailed analysis by I. Szabó ("Az 1351. évi 18. tc." [Article 1351:18], in *Szentpétery Emlékkönyv* [Sz. Festschrift] (Bp.: Dunántúli Nyomda, 1938), pp. 419–39; and "Az 1351. évi jobbágytörvények" [The Laws of 1351 Concerning the Tenants], *Száz.* 88 [1954]: 497–527; French resumé on pp. 743–44) an explicit extension

of it for the lesser nobility. The delicts listed in the article belong to those *causae criminales* which usually were not included in the jurisdiction of nobles without the right to "high justice." Neither were the lesser nobles, in contrast to the crown, the magnates and free cities, permitted to prosecute *pro pristinis factis* ("for ancient delicts"). Thus, the inclusion of these crimes into this article meant a widening of the juridical powers of the lesser nobility.

36. Cf. art. 10, above; while the notion of "collective guilt" was generally eschewed by the Christian Middle Ages, Louis referred to his decision of punishing only the guilty person in a charter of 1353 as a "privilege granted in grace" to the nobles (quoted by J. Holub, in his review of B. Hóman, Gy. Szekfü, *Magyar történet* vols. 1–3, *Száz.*, 69 [1935]: 194]. One may consider this issue in the light of the "collective property" of the Hungarian clans and see it as contrasting legal prosecution to rights of possession. Some historians have suggested that this passage was included expressly to bar the repetition of the horrible punishment of several dozen members of an entire clan, as was done in 1330 after the attempt by Felcian Záh on the life of the royal family, probably provoked by the seduction of his daughter serving at the royal court; see H. Marczali, "Le procès de Félicien Záh," *Revue historique* 107 (1911): 43–58.

37. Neither the wording nor the import of the article is clear. Although the recovery of estates was to be done "in three attempts" (Comp. c. 1300: 8, *DRMH* 1: 75) this article speaks about acquisition; the document issued by places of authentication in such "threefold attempts" was called a letter of *seisin* (see the Glossary) and not a letter of inquest (see the Glossary). Furthermore, it is not clear who is to be asked in the prescribed inquest "among nobles and churches." Bónis reads the last clause as referring to charters of privilege issued by the judges ordinary in the king's high courts.

38. This measure also aims at the control of the legal activity of the chapters as art. 3, above; cf. Eckhart, Glaubw. Orte, p. 493. The amount of per diem was earlier stipulated at twenty-four pennies, see: Comp. c. 1300: 19 (*DRMH* 1: 76–77).

39. Inquest as a means of producing evidence was introduced around 1300 (see Comp. c. 1300: 1–2, *DRMH* 1: 73). It could be held in different ways. The "simple" inquest could be ordered by many authorities on the initiative of a plaintiff who needed a letter of evidence on his being injured so that he could enter an action. (See Hajnik, *Bír. szerv.*, p. 287, who is probably wrong in making reference there to this article.) Here probably not the "simple" but the "common" inquest (*inquisitio communis*) is meant (see the Glossary).

40. If the party was convicted before a compromise could be reached, the 3 mark fine no longer sufficed; the judge had the right to collect 50 marks, i.e., a nobleman's composition (cf. above, art. 10).

41. Attempts at limiting the delay in suits are characteristic for the entire medieval legislation in Hungary; see already in Comp. c. 1300:8 (*DRMH* 1: 79).

42. On the use of *comes* as title, in contrast to the office of *ispán*, see the Glossary.

43. On the persons mentioned in the eschatocol, see the Index.

Notes to 22 June 1384
pages 14–15.

Incipit: *Eaque reipublice*

This decree was passed in a diet called by the government of the twelve-year old Queen Mary, which was in fact dominated by her mother, Queen Elizabeth, and Palatine Nicholas of Gara (Garai), in order to satisfy general dissatisfaction of the nobility with the new rulers. It was apparently hoped that by having the young queen confirm her father's 1351 decree, incorporating the Golden Bull of 1222—by this time regarded as the "cornerstone of noble liberty"—the opposition could be quelled. The proem does not include the prelates among those present, even though their names feature in the eschatocol, as was usual with charters of privilege.

MSS.: four contemporary originals, three in Hungary (OL Dl. 42297, 7052/2 and 7052/1) and one in Zagreb (Državni Archiv, Doc. Med. Var. 101); all on parchment with pendant seals lost or broken. (For details, see *DRH 1301–1457*, p. 142.)

EDD.: *MTvt/CJH* 1: 184–89 (cf. Kovachich, *Lectiones*, pp. 55–59, 542–57); Pray, *Annales* 2: 167–68; Fejér, *Cod. dipl.* 10/1: 148–51; *DRH 1301–1457*, pp. 142–45.

LIT.: Kovachich, *Vestigia* pp. 191–92; Bak, *Königtum*, p. 25.

1. Based on some contemporary unofficial comments, such as those in the *Memoriale* by the Zadar patrician Paulus de Paolo (ed. G. Schwandtner, *SS rer. Hung.* 3: 724), who, aware of the unusual case of female succession, speaks of Mary as "king," the Hungarian chronicler Thuróczy coined the term *rex foemineus*, and this anomaly came to be noted in historical scholarship even to our day. (Cf. E. H. Kantorowicz, *The King's Two Bodies* [Princeton: Princeton Univ. Press, 1956], p. 80, n. 93.) In fact no official, contemporary source refers to her except as *regina*, and this was already demonstrated by Mathias Bél in 1745; cf. Bak, p. 25, with nn. 100–04 on p. 93.

2. On the Angevin royal style, see above note 1 to 10 August 1324.

3. Louis I died 10 September 1382 and was buried in Székesfehérvár on 16 September. Mary was crowned on the following day.

4. Louis, of course, made elaborate arrangements for the succession of "one of his daughters" in his Polish kingdom, including the grant in 1379 of

the famous first charter of liberty for the lesser nobility, the "privilege of Kassa" (in Polish sources: Koszyce)—see J. Dąbrowski, *Ostatnie lata Ludwika Wielkiego 1370–1382* [The Last Years of Louis the Great] (Kraków: Akad. Umiejtnosći, 1918), pp. 351 f.—but there is no reliable evidence about any similar steps in Hungary, where he must have trusted in the loyalty of the new aristocracy to assure the succession of Mary, the only reigning queen in the medieval history of Hungary. That Mary does not refer even in passing, as Louis did in 1342, to any kind of "election," merely to her hereditary right, suggests that her party wanted to emphasize her legitimacy; cf. Bak, pp. 24 f.

5. The Latin *cetus et universitatis idemptitas*, though awkward, became a standing formula in chancellery documents; on the former see n. 3 to 1351.

6. As far as we know, it occurs here for the first time and was not to become usual until the sixteenth century that the estates presented their wishes by delegates (*nuncii*) to the ruler; cf. also below, n. 2 to 1385.

7. On these, see the Index; they were probably the delegates of the counties Somogy and Pozsega, respectively; Bónis (*DRH 1301–1457*, p. 142) saw it as significant that the two envoys came from that southwest corner of the country where the opposition to Mary's reign was soon to erupt in violent confrontation.

8. King Louis' first great seal was lost in 1363 during a campaign against Bosnia; Ozora (in the text *Uzura*, today: Osora) is a region in northern Bosnia, between the Drina and Bosna Rivers.

9. On the use of the term *comes* as a title and not the office of county *ispán*, see the Glossary, s.v.

10. Names like those of Nicholas and Blaise (below) in the form *Nicolaus dictus* (="called") *Zambo*, which has been rendered in translation as simply a Christian name and a "family name," indicate an early stage of the development of constant family names that were not always derived, as usual with the nobility, from their estate (which seems to have remained "official" as late as 1435, see below 8 March 1435:4).

11. On the persons listed in the eschatocol, see the Index.

Notes to 14 November 1385
pages 16–17.
Incipit: *Quod cum nos*

The dissatisfaction with the regimen of Queen Elizabeth, the queen mother, led to virtual civil war by 1384 despite the affirmations of peace in the decree of that year. Several barons supported Mary's fiancée, Sigismund of Luxemburg, margrave of Brandenburg, but the queen mother secretly engaged her to Louis of Orléans, brother of King Charles VI of France. A third party, apparently mainly of lesser nobles, opposed Mary's succession and supported the claims of Charles of Durazzo, her second cousin. In the summer of 1385, the two court parties came to an agreement and Mary was wed to Sigismund, but the margrave had to flee Buda to escape the advancing Charles. In these circumstances the diet convened; it is unclear, however, whether it was called by the queens to placate the opposition or in response to the insistence of the counties. While the decree contains merely a repetition of previously confirmed liberties, the diet was a historical one, for this was the first time that the presence of "four richer nobles" from each county, already referred to in the *decretum* of 1267 (*DRMH* 1: 43), is explicitly documented. That the privileges of liberty were not transcribed and the law promulgated (at least in both surviving originals) in the form of simple letters patent without the list of dignitaries, with the great seal *en placard*, may have been the consequence of the troubled situation.

MSS.: Two authentic originals: a copy for District Rábaköz in Co. Sopron, OL Dl. 61249, and a copy for the "Ten lances" noble community in Co. Szepes, now OL Dl. 38885.

EDD.: Kovachich, *Vestigia*, pp. LIX–LXII; Kovachich, *Sylloge*, pp. 53–56; Fejér, *Cod. dipl.* 10/1: 216–18; *DRH 1301–1457*, pp. 146–48.

LIT.: I. N. Bard, "Aristocratic Revolts and the Late Medieval Hungarian State A.D. 1382–1408," Ph. D. dissertation, Univ. of Washington, 1978.

1. 8 November 1385.

2. As the diet took place in Buda, where the queens were also staying, it is unclear why communication by envoys was necessary, but may have been customary in those years (see above, n. 6 to 1384). In view of the turbulent political situation, one may assume that Mary and her mother remained behind the walls of the castle, while the nobles assembled in the city.

3. References to the "holy kings," meaning above all St. Stephen, as founders of the noble privilege were common since the thirteenth century (see 1222: Pre., *DRMH* 1: 34). The Angevin rulers were particularly eager to underscore their continuity with the royal saints of the Árpád dynasty; see G. Klaniczay, "The Cult of Dynastic Saints in Central Europe (Fourteenth Century Angevins and Luxemburgs)," in *The Uses of Supernatural Power: The Transformation of Popular Religion in Medieval and Early-Modern Europe*, tr. S. Sigerman, ed. K. Margolis (Cambridge: Polity, 1990), pp. 111–28.

4. The *decretum* of 11 December 1351, and its transcript of 22 June 1384 are meant.

5. The scribe tried to use some classical allusions (probably) from Vergil (*Aeneid* 4.643) and, at first or second hand, from Cicero (*de natura deorum* 2.57.142, cf. Catullus 63. 56) which led to a rather complicated clause.

6. This might be an allusion to the Moravian border which was threatened at that time by an invasion of Sigismund's troops.

7. *Ex certa nostre maiestatis scientia* is a recurrent phrase of royal charters, but its exact meaning is not clear. The translation we chose is probable, not certain, but renders the traditional sense of the words, which is something like "according to our understanding of our authority. . . ." Zs. Teke's interpretation (*Decreta regni Hungariae 1458–1490* [Bp.: Akadémiai K., 1991], p. xix), according to which this clause was to refer to the king's special jurisdiction (*absoluta potestas*) does not explain its use here.

Notes to (1386 after 27 August)
pages 18–20.
Incipit: *Noverit presens etas*

It is difficult to define the exact legal character of this document. In essence, it is a peace treaty between the "court party," supported by a number of nobles, on the one hand, and the rebellious "Horváti-party" of southern Hungary and Croatia, who held Queen Mary and Queen Elizabeth captive, on the other. Contemporary sources are too contradictory to allow us to decide whether the peace was in fact concluded or remained a plan. The document was issued from a festive gathering of prelates and nobles, called by Palatine Nicholas of Szécs (Széchi) and dramatized by an oath sworn on the head reliquiary of the kingdom's founder. Some time around 1387 the palatine and the barons did constitute a "council of the realm" which had its own seal with the inscription *Sigillum regnicolarum regni Hungariae* in order to bridge the gap of the interregnum. If this decree was issued under that seal, it would certainly qualify as a "decree of the interim sovereign power." However, the sole surviving copy is fragmentary, incomplete, and unsealed. Hence, formally it cannot be classified as a *decretum.* Nevertheless, the highly significant statements about the conceptual separation of ruler and realm, expressed for the first time in such poignant words, make it constitutionally an important document for the development of political and legal thought. Therefore, we followed the editors of *DRH 1301–1457* and included this text among the *decreta.*

The date of this decision is also open to conjecture. John Nicholas Kovachich, who discovered the only copy, dated it as emanating from a diet that opened on 27 August 1386, but Imre Hajnik, who later edited it, dated it to 1387. István R. Kiss devoted a study to the diets of 1386 and accepted the date proposed by Kovachich, arguing that it is impossible that the murder of Queen Elizabeth in January 1387 would not have been known eight months later, when Queen Mary was already released, while the text speaks of her as still alive. This dating remains still problematic because of the equivocal formulation in art. 4, where "royal" and "reginal" majesties are separately referred to: as far as we know, Sigismund's acceptance as ruler of Hungary was not yet decided by summer 1386, hence the "king" implied here would have to be Mary (see below, note 9). A solution might be that the wording was meant in generic ("constitutional") terms: *regia serenitas* meaning any ruler, in general. Lacking more precise information on the turbulent events of the age, we accepted the dating of both Kovachich and R. Kiss.

MS.: Fragmentary copy on paper, from the Kállay Family Archives; OL Dl. 52575.

EDD.: J. N. Kovachich, *Notitiae praeliminares ad Syllogen decretorum* (Pest: Trattner, 1820), pp. 417–22; I. Hajnik, "Az 1387. évi székesfehérvári "országgyűlés" cikkelyei" [The articles of the Székesfehérvár "diet" of 1387], *Történelmi Tár* (1878): 173–76; *DRH 1301–1457*, pp. 149–53.

LIT.: Hajnik, as above; I. R. Kiss "Az 1386. évi országgyűlések" [The Diets of the Year 1386], *Száz.* 47 (1913): 721–35; F. Eckhart, *A szentkorona-eszme története* [History of the Idea of the Holy Crown] (Bp.: MTA, 1941), pp. 67–68; I. Szentpétery, *Magyar oklevéltan* [Hungarian Diplomatics] (Bp.: MTA, 1930), p. 211 (on the seal of the council).

1. For the preceding events, see Bard, "Revolts" (as above, Notes to 1385). After the forced abdication of Mary, the coronation of Charles of Durazzo on 31 December 1385, and his murder by the queens' men in February 1386 (see L. di Monaci, *"Carmen de Carolo parvo"* in F. Cornelius, ed., *Chronicon de rebus Venetis* [Venice, 1758], pp. 325–381), civil war broke out once more, this time between the supporters of Mary and of Charles's son, King Ladislas of Naples (1386–1414).

2. In Hungary, 20 August is observed as St. Stephen's Day.

3. On the tradition of judicial and political assembly in Székesfehérvár, since at least the early thirteenth century, see 1222:1, 1231:1 (*DRMH* 1:34, 38.).

4. The head-reliquary of St. Stephen, which, together with the crown adorning it, also played a role in 1440 (see below), was kept in the treasury of the collegiate chapter of Székesfehérvár and disappeared probably during the Ottoman siege of the city in 1543. It is not known even from a picture. However, in the eighteenth century a similar reliquary, maybe the same, was in the custody of the Dominicans in Dubrovnik and recovered from them by Maria Theresa in 1769.

5. It is not entirely clear whether the term "royal majesty" here and in the following refers to Queen Mary who was taken prisoner by the rebels on 25 July 1386, or rather to any ruler, perhaps to one (Sigismund of Luxemburg?) that was to be elected by the lords who took on themselves the protection of the "Holy Crown's" interest (see also below, notes 9). At any rate, the concept of a government that would resist even the actions of the ruler in the name of the "kingdom," is an important step towards the development of a transpersonal concept of the "state"; cf. Bak, *Königtum*, pp. 27–28, with notes on pp. 94–95, summarizing the research of Eckhart and others as well.

6. *Novitas* implied in medieval understanding some evil innovation, it was often used for heresy; cf. Du Cange, *Glossarium* 4:657, where reference is

made to the French legal term *nouvelleté*, meaning usurpation of rights or property.

7. This program of a noble council, formulated as early as 1298 (see 1298:7, *DRMH* 1: 51), did not become a reality until the late fifteenth century.

8. Cf. 1222:30. (*DRMH* 1: 36)

9. The meaning of the expressions *regia serenitas* and *reginalis maiestas* has been often debated: while the context here suggests that Queen Mary and her mother, Elizabeth, are meant, this usage would confirm the assumption that Mary was in fact addressed as "king" (cf. n. 1, to 1384). If, however, this decree already implied the impending election of Sigismund, the *regia* may refer to him, and the *reginalis* to Mary or to both she and her mother.

10. On John of Horvát (Horváti), see the Index nominum; he and his three bothers, one of whom was Paul, bishop of Zagreb, were, as main supporters of Charles and Ladislas of Naples, the leaders of the rebellion in the south.

11. On John of Palisna, ally of John Horváti, see the Index. Castle Vrana, near Zara in Dalmatia, was the seat of the prior of the Knights Hospitallers in Hungary and Croatia.

12. Apparently the booty was already distributed among the rebels and they were to recover it under the threat of oaths.

13. On Gara(i), see the Index; he was the chief supporter of the dowager queen and was killed in a skirmish near Gara (today: Gorjani, Croatia) when the queens were taken prisoner. See also *Biogr. Lex.* 2:7–9.

14. This was partly true, for the competition between the two factions went back to the time of Louis I and the rebellion of the Horváti began against the hegemony at court of their opponent, Palatine Garai. Thus, the revolt against the queens could reasonably be presented as a factional feud.

15. Felony implied the immediate loss of all property which was then usually distributed among the faithful. Therefore, the sentence of high treason not only had to be annulled, but the grants of confiscated estates also had to be revoked. These measures may be implied in the clause *aliis ad hec necessarie occurrentibus*.

16. The text ends in mid-sentence.

Notes to (October 1397)
pages 21–28.
Incipit: *Quod quia creberrimis*

This decree is the first piece of legislation that can be styled "dualist" in that it reflects a compromise between king and noble estates. It was also the first of many laws which attempted to strengthen the country's position against the growing threat of Ottoman advance from the south. After the disaster at Nicopolis (28 September 1396)—whence Sigismund returned to Hungary only with great difficulties, many months later—the king's position was anything but stable. During his absence the party of Ladislas of Naples gained new strength and the powerful Lackfi family was attempting a coup (see Bard, pp. 40–50). However, the king managed to rally support and put down the rebellion swiftly. When he called a diet to the center of the southern defense, Temesvár (today: Timişoara, Romania), his aims were to stabilize central authority with the help of faithful aristocrats and the county nobility, on the one hand, and to reform the defense of the country, on the other.

The decree contains, without explicitly referring to their original issue, most of the articles of the Golden Bull of 1222, and almost all of those added to it in 1351 by Louis I. In addition to these re-issued privileges, the edict contains another 25 articles. These are mixed in terms of *cui prodest*: some strengthen the hand of the king, e.g., in recovering royal property, others enhance the power of the counties, the seat of the lesser nobility's power, and a few have an anti-clerical character. The reform of the army—had it been fully implemented—could have helped the entire nation in its fight against the Ottoman Empire.

The diet was called for 29 September 1397 and lasted less than a month. On 26 October Sigismund issued charters already quoting passages from the decree passed at the meeting (Zs. O. 1, no. 5037) and the deputies of Traù, who arrived on that day, were too late to participate. No dated and formally-issued original of this decree has survived; the only text we have was discovered in the nineteenth century in a simple transcript probably prepared for some landowner. Reference is, however, made to a copy which the nobles of Co. Zagreb presented to the ban in 1398, regarding their rights (see below, art. 41); hence, we may assume that the county delegates received originals in Temesvár or were sent copies later, as was usual.

MS.: Parchment with octagonal privy seal *en placard*; seriously damaged. State Archives, Bratislava (Slovakia), County archives, Diaetalia 1/30.

EDD.: N. Knauz, "Az 1397-ki országgyűlés végzeménye" [Decree of the Diet of 1397], *Magyar Történelmi Tár* 3 (1857): 213–38; *DRH 1301–1457*, pp. 157–74.

LIT.: Knauz, *op. cit.*; J. Deér, "Zsigmond király honvédelmi politikája" [Defense policies of King Sigismund], *Hadtörténelmi Közelmények* 37 (1936): 1–57, 169–202; J. Held, "Military Reform in Early Fifteenth Century Hungary," *East European Quarterly*, 11,2 (1977): 129–39; A. Borosy, "The *militia portalis* in Hungary before 1526," in Bak-Király *Hunyadi*, pp. 63–80; Mályusz, *Sigismund*, p. 175 f.; Idem, "Die Zentralisationsbestrebungen König Sigismunds in Ungarn," in *Études historiques* (Bp.: Akadémiai, 1960) 1: 317–58 (also: Studia Historica Acad. Sc. Hung. 50, *ibid.*, 1960.) On the seal: L. B. Kumorovitz, "A magyar királyi egyszerű és titkos pecsét használatának alakulása a középkorban" [Development of the Use of the Hungarian Royal Simple and Privy Seal in the Middle Ages], *A Bécsi Magyar Történetkutató Intézet Évkönyve* 7 (1937): 105–506.

1. The missing word in the Latin can be assumed to have been *iniquorum* or *impiorum* from a very similar clause in charters from 1397, 1398, cf. Zs. O. 1, nos. 5101, 5598.

2. The word *convenire* is a conjecture of N. Knauz. The reference to full powers from the county nobles signals another step towards the diet's development to a representative institution; see Gy. Bónis, "The Hungarian Feudal Diet (13th to 18th centuries)," *Receuils de la Société Jean Bodin pour l'histoire comparative des institutions*, 25 (1965): 207–307.

3. 29 September 1379.

4. The preamble of the *decretum* is in essence repeated in the charter mentioned above, which suggests that a copy of the original was retained in the royal chancellery.

5. Cf. 1222:1. Articles of the Golden Bull—even if the original formulation did not make sense in 1397, as in the references to *servientes*, who had long ago become *nobiles*—and of 1351 are mostly repeated verbatim; in order to save space, we merely refer to the articles by number, unless major changes were made vis-à-vis 1222 (cf. *DRMH* 1:34–37) or 1351 (above), repectively.

6. With the exception of *capiant* for *capiamus*, identical with 1222:4.

7. Identical with 1222:5 but the last sentence is omitted.

8. Identical with 5:1222, only cases related to tithes are left out from those pertaining to comital jurisdiction.

9. So far identical with 1222:7; the last sentence of the article in the Golden Bull is replaced by the following elaborate arrangements.

10. For the meaning of honor, esp. in the context of border defense, see the Glossary.

11. This clause was to override explicitly the traditional privilege of the nobility, for "true nobles" of the realm had to serve only under the king's personal command (1222:7).

12. As all sons were entitled to an equal portion of an inherited estate, with the paternal house usually going to the youngest, division was often postponed for another generation or more. From a legal point of view, brothers or cousins who lived on still undivided estates were considered to form one family; cf. also above note 6 to 1351.

13. In the 1390s, pennies of different value were in circulation. A "new penny" (*nova moneta*) was first issued by Sigismund in 1392 and was to be worth three old pennies which also remained in circulation. 100 new pennies (or 300 old ones) were in fact exchanged for one gold florin at least until 1403, when the government began a new financial policy leading also to the debasement of the new pennies.

14. Three marks (see the Glossary) was the usual amount of different types of fines; in what pennies is it meant here is not clear. It would have been equal to 400 new ones.

15. The exact meaning of this article, in particular of the words *de quibusvis viginti jobagionibus*, has been much debated by historians. According to some it aimed at arming every twentieth tenant farmer and thus setting up a peasant militia, while others interpret it to mean that landowners had to hire and equip as many (professional?) soldiers as they held estates divided in 20 *portae* (see the Glossary). There is evidence for both; the closest in time is a mandate of Sigismund from 13 November 1398 to the nobles of Co. Pozsony commanding them to appear in camp *cum vicesima parte universorum iobagionum* ("with the twentieth part of all their tenants"), cf. Zs. O. 1, no. 5582. Several royal mandates, originally probably circulars, survived from the last years of the century in which Sigismund repeated the essence of this new military organisation and specified its implementation, cf. Zs. O. 1, nos. 5583, 5683; these orders define procedures of registering the landowners, their obligations in the *militia portalis*, and the mode of punishing those reluctant to fulfill their duty. See also Deér, pp. 20–21. The discussion is summarized, with reference to older literature in Borosy, but the debate is by no means closed. One may, of course, also assume that the contemporaries were not aware of the problem and all they had in mind was to mount nobles and peasants invariably, depending on local conditions.

16. Namely, to serve only in person, under the king's command, as stipulated in 1222:7.

17. Identical with the first part of 1222:8; the textual corruption of *habeant* in the plural instead of *habeat*, which survived in all versions of the *CJH*, was the source of total misinterpretation of the article, assuming that it prohibited all judges—not only the palatine—from having deputies.

18. By reformulating 1222:14 this article extended the circle of defendants to all major officeholders, and that of plaintiffs to a wide circle of the population.

19. Here the reference of 1222:18 to the king's son is again totally out of place, for Sigismund had no son; similarly in art. 17=1222:19 the term *iobagiones castri* is entirely anachronistic.

20. The two words given in the vernacular mean rather marshes or backwaters, at any rate in modern Hungarian. Actually, such a high seigneurial impost would have totally ruined the entire fishery; evidence suggests, however, that this measure was not implemented and rents for fishing were rendered according to customary practice; A. Degré *Magyar halászati jog a középkorban* [Hungarian fishing laws in the M. A.] (Bp.: Jogi szeminárium, 1939), pp. 106, 109.

21. Identical with the closing sentence of 6:1351.

22. Repeating the measures of 11–12: 1351 in a slightly different formulation.

23. The content is identical with 22:1351. In the early fifteenth century this article was understood to mean that the chapter or convent of authentication had to be in the same county as the estate in which *seisin* was established; Sigismund, however, frequently granted dispensation from this arrangement, see Zs. O. 2, nos. 1960, 5988, 7730; cf. Eckhart, Glaubw. Orte, p. 457.

24. This promise of the king responded to the repeated protest of the nobles against his "foreign" counsellors; Sigismund had agreed to dismiss these in the agreement with his electors in Hungary in 1387 (before 31 March); see *Monumenta Hungariae Historica, Acta Extera* (Bp.: MTA, 1876) 3: 620–22 (repr. in Bak, *Königtum*, pp. 132–33). While a certain element of proto-nationalism or rather xenophobia did play a role in these demands, the main issue was that the king's confidants were above all loyal to him and, not embedded in the network of clan, family, and party in Hungary. Hence, they threatened the access of the Hungarian aristocracy to power. However, as soon as they, too, were connected by marriage and custom to the "native" Hungarians, they became part of the local aristocracy. The editors of *DRH 1301–1457* (p. 167, n. XLVII, 1) pointed to the example of the Bohemian cleric John of Usk, who in fact lost his Transylvanian prebend, granted him by Sigsimund in 1392 *iuxta statuta regni Ungarie*, but received the rich Buda parish in 1398 (Zs. O. 1, nos. 5505, 5527).

25. On this staunch supporter of Sigismund, see the Index.

26. See the Index.

27. See the Index. Maternus was the tutor of young Sigismund in Brandenburg. In order to retain him as a trusted counsellor, the king procured him the bishopric of Transylvania.

28. That, is by New Year's Day; the term set for such an extensive measure was very short and obviously aimed more at demonstrating the diet's mood than actually achieving the explulsion of foreigners.

29. Apart from the conflicts with the pro-Neapolitan (Horváti) faction during 1386–94 (cf. note 10 to 1386), which cannot possibly be meant here, no armed rebellion against Sigismund before 1397 is known. The passage may refer to an obscure plot of unnamed "mighty prelates, barons and lords" some time in early 1388; according to a royal charter (Fejér, *Cod. dipl.* 10/1: 420 of 7 May 1388) the archchancellor, Archbishop John Kanizsai of Esztergom, succeeded in "reconciling the troubled hearts" by calling on the rebels "in

their own homes." Simultaneously with the present decree Sigismund issued charters for Stibor, the Kanizsai brothers and the Treutels in which the present article is expressly referred to and these barons are execepted from the measure, *constitutionibus . . . in Themeswar . . . editis . . . non obstantibus*. (*DRH 1301–1457*, p. 168 n. XLIX, 1 with ref. to Fejér, *op. cit.* 10/2: 438–55, 10/3:204–10). This makes Mályusz (p. 47 f.) assume that the Kanizsai-Stibor faction was behind the move and that it was to veil the confiscation of the estates of the former palatine, Leusták of Ilsva, who fell at Nicopolis. It is also possible that the opaque formulation came in handy for the king, who in these years tried to recover as much of royal property lost during the struggle for the throne as possible.

30. Sigismund made good use of this decision for the recovery of some of the losses in the royal domain. Several charters cite this article justifying the revocation of grants and mortgages (Zs. O. 1, no. 5037; 2, nos. 812, 4373). However, most of these charters were issued when the recovered estate was granted to some other landowner, hence, the over-all gain for the royal domain was limited. Also, Sigismund continued to grant royal property to his supporters in the subsequent decades as well, although usually only as mortgages, reserving the proprietary rights of the crown; cf. *DRH 1301–1457*, p. 169, n. XLIX, 2. On the decline and partial recovery of royal domain, in particular of castles, see Fügedi, *Castle*, pp. 125–28, where the results of P. Engel's and his own monographic studies are summarized.

31. On these delicts, see the Glossary.

32. On judicial oaths, see above, 1324.

33. On these, see the Glossary s.v. combat, judicial and inquest, common, respectively.

34. *Obligatio* usually meant something like a promissory note in medieval Hungarian legal usage; see Bartal, *Glossarium*, p. 148.

35. *Lacuna* of about 14 letters.

36. See the Glossary; occasionally the expression "judge ordinary of the case" is intended to underline that the decision be made by the court where the case was opened and not elsewhere.

37. Even though the text is not specific, for it has the general term *dicare* ("assess for taxes," see the Glossary s.v. "dicator"), the king's promise obviously referred to those extraordinary taxes, mostly called *subsidium*, which the Angevins began frequently to raise and Sigismund continued to do so. Article 70, below, proves that he did not intend to stop this practice and the taxation of estates, of both lay and ecclesiastical landowners continued; in general see also Bak, "Monarchie," p. 355.

38. On the negative implications of *novitas* see above, note 6 to 1386.

39. On the *alispán* (*vicecomes*), see the Glossary and J. Holub, "A főispán és alispán viszonyának jogi természete." [Legal Character of the Relationship Between *comes* and *vicecomes*. Contributions to the County Administration in the Middle Ages], in *Fejérpataky Emlékkönyv* [F. Festschrift] (Bp.: Franklin, 1917), pp. 186–211. The intention of the article is to empower the noble county to act against violent disturbers of the peace. While Mályusz ("Zentralisationsbestrebungen," p. 174) maintains that the counties were not strong enough to make use of this increased jurisdiction before the 1410s, there is evidence that as early as 1400 the palatine ordered the officers of Co.

Szatmár, referring to the present decree, to proceed against a violent offender (Zs. O. 2, no. 279). See also below 31 August 1405: 4.

40. This clause establishes the appellate jurisdiction of the court of the *personalis presentia regia* (for which, see n. 53 below, and the Glossary.)

41. See the Glossary s.v. "son's right." At the beginning, the privilege was granted even in cases where male heirs in the fourth, third or even second degree were alive, thus infringing on the rights of the collateral branches (cf. above note 12). This provoked wide dissension among the nobility which induced Louis I to declare void, some time before his death, all previous *prefectiones* if relatives up to the fourth degree could be found. He also promised to limit his future grants in this sense. Although Louis' decree on this matter has not survived, his widow, Queen Elizabeth, in a charter from 1385 refers to such a decision; the text of that charter was included in a letter of judgment by the count palatine dated 1399 which came down to us in a transcript of 1414; see *DRH 1301–1457*, p. 141. It was King Louis' promise that was renewed here by King Sigismund.

42. On these delicts, already specified as serious felonies in art. 50, above, see the Glossary.

43. That cases of *nota infidelitatis* (see the Glossary) were to be judged at the diet came to be a practice only some hundred years after this decree; what is meant here is to assure a fair and open trial, with the participation of lay barons and lords (for clergy were not allowed by canon law to hear criminal cases) in cases that seemed to be so frequent in court intrigues that a special term, *denigratio*, was coined for them, meaning in fact an accusation of high treason.

44. On *bullati*, see the Glossary and below, 6 April 1404; even earlier Sigismund had promised in the agreement at his election (see above, n. 24) to hinder the papal designation of clergy to Hungarian prebends and repeated this prohibition in a charter for the chapter of Pozsony in 1394; see Mályusz, Konzil, 65–67.

45. Cf. 1351:15.

46. Exempting merchants from paying duties at royal tolls and customs was, of course, a general and basic right of every ruler; however, the Angevin kings often granted exemptions from every toll in the kingdom or in a certain region, which was seen as infringment of seigneurial rights. That is what the king here promises to stop doing; nevertheless, we know of such grants by Sigismund in favor of the citizens of Bártfa in 1402 (Zs. O. 2, no. 1471), and of Szeged in 1405 (*Ibid.* 3972).

47. 1 May 1398.

48. Cf. Comp. c.1300: 17, *DRMH* 1: 76.

49. The article aims at strengthening the position of the nobles of Slavonia. From the 1380s onward the judicial records of the ban of Slavonia were sealed, with the clause *absentibus sigillis*, with the seal of the vice-ban, who was also ex-officio *ispán* of the counties of Zagreb and Körös. This practice implied the transfer of considerable jurisdiction to this official, in analogy to the *specialis presentia* at the royal court. Allegedly under Louis I the nobles of the region acquired the right to elect the keeper of the seal, the protonotary or notary of the ban's court; they had now this right included in a *decretum*. In the next year the nobles made the ban, Nicholas of Gara, confirm this

right (Fejér, *Cod. dipl.* 10/2:622–24; Zs. O. 1, no. 5220). A generation later, in 1438, the nobles even obtained the right to depose the protonotary; cf. Fejér, *loc. cit.*, 192–94.

50. The conjecture of Knauz, *inquirendis*, is legally impossible, for inquest was not held before the judges, but out of court; hence, the editors of *DRH 1301–1457* inserted the procedurally appropriate words into the *lacuna*.

51. See the Glossary, s. v. "Octavial court." The terms beginning on the eighth day after St. George's Day (on 1 May), and after Michaelmas (on 6 October), were called "major" octaves.

52. The nobles seem to have demanded, and the king agreed, to send magnates to the sessions because the increasingly professional administration of justice by learned jurists instead of the great men of the realm appeared unacceptable to the conservative nobility.

53. The quoted formula was used to cite parties before the king who would then judge the case with the barons of his retinue, while travelling through his several countries; this was called the court of the *personalis presentia regis*. According to L. B. Kumorowitz this section was not aimed at abolishing that court (which is referred to below in art. 53 and 56), but to reduce its jurisdiction to cases of high treason and appeals in cases of violent trespass. In fact, as Knauz (p. 233 n. 3) already noted, the court of "personal presence" did not cease to operate, and summons with *ubi tunc . . .* were issued even during the session of this very diet.

54. In the late fourteenth century the court of the *specialis presentia* went "out of court," with the archchancellor presiding and sealing its sentences with his judicial seal, *propter absentiam sigillorum*. In fact this court, too, was on its way to professionalisation: it was usually held not by the (clerical) archchancellor himself but by a legally trained *vicegerens* or *diffinitor*. The article (apparently once again bowing to the wishes of the noblity) aims at restoring the royal supervision through the use of the seal of majesty and the presence of magnates on the bench; see L. B. Kumorovicz, "A specialis presentia regis pecséthasználata Zsigmond korában" [The Sealing Practice of the *specialis presentia regis* Under Sigismund], in *Domanovszky Emlékkönyv* [D. Festschrift] (Bp.: Egyetemi Nyomda, 1937), pp. 422–23; Gy. Bónis, *A jogtudó értelmiség a Mohács előtti Magyarországon* [Professionals Learned in the Laws in Pre-Mohács Hungary] (Bp.: Akadémiai K., 1971), pp. 120–31; briefly also in his "Men Learned in the Law in Medieval Hungary," *East Central Europe–L'Europe de centre-est* 4:1 (1977): 186–87.

55. This fragmentary sentence suggests that the *specialis presentia* was attempting another modernization by citing parties within a short term, a fortnight, and not only for the quarter-annually held octaves. The nobility apparently objected to this move.

56. The collectors empowered by this act did in fact exact considerable contributions from ecclesiastical bodies in the subsequent years; however, Sigismund continued to tax the clergy throughout his reign, not only for the imminent war; see Deér, p. 78. Several mandates are known from the years 1398 and 1401 in which half the income of prebends was ordered to be submitted for defense (Zs. O. 1, nos. 5559, 5617; 2, no. 1005).

57. Knauz (p. 234, n. 5) assumed that there was another decree, now lost, but it is possible that the reference was to a charter to be issued, perhaps in the court of the personal presence.

58. See 1351:6 and 1222:20.

59. This principle was expressed in regard to the chamber's profit, as early as in 1351:6. It is to be noted that nobles in general were at this time not exempt from the tithe; this seems to have been granted to them some time in 1405, see *DRH 1301–1457*, p. 216.

60. Apart from a privileged minority in royal and Saxon cities, most Hungarian parish priests were subject to diocesan jurisdiction and taxation. Their annual tax, called *cathedraticum*, was to be paid to the archdeacon, but its amount was not fixed before the late fifteenth century. The general recommendation that "the rich [priest] should pay more and the poor less" could not cut short abuses, of course; see E. Mályusz, *Egyházi társadalom a középkori Magyarországon* [Ecclesiastical Society in Medieval Hungary] (Bp.: Akadémiai K., 1971), p. 124. Actually, this article was not initiated by the lower clergy which in Hungary did not play any role in politics, but by the lords and nobles who as patrons of churches were interested in the finances of their parishes.

61. The provision apparently brought no results. As late as 1450 the synod of Esztergom had to face the common abuse that archdeacons made their annual visitations to the parishes with a huge escort of twenty or more persons. It declared that the number should be limited to eight. We are also told that, besides chaplains, the escort used to consist of stable-grooms, huntsmen and other man-servants as well, see I. Batthyány, *Leges ecclesiasticae regni Hungariae et provinciarum adiacentium*, vol. 3 (Alba-Carolinae: Typ. episcopalibus, 1825), p. 481.

62. This important liberty of the tenant peasants (see the Glossary), in principle contained in Comp. c. 1300:13 (*DRMH* 1: 76) was spelled out in a decision of the royal council of 3 August 1397 (*DRH 1301–1457*, pp. 154–56). The full text from 3 August 1397 came to be a point of reference for a long time (virtually into the sixteenth century) and was included in later *decreta* as well (see below, 31 August 1405:14–16). Clearly, many a landowner tried to retain his tenants, especially when land-labor ratios were favorable for the peasants.

63. The reference to Louis I's regulation of fees cannot be to 1351:7, where fees for charters of donations are specified, but rather to some unknown order of the king or merely to the general practice of the fourteenth century.

64. It is remarkable that the diet did not object to the tax of 121d, merely ordered the assessors to render accounts by 13 January 1398. The origin of this tax is not clear. On 12 April 1394 the royal council levied a tax of 1/2 florin on every *porta* (Zs. O. 1, no. 3366); and on 25 January 1399 the king ordered another accounting of the "half florins and 21 pennies" (*ibid.* no. 5683); see also Deér, p. 77.

Notes to 6 April 1404
pages 29–30.

Incipit: *Quomodo nunnulli*

Following the unsuccessful bid of Ladislas of Naples for the Hungarian throne, in which he was supported by Pope Boniface IX against Sigismund, the king and his lords confiscated ecclesiastical income in Bohemia and Hungary. This decree (or rather decision of the royal council, for it does not seem to have been passed by a diet) aims at codifying these advances and, based on art. 57 of 1397, curtails significantly papal rights over Hungarian churches. It was intended to be a lasting arrangement, as the words about its validity "until expressly revoked," a notion borrowed from Roman legal jurisprudence, testify. Although motivated by political conflict, it should also be viewed in a broader European context. In the fourteenth and fifteenth centuries European monarchies attempted increasingly to place restrictions upon appeals to Rome, upon collection of papal revenues, and upon the collation of benefices. This decree, customarily cited as the *placetum regium*, should, thus, be seen as part of this larger movement which includes several English statutes of Provisors and Praemunire from the later fourteenth century, the French Pragmatic Sanction of Bourges of 1438, the German *Acceptatio* of Mainz of 1439, and others.

MS.: Original on paper with privy seal *en placard*, Archives of the Primate of Esztergom, Arch. Saec., Acta rad. fasc. 29, n. 44.

EDD.: I. Batthyány, *Leges ecclesiasticae regni Hungariae et provinciarum adiacentium* (Alba Carolinae-Claudiopoli: Typis episcopalibus, 1785–1827), 1: 471–74; Kovachich, *Vestigia*, pp. 199–203; Katona, *Hist. crit.* 11: 614–18; Fejér, *Cod. dipl.* 10/4: 303–06; Marczali, *Enchiridion*, pp. 235–37; *DRH 1301–1457*, pp. 180–82 (cf. also Zs. O. 2, no. 3094)

LIT.: V. Fraknói, *A magyar királyi kegyúri jog Szent Istvántól Mária Teréziáig* [The Royal Right of Patronage from St. Stephen to Maria Theresa] (Bp.: MTA, 1895); E. Mályusz, *Das Konstanzer Konzil und das königliche Patronatsrecht in Ungarn* (Bp.: Akadémiai K., 1959); Bard, "Aristocratic Revolts," pp. 94–113; for the European background, cf. F. Oakley, *The Western Church in the Later Middle Ages* (Ithaca-London: Cornell Univ. Press, 1979), pp. 53, 73–75.

1. For the term *bullatus*, see the Glossary. In the present context, however, it is clear that the reference is to collectors of papal revenues empowered to punish the recalcitrant with ecclesiastical sanctions including summons abroad (i.e., to Rome). Papal collectors were normally commissioned in Rome by the Camerarius (papal chamberlain) and once resident in a specific region they in turn would commission local clerics to serve as deputy collectors; see W. E. Lunt, *Papal Revenues in the Middle Ages*, 2 vols. (New York: Columbia Univ. Press, 1934, repr. Hamden, Conn.: Octagon Books, 1965) 1: 42–51, and the specimen letter of commission of a collector of annates from Pope Clement VI to Archbishop Cenadinus of Esztergom from 13 September 1343, *ibid.*, 2: 358–61. An excellent recent study of the work of the papal Camera and the collection of one particular form of income, papal spoil, is D. Williman, *The Right of Spoil of the Popes of Avignon, 1316–1415* (Philadelphia: Amer. Philos. Soc., 1988), esp. pp. 19–22, where the solitary Hungarian (as opposed to Dalmatian) reference is to the commission to the collector of Poland and Hungary following the death of Bishop John of Veszprém dated 1357.

2. On 1 June 1403, Pope Boniface IX recognized Ladislas, king of Naples (1386–1414), son of the hapless Charles of Durazzo, as king of Naples and Hungary, who claimed the crown of Hungary by hereditary right (cf. notes 1 and 10 to 1386).

3. The term *bullati* here appears to convey the more general meaning, see the Glossary.

4. The reference is obviously to 1397:57 (cf. also 1397:64).

5. On the right of patronage, see Fraknói, passim; Mályusz, pp. 65 ff..

6. The term *prophanis* is apparently used here in opposition to *criminalibus* as synonym for 'secular' to refer to those cases brought before ecclesiastical courts in which a layman was one of the litigants and where criminal behavior was not at issue. For a recent discussion of the theoretical underpinning of canonical criminal jurisprudence, see R. M. Freher, "Preventing Crime in the High Middle Ages: The Medieval Lawyers' Search for Deterrence," in J. R. Sweeney and S. Chodorow, eds., *Popes, Teachers, and Canon Law in the Middle Ages* (Festschrift for Brian Tierney) (Ithaca, NY: Cornell Univ. Press, 1989), pp. 212–33, esp. 219–21.

7. Mályusz (pp. 14–18) lists a whole series of cases which prove the implementation of this decree; most characteristic is a mandate of the voivode of Transylvania of 1405, in which he seized the tithe of a parish priest, because he called upon the Roman curia in a legal matter "in contempt of the decree of the royal majesty" (Zs. O. 2, no. 4132).

Notes to 21 December 1404
pages 31–34.
Incipit: *Quod quemadmodum*

This royal ordinance, just as its procedural predecessor and legal cause, Sigismund's letter of pardon for the rebels of 8 October 1403 (see *DRH 1301–1457*, pp. 175–79), could be classed as a regulation of particular and not general purport; hence, it might not qualify as a *decretum* proper. Also, it was issued as letters patent without the list of office-holders usual for charters of privilege. However, the text itself refers to "articles," which is usually a name for laws; the king called it in contemporary charters a *statutum*; and tradition also included it among the *decreta*. It is a regulation of elaborate procedures of *seisin* and of verification of claims to royal grants, following the widespread confiscations after the last major rebellion against Sigismund in 1402–03.

All earlier editions printed the text from a transcript, issued in all likelihood in February 1405 but erroneously dated to February 1404 which came to be the date of the "First Decree of Sigismund" in the *CJH* and other editions. The king's itinerary tallies well with the date of the original printed here (which is textually identical with the earlier editions, save for a few minor scriptorial errors) and so does the fact that Sigismund referred to this *statutum* a day before its issue on 20 December 1404. (Zs. O. 2, no. 3553).

The format is also quite confusing and caused earlier editors to introduce entirely misleading paragraph numberings. The preface and *narratio* end with a series of statements verbally numbered as "first," "second," and "third" but then the statutory parts and the final "articles" are again divided (as usual, without formal numbering) into articles. Whereas the introduction to this series of statements suggests that these are the complaints (*querelae*), this decree is in fact a summary of both the complaints and the specific remedies provided. The present numbering was introduced by the editors of *DRH 1301–1457*.

MS.: Original on parchment with the privy seal en placard, OL Dl. 8997.

EDD.: Pray, *Annales*, 2: 212–14; Katona, *Hist. crit.*, 11: 597–605; Fejér, *Cod. dipl.* 10/4: 276–83; *MTvt/CJH* 1: 203–09 (all dated Buda, 19 February 1404); *DRH 1301–1457*, pp. 183–88.

LIT.: Mályusz, *Sigismund*, pp. 66–69.

1. Sigismund of Luxemburg was elected king in 1387 by a league of barons and had to accept their control. Soon he began to build up his own party and follow his own policies which provoked growing discontent among the magnates (see above, notes to 1397). In 1401 he was temporarily arrested by the royal council. In early 1403, while Sigismund was fighting in Bohemia, an open revolt of the barons followed, led by Chancellor John of Kanizsa and Count Palatine Detric Bebek of Pelsőc in support of King Ladislas of Naples (see above, note 2 to 6 April 1404 and Bard, "Revolts," pp. 41–61). Sigismund spent most of the year 1402 (February-September, November-December) in Bohemia, where he had been named vicar by his brother Venceslas (4 February 1402). However, two months later Sigismund captured Venceslas and entrusted him to the Habsburg dukes of Austria with whom he made an alliance. In 1403 the king spent the first half of the year in Moravia, fighting against Margrave Jodok (Jobst) for his hereditary claims and in the last resort for his succession in the Holy Roman Empire.

2. On the attempts of King Ladislas to gain the throne of Hungary, see above, note 2 to 6 April 1404.

3. The reference is to John of Kanizsa, Nicholas of Csák and Nicholas of Marcali; on them, see the Index.

4. Such summonses to the court of the king's personal presence were supposed to be discontinued, see 1397:62.

5. Several summonses, referring to this *statutum* are known from 1405; cf. Zs. O. 2, nos. 3664, 3669, 3737, 3985.

6. On the form and meaning of *seisin*, see the Glossary.

7. In a letter of judgment, in 1419, Count Palatine Nicholas of Gara made reference to a royal *decretum* which seems to have completed this one on some points. It ordered that all persons claiming an estate from a rebel should lose their claims forever unless they could bring their action to a definitive sentence before the *nota infidelitatis* (see the Glossary) of their opponent was proclaimed (OL Dl. 100414, cf. *DRH 1301–1457*, p. 188, n. 1).

Notes to 15 April 1405
pages 35–45.

Incipit: *Sceptigera regalis dignitas*

This decree indicates King Sigismund's interest in the development of towns in Hungary, which may have had several reasons. His familiarity with the much more developed Bohemian and German urban scene was certainly one of them. His support given to the fortification of cities can also be explained by the fact that the number of royal castles had diminished drastically in the early years of his reign while royal control of the cities had been an important factor in the king's victory over the baronial revolt in 1403. Above all, however, Sigismund needed monetary income and was aware that florishing towns were the quickest source of revenues.

The assembly in which this decree was passed met in early April; a privilege issued by Sigismund for the town of Debrecen on 2 April 1405 (Zs. O. 2, no. 3767) already contains a number of articles from it. It was not a diet proper, because neither the aristocracy nor the counties were represented (see Mályusz, "Geschichte," p. 393), although the text of the decree was sent to some counties (the copy for Co. Pest. did survive), suggesting that the king wished to inform the nobility and win their support for his urban policies.

MSS.: Eleven originals survived, two deperdita were known before 1945: a copy for Debrecen, County archives, Dipl. no. 6; a copy for Eperjes, Archives of Pannonhalma no. 715; a copy for Hibe, Archives of Liptovsky Mikuláš (Slovakia), Chyba no. 5; a copy for Kassa, City Archives Košice (Slovakia), Coll. Schwartzenbach. no. 45; a copy for Korpona, OL Dl. 42840; a copy for Németlipcse, Archives of Liptovsky Mikuláš (Slovakia), Partizánska Lupča, no. 51; a copy for Rózsahegy, *Ibid.* Ružomberok, no. 9; a copy for Sárvár, OL Dl. 9031; a copy for Sopron, City Archives, Sopron, L, IV, 103; a copy for Szeged, OL Dl. 90552; a copy for Zsolna, City Archives Zilina (Slovakia), Dipl. no. 11. All had pendant seals, but all of those are lost now. (For details, see *DRH 1301–1457*, p. 190.)

EDD.: Pray, *Annales* 2:215–22; Katona, *Hist crit.* 11: 636–51; *MTvt/CJH* 1:211–29 ("II Decree of Sigismund"); *DRH 1301–1457*, pp. 189–213. (See also Zs. O. 2, no. 3791.)

LIT.: E. Mályusz, "Geschichte des Bürgertums in Ungarn," *Vierteljahrschrift für Sozial- und Wirtschaftsgeschichte* 20 (1928): 393; A. Kubinyi, "Der ungarische König und seine Städte im 14. und am Beginn des 15. Jahrhunderts," in W. Rausch, ed., *Stadt und Stadtherr im 14. Jahrhundert* (Linz: Wimmer, 1972), pp. 193–220; F. B. Fahlbusch, *Städte und Königtum im frühen 15. Jahrhundert. Ein Beitrag zur Geschichte Sigmunds von Luxemburg* (Köln-Wien: Böhlau, 1983), pp. 39–48.

1. Calling together burghers to a special meeting was not only an unprecedented, but in fact a unique event in the history of medieval Hungary. Actually, not all the important cities were represented, which is suggested by the fact that Kolozsvár received its copy of the statutes only seven months later (Fahlbusch, p. 34, n. 106). The difference between cities, towns and free villages is not easy to define because the terms were not always used in a consistent way (see E. Ladányi, "Libera villa, civitas, oppidum. Terminologische Fragen in der ungarischen Städteentwicklung," *AUSBp, Sect. hist.*, 18 [1977], pp. 3–43). It may be said on the whole, however, that fortified towns were called *civitates*, and this was the usual name also for some unfortified places like mining towns or episcopal cities. Apart from these, unfortified royal towns or privileged royal markets were generally termed *liberae villae* up to the late fourteenth and early fifteenth century when these words were gradually replaced by the term *oppidum*. This became common later for all categories of such privileged places, royal or not, which were not considered to be "free cities" (*civitates*). Characteristically enough, the Hungarian equivalent of *oppidum* was *mezőváros*, literally "a field town," implying any unwalled settlement with a privileged community (see E. Fügedi, "Die Ausbreitung der städtischen Lebensform: Ungarns *oppida* im 14. Jahrhundert," in *Kings*, ch. 13, pp. 165–92).

2. Increasing the number of fortified royal cities seems to have been a point of particular importance to Sigismund. By temporary exemption from taxes and other means he supported the completion of unfinished fortifications in royal cities. At the time of the 1405 assembly he granted extended liberties to a number of royal markets with the remarkable stipulation that they could enjoy them only after their walls were built up. On Sigismund's policies towards the cities, see Kubinyi, *passim* and the studies cited above.

3. The "chronicles of the Hungarians" obviously refers to the fourteenth-century compilation of different chronicles and gesta of the Árpádian period ("Chronici Hungarici compositio saeculi XIV," ed A. Domanovszky) preserved in the well-known Illuminated Chronicle of 1358 as well as in other redactions, ed. in Szentpétery, *Scriptores* 1, pp. 217–505. See J. Gerics, "Krónikáink szerepe a középkori jogéletben" [The Role of our Chronicles in Medieval Legal Life], *Levéltári Közlemények* 33 (1962): 11 ff. and E. Mályusz, "La chancellerie royale et la rédaction des chroniques dans la Hongrie médiévale," *Le Moyen Age* 75 (1969): 51–86, 219–54, esp. p. 241. The invasions of the Pechenegs took place in the twelfth century, those of the

"Tartars," i.e., of the Mongols in 1241/42 and 1285, while Ottoman raids had been a more or less usual phenomenon since 1390 or 1391. Despite the reasoning of the edict it is unlikely, however, that Sigismund's policies on this point were motivated by these invasions, for none of the cities to be fortified lay in the exposed region.

4. This ambitious attempt at the standardization of all measures, however favorable it might have been, had no practical consequences; see A. Kubinyi, "Budapest története a későbbi középkorban Buda elestéig" [The History of Budapest in the Late Middle Ages Until the Fall of Buda], in L. Gerevich, ed., *Budapest története* [History of Bp.], vol. 2 (Bp.: Fővárosi Tanács, 1973), p. 51, with a short summary of the Buda measures. Local measure systems, above all those of other important cities, such as Pozsony or Kassa, continued to prevail and were not definitely abolished before the nineteenth century.

5. For this wine-tax, see above, n. 15 to 1351. The Hungarian word "hegyvám" is a literal translation of *tributum montis*; the literal meaning of the German "Bergrecht" is "right of the mountain."

6. Restriction on foreign merchants (or merchants in general as opposed to cloth-cutters) selling cloth "en detail" was widespread in medieval Europe; see, e.g., "Charter of the Garment cutters of Stendal," *Source Book for Medieval Economic History*, R. C. Cave, and H. H. Coulson, eds. (Milwaukee: Bruce, 1936), pp. 246–47.

7. Few public notaries are known to have been working in Hungary, for their functions were fulfilled by other authorities, above all by the *loca credibilia* (see the Glossary). Their competence in ecclesiastical matters was not questioned, but their activity among laymen was restricted to cases reserved for canonical jurisdiction, such as wills and marriage contracts, a practice which this law intended to codify.

8. Royal cities had an unquestioned jurisdictional power over their territory, and their council functioned for the citizens as a place of authentication (*locus credibilis*); see M. C. Rady, *Medieval Buda: A Study of Municipal Government and Jurisdiction in the Kingdom of Hungary* (Boulder, Co.: East European Monographs, 1985), pp. 54–68. As a consequence, documents issued by other local authorities were not accepted as valid, and inquests against citizens were to be held by emissaries of the council and not, as usual, by a chapter or county magistrates. In 1435 the citizens of Zagreb refused to accept three letters of inquest not issued by urban authorities, explicitly referring to this article; whether they were successful or not is not known, for the ban sent the case to the royal court; see I. K. Tkalčić, *Monumenta historica liberae regiae civitatis Zagrabiae* (Zagreb: Albrecht, 1870) 2: 112–13.

9. The "list" of townsmen *cives, hospites, populi* suggests the differentiation of burghers in Hungarian cities. While *hospites* is frequently used for any townsman, the three categories may have indicated burgesses, other burghers and non-privileged urban dwellers: see Gy. Granasztói, *A középkori magyar város* [The Medieval Hungarian City], (Bp.: Gondolat, 1980), p. 107 f.

10. The Master of the Treasury is first mentioned as judge of the cities in the urban privilege for Szatmárnémeti in 1264. Until the end of the

fourteenth century he acted as royal judge delegate with noble jurors. Urban asesssors, first mentioned in 1383, were to gradually replace noble members of the court who are mentioned last in 1439. From the extensive literature (going back to G. M. Kovachich) see, Kubinyi, in Rausch, pp. 198–201, 204–06; I. Bertényi, "Die städtischen Bürger und das Gericht der königlichen Anwesenheit im 14. Jahrhundert," *AUSBp, Sect. hist.* 11 (1970): 10–14.

11. "Extradition" probably refers to those criminals who were captured by landholders not invested with high justice. They had to be extradited to a person or body authorized to pass and execute the capital sentence.

12. On the the privilege of high justice (*ius gladii*), see above, n. 6 to 1328.

13. This article expands on the brief regulation contained in 1397:68, based on the council decree of 3 August 1397 (see note 62 to 1397). On the condition of tenant peasants under Sigismund, see Mályusz, *Sigismund*, pp. 233–35.

14. The phrase is an isolated evidence for the special status of Slavonian tenants. It can be surmised from other sources that by about 1430 they already acquired the right to move freely (see Mályusz, as above).

15. This kind of action against a member of a community another member of which was indebted to a person was quite common; it was prohibted in 1290:10 (see *DRMH* 1:46, with n. 30 on p. 114).

16. On seigneurial jurisdiction, see above, n. 5 to 1328. Cf. also 1351: 18.

17. Here and in several subsequent articles the word *regnicola* (for which, see the Glossary) is used in reference to merchants; clearly, the more general meaning of "resident of the kingdom" is implied.

18. According to this article the court of the Master of the Treasury was to be the appellate court for all towns, whence appeals were allowed to a second instance, the court of the *personalis praesentia*. In fact the *ius tavernicale* was the law of the seven (later eight) "free royal cities" while other towns appealed to the royal presence; see M. G. Kovachich, *Codex authenticus iuris tavernicalis* (Buda: Universitas Scient., 1803), pp. 23ff; Rady, *Buda*, pp. 127–60.

19. The "ninth and tenth" (*nona et decima*) (worth 10 percent each, just as with tenants' dues) was the portion due to the judge from any monetary payment in any case brought before him. It is mentioned already in eleventh century laws, see, e.g., Ladislas III: 22 (*DRMH* 1: 22), see Hajnik, *Bír. szerv.* pp. 442–50, esp. p. 449.

20. The article sanctioned a royal decree issued in 1402. In the fourteenth century, staple right had been the privilege of four cities only: Buda and Győr since the thirteenth century, Lőcse was granted it by Charles I in 1321 and Kassa by Louis I in 1347; see S. Domanovszky, *A szepesi városok árúmegállító joga* [The Right of Staple of the Cities of Szepes] (Bp.: MTA, 1922). Owing to the central position of Buda, its staple right was of primary importance. Sigismund granted this right to five other cities in January 1402 as a reward for their "faithfulness in the time of our necessity," i.e., during his captivity in 1401, but he withdrew this grant in October of the same year. At the same time he restricted, however, the force of existing staple rights to foreign merchants and exempted all Hungarian citizens from it (see Mályusz, *Sigismund*, p. 37).

21. Sigismund confirmed or repeated the exemption from tolls for several cities in the subsequent years explicitly referring to this article (see *DRH 1301–1457*, p. 200, n. 1)

22. See above note 10; here, however, the typical medieval custom of first appeal to the "mother-town," i.e., the city of whose laws were granted to the new foundation (or newly privileged city) is emphasized. Hungarian cities were frequently granted the laws of Székesfehérvár (in the earlier period), of Buda or Korpona (later); see E. Fügedi, "Középkori magyar városprivilégiumok" [Medieval Hungarian Urban Privileges], *Tanulmányok Budapest múltjából* 14 (1961): 17–108, repr. in his *Koldulό barátok, polgárok, nemesek* [Mendicant Friars, Burghers, Nobles] (Bp.: Magvető, 1981), pp. 238–334; cf. Rady, *Buda*, pp. 141–59.

23. *Munera* ("gifts") were regular payments in kind, due to the landowners usually on three major feasts of the year. The New Year's gift *(donum* or *munus)* rendered by the royal cities to the king may have been, too, of seigneurial origin. It is attested in the fourteenth and fifteenth centuries and was paid most often in clothes (see Fügedi, *Koldulό*, p. 263).

24. These arrangements seem to be late sucessors of the early medieval *descensus*, originally a *droit de gîte*, which otherwise came to be a monetary tax before it vanished; see *DRMH* 1: 144.

25. The passage is technically unclear in its present form. The "presence," i.e., the court of any judge was called "special" if he administered justice not through his deputy, as usual, but in his own person. The king did it occasionally at any place within his realm where "by God's guidance" he happened to stay (on the opposition to this form of jurisdiction and summons, see above 1397:62). His "special presence" can be meant here only in this sense, because in the fourteenth-fifteenth century this form of royal jurisdiction was technically called "personal presence." The term "royal special presence" was at that time reserved for a high court which had been set up in the capital in about 1376 and functioned permanently under the presidence of the archchancellor until 1428 (see n. 54 to 1379 and the Glossary). Actually, one copy of this decree, the one for Körmöcbánya, has the correct *personalem in presentiam*, see Kovachich, *Lectiones*, p. 62. As to the gist of the matter, the expansion of royal jurisdiction vis-à-vis courts spiritual was an important concern of Sigismund and does not, properly speaking, belong to the purview of this *decretum*.

26. On the prohibition of precious metal exports, see CC 1342: 12.

27. This arrangement, of course, presupposes the existence and use of private seals among burghers, for which there is evidence from several towns of Hungary; see, e.g., E. Tompos, "Soproniak középkori pecsétei" [Medieval Seals of Sopron Burghers], *Soproni Szemle* 28 (1973): 289–306.

28. *Mázsa* was a cart of large capacity, used in long-distance trade from the thirteenth to the early sixteenth century; see S. Domanovszky, *Gazdaság és társadalom a középkorban*, [Economy and society in the Middle Ages] (Bp.: Gondolat, 1979), pp. 101–35. The Hungarian word itself now means "hundredweight."

29. The gold mark is used here as a money of account. Sixty-four florins were an enormous sum, amounting to about two year's pay of a mercenary soldier. By the "money" (*moneta*) the current pennies are meant whose value

fluctuated, see n. 13 to 1397. (In 1405, 132 or 133 "new" and 396 to 400 "small" pennies equalled one florin.)

30. Partnerships between merchants in Hungary and abroad were usually initiated in form of credits for merchandize or were arranged so that a member of a foreign trading family took out burgesses' right in a Hungarian city; see E. Lederer, *Középkori pénzüzletek Magyarországon* [Medieval Financial Transactions in Hungary] (Bp.: Kovács, 1936), pp. 89–109, who also noted that Sigismund's prohibition had little effect on such joint ventures.

31. On the thirtieth, see the Glossary and S. Domanovszky, "A harminczadvám eredete" [Origins of the Thirtieth], repr. now in his *Gazdaság*, pp. 49–99. Sigismund's "recent" decree to which reference is made in the text, has not survived.

32. *Tributum* or *teloneum* was a comprehensive term for any toll (see the Glossary) except the thirtieth. By royal grants, most tolls belonged to churches and lay lords, but a minority remained in the king's hands.

33. On Sigismund's monetary policies, see n. 13 to 1397, 31 August 1405:7, and below, 1427B; on measures against counterfeiters CC 1342: 7, 14, and 31.

34. On the royal money-changer, see CC 1342: 34.

35. Since the earliest times, both the mining and selling of salt had been royal prerogatives. Old salt mines were to be found in Transylvania (Dés, Szék, Kolozs, Torda, Vizakna) and new ones were opened up in Máramaros in the fourteenth and early fifteenth centuries. All of them were administered by the count of the royal salt chamber (*comes camerarum salium regalium*) who was also in charge of the salt trade. Cut into cubes, the salt was transported by his officers to special store houses (also called *camerae*) throughout the kingdom. Most of the salt was to be sold at fixed price but it often occurred that debts to the king's account were acquitted by paying in salt cubes. Income from the salt monopoly was estimated to amount to 100,000 florins per year in Sigismund's age and thus it became by that time the most substantial item in the king's annual revenues. See A. Kubinyi, "Königliches Salzmonopol und die Städte des Königreichs Ungarn im Mittelalter," in W. Rausch, ed., *Stadt und Salz* (Linz: Wimmer, 1988), pp. 227; Bak "Monarchie," pp. 359–60, 381.

36. On the monopoly of gold and silver trade, see n. 26 to CC 1342:11.

37. The phrase that follows explains this term; an *acus* is a touchstone: basanite, a type of jasper or black siliceous mineral, see R. J. Forbes, *Studies in Ancient Technology* 8, 2nd ed. (Leiden: Brill, 1971), pp. 175–76. What is unusual is the use of *acus*, a word normally designating needles, combs and other sharp instruments. The common Latin term (early and late) for a touchstone is *coticula* (see esp. Pliny *HN* 33.43.126). But *acus* as a synonym for *coticula* also appears in a Latin dictionary dedicated to Charlemagne (Paul the Deacon,, *Epitome of Festus de signficatu verborum*, p. 23, ed. Lindsay) and this usage may go back to the late first century B.C.

38. For the persons mentioned in the eschatocol see the Index.

Notes to 31 August 1405
pages 46–51.
Incipit: *Inter ceteras animi*

This formal *decretum*, written in full privilegial form, seems to have been issued in a regular diet, a few months after the "urban decree," which was passed in a special meeting with urban delegates. Its date, which is crucial in defining its aim and place in Sigismund's legislation, was long debated. Several sixteenth-century codices (see *DRH 1301–1457*, p. 218, n. 1) have different dates, from 12 March to 5 August 1405, while the chartulary of the convent of the Order of St. John (University Library, Budapest, Coll. Hevenessiana Ab 71, II: 183–87) has 31 August 1404. However the exemplar closest to the date of issue, the authentic transcript by the collegiate chapter of Székesfehérvár (see below, MS) of 23 April 1406 gives the most reliable date, and this was accepted by the editors of *DRH 1301–1457*, and us.

In the light of this, the decree is clearly an attempt at formalizing some of the more general measures of 15 April 1405, adding a number of regulations relevant to the nobility and altogether attempting to produce a law of lasting purport (see below, n. 1).

MS.: Parchment with a pinkish-green silk thread passed through four holes for the affixing of the now lost seal; from the archives of the Knights of St. John, OL Dl. 106238.

EDD.: Katona, *Hist. crit.* 11:625–27; Fejér, *Cod. dipl.* 10/4: 308–10, 564–65; Kovachich, *Vestigia*, p. 209; *MTvt/CJH* 1:230–41 ("III Decree of Sigismund"); *DRH 1301–1457*, pp. 218–25. (Cf. Zs. O. 2, no. 3902.)

LIT.: E. Ladányi, "Zsigmond 1405. évi törvényeinek keletkezési körülményeihez" [On the origins of Sigismond's laws of 1405 A. D.] in *Málуusz Elemér Emlékkönyv* [Festschrift E. M.], É. H. Balázs, E. Fügedi, F. Maksay, eds. (Bp.: Akadémiai K., 1984), pp. 269–76.

1. The attempt at replacing "diverse customs" by a *decretum* on major matters suggests a conscious interest in issuing systematic and long-term legislation for the realm. On this tendency in early fifteenth-century Europe, including Hungary, see A. Wolf, "Die Gesetzgebung der entstehenden Territorialstaaten," in H. Coing, ed., *Handbuch der Quellen und Literatur der*

neueren europäischen Privatrechtsgeschichte (München: Beck, 1973), 1: 554–55. A similar attempt at overriding an old custom and establishing uniform usages was made in the "urban decree" concerning measures and weights, see above, 15 April 1405: 1.

2. Members of the royal council and the household, travelling on royal affairs, seem to have required quarter and food without payment by force based on the ancient right of *descensus* (apparently sometimes exacted by violence, see 1279:[9], *DRMH* 1: 72 and 118, n. 32). The article was meant to stop this abuse. On a more practical level, it was probably directed against the usual acts of violence committed by people joining the royal army, and thus anticipated the overall measures taken in the decree of 17 March 1427 (1427A). It may be worthwhile to note that the somewhat awkward phrase *abs iuris tramite. . .* is an obvious borrowing from such late Antique or early Christian authors as Tertullian or Ammianus Marcellinus.

3. The formula is borrowed from the "summary procedure" of canon law. The language of this passage is borrowed from a decretal letter of Clement V of c. 1306/7, *Saepe contingit quod*, incorporated in that pope's supplement to the canonical collections, the *Clementines* V. 11. 2 (E. Friedberg, *Corpus Iuris Canonici* 2 [Graz: Akademische Verlagsanstalt, 1959], col. 1200), which reads: *de plano ac sine strepitu et figura iudicii.* For the background of the decretal *Saepe*, see St. Kuttner, "The Date of the Constitution "Saepe", the Vatican Manuscripts, and the Roman Edition of the Clemetines," now in his *Medieval Councils, Decretals and Collections of Canon Law* (London: Variorum Reprints, 1980), ch. 13, pp. 427-52. At the moment we lack any full-scale discussion of the impact of *Saepe* on the development of summary procedure in either the canonical or secular traditions. This will soon be remedied by K. Pennington in his *The Prince and the Law, 1200—1600: Sovereignty and Rights in the medieval Legal Tradition* (Univ. of California Press, forthcoming), ch. 5. The Editors express their gratitude to Professor Pennington for his guidance and helpful advice.

4. Instead of initiating a lawsuit, it seems to have been an old custom to take a "security" (*vadium*) arbitrarily, in goods or chattels, for a minor offense, real or presumed. It was obviously thought to be an advance or a substitute for expected fine (cf. above, n. 15 to 1320).

5. The word *regnicolae* is used variously in the preamble and articles of this decree. Sometimes it implies a wider or different stratum than "gentlemen of the realm" (see the Glossary). We have, therefore, translated the term in this decree, depending on the specific context as "gentlemen subjects" or "gentlemen of the realm."

6. On the privilege of high justice, see above, n. 6 to 1328.

7. This article was seen as a general confirmation of older measures against violent trespass (e.g., Comp. c. 1300:1; 1397: 53), and frequently cited by the king and other judicial organs in the subsequent years, see *DRH 1301–1457*, p. 220, n. 1. Until the enactment of detailed regulations in 8 March 1435: 3, 4, and 6 (see below) the courts acted on the basis of this article against "new violent trespassers."

8. By "public place" (*locus communis*) probably a place is meant where fairs used to be held.

9. Cf. 15 April 1405: 1. We have translated *cubulus*, a Hungarian measure for grains and wine (see below, n. 13 to 1427A, where a definite

amount of grain is meant), mentioned here with the other general terms for measures, for simplicity's sake as "bushel," without wanting to imply that it was identical with the measure of that name used in pre-modern England (where it, actually, did not have a uniform size either).

10. This article successfully suppressed the anarchy of local systems of account prevalent in the fourteenth century, see P. Engel, "A 14. századi magyar pénztörténet néhány kérdése" [Some questions of fourteenth-century Hungarian monetary history], *Száz.* 123 (1989) [forthc.]. After 1405 payments were to be—and came to be, indeed—defined either in effective florins or in "florins percent" (a money of account comprising one-hundred current pennies).

11. See 15 April 1405: 11.

12. According to ancient custom, a ban was proclaimed by the community against all the "thiefs and malefactors" (*fures et latrones*), i.e., all public criminals of a province convicted of a felony, such as robbery, arson, rape or counterfeiting money. In the fourteenth century, the procedure took the form of general assemblies held by the count palatine (or by a royal commissioner) for a county where a list of the proscribed criminals was drawn up und solemnly proclaimed. The *proscriptus*, that is, the person outlawed in this way, could not receive pardon but was to be captured by anyone and handed over to the authorities for execution. Those protecting the proscribed, called *hospites furum*, fell under the same punishment.

13. Cf. 1351: 18 (repeated in 1397: 40).

14. See above n. 3.

15. The article summarizes and specifies the articles 15 April 1405: 4, 8, and 9.

16. Cf. 1351: 13. On the mining dues (*urbura*), see n. 31 to 1351.

17. Cf. CC 1342: 15 and 15 April 1405: 15.

18. art. 14 is the verbatim repetition of 15 April 1405: 6 without the clause concerning the tenants beyond the Drava River. The two following articles repeat a charter of Sigismunds of 3 August 1397 (see *DRH 1301–1457*, p. 155 and above, n. 62 to 1397) concerning the free movement of the peasant tenants. These passages were frequently referred to in royal charters of the subsequent years (see the references in *DRH 1301–1457*, p. 224, n. XIV/1). An almost identical text was also issued as a royal mandate to the collegiate chapter of Pozsony, 20 January 1407, and as an order in council of 26 July 1409 (see *ibid.*, pp. 226–29.)

19. This measure, like many others in Sigismund's reign, was intended to enhance the competence of the county magistrates as possible supporters of the royal power, see Mályusz, *Sigismund*, pp. 183–86.

20. For the names included in the eschatocol, see the Index.

Notes to 1411 (before 18 March) pages 52–53.

Incipit: *Cum nos pridem*

This decree did not survive in the original form, only in several essentially identical mandates the earliest of which is dated 18 March 1411. This fact warrants a dating of this decree as "before 18 March." Several sixteenth-century collections contain it as a decree and the text itself refers to it as a *decretum generale*. Considering that the mode of collecting the chamber's profit and the tithe was relevant for the entire country, we accepted the decision of the editors of *DRH 1301–1457* to include it in the series of laws.

MSS.: [contemporary copy] Letters patent inserted in a transcript of 30 May 1412 issued by the Premonstratensian convent of Jászó, sealed *en placard*, in Státni archív Levoča, Archives of the chapter of Szepeshely, scr. 10, fasc. 2, no. 26. For other copies, see *DRH 1301–1457*, p. 232.

EDD.: *MTvt/CJH* 1:214-45 (from a 4 November 1411 copy); *DRH 1301—1457*, pp. 232-34 (from a 5 April 1411 copy).

LIT.: Kovachich, *Vestigia*, p. 217; Thallóczy, *A kamara haszna*, p. 68.

1. On the officer called *dicator*, see the Glossary.

2. The expression (already used this way in 1351:5) implies by the word *redemptio*, usually referring to documents, that the prohibited fees were asked for the quittance. The sixteenth-century copies have *literarum*.

3. On the "new pennies," see n. 13 to 1397. Because of the devaluation after 1402 between 1407 and 1410, 160 new pennies were worth a florin. We have no data of the exact value of "new pennies" in 1411.

4. Cf. 1397:29 and CC 1342: 19.

5. Cf. 1351:5; 1397:30.

6. That the lord has to declare merely *ad humanitatem suam*, i.e., on his word of honor, meant an acceptance of his higher social status, for usually legally binding declarations were made under oath (as the officials are bound to do). On the concepts of *honor* and *humanitas* in Angevin Hungary, see A. Kurcz, *Lovagi kultúra Magyarországon a 13.–14. században* [Chivalric culture in Hungary in the thirteenth and fourteenth centuries] (Bp: Akadémiai K., 1988), pp. 170, 188–192.

7. Cf. Syn. Szab.:40 (*DRMH* 1: 61).

8. Here again the role of the county is enhanced; cf. above 1405, note 21. The last two articles were repeated by King Matthias as 1464:24, see *DRMH* 3 (forthc.), which also warrants that the decision be regarded a law.

Notes to 23 July 1421
pages 54–55.
Incipit: *Quod nobis Posonii*

This royal decree, issued in a general meeting of Co. Pozsony, regulates the administration of justice in the county courts. The rise of their standing seems to have induced the officers of the counties to litigate in the local courts, where they served as party and judge at the same time. The decree seeks to end this abuse.

The text came down to us only in letters patent issued for certain individual families; the most complete one (see MS), for an unknown addressee, contains, however, references to the royal council's participation in the issue. Also, several records refer to this text as *decretum*, and, considering that it regulates matters relevant to the entire kingdom, it does qualify as a law of the realm.

MS.: Original on parchment with the privy seal *en placard*; OL Dl. 79687.

ED.: *DRH 1301–1457*, pp. 240–41.

1. According to a royal mandate of 6 February 1426 this decree was issued in a *congregatio generalis* of Co. Pozsony. Two copies of it, sent to the counties Fejér and Vas, in favor of noble families there, are published in I. Nagy *et al.*, eds., *Codex diplomaticus domus senioris comitum Zichy de Zich et Vásonkeő* (Bp.: Magyar Történelmi Társulat, 1895) [henceforth: *Cod. dipl. Zichy*] 8: 28–30 and in *Cod. dipl. patr.* 1: 315, respectively.

2. This legal maxim is a specific application of a principle of Roman civil law: "he who exercises jurisdiction ought not pronounce law in matters affecting himself or his household" (Ulpian [ca. A.D. 215], *Digesta Iustiniani* 2.1.10). This principle was made law by an imperial constitution of A.D. 376: "no one may be a judge in a matter affecting himself" (*Codex Iustinianus* 3.5.1).

3. On the court of the "special royal presence," see above, n. 54 to 1397 and n. 25 to 14 April 1405. Here it is unclear, whether the king's "personal presence" or the chancellor's court is meant. On the courts of the palatine and the judge royal, see the Glossary.

4. The numerous explicit and implicit references to this decree in royal charters are listed in *DRH 1301–1457*, p. 241, n. 4. Some of them aim at widening the purview of the decree so as to include county magistrates and the ban and vice-ban of Croatia.

5. This clause is typical for letters patent, the form in which this decree became known.

Notes to 17 March 1427 (a)
pages 56–59.
Incipit: *Quod nos frequentibus*

This military ordinance regulates more systematically matters regarding the movement of troops addressed in earlier laws. It was issued by the king and his council, perhaps in preparation for the two Walachian expeditions of Sigismund later that year.

MS.: Original on parchment, with remnants of the privy seal *en placard*; Archives of the convent of Lelesz, fasc. 47, Acta anni 1427, no. 22.

EDD.: Kovachich, *Supplementum*, 1:328–37; Fejér, *Cod. dipl.*, 10/6: 878–84; *DRH 1301–1457*, pp. 244–47.

LIT.: S. Kőszeghy, "Zsigmond király két honvédelmi szabályzata" [Two Military Ordinances of King Sigismund], *Hadtörténelmi Közlemények* 5 (1892): 587–91.

1. Damages caused by the military were a recurrent problem of the time, treated more than once in the laws; see 12 March 1435:6–8 and Prop. 1432/33: 3.

2. The oath taken by the noble magistrates at their accession was probably as old as their institution. As early as the mid-fourteenth century, the magistrates were occasionally called *iudices iurati*; see Gábor, *Megyei* (see above, p. 155), p. 85. Cf. also 8 March 1435:1.

3. On the octavial courts, see the Glossary.

4. On *litterae testimoniales* (or *fassionales*) and *litterae sententiales et praeceptoriae*, see the Glossary.

5. A seal was called authentic if it had legal force. Documents sealed in this way were accepted as evidence in lawsuits. Besides the royal seals, those of the high justices of the realm (the count palatine, the judge royal, the Master of the Treasury and the bans), and, of course, the seals of the places of authentication, were regarded "authentic" (see the literature in note 10 to 1351, above).

6. Estimation (see the Glossary) was an artificial means of assessing property, mobile and immobile, in course of a legal procedure. It was not made on current prices but according to a traditional key, and the amount given in a special "mark of estimation" remained far below the real value.

This law may have been intended to assure that damages were repaired in their actual worth. Another possible reading (by E. Fügedi) implies that the measure was to prohibit the practice of pledging cattle or land for major debts, instead of paying them in money or valuable objects. Such pledges were often defined not by amount but generally as *in condigna estimatione*. On the other hand, the text allows payment by "occupation of estates" and there is evidence for both land and cattle being pledged under Sigismund (see, e.g., Zs. O. 2, nos. 3421, 5275, 6996).

7. *Iuramentum corporale*: an oath in which the number of oath helpers depended on the amount of the damage. Usually for each mark of damage (in value of estimation, see note above) one person's oath was required. Cf. Hajnik, *Bír. szerv.*, p. 316.

8. The penalty of fourfold damages may be traced to Roman civil law. However, not in remedies for damages in property (for which twofold damages were the normal penalty), but for outright theft (*furtum manifestum*), see *Dig.* 47.2, esp. 47.2.89; *Codex Iustinianus* 6.2.11 and 18.

9. Threefold inquiry: an inquiry made in the same case by three different authorities in order to make the evidence more weighty. It was carried out by the county in question and by two *loca credibilia* in the neighborhood. Cf. *Ibid.*, p. 291.

10. On capital sentence, see note 25 to 1351, above, and the Glossary.

11. On composition, *homagium*, see the Glossary.

12. Up to the end of Sigismund's rule, the prelates and barons of the realm alone were entitled to use a banner (*vexillum* or *banderium*) as their sign when leading their retainers and other soldiers to war. Other nobles, however rich, were supposed to join the king's "banner"; hence the command of a *banderium* became the symbol of baronial status (see the Glossary, s. v. baron).

13. I.e., when the lord took part on the campaign in person. On many occasions the lord's *banderium* was led by his deputy.

14. The measure of grain is given in *cubulus Budensis*—according to E. Lederer ("Régi magyar űrmértékek" [Old Hungarian Measures of Volume] *Száz.* 57, 1923/24, 135–42) ca. 80 litres—consistent with Sigismund's efforts to make the the measures of Buda compulsory for the whole land (see above, 15 April 1405:1), although the "*cubulus* of Kassa" was the most widely used one. The difference between the two cannot be ascertained any more precisely.

15. About five words are missing.

16. Import of foreign salt had been prohibited many times before, most recently in 14 April 1405: 20.

17. Professional soldiers were mostly paid in salt (cf. with note 36 on p.193); hence the inclusion of the last two articles into this decree.

Notes to 17 March 1427 (b)
pages 60–62.

Incipit: *Cum inter ceteras*

This short decree introduced a new money of change which remained standard for decades. Although the surviving original lacks the usual privilegial form, it opens with full royal style and the text refers to a formal royal command. Since the contents also treat matters of national importance, it may count as a law of the land.

MS.: Paper original, sealed on the dorso with the great seal of the realm, *en placard*; City Archives, Cluj (Romania) M, 54.

EDD.: E. Jakab, *Oklevéltár Kolozsvár története a középkorban I. kötetéhez* [Diplomatarium to the First Volume of the History of Kolozsvár in the Middle Ages] (Bp.: Egyetemi Nyomda, 1870), pp. 164–66; Zimmermann-Werner, *Urkundenbuch* 4: 275–77; *DRH 1301–1457*, pp. 248–50.

LIT.: L. Huszár, *A budai pénzverés története a középkorban* [History of the Minting of Buda in the Middle Ages] (Bp.: MTA, 1958), pp. 69–81.

1. This is the only known law issued together by the king and his second wife, Barbara, countess of Cille (see the Index). Whether there was any special reason for this, cannot be ascertained.

2. Obviously, there was a parchment original with several seals pendant, now lost. The practice of appending the seals of magnates began in the fourteenth century, first only on international treaties, later on other important documents as well. For its origins in the Angevin age, see P. Engel, "Nagy Lajos bárói " [Barons of Louis the Great], *Történelmi Szemle* 28 (1985): 393–94, 410–13.

3. Counting the silver mark as the mark of Buda (245.5 g), the new "larger silver pennies" contained 0.4 g silver. Although their face value established by this decree was far above their intrinsic value in terms of the current price of silver (see below, n. 9), they remained in circulation for the rest of Sigismund's reign.

4. In this text *regnicolae* (for which see the Glossary) is consistently used in contrast to foreigners and sojourners in the kingdom; "residents" is, therefore, the proper translation in this decree.

5. 25 July 1427.

6. The editors of *DRH 1301–1457* emended here *curia* to *civitas* on the basis of the second mention of these office-holders, in same article, below.

7. *Obulus* was the name used for the smallest coins since the early fourteenth century. In the Angevin period *obuli* had the value of half a penny, but after the accession of Sigismund they rapidly lost value, which was reflected in their Hungarian name *fillér*, derived from German *Viertel* ("quarter"), meaning a farthing.

8. On the procedure and punishment of counterfeiting, see CC 1342: 31 (p. 137).

9. This price setting corresponds to a 1:12.5 ratio between gold and silver, 5.5 florins (=19.5 gold) being exchanged to a mark of 245.5 gold. The real price of silver in terms of Buda mark around this time was, however, 3.2 florins, i.e., the ratio was rather 1:21.

10. The export of unminted gold and silver was prohibited for centuries; see below, CC 1342: 12 with n. 28.

Notes to 8 March 1435
pages 63–76.
Incipit: *Inter cuncta que*

This major piece of legislation, conventionally referred to as the *decretum maius* of Sigismund, is essentially an elaborate attempt to make an end of abuses that emerged during the long absence of the king, under the government of baronial "vicars of the realm." It is seen as a decree favoring the lesser nobility of the counties, by giving them extensive powers against violent magnates, limiting the expenses of litigation, regulating the procedures of arrest and seizure. Also, the preamble contains the constitutionally significant clause about the county deputies representing "the entire body of the realm." It has been suggested that these reforms were elaborated by the royal advocate, Stephen of Arany, while in Siena with Sigismund in 1433, but this cannot be ascertained (Mályusz, *Sigismund*, pp. 183–84).

In the *CJH* this decree has been erroneously called the "second decree of 1435," even though it preceded the decree of 12 March 1435 by four days. Also, the division and numbering of the paragraphs in all the manuscript copies and older editions is inconsistent. The editors of *DRH 1301–1457* have changed the numbering in several places (see the Concordance).

MSS.: Six originals (two in the OL, as Dl.12672; one was in the Croatian National Archives, now lost, but copied by Dőry; one is in the Esztergom archiepiscopal archives Arch. saec., Acta radic. Lad. V. fasc. 1; one in the city archives of Trenčin, Slovakia, Cista 1, fasc. 1, no. 6; and one from the Zichy family archives, now also in the OL: Dl. 804498; for details, see *DRH 1301–1457*, p. 260), all on parchment, their double pendant seals lost or broken with the exception of the one in Esztergom.

EDD.: *MTvt/CJH* 1:254–76; *DRH 1301–1457*, pp. 260–76.

LIT.: Kovachich, *Supplementum* 1: 462–66; Mályusz, "Zentralisationsbestrebungen," p. 350; Idem, *Sigismund*, pp. 183–87.

1. This narrative summarizes the events of two decades: Sigismund was elected king of the Romans on 20 September 1410 by a split vote, and, after his accord with King Wenceslas IV, on 21 July 1411, unanimously; he was crowned king of Germany on 8 November 1414 in Aachen, king of the Lombards on 28 November 1431 in Milan, and emperor of the Holy Roman Empire on Whitsun, 31 June 1433, in Rome. Between 1410 and 1435

Sigismund was absent from Hungary about half the time (12 years: 1412–19, 1420–21, and 1430–34). During these years the kingdom was governed by vicars and lieutenants, initially two (the archbishop of Esztergom and the count palatine), in 1430 augmented by four more: the bishop of Eger, the judge royal, the Master of the Treasury and the treasurer (see Kovachich, *Supplementum* 1: 422–23, 449–56).

2. The clause about the diet's representing the *totum corpus regni cum plena facultate* is the first explicit statement of the noble deputies' claim to corporate sovereignty; see, among others, J. Holub, "La représentation politique en Hongrie au Moyen Age" in *Études présentés à la Commission Internationale pour l'Histoire des Assemblés d'États* 18 (Louvain-Paris 1958), pp. 104–6.

3. On these judges and officers, see the Glossary; the protonotaries mentioned in the higher courts, the deputies of the justices (also of the voivode and the ban as judges in their regions) were becoming ever more frequently the actual administrators of justice. They were laymen learned in the laws; see Bónis, *Jogtudó*, pp. 175–201.

4. The text of the oath is seen as having developed over a long period, F. Kovács, "Régi magyar eskümintàk" [Old Hungarian Oath Formulae], *Magyar Nyelv* 57 (1961): 290. The last words suggest that the oaths were sworn on a cross regarded as containing a relic of the Holy Cross.

5. The arrangements in this passage suggest that county administration had deteriorated in the preceding decades, so that better-off nobles (those later called *bene possessionati*) were often replaced by poor nobles (*unius sessionis*). The king's efforts to remedy the situation do not seem to have born fruit. Seals of noble magistrates (from the wealthy lesser nobility) are known from the early fourteenth century onwards. Having been usually attached *en placard*, they did not survive. The earliest extant exemplars are from the late fifteenth century.

6. The terms *nova occupatio, nova potentia* had emerged around 1400 in royal charters (see e.g., Zs. O. 2, nos. 1172, 1213) and became technical terms in the subsequent years. It cannot be decided whether they denoted a special group of violent deeds, or the adjective "new" or "recent" simply referred to crimes committed since the regulations passed earlier; see 1397: 53.

7. On *litterae querimoniales* (letters of complaint), see the Glossary.

8. In obvious cases of violent trespass a *proclamata congregatio*, verbatim: "announced assembly," which we translate as "extraordinary county assembly," was summoned on royal order. This kind of jurisdiction is first attested from 1404. In general, see the Glossary; also Hajnik, *Bír. szerv.*, pp. 303–6, and Mályusz, *Sigismund* p. 179. This procedure was often followed by the counties with reference to this paragraph, see e.g. OL Dl. 67797.

9. In cases involving estates, only noblemen had the right to give evidence. Since the nobility of certain witnesses was frequently contested, it was important for the court to know the principal estate (domicile) of the witnesses so that their status could be verified. Thus the use of the place of residence (estate) was a legal necessity; the form of "N. of M." replaced the earlier form referring to the origin of a nobleman, by "N. *de genere* M." By the end of the fifteenth century they came to be family names and were not altered even when the family's possessions changed.

10. This kind of efficient procedure was followed in cases preceded by an extraordinary county assembly (see n. 8, above). On capital oath, deciding the outcome of a suit, see above, 1324, n. 4.

11. Settling "out of court" was ancient custom, see, e.g., in the thirteenth-century *Regestrum Varadiense examinum ferri candentis ordine chronologico digestum*, J. Karácsonyi, S. Borovszky, eds. (Nagyvárad: Capitulum Varadiense, 1903), *passim*; also in Comp. c. 1300:8 (*DRMH* 1: 75). Bónis (*DRH 1301–1457*, p. 258) points out, however, that this custom also opened the way to forcing lesser men to settle with their powerful enemies without applying the full force of law to the trespassers.

12. There is no evidence that such inquiries against royal office-holders were ever held; it is, however, interesting to note that a kind of administrative court was envisaged.

13. The responsibility of lords of castles (great landowners) for the deeds of their castellans (noble retainers) was already decreed in Comp. c. 1300: 7 (see *DRMH* 1: 74); see also Fügedi, *Castles*, pp. 78–80.

14. The guarantee of free removal of tenants from their lord's land and the prohibition of their abduction was already decreed in 15 April 1405:6; see n. 13, there. Apparently there was still a shortage of labor in the mid-fifteenth century which might have encouraged illegal moves of peasants from one estate to another. It has been pointed out that lesser nobles were more vulnerable to such acts, for they could ill-afford to offer easier terms to their tenant, while greater lords could be more generous.

15. The matter of bringing a captured criminal to justice was already addressed in the legislation of the eleventh century; see, e.g., Lad. II:3, III:9, 19 (*DRMH* 1: 13, 20, 22). On the composition, see the Glossary.

16. This procedure and penalty goes back to the beginnings of the transformation of the chamber's profit to a direct tax; see CC 1342: 15–19.

17. On the payment of tithes, see the earlier decrees, e.g., Stephen II:[20]; Syn. Szab.:40 (*DRMH* 1:11, 61); and 1351:6, with note 18.

18. The judicial fines could amount to considerable sums; they started out with 3 marks (e.g., for a prorogation issued on the request of one party) but outstanding fines doubled every session.

19. The purpose of this measure, just as the one (further below in the same article) regulating the duties of the royal bailiff, is to assure the impartiality of official witneses at legal transactions; cf. the abolition of the authenticating function of lesser convents in 1351:3. See also Eckhart, Glaubw. Orte, pp. 449–62 and Mályusz, *Egyházi*, p. 72 ff. on higher clergy entrusting clerics in minor orders with important tasks.

20. The importance of witnesses, whose memory was often called upon, was emphasized by Fügedi, "Verba volant . . . ," in *Kings*, ch. 6. Actually, this is a rare case when a rule proclaimed by law was immediately followed by practice: records of proceeding according to this prescription abound in the time following its promulgation.

21. The fees for letters and charters issued by places of authentication and the expenses to be paid for their service as authentic witnesses were regulated earlier in Comp. c.1300:19 (*DRMH* 1: 76f) and 1351:21 (above) but not as extensively as here. For the different types of letters, see the Glossary.

22. *Moneta maior* refers to the silver coins (*denarii*), the exchange rate of which was regulated in 1427B. Additional measures relating to these coins

were passed both by the king and, in his absence, by the royal council in 1430 and 1432; see *DRH 1301–1457*, pp. 251–57. However, the new coins were soon displaced by debased emissions. In the 1430s, the actual small coin in circulation was the *quarting*, initially worth a quarter of *denarius* but by the end of Sigismund's reign 6000–8000 of them were worth a florin (instead of 400). Under such circumstances the regulation of fines and fees in stable money was most necessary.

23. On this kind of oath, see 1324, note 4.

24. These fees reflect old received practice of the courts; they were summarily regulated earlier in a charter of Sigismund of 21 July 1417 (*DRH 1301–1457*, pp. 235–37). Most of the types of documents are discussed in the Glossary.

25. The fees of the royal chancellery were regulated earlier in Comp. c. 1300:20 (cf. *DRMH* 1:77), 1351:7, and 1397:33.

26. See above, note 21.

27. On such arrests and "reprisals," see 1290:10 (*DRMH* 1:46); and 15 April 1405:8.

28. On public place, see 31 August 1405:5, with n. 8; in the present context it seems that merely such a place is meant, where the judge is "neutral" in the matter.

29. This paragraph is an unusually candid admission of the limits of public justice vis-à-vis powerful lords. A noble magistrate of humble origin or even the judge of a royal city were, indeed, not supposed to arrest a magnate. In these cases the king had to intervene. There is ample evidence that Sigismund was able to impose his will on all of his subjects, and did not hesitate to do so if his royal prerogative was at stake. Since the court of *specialis presentia* ceased to exist around 1429, it was at the *personalis presentia* where successful action could be implemented against violent nobles. For example, between 1433 and 1435, three powerful magnates received capital sentence for alleged misdeeds; see P. Engel, *Királyi hatalom és arisztokrácia viszonya a Zsigmond-korban* [Relationship of Royal Power and Aristocracy Under Sigismund] (Bp.: Akadémiai K., 1977), p. 62.

30. On the reeve (*villicus*), see the Glossary.

31. While estates were usually inherited only in the male line, there were exceptions. If it could be proven that the property was purchased or acquired through defaulted mortgage, daughters and their successors in both the male and female line had rights of inheritance. Purchase was rare, for noble land counted as inalienable (see 1351, note 6), but just because of that, mortgaging became a widespread practice. Female hereditary right might have also originated in royal grant of "son's rights" to sole surviving daughters (see the Glossary and 1397, note 74); daughters of women so privileged enjoyed the same rights and could pass on the estate to their daughters.

32. As far as the record permits to judge, this arrangement for guardianship of estates did not become general practice. The properties were usually either seized by the crown or retained by those (widows, kinsmen) in actual possession of it.

33. Dowry is only an approximate translation of the term *dos*. In Hungarian customary law the widow was entitled to a part of her husband's estates in return for her "cohabitation" (*concubitus*). Besides the *dos*, the

widow had also claim to her wedding-present (*res paraphernales*), consisting of goods and chattels that were given to her by the bridegroom, by her parents and other persons at the time of her marriage. In practice these claims had relevance only after the husband's death, at which time the widow's claims to immobile and mobile property had to be redeemed in money by his successors in the estate.

34. On the "filial quarter," see 1222:4, *DRMH* 1:34) with note 9; it was usually given to the daughters in money, but noble girls marrying unpropertied (non-noble) men received, exceptionally, a piece of land from the family estates.

35. The reference implies that young noblewomen served in the household of barons as ladies-in-waiting.

36. The royal right of patronage was not part of the *honores* granted to officeholders and interference in ecclesiastical prebends was always seen as an abuse; see Fraknói, *A magyar királyi kegyúri jog,* passim. The clause "without special permission of the king" calls attention to the fact that protection of ecclesiastical prebend had no power against the king. Actually, at the time of this decree, five out of fourteen bishoprics and other rich prebends (such as the priory of Vrana of the Knights Hospitallers) were vacant and governed by royal administrators (see Engel, *Királyi*, p. 80).

37. See the earlier regulation of tolls in 1351:7, above; in the course of the fourteenth century the originally royal tolls fell into the hands of private landowners and, on the other hand, royal exemptions from them also increased (see above, 1397: 58). This article legalised the practice of county assemblies which tried to clear up the situation by inquiring into the title of the tolls and their customary amounts. Such a list, drawn up by the noble assembly of Co. Nógrád, presided over by the palatine, is known from 1405 (Zs.O. 2, no. 3890); similar actions are recorded from 1412 and 1424; one of these documents was published by G. Wenzel, *Nyitra vármegyének XV. századbeli vámhelyei. Tanulmány hazánk közlekedési viszonyainak történetéhez* [Tolls in Ffifteenth-century Co. Nyitra: A Study on Conditions of Traffic in Hungary] (Bp.: Eggenberger, 1872).

38. The major commercial centres of the country were connected by customary roads, called *via recta, via iusta*, never formally codified but apparently well-known to travellers (see Map. # 2, p. 154, above). Tolls were levied, originally at least, where these roads crossed natural obstacles; hence the reference to bridges and ferries (on the peculiar abuse of "dry tolls," see above 1351:8). A road or detous avoiding the tolls was called *via falsa*. The lists of tolls drawn up by county assemblies (see note above) also contained references to these "illegal roads."

39. On proscription, see 31 August 1405: 12, with note 12; the peculiar custom of tolerating criminals in the border castles is not mentioned elsewhere, therefore, not easy to explain. It is possible that, considering the enormous burden which the defense of the southern frontier placed on the kingdom, criminals were not pursued if they were willing to serve in the castles of the defense lines. There is a possibility that some special fortified keeps are meant, for the word *metalis*, used here for the castles, also means "round tower," but is rarely used in that sense.

40. On these officeholders, see the Index.

Notes to 12 March 1435
pages 77–80.
Incipit: *Quod nos cuius*

This royal edict (as Kovachich called it, *mandatum edictale*), issued a few days after the *decretum maius*, may not have been a decree passed by the same diet, but rather a decision of the royal council based on the responses Sigismund received to his military propositions (see below, Prop. 1432–33). There is no precedent for two decrees issued by same diet and this document makes only perfunctory reference to the estates. Also, it was issued in non-privilegial form. In legal collections of the early modern centuries it is regularly referred to as a *manifestum* of the king. However, its main measures regulating military service by the major and lesser nobles remained the basis for the country's defense arrangements for a long time; hence, it is appropriate to include it among the laws of the realm.

The structure of this law is also unique for its time: the decree opens with royal promises about the crown's duties in the defense of the realm and continues in almost perfect dualist-corporate form, with the duties of the nobles in response. It essentially codifies the king's propositions of a few years earlier, however, without distinguishing between richer and poorer nobles, which may have displeased the nobility, insistent on its legal unity as one estate.

Earlier editions changed the sequence of the two decrees of 1435 and called this one the fifth of Sigismund's, placing it in front of the law of 8 March 1435; also the numbering of the articles was inconsistent and had to be corrected by the editors of *DRH 1301–1457*.

MSS.: Three originals; two in the OL (Dl. 12674 and 25064), one in the State Archives, Sibiu (Romania); all on parchment, only the last one has still the double pendant seal (for details, see *DRH 1301–1457*, p. 278).

EDD.: Fejér, *Cod. dipl.* 10/7: 619–21 (incpl.); *MTvt/CJH* 1:245–51; *DRH 1301–1457*, pp. 278–82.

LIT.: Kovachich, *Supplementum* 1:462–66; Deér, "Zsigmond király" (see above, p. 177), pp. 29–30, 32–34; Borosy, "The *militia portalis*" (see *ibid.*), p. 64.

1. Attacks by the Hussites, as a response to Hungarian troops fighting in the crusades against them, began in 1428, when the troops of Prokop the Great and Prokoupek advanced as far as Pozsony. Hussites waged several campaigns in the northeastern parts of the kingdom, and acquired some strongholds, such as Nagyszombat (Trnava) and Nagytapolcsány (Topolčiany) in 1432, whence they extended their control over considerable areas. These towns were later redeemed from them for money.

2. At that time the Margravate of Moravia was governed by Sigismund's son-in-law and ally, Duke Albert V of Austria (the later Albert I, king of Hungary), but some important Moravian fortresses, such as Brumov and Uherské Hradište, were, since the 1420s, temporarily in the hands of Hungarian garrisons.

3. Hungarian prelates (the archbishops, bishops, and the prior of Vrana of the Knights of St. John) had the obligation, as "ecclesiastical barons" (see n. 10 to 1397), to mount an army under their own banner and report to the king's call, as other barons holding honors, ever since Árpádian times. The specific arrangement of the northwestern border's defense being entrusted to the archbishop of Esztergom and the bishop of Eger was, however, recent; see below, Prop. 1432–33.

4. Cf. the original arrangement of the *militia portalis* in 1397:6, where the ratio was 1:20 (=5:100); the reason for the reduction of the numbers is not known. It may be worth noting that in 1397 Sigismund expressly promised to demand this kind of militia only for the impending war against the Ottomans.

5. This clause refers to those noble retainers (see the Glossary), who served in the *banderia* of barons and prelates.

6. See above, 1397:6, with note 12 on the undivided property.

7. In Sigismund's times the greatest lords began to organize households modelled after the king's. They created dignitaries (chancellor, marshal, and so on) from among their noble retainers and in records issued for their subjects used formulas typical for the royal chancellery. These can be seen as the first symptoms of a new social order, based on the predominance of the magnates, which was to be fully established by the end of the fifteenth century.

8. No such register survived. There exists a list of landowners in Co. Ung, from 1398. It was obviously the implementation of 1397:6, drawn up by the noble magistrates on the king's command.

9. Confiscation of property was the customary punishment of deserters; a charter of Sigismund of 21 April 1411 refers to such a procedure, based on a *generale edictum* of the king.

10. Cf. 1427A, passim. It is peculiar that this decree does not refer to the earlier legislation, which it repeats in essence in this and the following article.

11. This unique procedure of compensation based solely on the damaged party's oath, even if he was a peasant, was unprecedented and soon fell into oblivion. It was contrary to legal custom in many aspects: first, the oath of a nonnoble was never regarded valid against that of a nobleman; second, an unfree peasant was not considered able to act at law but had to request his lord to litigate for him.

Notes to 29 May 1439
pages 81–88.

Incipit: *Excellentissimo principe*

Shortly after the death of Sigismund, a group of barons "elected" his son-in-law, Duke Albert of Austria, as king of Hungary. The main opponent to the accession of Albert in Hungary seems to have been Queen Barbara, but Sigismund had her incarcerated shortly before his death, thus the accession of their daughter Elizabeth's husband was unproblematic. Nevertheless, the barons compelled the "elected king and queen" to issue a set of election promises—just as Sigismund had done in 1387, and as was to become general practice at Hungarian successions—in which a number of centralising reforms were rescinded and the role of the "royal council", that is, of the magnates holding baronial offices, was enhanced. (Undated, between 17–31 December, 1437; edited from a sixteenth-century copy in Wostry, pp. 145–49; repr. with corrections in Bak, pp. 136–38.) However, King Albert's long absence on imperial and Bohemian business during the following years and a major Ottoman campaign that devastated southern Hungary caused such disaffection among the nobles that a diet had to be called to pacify them. The meeting took place under circumstances very disadvantageous to the king and his barons: a popular rebellion against foreigners in Buda (on 23 May 1439) made Albert and his entourage virtual prisoners in the royal castle. This situation was well exploited by the nobility who managed to change a good number of the election promises to their own advantage, reducing the magnates' codified influence on the central authority.

Although the decree is not issued in a full-dress privilegial form, no historian doubts its formal legal character; also, King Matthias referred to it as a *decretum* (1458:1). There is, however, an entirely new element, pointing to the gradual emergence of corporate dualism: a day after the royal edict—which was, as usual, sent in several copies to the counties (see below, MSS)—the nobility issued a promise in return, not to request further privileges and to keep the law of May 1439. This was done through a charter, signed and sealed by more than fifty individuals (see *DRH 1301–1457*, pp. 301–02). M. G. Kovachich, who edited the charter from a copy (*Vestigia*, p. 232), compared the pair of the royal diploma and the nobility's "charter in return" to a "mutual pact and convention" as between parties to a contract. A few months

later this procedure was repeated in an even more explicitly "contractual" style, however this time not with county deputies, but merely with magnates. The decree about a general tax for a major campaign against the Ottomans of 17 September 1439 begins with the decision of the king and his council and continues with the obligation of several dozen barons, prelates and major nobles, some of whom sealed the charter next to the king's seal, to support the measure and help levy the subsidy (see *DRH 1301–1457*, pp. 304–07.)

The numbering of the articles 1439: 23–34 in the older editions is illogical. Döry and the others editors of *DRH 1301–1457* introduced a new count, which we follow. (See the Concordance).

MSS.: Eight authentic originals survived: in Hungary the charters OL Dl. 103590, 88151, 13381/1–2, 59249, 64340, copies sent to known or unknown counties, all on parchment, two still having their pendant seals; one in Zagreb (Državni Archiv, Doc. Med. Varia 256), one in Košice (City Archives, Coll. Schwartzenbachiana 220) both on parchment with seals broken or lost; and the transcript included in the charter of the nobles (Wien, State Archives, Ung. Urkk. 96). For details, see *DRH 1301–1457*, pp. 285 and 301.

EDD.: Katona, *Hist. crit.* 13:882–900; Fejér, *Cod. dipl.* 11: 244–56; *MTvt/CJH* 1:278–99; *DRH 1301–1457*, pp. 283–304. The nobility's charter was first edited by M. G. Kovachich, *Vestigia*, pp. 228–30; now in *DRH 1301–1457*, pp. 302–03.

LIT.: W. Wostry, *König Albrecht II. (1437–1439)* (Prag: Rohliček, 1907) 2:146 ff.; D. Szabó "Albert királlyá választása" [Election of Albert to King], in *Fejérpataky Emlékkönyv*, pp. 312–25; F. Eckhart, *Magyar alkotmány- és jogtörténet* [History of Hungarian Law and Constitution] (Bp.: Politzer, 1946), p. 42; Mályusz, "Rendi állam," pp. 70–74; Bak, *Königtum*, pp. 39–41.

1. Albert of Habsburg (born 1397), son of Albert IV, Duke of Austria, succeeded his father in 1404. Assuming government in 1411 as Albert V, Duke of Austria, he received the margravate of Moravia in 1422 as a Bohemian fief from Sigismund whose daughter, Elizabeth, he married on 28 Sept. 1421. The couple was "elected" king and queen of Hungary on 18 December 1437 and crowned on New Year's Day 1438. His wife's claim to the throne of Hungary was not accepted by the estates. While Albert was crowned by the archbishop of Esztergom with the "Crown of St. Stephen," Elizabeth was crowned, as queens as consorts usually were, by the bishop of Veszprém with a private crown. She was not considered a reigning queen, therefore, this decree bears only Albert's name, while the election patent was still issued and signed by both the future queen and the king. Albert was

elected King of the Romans (as Albert II) on 18 March 1438 and king of Bohemia by the Catholic majority of barons on 5 May 1438.

2. Sigismund of Luxemburg died on 9 December 1437 in Znaim (today: Znojmo, Czecho-Slovakia).

3. The references here and in several subsequent articles (e.g., art. 7, 9) to King Louis I imply the opposition of the diet (and the barons) to the "harmful novelties" of Sigismund (see explicitly art. 4, below). Here, of course, the immediate reference is to the decree of 1351.

4. There was no such "ancient custom," as F. Eckhart ("Alkotmánytörténet," in *A magyar történetírás új útjai* [New Trends in Hungarian History Writing], ed. B. Hóman [Bp.: Egyetemi Nyomda, 1931], p. 284) has convincingly demonstrated. The consent of the *regnum* was, however, stipulated as early as thirteenth century, which, depending on the interpretation of the term (see the Glossary), may be understood as the estates' participation in the selection of a palatine.

5. Cf. 1379:6; 1427A:1–4; 12 March 1435:6–8.

6. Cf. 1222:7, as renewed in 12 March 1435:6.

7. Mályusz (p. 72) pointed out that in contrast to the election patent, which had only stipulated that such offices should not be granted to foreigners without the council's approval, this article imposed an absolute prohibition and underlined it with the clause "only Hungarians." See also *ibid.*, p. 556, n. 418.

8. On most of these types of royal revenues, see the Glossary. The "fiftieth" was an old type of tax, collected in Transylvania (see art. 7, below). Not much is known about this tax, apparently rendered by mainly Romanian shepherds living on the lands of Transylvanian nobles, in cattle or sheep; see Gy Székely, "Az erdélyi románok feudalizálódása" [Feudalization of Romanians in Transylvania], in Idem, ed. *Tanulmányok*, pp. 240–77, here p. 244; for its earlier history, see Eckhart, *A királyi adózás története Magyarországon 1323-ig* [History of Royal Taxation in Hungary to 1323] (Arad: Réthy, 1908), pp. 12–13. It is to be distinguished from the *quinquagena*-tax introduced by King Sigismund on the authorisation of the Council of Basle, but not collected regularly in Hungary.

9. The word *officiolatus* meant something similar to *honor* (for which see the Glossary), only for lesser officeholders; that is, it implied the income from the office as well as the administrative and judicial tasks. This is a rare reference to what may have been, albeit marginal, venality of offices in medieval Hungary, for which there is no firm evidence.

10. This article was changed in a similar sense as art. 6; the formulation "subjects of the Crown of Hungary" may have been chosen in order not to exclude the (German) burghers of royal cities from farming the royal revenues (cf. Mályusz, p. 72).

11. This article was addressed against the increased taxation under Sigismund, about which, however, few details are known. We know, for example, that the chamber's profit, previously paid in silver pennies, was under Sigismund collected at the rate of a gold florin from every five *portae*; see Mályusz, p. 114; also Mályusz, *Sigismund*, p. 246.

12. Cf. 1222:30.

13. No legislation of Louis I on this matter is known. The measures implied here are more similar to the grant of right of staple to towns other than Buda by Sigismund, which was, however, rescinded in the decree of 15 April 1405:11.

14. In the decree of 1427B and again on 20 January 1432 (see *DRH 1301–1457*, pp. 255–57) Sigismund had decreed the same exchange rate for pennies. The quality of halfpennies (*obulus*, see 1427B, n. 4) needed regulation probably because of the inflated copper *quartings* ("farthings"), issued in the 1430s (cf. 8 March 1435: 12 with n. 26). The election pact was here, once again, changed in favor of the nobility by granting the diet the right of approving the coinage (cf. Mályusz, p. 71), a major right of estates in all medieval parliaments, but one which did not become reality in Hungary until much later.

15. According to the cameral contracts of the fourteenth century, the archbishop of Esztergom (because of his claim to the *pisetum*, the remnant of the archbishopric's claim to the tithe of royal revenues) and the Master of the Treasury had an agent each for supervising the coinage (see below, CC 1342:22, 23). This article seems to have aimed at having a deputy of the diet also involved in the minting. Nothing is known about the implementation of this demand.

16. Cf. 15 Apr. 1405:20; 5 Aug. 1405:8; 1427A:8.

17. Elizabeth of Luxemburg, only offspring of Sigismund and Barbara of Cille, born in 1409, was by unwritten Hungarian custom regarded as heiress of the kingdom or rather, as the suitable transmitter of dynastic claims by marriage. Her father obtained the throne as the spouse of a reigning queen (Mary), now it was Elizabeth's husband who *de facto* (if not *de iure*) inherited the kingdom. It has been recently pointed out that this kind of transmission of inheritance through the female line (even where succession of women was not accepted) was much more widespread in medieval Europe than hitherto noted; see A. Wolf, "Prinzipien der Thronfolge in Europa um 1400," in *Vorträge und Forschungen* 32 (1987): 233–78. The queen's properties were extensive for she took over her mother's domains (for these, see Engel, *Királyi hatalom*, pp. 197–99), apparently as a temporary arrangement. Shortly after this decree, on 11 June 1439, she was generously provided for by her husband with estates that were more modest than Barbara's, but still included at least nine castles and their appurtenances (see, J. Teleki, *A Hunyadiak kora* [The Age of the Hunyadis] [Bp.: MTA, 1853], 10: 43–55).

18. In contrast to the election patent, the baronial council was left out from this article; see Mályusz, p. 71, n. 107.

19. While art. 5, above, merely stipulated the exclusion of "foreigners" from all offices, here the exclusive prerogative of the king to make exceptions on his own was codified, clearly reducing baronial control on this matter; see Mályusz pp. 72–73, nn. 113–14. Whether the expression *advena* ("newcomer") means here something different from the foreigners, otherwise generally described as *forenses*, is unlikely.

20. While neither Sigismund, nor, as a matter of fact, Albert, were able to stop giving away estates from the dangerously shrunken royal domain, it became usual that the king mortgaged these properties and even if he was unable to recover them (which was usually the case), at least some of the

monetary burden on the royal purse was thus alleviated. The last major portion of the royal domain—some twenty to twenty-five royal castle estates—was lost to private lords under Albert.

21. Since Albert was duke of Austria and margrave of Moravia, the border betweeen his realms needed special attention by the Hungarian estates. The "previous arrangements" mentioned here are not known, for these borders seem not to have been disputed ever since the mid-fourteenth century.

22. The *descensus violentus*, the forced exaction of hospitality (*droit de gîte*), was prohibited as early as in 1222:3, but seems to have become a renewed abuse under Sigismund.

23. Since 1397 the churches were obligated to pay half of their income to the royal treasury (see 1397: 63). This "extraordinary measure for the duration of the present war" seems to have remained in force until Sigismund's death. For the military obligations of the prelates, see above, 12 March 1435:1, with note 3.

24. The demand of the estates for a voice in the marriage of the king's daughters (Albert and Elizabeth had two daughters, Anna, born 1432, who later married William, Duke of Saxony, and Elizabeth, born 1437, queen of Poland 1454–1505) implies that the diet assumed that their husbands might claim rights to the throne of Hungary; see note 17, above.

25. Cases between the king (or the queen) and gentlemen of the realm were judged as a rule by the count palatine, whose bench, like all central courts (with the exception of that of the Master of the Treasury), consisted of members of the royal council. Under Sigismund, some of the king's advocates were at the same time influential royal councillors (e.g., Stephen of Arany, see the Index, cf. Mályusz, "Zentralisationsbestrebungen," p. 350; Idem, *Sigismund*, pp. 233–34) and were entitled, by this fact, to judge in cases where the king himself was an interested party.

26. This reference is to the *magistri protonotarii*, those practically trained lawyers who became in the fifteenth century ever more frequently the actual judges on royal and palatinal courts of justice; cf. Bónis, "Men trained . . .,"p. 187. The expression "masters of judgment" seems to be the verbatim translation of their Hungarian name (*ítélőmester*), which, however has not been recorded before the sixteenth century.

27. For royal rights, see the Glossary s.v. "rights, royal." The concept in its initial form emerged in the fourteenth century as a legal device for expanding royal power and was amply developed later by Sigismund's legal experts. Any landowner could be the victim of such a process and those who could not prove the legality of their dominion ran the risk of losing it, even if it happened to be their ancestral home. The danger could safely be averted only by a new royal confirmation of ancient rights. Such charters were sought for and were issued indeed in great number, as a kind of reward for services, by Sigismund's chancellery since the 1410s. They either contained a "new royal grant" (*nova donatio regia*) on the ancient property, or invested the privileged person in advance "with all royal rights that might be hidden in it."

28. On estimation, see the Glossary.

29. George Branković, despot (ruler) of Serbia (see the Index) and Frederick, count of Cille, Ortenburg und Zagorje (d. 1454), the queen's uncle, counted among the four greatest landowners of the realm. Both of them being foreigners, they were—with good reason—suspected, more than others, of having officials of foreign birth in their service.

30. Unlike his predecessors who conferred royal honors (see Glossary) "in the usual way," Sigismund appointed royal castellans who probably were not entitled to keep the entire revenue of their *honor* for themselves (cf. Engel, "Honor," p. 14). This article aims at suppressing this new usage.

31. Cf. 1222:2.

32. The exemption of nobles from paying the tithe was contained in a now lost edict of Sigismund of 23 June 1405, referred to in a charter of 1 August 1421, see *DRH 1301–1457*, pp. 216–17. In 1415, Pope John XXIII confirmed this exemption based on the service of the nobles "in the defense of the faith," see J. M. Kovachich, *Monumenta vet. leg.* 2:8–9.

33. With the exception of the reference to Sigismund's *decretum maius*, this art. repeats 8 March 1435:3–4; the last sentence of art. 4 wandered to the end of the following article.

34. On the "extraordinary county assembly," see the Glossary. Mályusz (p. 64, n. 75) cites several examples of such *proclamatae congregationes*. The prerogative of the county nobles to judge violent trespassers was defended even against the crown: in 1440, Stephen of Rozgony, *ispán* of Co. Pozsony, protested against a judgment of the queen against the brothers of Tarkő "by edict" and requested that such matters be tried and judged by the county, "according to the law and custom of the realm" (OL Dl. 13522).

35. This formula seems to mean "give permission to hold an extraordinary county assembly," but is not otherwise known from records of the royal chancellery.

36. See above, n. 33.

37. Reference to 8 March 1435:10–12, 20–21.

38. On the form of these summons, see the Glossary.

39. Note the assumption of joint property of (or at least common interest in) estates by several members of a clan; see above n. 6 to 1351. As each defendant (and also claimant) had to be summoned three times (see the Glossary, s.v. "summons"), they could prolong a lawsuit almost infinitely by remaining absent alternately on some excuse. There is ample evidence for this practice.

40. On the composition, see the Glossary.

41. Cf. 1351:1.

42. Cf. Ps. 16:6, 30:3; Prov. 5:1; and so on

43. On this somewhat enigmatic clause, see note 7 to 1385.

44. Albert was the only king of Hungary in the late Middle Ages who did not have a great seal of majesty. This puzzling fact has not been explained yet in a satisfactory way. (Cf. E. Mályusz, "A kancelláriai tevékenység Albert király uralma alatt, 1438–1439" [Activity of the Chancellery Under King Albert], in *Opuscula classica mediaevaliaque in honorem J. Horváth composita*, ed. J. Bollók [Bp.: ELTE BTK Latin nyelvi tanszék, 1978], pp. 287 ff.)

Notes to 20 July 1440
pages 89–92.
Incipit: *Preesse feliciter*

The background history of this coronation patent is only tangentially similar to that of 1439, insofar as Wladislas I agreed to a set of conditions at his election in Cracow, and these obligations were to be included in a decree issued at his inauguration. But Wladislas's election was not accepted by the widowed queen Elizabeth. Her party decided to place Albert's posthumously born son, Ladislas, on the throne and crowned the infant on 14 May 1440 with the traditional "Crown of St. Stephen," cunningly removed from its custody in Visegrád. Thereupon the adherents of Wladislas—the so-called soldier barons and a good part of the lesser nobility—assembled in Buda, confirmed the election in Cracow and declared the coronation of the Habsburg child null and void (29 June 1440; see Katona, *Hist. crit.*, 13:70; cf. Bak, n. 27, p. 102). However, before proceeding to crown their own candidate on 20 July 1440 in Székesfehérvár the estates had to bridge the gap caused by the lack of the venerated crown of the kings of Hungary. In the dietal decision of 17 July 1440 (Bak, pp. 141–43), the nobility declared that the force, efficacy, and mystery of the crown did not rest in the object itself but "in the will of the *regnum*" and transferred all power to the reliquary crown of St. Stephen which was to be used for the inauguration of king Wladislas I. Three days later the king issued this coronation patent, in which parts of the charter of the estates were repeated.

MS.: a unique original from the possession of a nobleman of Co. Ung, now OL Dl. 13894; a somewhat careless contemporary copy on two pieces of parchment sewn together, the seal is missing but its cord survived (for details see *DRH 1301–1457* p. 309).

EDD.: Katona, *Hist. crit.* 13:101–02; Kovachich, *Supplementum* 1: 474–500; J. N. Kovachich, *Sylloge decretorum comitialium regni Hungariae* (Pest: Trattner, 1818) 1:60–73.

LIT.: Eckhart, *A szentkorona-eszme*, pp. 96–99; L. Szilágyi, "III. Endre" (see p. 155), pp. 135–41; Mályusz, "Rendi állam," pp. 75–79; J. Deér, *Die heilige Krone Ungarns* (Wien: Böhlaus Nachf., 1966), pp. 231–39; J. Dąbrowski, *Władisław Jagiełłończyk w Węgrzech* [W. J. in Hungary] (Warszawa: Gebethner & Wolff, 1923); Bak, *Königtum*, pp. 42–47.

1. Wladislas (Władisław III of Poland, called Jagiellończyk) succeeded his father, Władisław II Jagiełło (Jogaila), king of Poland, formerly grand prince of Lithuania, in 1434; his title as "heir of Russia" rested on the Lithuanian rulers' claim to western Russian territories.

2. Some 15 letters are missing. (There are several gaps in the text which the editors have filled in if the context allowed unequivocal emendation. We have not noted every lacuna.) This is the place to express our thanks to Angéla Zsolt whose help in disentangling the obscure and fragmented sentences of the arenga was of great value.

3. King Albert died in an epidemic that broke out in the camp while planning a campaign against the Ottomans, on his way to Vienna on 27 October 1439.

4. With the fall of Serbia (its last major fortress, Smederevo, capitulated on 18 August 1439) the Ottoman Empire reached the southern Hungarian border virtually along its entire length. In the spring and summer of 1440, Sultan Murad besieged Belgrade, the linchpin of the Hungarian defense system, for many months. The Ottoman threat was the main reason that a major part of great lords and nobles looked for a king who could defend the country. Albert's widow, Elizabeth, was still pregnant when a delegation of the Hungarian estates, consisting of five barons, was sent to Poland in January 1440, to invite King Wladislas III to the throne, then considered vacant. Having won him for the plan, the delegates, in the name of the estates, elected him king of Hungary in Cracow on 8 March. It is worth noting that he was the first king of Hungary who was in no way related to any of his predecessors. Though his father, Wladislas, in 1386 had married Hedwig/Jadwiga (d. 1399), the younger daughter of King Louis I of Hungary, Wladislas III himself was born in 1424 from the fifth marriage of the king with Zofia (Sonka) Holczańska; see Jan Długosz, *Historiae Poloniae libri XII*, A. Przezdziecki, ed. (Kraków: Kirchmayer), vol. 4 (1877) p. 614 ff.

5. The queen's lady-in-waiting, Helene Kottaner, managed to get hold of the crown, smuggled it out of its custody in the castle Visegrád in February 1440 (see *Die Denkwürdigkeiten der Helene Kottanerin*, K. Mollay, ed. [Wien: Bundesverlag, 1971]) and delivered it to Queen Elizabeth in Komárom, where Ladislas Posthumus was born on 22 February 1440. An extract from H. Kottaner's memoir describing the theft of the crown has been translated into English and appended (pp. 337–48) to M. C. Bijvoet, "Helene Kottaner: The Austrian Chambermaid," in K. M. Wilson, ed., *Women Writers of the Renaissance and Reformation* (Athens, Ga.: Univ. of Georgia Press, 1987), pp. 327-49.

6. Some 28 letters missing or illegible.

7. See the charter of 17 July 1440 in Bak, pp. 141–43. It is noteworthy that in spite of the sophisticated legal construct of the diet, based on the late Roman or Byzantine notion of the *lex regia* about the ultimate right of the *populus* to transfer power to the prince (see W. Ullmann, *Law and Politics in the Middle Ages* [Ithaca, NY: Cornell Univ. Press, 1975], p. 56f.), the estates chose a diadem symbolically connected to the founding holy king of the country. (On crowns placed on head-reliquaries of saintly kings, such as Emperor Frederick II's or the Bohemian "Crown of St. Wenceslas," see Bak, n. 37, p. 105–06 with literature. On the Székesfehérvár reliquary crown, which played a role in an earlier interregnum, see n. 4 to 1386, above.) Much

was made of this declaration of "popular sovereignty" (e.g., by Deér, pp. 244 ff.; cf. Bak, p. 44), but in fact it was, as Deér correctly formulated it, nothing but "an emergency solution." It should also be noted that the construct did not stand up against political realities and symbolical tradition: after the death of Wladislas, when Ladislas V (Posthumus) came of age, the estates tacitly recognized his coronation and annulled the acts of Wladislas (see below, 1453).

8. This *libellus* may have been an older collection of laws, or was compiled for this occasion from different sources, including a formulary (see notes to Comp. c. 1300, *DRMH* 1:136). The selection of the texts was certainly well considered, for it contained long forgotten texts that favored the position of lesser nobles.

9. That is, the Golden Bull of 1222; see *DRMH* 1:34–37).

10. That is, the decree of 1351; see above.

11. The description is erroneous: the decree was not Andrew III's coronation decree (1290, see *DRMH* 1:44–47) but one passed by a diet in 1298 (see *ibid.*, 48–53), augmented by a number of legal norms which are now seen as having originated around 1300 (Comp. c. 1300, *ibid.*, 73–77).

12. Here follows the copy of 1222:1–30.The final clause on the right of resistance and the dating were omitted.

13. Complete copy of 1298 and—without any transition—of Comp. c. 1300, the origin of which seems not to have been known (cf. Szilágyi, p. 138).

14. Copy of 1351, without preamble, transcript and concluding formulae of 1222, containing all the additional articles 1351:1–25.

15. On the translation of this enigmatic clause, see n. 7 to 1385.

16. Cf. 1439:28.

17. The connection between the nobility's exemption from the tithe and their military service was explicitly mentioned in the papal letter of 1415 (see above, n. 32 to 1439, p. 215); freedom from taxation also followed from the early medieval understanding of *servitium* and *libertas*; see J. Szücs, "Az 1267. évi dekrétum és háttere" [The Decree of 1267 and its Background], in *Mályusz Elemér Emlékkönyv*, pp. 341–94, esp. p. 351; on the assumption that the nobles' belonging to the kings' *familia* was the basis of their judicial immunity and freedom from taxation, see also *DRMH* 1: 108.

18. The existence of such practice under Sigismund's reign can indeed be documented.

19. This article extends the general rule of *res sequitur reum* to a special case which previously seems to have been handled differently. This article grants the right to seigneurial courts to prosecute in the first instance injury-trials which were earlier handled immediately by courts spiritual. It can be seen as an advance for the secular landlords.

20. The measure seems to apply to all subjects, hence it appeared better to translate *regnicolae* here as "people."

21. Cf. 8 April 1404, above.

22. The only surviving copy lacks the usual eschatocol, although the elaborate *arenga* would suggest that originally a full-dress privilege was issued.

Notes to 1443 (March or April) pages 93–97.

Incipit: *Cum a primevo*

The assembly, in which this decree was issued, must have taken place in the first days of April (according to Mályusz, p. 83) or at the end of March (according to *DRH 1301–1457*, p. 318, n. 1). It cannot be considered a diet, for no delegates of the counties seem to have been present. In the face of imminent Ottoman threats, the king called together his leading generals, his council and some major lords in order to prepare a campaign, the so-called long campaign, deep into the Balkans. Its legal significance is above all the introduction of "terminal summons" (*evocatio cum insinuatione*), a procedure modelled after similar canonical legal practice, which was to enhance the swift administration of justice against widespread violence in the country.

MS.: Contemporary copy on paper, damaged and faulty; OL Dl. 80798.

ED.: *DRH 1301–1457*, pp. 317–23.

LIT.: Mályusz, "Rendi állam," pp. 83–84, 100–12.

1. These two persons (on whom see the Index and *Biogr. Lex.* 2: 193–96) were the mightiest magnates of Hungary in their time. Besides the voivodate of Transylvania which was their most important office after 1441, they held jointly a number of other honors including all the frontier castles from Severin to Belgrade, and were thus responsible for the defense of the kingdom along its entire southeastern border.

2. Mályusz (p. 83) has convincingly demonstrated that this was not a diet proper, for the lesser nobles did not attend.

3. One of these letters, sent to the county of Közép-Szolnok, has survived, unfortunately mutilated like the copy of the decree and therefore also having no date (cf. *DRH 1301–1457*, p. 318, n. 1). However, on 11 April 1443, the king issued an additional order, raising the demanded contribution to one gold florin (OL Dl. 65057). The tax seems to have been collected, as we have records about parts of it being handed over as *dispositio* (stipend for soldiers) to Hunyadi and Ujlaki (Mályusz, p. 111).

4. 8 May.

5. Note the implication that victory is seen as granted by God to the righteous, hence the sinful would endanger the success of the campaign; the idea behind this is may be the equation of war and battle with ordeal, a common idea in the Middle Ages. It may also be derived from the concept

that a *bellum iustum* may not be successfully waged by the impious, which may go back through St. Augustine to Roman reflections on civil wars during the first century B.C.; for some apposite comment, see P. Jal, *La guerre civile à Rome* (Paris: Presses universitaires de France, 1963), pp. 473–88.

6. On terminal summons, mentioned here the first time, see the Glossary s.v. summons, terminal.

7. 16 June.

8. Lacuna of some 10 letters.

9. In the same way as Hunyadi and his colleague Nicholas of Ujlak were responsible for the defense of the south (see above, note 1), other parts of the kingdom were committed to other persons who in the 1430s began to be titled "captains" or "captains-general" (*capitaneus generalis*). The title *capitaneus* has been used for the commanders of the most important royal castles (cf. 1439, note 30). The new captains-general held their office in pairs (cf. below, art. 6) and were invested with exceptional authority, including the appointment of the *ispánok* in the counties of their areas.

10. Lacuna of some 20 letters; another lacuna at the end of the same sentence (of some 8–10 letters) does not seem to distort the meaning.

11. On noble retainers, see the Glossary.

12. The text is corrupt and partly illegible.

13. Lacuna of about 5 letters.

14. 8 May.

15. The fighting to which reference is made here was the civil war between the followers of King Wladislas and the infant King Ladislas V. The war broke out in summer 1440 and lasted, with interruptions, until after Wladislas' death in 1444. The greater part of the kingdom with the capital was controlled by Wladislas, but extended regions of northern and western Hungary, including many royal cities and mining-towns, remained faithful to his rival. After his mother's death in December 1442, Ladislas' case was supported by his distant cousin and guardian, Emperor Frederick III of Germany who, of course, largely depended on German and Czech mercenaries. Hence the many allusions, as here, to the enemy as "foreigners" in the contemporary propaganda of Wladislas' party.

16. The term *hold* does not seem to refer here to the Hungarian measure of land, but to an exaction of tribute, widespread in Bohemia, the name of which probably goes back to the German term *Huldigung*, homage; see H. Toman, *Husitské válečnictví za doby Žižkovy a Prokopovy* [Hussite Warfare under Žižka and Prokop], Praha: Král. České Společnost Nauk, 1898, pp. 62-64. Thus, this type of forced exaction, probably comparable to the *descensus violentus* of the Hungarian sources, may have been introduced to Hungary by the Czech Hussite troops who occupied the northern counties for decades.

17. The surviving copy ends here in mid-sentence.

Notes to 18 April 1444
pages 98–105.
Incipit: *Quod quamvis hoc*

This decree originates from a diet held by King Wladislas I in April 1444 and was aimed at restoring order and strengthening royal authority after years of open civil war between the Habsburg and Jagiello factions.

It seems to have been issued in different forms, by the king and by the estates. The text refers to 218 aristocrats and nobles who had committed themselves, just as the king did, to observe the articles, and had sealed an exemplar with their seals. No such sealed exemplar survived. Two of the surviving originals issued under the king's seal contain the clause and the list of names, the third omits both. All three, however, contain art. 32, added after the dating clause, in which the decision of the estates about foreign office-holders is contained. It is assumed that the *reversalis* of the noble estates was issued a few days later and added to some copies of the royal diploma.

MSS.: Three originals: two on parchment, one with royal pendant seal, OL Dl. 13827, one with royal seal on simple cue, Archives of the Archabbey Pannonhalma, Caps. 1044; one on paper, damaged, with royal seal *en placard.* (For details, see *DRH 1301–1457*, p. 325.)

EDD.: J. N. Kovachich, *Monumenta veteris legislationis Hungaricae* (Claudiopolis: Collegium, 1815) 1: 30–55; Idem, *Sylloge* 1: 74–93; *DRH 1301–1457*, pp. 325–37.

LIT.: Mályusz, "Rendi állam," pp. 66, 84, 536–37; P. Engel, "János Hunyadi: The Decisive Years of His Career, 1440–1444," in Bak-Király, *Hunyadi*, pp. 103–24; Dąbrowski, *Władisław Jagiełłończyk*, pp. 138 ff.

1. On the civil war that raged almost continuously from the election of Wladislas I to the issuing of this decree, see n. 15 to 1443, above.

2. The so called "Long Campaign," led by the king and János Hunyadi, started on 22 July 1443 and lasted unusually long: the army did not return to Belgrade until 25 January 1444. The Hungarian and allied forces reached

the passes of the Balkans beyond Sofia and defeated Ottoman armies in three major battles, but the campaign, while a military feat of great moral success, brought no tangible gains; see: F. Szakály, "Phases of Turco-Hungarian Warfare before the Battle of Mohács, 1365–1526," *Acta Orientalia Acad. Sc. Hung.* 23 (1979): 88–91; J. Fine, *The Balkans in the Late Middle Ages* (Ann Arbor: Univ. of Michigan Press, 1987), pp. 548–51; cf. pp. 478–79.

3. A formal profession of allegiance demanded from all present and obviously directed against the infant King Ladislas' party.

4. In this context *regnicola* clearly emphasizes the opposite of "aliens."

5. On the chamber's profit, *mardurina*, see the Glossary. On the salt revenue, see April 1405, note 36.

6. The use of both forms of reference to the crown in one paragraph is worth noting: *corona regia* (royal crown) is the older formulation implying the exclusive rights of the king to the power and property attached to the kingship; the other, *corona regni* (crown of the realm) came to be used in the fifteenth century with the intention of implying that the *regnum*, that is, the community of the estates was the depository of these rights and properties; see Bak, *Königtum*, pp. 33–35; idem, "Corona," in *Lexikon des Mittelalters* 3:256 (München: Artemis, 1988) with literature. On the inalienability of royal rights and possessions, see 1222:16, and the discussion in J. R. Sweeney, "The Decretal *Intellecto* and the Hungarian Golden Bull of 1222," in *Album Elemér Mályusz* (Bruxelles: Librairie Encyclopédique, 1976), pp. 89–96.

7. On mining dues (*urbura*), see the Glossary

8. On the thirtieth, see the Glossary.

9. In Hungarian Latin, the Biblical name Philistine denoted the Jász tribes (Pl.: Jászok), a semi-nomadic people who settled in Hungary in the thirteenth or early fourteenth century in the north of the Great Plain, close to the Cumans. Both people were long considered royal subjects of free status and owed the royal treasury an annual tax, payed in cash as well as in kind (cf. Bak "Monarchie," pp. 356, 382). Owing to this fact most of them were held later to be unfree tenants of the king. As late as the fifteenth century the Jászok still spoke their original language of Iranian (Alanian) origin, as has been proven by a unique find: a list of Jász words scribbled on the verso of a document from 1419; see Gy. Györffy,"A jászság betelepülése" [Settlement of the Jász People], in *A magyarság keleti elemei* [Oriental Elements of the Hungarian People] (Bp.: Gondolat, 1990), pp. 312–15.

10. Jews in Hungary, as in many other medieval kingdoms, lived under the protection of the royal chamber, for which they paid a regular fee that was frequently farmed out by the king. This article intends to recover this income for the crown, which in 1453 amounted to some 4000 gold florins; see I. Hajnik, *A zsidók Magyarországon a vegyes házakbeli királyok alatt* [The Jews in Hungary Under the Kings of Different Dynasties] (Bp.: Emich, 1866), pp. 5–8.

11. See n. 6, above.

12. After the virtual dissolution of the royal domain, royal grants could only entail land that escheated to the crown, when all male heirs in a given clan had died out.

13. 31 May 1444.

14. On high treason, see Glossary, s.v. nota infidelitatis. Since the beginning of the civil war both parties had generously rewarded their followers with estates confiscated from partisans of the other party. Many lords changed side during the war for different reasons but, in spite of promises made here and also later, they often did not succeed in recovering their lost possessions. Exceptionally we have evidence that they did: a charter of Wladislas I of 12 July 1444 (OL Dl. 13788) refers to this law when restoring the estates of Michael Nodlar.

15. In 1441, King Wladislas invested some of his partisans with the right of minting, which had been a royal monopoly at all times (cf. Mályusz, p. 11). This unprecedented measure might have contributed to the monetary disorder which, though otherwise unknown, is referred to here definitely and is plausible in view of the fact that most of the gold and silver mines were held by Ladislas' captains.

16. The same exchange rate was fixed in 1427B, cf. also 1439:8 with note 14.

17. This measure was a significant attempt at introducing appeal as an ordinary judicial procedure. Earlier the lower (provincial or county) courts were not obligated to transfer cases to the royal court, except on a specific mandate (*introductoria causa*) from the chancellery.

18. The meaning of this clause is not unequivocal, but may refer to the *privilegium fori* of clergy to be tried in courts spiritual.

19. Mályusz (pp. 65–66) demonstrated that this clause was introduced on the initiative of the delegates from Co. Somogy, in western Hungary. The activity of such elected nobles in the neighbouring county, Zala, is documented for the years 1444 and 1445 (*ibid.*).

20. Cf.1439:32, above.

21. On this term, see above, note 16 to 1443.

22. This clause refers to the procedures *in contumaciam*, ordered in 1443: 2.

23. Cf. above, art. 5 and 6.

24. Secular protector (*gubernator*) was the official title of lay administrators appointed by the king to major ecclesiastical benefices in case of a vacancy. During the civil war, a number of churches were occupied by Wladislas' adherents who pretended to be their protectors and refused to hand them over to the lawful claimant.

25. During Wladislas' reign, the tax was mostly collected by the captains-eneral and other magnates who had it exacted without mercy but were seemingly not so eager to hand it over to the treasury. (Cf. Mályusz, p. 111 f.)

26. At this time, the four usual octavial terms were those of Epiphany (from 13 January), St. George (from 1st May), St. James (from 1st August) and Michaelmas (from 6 October).

27. Damages caused by the military were regulated previously in the art. 1439: 3 and 18. For earlier laws, see there, with note 5.

28. On the right of tenants to change lords, see 1397:6; 15 April 1405: 14–16, but these laws do not contain the clause about the duty to return illegally absconded tenants.

29. The measure seems to aim at lords who did not join either party but tried to remain neutral, an attitude always dangerous in a civil war. The last sentence makes sense—considering the wording of relevant charters (e.g., OL Dl. 13782)—if the word *iudicata* is emended to *iuramenta*.

30. There are many examples known (see *DRH 1301–1457*, p. 331, n. 3) in which usurped possessions were returned; also, several charters of the royal chancellery survived that refer to this article, pass summary judgment, and emphasize that the usurpation happened after this decree (*ibid.* n. 4).

31. See above, 8 March 1435: 10–12,20–21 and 1439:31.

32. On the *descensus*, see above 1439:8; for the collection of fines (*birsagia*), as an exceptional case of exacting hospitality, see *ibid.* art. 7.

33. On terminal summons, see the Glossary. This institution, introduced in 1443, became general practice after 1444 (see the examples of charters referring to this decree in *DRH 1301–1457*, p. 332, n. XXV/1), so much so that in 1447 in a suit at the king's court, extensive debate was held as to whether a certain violent trespass was perpetrated before or after the issue of this law (OL Dl. 14067).

34. 1 August 1444.

35. It cannot be even surmised to what extent the ecclesiastical places of authentication were influenced by those secular lords who promoted themselves to their protectors (cf. above note 24). There is evidence for quite open misuse of such power, for example in a papal letter that tells us how Nicholas of Perény (d. 1444, see Index), Wladislas' captain in Késmárk, ousting the chapter of Szepeshely from its seat and obtaining its seal, compelled a canon to forge two documents for him in the chapter's name, one attesting that the late George of Somos, a local lord, had mortgaged to him his castle and all of his estates, and another testifying that he was duly granted *seisin* to the same goods. The canon was punished by excommunication but was later absolved by Pope Nicholas V; see P. Lukcsics, *XV. századi pápák oklevelei* [Charters of Fifteenth-Century Popes] (Bp.: Római Magyar Intézet, 1931), no. 997.

36. In view of what was said about king Ladislas' "foreign" support (see 1443, note 15), virtually all of his followers were threatened with capital sentence by the force of this article.

37. Apart from several major campaigns led by the king in person or his generals, the civil war was fought by local potentates who often made treaties with the other side. So on 22 November 1443 John of Rozgony, one of the leaders of Frederick's party in West Hungary (see the Index), dissolved his former truce with the brothers of Gerse, ardent partisans of Wladislas, and he even informed them obligingly that he would henceforth make himself a perfect nuisance to them (*vobis scire damus non velle tenere ulterius aliquam treugam, sed in omnibus quibus nos possumus vobis ac partem vestram faventibus nocere seu contrarium facere*, OL Dl. 92955).

38. For Matthaeus Polonus, that is, Matthew of Łabiszyn/Labischin (often referred to erroneously as "de la Bischino"), see the Index.

39. This paragraph was obviously inserted after the initial issue of the decree in privilegial form.

40. The signatories are identified in the Index.

Notes to 7 May 1445
pages 106–11.
Incipit: *Quod cum occulto*

After the disaster at Varna, about which only incomplete news reached Hungary during the winter of 1444/45, the magnates established first an informal and soon after a formal council of regency. In their meeting in February 1445, they called a diet for 4 April at Pest. The deliberations began only in late April and the decree was not issued until 7 May 1445. Waiting for definite news of the fate of King Wladislas, the estates issued the *decretum* in their own name and decreed, among others, that a seal of the realm be cut. While the original was issued under the seal of several magnates, the surviving copies are sealed by this corporate seal.

Even though the decree did not formally name captains for the regional enforcement of its measures, the magnates entrusted with its implementation acquired such a position. In July 1445 a meeting in northern Hungary—representing the powerful magnate Giskra, the counties of present-day Slovakia and the cities of Upper Hungary—passed decisions about the implementation of this decree.

MSS.: Three originals: one on parchment (OL Dl. 13848/1), one on paper (OL Dl. 13848/2) and another on paper in the City Archives of Trenčin (Cista 3., Fasc. 10, No. 12), all three sealed with the *Sigillum regnicolarum regni Hungariae; en placard.* (For details see *DRH 1301–1457* p. 339.)

EDD.: Kovachich, *Supplementum* 2: 9–36; Kovachich, *Sylloge* 1: 94–107; *MTvt/CJH* 1:302–07; *DRH 1301–1457*, pp. 338–48.

LIT.: Knauz, *Az országos tanács és az országgyűlések története, 1445–1452* [History of the Royal Council and the Diets between 1445 and 1452] (Pest: Eggenberger, 1859), pp. 20–27; Gábor, *A kormányzói méltóság a magyar alkotmányjogban* [The Dignity of Regent in Hungarian Constitutional Law] (Bp.: Athenaeum, n.d.[1932]), pp. 46–47; Mályusz, "Rendi állam," pp. 85, 543, 559–60; Bak, *Königtum*, pp. 49–51; J. Held, *Hunyadi: Legend and Reality* (Boulder, Co.: East European Monographs, 1985), pp. 113–18.

1. The notion of Hungary as the "bulwark" of Christianity goes back to 1250 when King Béla IV, in his letter to Pope Innocent IV, hinted at his lonely fight *propter bonum Christianitatis* against the Mongols. Similarly, Louis I was admonished by Pope Gregory XI to continue being a defender of Christendom, and Sigismund was addressed by Pope John XXIII in 1410 as *athleta invictissimus orthodoxae fidei*. However, as J. Deér pointed out (*A magyar nemzeti öntudat kialakulása* [Development of Hungarian National Consciousness] [Bp.: J. Deér, n.d. (1936)], pp. 8–10; briefly also summarized in his "Le sentiment national hongrois au moyen âge," *Nouvelle Revue de Hongrie* 19 [1936]: 418), this idea was for a long time restricted to the ruler, and did not refer to the nation until the later Middle Ages. It became a commonplace in the rhetoric of the chancellery under Matthias Corvinus; hence, the formulation here may count as an early example of this perception as a "Hungarian mission."

2. The battle of Varna, in Bulgaria, on 10 November 1444, where the Hungarian army was routed by Sultan Murad II and King Wladislas I killed. Cf. B. Tsvetkova, *La bataille mémorable des peuples* (Sofia: Sofia-Presse, 1971), with previous literature; also Fine, *Balkans*, pp. 548–50.

3. 30 May 1445.

4. On 25 February 1441, the Hungarian crown was pledged by Queen Elizabeth for 8000 gulden to King Frederick III of Germany, then head of the House of Habsburg, who, after her death in December 1442, became also the guardian of her infant son, King Ladislas V. Cf. the introduction to 20 July 1440, and note 15 to 1443.

5. That is, from the beginning of the civil war in Summer 1440 to 30 May 1445.

6. This article was frequently quoted during the subsequent months in cases against powerful lords, forcing them to return usurped possessions. The governing council of the realm issued several final summonses based on this and the following articles (see e.g., OL Dl. 13846, 13851, 13857, 66910).

7. Namely: Wladislas I Jagiello and Queen Elizabeth of Luxemburg.

8. See also below, 23:1445.

9. 30 May 1445.

10. Later evidence implies that in response to Ottoman raids, a number of places were fortified by local lords in the southern parts of the kingdom, mostly between the Sava and Drava Rivers. However, no such construction work is know from Transylvania.

11. The still extant castle of Várpalota, in Co. Veszprém.

12. Verőce, today: Vitrovica in Croatia.

13. Vámos, today Sajóvámos, in Co. Borsod, and Nána, today Kisnána, in Co. Heves. Remnants of castle Nána have been recently excavated.

14. Pelsőc in Co. Gömör, today: Plešivec, Slovakia.

15. A meeting of several counties in Szina in July 1445 repeated these injunctions and requested the region's captain, John Giskra (or: Jiskra) z Brandýsa (on whom see *Biogr. Lex.* 2:263f.), to act accordingly; in 1452 Hunyadi himself referred to this passage (or to 1446:2) in a mandate ordering the razing of the castle of the noble family of Martonfalva (OL Dl. 88266).

16. The list of the elected captains and their regional jurisdiction has been critically evaluated by Kovachich (*Supplementum*, 2: 20–24) and others.

The two voivodes are, of course, Ujlaki and Hunyadi; the companion of Michael Országh was Pancrace of Szentmiklós; for all of the persons mentioned, see the Index. It has been debated, whether Giskra was from the outset one of the captains, or was named only in the Szina regional meeting, as the *de facto* lord of northern Hungary. One of the original charters lists him among the captains, two others do not; however, since the record of the Szina meeting (OL Dl. 105552), which otherwise gives the best text of the decree, included Giskra, the editors of *DRH 1301–1457* opted for that version; see also Mályusz, pp. 559–60.

17. See the decree of 18 May 1444.

18. 1 August 1445.

19. Cf. 1444:16.

20. Cf. 1439:3

21. Cf. 1444:7

22. On the amounts paid to the major barons, who had to hire troops for the defense of the realm, we have some indication in a "reform proposal" submitted in 1453 to King Ladislas V. That plan foresaw six thousand florins to the commander-in-chief, Hunyadi, 4,600 florins to the palatine and 1,400 florins each to the commanders of the southern defense; see Bak "Monarchie," p. 361 f..

23. Cf. below, 1445:23

24. The invitation to the diet was issued on 8 February (see Mályusz, pp. 84–85); that *regnicolae* here means explicitly the lesser nobles (or their deputies), suggested by Mályusz (*ibid.*) is now supported by the emended text of the decree, as printed in *DRH 1301–1457*, p. 345.

25. In a case before the council of regency the counsel for Ladislas of Marót expressly noted that the accused committed his alleged crimes before the deadline set in this article; hence, the attempt of the diet to curb violence seems to have had a beneficial result.

26. No Ottoman attack is known from this year, rather an unsuccessful siege by Hunyadi and his allies of Little Nicopolis on the Lower Danube in September 1445. Actually, no major Ottoman campaign reached Hungary's borders until after the fall of Constantinople in 1453.

27. Cf. 1397:6, 1439:3, and Prop.1432/3: 1, 4.

28. Cf. 1444:32

29. Mályusz points out (pp. 48–49) that through this measure the diet wished to assure the implementation of 1439:19, which aimed at abolishing Sigismund's practice of diverting ecclesiastical revenues for government expenditures. The diets did not object to the emperor-king's anti-Roman policies, but wished to restore the domestic position of the prelates; hence, the military "obligation" was, in fact, perceived of not as a burden on the churchmen, but rather as their right to field ecclesiatical banderia, and thus be equal to secular magnates.

30. This was the only article of this decree that found its way into Werbőczy's *Tripartitum* (Pars II, tit. 14: 36) and the *CJH*. The cutting of a seal of the *regnum*, independent of king or regent was a significant symbolic act in the development of corporate political ideas. The design of the seal followed that of the seal cut by the council of barons in 1401, during Sigismund's captivity, of which several good impressions survived (see fig. 4,

on the rear endpaper). The cross—actually the double cross—was regarded as the sign of the kingdom since the thirteenth century and featured also on the seal of the *regnicolae*, cut in 1386 (see above p. 173). See: L. B. Kumorowitz, "Die Entwicklung des ungarischen Mittel- und Großwappens," in *Nouvelles études historiques publiées à l'occasion du XIIe Congrès International des Sciences Historiques* (Bp.: Akadémiai K., 1965) 2:319–56.

31. Cf. 1440:4–6

32. Cf. 1444:22.The measures decreed here seem to have been interpreted in an extended manner; Mályusz (p. 543, n. 366) cites a case, where a nobleman suspends his grant for a market beacuse of this paragraph. The charter of the Szina regional meeting also includes all, even urban, tolls in the prohibition.

33. Mályusz (p. 560) sees in this measure, suspending the commercial limitations of 30 May 1439:9, a minor victory for the urban delegates present at the diet. Actually, the deputies of royal cities were most active in the diets of the interregnum; their counsel was sought even at the election of the regent, see Bak, p. 50.

34. See above, n. 24.

35. Cf. 30 May 1439:3, with reference to earlier legislation.

36. Cf. Prop. 1432/3 below.

37. Cf. 1397:68 (with n. 62 on p. 183 and 1405:14–16. This time the Judge Royal Ladislas of Pálócz ordered a special investigation of tenants hindered in their movement, see OL Dl. 13943 of 29 July 1446.

38. See articles 2 and 11, above.

39. This clause referred to a way of sealing as used on the decree of 1444, and may have been used on some of the now lost originals. By the time the now surving copies were issued, the new seal (1445:15) was ready and applied to the charter; however, the sealing clause was not corrected to match the actual situation, save on the one copy, now in Trenčin, which has *sigillo universitatis regni Hungariae consignatarum* at this place.

Notes to 13 June 1446
pages 112–15.
Incipit: *Quod cum universitate*

This decree, passed in a diet that met in early June, 1446, consists of three parts: the first five articles contain the intention of the "Hunyadi-party" to elect John of Hunyad regent of the kingless country; the following nine articles define the limits of the regent's power and jurisdiction; in a paragraph connecting the two (and also in the eschatocol) the elected regent accepts the office with the limitations imposed upon him. Actually, the "program" of Hunyadi's adherents (as Mályusz, p. 87, calls it) was apparently already circulated before the meeting (a copy of these articles survived as OL Dl. 55325). The final text was issued by the regent under his own seal.

The text of this *decretum* was transcribed verbatim into the decree of 1447; that version was also considered for the edition.

MSS.: One original, on parchment with pendant seal (missing), OL Dl. 13938; two transcripts in the text of 1447 and a copy of Artt. I–V separately (see above). For details, see *DRH 1301–1457*, p. 354.

EDD.: Kovachich, *Vestigia* pp. 253–61; Kovachich: *Sylloge* 1:108–16; Marczali, *Enchiridion*, pp. 260–65; *DRH 1301–1457*, pp. 354–59.

LIT.: Knauz, *Az országos tanács*, pp. 40–46; Gábor, *A kormányzói méltóság*, pp. 49–53; Mályusz, "Rendi állam," pp. 87–88, 113–14, 561; Held, *Hunyadi*, pp. 120–24.

1. See the introduction to 20 July 1440. Calling Ladislas a *rex electus* implied that at this time his 1440 coronation was not (yet) seen as valid.

2. A diet was held in early Spring 1446; its decrees, issued on 14 March survived only in a badly mutilated copy (see *DRH 1301–1457*, pp. 349–52), which we omitted.

3. There are indeed several cases known from the months following this diet in which usurped rights and estates were returned to their legal owners (see the examples listed in *DRH 1301–1457*, p. 355, n. II/1 and in Mályusz, p. 88, n. 177). Bónis (*loc. cit.*) assumed that the diet issued another decree about restitution as well, for in a reference in a sentence of the council of regency from 6 August 1446 the obligation of returning estates is more elaborate; see also Knauz, p. 53.

4. Cf. 1445:5.

5. Cf. 1445:4.

6. A letter of protection by Hunyadi for the family Rikolf of Tarkő (OL Dl. 68996, 68997 of 6 August 1447) suggests that many nobles were in fact forced to raze their illegal castles.

7. The text of this oath in the vernacular survived in the Codex Nádasdy and belongs to the stock of early Magyar vernacular official texts, ed. by M. G. Kovachich, in *Supplementum* 2:44. A literal English translation of the main formula is, in comparison to the elegant archaic language of the original, rather pedestrian: "God so help you, the Holy Virgin so win you mercy, God's all saints so support you, the holy body of God so may lead you to salvation at the moment of your death, the earth so received your corpse and so not eject it on the third day, your seed may so multiply, so you may see God's holy countenance on Judgment Day and avoid eternal hell . . . ." The oath formulated in the Pest diet became a point of reference in subsequent years, and was used, for example, in the treaty of alliance sworn between Hunyadi, Ujlaki and Palatine Ladislas of Gara in 1450 (OL Dl. 14379).

8. The election took place on 5 June 1446. Apparently the first five articles were passed preceding this date, the rest after it.

9. Not all royal castles were handed over to the regent immediately. Buda, for example, was held by Palatine Lawrence of Hédervár until his death in September 1447. It was only then resigned by his son to Hunyadi, with reference to the present decree; see Mályusz, pp. 529–36.

10. This meant that the regent was not authorized to pronounce sentence in person, a royal prerogative, but only to hear the cases, and even in this judicial function he was to be assisted by a small council of four persons representing the estates.

11. It is noteworthy that several clauses of these articles, defining the new institution of regent, found their way into Werbőczy's *Tripartitum* (Pars II, tit. 14).

12. The procedures referred to here are instruction (*relatio*) and the issuing (*expeditio*) of judicial mandates, written by the chancellery on the basis of the parties' statements at law.

Notes to 25 March 1447
pages 116–22.

Incipit: *Quoniam in novissima*

As the proem of this decree describes, the estates had postponed the detailed regulation of government under the regency from the election diet of 1446 to one planned for Whitsun 1447. However, the diet met already in the spring and passed a fairly inclusive decree on 25 March. By transcribing the decree of 1447, expressly confirming the validity of decisions from the preceding diets, and including a number of longterm measures (such as fees for records, and so on), the nobility seems to have aimed at a general codification of its newly-acquired powers. This decree may, therefore, count as one of the earliest elaborate statements about corporate government (*Ständestaat*) in fifteenth-century Hungary. Many articles aim at reducing the power of the magnates, some limit clerical jursidictions, and a few intend to curtail burgher liberties, thus, clearly expressing the political priorities of the county nobility.

MSS.: One original (OL Dl. 80877), from the Zichy family archives, on parchment, the pendant seal (originally on a simple cue) is now lost; one transcript by the collegiate chapter of Pozsony from 18 May 1447 (OL Dl. 14071).

EDD.: Kovachich, *Supplementum* 2: 52–102; Kovachich, *Sylloge* 1: 116–35; Nagy, *Cod. dipl. Zichy*, 9:155–59; *DRH 1301–1457*, pp. 361–73.

LIT.: Knauz, *Az országos tanács*, pp. 57–66; Gábor, *A kormányzói méltóság*, pp. 54–57; Mályusz, "Rendi állam," pp. 89–90, 114.

1. 13 June 1446.

2. Here follows a verbatim transcript of 1446: 2–14, without, of course, the inserted declaration of elected regent (after art. 5); also, expressions referring to the election in the future tense were changed to past.

3. Cf. 1445:3.

4. The meeting was held on 8 February 1445, in preparation of the diet of that year; summary proceedings were ordered against violent trespassers in 1445:12.

5. While a few prelates acquired the position of "perpetual *ispán*" of the county of their see as early as Árpádian times, the honors (for which see the Glossary) of secular lords usually remained limited to the "king's pleasure." However, some of them were held, at least in practice, by magnate families. The *ispán* of Varaždin was appointed, for example, by the counts of Cille who were perpetual lords of the town.

6. Cf. 1445:9

7. This demand of the nobles has been repeatedly expressed ever since King Sigismund's times (see, e.g., 1397:48) and was also codified in 1445:14.

8. Cf. 1222:7 (*DRMH 1: 35).*

9. *For calumnia* and *potentia*, see the Glossary.

10. Cf. 1439: 38. On the "composition" (*homagium*), see the Glossary. There are examples for the application of this measure, e.g., in a charter of Judge Royal Ladislas of Pálóc of 28 November 1453, see: OL Dl. 14754.

11. See 1445:5.

12. These *litterae annuales* were special royal permissions allowing the grantee to call on the services of any place of authentication for a year, without having to seek a royal mandate every time. Such annual letters were granted to ecclesiastical bodies ever since the mid-fourteenth century; see Fejér, *Cod. dipl.* 8/2:612–15, 9/1:208, 9/3:573 from 1344 and 1366. The measures seeking their abolition do not seem to have been successful, for the practice is included in the *Tripartitum* (Pars II, tit. 50) as still existing in the sixteenth century.

13. On the octavial courts, see the Glossary. Evidence suggests that during the interregnum octavial court sessions were not held regularly.

14. The reference is to the decree of 1446. On terminal summons, see the Glossary. The regent and his council issued many mandates and passed capital judgment against violent offenders in the years 1447–48 on the basis of this decree (see *DRH 1301–1457* p. 364, n. XV/3). However, charters from 1449 ff. seem to refer to another, now lost, decree on the same matter; see *ibid.*.

15. The statutes referred to are 1446 (above) and another dietal decree, which survived only in fragments, from (March) 1446 (see *DRH 1301–1457*, pp. 349–52).

16. See the earlier prohibitions of violent extraction of pledges: 31 August 1405:2, 5; 8 March 1435:4; 1439:29 and 1445:11.

17. See the regulation for collecting fines in (1320).

18. This article is the renewal of 1444:22, 1445:17, 8 March 1435:21, Comp. c. 1300:17 (*DRMH* 1:76) and 1379:40.

19. The only "legal" regulation concerning the time of paying the chamber's profit is in CC 1342:14, where it is prescribed that the tax must be paid 15 days after its assessment. The stipulation of not levying taxes except in the current coinage was frequently decreed, but in the 1410s it seems to have been a practice to demand the tithe in gold florins; see Mályusz, *Sigsimund*, pp. 246–48.

20. Considering the exchange rate defined in art. 37, below, this measure made a "mark of fines" equal to a half florin, while the silver mark usually had the value of four florins.

21. While the decree of 1440 (and the dietal decision preceding it) stated that the power of the crown rested in the will of the estates, there was no previous law about the nobility's right to participate, by delegates, in the "election" of a king. This article set the stage for the mass participation of nobles in the election of Matthias Hunyadi (Corvinus) in 1458; see Bak, *Königtum*, p. 54.

22. Cf. 1446:3; this formulation puts in writing a practice which must have been observed for some time, namely, that the poor nobles did not attend the diets. Regent Hunyadi referred to this article in his call for a diet on 12 April 1448; see Nagy, *Cod. dipl. Zichy*, 9: 184.

23. On the letter of *seisin*, see the Glossary.

24. See 1440:4, going back to 4 April 1404.

25. The issue of rendering the tithe in kind or money goes back to the thirteenth century (see 1222:20 with n. 29; *DRMH* 1:36, 101), and came up in 1351:6 and again in 1397:46. On the mode of its collection, see Syn. Szab. 40 (*DRMH* 1:61) and 1397:17.

26. On the nobles' exemption from the tithe, see 1439:28. On their exemption from the chamber's profit no decree survives; CC 1342:14 does not mention it, while 1351:12 explicitly codified its opposite. There is sporadic evidence for both practices, but poor nobles seem to have been increasingly obligated to pay the chamber's profit; see Thallóczy, *A kamara haszna*, pp. 83, 92.

27. The measure seems to aim at demanding payments in the better (larger) pennies of which 100 was worth a gold florin. Two-third fineness was the usual alloy for silver coins ever since the monetary reforms of King Charles I.

28. Cf. 15 April 1405:14.

29. Cf. 1445: 14 and 1446: 6; there is, however, no known Hungarian case of imposing an abbot of another order on a religious house. The transfer of monasteries or convents from one order to another (for example, from conventual to observant Franciscans), which happened frequently, does not seem to have been meant here.

30. See above, 1445:7 and 20.

31. See 1444: 17.

32. The original was apparently sealed by the seal cut according to 1445: 15.

Notes to 29 January 1453
pages 123–24.
Incipit: *Quod cum nobis*

Since Ladislas V was not formally elected or crowned king at any diet, he did not issue a coronation patent, similar to those of his father and grandfather. Rather, after his release from the guardianship of Emperor Frederick III, he approved in decretal form the submissions and requests of the barons and nobles, who had gathered at a diet in Pozsony. This decree does not contain the usual detailed confirmation of noble privilege, yet assures the estates of their liberties and of the integrity of the realm, besides containing several measures that were necessary after the long interregnum. Remarkably, Ladislas always referred to this decree as that of the "prelates and barons" (e.g., in the charters OL Dl. 73119, 88272). The delegates seem to have planned to regulate details in a diet at Székesfehérvár, which, however, never took place.

MS.: A single original, on parchment with privy seal *en placard*, OL Dl. 44653.

EDD.: *MTvt/CJH* 1:310–15 (erroneously dated 6 February 1453); *DRH 1301–1457*, pp. 373–77.

LIT.: Mályusz, "Rendi állam," pp. 95–96, 543–43; Bak, *Königtum*, pp. 52–53.

1. Ladislas used the style which all Habsburg rulers had since 1282, regardless of whether they actually reigned in Austria or Styria; his Bohemian royal title was in fact confirmed by the Czech estates only ten months later, when, on 28 October 1453, he was crowned king of Bohemia.

2. After several years of negotiation and, finally, threatened by an alliance of Austrian, Czech and Moravian estates and the powerful counts of Cille, on 4 September 1452, Emperor Frederick released his nephew Ladislas into the hands of Ulrich of Cilli. He was greeted by the Hungarian magnates on 7 October and at the end of the year accepted Hunyadi's resignation from the regency. King and barons agreed on several governmental reforms, such as the separation of major and a minor (secret) chancellery, with their own seals and courts of law (the "special" and the "personal royal presence," for

which see the Glossary). The estates tacitly dropped the constitutional claims enunciated in the decree of 1440.

3. This summary promise became the model for the "constitutional oath" of subsequent kings of Hungary; see Bak, p. 53.

4. The oft-mentioned diet at Székesfehérvár never materialized; see Mályusz, p. 96. The formal obligation of the king to send out invitations forty days in advance was codified here for the first time. The stipulation that the kings should observe the future decisions of a diet sounds peculiar and suggests that the royal chancellery did not care to scrutinize this document before its issuance.

5. Such pardons were, in fact, issued, with reference to this article; see e.g., OL Dl. 102842 of 31 January 1454 in favor of Oswald of Bucsán.

6. The wording of this article implictly denies the legitimacy of Wladislas I's Hungarian kingship, even if by cancelling the donations of both sides in the civil war of 1439–43 it appears to be impartial.

7. The relevant dates are 13 February and 14 March 1453.

8. On razing the castles, see 1446: 2.

9. While the royal chancellery issued summonses and threatened trespassers with the charge of high treason on the basis of this decree (see OL Dl. 14665, 14761, 83242, 88272), legal practice rested more frequently on older and more detailed regulations. The problematic standing of the present decree is obvious from an order of King Ladislas of 6 May 1453 in which he expressly mandates that judgment be passed "not according to the said decree of Pozsony, but according to the ancient custom of the realm," where ancient custom is defined as "old law" (*antiqua lex*); OL Dl. 73119.

10. See 1446:10–11.

11. These short-term "terminal summonses" (see the Glossary) were last regulated in 1447:14 and 40.

Notes to 25 January 1454
pages 125–29.

Incipit: *Crebrarum a dudum*

This last extant decree of King Ladislas V, aimed at the preparation of a major campaign against the Ottomans, who had taken Constantinople the year before, survived only in a mandate of the king addressed to the nobles of Co. Szabolcs. Since the king was at the time of this meeting in Prague, the diet was most likely called and presided over by Hunyadi. A few months later (probably in March 1454) a diet discussed the propositions sent by the king but its decree did not survive (see *DRH 1301–1457*, p. 431). The last known diet of Ladislas was held in January 1455, when additional arrangements were made for the campaign, but its decree did not survive, save in fragmentary references (see *Ibid.*, pp. 384–86.)

MS.: Original on paper, with rests of a signet seal *en placard*. OL Dl. 55565, from the family archives of the Kállay.

EDD.: *MTvt/CJH* 1:317–25; *DRH 1301–1457*, pp. 378–83.

LIT.: Mályusz, "Rendi állam," pp. 97, 118; Held, *Hunyadi*, pp. 148–54.

1. As noted above, the surviving text is the copy sent to the noble community of Co. Szabolcs in northeastern Hungary.

2. Actually, during the following summer Sultan Mehmed II besieged unsuccessfully Smederevo, the residence of George Branković, despot (ruler) of Serbia. Hunyadi led a campaign into Serbia and defeated the rear-guard of the Ottomans at Kruševac on 2 October 1454.

3. Constantinople fell to the Ottomans on 29 May 1453.

4. The exact dates of the diet are not known.

5. Hunyadi was given the title of *comes perpetuus* by the young king. Although this title had been borne by other prelates and barons who were perpetual *ispánok* of a county, this time the title was to be similar to German-imperial title of *Graf*. That is why we chose to translate it not by the otherwise-used Hungarian term, but rather by the European-style "count." Actually, it was Hunyadi's son, King Matthias I, who legalized the existence of such formal titles, when he created several perpetual comital families and in 1487 (Peace of St. Pölten) wrote about *barones naturales*, in contrast to *barones ex officio*; see E. Fügedi, "The Aristocracy in Medieval Hungary,", in *Kings*, ch. 4, p. 14.

6. This meant that he was charged with both hiring a mercenary force and commanding the *banderia* and comital contingents. Hunyadi's right to dispose of the royal revenues was challenged by the king's propositions in (March) 1455, but the diet confirmed the captain-general's powers against the young king's opposition (see *DRH 1301–1457*, p. 432, n. III.1).

7. This decision is an attempt of the estates to gain control over the royal finances, a recurring program of the diet, but rarely successful until the early sixteenth century; see E. Mályusz, "Les débuts du vote de la taxe par les ordres dans la Hongrie féodale," *Nouvelles études historiques* 1:55–82, and Gy. Bónis, "Ständisches Finanzwesen in Ungarn im frühen 16. Jahrhundert," *ibid.* 83–103, esp. 83f.

8. "Approved custom" refers to the traditon as contained e.g., in Prop. 1432/33 (below).

9. See 8 March 1435:1 and 1439: 19.

10. By this time the southern regions of the country had suffered so much from some sixty years of Ottoman incursions that, for example, the bishop of Bosnia, once one of the richest prelates of the kingdom, was now one of the poorest. Another indicator of the devastation of the region is that by the 1450s virtually all fourteen Franciscan convents of southern Hungary and Croatia had disappeared.

11. The "register" is clearly what we know as Prop. 1432/33.

12. As prescribed e.g., in 8 March 1435:4.

13. This quota is higher than the earlier ones for the *militia portalis*: 1397:6 had stipulated 5, but 12 March 1435:2 only 3 mounted archers for every 100 tenants.

14. The restriction to serve only within the territory of the realm, earlier valid only for the feudal levy, is new and is in contrast to Prop. 1432/33:5.

15. By the law of 8 March 1435:4 the *ispán* was entrusted with the command of the county's levy, which seems to have been established custom (see also the "historical" argument in Prop. 1432/33:2). The reason for the change proposed here is not known.

16. Cf. Prop. 1432/33:2, 6, and 8 March 1435: 3.

17. Note the assumption of still undivided clan-properties, cf. above n. 12 to 1397.

18. Cf. 1397:6 and 8 March1435:5.

19. Cf. 8 March1435: 4–5.

20. See above, n. 18.

21. The wording here (*jobagiones exercituantes*) is one of the few explicit references to peasant tenants actually going to war in the so-called portal militia. On the debate about this issue, see n. 15 to 1397.

22. On the noble retainers, serving in their lords' armies, see the Glossary.

23. This archaic formulation means capital punishment, for which see the Glossary.

24. This procedure has been regulated many times, see, e.g., 1427B:2; 8 March 1435:8–9; 1445:7, 20; 1447:40.

25. For George Branković and Ulrich of Cille, see the Index.

26. The inhabitants of Slavonia usually paid the *mardurina*; see above, n. 30 to 1351 (p. 166 f.).

27. On semi-dependent Jász warriors (*Philistei*,) see above n. 9 to 1444; on the Cumans *DRMH* 1: 69–72. It is not quite clear, which people are meant under "Wallachs," most probably those who lived in the border districts between Severin (Szörény) and Temesvár. They were subject to royal border fortresses and registered for military service. (In a list from around 1430 there were 643 *kenezi*, i.e., local leaders, 2066 peasants and 108 other servants in the three districts of Mehadia, Halmas and Ilidia.) Tartars are mentioned occasionally in the early fifteenth century along with Cumans and Jászok; they probably lived in the same region, but nothing is known about their origin and date of settlement in the Hungarian Plain.

28. 1 May 1454.

29. 11 November 1454. This clause may have had something to do with the mobilization of tenant militiamen, see above, n. 22.

30. Cf. 12 March 1435:7 and Prop. 1432/33: 11.

31. On capital sentence, see the Glossary.

32. On desertion, see above, n. 9 to 1411, 12 March 1435:5 and Prop. 1432/33:12.

33. It may be worth noting that Sigismund promised a similar return to "ancient custom" half a century earlier (1397:6).

34. A charter of King Ladislas of 15 May 1454 (Nagy, *Cod. dipl. Zichy*, 9:437), addressed to the elected men of Co. Bodrog in a matter of compensation, suggests the implementation of this ordinance.

35. Several charters of the subsequent years refer to this decree ordering the procedure set out in the last article, e.g., Nagy, *Cod. dipl. Zichy*, 9:459; OL Dl. 61662, 88302, 90015, 15108, 93265.

36. If a document of some importance was to be issued in the name of the king, the chancellor usually noted, by a remark on the margin of the charter, the way the king's command was transmitted to him. If he received it from the king in person, he wrote *commissio propria domini regis*. If a member of the court (a baron, a prelate, a knight of the court) presented to him the mandate, the notice read: *relatio* (or: *ad relationem*) *N*. In the present case, in view of the particular weight of the charter, it was issued on the collective instruction of the royal council, a practice which, though uncommon, had its precedents under Sigismund.

Notes to 2 February 1342
Cameral contract
pages 131–40.

All older collections of medieval laws contain one or more of those contracts which King Charles I and his son Louis I made with entrepreneurs who farmed the chambers of mines and mint. While they cannot be classed as *decreta*, they are, in fact, the most informative sources on the extensive monetary and fiscal reforms of Charles and thus, on major decisions that influenced the country's economic boom in the fourteenth century. Therefore, we decided to include in the Appendix of this volume one of the last and most extensive contracts, the one which was also printed in *MTvt/CJH*.

The monetary reforms of Charles began in 1323 (see *DRH 1301–1457* , pp.76–77, but did not lead to results until a decade later. In 1327 the king issued an order about sharing the income of mines with the landowners, which enhanced the exploration and exploitation of precious metal resources; see *ibid.,* pp. 80–81. The first surviving cameral contract, with Master Hyppolit of Körmöcbánya, was signed on 26 March 1335 (see *ibid.*, pp. 85–89). It was followed by a contract with Master Andrew Nagy in 1336 (see *ibid.*, pp. 90–95) and one with Master Frichko of Buda in 1338 (see *ibid.*, pp. 95–102). The contract of 1342, printed below, reflects those financial measures of Charles I which proved to be durable. Its content was not significantly changed by Louis I, whose extant contract with Nicholas of Szatmár, of 25 March 1345 (see *ibid.*, pp. 118–123) differs little from it.

An almost identical contract was signed on the same day with Master Hyppolit; the editors of *DRH 1301–1457* used it (as Variant B, *ibid.*, pp. 116–17) to emend errors in the surviving text of the contract with Master Andrew (Variant A).

MSS.: Original on parchment with remnants of the great seal on the dorso; Primatial Archives, Esztergom, Arch. saec. Acta rad. Lad. B. fasc. 1, no. 5. Variant B is known from copies only, see *DRH 1301–1457*, p. 106.

EDD.: Gy. Szekfü, ed., "Oklevelek I. Károly pénzverési reformjához" [Records on the coinage reform of Charles I], *Történelmi Tár* (1911): 24–35; Knauz, *MES* 3: 412–19; *MTvt/CJH* 1: 150–63; *DRH 1301–1457*, pp. 106–15.

LIT.: Thallóczy, *A kamara haszna*, pp. 38–39; B. Hóman, *Magyar pénztörténet 1000–1325* [Hungarian monetary history, 1000–1325 A.D.] (Bp.: MTA, 1916), pp. 450, 470; Idem, *A magyar királyság pénzügyei és gazdaságpolitikája Károly Róbert korában* [Monetary conditions and economic policies of the kingdom of Hungary in the age of Charles Robert] (Bp.: Budavári Tudományos Társaság, 1921), pp. 109–28 *passim*, 212–37; O. Paulinyi, "The Crown Monopoly of the Refining Metallurgy of Precious Metals and the Technology of the Cameral Refineries in Hungary and Transylvania in the Period of Advanced and Late Feudalism (1325–1700), with Data on the Output," in *Precious Metals in the Age of Expansion*, H. Kellenbenz, ed. (Stuttgart: Klett-Cotta, 1981), pp. 32–43.

1. For Csempelényi, see the Index; cf. also the discussion of the personnel of the chambers in W. von Stromer, "Die ausländischen Kammergrafen der Stefanskrone," *Hamburger Beiträge zur Numismatik* 16 (1973/75): 85–106, where Csempelényi and another count of the chamber are identified as the only two ethnic Hungarians in contrast to the many Italian, south German, and German-Hungarian cameral entrepreneurs.

2. On this office, see the Glossary.

3. The first four counties belonged to the chamber of Szerém (Srem), the other four to Pécs.

4. According to ancient custom, 10 percent of the royal chambers' income went to the archbishop of Esztergom, primate of Hungary, who also had various rights in the mining and minting (see below art. 2 and *passim*.)

5. The value of the farm seem to have varied considerably. In 1345 the same chambers were farmed for 3300 marks; see *DRH 1301*, p. 119.

6. Gold florins began to be minted under Charles I, around 1325 (first mentioned in Moravia in 1326). They followed the model of the Florentine *fiorino d'oro*, their gold content was also the same (3.52 g) but they were slightly heavier (3.56 g) because the alloy was less fine. Hungarian gold florins were minted throughout the Middle Ages; see Hóman, "La circolazione," pp. 8–14; A. Pohl, *Ungarische Goldgulden des Mittelalter, 1325–1540* (Graz: Akademische Verlagsanstalt, 1974), pp. 3–18.

7. *Integros denarios* meant that half-pennies or *obuli* were not to be minted.

8. The text consistently says "the money of the past, third and fourth past years," but for simplicity's sake we translate this formula as "the past four years." Since 1338 the royal penny had been issued in the same weight and alloy.

9. The *pensa* was a money of account, equal to forty *denarii*, i.e., pennies. Thus 12 x 40 = 480 pennies were to contain a (Buda) mark of pure silver. "Third firing" meant two-third (0.666) fineness, i.e., 320 pennies (eight pense) were to be minted from one Buda mark of this fineness.

10. The Buda mark was equal to the Troy weight of ca. 245 g. Thus a new penny weighed ca. 0.77 g and contained 0.51 g silver.

11. The royal mining towns *(montanae)* enjoyed immunity from the county courts and were administered by the counts of the chambers. The most important ones were Körmöcbánya (Kremnitz) as the center of gold mining, Selmecbánya, Besztercebánya in the northwest, Gölnicbánya and Szomolnok in the northeast and Nagybánya in the east. There were also some less important silver and gold mines in Transylvania (see A. Pohl, "Die Münzkammer Siebenbürgens 1325–1526," *Südost-Forschungen* 13 [1970]: 24 ff). By virtue of the royal monopoly of gold and silver, these metals were purchased by the royal chambers *in montanis* on an imposed low price. For one mark of pure silver only 320 pennies were paid which had the worth of only two thirds of a mark. The remaining one third was the traditional rate (33 per cent) of the chamber's profit (see below n. 31).

12. See above, n. 4.

13. On this officer, see the Glossary.

14. On these officers, see the Glossary.

15. The "broad" Vienna pennies had about the same silver content as the Hungarian pennies of 1338 to 1342. Thus, by the exchange, the chamber had a profit of ca. 37 p.c., slightly above the usual rate of 33 p.c..

16. The *grossus*, in German *Groschen*, Hung. *garas*, was a silver currency of good quality, with a fineness of "sixteeenth firing" (0.9375) minted in Hungary from 1329 to 1338. Eighty groats equalled one Buda mark of pure silver. Even after the minting stopped, the term survived as a money of account.

17. In Hungary, the mark of payment i.e., of account traditionally amounted to 10 *pense* (400 pennies). Here, the value of the mark of payment, i.e., of the mark of account, is fixed at the value of 336 pennies (or 56 groats) equalling 0.7 Buda mark of pure silver.

18. Counterfeiting royal money was considered a felony (*infidelitas*) and punished by capital sentence (on which see Glossary).

19. "Clipping" of coins meant the systematic selection of heavier pieces and cutting of their rim so that only lighter coins are circulated and illegal profit obtained from the remaining silver. This practice, usually done by money-changers, was widespread in medieval Europe and everywhere regarded as counterfeiting.

20. The setting of a minimum of new money to be minted was an innovation in 1342, not included in the earlier cameral contracts (see *DRH 1301–1457*, pp. 85–105. See also below, art. 178.

21. No such case is known from the surviving records, nor can be asssumed on the basis of extant coins from this age.

22. This formulation seems to be tantamount to capital punishment (see Glossary).

23. This measure can be interpreted in two different ways. Either the legal course of the gold florin throughout in the kingdom was fixed thereby in 90 pennies. In terms of actual silver price, the florin was worth about 108 to 111 pennies, depending on how one calculated the exchange rate of gold and silver (then fluctuating between 1:15.5–16). Thus the official price invested the pennies with a nominal value, exceeding their intrinsic value by 15 to 23 percent. (This meant, of course, a corresponding devaluation of the florin.) Or the price of 90 pennies was prescribed for official money-changers only who

sold the new pennies to the towns and other communities with the legal reduction of 33 percent. Without this measure, the legal price would have been 72 or 74 pennies, i.e., two-thirds of the market price, one-third being the chamber's profit (see below, n. 31). By the new regulation, the course of the florin was fixed well above the market value (by 21 to 25 percent), a measure encouraging the towns and others to pay their taxes in florins rather than in silver. The stipulation included in the text that the florin must be "accepted" by the officials of the chamber at this imposed high price and should not be "refused" speaks in favor of the second interpretation.

24. In view of the market exchange rate of gold and silver (see note above), this imposed price for unminted gold was highly profitable for the chamber. The profit realized in this way must have been well above 60 percent.

25. The prohibition of exchange by count (*numerando*) and not by weight (*ponderando*) is recurrent in the cameral statutes of King Charles. It was aimed at eliminating the sorting out of heavier pieces and of "clipping" (see above, art. 5).

26. This categorical prohibition of other than royal cameral coins did not work. Already in 1345 Louis I faced reality and did not include such a clause in the cameral statutes; see *DRH 1301–1457*, pp. 118–23.

27. At this time Buda, Győr and Lőcse (today: Levoča, Slovakia) enjoyed right of staple; see Domanovszky, *Gazdaság*, pp. 158 ff.

28. See below, art. 30.

29. Lead was needed for the parting of silver during the first stage of silver ore metallurgy, the so-called cupellation. See G. Agricola, *De re metallica*, tr. H. C. and L. H. Hoover, 2nd ed. (New York: Dover, 1950) Book X, pp. 476–83; cf. Paulinyi, "Crown Monopoly," p. 35.

30. This reference to the "gate" is one of the earliest mentions of the *porta* (on which see the Glossary), the original unit of peasant tenancy and direct taxation. The sentence, however, suggests that by this time more than one household lived on these plots, which, in the course of time, were often divided down to the "quarter-virgate" size; see I. Szabó, "Magyarország népessége az 1330. és 1526. évek között" [Population of Hungary Between 1330 and 1526 A.D.], in *Magyarország történeti demográfiája* [Historical Demography of Hungary], J. Kovacsics, ed. (Bp.: KSH, 1963), pp. 63 ff.

31. Originally, the *lucrum camerae* or chamber's profit (see also Glossary) was the income arising from the exchange of coins, the *renovatio monetae*. By this measure, the royal chamber issued silver pennies of new minting year by year and withdrew the old ones simultaneously. The amount of silver which each town and county had to exchange was fixed in view of their economic capacity. Accordingly a quantity of new pennies was sent to the spot to be "exchanged" by the officials of the chamber either for old money or foreign currency and also for unminted silver. The usual exchange rate was 66.6 percent, i.e., for each mark of silver only two-thirds of the real value was paid, while the remaining one-third made out the profit of the chamber, or, more precisely, of those who farmed its revenues. Thus the chamber's profit equalled, in practice, a heavy annual tax imposed on the cities and the peasant households of free status. The tax of the latter was substituted, in 1336, by a direct tax, also called "the chamber's profit,"

amounting as a rule to one-fifth of a gold florin per "gate." The cities, however, were obligated to pay their share in the same way as earlier; see art. 25.

32. The term *conditionarii* refers here to that group of peasants on royal estates—elsewhere called *udvornici* (see Glossary)—who, because of their unfree origin, were traditionally exempt from royal taxation.

33. On the "gate" as the unit of taxation, see above, n. 30 and the Glossary s.v. *porta*. The statute here takes cognizance of the fact that the typical wide gate of the farmyard, still usual in many parts of Hungary, was not the only arrangement in rural settlements.

34. The special arrangements for the cities and their burghers are detailed below in art. 25.

35. See above, art. 6. Here the specific penalty is added for fraudulent collection of the chamber's profit.

36. One of the purposes of the monetary reform was to suppress the circulation of foreign currencies which were widespread in Hungary because of the lack of good local money; see Hóman, *Magyar pénztörténet*, pp. 104 ff.

37. The standard penalty of 3 marks for non-payment of the chamber's profit was established in 1335 (see *DRH 1301–1457*, pp. 88) and remained valid throughout the Middle Ages (see Thallóczy, *passim*).

38. This sentence underlines the meaning of the oft-repeated *multiplicando*-formula of this document (see above, n. 25).

39. These cities (for which see also the Index) were the most important urban settlements of southern Hungary in the mid-fourteenth century. With the exception of Pécs they lost their importance in the later centuries; owing to the destructions of Ottoman occupation and the Turkish wars some (such as Eng and Esztyén) were destroyed to the point that they cannot now be located; cf. D. Csánki, *Magyarország történelmi földrajza a Hunyadiak korában* [Historical Geography of Hungary in the Age of the Hunyadi] vol. 2 (Bp.: MTA, 1894), pp. 281, 482. However, Gy. Győrffy, *Az Árpád-kori Magyarország történeti földrajza* [Historical Geography of Árpád Hungary], vol. 1 (Bp.: Akad. Kiadó, 1987), p. 301 identifies Esztyén (Istyén, Sztyén) as a location in Co. Baranya first noted in 1093 and twice in the fourteenth century. According to the map in the same, Esztyén lay to the southeast of Pécs, south of Nyárad, south of the Borza River. Today Ustine in Croatia.

40. For their part of the chamber's profit, the cities continued to pay a sum assessed according to their size and wealth. The peasant population of the counties paid its tax in the same way until 1336 (cf. note 31 above).

41. See the Glossary. The fee of a groat (see note 16 above) was levied only once even if a nobleman had several estates, which was the usual case.

42. This clause specifies the procedure by which the royal monopoly in the traffic of gold and silver, introduced by Charles I in the 1320s and retained into modern times, was to be implemented. See, Paulinyi, "Crown monopoly," *passim*.

43. This article aimed at enhancing the crown's monopoly; see above.

44. Even some time before this regulation, the counts of the chamber usually put their mark on the gold and silver coins issued by them. As a rule, the mint was marked by a letter, e.g., B for Buda, K for Körmöcbánya, and the moneyer by a symbol. The Paduan banker Giacomo Saraceno, in charge

of Hungary's finances in the 1360s and 1370s, marked his coins with a "Saracene" head (a face with pronounced African features). In other cases the identification is not so easy as that; see E. Mályusz, "Az izmaelita pénzverőjegyek kérdéséhez" [On the Marks of Ishmaelite Minters], *Budapest Régiségei* 18 (1958): 301–11.

45. On such tools, see A. Luschin von Ebengreuth, *Allgemeine Münzkunde und Geldgeschichte des Mittelalters und der neueren Zeit*, 2nd ed. (München-Berlin: Oldenbourg, 1926), pp. 82–93.

46. The cameral statute of 1338 specifies that forty pennies both of new minting and of the Viennese type are to be melted down, obviously for comparison of their fineness; see *DRH 1301–1457*, p. 99.

47. On the thirtieth, a customs duty, see the Glossary.

48. For similar attempts at eliminating the delay of judicial procedures through several postponements from term to term, see above 1351: 25.

49. This forty-eighth part due to the archbishop from minted silver and gold (which is not to be confused with the tenth part due from the revenue of the royal chamber, see above, note 4), was called *pisetum* and was collected by the primate until the nineteenth century; see S. Kazimir, and J. Hlinka, *Kremenická mincovna 1328–1978* [The Mint of Kremnitz 1328–1978 A.D.] (Martin Osveta, 1978), p. 40.

50. A *ferto*—as its name, derived from German *Viertel*, Hungarian *fertály*, meaning a quarter, suggests—was one-fourth of a mark; hence, 2 oz.

51. See above, n. 18.

52. The precise legal meaning of the expression *ratione fororum*, verbatim: by reason of markets, is not quite clear. Apparently the *ispánok* had a claim to any market revenue of their county because of the honor they held and the sum specified here was set as the maximum of such payments.

53. This clause was to prevent the sub-leasing of the royal and archiepiscopal fractions of the minting revenue; however, no evidence has survived about such attempts.

54. See art. 25.

55. The *pondus* (1/48th of a mark as a weight) was made often equal to the groat (1/56th of a mark as a money of account, see above, nn. 16–17).

56. The dates of payments varied in the course of time; they were different, for example, in 1335 (see *DRH 1301–1457*, p. 89). The present contracts stipulated terms for 1 July, 15 September, 18 November, and 8 January.

Notes to Propositions of (1432/33) pages 141–53.

Very few royal proposals for discussion at diets or royal council meetings have come down to us from the Middle Ages. *DRH 1301–1457* contains, besides this one, a brief one from Sigismund, dated ca. 1415/17 (pp. 397–404), and a short document from Ladislas V from ca. 1454. (pp. 431–34). We decided to include the longest text in the Appendix, for it served clearly as a basis of the decree of 12 March 1435 and was referred to as "King Sigismund's Register" (see art. 6) as late as 1518.

The surviving copies are not dated, but the contents allow us to conjecture a fairly exact date. Sigismund refers to the loss of Nagyszombat, which was captured by the Hussites around 24 June 1432; it must have taken some time for the news to reach the king and emperor who was at that time detained in Siena. From there Sigismund sent orders for a campaign against the Venetians on 28 October 1432, but revoked it, having made a truce with the Signoria, on 21 January 1433. Actually, in the latter command to Ladislas of Kanizsa, Sigismund refers to "other dispositions sent to you," which most likely mean the present military arrangement, for he still expects a war in Friuli, but expresses hope to avoid it (art. 23). These and other minor indications speak for a dating "between November 1432 and 20 January 1433," as was already proposed by M. G. Kovachich (*Supplementum* 1: 350, 361).

Two of the sixteenth-century codices which contain this "Register" also contain a slightly different list of *banderia*, augmenting art. 21–22 of the ordinance. They seem to have been drawn up after the death of Sigismund, as their preface suggests, but before the mid-sixteenth century, when they were copied into three manuscript collections of legal texts. The heading runs:

> In the time of king Sigismund of Hungary, who was also emperor of the Romans, the kingdom of Hungary had many enemies from different lands, and so because of this the king, with the counsel of his lords and the gentlemen of the realm, has divided all his people and those of the lords gentlemen of the realm, who were able to go on campaign from the kingdom, in the following order. . . .

The textual transmission of this list (see *DRH 1301–1457*, pp. 425–30) must have been different from that of the Propositions. The two texts

are included in the codices at entirely different places; the later list is also contained in a codex from 1588, while it is missing from one that has the Register. We took the liberty of adding the data contained in that list to the English translation of the propositions, in brackets, because they usually clarify the size of military units assigned to the different borders. In the rare cases where the list does not contain a region or person mentioned in the Register, a note refers to this fact; persons not mentioned in the Register but in the list appear in brackets.

MSS.: No original survived; copies are in Cod. Festetich (pp. 217–31 and 391–95); Cod. Debrecen (11 pp. unnumbered); Cod. Nádasdy (foll. 190v–92v, list only). It was also copied into the now lost Cod. Szapáry, see below, EDD.

EDD.: Kovachich, *Supplementum* 1: 374–441 (from the Cod. Szapáry); Kovachich, *Sylloge*, pp. 416–40 (list only); *DRH 1301–1457*, pp. 405–30.

LIT.: Kovachich, *Supplementum* 1:348ff.; Kőszeghy, "Zsigmond király" (see above, p. 199) pp. 592–608; Deér, "Zsigmond" (see above, p. 177), pp. 15–16, 25–30, 34.

1. These countries, listed in the royal style ever since late Árpádian times, were glossed by the sixteenth-century editors (John Sambucus and Nicholas Telegdi) as follows: "Rama means Bosnia, Serbia means Rascia, Galicia is greater Walachia, Lodomeria is Russia, Cumania has its name from the land of Walachia, earlier inhabited by the black Cumans, which lies between the Alps and the Danube, from the river Olt towards Tartary and is now inhabited by the Wallachs and is called a part of the Transalpine and Moldavian lands." By Alps, of course, the Carpathian Mountains are meant. Galicia, a Russian principality belonging to Poland since the 1340s, was erroneously identified with Walachia.

2. It is believed that a report by the Grand Master of the Teutonic Order in a letter of 1422, where he speaks about many thousand "peasants" (*gebawer*) in Sigismund's army, was in fact a reference to the rather shabby noble levy; see František Palacký, *Urkundliche Beiträge zur Geschichte des Hussitenkrieges* (Prag: Tempsky, 1873) 1, pp. 191.

3. The meaning of "men of property" was practically identical with "noble," for almost all landowners were of noble origin.

4. The reference is to the chronicle text now known as *Chronici Hungarici compilatio saeculi XIV*, well-known in the later Middle Ages in several versions (ed. A. Domanovszky, in Szentpétery, *Scriptores* 1: 217–506). The war against the Pechenegs and Greeks of 1071–72 is described in cap. 103 (*ibid.*, pp. 368–69). The "testimony" of the chronicle is here adduced to convince the nobles of the legitimacy of local leadership (of the *ispán*) in contrast to their codified right to go to war only under the king's command.

5. On the harm done by soldiers of the levy, see above, 1427A: 1–6.

6. The extension of the duty of service was in fact an innovation in contrast to customary limitation of noble service.

7. The letter of Sigismund from Siena did not survive; the vice-chancellor in question was Andrew of Szentgyörgy, for whom see the Index.

8. The vicars of Sigismund in 1430–34 were Palatine Nicholas of Gara; Judge Royal Matthew of Pálóc, Master of the Treasury Peter of Berzevicze, Treasurer John of Rozgony, George of Pálócz, archbishop of Esztergom, Clement of Molnár, bishop of Győr, and Peter of Rozgony, bishop of Eger.

9. Filippo (Pipo) Scolari of Ozora, *ispán* of Temes, and Stephen Lazarević, Despot (Prince) of Serbia, are meant; on them, see the Index.

10. The price of salt under Louis I is not known; this passage was included here because many a professional soldier was paid in salt; cf. 1427A:8–9.

11. Rock salt from the mines in Máramaros and Transylvania was sold widely in East Central Europe both in blocks (*lapis, petra salis*) and in smaller pieces as well, contrary to what R. L. Multhauf in the *Dictionary of the Middle Ages* (New York: Scribner, 1986) 10: 634 maintains. The royal income from this monopoly was in fact one of the main items in the Hungarian "budget"; see Bak "Monarchie," pp. 356–59.

12. On the procedures at the Council of Basle, see the chronological overview by R. W. Cook "Negotiations between Hussites, the Holy Roman Emperor, and the Roman Church, 1427–36," *East Central Europe-L'Europe de centre-est* 5 (1978): 90–104, esp. pp. 95 ff. with references to the sources and literature.

13. The Republic of Florence was an ally of Venice in her war against Sigismund (see below, n. 26) and hindered the emperor-elect in reaching Rome, where he was to be crowned. Sigismund was supported only by Siena, Florence's arch-enemy, and had to stay there for nine months in 1432–33, incurring enormous debts, surrounded by enemies.

14. The word *passagium*, although usually meaning "passage" or "travel" in general, must refer here to the safe conducts issued to the Hussite delegation by the Council and, later, by the Czechs to the conciliar envoys to Prague; on these see Cook, "Negotiations," pp. 94, 96.

15. These towns, together with several castles, were taken by the Hussites in 1432 and were redeemed from them only in 1434, when Hussite invasions into northern Hungary ended. The six years of incursions of the Hussites into northern Hungary caused extensive damage: they sacked the royal cities in the Szepesség/Spís and (in 1433) the mining and minting centre Körmöcbánya.

16. There is no evidence that the king's call on the peasants to fight against the Hussites had any consequences; see P. Tóth-Szabó, *A cseh-huszita mozgalmak és uralom története Magyarországon* [History of Bohemian-Hussite Movements and Domination in Hungary] (Bp.: Hornyánszky, 1917), pp. 130–32.

17. These arrangements are contained in the "Division," below.

18. These measures offer a rare insight into the internal workings of county assemblies, where, apparently, the barons and their retainers, together with the major landowning nobles, dominated the discussions; the king attempted to protect the rights of the lesser nobles.

19. The region of Chulm in West Bosnia, with the county (župa) Livno and its chief castle Bistrica, roughly equal to Hercegovina (see H. Kreševljaković, "Stari bosanski gradovi" [Ancient Bosnian Castles], *Naše Starine* 1 [1953], 41), was annexed by Hungary under King Louis I in 1357 but was lost after his death. Prior to this Hum/Chulmia/Zachulmia was subject to Hungary in the twelfth Century, especially to the future Andrew II in his capacity as Duke of Croatia. But at this time they were under the rule of King Tvartko II of Bosnia (1420–43); see Fine, *Balkans*, pp. 463–79; P. Živković, *Tvrtko II Tvrtković. Bosna u prvoj polovini XV stoljeća* [Tvartko II: Bosnia in the First Half of the Fifteenth Century] (Sarajevo: Inst. za ist. u Sarajevo, 1981).

20. Castle Greben in northwestern Bosnia had been in Hungarian hands since 1358 but returned to Bosnia after 1382.

21. The bishop of Bosnia, in spite of his name, had his seat in the Hungarian town Diakovár/Djakovo ever since the foundation of the see in the thirteenth century. The other countries named here were traditionally listed in the Hungarian royal style (see above, n. to 1328, p. 160). The banate of Severin, founded ca. 1250, subsisted until the Ottoman conquest in 1524, but most of its former territory had become part of Walachia; see Sweeney, "Walachia-Moldavia," in *The Dictionary of the Middle Ages*, 12:505f.

22. The additions in brackets are taken from the later, extended version of the list; the sequence follows the format of the Propositions, but, for practical reasons, not its two-column arrangement. Typographical considerations suggested that the English translation be set in smaller type.

23. Not listed in the later list.

24. The special position of Pozsony, the major border towards the West is emphasized by this special arrangement; it is to be noted that the *ispán* of Pozsony is always included among the barons listed in the eschatocol of privileges.

25. It is unclear what is meant by *Turcia* here, unless it is a scribal error. A few years later, after the conclusion of the Hussite wars Sigismund organized a campaign against the Ottomans, together with a former Taborite captain, which was quite a symbolic success, but worthless in military terms; see Mályusz, *Sigismund*, p. 127.

26. The war with Venice was, as usual, about the control of Dalmatia. King Louis I had reasserted there Hungarian sovereignty (acknowledged by Venice in the Peace of Torino, 8 August 1381), but Venice recovered the towns between 1409 and 1420, and succeeded in holding them against Sigismund's attacks in 1410–13, 1418–20 and 1431–33. The Venetian annexation of the Patriarchate of Aquileia in 1420 widened the conflict, for that was imperial territory. Sigismund planned to break the Serenissima's resistance by a commercial blockade, but that, too, failed. The conflict ended with a long-term truce between Sigismund and Venice signed on 5 June 1433, on the worst possible terms for Hungary and the Empire: it left Dalmatia and Friuli in the hands of the Republic with no reparations in return. The kings of Hungary made no more attempts to regain their Adriatic foothold. See Mályusz, *Sigismund*, pp. 108–22.

GLOSSARY

abutter (*commetaneus*). The owner of land adjacent to another person's (or family's) estate. The testimony of abutters was given preference at common inquests (q.v.).

alispán [Pl. *alispánok*] (*vicecomes*). Deputy of the county's *ispán* (q.v.); from the 1300s usually a *familiaris* (q.v.) of the latter, president of the county court (*sedes iudiciaria*), administrative head of the noble county (q.v.), often castellan of the central castle in the county.

astatio falsi termini—see false court appearance.

bailiff, royal (*homo regius*). Nobleman from the same county, representing the king or a royal judge, when officiating, together with the witness of the chapter of authentication (q.v.) at *seisins* (q.v.), surveys of boundaries, and summons (q.v.). From ca. 1450, royal clerks were often commissioned as specially delegated royal bailiffs with powers more extensive than regular royal bailiffs.

ban (*banus*) 1. Viceroy governing the kingdom of Croatia and Dalmatia (part of the kingdom of Hungary since the early twelfth century), or the region called Slavonia (between the Drava and Sava Rivers). The military and political importance as well as the income of the ban was considerable.
2. Royal officer in charge of one or more of the territories ("banates") claimed and in parts (depending on the political and military strength of Hungary's southern neighbors) held by the kingdom south of the Sava River or at the lower Danube. These bans were members of the royal council, royal judges of their banates and, with the increase of the Ottoman threat in the fifteenth century, holders of crucial strategic positions.

banderium (from Italian *bandiera*: "banner") Military unit of 50-400 men, serving under the banner of the king, the queen, prelates, barons and great lords. This thirteenth-century arrangement remained in force until the end of the Middle Ages.

baron (*baro*). Collective term, from ca. 1230, for those lords who held national offices or positions at court (*veri barones*) and therefore enjoyed legal privileges. Barons holding honors (q.v.) were appointed by the king and held their office "during the king's pleasure," with complete civil and military authority in their province, and enjoying the revenues of the royal domains lying within it. Barons had the special privilege of commanding their retainers under their own banner (see - *banderium*). Bishops of the kingdom had the same prerogative, and were sometimes called "ecclesiastical barons." From the mid-fourteenth century the barons usually retained their title (*magnificus vir*) and privileges even after they left office, and from the mid-fifteenth century, great landowners were also granted this status, without having served in any office.

birsagium—see fine.

boundaries, inspection of (*reambulatio*). A landowner was entitled to request the inspection of the boundaries of his estate in company with a royal bailiff (q.v.) and the presence of abutters (q.v.) and neighbors. The chapter of authentication (q.v.) whose witness was also present described in writing the landmarks and boundaries in a letter of inspection (*litterae reambulatoriae*) and also whether any abutters and neighbors objected (*contradictio*). In the mid-fourteenth century specially delegated royal bailiffs (q.v.) were fully empowered to do such inspections.

bullatus. Clergy claiming an ecclesiastical benefice on the basis of papal grant (a "bull"); occasionally also used for papal collectors.

calumnia—see frivolous prosecution.

chancellor (*cancellarius*). From 1320 the Angevins had two chancellors. The chancellor of the royal court, usually an archbishop, was the keeper of the great or double seal of the realm. After 1376, he was styled "high chancellor" (*summus cancellarius*), his office became the major chancellery and he (or his deputy) the president of the court of the *specialis presentia regia* (q.v.). The keeper of the privy seal, called "secret chancellor," head of the royal chapel, came to lead, from 1376, the lesser chancellery, which became, in the late fourteenth century, an ever more important office, issuing significant decisions under the privy seal. With the exception of the period 1405-23, when Sigismund had lay secret chancellors, this office was also held by prelates. The queen's chancellor was usually the bishop of Veszprém.

capital punishment. Loss of life and property, in fact only one of the two, for this punishment included the ancient obligation of satisfaction: if the condemned person was executed, his estates were not confiscated, and vice versa. Sons of the condemned had to be given their part even in the case of confiscation. Royal pardon relieved the condemned from either death or confiscation.

castellan (*castellanus*). Royal (or seigneurial) officer in charge of a castle. Under the Angevin kings the royal castellans were powerful men, controlling the estates (appurtenances) of the castles, fulfilling economic, legal, and administrative functions. Some castellans controlled more than one castle or combined their office with that of a county *ispán* (q.v.).

chapters and convents of authentication (*loca credibilia*). Cathedral or collegiate chapters (*capitula*) and—mostly Benedictine and Premonstratensian—convents; from the thirteenth century they replaced in Hungary the notaries public of medieval Europe. They issued under their authentic seal documents about private legal transactions, and witnessed the actions of the royal bailiff (q.v.). In 1351, their number was reduced.

citatio cum insinuatione—see summons, terminal.

clan. Social unit of families who claimed patrilinear descent from a common ancestor and frequently held common legal, property, and religious interests. In Hungary, many clans founded their own monastery for burial and cultic purposes. The institutions and customs of the clan, especially division of property among male descendants, survived the transformation of nomadic tribes into settled communities. They were also taken over by western immigrants and families who rose into the nobility during the high Middle Ages.

combat, defeat in judicial (*succubitus duelli*). Judicial combat or duel, as a form of ordeal, survived in Hungary into the late Middle Ages, despite ecclesiastical protests. Until the fourteenth century, judges could order duels for major criminal cases (e.g., murder, arson); likewise for civil suits, where testimony conflicted. The duel was usually fought by semiprofessional champions. The defeated party was irrevocably convicted, and the losing of a civil suit or a case of violent trespass involved capital sentence (q.v.). The term "defeat in duel" (without fighting one) came to be used by chosen arbitrators, even private persons, as a sanction of contracts and similar transactions, implying that the party which would break it should be considered as though he had lost a case of violent trespass by duel.

comes camerae—see count of the chamber

comes palatinus—see palatine.

comes 1. *Ispán* (q.v.), head of a county;

2. Title ("count") given to men from families usually holding comital office, or of similar status.

3. Latin equivalent of the imperial or West European "count," "Graf."

comitatus—see county.

commetaneus—see abutter

composition (*homagium*). Remnant of the archaic system of justice in which composition replaced revenge: a monetary payment usually due for murder, the amount of which depended on the social status of the victim: the composition of barons was 100, of nobles 50 and of burghers 25 Marks.

congregatio, generalis—see diet.

congregatio, proclamata—see extraordinary county assembly.

council, royal. Usually an informal body of viceroys (bans [q.v.], voivode [q.v.]), major household officers and prelates who happened to be in the king's court; usually referred to as *prelati et barones*. More formal gatherings for the purpose of legislation, however, are also documented. The witnesses to royal charters of privilege or the list of names of spiritual and secular office-holders appended to diplomas (from c. 1270 to c. 1435—see "eschatocol," below) suggests the circle of men who probably belonged to the council.

count of the chamber (*comes camerae*). Responsible keepers of the *regalia*, such as mint, customs, precious metal and salt mines, appointed by the king or farming them from the crown; usually burghers. Until ca. 1376 they were subject to the jurisdiction of the Master of the Treasury (q.v.), afterwards to his independent deputy, the treasurer.

county (*comitatus*). The self-governing corporation, initially of lesser nobles called *servientes regis* that emerged after c. 1230 to serve in the self-defense of the lesser knights against powerful barons. Its elected officers (see—magistrate) and their regular assemblies became the main seats of local adminsitration and of justice. The deputies of the counties attended the national assemblies (q.v., s.v.: diet) called by the king.

courts of justice—see judge royal; justice ordinary; magistrate, Master of the Treasury; palatine; personal presence; special presence.

dicator—see tax collector.

diet (*diaeta, dieta*). From c. 1430, the meeting of the estates, probably with reference to their "set date." The expression remained the name of the noble assembly until the end of old Hungary.

eschatocol (from the Greek for "last glued," i.e., last attached piece of papyrus or parchment). The closing formulae of charters. Hungarian royal charters of privilege contained, from the late thirteenth century onward, a long list of ecclesiastical and secular office-holders, not as witnesses, but rather as an extended dating clause. They do not appear in the *decreta* after 1439, but during the interregnum and in some documents issued by the estates, a list of signatories or witnesses take their place.

estimation, judicial (*estimatio, aestimatio*). Estimate of the value of real and mobile property, usually on the traditional basis (*est. communis*), but occasionally a tenfold (*est. perennalis*) valuation for real estate was used.

exercitualis—see soldier.

extraodinary county assembly (*proclamata congregatio*). In major criminal cases, mainly violent trespass, the king often ordered such assemblies in which his delegate (from 1435 the county magistrate) called together the nobles of the county, in the presence of the parties, a witness of the chapter of authentication (q.v.) and a royal bailiff (q.v.), under the penalty of 3 Marks (q.v.) and examined them under oath.

false court appearance (*astatio falsi termini*). A serious delict committed by someone who appeared in court instead of another person (without a letter of advocacy, q.v.), summoned an adversary to a false term so as to mislead him and the court, and similar offenses of willfuly obstructing the administration of justice.

familiaris—see noble retainer.

famulus—see noble retainer.

ferto ("quarter," from the German *Viertel*). A quarter of a mark of silver, according to the different marks, c. 56-60 gr.

fine (*judicium*, or *birsagium*, from the Hungarian *bírság*=fine). Monetary fines paid by parties at law for missing some obligation or trespassing against rules. Fines were doubled in case of late payment. Two-thirds went to the judge, one-third to the opposing party.

florin (*florenus*,, Hung.: *forint*). Gold florins began to be minted under Charles I, c. 1325 (first mentioned in Moravia in 1326). They were modelled after the Florentine *fiorino d'oro* (hence the name) and their gold content was the same (3.52 g), but the coins were slightly heavier (3.56 g) because the alloy was less fine.

free village (*libera villa*). Those villages of *hospites*-settlers (q.v.) which were given either free royal city status in the thirteenth, or market (*oppidum*) status in the fourteenth century.

frivolous prosecution (*calumnia*). In contrast to its classical Roman legal meaning, Hungarian law used the term for unfounded litigation, useless vexation of the opposing party (*patvarkodás* in Hung.). Such offenses as prosecuting the same case in two different courts, acquiring satisfaction twice (*dupplex via*), claiming a due already settled (*dupplici sub colore*) were classified as *calumnia*. Anyone so convicted had to pay the composition (q.v.).

genus, generatio—see clan.

gentleman (gentlemen) of the realm (*regnicola*, Pl.: *regnicolae*). The term generally—but not exclusively—used for those inhabitants who as owners of land and lords of tenant peasants (q.v.), enjoyed political rights. As late as 1437, the term could also occasionally include peasants and free settlers, but came to be restricted to the noble estate in the later Middle Ages. (In *DRMH* 1, this term was translated as "landed resident/s.")

groat (*grossus*, Germ.: *Groschen*). A silver coin of good quality (with a fineness of "sixteenth firing," i.e., 0.9375), minted in Hungary from 1329 to 1338. 56 groats had then the value of one Buda mark (q.v.) Even after its minting was suspended, the term groat (Hung. : *garas*) remained in use for long as a money of account.

high treason (*nota infidelitatis*). Capital punishment (q.v.) meted out for crimes against the person of the king, the interests of the realm and certain other serious offenses (heresy, forgery and counterfeiting, violence against private persons and property).

homagium—see composition.

homo regius—see bailiff, royal.

honor (*honor*). Designation of different kinds of royal offices, of lesser and higher standing, granted "at the pleasure" of the ruler, i.e., for a limited, but not in advance specified, time. Honor was also the comprehensive term for those rights, estates and incomes which went with these offices. The holder of an honor was termed a baron (q.v.) .

hospes—see settler.

impignoratio—see security.

inquest, common (*inquisitio communis*). Procedure of material proof introduced by King Charles I in which abutters, neighbors and other nobles from the county (*comprovinciales*) swore an oath on their faith and "fidelity to the Holy Crown" regarding the truth of their testimony usually in matters of property rights. The inquest, as ordered by a higher court, had to be held where the disputed estate was located.

insinuatio—see *citatio cum insinuatione*.

installatio—see *seisin*.

iobagio—see tenant peasant.

ispán [Pl. *ispánok*] (*comes*, *c. parochialis*). The royal officer in charge of a (noble) county. With the development of the corporation of the noble county (q.v.), the *ispán* (later called *főispán*, in modern texts often translated as "lord lieutenant") exercised his office in concert with the county magistrates (q.v.) and left the daily administration to his noble retainer (q.v.), the *alispán* (q.v.). The title of perpetual *ispán* of their see's county was granted to several prelates, and in a few exceptional cases to secular barons (e.g., Hunyadi).

iudex Comanorum—see judge of the Cumans.

iudex curiae regis—see judge royal.

iudex nobilium—see magistrate.

iudex ordinarius —see justice ordinary.

ius regium—see right, royal.

judge of the Cumans (*iudex Cumanorum*). Chief justice of the Cumans, who had settled in Hungary in the mid-thirteenth century and remained privileged soldiering people until the late Middle Ages; the count palatine listed this office in his title from 1323.

judge royal (*iudex curiae regis*, Hung.: *országbíró*). After the palatine (q.v.) the second highest judge of the land, the king's deputy in matters of justice. The judge royal held a separate court in the royal *curia*, where he tried cases of the nobility. Some towns came to be subject to the judge royal's jurisdiction in the fourteenth century.

justice ordinary (*judex ordinarius*). Royal judge, who by his office was authorized to administer justice to free persons, in contrast to others who received such an authority by a definite commission. Usually the reference is to the king, the palatine (q.v.), the judge royal (q.v.), and (for burghers) the king's or the queen's Master of the Treasury (q.v.); in Transylvania the voivode (q.v.), in Croatia and the banates the ban (q.v.) had the same authority. Occasionally the laws use the expression for the judge of a specific case.

letter of advocacy (*litterae procuratoriae*). Any party was allowed to name his legal representative (*procurator*) at a chapter of authentication (q.v.) and empower him to act in all stages of the litigation. (Minors were represented by their guardians without written powers.) The person so specified identified himself with a letter of advocacy.

letter of complaint, royal (*litterae querimoniales regales*). Royal mandate specifying the complaint for initiating a suit and ordering an extraordinary county assembly (q.v.).

letter of final summons (*litterae proclamatoriae*). If a party failed to appear after five (later three) summons, the judge could order that the summons be announced at the weekly fair held in three places in the county (usually on three consecutive days) (*trineforensis proclamatio*).

letter of protest (*litterae prohibitoriae et protestatoriae*). A party suffering legal wrong (e.g., in connection with the establishment of boundaries, at a *seisin* (q.v.)) could protest and contradict either on the spot, in the presence of his opponent (*facie ad faciem*) or at a chapter of authentication (q.v.), about which such a record would be issued. This letter would prohibit any person from granting, selling, mortgaging or damaging the property in any way.

letter of record (*litterae fassionales*). Record of any declaration (*fassio*= "confession") made in a legal matter at a chapter of authentication (q.v.).

letter of *seisin* (*litterae statutoriae*). Record by a place of authentication about the installation, in the presence of a royal bailiff (q.v.), of a new grantee (or purchaser) into an estate. As a rule, the grantee was obligated to take *seisin* and procure such a letter within a year from the grant's date, lest he forfeit his claim.

letter of sentence (*litterae sententionales*). The legal record of a final sentence in a trial.

letter of summons (*litterae evocatoriae*). Mandate (*mandatum evocatorium*) sent by the king or a royal justice to a chapter of authentication (q.v.) ordering that a designated royal bailiff (q.v.) should summon a certain plaintiff in the case raised by him to a given term, usually the next octavial court (q.v.). The summons had to be delivered at the nobleman's residence (*locus solitae residentiae*), or in his absence handed to his steward or a tenant. If the party failed to appear, he was summoned five

more times. (Thus, in the fourteenth century; later only twice more.) See also: summons, terminal.

libera villa—see free village.

litterae evocatoriae—see letter of summons.

litterae fassionales—see letter of record.

litterae proclamatoriae—see letter of final summons.

litterae procuratorie—see letter of advocacy.

litterae prohibitoriae—see letter of protest.

litterae querimoniales regales—see letter of complaint.

litterae reambulatoriae—see boundaries.

litterae sententionales—see letter of sentence.

litterae statutoriae—see letter of *seisin.*

loca credibilia—see chapters.

lords (*proceres*). Our translation for the elusive term used in the later fourteenth and early fifteenth century for those prestigious nobles who participated in the administration of the realm. Their title in the fourteenth century was *strenuus miles*, later *egregius vir/miles* Some historians tend to identify this group with the similarly elusive stratum of "knights."

magister tave[a]rnicorum—see Master of the Treasury.

magistrate, noble (*judex nobilium, judex servientium*, hence Hung.: *szolga-bíró*=judge of servitors). One of the elected (usually four) judges and administrative officers of a noble county (q.v.) with responsibilities in a defined quarter of the county.

mark. A measure of silver, often the unit of fines. A Buda mark in the fourteenth-fifteenth centuries was 245.54 gr.

Master of the Treasury (*magister tavernicorum*). The title of the chamberlain, originally responsible for the king's finances, derived from the Hungarian name of the guards of royal magazines of the early Middle Ages (*tárnok*); from ca. 1376, presiding judge of the court treating the cases of major royal cities (*sedes tavernicalis*), when the treasurer supervised royal finances.

mining dues—see *urbura.*

noble retainer (*familiaris, famulus*). A lesser nobleman who chose (or, occasionally, was forced) to accept military or administrative positions in the service of a baron or a major landowner; he retained his noble privilege and was subject to his senior (*dominus*) only for service, for which he received monetary compensation (occasionally land). He was obliged to escort his lord, to supervise his affairs, to govern his domains and, to perform military service under his banner. The institution resembled superficially West European vassallage, but was less formalized, less mutual, and was not passed on to descendants.

nobleman (*nobilis*). By the mid-fourteenth century almost all landowners were regarded as nobles and claimed the privileges guaranteed in the Golden Bulls of 1222 and 1231, originally granted to magnates; the nobles enjoyed freedom from taxation in return for military service.

nota infidelitatis—see high treason.

notary (*notarius*). In Hungarian-Latin usage: scribe; scribes were clergy in the royal chancellery from its beginnings in the thirteenth century; in the

counties they were first members of the *ispán*'s retinue, from the fourteenth century secular employees; in the chapters of authentication (q.v.) secular persons were in charge of the writing office from the mid-fourteenth century onward. Town notaries were always urban employees and laymen.

novelty (*novitas*), also specified as "new seizure" "recent violent act" (*nova occupatio, potentia*, and so on). A general negative term for trespasses against customary possessions or rights. Gradually this word became something of a technical term, comparable to medieval French *nouvelleté*, meaning usurpation or seizure of estates in detriment to the rightful owner or heir. (While in essence similar to the English legal concept of *novel disseisin*, it does not seem to have been as clearly defined; hence, we found it inappropriate to translate it thus.)

octavial court (*octava*). Royal courts of justice were in session usually four times annually, beginning on or around the eighth day of major feasts (such as St. George's Day, St. James's, Michaelmas, Epiphany) and lasting 30-40 or more days. In the fourteenth century the courts often met a fortnight after the "return of the general levy" (*descensus* or *residentia exercitus*).

palatine, count palatine (*comes palatinus*). The highest officer of the kingdom, the ruler's deputy, commander of the royal host, highest judge (mostly itinerant) of the nobility, judge of the Cumans (q.v.) and ex-officio *ispán* of Co. Pest. The palatines were among the closest followers of the king and came from the greatest magnate families.

personalis presentia regia, court of royal personal presence. After the establishment of the *specialis praesenti regia* (q.v.) this was the name of the late medieval version of the itinerant royal court. Summons were issued to appear wherever the king and his court might be. Until ca. 1430 all cases of political import were decided in this supreme court. In 1435 this court was abolished, and its name transferred to a permanent high court sitting in Buda.

pondus. A measure of weight of silver, being one-twelfth of a *ferto* (q.v.); in Buda the *pondus* was c. 5.12 gr. According to the cameral contract of 1342 its value was equivalent to a groat (q.v.).

porta. Basic unit of the direct tax introduced in 1336 by Charles I, originally identical with a tenant's holding, the unit of seigneurial dues (*porta seu mansio*). Later, other taxes, such as the war tax (*subsidium*), were also levied on the *porta*.

potentia—see violent trespass.

prefectio in filium—see son's right, grant of.

proceres—see lords.

proclamata congregatio—see extraordinary county assembly.

proscription (*proscriptio*). A list of criminals (*publici malefactores*): e.g., thieves, forgers and counterfeiters) compiled by the county assemblies where the palatine (q.v.) usually presidied, later by the magistrates with twelve elected jurors. Criminals failing to appear were proscribed according to Roman practice (i.e., their properties, and sometimes their lives, were forfeit).

reeve (*villicus* or *vilicus*). Elected head of the villagers, judge of the first

instance and representative of the tenant peasants (q.v.) at the assessment and levy of taxes and tithes.

regnicola ("inhabitant of the kingdom") —see gentleman of the realm. In rare cases the word seems to have been used in the literal sense meaning all inhabitants of the kingdom or "residents," in contrast to "foreigners."

regnum ("kingdom," "realm," Hung.: *ország*). Used not only in the general sense denoting the area of the kingdom or the complex rights of the ruler, but also referring in particular to the king's council or (from c. 1440) to the estates.

rent (*terragium*). Ground rent payed in coin by the tenant peasant (q.v.) for his plot held in perpetual lease; the most important part of seigneurial dues in the fourteenth and fifteenth centuries.

right, royal (*ius regium*) comprised, apart from the royal demesne proper, any estate which, though actually not possessed by the king, was supposed or claimed to belong to him. It was extended to estates held by royal grant which, therefore, were to escheat to the crown if no male heir was apparent. From the 1370s onward, actions were moved by or in the name of the crown against persons accused of "hiding royal rights" (*celatores iurium regalium*) i.e., allegedly usurping a royal estate.

security, pledge (*impignoratio*). Landowning nobles frequently pledged all or part of their estates to their creditors, retaining possession, while the income belonged to the creditor. Such pledging could also be ordered by a judge for the benefit of a plaintiff entitled to satisfaction or in matrimonial suits (dowry, filial quarter [q.v.]). The contract of pledge was to be authenticated by a chapter or convent (q.v.). Relatives had preemptory rights to securities. The creditor had full rights to the usufruct of the pledged property and could pledge it further but had to return it at a set date (32 years was the usual maximum term). This practice basically followed the Roman legal institution of *pignoratio* and *antichresis*.

seisin (*introductio* or *statutio*) was the formality required to validate the acquisition of property. Grantees of royal donations or new owners of purchased, inherited, exchanged or divided estates were expected to take *seisin* within a year, with the assistance of a royal bailiff (q.v.) specified in the charter, witnessed by a specified chapter or convent of authentication (q.v.) in the presence of abutters (q.v.) and neighbors. *Seisin* could be thwarted by anyone within the estate, who made a *contradictio*, i.e., opposed the execution. Moreover, any interested party could object to the *seisin* by announcing his protest (*prohibitio*) within two weeks and thus initiating a lawsuit. (See also letter of *seisin*, letter of protest, above.)

settler (*hospes*). Originally used for all foreigners who came to the kingdom, from the late thirteenth century, also those personally free peasants who enjoyed liberties similar to peasants from abroad regardless of their ethnic origin—those styled in the fourteenth century tenant peasants (q.v.). Thereafter, urban dwellers were so called, frequently in the combination *cives et hospites*.

soldier (*exercitualis*). Any member of the general levy, regardless of the arrangement of his service, i.e., whether noble retainer, professional soldier or a freeman obligated to personal military duties.

son's right, grant of (*prefectio in filium in heredem masculinum*, Hung.: *fiú-*

sítás) Beginning in the 1330s, the Angevin kings dispensed a new privilege in which they "promoted" the daughter (or daughters) of a nobleman, deceased without male heir in the third (after 1397 fourth) degree, to a son, i.e., they authorized her to inherit the paternal fortune just as if she were a son. The purpose was to favor nobles who served at court, both those without sons and those wishing to marry daughters so privileged. The privilege, once granted, descended in the female line.

specialis presentia regia, royal court of special presence. The central court of justice that developed, in the fourteenth century, for persons and institutions granted the privilege of being judged only before the king. From 1376 to 1429 (and again from 1453 to 1464) this court was presided over by the (arch)chancellor and passed sentences under his or the vice-chancellor's seal. Its judges were among the first legally-trained professionals in a royal court.

succubitus duelli—see combat.

summons, terminal (*citatio cum insinuatione*). In the fourteenth century third summons were often issued with the clause that judgment would be passed regardless of the appearance of the party cited; in the fifteenth this clause was frequently included in the first summons. This kind of summons was issued particularly against violent trespassers (q.v.).

tax collector (*dicator*). An officer (usually a nobleman or burgher) sent by the treasurer or a count of the chamber to an administrative unit, who, together with the delegate of that unit (in the counties with the magistrate, q.v.) assessed and collected the direct tax (*dica*, see *porta*). The tithe-collector of a prelate (*decimator*) was often also called *dicator*.

t(h)elonium—see toll.

tenant peasant (*iobagio*, Hung.: *jobbágy*). Peasant with personal liberty, bound to the lord of the land by having to render dues in kind, in money (see—rent) and, rarely, in labor. Tenants were free to move, but subject to seigneurial jurisdiction. In the late Middle Ages tenants' liberty, achieved in the thirteenth-fourteenth centuries, was restricted in favor of service, but not replaced by hereditary servitude until the sixteenth century.

term, judicial (*terminus*)—see octavial court.

terragium—see rent.

thirtieth (*tricesima*). A royal duty levied on trade, fixed by Charles I to 1 percent of the imported and exported value, increased to a true thirtieth (3.33 percent) around 1380-1400, when it took the form of a customs duty, levied at the frontier gates.

toll, internal (*t(h)elonium*). Payment collected on the basis of custom or royal license from merchants at fairs or for the passage by bridge or ferry in ratio to the value of the goods transported. In the fifteenth century distinction was made between tolls at fairs (*tributum fori*), at ferries (*portus*) and "dry tolls" (*th. terrestrium, siccum*), collected on certain roads. Initially tolls were attached to royal castles and shared by king and *ispán*. By the fifteenth century most of them were in private hands, granted them by the crown. Clergy, burghers, and nobles enjoyed full or partial exempiton from all internal tolls.

tricesima—see thirtieth.

udvarnok (Pl. *udvarnokok*, from Hung. *udvar*, "court," also Latinized as

udvo[a]rnicus). Originally unfree peasants on scattered settlements attached to the royal court, who remained servitors of special standing. Such people living on royal estates are mentioned until the late fourteenth century as being subject to their own *ispán* and exempt from certain taxes (chamber's profit, tithe) which were originally levied only on free men. However, we know close to nothing about their exact legal status, duties, or organization after the decline of the servile system.

urbura. The king's portion from the mining of precious metals which amounted to 1/10 for gold and 1/8 for silver; one-third of the dues went to the owner of the land over the mine.

vice-chancellor (*vicecancellarius*). The vice-chancellor of the royal court was, after 1320 (except between 1356-71) the head of the writing office, the chancellery of the great seal; until 1351, the post was always held by the provost of Székesfehérvár, later also by other lesser prelates.

vicecomes—see *alispán*.

villicus—see reeve.

violent trespass (*potentia, factum potentiae*). Delicts, committed by noblemen, against persons and property in a violent manner; in the late Middle Ages distinction was made between "major" and "minor" acts of violent trespass for which precise judicial procedures were prescribed, including judicial combat.

voivode. (Probably of Slavic derivation.) From 1199, viceroy of Transylvania; also used of the rulers of Wallachia and Moldavia.

CHRONOLOGY

General	Legal-administrative
1301 (May) Charles I of Anjou-Sicily's first coronation as king of Hungary (ruled until 1342)	
1301–05 Wenceslas-Ladislas of Bohemia king of Hungary	
1305–07 Otto of Lower Bavaria (Wittelsbach) king of Hungary	
1307 Charles acclaimed king at the diet, second coronation	
1310 Third coronation of Charles I	
1312 Battle of Rozgony	
1317 Defeat of Borsa Kopasz	1318 Diet, no decree survived
	ca. 1320 Decree on collecting fines
1321 Defeat of Matthew Csák	
1322 Fall of Subić	
1323 Charles moves royal residence to Visegrád	1324, 1328 Decrees on oath-taking
1326 Hungarian gold florins first mentioned	1327 Charles grants mining rights to landowners
1328 Foundation of Körmöcbánya	
1330 Attempt on the life of the royal family by Felician Záh	1332–37 Papal tithe lists compiled
1335 Hungarian–Czech–Polish–Prussian congress in Visegrád	1335–45 Cameral contracts between Angevin kings and counts of the chamber
	1336 *Lucrum camerae* becomes direct tax
1342–82 Louis I of Anjou, king of Hungary	
1345 Murder of Prince Andrew in Naples	
1347–48 First Neapolitan campaign	
1349 Black Death reaches Hungary	
1350 Second Neapolitan campaign	1351 Dec. 11: Louis I's only decree confirming the Golden Bull

1358 Peace of Zara: Dalmatia returned to Hungary	
1359 Second wave of plague	
1370(–82) Louis I king of Poland	
	1376 (–1429) Court of special royal presence, chaired by the arch-chancellor, established 1376 Master of Treasury becomes head of appellate court for royal free cities
1382 (–98) Mary of Anjou queen of Hungary	1384 Mary confirms the Golden Bull
1385 Charles II of Durazzo-Naples, king of Hungary	1385 Diet with deputies; general renewal of noble liberties 1386 Barons' decree attempting to settle civil war with Horváti party
1387–1437 Sigismund of Luxemburg king of Hungary	
1390 Beginning of Ottoman raids against Hungarian territory	
1396 Defeat of Crusaders at Nicopolis	1397 Temesvár diet passes decree with renewal of Golden Bull and military reform
1401 Conspiracy against Sigismund	
1403 Ladislas of Durazzo claims Hungary; baronial revolt against Sigismund	1403 Letter of pardon for the rebels (1404 additional measures about amnesty) 1404, Apr. 6: Decree ("Placetum regium") 1405, Apr. 15: Decree about cities
1408 Foundation of the Order of the Dragon	
1410 (1411)-37 Sigismund as Holy Roman emperor	
1410–13 First war with Venice for Dalmatia 1414–18 Council of Constance	1411 Decree on collection of taxes
1418–20 Second war with Venice over Dalmatia	
1420 Sigismund crowned king of Bohemia (entry to Prague 1436)	1421, July 23: Decree on local administration of justice
1420–34 Hussite wars including raids into Northern Hungary (1428–33)	

1427 Belgrade ceded to Hungary	1427, March 17: Decrees: about damages connected with general levy and new rate of exchange
	1432/33 Sigismund's proposal for military reform ("Siena Register")
1433 Truce with Venice. Dalmatia lost to Hungary	1435, March 8: "Decretum maius" March 12: Decree on military service
1437–38 Rural rising in Transylvania	
1437–39 Albert I of Habsburg. king of Hungary (and Bohemia, emperor 1438–39)	
	1439, May 29: Decree altering coronation promises (of 18 Dec. 1437) in favor of lesser nobles Sept. 17: Council decree about anti-Ottoman campaign
1440–44 Wladislas I (Jagiello), king of Hungary (and Poland)	1440, July 20: Coronation decree with renewal of Golden Bull and laws of Andrew III
	1443 Council decree against violent trespassers
1440–57 Ladislas V (Postumus) of Habsburg, king of Hungary	
1443–44 "Long campaign" on the Balkans	
1444 Nov. 10 Battle of Varna	
	1445, May 7: Dietal decree about royal succession and the keeping of the peace
1446–53 János Hunyadi regent of Hungary	1446, March 25: repetition of regent's electoral decree, arrangements for regency council
1448 Second Battle of Kosove Polje	
	1453, Jan. 29: Ladislas' decree about regaining government in Hungary
	1453 Re-establishment of the court of special royal presence (-1464)
	1454 Last extant decree of Ladislas
1456 Siege and relief of Belgrade. Death of Hunyadi and Capestrano	
1457 (23 Nov.) Ladislas V dies in Prague	

CONCORDANTIA
CONCORDANCE

This table compares the article numbers of this edition (*DRMH II*) with those of older editions whenever differences exist.

21 Decembris 1404

MTvt/CJH	*DRH 1301–1457/DRMH II*
I-VIII	Pr.
IX	I
X	II
XI	III
XII-XIV	IV
XV-XVII	V
XVIII–XX	VI–VIII

8 Martii 1435

MTvt/CJH	*DRH 1301–1457/DRMH II*
I	I
II-III	II
IV	III
V	IV-V
VI–XVII	VI–XVII
XVIII-XX	XVIII
XXI	XIX
XXII	XX
XXIII	XXI
XXIV	XXII-Esch.

12 Martii 1435

MTvt/CJH	*DRH 1301–1457/DRMH II*
Pr.	Pr.-I
I	I
II-IV	II
V–X	III–VIII

29 Maii 1439

MTvt/CJH	*DRH 1301–1457/DRMH II*
I–XXIX	I–XXIX
XXX-XXXI	XXX

XXXII	XXXI
XXXIII-XXXVII	XXXII
XXXVIII	XXXIII
XXXIX	XXXIV

18 Aprili 1439

MTvt/CJH	*DRH 1301–1457/DRMH II*
I–XVI	I–XVI
XXVII-XXVIII	XVII
XIX	XVIII
XX	XIX
XXI-XXII	XX
XXIII–XXXIV	XXI–XXXII

13 Junii 1446

Kovachich *Sylloge*	*DRH 1301–1457/DRMH II*
I	I
II-III	II
IV–VII	III–VI
VIII-IX	VII
X–XVI	VIII–XIV

25 Martii 1446

Kovachich *Suppl.*	Kovachich *Sylloge*	*DRH 1301–1457/DRMH II*
XV–XX	I–VI	I–VI
XXI-XXII	VII-VIII	VII
XXIII-XXIV	IX-X	VIII
XXV–XXXVI	XI–XXII	IX–XX
XXXVII-XXXVIII	XXXIII-XXIV	XXI
XXXIX–LII	XXV–XXXVIII	XXII–XXXV
LIII-LIV	XXXIX-XL	XXXVII
LV	XLI	XXXVIII
LVI-LVII	XLII-XLIII	XXXIX
LVIII-LIX	XLIV-XLV	XL
LX	XLVI	XLI
LXI	XLVII	XXXVI

25 Januarii 1454

MTvt/CJH	*DRH 1301–1457/DRMH II*
I–XV	I–XV
XVI-Esch.	Esch.

2 Februarii 1342 in Appendice

MTvt/CJH	*DRH 1301–1457/DRMH II*
I	Pr.
II–VII	I–VI
VIII-XI	VII
X–XIII	VIII–XI
XIV-XV	XII
XVI	XIII
XVII-XVIII	XIV
XIX-XX	XV
XXI–XXVI	XVI–XXI
XXVII-XXVIII	XXII
XXIX–XXX	XXIII–XXIV
XXXI-XXXII	XXV
XXXIII–XXXVIII	XXVI–XXXI
XXIX-XL	XXXII
XLI	XXXIII
XLII-XLIII	XXXIV
XLIV-XLV	XXXV
XLVI-XLVII	XXXVI
XLVIII–LI	XXXVII–XL
LII-LIII	XLI

[1432/1433] in Appendice

Kovachich *Suppl.*	*DRH 1301–1457/DRMH II*
Pr.-I	I
II-V	II
VI	III
VII	IV
VIII-IX	V
X–XII	VI–VIII
XIII	IX-X
XIV–XVI	XI–XII
XVII-XIX	XIV
XX-XXII	XV
XXIII–XXV	XVI–XVIII
XXVI-XXVII	XIX
XXVIII	XX
XXIX-XXX	XXI
XXXI-XXXII	XXII
XXXIII	XXIII
XXXIV-XXXVI	XXIV

SELECT BIBLIOGRAPHY

This bibliography contains those titles, referred to in the critical apparatus (Introduction, Notes), which are relevant to fourteenth-fifteenth century Hungarian institutional and legal history. Generally, titles referred to more than once have been included, but not those which were adduced merely for comparative or explanatory purposes. The editors made every effort to list all relevant foreign-language publications. Readers familiar with the Hungarian language will find extensive bibliographies on these subjects in the standard reference works on Hungarian history.

Bak, J. M. "Hungary," in *Dictionary of the Middle Ages*. 6. New York: Scribner, 1985, pp. 337–51.

———. *Königtum und Stände in Ungarn im 14.-15. Jahrhundert*. Wiesbaden: Steiner, 1973.

———. "Monarchie im Wellental: Materielle Grundlagen des ungarischen Königtums im späteren Mittelalter," in R. Schneider, ed. *Das spätmittelalterliche Königtum im europäischen Vergleich*. Sigmaringen: Thorbecke, 1987, pp. 347–87.

———. "Sankt Stefans Armreliquie im Ornat König Wenzels von Ungarn," in *Festschrift Percy Ernst Schramm zu seinem siebzigsten Geburtstag von Schülern und Freunden zugeeignet*, P. Scheibert, C. P. Classen, eds. Wiesbaden: Steiner, 1964, vol.1, pp. 175–88.

———, and B. K. Király, eds. *From Hunyadi to Rákóczi: War and Society in Medieval and Early Modern Hungary*. Brooklyn, N.Y.: Social Science Monographs, 1982.

Bard, I. N. "Aristocratic Revolts and the Late Medieval Hungarian State A.D. 1382–1408." Ph. D. dissertation, Univ. of Washington, 1978.

Bartal, A. *Glossarium mediae et infimae latinitatis Regni Hungariae*. Budapest: Franklin, 1901; repr. Hildesheim-New York: Olms, 1970.

Batthyány, I. *Leges ecclesiasticae regni Hungariae et provinciarum adjacentium*. 3 volumes. Alba-Carolina: Typis episcopalibus, 1785–1827.

Bernath, M., ed. *Historische Bücherkunde Südosteuropa*. München: Oldenbourg, 1980.

Bertényi, I. "Die städtischen Bürger und das Gericht der königlichen Anwesenheit im 14. Jahrhundert." *AUSBp, Sect. hist.*, 11 (1970), 3–31.

Biographisches Lexikon zur Geschichte Südosteuropas. M. Bernath *et al.*, eds. 4 volumes. München: Oldenbourg, 1974–81.

Bónis, Gy. *A jogtudó értelmiség a Mohács előtti Magyarországon* [Professionals Learned in the Law in Pre-Mohács Hungary]. Bp.: Akadémiai K., 1971.

———. "A Somogyvári Formuláskönyv," in *Emlékkönyv Kelemen Lajos születésének 80. évfordulójára* [Festschrift for the Eightieth Birthday of L. Kelemen] (Bucharest: Tudományos K., 1957) pp. 117–33.

Bónis, Gy. *Die Einflüsse der römischen Rechts in Ungarn*. Ius Romanum Medii Aevi V, 10. Milano: Giuffre, 1964.

———. "Die Entwicklung der geistlichen Gerichstbarkeit in Ungarn vor 1526." *Zeitschrift der Savigny-Stiftung für Rechtsgeschichte*, 80, Kanonistische Abteilung 49 (1963), 174–235.

———. *Hűbériség és rendiség a középkori magyar jogban* [Feudalism and Corporatism in Medieval Hungarian Law]. Kolozsvár: Erdélyi Tudományos Intézet, n.d. [1947].

———. *Középkori jogunk elemei: Római jog, kánonjog, szokásjog* [Elements of Our Medieval Law: Roman Law, Canon Law, and Customary Law]. Bp.: Közgazdasági K., 1972.

———. "Men Learned in the Law in Medieval Hungary." *East Central Europe/L'Europe de centre-est*, 4, pt. 1 (1977), 181–91.

———. "Petrus de Vinea leveleskönyve Magyarországon," [The Letter-Book of P. de V. in Hungary]. *Filológiai Közlöny* 4 (1958), 1–26, 73–193.

———. "Ständisches Finanzwesen in Ungarn im frühen 16. Jahrhundert." *Nouvelles études historiques publiées à l'occasion du XIIe Congrès International des Sciences Historiques*. (Bp.: Akadémiai K., 1965) 1: 83–103.

———. "The Hungarian Feudal Diet (13th to 18th Centuries)." *Receuils de la Société Jean Bodin pour l'histoire comparative des institutions*, 25 (1965), 287–307.

———. "Uzsai János Ars Notariaja" [The Ars Notaria of J. Uzsai]. *Filológiai Közlöny*, 7 (1961), 229–60.

Budapest története [History of Budapest]. L. Gerevich, ed. 5 volumes. Budapest: Fővárosi Tanács, 1973–80.

Csánki, D. [and A. Fekete Nagy] *Magyarország történeti földrajza a Hunyadiak korában*. [Historical Geography of Hungary in the Era of the Hunyadis]. 5 volumes. Bp.: MTA, 1896–1941; repr. Bp.: ÁKV, 1985.

Dąbrowski, J. *Ostatnie lata Ludwika Wielkiego 1370–1382* [The Last Years of Louis the Great]. Kraków: Akad. Umiejtnośći, 1918.

Deér, J. *A magyar nemzeti öntudat kialakulása* [Development of Hungarian National Consciuosness]. Bp.: J. Deér, n.d. [1936]

———. *Die Heilige Krone Ungarns*. Graz: Böhlaus Nachf., 1966.

———. "Le sentiment national hongrois au moyen âge." *Nouvelle Revue de Hongrie* 19 (1936) 411–19.

———. "Zsigmond király honvédelmi politikája" [Defense Policies of King Sigismund]. *Hadtörténelmi Közelmények*, 37 (1936), 1–57, 169–202.

Die Denkwürdigkeiten der Helene Kottanerin. K. Mollay, ed., Wien: Bundesverlag, 1971.

Długosz, Jan *Historiae Poloniae libri XX*. A. Przezdziecki, ed. Kraków: Kirchmayer, 1873–78.

Domanovszky, S. *A harminczadvám eredete* [Origins of the Thirtieth-Toll]. Bp.: MTA, 1916.

———. *A szepesi városok árúmegállító joga* [The Right of Staple of the Cities of Szepes]. Bp.: MTA, 1922.

———. *Gazdaság és társadalom a középkorban* [Economy and Society in the Middle Ages]. Bp.: Gondolat, 1979.

Dőry, F., Bónis, Gy., Bácskai, V., eds. *Decreta regni Hungariae: Gesetze und Verordnungen Ungarns 1301–1447*. Bp.: Akadémiai K., 1978.

Dőry, F., Bónis, Gy., Érszegi, G., Teke, Zs., eds. *Decreta regni Hungariae: Gesetze und Verordnungen Ungarns 1448–1490.* Bp.: Akadémiai K., 1990.

Eckhart, F. "Alkotmánytörténet" [Constitutional History], in *A magyar történetírás új útjai* [New Trends in Hungarian History Writing]. B. Hóman, ed. Bp.: Egyetemi Nyomda, 1931, pp. 269–320.

———. *A szentkorona-eszme története* [History of the Idea of the Holy Crown]. Bp.: MTA, 1941.

———. "Die glaubwürdigen Orte Ungarns im Mittelalter." *MIÖG*, Ergänzungsband 9 (1913/15), 395–558.

———. *Magyar alkotmány- és jogtörténet* [History of Hungarian law and constitution]. Bp.: Politzer, 1946.

Engel, P. "A 14. századi magyar pénztörténet néhány kérdése" [Some Questions of Fourteenth-century Hungarian Monetary History]. *Száz.*, 123 (1989), [forthc.].

———. "A honor. (A magyarországi feudális birtokformák kérdéséhez)" [The *Honor:* Questions Regarding Feudal Property in Hungary]. *Történelmi Szemle*, 34 (1981), 1–19.

———. "Honor, vár, ispánság: Tanulmányok az Anjou-királyság kormányzati rendszeréről" [*Honor*, Castle, *Ispán*: Studies on the Governmental System of the Angevin Monarchy]. *Száz.*, 116 (1982), 880–922, French summary p. 922.

———. *Királyi hatalom és arisztokrácia viszonya a Zsigmond-korban* [Relationship of Royal Power and Aristocracy under Sigismund]. Bp.: Akadémiai K., 1977.

———. "Ozorai Pipo," in *Ozorai Pipo emlékezete* [In Memory of Pipo of Ozora] F. Vadas, ed., Szekszárd: Béri Balogh Múzeum, 1987, pp. 53–88.

Fahlbusch, F. B. *Städte und Königtum im frühen 15. Jahrhundert. Ein Beitrag zur Geschichte Sigmunds von Luxemburg.* Köln-Wien: Böhlau, 1983. pp. 39–48.

Fejér, G. *Codex diplomaticus Hungariae ecclesiasticus ac civilis.* 11 volumes in 43 parts. Buda: Regia Univesitas, 1829–44.

Fine, J. V. A., Jr. *The Late Medieval Balkans: A Critical Survey from the Late Twelfth Century to the Ottoman Conquest.* Ann Arbor: The University of Michigan Press [1987].

Fraknói, V. *A magyar királyi kegyúri jog Szt. Istvántól Mária Tereziáig* [The Right of Hungarian Royal Patronage from St. Stephen to Maria Teresa]. Bp.: MTA, 1895.

Fügedi, E. *Castle and Society in Medieval Hungary (1000–1437)* transl. J. M. Bak . Bp.: Akadémiai K., 1986.

———. "Die Ausbreitung der städtischen Lebensform—Ungarns *oppida* im 14. Jahrhundert," in *Stadt und Stadtherr im 14. Jh.* W. Rausch, ed. Linz: Wimmer, 1972, pp. 165–92, repr. in *Kings* as ch. 13.

———. *Kings, Bishops, Nobles and Burghers in Medieval Hungary.* J. M. Bak, ed. London: Variorum Reprints (CS 229), 1986.

———. "Királyi tisztség vagy hűbér?" [Royal Office or Fief?] *Történelmi Szemle* 25 (1982), 438–509.

Fügedi, E. *Kolduló barátok, polgárok, nemesek* [Mendicant Friars, Burghers, Nobles]. Bp.: Magvető, 1981.

———. "Középkori magyar városprivilégiumok" [Medieval Hungarian Urban Privileges]. *Tanulmányok Budapest múltjából*, 15 (1959), 81–104, repr. in his *Kolduló barátok* pp. 238–310.

———. "The *avus* in the Medieval Conceptual Framework of Kinship in Hungary." *Studia Slavica Acad. Sc. Hung.* 25 (1979), 137–42, repr. in Fügedi, *Kings*, as ch. 4.

———. "Tourniere im mittelalterlichen Ungarn," in *Das ritterliche Turnier im Mittelalter.*, J. Fleckenstein, ed. Göttingen: Vandekhoek & Ruprecht, 1986, pp. 390–400.

Gábor, Gy. *A megyei intézmény kialakulása és működése Nagy Lajos alatt* [Development and Functions of the County under Louis the Great]. Bp.: Grill, 1908.

———. *A kormányzói méltóság a magyar alkotmányjogban* [The Dignity of Regent in Hungarian Constitutional Law]. Bp.: Athenaeum, n.d. [1932].

Gerics, J. "Krónikáink szerepe a középkori jogéletben" [The Role of our Chronicles in Medieval Legal Life]. *Levéltári Közlemények*, 33 (1962), 3–12 [French summary, pp. 13–14].

Glossarium mediae et infimae latinitatis ... conditum a Carolo Du Fresne domino Du Cange. G. A. L. Henschel, ed. 4 volumes. Paris: Didot, 1846–50.

Györffy, Gy. "A jászság betelepülése," in his *A magyarság keleti elemei* [Oriental Elements of the Hungarian People]. Bp.: Gondolat K., 1990, pp. 312–15.

Hajnik, I. *A magyar bírósági szervezet és perjog az Árpád- és a vegyesházi királyok alatt* [The Hungarian Judicial System and Procedural Law under the Kings of the Árpád and Diverse Dynasties]. Bp.: MTA, 1899.

———. "Az 1387. évi székesfehérvári 'országgyűlés' cikkelyei" [The articles of the Székesfehérvár "Diet" of 1387.]. *Történelmi Tár* (1878), 173–76.

———. *A zsidók Magyarországon a vegyes házakbeli királyok alatt* [The Jews in Hungary under the Kings of Diverse Dynasties]. Bp.: Emich, 1866.

Halecki, O. *Jadwiga of Anjou and the Rise of East Central Europe*, T. V. Gromada, ed. Boulder, Co.-Highland Lakes, NJ.: Social Science Monographs-Atlantic Research and Publications, 1991.

Handbuch der europäischen Geschichte. Th. Schieder, ed. 7 volumes. Stuttgart: Klett, 1976–87.

Handbuch der Quellen und Literatur der neueren europäischen Privatrechtsgeschichte. H. Coing, ed. München: Beck, 1973.

Hay, D. *Europe in the Fourteenth and Fifteenth Centuries.* 2nd ed. London: Longman, 1988.

Held, J. *Hunyadi: Legend and Reality* Boulder, Co.: East European Monographs, 1985.

———. "Military Reform in Early Fifteenth Century Hungary." *East European Quarterly*, 11/2 (1977), 129–39.

Holub, J. "A főispán és alispán viszonyának jogi természete" [Legal Character of the Relationship Between *comes* and *vicecomes*. Contributions to the County Administration in the Middle Ages], in *Fejérpataky Emlékkönyv* [F. Festschrift]. (Bp.: Franklin, 1917), pp. 186–211.

———. "La représentation politique en Hongrie au Moyen Age," in *Études présentés à la Commission Internationale pour l'Histoire des Assemblés d'États*, 18 (Louvain-Paris 1958), pp. 79–121.

———. "Quod omnes tangit." *Revue historique de droit français et étranger*, 4, No. 29 (1951), 97–102.

Hóman, B. *A magyar királyság pénzügyei és gazdaságpolitikája Károly Róbert korában* [Monetary Conditions and Economic Policies of the Kingdom of Hungary in the Age of Charles Robert]. Bp.: Budavári Tud. Társ., 1921.

———. *Gli Angioini di Napoli in Ungheria, 1290–1403*. Roma: Reale Academia, 1938.

———. "Hungary 1301–1490." in *The Cambridge Medieval History* J. B. Bury, ed. Vol. 7. Cambridge: Cambridge Univ. Press, 1936, pp. 587–619 with bibliography on pp. 961–64.

———. "La circolazione delle monete d'oro in Ungheria dal X als XIV secolo e la crisi europea dell'oro nel secolo XIV." *Rivista Italiana di Numismatica* 35 (1922), 109–56.

———. *Magyar pénztörténet 1000–1325* [Hungarian Monetary History 1000–1325]. Bp.: MTA, 1916.

Huber, A. "Ludwig I. von Ungarn und die ungarischen Vasallenländer." *Archiv für österreichische Geschichte*, 66 (1885), 1–44.

Huszár, L. *A budai pénzverés története a középkorban* [History of the Minting of Buda in the Middle Ages]. Bp.: MTA, 1958.

Illés, J. *Az Anjou-kori társadalom és az adózás* [Society and Taxation in the Angevin Era]. Bp.: Politzer, 1900.

Jakab, E. *Oklevéltár Kolozsvár története a középkorban I. kötetéhez* [Diplomatarium to the First Volume of the History of Kolozsvár in the Middle Ages]. Bp.: Egyetemi Nyomda, 1870.

Karpat J. "Die Idee der heiligen Krone Ungarns in neuer Beleuchtung," in *Corona regni. Studien über die Krone als Symbol des Staates im späteren Mittelalter*. M. Hellmann, ed. Darmstadt: Wiss. Buchges., 1961, pp. 349–98 [from *Carpatica Slovaca* 1–2, 1943–44, 501–32].

Katona, St. *Historia critica regum Hungariae*. 42 volumes. Pest: Weingand, 1779–1817.

Kiss I. R. "Az 1386. évi országgyűlések" [The Diets of the Year 1386]. *Száz.*, 47 (1913), 721–35.

Klaić, V. "Marturina, Slavonska daca u srednijem vijeku" [The Mardurina: A Slavonian Tax of the Middle Ages]. *Rad Jugoslavenske Akademije Znanosti i Umjetnosti*, 157 (1904), 114–23.

Klaniczay, G. "The Cult of Dynastic Saints in Central Europe (Fourteenth Century Angevins and Luxemburgs)," in *The Uses of Supernatural Power: The Transformation of Popular Religion in Medieval and Early-Modern Europe*. Tr. S. Sigerman, ed. K. Margolis (Cambridge: Polity, 1990) pp. 111–28.

Knauz, F. "Az 1397-ki országgyűlés végzeménye" [Decree of the Diet of 1397]. *Magyar Történelmi Tár*, 3 (1857), 213–38.

Knauz, F. *Az országos tanács és az országgyűlések története, 1445–1452*. [History of the Royal Council and the Diets between 1445 and 1452]. Pest: Eggenberger, 1859.

Knauz, F. [N.], ed. *Monumenta ecclesiae Strigoniensis*. 2 volumes. Esztergom: Horák, 1874–82.

Knoll, P., *The Rise of the Polish Monarchy: Piast Poland in East Central Europe, 1320–1370*. Chicago-London: Univ. of Chicago Press [©1972].

Kovachich, J. N. *Formulae solennes styli in cancellaria curiaque regum, foris minoribus ac locis credibiliis Regni Hungariae usati*. Pest: Trattner, 1799.

———. *Lectiones variantes decretorum comitialium in regni Hungariae, in Corpore Iuris Hungarici editorum, quas ex collatione textus eorum cum originalibus authenticis eruit.* . . . Pest: Trattner, 1816.

———. *Monumenta veteris legislationis Hungaricae*. Claudiopolis: Typis Coll. Reform., 1815.

———. *Notitiae praeliminares ad syllogen decretorum comitialium*. Pest: Trattner, 1820.

———. *Sylloge decretorum comitialium inclyti regni Hungariae, quae in vulgato corpore juris hungarici, hactenus, aut penitus desiderabantur, aut aliqua sui parte, manca referebantur. et oblivioni postliminio, recenter erepta sunt.* . . . Pest: Trattner, 1818.

Kovachich, M. G. *Supplementum ad vestigia comitiorum apud Hungaros ab exordio regni eorum in Pannonia, usque ad hodiernum diem celebratorum*. 3 volumes. Buda: Regia Universitas, 1798–1801.

———. *Vestigia comitiorum apud Hungaros ab exordio regni eorum in Pannonia, usque ad hodiernum diem celebratorum.* . . . Buda: Regia Universitas, 1790.

Kovács, F. "Régi magyar esküminták" [Old Hungarian Oath Formulae]. *Magyar Nyelv*, 57 (1961), 285–95.

Kőszeghy, S. "Zsigmond király két honvédelmi szabályzata" [Two Military Ordinances of King Sigismund]. *Hadtörténelmi Közlemények*, 5 (1892), 587–91.

Kring, M. "Kun és jász társadalomelemek a középkorban" [Cuman and Jazyg Social Elements in the Middle Ages]. *Száz.*, 66 (1932), 35–63; 169–88.

Kubinyi, A. "Budapest története a későbbi középkorban Buda elestéig" [History of Budapest in the Late Middle Ages Until the Fall of Buda], in *Budapest története*, Vol. 2, pp. 9–240.

———. "Die Nürnberger Haller in Ofen. Ein Beitrag zur Geschichte des Südosthandels im Mittelalter." *Mitteilungen des Vereins für die Geschichte der Stadt Nürnberg* 52 (1963/64), 80–128;

———. "Der ungarische König und seine Städte im 14. und am Beginn des 15. Jahrhunderts," in *Stadt und Stadtherr im 14. Jahrhundert*. W. Rausch, ed. Linz: Wimmer, 1972, pp. 193–220.

———. "Königliches Salzmonopol und die Städte des Königreichs Ungarn im Mittelalter," in *Stadt und Salz*. W. Rausch, ed. Linz: Wimmer, 1988, pp. 213–32.

———. "Soziale Stellung und Familenverbindungen des deutschen Patriziats von Ofen in der ersten Hälfte des 14. Jahrhunderts." *Archiv für Sippenforschung* 36 (1970), 446–54.

Kumorovitz, L. B. "A magyar királyi egyszerű és titkos pecsét használatának alakulása a középkorban" [Development of the Use of the Hungarian Royal Simple and Privy Seal in the Middle Ages]. *A Bécsi Magyar Történetkutató Intézet Évkönyve*, 7 (1937), 69–112.

———. "A specialis praesentia regis pecséthasználata Zsigmond korában" [The Sealing Practice of the *specialis presentia regis* under Sigismund], in *Domanovszky Emlékkönyv* [D. Festschrift]. Bp.: Egyetemi Nyomda, 1937, pp. 422–39.

———. "Az authentikus pecsét" [The Authentic Seal]. *Turul*, 50 (1936), 45–68.

Kurcz, Á. *Lovagi kultúra Magyarországon a 13.-14. században* [Chivalric Culture in Hungary in the Thirteenth and Fourteenth Centuries]. Bp.: Akadémiai K., 1988.

Ladányi, E. "Libera villa, civitas, oppidum. Terminologische Fragen der ungarischen Städteentwicklung." *AUSBp, Sect. hist.* 18 (1977), 3–43.

———. "Zsigmond 1405. évi törvényeinek keletkezési körülményeihez" [On the Origins of Sigismund's Laws of 1405 A.D.], in *Mályusz Elemér Emlékkönyv*. pp. 269–76.

Léonard, E. G. *Les Angevins de Naples*. Paris: Presses Univ. de France, 1954.

Magyar Törvénytár: Corpus Juris Hungarici. D. Márkus *et al.*, ed. Budapest: Franklin, 1896.

Maksay, F. *Les pays de la noblesse nombreuse*. Bp.: Akadémiai K., 1980.

Mályusz, E. "A kancelláriai tevékenység Albert király uralma alatt, 1438–1439" [Activity of the Chancellery under King Albert], in *Opuscula classica mediaevaliaque in honorem J. Horváth composita*. ed. J. Bollók. Bp.: ELTE Latin nyelvi tsz., 1978, pp. 287–357.

———. "A magyar rendi állam Hunyadi korában" [The Hungarian Corporatist State in the Age of Hunyadi]. *Száz.* 91 (1957) 46–123, 529–602.

———. *Das Konstanzer Konzil und das königliche Patronatsrecht in Ungarn*. Bp.: Akadémiai K., 1959.

———. "Die vier Gebrüder Tallóci." *Studia Slavica Acad. Sc. Hung.* 28 (1982), 1–66.

———. "Die Zentralisationsbestrebungen König Sigismunds in Ungarn," in *Etudes historiques*. Bp.: Akadémiai K., 1960, 1, pp. 317–58.

———. "Geschichte des Bürgertums in Ungarn." *Vierteljahrschrift für Sozial- und Wirtschaftsgeschichte*, 20 (1928), 356–407.

———. "La chancellerie royale et la rédaction des chroniques dans la Hongrie médiévale." *Le Moyen Age*, 75 (1969), 51–86, 219–54.

———. "Les débuts du vote de la taxe par les ordres dans la Hongrie féodale," in *Nouvelles études historiques publiées à l'occasion du XIIe Congrès International des Sciences Historiques*. Bp.: Akadémiai K., 1965, 1:55–82.

———. *Egyházi társadalom a középkori Magyarországon*. [Clerical Society in Medieval Hungary]. Bp.: Akadémiai K., 1971.

———. *Kaiser Sigismund in Ungarn 1386–1437*. Trans. A. Szmodits. Bp.: Akadémiai K., 1990.

Mályusz Elemér Emlékkönyv [Festschrift Elemér Mályusz]. É. H. Balázs, E. Fügedi, F. Maksay, eds. Bp.: Akadémiai K., 1985.

Marczali, H. *A magyar történet kútfőinek kézikönyve. Enchiridion fontium historiae Hungarorum*. Bp.: Athenaeum, 1901.

Murarik, A. *Az ősiség alapintézményeinek eredete* [Origin of the Basic Institutions of Aviticitas]. Bp.: Sárkány, 1938.

Nagy, I. and Gy. Tasnádi Nagy, eds. *Anjou-kori okmánytár. Codex Diplomaticus Hungariae Andegavensis*. 7 volumes. Bp.: MTA, 1879–1920.

Nagy I. *et al.*, eds. *Codex diplomaticus domus senioris comitum Zichy de Zich et Vásonkeő*. 12 volumes. Bp.: Magyar Történelmi Társulat, 1871–1931.

Nagy, I. *et al.*, eds. *Hazai Okmánytár. Codex diplomaticus patrius*. 8 volumes. Győr–Bp.: MTA, 1865–1891.

Palacký, F. *Urkundliche Beiträge zur Geschichte des Hussitenkrieges*. Prague: Tempsky, 1873.

Paolo, Paulus de. "Memoriale," in G. Schwandtner, *Scriptores rerum Hungaricarum veteres ac genuini*. Wien: Kraus, 1748, 3: 732–54.

Paulinyi, O. "A sóregálé kialakulása Magyarországon" [The Development of the Salt Monopoly in Hungary]. *Száz.*, 57/58 (1923/24), 627–47.

———. "The Crown Monopoly of the Refining Metallurgy of Precious Metals and the Technology of the Cameral Refineries in Hungary and Transylvania in the Period of Advanced and Late Feudalism (1325–1700), with Data on the Output," in *Precious Metals in the Age of Expansion*, H. Kellenbenz, ed. Stuttgart: Klett-Cotta, 1981.

Pray, G. *Annales regum Hungariae ab anno Christi CMXCVII ad annum MDLXIV deducti. . . .* 5 volumes. Wien: Schulz/Trattner/Bernard, 1763–1770.

Rady, M. C. *Medieval Buda: A Study in Municipal Government and Jurisdiction in the Kingdom of Hungary*. Boulder, Co.: East European Monographs, 1985

Schwandtner, G. *Scriptores rerum Hungaricarum veteres ac genuini ... in nitidissimam hanc formam redacti*. 3 volumes. Wien: Kraus, 1746–48.

Smičiklas, T. *Codex diplomaticus regni Croatiae, Dalmatiae et Slavoniae*. Zagreb: Academia Scientiarum, 1904.

Sugár, P. F., and P. Hanák, eds. *A History of Hungary*. Bloomington: Indiana Univ. Press, 1989.

Sweeney, J. R. "The Decretal *Intellecto* and the Hungarian Golden Bull of 1222." in *Album Elemér Mályusz*. Brussels: Librairie Encyclopédique, 1976, pp. 89–96.

———. "Walachia-Moldavia," in *The Dictionary of the Middle Ages*. New York: Scribner, 1989, 12:497–507.

Szabó D. "Albert királlyá választása" [Election of Albert to King]. in *Fejérpataky Emlékkönyv* [F. Festschrift]. Bp.: Franklin, 1917, pp. 312–25.

Szabó I. "Az 1351. évi 18. tc." [Article 1351:18]. in *Szentpétery Emlékkönyv* [Sz. Festschrift]. Bp.: Dunántúl, 1938, pp. 419–39.

———. "Az 1351. évi jobbágytörvények" [The Laws of 1351 Regarding the Tenants]. *Száz.*, 88 (1954), 497–527. French resumé on pp. 743–44.

———. "Magyarország népessége az 1330-as és 1526-as évek között" [Population of Hungary between 1330 and 1526 A.D.], in *Magyarország történeti demográfiája* [Historical Demography of Hungary]. J. Kovacsics, ed. Bp.: KSH, 1963, pp. 63–113.

Szakály, F., "The Hungarian-Croatian Border Defense System and Its Collapse," in Bak-Király, *Hunyadi*, pp. 141–58.

———. "Phases of Turco-Hungarian Warfare before the battle of Mohács (1365–1526)," in *Acta Orientalia Acad. Sc. Hung.*, 33 (1979), 65–111.

Székely, Gy., ed. *Tanulmányok a parasztság történetéhez Magyarországon a XIV. sz.-ban* [Studies in the History of Peasantry in Hungary in the 14th Century]. Bp.: Akadémiai K., 1953.

Szekfű, Gy., ed. "Oklevelek I. Károly pénzverési reformjához" [Records on the Coinage Reform of Charles I]. *Történelmi Tár,* 1911, pp. 24–35.

Szentpétery, I., jr. "A tárnoki ítélőszék kialakulása" [Development of the Tavernical Court]. *Száz.*, 68 (1934), 510–90.

Szentpétery, I. *Magyar oklevéltan* [Hungarian Diplomatics]. Bp.: MTA, 1930.

Szentpétry, E. [I.], ed. *Scriptores rerum Hungaricarum tempore ducum regumque stirpis Arpadianae gestarum.* 2 volumes. Bp.: MTA, 1937–38.

Szilágyi, L. "III. Endre 1298. évi törvénye" [The Law of Andrew III of 1298]. *AUSBp, Sect. hist.* 20 (1957), 135–71

Szoika, K. *A földesúri bíráskodás az Árpádkori Magyarországon* [Seigneurial Jurisdiction in Árpádian Hungary]. Bp.: Faculty of Law, 1944 [German summary pp. 75–78].

Teleki, J. *A Hunyadiak kora Magyarországon* [The Era of the Hunyadis in Hungary]. 12 volumes (vols. 6–9= Csánki, q.v.). Pest: Emich, 1852–57.

Thallóczy, L. *A kamara haszna (Lucrum camerae) története...* [History of the Chamber's Profit (*lucrum camerae*) in the Context of Taxation in Hungary]. Bp.: Weiszmann, 1879.

Theiner, A. *Vetera monumenta historica Hungariam sacram illustrantia.* Roma: Typis Vaticanis, 1859; repr. Osnabrück: Zeller, 1968.

Tkalčić, I. K. *Monumenta historica liberae regiae civitatis Zagrabiae.* Zagreb: Albrecht, 1889.

Vardy, S. B., G. Goldschmidt, L. S. Domonkos, eds. *Louis the Great, King of Hungary and Poland.* Boulder, Co.: East European Monographs, 1986.

Vierhaus, R., ed. *Herrschaftsverträge, Wahlkapitulationen, Fundamentalgesetze.* Göttingen: Vandenhoek, 1977.

Werbőczy, I. *Tripartitum opus iuris consuetudinarii regni Hungariae.* ed. K. Csiky. Bp.: Eggenberger, 1894.

Wolf, A. "Die Gesetzgebung der entstehenden Territorialstaaten. . .," in *Handbuch der Quellen und Literatur der neueren europäischen Privatrechtsgeschichte.* H. Coing, ed. München: Beck, 1973. 1:721–62.

Wolf, A. "Prinzipien der Thronfolge in Europa um 1400," in R. Schneider, ed. *Das spätmittelalterliche Königtum im europäischen Vergleich.* Sigmaringen: Thorbecke, 1987, pp. 233–78.

Wostry, W. *Albrecht II (1437–1439).* 2 volumes. Prague: Rohlicek, 1907.

Zimmermann, Franz and Carl Werner. *Urkundenbuch zur Geschichte der Deutschen in Siebenburgen.* Volume 1. Hermannstadt: Michaelis, 1882.

Zsigmondkori Oklevéltár [Calendar for the Age of Sigismund]. E. Mályusz, *et al.*, ed. Bp.: Akadémiai K., 1951- (vols. 1 ff.)

INDEX NOMINUM PROPRIUM–INDEX OF PROPER NAMES

(*A general subject index will be printed in the last volume of the series*)

PERSONAL NAMES

This index contains the names of persons mentioned in the text of the laws, but not those in notes or the introduction. The prevailing usage in the Latin documents of the fourteenth-fifteenth century was to add the name of the property (or origin) to the person's Christian name, e.g., *Georgius de Agard*. In Hungarian the same person was probably called *Agárdi György*, for the syntax of the language demands that the adjective (in this case the property or "family" name) be placed in front of the substantive (the surname or Christian name) with the suffix -i, the Hungarian way of forming adjectives. In certain cases other types of names were also used, in our sources usually prefaced by *dictus* ("called"), pointing towards the development of "true" family names. In the preparation of this index we used either the Christian names or—if we felt that the "family" name was reasonably stable—the name of the family's property or origin. Christian names were "Anglicized" if unequivocally identical with accepted names from the Christian calendar. The only major exception is János Hunyadi (John of Hunyad), well-known in this form. In case of foreigners, if known, their original vernacular name was applied. Since no good biographical dictionaries are available for medieval Hungary, we gave extensive biographies for all major figures. Medieval and modern variants of geographical terms used in this index are listed in the Gazetteer, below, page 294.

GEOGRAPHICAL NAMES

Only such placenames are included in this index which refer to the location itself and not to a ruler or secular or spiritual office holder of that place or region. Placenames as part of the name of a nobleman are also omitted. All these are listed in the Index of personal names, above. The names are given in the form used at the time (Hungarian, Latin, and so on). Modern and medieval variants are given in the Gazetteer, below, page 294.

GAZETTEER OF PLACE-NAMES

Abbreviations:

Cr = Croatia
Sl = Slovakia (Czech and Slovak Republic)
R = Romania
Slo = Slovenia

Medieval name	*Present-day name*	*Other variants*
Aurana	Vrana (Cr)	
Árva	Orava (Sl)	
Bolondóc	Beckov (Sl)	
Brassó	Braşov (R)	Kronstadt
Cilli/Cille	Celje (Slo)	
Corbavia	Krbava (Cr)	
Csanád	Cenad (R)	
Diakó	Djakovo (Cr)	
Fara	Hvar (Cr)	Lesina
Hlevna	Livno (Cr)	
Kassa	Košice (Sl)	Kaschau
Macaria	Makarska (Cr)	
Macsó	Mačva (Serbia)	
Nagyolasz	Mandjelos (Cr)	Francavilla
Nagyszeben	Sibiu (R)	Hermannstadt
Nagyszombat	Trnava (Sl)	Tyrnau
Nona	Nin (Cr)	
Nyitra	Nitra (Sl)	
Pelsőc	Plešivec (Sl)	
Pozsony	Bratislava (Sl)	Pressburg
Ragusa	Dubrovnik (Cr)	
Scardona	Skradin (Cr)	
Sebenico	Šibenik (Cr)	
Spalato	Split (Cr)	
Szalánkemén	Slankamen (Serbia)	
Szávaszentdemeter	Sremska Mitrovica (Serbia)	
Szerém(ség)	Srem (Serbia)	Syrmium
Temesvár	Timişoara (R)	
Tinnin	Knin (Cr)	
Trau	Trogir (Cr)	Traù
Trencsén	Trenčin (Sl)	
Várad	Oradea (R)	
Verőce	Virovitica (Cr)	
Veglia	Krk (Cr)	
Zengg	Senj (Cr)	Segnia
Zólyom	Zvolen (Sl)